Introduction

to the 1992 facsimile edition

Commercial Directories are one of the major sources of social, economic and genealogical information from the eighteenth to the mid-twentieth centuries. They help to illuminate some tangled historical undergrowth previously shaded by the tall trees of the gentry and politics which have already been subject to much investigatory light. There is still considerable scope however, for research on the *common people* especially at local level. As most of the commercial directories are arranged and designed for local use they are of particular help in this respect.

The directories of most interest are the earlier ones, where alternative sources are more limited. The best early directory for Scotland is Pigot and Co's **National Commercial Directory of the whole of Scotland...** of 1825-26, which provides a detailed view of commerce and society. Subsequent revisions included Pigot's 1837-38 directory and Slater's **Royal National Commercial Directory and topography of Scotland** of 1852. All of these works are now extremely difficult and expensive to find in the antiquarian book market. Even in libraries and similar institutions they are uncommon.

With this in mind, the Regional Library Service decided to republish the local sections from each of their Pigot and Slater directories - the old areas of Dumfriesshire, Stewartry of Kikrcudbright and Wigtownshire - in one cloth-bound volume. Whilst each individual directory provides a *snapshot* image of local life, the three together form a moving picture during a period of considerable change. The introduction of railways and the rise of the measured population of Dumfries and Galloway to its 1851 peak of 164,633 are only two examples of such change.

It should be remembered that the original directories were first published well over 100 years ago as instant reference books. They have been in constant use ever since and despite surviving in remarkably good over-all condition, a limited number of pages have become badly worn and faded. The printers of the present facsimile, to their credit, have worked marvels in improving the legibility wherever possible. The original directories are part of the Regional Library Service's 80,000 strong Dumfries and Galloway Local Studies Collection which is principally housed in the Ewart Library, Catherine Street, Dumfries. All local libraries within Dumfries and Galloway have Local Studies sections.

This edition has been arranged in three chronological sections representing the 1825-26, 1837-38 and 1852 directories. Within each section Dumfriesshire is followed by the Stewartry of Kirkcudbright and then Wigtownshire.

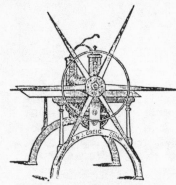
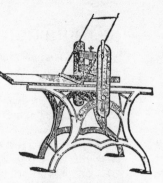
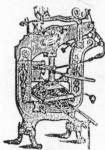
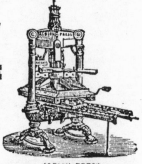
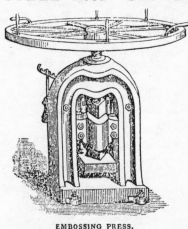
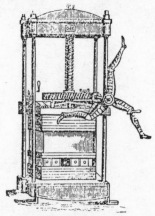

Pigot & Co.'s Directory
1825–26

DUMFRIES-SHIRE,

IS bounded on the north by the counties of Lanark, Peebles, and Selkirk; on the east by Roxburghshire; on the south by the stewarty of Kircudbright, and by the Solway Frith, which separates it from England; and on the west by Ayrshire. This area of land measures about 60 miles from N. W. to S. E. and 30 in a transverse direction. A great part of this county is mountainous, particularly towards its north, north-east, and western confines, where the eminences are lofty, and assume a sterile appearance. However, numerous flocks of sheep and black cattle feed on them, and they abound with game. The vallies are pleasant and fertile, and in these the chief towns, villages, and seats are to be found. In ancient times this district is said to have been inhabited by Selgoræ, a tribe of the Cumbri, the most ancient inhabitants of the middle and southern parts of Britain, who were found here by the Romans, when they established the province of Valentia. After the departure of the Romans, a new kingdom was established by Ida, and the Angles, in 547. About the beginning of the ninth century, the Picts and Scots established themselves here, and made frequent irruptions into England; and, during the subsequent border-wars, the inhabitants of Dumfries-shire, and of Cumberland, were subjected to all the horrors of savage cruelty by their neighbouring enemies. This county contains four royal burghs, Dumfries, Annan, Sanquhar, and Loch-maben; 1253 square miles of land, 10 square miles of lakes; 232,557 acres of cultivated, and 569,363 acres of uncultivated land. Three rivers give their names to different districts of the county, viz. the Nith, Annan, and Esk; hence Nithsdale comprehends the west, Annandale the middle, and Eskdale the east division; but they are unequal in point of extent, though the rivers run nearly in parallel directions, at about 12 miles distance from each other.

NITHSDALE. The river Nith rises in the eastern hills of Ayrshire, enters Nithsdale by the foot of Carsoncone hill, in the parish of Kirkconnel, and descends into the valley of Sanquhar: having forced its way through the hills, which surround this valley, it receives the Crawick water from the north, and the Euchan from the south. N. E. of Sanquhar is Wenlockhead, with its lead mines, the property of the Marquis of Queensberry. A little southward the country becomes flatter, and farther on the valleys are well cultivated, and the hills afford good pasture for sheep. Near Jarborough castle, on the banks of the river Cairn, are to be seen those earthen mounds, called Bowbutts, where the barons of Glencairn, with their vassals, used to practise archery; The river Cairn, which forms the western boundary of the county, unites its stream with the Nith a little above Dumfries, a little to the southward of which the latter river empties itself into the Solway Frith. Eastward from Dumfries lies Locher Moss, twelve miles in length, and three in breadth.

ANNANDALE. The river Annan, as well as the Tweed and Clyde, takes its rise in the mountains above Moffat, and runs through the flat part of the vale of Annan, for upwards of 23 miles. In this course it receives the Evan and Moffat waters, as well as the Wamphray, which irrigates a pleasant valley of that name. Passing Johnstone, it receives some other tributary streams; at Loch Maven it is joined by the Ae, and a little below by the Dryfe, which runs through the vale of Dryfesdale, or Drysdale. When it approaches the Kirk of St. Mungo, the Annan flows over a rocky bed, which may be considered the termination of the vale of Annan.

ESKDALE is the eastern division of the county; the higher part, for near 20 miles, is mountainous, but affords fine pasturage for sheep. During this part of its course it is joined by the Black Esk, the Meggot, the Ewes, and the Wauchope. Almost the whole of this district belongs to the noble family of Buccleugh. After reaching Broomholm, it flows through a flat country, and a part of Cumberland, before it reaches the Solway Frith; during this part of its course it receives the Liddal from Roxburghshire, and the Line from Cumberland. Its course is about 38 miles, 30 of which are in the shire of Dumfries. Limestone is found in various parts of the county, as well as coals; and the lead mines at Leadhills and Wanlockhead are among the most cosiderable in Britain. The greatest elevations in Dumfriesshire are Auchinleck 1500. Blacklarg 2890, Cairnkinnow 2080, Hartfell 2629, Queensberry hill 2259, and Tennis hill 1346 feet above the level of the sea.

POPULATION OF THE SHIRE OF DUMFRIES.

B. Burgh ; P. Parish ; T. Town.

	Houses	Males	Fe-males	Total.		Houses	Males	Fe-males	Total.
Annan ....b & p	808	2161	2325	4486	Kirkmahoe ....p	312	743	865	1608
Applegarth.........................p	141	474	469	943	Kirkmichael ....p	210	571	631	1202
Canonby...........................p	611	1491	1593	3084	Kirkpatrick—Fleming ......p	318	821	875	1696
Carlaverock ....p	253	657	649	1296	Kirkpatrick—Juxta ....p	160	436	476	912
Closeburn ....p	285	807	875	1682	Langholm ....p	439	1125	1279	2404
Cummertrees ....p	296?	748	813	1561	Lochmaben..............b and p	591	1260	1391	2651
Dalton..............................p	139	369	398	767	Middlebie ....p	380	881	993	1874
Dornock ....r..p	162	359	381	743	Moffat ....p	365	1091	1127	2218
Dryesdale ....p	392	1066	1185	2251	Morton ....p	338	872	974	1806
Dumfries.....................b & p	1436	5019	6033	11052	Mousewald ....p	165	386	409	795
Dunscore ....p	276	732	759	1491	Mungo, St..................p	130	341	388	709
Durisdeer ....p	231	770	831	1601	Penpont ....p	294	516	566	1082
Eskdalemuir ....p	117	339	312	651	Ruthwell ....p	246	616	669	1285
Ewes ....p	61	153	161	314	Sanquhar.................b and p	420	1084	1236	2320
Glencairn ....p	383	884	997	1881	Wanlockhead ....t	145	323	373	696
Graitney ....p	363	914	1031	1945	Tinwald ....p	223	598	650	1248
Halfmorton ....p	127	272	291	553	Tortborwald ....p	248	574	631	1205
Hoddam ....p	314	767	873	1610	Tundergarth ....p	98	235	283	518
Holywood ....p	180	472	532	1004	Tynron ....p	100	251	262	513
Hutton and Corrie ....p	137	391	413	804	Wamphray ....p	99	261	293	554
Johnstone ....p	197	583	596	1179	Westerkirk ....p	116	311	361	672
Keir................................p	166	477	510	987					
Kirkconnel ....p	296	569	509	1075	Total........	12518	33573	37306	70878

ANNAN,

THE capital of Annandale, distant from Edinburgh 79 miles, Glasgow 89, Dumfries 16, Ecclefechan 6, Kircudbright 43, and Moffat 27, situated on the left bank of the river of the same name, is one of the most ancient burghs in Scotland, and in conjunction with Dumfries, Kircudbright, Lochmaben and Sauquhar sends one member to parliament; the charter was granted by James VI. of Scotland, and is dated July 12, 1612. Annan was a Roman station, and the reromum of the geography of Ravenna. It seems to have been held by the Britons after the departure of the Romans, till they were subdued by the Saxons of the Northumbrian kingdom, when it came to the Scotch. It afterwards became a principal port, and was granted with the territory of Annandale, and the port of Lochmaben to the ancestors of Robert Bruce, some of whom a castle was erected, which was once occupied as a church, but afterwards went to ruin, and the original wall now forms part of the gaol and town hall. By the accession of the Bruce family to the throne it became a royal burgh. Upon the death of David II. in 1371, this castle, Lochmaben, and the lordship of Annandale came to Thomas Raudolph, earl of Murray, and went with his sister Agnes to the Dunbars, earls of March; after their forfeiture it went to the Douglasses who also lost it by similar conduct, and then having come to Alexander duke of Albany, he, for rebelling against his brother, King James III. and plundering the fair of Lochmaben, in 1484, also forfeited it. Since that period it continued in the hands of the King, and became the great key of the western border. Vessels of 250 tons can come within half a mile of the town. The old bridge, which consisted of five arches, has been removed and a new one is now erecting on its scite, towards which a grant of 3000l. has been obtained from government, and the remainder supplied by the county; the whole expense will be about 7000l. Annan has been of late much improved by new streets and buildings; at its east end is a fine new church built of stone, with a tower and spire; and on the west are the town house and market places. A manufactory for spinning cotton has been established by a company at Manchester, which has greatly added to the prosperity and population of the town. Cured bacon, hams, and between 20 and 30,000 bushels of corn are annually exported. The revenue of the burgh arising from fisheries, tolls, and feu duties, is about 300l. per annum. The parish of Annan is about eight miles long and from one to three broad; the surface is generally level, and the soil fertile. Potatoes are much cultivated here, and they are found to be of so excellent a quality as to be much sought after for seed. The river Annan intersects this parish, and forms an excellent harbour at its influx into the Frith. The side of the river, and the elevated parts of the parish, are adorned with tracts of planting. Limestone, granite, and freestone are abundant. The town is governed by a provost, two bailies, fifteen councillors, a treasurer, dean of guild, and town clerk. A very elegant academy was erected in 1820, in which are taught most of the elegant and useful branches of education; it is governed by the magistrates, and a committee of heritors; the present masters are a rector and assistants. There are also a subscription library, and several benevolent societies. The market is held on Thursday, at which large quantities of pork are sold. There are fairs on the first Thursday in February, the first Thursday in May, the third Thursday in August, first Tuesday after the 29th of September, third Thursday in October, and the first Tuesday after the 11th of November.

POST-OFFICE. High-street.—Post Master, Mr. George Pool, jun. The mail from the South arrives every day at half-past twelve, and is despatched every night at half-past eight. The mail from the North arrives every night at half-past eight, and is despatched every day at half-past twelve.

PLACES OF WORSHIP.

ESTABLISHED CHURCH.—Rev. James Monilaws, Minister
UNITED SECESSION CHAPEL.—Rev. James Dobbie, M. A. Minister

Mr. Benjamin Irving, Elder Bailie
Mr. Isaac Hope, Younger Bailie
Mr. Richard Graham, Town Clerk
Mr. Charles Graham, Treasurer
Mr. John Ferguson, Dean of Guild

Magistrates.
Benjamin Nicholson, esq. Provost

PAROCHIAL SCHOOL.
Mr. Richard Forest, Teacher

RESIDENT GENTRY.

Armstrong Mr. John, High st
Bell Mrs. High st
Blake Mr. George, Bruce's Moat
Burgess Mr. James, Edman st
Carruthers John, esq. Warmanby
Dirom Major General, Mount Annan
Dobbie Rev. James, A. M. Edman street

Douglas Lieut. Col. W. of Netherkirkton
Gracie Miss, Butt st
Hannah Miss Jane, George st
Irving Miss Janet, the Lodge
Irving Mr. Gavin, Butt st
Johnston Mrs. Dr. Scotch st
Little Mrs. Margaret, Edman st
Lowther Miss, Wellington st

Moncrief Mrs.
Monilaws Rev. James, Manse
Pattie Peter, esq. Gill
Peter Gen. Thomas, Green-croft
Stewart Mrs. Bruce's Moat
Thomson Jno. esq. Northfield
Wright Mrs. Agnes, Wellington st

MERCHANTS, TRADESMEN, &c.

ACADEMIES.
(LADIES')
Johnston Miss Jane, High st
Liddersdale Misses, Edman st

AUCTIONEERS.
Hill Thos. Butt st
Kerr Geo. High st
Richardson John, Butt st

BAKERS AND FLOUR DEALERS.
Brysou Alex. High st
Gullen John, High st

Johnston Euphemia, High st
Ker Ann, (& grocer) High st
Reidford Wm. Lodge lane
Richardson Rt. (& grocer) High st
Scott Wm. Murray st
Waugh Geo. High st
Weild Wm. High st

BANK.
Commercial Bank of Scotland, High st. James Scott, agent

BLACKSMITHS.
Cock James, George st

Johnston Thos. High st.
Moffat Wm. High st

BOOKSELLERS AND STATIONERS.
Forrest Peter, (& circulating library, and letter-press printer) High st
Norvel John, High st

BOOT & SHOEMAKER.
Dalgleish George, High st
Harrison Wm. Murray st
Irving John, Morris st
Irving Wm. High st

Jardine Geo. George st
Johnston James, High st
Mc Neish Wm. Murray st
Morton Thos. High st
Reid Wm. Edman st
Roxburgh Joseph, High st
Thomson John, High st
Thomson John, High st

CLOG MAKERS.
Beattie Simon, Scotch st
Burnie William
Irving John, Lodge lane
Johnston James, High st
Turnbull John

COOPERS.
Crawford David, High st
Johnston Wilson, Port st
Mc Connochie Thos. High st
Mc Lauchlan Wm. High st
Rome Geo. High st
White Robt. Scotch st

COTTON SPINNERS.
Douglas Wm. & Co. Annan Mill

DRESS MAKERS.
Armstrong Mary Tayler, High st
Corrie Eliz. High st
Jackson Margaret, High st
Little Ellen, High st
Nicholson Ann, High st

**FIRE
OFFICES AND AGENTS.**
County, Jas. Richardson, High st
Insurance Co. of Scotland,
Andrew Irvine, High st
North British, Jas. Simpson,
High st
Phœnix, Chas. Graham, High st

FLESHERS.
(IN THE FLESHMARKET.)
Anderson James
Anderson James, jun.
Burnett Robert
Douglas John
Douglas William
Forster Wilfred
Gass George
Gass William
Gleasby John
Hamilton John
Irving John & George
Johnstone Bryce
Lindsay Daniel
Lindsay John
Parker Thomas
Porteous John
Robinson Robert
Robinson William
Sword John
Thomson David

**GROCERS
AND SPIRIT DEALERS.**
Anderson James, High st
Bell John, High st
Cartnea Thos. High st
Cowen Jane, High st
Douglas Jas. High st
Dudson Thos. High st
Ferguson John G. High st
Graham Charles, High st
Inglis Alex. Port st
Irving Benj. High st
Jardine James, High st
Mc Lean James, Port st
Mc Vitie John, High st
Nelson Humphrey, High st
Norvel John, High st
Pool Geo. High st
Pool Geo. jun. High st

Pool Jno. (& flour dealer) High st
Pool Robt. High st
Rae Mary G. High st
Roxburgh James, High st
Rule Thos. High st
Scott Gideon, High st
Sloan Nicolas, High st
Williamson Thos. High st
Wright Geo. High st

HAIR DRESSERS.
Blaycock John, High st
Brisben James, High st
Teasdale John, High st

**HAT
MANUFACTURERS.**
Dockray John, Battery
Howe Robt. High st

INNS.
Buck, Ellen Robison, High st
Globe, John Elliot, High st
Queensberry Arms, (and posting house) Joseph, Benson, High st

IRON MERCHANTS.
Forrest John & Wm. High st
Irvine Andrew, High st

IRON MONGERS.
Carruthers Wm. High st
Gunning John, High st
Irvine Andrew, High st

**JOINERS
AND CARPENTERS**
Aitcheson Jas. Port st
Forsyth John, High st
Gass James, High st
Graham Geo. Edman st
Irving Robt. Vine st
Oliver Geo. Edman st
Rome Wm. High st
Williamson James, High st

**LINEN AND
WOOLLEN DRAPERS.**
Bell John, High st
Carson John & Co. High st
Ewart James, High st
Farrish Francis, High st
Little John, High st
Nelson Senhouse, High st
Weild David, High st

MASONS & BUILDERS.
Brown Robt. Port st
Kerr Hugh, Johnston st
Kerr James, Johnston st
Laidlaw Wm. High st
Steel David, Butt st

MEAL DEALERS.
Dickson James, Murray st
Glocester Wm. Edman st
Scott James, Butt st

**MERCHANTS
AND SHIP OWNERS.**
Nelson Edwd. Annan Well
Nicholson Benj. Annan Well

MESSENGERS AT ARMS.
Dickson George, Town Office, High st
Hill Edward, High st

NAIL MAKERS.
Baxter Wm. Port st
Forrest John & Wm. High st
Irving James, George st

NURSERY & SEEDSMEN.
Dickson Robt. High st
Little John, English st

PAINTERS.
Gunning John, High st
Kerr Hugh, Murray st
Waddeson John, Vine st

PLASTERERS.
Dalziel David, Foothill
Park Walter, Port st

PUBLICANS.
Bell Margaret, (Mason's Arms) High st
Bell Wm. (King's Arms) High st
Bell Wm. (Britannia) Annan well
Forster Wilfred, (Mason's Arms) Port st
Graham Wm. (Coach & Horses) High st
Graves Thos. (Ship) Port st
Hetherington Fras. (Commercial) High st
Holliday John, (Cross Keys) Scotch st
Hope Isaac, (Blue Bell) High st
Irving Janet, High st
Irving Richd. (and salt dealer) High st
Little Geo. High st [High st]
Lockyer John, (Horse & Jockey)
Richardson Christopher, (Red Lion) Scotch st
Roxburgh Joseph, High st
Scott Jno. (Turk's Head) High st
Torbron And. (Crown & Thistle) High st
Turnbull Geo. Close Head
Wood Francis, High st

ROPE MAKERS.
Lawson John, Scotch st
Wilkin John, Scotch st

SADDLERS.
Bell Wm. High st
Bell Wm. Port st
Kinley John, High st

STOCKING MAKERS.
Farrish Francis, High st
Mundell John, High st
Rogerson David, Windmill
Little & Johnston, Windmill

STRAW HAT MAKERS.
Corrie Ellen, High st
Nicol M. High st
Rome Janet, High st

SURGEONS.
Grierson David, High st
Irving John, High st
Thorburn James, Port st
Waugh John, M. D. High st

TAILORS.
Finis Andrew, Wellington st &
Hill James, High st
Irving Geo. High st
Jardine Jas. Morris st
Leishman John, High st
Richardson Jas. Scotch st

TEACHERS.
Heslop Thos. (languages) Johnston st
Irving Jonath. (English) Scotch st
Lattimer Matth. (English) Butt st
Purdie Wm. (English) Butt st
Smith Wm. (English) Johnston st
Thomson Fras. (English) High st

TIMBER MERCHANTS.
Irving David, (& slate) Scotch st
Little Wm., Geo. & Wm. (& brewers) Port st
Nelson Benj. (& slate) Port st
Nicholson Benj. Port st

TIN PLATE WORKERS.
Moffatt Joseph, High st
Sinclair Alex. High st

WATCH AND CLOCK MAKERS.
Armstrong Thos. High st
Hodgson John, High
Little James, High st

WRITERS & NOTARIES.
Dalgleish George, (writer only) High st
Farrish John, High st
Foot John, High st
Graham Richd. High st
Hill Edw. (writer only) High st
Little James, High st
Little John, High st

Miscellaneous.
Baxter Jas. tallow chandler and earthenware dealer, High st
Baxter Wm. currier and leather seller, Edman st
Bryden John, tanner, Butt st
Clark John, miller, North st

Duncan Wm. gardener and seedsman, North st
Elliot Robt. plumber, High st
Gillead John, sail maker, Annan Well
Healy John, spirit merchant, High st
Johnston Douglas, turner, & cart and wheelwright, Scotch st
Kinen Patrick, flax dresser, Wellington st
Richardson Janet, glover, High st
Thomson Geo. slater, Toothill

CUSTOM HOUSE,
HIGH-STREET.
John Dalgleish, collector
—Two Officers

STAMP OFFICE,
HIGH-STREET.
Geo. Pool, jun. distributor

COACHES.
CARLISLE, the Robert Burns, from the Buck, every night at seven, and returns for Dumfries at the same hour.

LONDON and Carlisle, the Royal Mail, from the Queensberry Arms, every night at half-past eight, and returns for Dumfries, Stranraer, and Portpatrick, every day at half-past twelve.
LONDON and Carlisle, the Independent, from the Globe, every night at half-past seven, and returns for Dumfries, Kilmarnock, and Glasgow every morning at six.
LONDON, Carlisle, and Manchester, the New Times, from the Queensberry Arms, every night at half-past seven, and returns for Dumfries, Kilmarnock, and Glasgow, every morning at six.

CARRIERS.
CARLISLE, James Baxter, from the Buck, every Friday, and returns for Dumfries on Tuesday.
CARLISLE, Peter Johnston, Port st, every Friday and Monday, & returns on Saturday and Tuesday.
DUMFRIES, Peter Johnston, every Wednesday morning, and returns at night.
EDINBURGH, through Lockerbie & Moffatt, John Johnston, every Monday, and returns on Wednesday.
GLASGOW, Lockerbie, and Moffat, Hugh Crichton, from the Horse and Jockey, every other Monday.

APPLEGARTH,
CANONBY, DALTON, ESKDALEMUIR, EWES, HUTTON, ST. MUNGO, TUNDERGARTH, AND WESTERKIRK.

APPLEGARTH lies on the great road from Carlisle to Edinburgh and Glasgow. Sir Wm. Jardine, bart. who has an elegant mansion here, is the principal proprietor of the parish. It is in the district of Annandale, and on the banks of the river Annan.

CANONBY, on the southern borders of the county, is separated from England by the rivers Liddal and Tarus, whose romantic banks present some pleasing v. This parish is about nine miles long, and six broad.

DALTON is a small parish in Annandale. Great improvement has been made in it by the cultivation of several moors and commons.

ESKDALEMUIR, a mountainous parish on the east side of the county, and in the district of Eskdale, is adapted for sheep pasturage, and a very small part only is under cultivation.

EWES, in the district of Eskdale, is a most romantic parish, being composed chiefly of ranges of hills, many of which are covered with verdure to their very summits; numerous plantations add beauty to their appearance.

HUTTON is watered by the rivers Milk, Dryfe, and Corrie. The pasturage of sheep is here extensive, and the principal object of the farmer.

ST. MUNGO is in the district of Annandale, thro' which the road for Glasgow and Carlisle passes, and at a short distance from the villages of Ecclefechan and Lockerbie. Castlemilk, the residence of Major Hart, is one of the most beautiful mansions in this part of Scotland, being romantically situated in the midst of ornamental pleasure grounds, and in the bosom of a fine valley.

TUNDERGARTH is a parish, in which a great number of sheep are pastured. The old castle, now in ruins, is deserving of notice, as it was formerly the residence of the Marquisses of Annandale. There are also two encampments, supposed to be Roman.

WESTERKIRK, on the eastern borders of the county, pastures many sheep and black cattle. Several elegant villas, together with its having been the birth place of Sir Robert Walpole, renders this parish not a little interesting.

PARISH CHURCHES.
APPLEGARTH—Rev. Wm. Wm. Dunbar, Minister
CANONBY—Rev. James Donaldson, Minister
DALTON—Rev. James Cririe, D.D. and Rev. Thos. H. Thomson, A. & S. Ministers
ESKDALEMUIR—Rev. Wm. Brown, D. D. Minister
EWES—Rev. Robt. Shaw, Minister
HUTTON—Rev. Jacob Wright, Minister
ST. MUNGO—Rev. Andrew Jamieson, Minister
TUNDERGARTH—Rev. Richd. Paxton, & Rev. Thos. Little, AM. A. & S. Ministers
WESTERKIRK—Rev. James Green, Minister

PAROCHIAL SCHOOLS.
APPLEGARTH—John Brown, Master
CANONBY—Wm. Paterson, Master
DALTON—George Rose Master
ESKDALEMUIR—James Yool, Master
EWES—John Little, Master
HUTTON—James Wright, Master
ST. MUNGO—Thomas Byers, Master
TUNDERGARTH—George Bell, Master
WESTERKIRK—Archibald Graham, Master

RESIDENT GENTRY.
Beattie Thos. esq. (of *Muccledull*) Ewes
Bell Thos. esq. (of *Skellyholm*) St. Mungo
Bell Thos. esq. (of *Strands*) St. Mungo
Carmichael Miss, (of *Kirkbank*) St. Mungo
Carruthers John, esq. (of *Brecon Hill*) St. Mungo
Carruthers Wm. esq. (of *Nutholm*) St. Mungo
Curll William, esq. (of *Belholm*) Westerkirk
Graham George, esq. (of *Shaw*) Hutton
Hart Major Thos. (of *Castlemilk*) St. Mungo

R R   **313**

Irving John Bell, esq. (of *White Hill*) St. Mungo
Jardine Sir Wm. (of *Applegarth*) Applegarth
Johnstone Lady, Wester Hall, Westerkirk

Macrae J. C. esq. (of *Holmains*) Dalton
Martin James, esq. (of *Highlaw*) St. Mungo
Rogerson Samuel, esq. Borlands, Hutton

Rogerson Wm. esq. Gillesple, Hutton
Sommerville W. D. Wightman Henderson, esq. (of *Fingask*) Dalton

---

CLOSEBURN,

DURISDEER, GLENCAIRN, KEIR, KIRKCONNEL, KIRKMICHAEL, AND PENPONT.

CLOSEBURN, in the Nithsdale district and county of Dumfries, is a parish of great extent, nearly ten miles in length and about the same breadth. The ancient castle of Closeburn forms an interesting object; it is the property of Charles G. Monteith, esq. and about two miles from the castle are some beautiful waterfalls. An excellent free grammar school, supported by property left by — Wallace, esq. of Closeburn, amounting to near 600*l.* annually affords a superior education to numerous pupils.

DURISDEER, is bounded on the north-west and west by the parish of Sanquhar, on the north-east by that of Crawford in Lanark, and on the east by Penpont. Being surrounded by hills it exhibits fine scenery, and freestone is abundant.

GLENCAIRN parish contains 21,795 Scots acres, or nearly forty-three square miles. Several small rivulets meander beautifully through it, and form much pleasing scenery, to which the elegant mansion of H. Fergusson, esq. of Orrolands, contributes much. Loch Orr or Urr, is in this parish, and from it rises the river of the same name. It is bounded on the east by Keir, on the south by Dunscore, on the north by Tynron, and on the west by Carsphairn in Kircudbright.

KEIR, a parish possessing a considerable quantity of plantation and limestone, is bounded on the east by Closeburn, on the north-west and north by Tynron and Penpont, and on the south by Dunscore; it is about three miles in breadth and eight in length.

KIRKCONNEL parish forms part of the district of Nithsdale; it is very mountainous, and abounds with limestone and several mineral springs; Rigburn spa is particularly deserving of notice.

KIRKMICHAEL, united with Garrell, in the district of Nithsdale, is about ten miles long, and four broad. The parish of Kirkpatrick-juxta bounds it on the north-west, Johnstone on the north-east, Lochmaben on the south-east, Tinwald and Kirkmanse on the south, and Closeburn on the west. Many remains of ancient fortifications and Roman roads are visible.

PENPONT is a very extensive parish, being upwards of twenty-one miles long and averaging about five broad; many parts of it are mountainous, intersected with romantic glens and streams of water; large quantities of cattle are pastured. The great Glenquhargen craig, rising perpendicularly 1000 feet, and one of the greatest natural wonders in Scotland, is in this parish. There are also the remains of Roman encampments, causeways, and a castle; freestone is abundant.

PARISH CHURCHES.

CLOSEBURN—Rev. Charles Anderson, Minister
DURISDEER—Rev. George Wallace, Minister
GLENCAIRN—Rev. John Brown, Minister
KEIR—Rev. James Keyden, Minister
KIRKCONNEL—Rev. James Richardson, Minister
KIRKMICHAEL—Rev. James Smaill, Minister
PENPONT—Rev. John Nevison, Minister

PAROCHIAL SCHOOLS.

CLOSEBURN—Robert Mc Murdy, Master
DURISDEER—Wm. Mouncie, Master
KIRKCONNEL—Andrew Turner, Master
KIRKMICHAEL—John Burnett, Master

GRAMMAR SCHOOL.

CLOSEBURN—Robert Mundell, Teacher

NOBILITY AND GENTRY.

Buccleugh, his Grace the Duke of, (of *Drumlanrig Castle*) Durisdeer
Fergusson Henry, esq. (of *Orrolands*) Glencairn

Hoggan James, esq. (of *Waterside*) Keir
Hunter W. F. esq. (of *Barjarg*) Keir
Kirkpatrick Sir Thos. bart. (of *Capenoch*) Keir

Laurie Sir Robt. bart. (of *Maxweltoun*) Glencairn
Monteith Charles G. S. esq. (of *Closeburn*) Closeburn
Mundell Robt. esq. Wallace Hall, Closeburn

CUMMERTREES,

DORNOCK, GRAITNEY, OR GRETNA GREEN, KIRKPATRICK-FLEMING, MIDDLEBIE, MOUSEWALD, RUTHWELL, TINWALD, AND TORTHORWALD.

CUMMERTREES parish lies on the banks of the river Annan, which bounds it on the east. The village is one of the prettiest in this part of Scotland, and the houses are remarkable for their clean appearance.

DORNOCK is pleasantly situated upon a gentle eminence, about a mile from the sea, and has a very commanding view of the Solway Frith. This parish is nearly a square of two miles and a half, with the river Kirtle running through it. Fishing in the Frith forms the chief employment of the inhabitants.

GRAITNEY, OR GRETNA GREEN, is the first stage in Scotland from England, and has been long famous in the annals of matrimonial adventure for the clandestine marriages of runaway lovers' from England. The ceremony is performed by several persons, but principally by a tobacconist, and not by a blacksmith, as is generally believed. It is about 70 years since these marriages were first solemnised, and it is considered, that not less than sixty or seventy couples annually pay a visit to this much talked-of shrine. The usual fee is fifteen guineas for each pair of love sick swains, which affords the clergyman no inconsiderable yearly income. The village of Graitney is in a pleasant part of the county, and, from the circumstances just mentioned, is viewed with considerable interest by all travellers.

KIRKPATRICK-FLEMING is one of the most beautiful parishes in the south of Scotland, presenting scenery in many parts bold and romantic; the different elegant mansions, surrounded with trees and shrubs, give considerable effect to the whole. Lime and free stone abound, and there are several mineral springs, possessing qualities similar to those of Hartfel spa, near Moffat.

MIDDLEBIE abounds with red free stone, and considerable quanties of lime stone are also found. The parish is nine miles in length, and about five in breadth, it lies between Ecclefechan and Langholm, and in the midst of beautiful scenery.

MOUSEWALD is the second parish on the road from Dumfries to Annan. The church is built in a superior manner to most in this part of the country, and is placed on an elevated situation; the bell tower is particularly neat. Sir Robert Grierson, bart. of Lagg, has a noble mansion here.

RUTHWELL parish extends about six miles in length along the banks of the Solway Frith, and the great read from Carlisle to Dumfries runs through it. The village bears a respectable appearance, and there is a good parish school. The church is pleasantly situated, and many memorials of the departed adorn the burial ground around it.

TINWALD parish is famous for having given birth to Paterson, the planner of the bank of England, and of the unfortunate Darien scheme; he represented the burgh of Dumfries more than once in the Scottish parliament.

TORTHORWALD.—The junction of the old and new roads, between Dumfries and Annan, commences in this parish. The ruins of Skrimple castle, which is supposed to have been built in the twelfth century, are to be seen here.

PLACES OF WORSHIP.

CUMMERTREES—Rev. Thomas Gillespie, Minister
DORNOCK—Rev. Nicolas Sloan, Minister
GRAITNEY—Rev. John Morgan, Minister
KIRKPATRICK-FLEMING—Rev. Alexdr. Monilaws, Minister
MIDDLEBIE—Rev. Richard Nevison, Minister
MOUSEWALD—Rev. Duncan Stewart Singer, Minister
RUTHWELL—Rev. Henry Duncan, D.D. Minister
TINWALD—Rev. George Greig, Minister
TORTHORWALD—Rev. John Yourston, Minister

PAROCHIAL SCHOOLS.

CUMMERTREES—John Owen, Master
DORNOCK—John Reid, Master
GRAITNEY—John Stodhart, Master
KIRKPATRICK-FLEMING—William Stewart Smith, Master
MIDDLEBIE—John Lowrie, Master
MOUSEWALD—Francis Halliday, Master
RUTHWELL—Thomas Ferguson, Master
TINWALD—Theodore Edgar, Master
TORTHORWALD—Irvine Barton, Master

RESIDENT GENTRY.

Barker John, esq. Lanshaws, Kirkpatrick-Fleming
Borthwick Captain, R.N. (of Lockerwoods) Ruthwell
Dickson Mr. Abraham, Mousewald
Dickson Miss Isabella, Clarence Cottage, Ruthwell
Douglas Lady, Glen Stewart, Cummertrees
Grierson Sir Rob. bart. (of Lagg) Mousewald

Irving Sir P.E. bart, Woodhouse, Annandale
Lowther Tristram, esq. (of Rosehall) Dornock
Mc Clelland Miss Elizabeth, Bries, Middlebie
Mair Hugh, esq. Wiseby, Kirkpatrick-Fleming
Maxwell Lieutenant Col. Christopher, Graitney Hall, Graitney

Maxwell Sir John Heron, bt . Sprinkell, Kirkpatrick-Flemin
Murray John Dalrymple, esq. (o Murraythwaite) Cummertrees
Nicholson Jas. esq. Torthorwald
Queensberry, The Marquis of, Kenmount, Cummertrees
Sharp General Matthew, (of Hoddam) Cummertrees
Smith Joseph, esq. Comlongon Castle, Ruthwell

DUMFRIES

Is situated along the north east bank of the river Nith, about nine miles above the confluence of that river, with the Solway Frith, and distant from Edinburgh 72 miles, Glasgow 80, Carlisle 34, Ayr 60, Sanquhar 26, Cumnock 34, Kilmarnock 48, Castle Douglas 20, Kirkcudbright 27, Annon 16, Thornhill 14, Lockerby 12, Lochmaben 8, Ecclefechan 16, Langholm 30, and London by way of Manchester 341. Of the precise period, at which it was founded, no record has been preserved. Antiquarians, without recurring to the Celtic, have bewildered themselves in endeavouring to settle the etymology of its name, which, in fact, has undergone little change, from what it was originally, viz. Druim-a-Phrish, afterwards altered to Drumfries, and within those 50 or 60 years changed to Dumfries, for the sake of euphony. Druim-a Phrish, in the celtic, signifies the back, or ridge, of a woody eminence, which is very descriptive of the situation of Dumfries rising gradually from the river side, and enbosomed in one of the finest and best sheets of dale country in Scotland. The prospect, which is terminated at the distance of a few miles, by a continued chain of hills, covered with wood, or cultivated to their summits, is altogether one of the grandest scenes in Britain. Serving as a kind of capital, not only to its own shire, but to the whole district of Galloway, and possessing an easy and frequent intercourse with London, Edinburgh, and Glasgow, it is a place of great resort for the nobility and gentry of the neighbouring counties. Independently of those, who have amusement only in view,

many families are attracted hither by the cheapness of living, the salubrity of the air, and above all, by its excellent seminaries of education; society, therefore, possesses a greater share of elegance and gaiety here than can probably be found in any other town of its size in Scotland. The Municipal Government is vested in a provost, three bailies, a dean of guild, a treasurer, two town clerks, and twelve councillors, to whom the whole jurisdiction of the burgh is confided. The craftsmen are divided into seven corporations with each a deacon, chosen from their respective trades, and who elect one of their own number to be convener, and another to be general box master, all of whom form what is called a grand committee of the seven trades. The places of worship consist of two churches of the establishment, one of Relief, two of the United Secession, an Episcopal, a Catholic, a Methodist and an Independent Chapel. St Michael's or the parish church, claiming particular notice, on account of its cemetry, which contains numerous elegant and curious monuments, many of them very ancient; but the chief is the fine mausoleum raised to the memory of the Scotish Bard Burns. By the erection of this monument it may be said that Scotland has repaid the debt so long due to the memory of him, of whose natural genius Scotsmen may well be vain. But while, as Scotsmen, they justly exult, that it was reserved for their country to give birth to such a poet, the hard fate of Burns, while living, and the comparative obscurity, in which he closed his days prove also, that he was not sufficiently valued in

315

" At length we hail him, cenotaph'd, inurn'd ;
At length we mourn him, as he should be mourn'd;
Art awaits at length upon his honour'd tomb,
And poesy recording, weeps his doom."

Burns died at Dumfries, on the 21st of July, 1796, aged 36 years and about seven months, and his remains were deposited in the church yard of St. Michael; but it was some time, before even a stone was raised over the sod, that covered the relics of departed genius, and this was but a plain memento, reared by a widow's affections, and dewed with a widow's tears. It was not until 1813, that any decisive plan was adopted ; and it was then chiefly owing to the indefatigable perseverance of Wm. Grierson, esq. of this town, that a public meeting was convened on the 6th January 1814, at which General Duplop, M. P. presided. A public subscription was immediately commenced, the amount of which soon proved that it only wanted a spark to kindle into a flame, the generous sentiment of paying due honour to their immortal countryman. His present Majesty, then Prince Regent, graciously sent a donation of 50 guineas. The design of the mausoleum was furnished by Thos. F. Hunt, esq. of London, and a most classic model by Peter Turnerelli, esq. was chosen for the marble sculpture to be placed in the interior. The subject is happily taken from words which occur in the dedication of an early edition of the bard's own poems, to the noblemen and gentlemen of the Caledonion Hunt. "The Poetic Genius of my country found me, as the Prophetic Bard Elijah did Elisha at the plough, and threw her Inspiring Mantle over me :" The foundation stone was laid June 5th, 1815, and the body removed from the place in which it was originally interred, on the 19th of the September following. It is surrounded with handsome iron palisades and evergreens, which add greatly to the beauty of its appearance. The whole expense amounted to about 1500l, and it is certainly a cemetery worthy of Caledonia's highly gifted bard.
"Where still that fresh, that unforgotten name
Shall pay the arrear of monumental fame,
As oft the traveller, oft the poet turns
To muse, and linger o'er the tomb of Burns."
With a further desire to do honour to the memory of Burns, a number of gentlemen have formed themselves into a club, and meet annually to celebrate his natal day.

CHARITABLE INSTITUTIONS.

The Infirmary was founded in 1776, at a period when very few charities of a similar nature, were in Britain; and this is still the only one in the south of Scotland. Medical advice and medicine are gratuitously afforded to every applicant who is an object of charity. It is supported by annual subscriptions, legacies, donations, benefactions, &c. and is under the management of governors. There is also a Lunatic Asylum connected with it. The Poors' Hospital is for the purpose of supporting aged and indigent poor, and destitute children, who are taught to read and write. It is governed by the Magistrates and Town Council, &c. and it is supported by part of the collections from the church doors, numerous benefactions, donations and annual subscriptions; the health, morals, and comfort of its poor inmates are studied with the greatest care. It was founded in 1753, by Messrs. J. & W. Moorhead's, merchants. Dumfries also contains a Society for Promoting education in the Highlands, a Missionary Society, a Society for Promoting Christianity amongst the Jews, a Bible Society, a Local Sabbath School Society, a Ladies' Free School, a Juvenile Society, a Branch of the Scottish Missionary Society, and a Penny-a-week Bible and Missionary Society.

ACADEMY. This elegant and useful seminary was founded in 1802, on one of the most delightful and healthy situations to be found in the town or neighbourhood. The expences of the ground, and of building and finishing the fabric were entirely defrayed by voluntary subscription. A committee of management having been chosen by a general meeting of the subscribers, the whole operations were carried into execution under their superintendence, and in October, 1814, the structure was formally delivered over to the magistrates, as patrons and guardians of the institution, who, along with the other members of the town council, have the exclusive privilege of appointing the masters.

The THEATRE is rather a handsome building of stone with a projecting portico ; the interior which is tastefully decorated, has been lately lighted with gas, and the performances are superior to most in Scotland ; it is generally open a few weeks in the winter.

The COURT HOUSE is a large elegant structure, containing a very spacious court room, and other offices; nearly opposite stands the Gaol, whence the prisoners are conveyed for trial through a subterraneous passage, which communicates with the court room. Courts are held in April and September, for Dumfriesshire and the stewartry of Kirkcudbright; there are also a small debt, Sheriff, and Borough Courts. There are two subscription, reading and news rooms, supplied with London and Provincial papers, magazines, &c.; the principal one has an excellent billiard table. Two Libraries are supported by subscription. A coursing club has two meetings during the summer ; Races are held in October, and the Caledonian Hunt once in five years. A variety of ancient customs formerly observed in Dumfries, are now relinquished; but one still exists, called shooting for the silver gun, and is celebrated with great enthusiasm. The silver gun, which is still preserved, derives great importance from being the gift of James VI, of Scotland, who ordained it as a prize to the best marksman among the Incorporations of Dumfries. The contest was by Royal Authority to take place every year, but from the great trouble and expense it has become a
" ance in seven year's jubilee,"
and the birth day of the reigning monarch is the day invariably for the celebration ; the last festival took place April 23rd, 1824. The principal inns are the King's Arms, the Dumfries and Galloway Hotel, and the Commercial, kept by Mrs. Williamson, which has been lately very much improved by an addition of twenty sleeping apartments ; it is now one of the most comfortable houses of entertainment in the south of Scotland, and is particularly deserving the attention of every traveller from the circumstance of its having been the head quarters of the Pretender Stuart, in December, 1745. A spirit of improvement has been shewn by the inhabitants, assisted by the commissioners of police, in numerous alterations, public structures, &c. and many are still in a state of forwardness, amongst which may be named the erection of a new suite of assembly rooms, lighting the town with gas, new market places, a timber bridge over the Nith, and the widening of Bank-street. A spacious quay is also immediately to be built along the side of the town, and a company is forming to supply water by pipes. A fine doric pillar erected by the county of Dumfries to the memory of the late Duke of Queensberry adorns the centre of the town. A new clock has been lately put up in the mid steeple of the old town house, which cost about 140l. raised by subscription. It was manufactured by Messrs. Law and Son, Castle Douglas, and Mr. Wm. Law, of Kirkcudbright. The commercial advantages have lately been much increased by obtaining an act of parliament, empowering a certain number of commissioners to be annually chosen to conduct the shipping business of the river, since which period great and important improvements have been effected ; the dangerous sand banks in the Solway Frith, have been made comparatively safe, by placing buoys in the Scotch and English Channels ; obstructions of every kind have been removed ; the river Nith has been confined by great and solid embankments and stone jetties; new cuts have been made, where necessary ; and now most of the vessels may discharge their cargoes close to the town, which were formerly obliged to unload at a considerable distance down

the river. In 1808 and 1809 the river dues from the shipping were only about 300*l.* annually; at this period they are not less than 1000*l.* and the whole tonnage of the vessels amounts to upwards of 4000 tons. The principal imports are timber, hemp, tallow, coal, slate, iron and wine; the exports consist of wheat, barley, oats, potatos, wool, and free stone. Considerable business is done in the manufacture of hosiery, principally lamb's wool, to a very great extent, the making of hats, extensive breweries, tan yards, and a distillery. Two newspapers are printed every Tuesday, both of which are conducted in a most respectable manner and each has an extensive circulation. The market days are Wednesday and Saturday for domestic purposes; on Wednesday the cattle market is the largest in Scotland, and during the season many thousand carcasses of pork are sold. Fairs are held on the first Wednesday in February, O. S. (this is peculiar for the immense quantities of hare, skins sold at it, as during one season skins to the amount of 6000*l.* were disposed of, and from two to three thousand *perfect* skins are annually shewn) 26th of May or the Wednesday after the 25th of September, or Wednesday after; and the 22d of November, or Wednesday after. These are chartered fairs and at each large quantities of horses are shewn.

MAXWELLTOWN, formerly a village, is now a burgh of barony, in the stewartry of Kirkcudbright, and connected with Dumfries by two bridges across the Nith. In no instance have the good effects of erecting a village into a Burgh of Barony been more conspicuous than in Maxwelltown. The charter was obtained from the crown, in 1810, and since that time, from being a poor village, notorious for disorderly conduct; for it was a remark of the late Sir John Fielding's, that he could trace a rogue over the whole kingdom, but always lost him at the bridge end of Dumfries, now Maxwelltown, it has improved in the value and extent of houses; and increased considerably in the number and respectability of its inhabitants. It is governed by a prevost, two bailies, and councillors.

POST OFFICE, Castle street.—*Post Master,* Robert Threshie, esq; Mr. David Dalgleish, *Clerk;* John Drummond, *Letter Carrier.* Mail from London and Carlisle, arrives every afternoon at three and is despatched every night at a quarter before seven. Mail from Edinburgh arrives every morning at eight, and afternoon at half past three, and is despatched every morning at seven and half past ten. Mail from Portpatrick and Ireland arrives every evening at six, and is despatched every afternoon at four. Mails from Glasgow and Lockerby arrive every morning at eight, and are despatched every morning at half past ten. Mails from Thornhill, Minihive, and Sanquhar arrive every afternoon at three, and are despatched every afternoon at ten minutes past four.

Note.—No letters are received from London on Tuesdays, nor any despatched on Thursdays. The Office opens for delivery about half an hour after the arrival of the different mails, and letters must be put into the office half an hour previous to the departure; and those for the Edinburgh seven o'clock morning mail, before ten the previous night.

PLACES OF WORSHIP.

ST. MICHAEL'S CHURCH, St. Michael's street.— Rev. Alex. Scot, D. D. Minister.
NEW CHURCH, Head of High street.—Rev. Thos. T. Duncan, M. D. Minister; Rev. —— Miller, Evening Lecturer.
FIRST UNITED SECESSION CHAPEL, Lowerburn st.— Rev. Wm. Inglis, and Rev. Jas. Clyde, Ministers
SECOND UNITED SECESSION CHAPEL, Buccleugh street.—Rev. Walter Dunlop, Minister.
RELIEF CHAPEL, New st.—Rev. And. Fyfe, Minister
SCOTCH EPISCOPAL CHAPEL, Buccleugh street.—
Rev. Charles Murray Babington, M. A. Minister.
INDEPENDENT CHAPEL, Irish street.—Francis Dick, Preacher of the Gospel.
METHODIST CHAPEL, Queen st.—Ministers, various
ROMAN CATHOLIC CHAPEL, Shakespeare street.—
Rev. James Carruthers, Priest.

MUNICIPAL GOVERNMENT.

William Thomson, esq. Provost.
Messrs. John Mc George, Henry Mc Minn, and Robert Armstrong, Bailies
Mr. Christopher Armstrong, Dean
Mr. John Barker, treasurer and chamberlain
Messrs. Francis Shortt, & Rbt. Locke, Town Clerks
Mr. Thomas Fraser, Procurator Fiscal.

INCORPORATED TRADES.

Mr. Allan Anderson, Convenor
Mr. Alexander Howat, Box Master General
Deacons.

Hammermen,	Mr. Robert Mc Kinnel
Squaremen,	Allan Anderson
Weavers,	Samuel Inman
Tailors,	Wm. Richardson
Shoemakers,	James Nibloe
Skinners & Glovers,	John Woodmas
Fleshers,	Alexander Howat

COMMISSIONERS OF POLICE.

The Provost, three Bailies, and Convener of Trades, *ex-officiis.*

Messrs. J. Thomson,	Messrs. T. Milligan
T. Mc Caig	J. Martin
J. Bendall	J. Mc Whir
Wm. Grierson	R. Dinwiddie
S. Primrose	A. Rankine
J. Reid	J. Sinclair

DUMFRIES AND GALLOWAY ROYAL INFIRMARY.

The Marquis of Queensberry, President
Sir Thos. Kirkpatrick, bart. Vice President
R. Jardine, esq. Chairman of the Weekly Committee
James Shortridge & Robert Murray, esqs. Inspectors
Drs. Gilchrist & Melville, Honorary Physicians
Drs. Shortridge and Laing, Physicians
Mr. William Gordon, Treasurer
Messrs. Robson and Spalding, Surgeons
Mr. Joseph Crichton, House Surgeon & Clerk.
Mrs. Wright, Matron.

POORS' HOSPITAL.

ST. MICHAEL'S-STREET.

Provost William Thomson, President

Bailies Mc George, Mc Minn, & Armstrong, & the Convener, and Deacons of Trades, assisted by eight gentlemen from the Kirk Sessions, and eight from the Community form the members
A committee of ten gentlemen conducts the necessary business of the year.
Mr. John Mc Minn, House Surgeon

ACADEMY.

INSTITUTED IN 1802.

Teachers.
Mr. Alex. Harkness, Latin and Greek
Mr. Thos. White, Mathematics, Arithmetic, &c.
Mr. John Kennedy, Writing
Mr. James Mc Robert, English and Grammar
Mr. A. Fouchard, French

LADIES' FREE SCHOOL.

Walter Cummins, Teacher

CUSTOM HOUSE.

SHAKESPEARE-STREET.

John Staig, esq. Collector
Mr. James Locke, Comptroller and Surveyor
Ten Officers

EXCISE OFFICE.

KING'S ARMS INN.

John Wharton, esq. Collector
J. Lewars, Robert Porteous, and Thomas Lawson, Supervisors—Twenty Officers

COUNTY TAX OFFICE
1, GREY FRIARS' STREET.

Roger Kirkpatrick, esq. Collector.
Messrs. Wm. Gouldie, George Henderson and Jas. Gouldie, Surveyors
James Gouldie, esq. Inspector.

TOWN TAX OFFICE.
IRISH STREET.

John Barker, esq. Collector
Robert Locke, esq. Collector of Land Tax

STAMP OFFICE.
BANK-STREET.

Wm. Syme, esq. Distributor for Dumfries
The Stewartry of Kirkcudbright, and County of Wigtonu
Mr. Alexander Crawford, Clerk

SUBSCRIPTION READING ROOMS.
131, HIGH-STREET.

Mr. Thomas Glendinning, Keeper

READING ROOM.
113, HIGH-STREET.

Mr. James Broom, Manager

DUMFRIES AND GALLOWAY HORTICULTURAL SOCIETY.
The Most Noble the Marquis of Queensberry, President

Vice Presidents.

Viscount Kenmure
Sir John H. Maxwell, bart.
Sir Robert Laurie, bart.
Lieutenant General Dirom, of Annandale
William Maitland, esq. of Auchlan
Major Crichton, of Dalton
Wm. Grierson, esq. of Baitford, Secretary
P. Primrose, esq. Treasurer
Rev. J. Wightman, Chaplain

MAGISTRATES OF MAXWELLTOWN.
James Shortridge, esq. Provost
Messrs. John Walker and Joseph Pagan, Bailies
Messrs. Philip Forsyth, James Locke, Adam Dickson, and John Hunter, Councillors.

RESIDENT GENTRY.

Airth Alex. esq. of Craigs
Babington Rev. C. M. Summer Hill, Maxwelltown
Babington Miss Mary, Castle-st
Baillie Wm. esq. Nun Holm
Barker Mrs. Margaret, Troqueer
Bell Mrs. Eliz. Shakespeare st
Bell Miss Jane
Bell Mrs. Jessie, George st
Bevau Mr. Robt. Nith Place
Bevau Mrs. High st
Beon Mr. Saml. 22 Lowerburn st
Black Miss Jane, Albion place
Blair Mrs. Janet, Maxwelltown
Blount David, esq. Mid park
Brand John, esq. Mountain hall
Broom Mrs. High st
Brown Mrs. Agnes, Brown hall
Brown Mrs. Irish st
Burus Mrs. Jane, Burns st
Burnside Mrs. 12, Buccleugh st
Carruthers Miss Henrietta, (of *Dormont*) 2, Castle street
Carruthers Rev. J. Shakespeare st
Carruthers Mrs. Mary, (of *Warmanby*) 20, Buccleugh street
Clarke Miss, Queen st
Clarke Mrs. W. Queen st
Colton Mrs. Irish st
Covens James, esq. Stone house
Clyde Rev. Jas. 5, Lowerburn st
Copland Miss, Bank st
Creighton Mrs. Ann, Castle st
Crosbie Mrs. Thomas, Shakespeare st
Dalzell Dougal, esq. of Glenae
Dalzell Lady Elizabeth, 1, Albion place
Dalzell Mr. Jas. Castle st
Dalzell Major Stewart, 16, Buccleugh st
De Peyster Mrs. Colonel, Irish st
Drummond Major John, 22, Castle st
Duncan Rev. T. Thomas, Buccleugh st
Dunlop Rev. Walter, Buccleugh st
Evans Mrs. High st
Ferguson Mrs. 8, Grey Friars st
Forsyth Mr. Joseph, Wallgreen house
Forsyth Philip, esq. Nith side, Maxwelltown
Fyfe Rev. Andrew, Old Fleshmarket st
Gibson Mr. Wm. Nith bank
Gilchrist John, M. D. Irish st
Gillespie John, esq. Rose hall
Gillespie John, esq. Stone house
Glenn Miss Jessie, Irish st
Glenn Miss, 11, Townhead st

Goldie Mrs. Mary, 15, Buccleugh st
Gordon Mr. James, Maxwelltown
Gordon Miss Janet, (of *Campbletown*) 21, Buccleugh st
Gordon Miss, 7, Buccleugh st
Gordon Mrs. Thomas, Maxwelltown
Gordon Miss Wm. Maxwelltown
Gracie Miss, Bank st
Graham Miss Margaret, Irish st
Grierson Mrs. 5, Buccleugh st
Grierson Captain Wm. St. Michael st
Haig Mrs. Shakespeare st
Hainning Mrs. Mary, Loch bank
Halliday James, esq. Green brae
Halliday Mrs. Rose bank
Hamilton Miss, Bank st
Hannah John, esq. Hannah field
Harkness Mr. Alexander, Irish st
Harkness Mrs. Assembly st
Heron Mrs. Wm. 96, High st
Heslop Miss Isabella, Maxwelltown
Hewetson Mrs. Margaret, 16, Castle st
Hunter Mrs. A. 70, English st
Hutcheson Mrs. Queen st
Hyslop Misses, Irish st
Hyslop Mr. Wm. Shakespeare st
Inglis Rev. Wm. 12, Lowerburn st
Inman Mr. John, St. Michael's st
Jardine Mr. James, Carsewell
Jardine Mr. Robert, 11, Buccleugh st
Johnston Mr. And. jun. Shakespeare st
Johnston Miss Mary, 13, Buccleugh s
Kennedy Mr. John, Academy st
Key Miss Jane, Castle st
Kirkpatrick Miss Isabella, Albion place
Lawson Mrs. Assembly st
Longley Captain John, Maxwelltown
Lowden Miss, Nith bank
Mc Caskie Mrs. Elizbeth, 4, Buccleugh st
Macourtie Mrs. 12, Castle st
Mc Culloch Alex. esq. (of *Ardwell*) St. Michael's st
Mc Culloch Miss Janet, 4, Buccleugh st
Mc Doole Captain Robt. Castle st
Mc Ghie Mrs. Friars Vennel
Mc Kean Mrs. Thos. 21, Castle st
Mc Murdo Colonel Bryce, Irish st
Mc Murdy Mrs. Jane, 17, Buccleugh st
Mc Murphy Colonel Archibald, 9, Castle st
Mc Robert Mr. Jas. 38, High st
Manuel Captain George, Albion place
Martin Miss Agnes, Maxwelltown
Maxwell Mrs. Edward, Irish st
Maxwell Miss Margaret, 1, Castle st

RESIDENT GENTRY.

Maxwell Wellwood, esq. Irish st
Melville Mr. Andrew, Castle st
Miller Major Wm. Nunfield cottage
Mitchelson Miss, 160, High st
Moffat Mrs. Grace, Nith bank
Moffat Mrs. Queen st
Monies Wm. esq. Upper Netherwood
Newall Mrs. Agnes, 21 Castle st
Newall Mrs. David, Lowerburn st
Nicholson Mrs. Queen st
Pagan Miss Mary, Albion place
Paterson Mrs. Elizabeth, Maxwelltown
Porteous Mrs. 62, High st
Potter Mrs. 54, High st
Richardson Mrs. Ann, Rose bank
Richardson Mrs. Elizabeth, Irish st
Roan Mr. James, 44, Queensberry st
Robertson Mrs. Assembly st
Rogerson Mrs. Dawson's Cottage
Ross Miss, St. Michael's st
Sanderson Mrs. Lower Netherwood
Scot Rev. Alexander, D. D. St. Michaels st
Silver Mrs. Major, Shakespeare st
Simson Mr. John, Maxwelltown

Simson Mr. Simon, Pleasauce
Smith Miss, Irish st
Smith Misses, Troqueer
Spalding Mrs. 14, Buccleugh st
Staig David, esq. St. Michael's st
Staig John, esq. Huntingdon lodge
Stewart Mr. John, 70, English st
Stott Ebenezer, esq. Castle dyke
Sutherland Alex. esq. 9, Buccleugh st
Swainson Captain Francis, Troqueer
Sweetman Mrs. Irish st
Thomson William, esq. George st
Thorburn James, esq. Kalton
Walker Mrs. Margaret, Kalton manse
Wallace Miss, 4, High st
Watson Mrs. Mary, Maxwelltown
Welch Mrs. Eliz. Albion place
White Mr. Thomas, St. Andrew st
Whiteley Mrs. 159, High st
Whyte Mrs. Moss lane end
Wight Miss, Waterloo st
Williams Mrs. Castle street
Winlaw Mrs. Shakespeare st

MERCHANTS, TRADESMEN, &c.

ACADEMIES.
(Ladies Boarding and Day.)
Bushby Mrs. 24, Castle street
Laidlaw Misses, Nith place
Riddick Miss, High street
Ridley Miss, 10, English street
Roberts Miss, 44, High street

ARCHITECTS.
Newall Walter, High street
Thomson Jas. (& builder) Moat

AUCTIONEERS.
Anderson Robt. 20, Fleshmarket st
Dawson John, King street
Johnston George, Whitesands
Kerr James, King street
Richardson John, High street

BAKERS & FLOUR DLRS.
Barber John. 2, Friars vennel
Beveridge David, Maxwelltown
Chalmers Wm. St. Michael street
Chambers James, St. Michael st
Corson James, jun. 88, High st
Grierson Samuel, 18, English st
Hume John, 13, English street
Mc Kune Kenneth, 143, High st
Mc Lachlan Margaret, 13, High st
Mc Niel James, 25, High street
Montgomery Andrew, 103, High st
Murray Francis, 79, High street
Murray Roger, 12, Queensberry st
Newbigging Robert, 24, English st
Nicholson Joseph, St. David st
Shorthouse James, Maxwelltown
Shortridge Robert, Maxwelltown
Smith John, 60, High street
Wright Margaret, 9, High street

BANKS.
(Open from ten to three.)
Bank of Scotland, Irish st ; John
 Barker esq. agent ; draw on
 Coutts & Co. London
British Linen Co. High street ;
 John Commelin esq. agent ;
 draw on Smith, Payne and Co.
Commercial Bank of Scotland ;
 J. Mc Diarmid esq. 117, High
 street, country agent.
Galloway James, John Napier esq.
 attends at the King's Arms Inn
 every Wednesday and Thursday.

BLACKSMITHS.
Chalmers J. Maxwelltown
Hainning Wm. 40, High street
Haugh George, Whitesands
Hiddlestou Robt. 5, Fleshmarket st
Johnston Robert, Maxwelltown
Kirkpatrick Chas. 1, St. Andrew st
Lightbody James, Townhead st
Mc Nay Robert, Maxwelltown
Moffat William, Maxwelltown
Muir James, Shakespeare street
Muir Robert, Lowerburns street
Shanks Andrew, Brewery street
Smart Wm. 36, St. Andrew street
Thomson John, Muirs close, 136,
 High street

BLEACHERS.
Cruickshank John & Son, Trailflat ;
 John Millar, agent, High st
Cruickshank John, jun. Closeburn ;
 Jas. West, agent, Council stairs
Henry John, Sandbed ; Joseph
 Welsh, gent, 5, English street

BOOKBINDERS.
Dunbar John, 77, English street
Dunlop Charles, Maxwelltown
Henry James, 28, Buccleugh st

BOOKSELLERS, BINDERS AND STATIONERS.
Anderson Allan, (& library) 69,
 High street
Anderson John, (and library) 74,
 High street
Fraser Wm. 107, High street
Halliday David, 163, High street
Johnston John, (and library) 33,
 High street
Sinclair James, 90, High street
Sinclair John, 132, High street

BOOT & SHOE MAKERS.
Anderson Peter, 162, High street
Ballantine Wm. 74, Queensberry st
Gordon John, 39, Friars vennel
Henderson Peter, 139, High st
Henderson Wm. Bank street
Hunter John, Maxwelltown
Irving Peter, 90, Friars vennel
Irving Walter, 32, Friars vennel
Irving William, 64, High street
Kelly John, Maxwelltown
Mc Clellan Alex. 140, High st

Mc Clellan James, 17, High st
Mc Clellan Jno. 14, Friars vennel
Mc Clellan Robert, Nith place
Mitchell John, 168, High street
Murdoch James, 9, English street
Nibloe James, 26, Friars vennel
Primrose Saml. 80, Friars vennel
Roan John, Shakespeare street
Scott Robert, 60, English street
Scott Walter, 50, Friars vennel
Shanks James, 2, Brewery street
Shanks Walter, Friars vennel
Shaw John, 65, Queensberry st
Shortridge John, Maxwelltown
Smith Charles, 70, English street
Spence Samuel, 23, New Flesh
 Market street
Underwood James, 11, High st
Wilson John, 42, English street
Wilson Joseph, 30, English street
Wilson Wm. 4, Friars vennel

BRASS FOUNDERS.
Aitken William, 56, High street
Stafford John, Maxwelltown

BREWERS.
Corson James, 28, Irish street
Grierson Samuel, 18, English st
Lammie William, Whitesands
Richardson Wm. St. Michael st
Shortridge James, Maxwelltown
Shortridge Robert, Maxwelltown

CABINET MAKERS.
Donaldson Geo. 74, Queensberry st
Gregan & Creighton, (& uphol-
 sterers) 163, High street
Halliday John, Maxwelltown
Howat James, Maxwelltown
Kerr & Gibson, (& upholsterers)
 17, Queensberry street
Mc Gowan John, 26, High street
Mc Lean Wm. Maxwelltown
Mitchell John, 38, Irish street
Reid Thomas, 86, English street
Robb Charles, St. David street
Robb Charles, jun. Castle street

CARTWRIGHTS.
Gillies William, Maxwelltown
Mc Corty John, Troqueer

CARVERS AND GILDERS.
Mc Pherson James, High street
Mc Pherson Robert, High street

Roberts Thomas, Assembly street
Stott James, Church place

CHAIR MAKERS.
Black Samuel, Maxwelltown
Nicholson Wm. 4, Queensberry st

CLOTHES DEALERS.
Love John, Brewery street
Mc Cluskey Peter, Brewery st
Michael James, 89, Friars vennel
Morgan Thomas, Brewery street
Wemyss James, New Bridge st

CLOG & PATTEN MAKERS.
Carruthers Wm. 93, Friars vennel
Cunningham Jas. Maxwelltown
Cunningham Jos. 11, Academy st
Graham Robert, Maxwelltown
Grierson Alex. Maxwelltown
Kennedy Andrew, Maxwelltown
Locke Thomas, Maxwelltown
Moffat Joseph, Friars vennel
Moffat Thomas, High street
Richardson Wm. 33, Irish street

COACH MAKERS.
Beck Joseph, English street
Bell William, Irish street

CONFECTIONERS.
Bell Euphemia, 135, High street
Dick William, 76, English street
Taylor William, 63, High street

COOPERS.
Beattie Robt. Long close, High st
Mc Bornie John, Maxwelltown
Maxwell Jas. 68, Queensberry st
Moffat William, Irish street
Scott Robert, 25, Queensberry st

CORK CUTTERS.
Armstrong James, Brewery st
Leighton Miles, (and drysalter) Assembly street
Turner James, 44, High street

CURRIERS & LEATHER CUTTERS.
Holmes Ths. & Co. Shakespeare st
Nicholson James, High street
Nicholson John, 136, High st
Primrose Jas. 100, Friars vennel
Wemyss John, 21, English street

CUTLERS.
Hinchsliffe Mark, 3, English st
Rae William, Maxwelltown

DISTILLERS.
Barry Wm. & Son, 2, Buccleugh st

DRESS MAKERS.
Bruce Mary, 10, High street
Byers Ann, 66, High street
Dalzell Sarah, Grey Friars street
Dick Jane, 2, Grey Friars street
Fraser Miss, 17, Academy street
Haig Margaret, Assembly street
Hogg Miss, Bank street
Howat Misses, 82, High street
Ramsay Miss, Queen street
Smith Miss, 141, High street
Wallace Miss, Castle street
Wilson Miss, Shakespeare street
Young Miss, Irish street

DYERS.
Armstrong Robert, 3, Whitesands
Brown James, Maxwelltown
Holliday George, (& tea dealer) 8, English street
Lowrie John, Maxwelltown
Thomson Andrew, St. Michael st
Wilson Robert, 36, Irish street

EARTHENWARE & CHINA DEALERS.
Adams Wm. 62, Friars vennel

Billington Mary, 12, St. Andrew st
Bryden Joseph, 16, High street
Carruthers John, Church place
Crosbie Janet, 122, High street
Doherty Peter, 63, Friars vennel
Grainger Robert, 45, High street
Hume George, (& draper) Friars vennel
Rodick John, 14, English street
Waugh Thomas, 27, High street

FIRE & LIFE INSURANCE AGENTS.
ALLIANCE, Jas. Broom, 54, High st
ATLAS, Jas. Wright, 12, English st
EAGLE, Wm. Carson, 85, English st
EDINBURGH LIFE ASSURANCE Co. Gordon & Harkness, 5, High st
GLOBE, James Richardson, 7, English street
HERCULES, James Keddie, Bank of Scotland, and J. H. Affleck, Bank street
INSURANCE Co. OF SCOTLAND, John Richardson, 4, Church pl
NORWICH UNION, J. Mc Diarmid, 117, High street
PHOENIX, Wm.Grierson,51,High st
SCOTTISH UNION, Wm. Thomson, jun. Queen street
SUFFOLK, Gregan and Creighton, 163, High street
UNITED EMPIRE, David Johnston, writer, Castle street, and John Johnston, bookseller, High st
WEST OF ENGLAND, Archibald Hamilton, 72, English street

FLAX DRESSERS.
Bryden Joseph, 16, High street
Hepburn Andw. 4, St. Andrew st
Knight Edw. 34, Friars vennel
Little George, 70, Friars vennel
Thomson Robt. 80, Friars vennel

FLESHERS.
Cameron Richard, Maxwelltown
Dalrymple Wm. Maxwelltown
Davidson Gilbert, Maxwelltown
Gibson Robert, Maxwelltown
Howat Alexander, Fleshmarket
Mc Kune John, Maxwelltown
Mc Kune Joseph, Maxwelltown
Mason John, Maxwelltown
Morrine James, Fleshmarket
Musgrave Wm. Brewery street
Paxton John, Maxwelltown
Roan James, Fleshmarket
Roan James, jun. Friars vennel
Selkirk Alex. Friars vennel
Selkirk David, Friars vennel
Selkirk Wm. Fleshmarket
Steell Robert, Maxwelltown
Sturgeon James, Fleshmarket
Sturgeon Wm. Fleshmarket
Thomson Benjamin, Maxwelltown
Thomson Benj. jun. Maxwelltown
Thomson James, Maxwelltown
Thomson Wm. Maxwelltown

GLOVERS.
Kennedy Ann, 161, High street
Woodmas John, 165, High street

GLUE MANUFACTURERS.
Affleck Thomas, Bank street
Watt Wm. Mill street

GROCERS AND SPIRIT DEALERS.
Affleck Thomas, (and salt and oil merchant) Bank street
Armstrong Christ. 11, High st
Armstrong Christ. jun. Brewery st
Bairden Thomas, 74, English st
Beck Thomas, 28, Queensberry sq
Bell John, (& meal) Maxwelltown
Bendall James, 68, Friars vennel

Black John, 64, English street
Blair Robert, 78, Queensberry st
Brand John, 48, High street
Brown Wm. 58, Queensberry st
Craig Janet, Maxwelltown
Crosbie David, 125, High street
Crosbie James, 17, English street
Currie James, 5, Queensberry sq
Dickson George, 3, Friars vennel
Dinwiddie David, 41, English st
Dinwoodie Rbt. 13, Queensberry st
Edgar John, 29, Friars vennel
Farrish Wm. St. Michael street
Ferguson James, Maxwelltown
Ferguson Jos. 43, Queensberry st
Ferguson Thos. 5, Queensberry st
Fleming Andrew, Maxwelltown
Fraser Wm. (& snuff dealer) 95, High street
Gaws William, Maxwelltown
Gordon James, 94, Friars vennel
Hagget Jane, 1, Queensberry st
Hope John, 37, Queensberry st
Inman Robert, 45, Friars vennel
Jamieson John, Maxwelltown
Johnston James, Maxwelltown
Little James, 35, High street
Loban Barbara, 11, New Bridge st
Locke Thomas, Maxwelltown
Lookup Wm. Maxwelltown
Mc Burnie Thos. Maxwelltown
Mc Dougall John, Maxwelltown
Mc George Jn. 32, Queensberry sq
Mc George John, 2, Nith place
Mc George Wm. 30, Queensberry sq
Mc Gowan Mary, 59, Englishst
Mc Harg Robt. 50, Queensberry st
Mc Kean Adam, 13, New Bridge st
Mc Knoe Susan, 50, English st
Mc Lean David, 59, Friars vennel
Mc Michael Alex. 80, High street
Mc Minn John, 14, Townhead st
Mc Quhae William, 3, Chapel st
Mc Vitie John, 61, Queensberry st
Mc Vitie Wm. 59, Queensberry st
Mc Whir James, 70, English st
Martin James, 13, Church place
Millar George, 29, Queensberry sq
Miller Ann, Friars vennel
Milligan John, 38, Friars vennel
Mitchell John, Maxwelltown
Mundell Wm. 158, High street
Murray Thomas, 120, High street
Nairman Thomas, 48, English st
Newall James, St. Michael street
Nicholson Jonah, 142, High st
Osburn Robert, Maxwelltown
Park Wm. 71, English street
Parkins Joseph, St. Michaels st
Paterson Samuel, 11, English st
Paterson Wm. Maxwelltown
Richardson James, 7, English st
Robertson Geo. 1, Fleshmarket st
Scott George, 2, Church place
Sloan Jas. & Rbt. 2, Queensberry sq
Smith James, Maxwelltown
Spencer John, 68, Queensberry st
Stewart Ann, 68, English street
Thomson Ann, St. Michael street
Thompson John, 81, High street
Thomson John, 12, Friars vennel
Thomson Robert, (grocer and seedsman) 57, High street
Thomson Wm. 95, High street
Thorburn Jas. 15, Queensberry st
Towns William, 75, English st
Walker John, Maxwelltown
Watson Edward, 22, English st
Will Andrew, Maxwelltown
Wilson Elizabeth, Maxwelltown
Young Janet, 7, St. Andrew st

GUNSMITH.
Bell David, 17, Castle street

Johnston Thos. 10, New Flesh-market street
Kennan John, 27, Bucclengh st
Kerr Thomas, St. David street

HAIR DRESSERS.
Campbell Andrew, (& perfumer) 137, High street
Dickson Samuel, 145, High street
Hope James, (and perfumer) 6, English street
King Peter, 23, Queensberry st
Mc Caskie Robt. 17, Friars vennel
Mc Donald Jno. 55, Friars vennel
Robertson Andw. Shakespeare st
Simpson Jas. 19, Queensberry st
Smith William, (and perfumer) 2, English street
Stewart John, 16, New Bridge st

HAT MANUFACTURERS. AND DEALERS.
Bailieff Joseph, 123, High street
Bailieff Wm. & Son, St. David st, and 22, High street
Beattie John & Co. St. Michaels st
Nicholl Robert, 15, English st
Thomson John, 15, High street

HOSIERY MANUFACTURERS.
Burgess Robert, 13, High street
Milligan Jas. 10, New Bridge st
Pagan John, 10, English street
Scott & Dinwiddie, 37, English st
Shore George, 22, English street
Wright Wm. 2, St. Andrew st

INNS.
Commercial, Jane Williamson, 21, High street
Crown, Edward Dove, High st
Dumfries and Galloway Hotel, Ambrose Clarke, Assembly st
Globe, James Ewan, 138, High st
Kings Arms, John Fraser, High st
Kings Arms, Joseph Pagan, Glasgow street, Maxwelltown

IRON FOUNDERS.
Affleck John, Maxwelltown
Porter R. W. & R. Maxwelltown

IRON MERCHANTS.
Affleck Thomas, Bank street
Blair Robert, 78, Queensberry st
Paterson & Son, 28, High street
Sloan John & Robert, 3, Queensberry square

IRONMONGERS.
Bell John, 109, High street
Bell Robert, English street
Clark John, (& hosier) Maxwelltown
Gray David, High street
Lonsdale & Co. 29, High street
Watt Robert, (and smith and bell hanger) 37, High street

JEWELLERS AND SILVERSMITHS.
Hinchsliffe Jos. Walker, 126, High st
Hinchsliffe Mark, 3 English st

JOINERS & CARPENTERS
Bell John, Burns street
Colvin & Sons, 50, Queensberry st
Dickson Adam, Maxwelltown
Forsyth John, Maxwelltown
Gregan & Crighton, 163, High st
Grierson Edward, White sands
Johnston Christopher, High st
Kerr Jas. Turnpike, Maxwelltown
Laurie Wm. Long close, Irish st
Mc Clellan Robert, (ship) Kalton

Mc Cubbin & Geddes, Maxwelltown

LINEN AND WOOLLEN DRAPERS.
Anderson Andrew, 101, High st
Anderson James, 41, High street
Berwick John, 59, High street
Bland Samuel, 92, High street
Bland Robert, 1, Queensberry sq
Corrie Jno. & Robt. 114, High st
Gracie Thomas, 118, High street
Grierson Willam, (and dealer in upholstery articles) 51, High st
Hair John, 55, High street
Hogg James, 52, High street
Howat William, 104, High street
Mc George John, 81, English st
Mc Kay Robert, 61, High street
Mc Kay Wm. Maxwelltown
Montgomery George, 100, High st
Reid James, 72, High street
Richardson James, Behind Mid Steeple, High street
Riddock John, Castle street
Shaw Wm. & James, 98, High st
Swan James, 49, High street

MANUFACTURERS.
Kerr Isaac, (damask) Lowerburn st
Mc Kay Jno. (cotton) Maxwelltown
Morrison John, (damask) Maxwelltown
Sloan John, (damask & carpets) Dock head

MASONS & BUILDERS.
Affleck Robert, Chapel street
Aitken John, 13, Academy street
Herries & Edgar, Maxwelltown
Mc Craken John, Queen street
McCubbin & Geddes, Maxwelltown
Mc Gowan William, High street
Roxburgh Edward, High street
Samson & Mc Caig, Maxwelltown
Smith Robert, St. David street
Stewart John, High street

MEAL DEALERS.
Dickson David, Maxwelltown
Rae John, 73, Queensberry street
Russel James, Maxwelltown

MESSENGERS AT ARMS.
Baird Charles, High street
Dawson Edward, High street
Haining Thomas
Hamilton Archd. 72, English st
Hannay Alex. (& notary) Bank st
Irving John, jun. Bank street
Johnston Dav. (& notary) Castle st
Kemp Robt. (& notary) High st
Lowden John, Assembly street
Wallace Robert, 141, High street

NAIL MAKERS.
Boyd William, Maxwelltown
Graham John, 5, Fleshmarket st
Holden Andrew, Maxwelltown
Lewis George, St. Michael street
Mc Kinnell John, Queensberry st
Maxwell William, 4, High street
Russel John, 40, Queensberry st
Russel Joseph, 18, Queensberry st
Russel Thomas, 51, English street
Thomson Wm. 28, English street
Wood Robert, 76, Queensberry st

NEWSPAPERS.
Dumfries and Galloway Courier, published every Tuesday by Jno. Mc Diarmid & Co. 117, High st
Dumfries Weekly Journal, published every Tuesday by Wm. Carson, 85, English street

NURSERY & SEEDSMEN.
Hood Thomas, Pleasance
Hood William, 110, High street
Irving Robert, Maxwelltown
Learmont John, English street
Mc Ken Thomas & Robert, Maxwelltown

OPTICIAN AND LOOKING GLASS MAKER.
Stott James, 6, Church place

PAINT MANUFACTURER
Affleck Thomas, Bank street

PAINTERS & GLAZIERS.
Marked thus * are Painters only.
Anderson Allan, St. David street
*Carruthers Francis, (sign and portrait) 87, High street
Crosby John, Maxwelltown
Dinwiddie Jas. 42, Friars vennel
*Mc Diarmid Jas. K. (& japanner) 121, High street
*Mc Kinnell James, Bucclengh st
Mc Pherson Thomas, 14, High st
Martin David, 23, English street
Thomson James, 1, Church place
Wightman Wm. 63, Queensberry st

PAVIERS.
Bigham Wm. 73, Queensberry st
Mc Guffie James, King street

PHYSICIANS.
Laing John, 14, Castle street
Maxwell William, Castle street
Melville Alexander, Castle street
Symons John, 6, High street

PLASTERERS.
Crockett Thos. 7, Friars vennel
Kerr James, High street

PRINTERS. (LETTER-PRESS.)
Bruce Norman Mc Leod, (& copper plate) 26, Queensberry sq
Carson William, 85, English st
Mc Diarmid Jn. & Co. 117, High st
Mc Lauchlan Isabella, 34, High st

PUBLICANS.
Armstrong Geo. 22, Queensberry st
Benson John, 20, High street
Brown John, 42, Brewery street
Buchanan John, 18, King street
Campbell Robt. 26, Queensberry st
Carrick James, High street
Corrie William, New Bridge st
Crosbie Robert, 40, Queensberry st
Dalziel Martha, 36, Queensberry st
Dickson Allison, 44, Queensberry st
Dobson Jn. Carruthers, 156, High st
Farries John, 62, High street
Fergusson John, 80, English st
Gowanlock Ths. 16, Queensberry st
Graham Mary, 42, Queensberry st
Harris Margaret, 11, High street
Hetherington John, High street
Hunter Ellen, 40, Queensberry st
Huntington Thos. 9, Assembly st
Hyslop James, White sands
Irving John, 24, High street
Johnson John, 12, Chapel street
Johnston Arch. 40, Queensberry st
Johnston George, 4, Whitesands
Johnston James, 36, High street
Johnston Mrs. 44, Queensberry st
Johnston Thomas, White sands
King Charles, Waterloo street
Mc Gill David, 91, Friars vennel
Mc Kinnell Rbt. 36, Queensberry st
Mc Kune Jno. Long close, High st
Mc Lachlan Wm. 72, English st
Mc Naught Eliz. 97, Friars vennel
Moffat Archd. 41, Friars vennel
Muirhead Janet, St. Michael st

Nairne Mary, 12, High street
Neilson Robert, Nith place
Osmotherlay Wm. 136, High st
Papple Robert, 1, Brewery street
Paterson Edw. 14, Queensberry st
Powell John, Friars vennel
Quaile Edward, 136, High street
Rae Jno. (& grocer) St. Michael st
Ralton Isabella, 117, High street
Rawline Thomas, 12, High street
Richardson Fraser, 119, High st
Richardson Rbt. 48, Queeusberry st
Rigg Mary, 40, High street
Scott Deborah, 1, Academy street
Sinclair James, 93, High street
Sinnock John, (& livery stables)
Whitesands
Sloan John, Friars vennel
Smith John, Maxwelltown
Smith Marion, 24, High street
Thomson John, Brewery street
Thomson John, 30, High street
Weems William, Maxwelltown
Wells Thos. 29, Queensberry st
Wood John, Mill street

ROPE & TWINE MAKERS.
Armstrong George, Queensberry st
Fearon Thomas, Maxwelltown
Knight Edwd. 31, Friars vennel
Turner George, Maxwelltown

SADDLERS.
Anderson Charles, 17, High street
Black John, Maxwelltown
Coulthard John, 78, English st
Findlater Peter, 1, Friars vennel
Lancaster Jos. 58, Friars vennel

SHERIFF OFFICERS.
Neilson David, Queensberry st
Richardson John, High street
Ross Robert, High street

SHIP OWNERS.
Allan John
Gillespie John
Hair George
Locke James
Mc Harg Robert
Mc Whir James
Miller George
Neilson Robert
Pateron James
Sinclair John
Thomson George
Thomson John
Thomson Robert
Thomson William
Walker James

SKINNERS.
Lookup Alexander, Mill street
Watt William, Mill street
Woodmas Hugh, Mill street

SLATERS.
Baxter Walter, English street
Bridges Audw. 40, Queensberry st

SPIRIT DEALERS.
Bendall Edwd. 76, Queensberry st
Dickie Wm. (& ale) 67, English st
Glover George, 79, Queensberry st
Kerr William, 100, High street
Mc Naught Isabella, 79, English st
Mc Naught Wm. 98. Friars vennel
Neilson Thos. 52, Friars vennel

STRAW HAT MAKERS.
Campbell Martha, 5, Church place
Irving Janet, 31, Irish street
Kerr Jane, 31, Lowerburn street
Phillips & Preston, 70, High street
Thomson Mary, 108, High street

SURGEONS & DRUGGISTS.
Marked thus * are Surgeons only.
*Blacklock Arch. R. N. 32, Castle st
Corrie Robert, 85, High street
Fraser James, 111, High street
*Haugh Thomas, Irish street
Mc Craken Wm. 46, High street
*Mc Ghie John, Friars vennel
Mc Lauchlan James, 1, English st
*Mc Minn John, 18, Buccleugh st
*Maxwell Wm. 54, High street
Neilson Peter, 134, High street
Primrose John, 167, High street
Robson Alexander, 25, Castle st
*Shortridge Sml. M. D. 18, High st
*Spalding James, Buccleugh st

TAILORS.
Borthwick Geo. Long close, High st
Costin Robert, Maxwelltown
Hanning Edward, (& clothier) 56, Friars vennel
Johnston Alex. 16, English street
Kerr John, 57, Queensberry st
Kerr Samuel, 60, Friars vennel
Mc Connell R. Maxwelltown
Mc Keand Wm. Friars vennel
Mc Kerr Nathaniel, 20, Castle st
Maxwell Alex. Maxwelltown
Montague James, Maxwelltown
Parker James, Friars vennel
Richardson Wm. B. 12, Church pl
Thomson William, 2, Chapel st

TALLOW CHANDLERS.
Riddick John, 23, St. Andrew st
Riddick Samuel, Friars vennel
Smith Wm. Friars vennel

TANNERS.
Crosbie Thomas, Shakespeare st
Hairstens Ths. & Jn. Maxwelltown
James John, Shakespeare street
Kennedy Robert, Nith place
Lookup Alexander, Mill street
Primrose Jas. 106, Friars vennel
Thomson John, Maxwelltown
Thorburn Thomas, Clerk hill
Watt William, Mill street

TEACHERS.
Affleck Alex. (English) Lower-burn street
Borthwick ——, (dancing) High st
Gemmill Wm. (English) 2, Grey Friars street [welltown
Halliday John, (English) Max-
Heslop Joseph, (gentlemen's day academy)19, NewFleshmarket st
Manners Jno. Christopher, (music) New Fleshmarket street
Neilson Robt. (English) Irish st
Tillock James, (dancing) Irish st
Wall Thomas, (English) 3, St. Andrew street
Wright James, Maxwelltown

TIMBER MERCHANTS.
Hair George, White sands
Neilson & Mc Whir, White sands
Reid Thomas, White sands
Sloan James & Robt. White sauds
Thomson & Dunn, White sauds
Walker John & Son, Bank street

TIN PLATE WORKERS AND PLUMBERS.
Clark John, 106, High street
Milligan Thomas, 89, High street
Wilson John, 37, Friars vennel

TOBACCO MANUFACTURERS.
Mc Vicar Jno. 29, Queensberry st
Mitchell Nelson, Queen street
Mundell Robt. (dealer) 19, High st

TURNERS.
Beattie David, Maxwelltown
Bell William, 148, High street
Charters James, Mill street
Duncan William, Queensberry st
Strong William, 66, High street

UMBRELLA MAKERS.
Dickson David, 8, Castle street
Mc Clellan Hugh, 34, Friars vennel

UPHOLSTERERS.
Heron David, 7, Fleshmarket st
Reid George, 48, High street

WATCH AND CLOCK MAKERS.
Charters William, 67, High street
Chisholm & Son, 5, St. Andrew st
Ingram Richard, 156, High street
Mc Adam Robt. 94, Friars vennel
Mc Lachlan John, Friars vennel
Taylor William, 96, High street

WINE AND SPIRIT MERCHANTS.
Bryden John, 25, English street
Grive Thomas, 36, High street
Rankine Adam, Nith place, and New Bridge street
Reddick Alexander, 59, Irish st
Walker John & Son, Bank street

WOOLLEN DRAPERS AND CLOTHIERS.
Kerr James, (& merchant tailor) 130, High street
Kirkpatrick John, 87, High st
Oney Benjamin, 82, English st
Richardson B. 10, Church place
Richardson Wm. 12, Church place

WRITERS.
Marked thus * are also Notaries.
*Adamson Robert, Assembly st
*Armstrong & Martin, Irish street
Broom James, 54, High street
Dawson George, King street
Forsyth Philip, 34, High street
*Fraser Thomas, Irish street
*Gordon & Harkness, 5, High st
*Gordon & Primrose, 8, Buccleugh street
Gracie John F. 27, Queensberry st
Halliday William, 18, Castle st
Hamilton Archd. 72, English st
*Haenay Alexander, Bank street
Harkness Thos. junr. Assembly st
Laidlow William, Nith place
Locke Robert, 141, High street
Mc George Chas. 3, Queensberry sq
Mc Gowan William, Bank street
Moyses James Wm. 30, Irish st
*Murray Robert, 10, Castle st
Primrose Peter, 22, Friars vennel
Richardson John, 4, Church-place
Sanders John, Queen street
*Shortt & Johnstone, 11, Castle st
Smith Christopher, 65, English st
Spalding James, Buccleugh street
*Thomson James, Irish street
*Thomson Wm. jun. Queen st
*Thorburn John, High street
Threshie Robert, Court house
Threshie Robert, jun. Court house
*Wallace Robert, 141, High st
Wright James, 12, English street
*Young Alexander, Nith place

Miscellaneous.
Barnes Jno. stay maker, 36, Irish st
Carruthers John, wholesale merchant & brace maker, Church pl
Charters Jas. wool carding mill, Mill street [vennel
Coilart David, millwright, Friars

Cowan Saml. land surveyor, High st
Daniel Thomas, blacking maker, Friars vennel
Forsyth Saml. maltster, Ladyfield
Gillies Bryce, engraver, 89, High st
Hammond Jos. basket maker, 86, High street
Hogg Thomas, stamp-master, 24, Lowerburn street
Howat John, fishing-tackle maker, Maxwelltown
Hunter James, leather merchant, 144, High street
Mc Kinnell Wm. miller, Troqueer
Marshall & Son, plumbers, St. David street
Richardson Samuel, gardener and seedsman, English street
Steel James, pump borer, Maxwelltown
Wilson Charles, manufacturers agent, Maxwelltown

COACHES.

CARLISLE, the Robert Burns, from the Dumfries and Galloway Hotel, every Monday, Wednesday, and Friday afternoon at four, and every Tuesday, Thursday, and Saturday evening at half past five through Annan.

EDINBURGH, The Royal Mail, from the Kings Arms, High street, every morning at quarter before seven, through Moffat, &c. and returns every afternoon at half past three, in time for the mail to Castle-Douglas, Stranraer, and Portpatrick.

EDINBURGH, the Robert Burns, from the Dumfries and Galloway Hotel, every Monday, Wednesday, and Friday morning at eight, and returns the following afternoon at 5.

KILMARNOCK, the Robert Bruce, from the Dumfries and Galloway Hotel, at eight in the morning, during the Summer months.

LONDON and Carlisle, the Royal Mail, from the Kings Arms, High street, every evening at a quarter before seven, through Annan, and returns for Castle-Douglas, Stranraer, and Portpatrick, every afternoon at four.

LONDON, Carlisle, and Liverpool, the New Times, from the Kings Arms, High street, every evening at five, through Kendal, Lancaster, and Preston, and returns for Thornhill, Sanquhar, Mauchline, and Kilmarnock, every morning at eight.

LONDON, Carlisle, and Manchester, the Independent, from the Commercial Inn, every evening at five, through Kendal, Lancaster, Preston, Buxton, Derby, Leicester, Northampton, and St. Albans, and returns for Thornhill, Sanquhar, Cumnock, Mauchline, Catrine, Kilmarnock, and Glasgow, every morning at eight.

NEWTON-STEWART, the Express, from the Dumfries and Galloway Hotel, every Tuesday, Thursday and Saturday morning at ten, and returns the following afternoon at half past four.

CARRIERS.

ANNAN, Peter Johnston arrives and departs every Wednesday.
AUCHENCAIRN, Robt. Adamson from Castle st. every Wednesday.
CARLISLE and Newcastle, Jas. Baxter from High st. arrives every Wednesday, and departs same day.
CARLISLE, Peter Johnston, from High st. every Wednesday.
CASTLE-DOUGLAS, James Nash, and Wm. Anderson, every Wednesday.
CAUSEYHORN, Peter Cassidy, every Wednesday.
CRIEF, John Davidson, from 80, English st every Wednesday.
DALBEATIE, Robert Adamson, from Castle st. every Wednesday.
DALBEATIE, Thomas Button, from High st. every Wednesday.
DALRY, Alex. Good, from John Farries, every Wednesday.
ECCLEFECHAN, T. Nutman, from High st. every Wednesday.
EDINBURGH, Jas. Dickson, from 23, Queensberry st. arrives Monday, and departs on Thursday.
EDINBURGH, Walter Bell, from 26, Queensberry st. arrives on Wednesday, and departs on Saturday.
EDINBURGH, George Turner, from 14, Queen st. every Wednesday.
EDINBURGH, Wm. Butters, from Farries, High st. every Wednesday.

EDINBURGH, Thos. Buck, from 7, Assembly st, every Thursday.
EDINBURGH, John Dickson, from 33, Queensberry st. every Thursday.
EDINBURGH, Thomas Niven, from 17, Queensberry st. every Thursday.
EDINBURGH, Wm. Davidson, from 89, English st. every Saturday.
GATEHOUSE, Mrs. Rorison, from High st. every Wednesday.
GLASGOW, Wm. Black, from 26, Queensberry st. every Saturday.
GLASGOW, Robert Porteous, from High st. every Saturday.
KILPATRICK, Joseph Currie, from Papples, Brewery st. every Wednesday.
KILPATRICK, John Barclay, from G. Johnston's, Whitesands, every Wednesday.
KIRKCUDBRIGHT, Andrew Austin, from High st. every Wednesday.
KIRKBEAN, Joseph Copeland, from Farries, High st. every Wednesday.
KIRKBEAN, Mark Jardine from Johnston's Whitesands, every Tues. & Sat.
LOCHMABEN, James Hall, George Ellison, Gabriel Brown, every Wed.
LOCHERBIE, Wm. Mundell, from 80 English st. every Wednesday.
MOFFAT, John Kirkpatrick, from High st. every Wednesday.
NEW ABBEY, James Turner, from High st. every Wednesday.
NEW GALLOWAY, Wm. Clement, from High st. every Wednesday.
NEW GALLOWAY, Wm. Clement, from Farries, High st every Wednesday.
NEWTON-STEWART, John Gill, from High st. every Wednesday.
PARTON, John Thomson, from Farries, High st. Wednesday.
SANQUHAR, & Thornhill, John Walker, from 26, Queensberry st. arrives every Wednesday, and departs Saturday.
SOUTHWICK, John Carson, from Johnston's Whitesands, every Wednesday.
THORNHILL, & Sanquhar, Andrew Watson, from 22, Queensberry street, every Saturday.
THORNHILL, from 14, Queensberry st. every Saturday.
WIGTON, John Gill, from High st. every Wednesday.
WIGTON, Wm. Gibson, from High st. every Wednesday.

DUNSCORE,

HOLYWOOD, JOHNSTONE, KIRKMAHOE, KIRKPATRICK-JUXTA, WAMPHRAY.

DUNSCORE is a parish in the district of Nithsdale. The poet Burns rented a farm here for some years. Sheep and black cattle are reared for the southern markets. The river Nith runs through a part of it.

HOLYWOOD, an interesting parish, a short distance from Dumfries, is in a most delightful part of the county. The church is an exceedingly neat erection and much admired. In the church-yard are vestiges of an old abbey, built in the twelfth century.

JOHNSTONE parish is in the district of Annandale, joining that of Kirkpatrick-Juxta, and belongs to John Hope Johnstone, esq. of Raehills, whose elegant mansion, the only one in the parish, is the admiration of all who see it.

KIRKMAHOE parish, which is of a very irregular form, contains many small villages, and some pleasing scenery.

KIRKPATRICK-JUXTA is a parish near Moffat,

bounded on the north and east by the river Annan. It is of a triangular form, each side being about eight miles long, and the great road from Edinburgh to Dumfries passes through it. There are several interesting ruins of fortified places; as Auchincass castle, once the residence of Thomas Randolph, Earl of Murray, and Regent of Scotland in the minority of David Bruce; Loch House, formerly the residence of the Johnstones, of Corihead; the old tower of Kinnelhead, once belonging to the family of Chartres; and an old tower at Boreland, now the property of Hope Johnstone, esq. of Annandale.

WAMPHRAY.—The scenery in and around this parish is most beautiful, combining hills and wood, and several waterfalls add much to the general effect. The village and church have long been objects of interest, being romantically situated on the banks of the small river Wamphray, which meanders through the parish.

PLACES OF WORSHIP.

DUNSCORE—Rev. Robert Bryden, Minister
HOLYWOOD—Rev. Robert Kirkwood, A.M. Minister
JOHNSTONE—Rev. Robert Colvin, D.D. Minister

KIRKMAHOE—Rev. John Wightman, Minister
KIRKPATRICK-JUXTA—Rev. Wm. Singer, D.D. Minister
WAMPHRAY—Rev. Charles Dickson, Minister

PAROCHIAL SCHOOLS.

JOHNSTONE—Wm. Johnston, Master
KIRKMAHOE—Adam Robson, Master
KIRKPATRICK-JUXTA—Robert Mitchell, Master
WAMPHRAY—John Chartres, Master

RESIDENT GENTRY.

Anderson R. esq. of *Stroquhan*, Dunscore
Brown Mr. Alex. Dyke, Kirkpatrick-Juxta
Brown Mr. Wm. Cauldholm, Kirkpatrick-Juxta
Bryden Mr. Thomas, Kinnelhead, Kirkpatrick-Juxta
Johnston Geo. esq. (of *Cowhill*) Holywood
Johnston P. esq. (of *Carnsalloch*) Kirkmahoe
Johnstone Mr. James, Bearholm, Kirkpatrick-Juxta
Johnstone John Hope, esq. (of *Raehill*) Johnstone
Leny James Macalpine, esq. (of *Dalswinton*) Kirkmahoe
Lockhart W. E. esq. (of *Meikledale*) Kirkmahoe
Maxwell Alexander Harley, esq. (of *Portrack*) Holywood
Morin John, esq. (of *Carzeild*) Kirkmahoe
Paterson James, esq. (of *Langbedholm*) Kirkpatrick-Juxta
Renwick Mr. Herbert P. (of *Dumgree*) Kirkpatrick-Juxta
Renwick Mr. Herbert, Beattock, Kirkpatrick-Juxta
Renwick Mr. James, Cogrie, Kirkpatrick-Juxta
Scott Walter, esq. Palacekrow, Kirkpatrick-Juxta
Singer Rev. Dr. Minister, & Justice of Peace, Kirkpatrick-Juxta
Tod Mr. Wm. Chapel, Kirkpatrick-Juxta
Whigham G. esq. of Halliday-Hill, Dunscore
Younger Wm. esq. of Craiglands, Kirkpatrick-Juxta
Young S. D. esq. of Gullyhill, Holywood

BEATTOCK INN AND POSTING HOUSE

Kirkpatrick-Juxta two miles from Moffat,
Mr. Thos. Wilson, Proprietor

COACHES.

LONDON and Carlisle, The Royal Mail, from the Beattock Inn, every morning at one, and returns for Glasgow, every afternoon, at half-past three.

EDINBURGH, The Royal Mail, passes the Beattock Inn, every morning at nine, and returns for Dumfries, every afternoon at one.

ECCLEFECHAN,

DISTANT from Edinburgh 71 miles, from Glasgow 78, from Dumfries 16, from Carlisle 20, from Annan 6, from Moffat 22, from Lockerbie 6, from Lochmaben 10, from Thornhill 31, from Langholm 10, and from Sanquhar by Lochmaben and Thornhill 43, is a considerable village in the parish of Hoddam. It lies on the great mail road from Carlisle to Glasgow, and is much noted for its extensive fairs for cattle, &c. which are held on the first Friday after the 11th of January, the first Friday after the 11th of February, the first Friday after the 11th of March, the first Friday after the 11th of April, the first Friday after the 11th of May, the first Tuesday after the 11th of June, the first Friday after the 11th of July, the 26th of August, the 18th of September, (or the Friday before) the 26th of October, the Friday after the 11th of November, and the Friday after the 11th of December. A distillery is the only manufactory in the place, which otherwise contains only a few shops, &c. for the accommodation of the inhabitants and strangers. A small stream runs through the village, over which are thrown several small bridges or arches, for the purpose of crossing from one side of the street to the other.

POST OFFICE—Post Master, Mr. William Johnstone. The mail arrives from the South every day at half-past twelve, and is despatched every morning at half-past three. The mail arrives from the North every morning at half-past three, and is despatched every day at half-past twelve.

PLACES OF WORSHIP.

ESTABLISHED CHURCH—Rev. James Yourston, Minister, Hoddam, Manse

UNITED SECESSION CHAPEL—(No Minister)

PAROCHIAL SCHOOL.

William Gullen, Master

RESIDENT GENTRY.

Corrie Alex. esq. Newfield
Little William, esq. Crassfield
Miller Miss, Ecclefechan
Scott Alexander John. esq. Knock Hill

MERCHANTS, TRADESMEN, &c.

PROFESSIONAL GENTLEMEN.

Bell George, writer, notary, and messenger
Little George, surgeon
Simpson John, surgeon and apothecary

SHOPKEEPERS, TRADERS, &c.

Bean David, shoe maker
Beattie Wm. cotton manufacturer
Bell & Son, tailors
Bell George, publican & flesher
Bell George, mason & builder
Bell John, grocer, &c.
Bell Thos. publican & auctioneer
Brand James, carpenter
Brand Wm. tallow chandler and grocer

Carruthers A. mason and builder
Euston Peter, mason & builder
Farries George, publican
Farries Robert, flesher
Farries William, publican
Garthead John, tailor
Graham John, linen and woollen draper
Johnstone James, blacksmith
Johnstone Margaret, linen and woollen draper
Johnstone Wm. grocer & spirit dealer
Ker James, clog maker
Little Charles, Grapes & Commercial Inn
Mc Ghie Mary, grocer
Marshall James Robert, distiller
Marshall Wm. saddler & sheriff's officer

Miller John, shoe maker
Moffat H. clog maker
Park James, baker
Paterson Mary, grocer
Rae John, grocer
Reid John, carpenter & wheelwright
Scott Mrs. mail contractor
Scott Robert, blacksmith
Short Matthew, baker
Tait William, blacksmith
Weild Edwd. carpenter & glazier
White Robert, tailor
Wright John, tailor
Wright Walter, watch and clock maker

COACH.

GLASGOW, the Royal Mail, every day at half-past twelve, through Lockerbie and Beattock Bridge, and returns for Carlisle and the South, every morning at half-past three

CARRIERS.

CARLISLE, Wm. Johnston and James

Rae, every Friday, and return on Saturday.

DUMFRIES, Wm. Johnston, every Wednesday morning, and returns at night.

EDINBURGH, George Farrish, (occasionally) through Moffat and Lockerbie.

LOCKERBIE, James Rae, every Monday, and returns the same night.

LANGHOLM,

A Market town and parish in Dumfriesshire, 30 miles from Moffat, 21 from Carlisle, 12 from Longtown, 18 from Annan, 30 from Dumfries, 18 from Lockerbie, 70 from Edinburgh, and 322 from London by Carlisle and Borough Bridge, is delightfully situated on the banks of the Esk, which runs through the town, and over which there is a stone bridge of three arches. Langholm is a burgh of barony, the proprietor of which is his Grace the Duke of Buccleugh. That part of the town, which is situate on the left bank of the river, is called the New Town; in the market-place of the Old Town stands the town-hall and gaol, with its neat spire and clock. The church, which is built on a rising ground in the rear of the town, has nothing particular to recommend it, but the beauty of the surrounding scenery.

Langholm, which is governed by a baron baillie, appointed by the noble proprietor, contains a number of good shops, a banking house, a savings' bank, a worsted mill, a brewery, a distillery, dye-houses, &c. with two extensive libraries, and a well conducted parochial school. A court of request is held on the first Wednesday in each month, for the recovery of debts under forty shillings; and, on the same day, the Eskdale farmers' club meets at the Crown inn, for the discussion of agricultural topics. The market is held on Wednesday, and there are fairs on the 16th of April, the last Tuesday in May, old style, the 26th of July, the 18th of September, and in November; at the July fair are disposed of vast quantities of lambs; there are also two annual fairs for the hiring of servants.

POST OFFICE, Charles-street, New Town.—*Post Master*, Mr. James Little. The south mail arrives every day at half-past twelve, and is despatched every morning at three. The north mail arrives every morning at three, and is despatched every day at twelve.

PLACES OF WORSHIP.

ESTABLISHED CHURCH—Rev. W. B. Shaw, Minister
UNITED SECESSION CHAPEL—Rev. John Dobie, Minister
RELIEF CHAPEL—(No Minister)

PAROCHIAL SCHOOL.

NEW TOWN.

Thomas Scott, Master

NOBILITY AND GENTRY.

Bogie Mrs. Jane, High st
Borthwick Mrs. High st
Buccleugh, His Grace the Duke of, Langholm Lodge
Curll Mrs. Margaret, New Town
Dobie Rev. John, New Town
Henderson George, esq. High st
Henderson Geo. esq. baron bailie and surveyor of taxes, High st
Irvine Mrs. Thos. New Town
Irving Miss Janet, Market-place
Lawrie Mrs. Ann, New Town
Little Mr. Matthew, The Brow
Lundie Walter, esq. New Town
Malcolm Admiral Sir Pulteney, Irvin
Maxwell Captain Geo. High st
Maxwell George, esq. Broom Hall
Murray Mrs. Sarah, New Town
Shaw Rev. Wm. B. Manse

MERCHANTS, TRADESMEN, &c.

BAKERS.

Hume Wm. High st
Irving John, (& grocer) High st
Laidlow Wm. New Town
Thompson Wm. High st

BANK.

Leith Bank, High street; Archd. Scot, esq.; draw upon Hoare, Barnett, Hoare & Co. London

BLACKSMITHS.

Anderson Wm. New Town
Dalglish Thos. Drove st
Fletcher Thos. New Town
Scoon Walter
Welsh Thos. New Town

BOOT & SHOE MAKERS.

Aitchison Thos. (& clogger) New Town
Anderson Walter, New Town
Harestones Charles, New Town
Manderson Wm. High st
Martin Thos. New Town
White John, High st
Wilson John

BREWERS.

Irving & Scot, Drove st

CLOG MAKERS.

Armstrong John, Church Wynd
Elliot John, New Town
Grieve Archibald, High st
Scott Francis, (and last maker) High st

DISTILLERS.

Arnot John & Co.

DRESS MAKERS AND MILLINERS.

Armstrong Mary, Church Wynd
Browu Janet, Market-place
Donaldson Ellinor, High st
Hope Jane, (& straw hat) Market-place
Martin Frances, New Town
Roberts Elizabeth, High st

DYERS.

Bowman James, (& thread manufacturer) New Town
Brown Wm. Mill Town

FIRE OFFICES & AGENTS

CALEDONIAN, Andrew Irving
COUNTY, George Scott, jun.

FLESHERS.

Anderson Christopher, New Town
Clark David
Elliot John, High st
Hill John, High st

GROCERS AND SPIRIT DEALERS.

Anderson Elizabeth, New Town
Coulthard John, New Town
Elsdon Anthony, High st
Glendining John, (& ironmonger) High st

Grieve Archibald, High st
Grieve Wm. High st
Hervey Jane, (& meal dealer) New Town
Hogg Margaret
Hope Walter, High st
Irving Andrew, High st
Irving George, Market-place
Johnstone Mary, High st
Little George, High st
Park Thomas, High st
Reay Wm. (& baker) High st
Reid Thomas, New Town
Reid Walter, New Town
Thompson Joseph, New Town
Thorburn John, High st
Scott George, jan. Market-place
Warwick Walter, New Town
Warwick Wm. New Town
Young Mary, High st

HAIR DRESSERS.

Asplin Alexander
Scott Robert

INN.

Crown, Andrew Dow

JOINERS.

Armstrong Thos. (& cabinet maker) High st
Crowther James
Foster Walter, (& glazier) New Town
Johnston Wm.
Knox John, New Town

325

Mc Allister John, High st
Nichol Robert, New Town
Wilson Ninian, (& wheelwright) New Town

LINEN AND WOOLLEN DRAPERS.

Armstrong Elizabeth, High st
Irving Andrew, High st
Irving George, Market-place
Park Thos. High st
Scott Geo. jun. Market place
Somerville Hugh & Co.
Thorburn John, High st

MANUFACTURERS.

Reid David, (cotton) New Town
Reid Thos. (cotton) New Town
Yeoman Wm. & James, (stockings and lamb's wool) New Town

MASONS & BUILDERS.

Byers Christian, New Town
Hudson Alexander
Hudson John, New Town
Hudson John, jun. New Town
Scott Robert, New Town
Scott Robert, jun. New Town

MEAL DEALERS.

Armstrong James, New Town
Douglas Thomas, New Town
Tudhope James, High st
Veitch James, (& grocer)

MILLERS.

Beattie John, New Town
Graham Archibald, Langholm Mill

NAIL MAKERS.

Glendining John, High st
Lightbody Wm.
Thwaites John, High st

PHYSICIAN

Moffat James, High st

PUBLICANS.

Beattie Margaret, (Royal Oak) High st
Clark David
Elsdon Anthony, (Ship) High st
Hill John, (Shoulder of Mutton) High st
Jardine Eliz. (Globe) High st

Laidlow Wm. New Town
Little Peter, (Buck) High st
Lund Robert, High st
Reid Elizabeth, New Town
Reid James, High st
Rutherford Thomas, (Crown and Thistle) High st
Scott Robert
Smith Alex. High st
Telford Ptr. (King's Arms) High st
Thomson Elizabeth, High st
Thomson Marion, Market-place
Young John, (Salutation) High st

STRAW HAT MAKERS

Donaldson Ellen, High st
Miller Mary, High st

SURGEONS.

Little Peter, (& druggist) High st
Maxwell Wm. High st

TAILORS.

Anderson Robert, New Town
Beattie James, High st
Foster Thomas
Foster Thomas, jun.
Harkness George
Hunen William

TALLOW CHANDLERS.

Hope James, Drove st
Richardson Charles, High st

TANNER.

Paisley Walter, New Town

TIN PLATE WORKERS.

Coulthard John, (& plumber)
Duncan David, (& painter) High st

WATCH AND CLOCK MAKERS.

Carruthers George, High st
Graham John, High st
Johnston Samuel

WRITERS & NOTARIES.

Henderson & Scott, High st
Nichol Jno. (& messenger) High st

Miscellaneous.

Brown ——, nursery & seedsman, Home Head

Byers Andrew, hosier, New Tov
Clark John, saddler, High st
Dalglish Wm. auctioneer.
Fletcher Wm. cooper
Hope Walter, tobacconist, High st
Little Wm. teacher, New Town
Richardson Wallwood, bookseller and stationer, High st
Scott Geo. woollen draper, High st
Sinclair Wm. flax dresser, New Town

EXCISE OFFICE,

SALUTATION INN, HIGH-ST.

Mr. Wm. Gillispie, Collector
And two officers

STAMP OFFICE,

Wallwood Richardson, Distributor

COACHES.

LONDON and Carlisle, The Royal Mail, from the Crown Inn, every morning at three, and returns for Edinburgh every day at half-past twelve.
EDINBURGH, The Sir Walter Scott, from the Crown Inn, every Monday, Wednesday, and Friday evening at five; and to Carlisle the same mornings at ten.

CARRIERS.

EDINBURGH, and all intermediate places, John Hargreaves, from High-street, every Monday and Thursday morning.
EDINBURGH and all intermediate places, Anthony Welch, from New Town, every Monday and Thursday morning.
ANNAN, John Anderson, from the King's Arms, arrives on Monday, and departs the same day.
CARLISLE, John Little, from High-st arrives on Monday & Thursday, and departs the same days.
CARLISLE, Manchester, and all intermediate places, John Hargreaves, from High-street, every Wednesday and Saturday.
CARLISLE, Manchester, and all intermediate places, Anthony Welch, from New Town, every Wednesday and Saturday morning.

LOCHMABEN,

ON the borders of Castle-loch, and surrounded by a beautiful amphitheatre of hills, stands the ancient burgh of Lochmaben, distant from Edinburgh 65 miles, from Glasgow 70, Dumfries 8, Carlisle 30, Moffat 15, Lockerbie 4, Ecclefechan 10, Thornhill 21, Annan 13, Langholm 20, and Sanquhar 33. The period of its first erection into a royal burgh is of too remote a date for conjecture; its present charter was granted by James VI. and bears date 16th of July, 1612; from which it appears, that the town was more than once destroyed and burnt during the civil wars, its public edifices plundered, and its ancient records, &c. totally lost; but altho' the whole of the former privileges have been regained, the place itself has never recovered its former consequence. The remains of the once magnificent castle, which stood on a peninsula formed by the loch, and which was considered the strongest border fortress, next to that of Carlisle, are very extensive. In the year 1384 it was captured by Archibald Douglas, lord of Galloway, and it became the occasional residence of Robert Bruce, afterwards king of Scotland. In its present state sufficient remains to convince us, that it was a place of great strength, many of the walls being twelve feet thick, and the whole presents a beautifully picturesque mass of ruins. The loch which is about three miles in circumference, abounds with several sorts of fish; and it is a singular fact, that the vendish is not to be found any where else in Britain. The parish church is a handsome and convenient building in the pointed style, with a bold square tower, in which are two well toned bells. The first stone was laid on the 10th of April, 1818, and the church was opened for divine worship in July 1820. The expense of its erection amounted to about 3000l. it contains sittings for 1200 persons, but is capable of holding 1400. There is also a chapel for the united secession congregation and one for the Cameronians. The town house, with its tower and clock, stands at the end of the principal street. A subscription library affords literary and other information to the gentlemen by whom it is supported, and St. Magdalen's lodge of free masons is held here, as well as a royal arch lodge, which was chartered by Bruce, king of Scotland; there is also a savings' bank. The municipal government is vested in the hand of a provost, three bailies, a dean of guild, a treasurer, and 15 councillors. The market is discontinued, but fairs are held on the first Tuesdays of January, April, July, and October, all old style.

POST OFFICE.—*Post Master*, Mr. James Richardson. The mail from London and Edinburgh arrives every morning at six, and is despatched every day at twelve. The mail from Dumfries and the West arrives every day at twelve, and is despatched every morning at six.

Note. No letters are received from London on Tuesdays, nor any despatched on Fridays; and none are sent to Edinburgh on Saturdays.

PLACES OF WORSHIP.

ESTABLISHED CHURCH—Rev. Thos. Gibson, Minister
UNITED SECESSION CHAPEL—Rev. Andrew Young, Minister
CAMERONIAN CHAPEL—Rev. — Jeffrey, Minister

PAROCHIAL SCHOOL.

David Glover, Master

Municipal Government.

Robert Henderson, esq. Provost
Mr. John Wells
Dr. Thomas Brown ⎱Bailies
Mr. Robert Bryden ⎰
Mr. John Feadie, Dean of Guild
Mr. James Jardine, Treasurer and Town Clerk
And Ten Councillors

GENTRY AND CLERGY.

Bell Wm. esq. of Rammerscales
Brown Capt. James, of Mayfield
Brown Mr. Robert
Brown Wm. esq. of Newmains
Bryden Mr. Robert
Carruthers Miss Elizabeth
Carruthers Wm. Thomson, esq. of Dormont
Cruickshanks John, esq. of Trailflat
Dickson John Edgar, esq. Elshields
Farrish David, esq. (of *Todlamour*) Bankhead
Feadi Mr. John, Lochmaben
Gibson Rev. Thomas, Manse
Gordon Major Archibald, of Halleaths   [Excise]
Graham Mr. James, (late of the Excise]
Graham Mr. John   [head
Graham Matthew, esq. of Priesthead
Harkuess Mr. William
Henderson Capt. of Riggheads
Henderson Robert, esq.
Huggin Mrs.
Irving Mr. Francis
Jardine Sir William, bart. Jardine Hall
Mc Rae J. Charles, esq. of Holmains
Neilson Mr. William
Richardson Miss
Robertson Mr. John
Smaile Thos. esq. of Hightoe
Young Rev. Andrew

MERCHANTS, TRADESMEN, &c.

PROFESSIONAL GENTLEMEN.

Brown Thomas, surgeon
Dickson John, writer, messenger, and auctioneer
Jardine James, writer and messenger
Lindsay James, surgeon
Mc Donald John, architect

INNKEEPERS.

Crown, William Mitchell
Crown & Thistle, Wm. Smith
Sun, William Wilson

SHOPKEEPERS, TRADERS, &c.

Burgess Robert, flesher
Crimean Robt. grocer & spirit dlr.
Cruickshank John & Son, bleachers, Trailflat
Fraser John, painter and flax dresser
Gibson Robt. flax dresser
Gibson Wm. slater & town officer
Gibson Wm. ju n. slater

Graham John, flesher
Halliday Wm. clog maker
Henderson John, carpenter
Henderson Ths. boot & shoe mkr.
Hetherton John, grocer, draper, spirit dealer, agent for the Insurance Co. of Scotland
Inglis Wm. baker
Irving David, blacksmith
Jardine Walter, boot & shoe mkr.
Johnstone David, carpenter
Johnstone James, carpenter and millwright
Johnstone James, tailor
Johnstone Janet, dress maker
Johnstone Wm. stocking manufacturer
Kerr Wm. stocking manufacturer
Laurie Misses, dress makers
Lawson David, mason & builder
Lindsay Janet, dress maker
Lindsay J. stocking manufacturer
Lotimer J. grocer
Mc Caig Andrew, teacher, and watch & clock repairer
Mc Whirter John, stocking manufacturer

Maxwell John, stocking manufacturer
Miller Wm. tanner & skinner
Miller Wm. boot & shoemaker
Palmer Geo. mason & builder
Paterson Geo. carpenter
Richardson Jas. grocer & draper
Robertson Jane, straw hat maker
Smaile James, blacksmith
Smith Archibald, turner & wheelwright
Thomson John, blacksmith
Thorburn Jas. mason & builder
Thorburn Robert, tailor
Watt John, tailor
Wells John, painter & plasterer
Wells John, cooper
Wells Wm. boot & shoemaker
Wells Wm. cooper

CARRIERS.

DUMFRIES, James Hall, Geo. Ellison, and Gabriel Brown, every Wednesday, and return the same day.
GLASGOW, Geo. Green, once a fortnight.

LOCKERBIE,

SITUATED in the parish of Drysdale, and on the great mail road from Carlisle to Glasgow, is distant from the former 26 miles, from the latter 72, from Edinburgh 65, Dumfries 12, Annan 11, Ecclefechau 6, Moffat 16, Lochmaben 4, Langholm 18, Thornhill 20, and Sanquhar 32. It covers a considerable space of ground, the buildings possess a very neat appearance, and the surrounding country presents some fine scenery. The parish church is a very neat and convenient edifice, and the chapel belonging to the united secession congregation is a commodious building. A savings' bank, instituted in the year 1824, has been tolerably successful; there is also a masonic lodge; two friendly societies, and a circulating library have lately been opened. The market is held on Thursday, and from the commencement of October till the end of April it is extensively supplied with pork, at which not less than about 1800 carcases are sold during the season; there is also a market for the hiring of servants on the Thursday before old Martinmas. Fairs are held on the second Thursday in January, the second Thursday in February, the second Thursday in March, the second Thursday in April, the second Thursday in May, the third Thursday in June, and the second Thursday in August; (the last fair, which is for lambs, is the largest and last lamb fair in Scotland); a new one lately established for the sale of cattle in September, the second Thursday in October for cattle and horses, the second Thursday in November, and the Thursday before Christmas; all old style. These fairs add much to the prosperity of the town, most of them being well attended; the new one in September takes place the Thursday before the large fair, on Brough Hill, and is likely to become considerable.

POST OFFICE.—*Post Master*, Mr. John Johnstone. The mail arrives from the South every day at one, and is despatched every morning at three. The mail from the North arrives every morning at at three, and is despatched every day at one. The mail from Dumfries arrives every day at a quarter before one, and is despatched every morning at half past five.

PLACES OF WORSHIP.

ESTABLISHED CHURCH—Rev. John Henderson, Minister

UNITED SECESSION CHAPEL—Rev. J. Taylor, Minister

PAROCHIAL SCHOOL.
Alexander Fergusson, Master

GENTRY AND CLERGY.

Carruthers Wm. esq. (of *Dormont*)
Dalton Parish
Douglas John, esq. of Lockerbie
Halliday John, esq. of Dam

Henderson Rev. John, Drysdale Manse
Jardine John, esq. of Ladyward
Jardine Sir Wm. bart. (of *Applegirth*) Jardine Hall

Rae Mr. John, of Lockerbie
Stewart Chas. esq. of Hillside
Taylor Rev. Joseph, Lockerbie

MERCHANTS, TRADESMEN, &c.

AUCTIONEERS
AND SHERIFF OFFICERS.
Bell Francis, (& messenger, officer only)
Gifford Thomas
Jamieson Andrew
Jamieson John
Mundell Andrew, (officer only)
Wright George

BAKERS.
Dickson James
Shankland Robert
Wright John

BLACKSMITHS.
Black William
Hawkins Robert
Johnston Robert
Steel John

BOOT & SHOEMAKERS.
Dinwoodie William
Johnstone James
Johnstone John
Johnstone William
Kennedy & Mc Dowall

CARPENTERS & JOINERS.
Davidson Walter, (& cartwright)
Donaldson Robt. (& cabinet mkr)
Rae Robert
Williamson Robert, (& glazier)

CARTWRIGHTS.
Kerr John
Paterson John
Scott John

CLOG MAKERS.
Rae George
Wypers & Johnston

COOPERS.
Dickson James
Welsh John

DRESS MAKERS.
Dobie Jane
Linton Georgiana
Mundell Misses

FIRE OFFICES AND
AGENTS.
CALEDONIAN—Wm. Martin, writer
INSURANCE CO. OF SCOTLAND, Andrew Wright, writer

FLESHERS.
Dinwodie James
Dinwoodie John
Richardson John
Smith William

GROCERS
AND SPIRIT DEALERS.
Brand Robt. (& tallow chandler)
Gillespie James, (& publican)
Irving Wm. (& tallow chandler)
Jardine Mary
Johnston Janet, (and stamp office, and hardware dealer)
Johnstone John
Johnstone Wm. (& publican)
Johnston William
Little John, (& publican)
Pool Wm. (& hardwareman)

INNS.
Blue Bell, Eliz. Watters
King's Arms, Thos. Lawrence

LINEN AND
WOOLLEN DRAPERS.
Dobie William
Pagan John

MASONS & BUILDERS.
Gladstanes James
Masterton James
Murray Walter

MESSENGERS.
Martin William
Richardson William
Wright George

NAIL MAKERS.
Johnstone John
Mc Intosh John
Shennan Francis

PUBLICANS.
Dickson James
Dinwoodie James
Dinwoodie John
Dobie Mary
Jamieson John
Johnston Francis
Johnston John
Mc Queen Geo. Toll Bar
Richardson John
Shankland Robert
Smith William

SURGEONS.
Imrie John
Nwebigging Robert, MD. (& apothecary)

TAILORS.
Ferguson James
Murray James
Richardson Johnston
Thomson Samuel

TEACHERS.
Broadfoot Walter
Dobie William
Johnstone Misses

TURNERS
AND WHEEL MAKERS.
Jardine Alexander
Linton Alexander

WATCH & CLOCK
MAKERS.
Blacklock James
Forster Charles
Young George

WRITERS & NOTARIES.
Martin & Thomson
Richardson William
Wright George & Andrew

Miscellaneous.
Brown James, excise officer
Cairns — nurseryman, St. Mungo
Irving Misses, straw hat makers
Rae Andrew, tanner
Turner Wm. saddler
Walker Thos. bookseller, stationer, binder, and circulating library.

COACH.
GLASGOW, the Royal Mail, every day at one, and returns for Carlisle and the South, every Morning at three.

CARRIERS.
DUMFRIES, Wm. Mundell, every Wednesday.
EDINBURGH and Moffatt, Jas. Johnston, and Wm. and Andrew Smith once a fortnight.
EDINBURGH, Moffat, and Dalkeith, Wm. Hogg, and Thos. Ainslie, once a fortnight.
ECCLEFECHAN, James Rae, every Monday.

MOFFAT.

THIS delightful village is situated on a rising ground at the head of a valley, which extends more than 20 miles along the banks of the Annan. Moffat has long been celebrated for its mineral waters; these, together with the pleasantness of the situation, and the salubrity of the air, cause it to be much resorted to by invalids from Glasgow, Edinburgh, and various other quarters, during a great part of the summer season. The springs are three in number; one sulphureous, and two chalybeate. The sulphureous spring, which is about a mile and a half from the village, and is called the Moffat water, has a strong smell, resembling the waters of Harrowgate, but not quite so strong; the water has a slight saline taste, and sparkles in the glass, when taken fresh from the spring. Hartfell spa, the stronger of the two chalybeate springs, issues from a rock of alum slate in the side of the mountain of Hartfell, five miles from Moffat. The waters of the other chalybeate spring, which is near Evan Bridge, are different from the last, and nearly the same with the Harrowgate water. To the Moffat well there is a good carriage road, and accommodations have been erected for company and their horses. In the vicinity of Moffat is the celebrated cascade, called the Grey Mare's Tail, from its appearance when seen at a distance; the height of the various falls, which appear almost united, when the stream is full, is near 400 feet. The church is a neat erection, surrounded with trees. The village also contains a mason's lodge, with a subscription library; and debts to the amount of 5l. 6s. 8d. may be recovered at the court of requests, which is held in the town-hall once a month.

POST OFFICE.—Post Master, Mr. Thomas Grieve. The mail from Edinburgh arrives every afternoon at one, and is despatched every morning at nine. The mail from Dumfries and Portpatrick arrives every morning at nine, and is despatched every afternoon at one. The mail from London and Carlisle arrives every afternoon at three, and is despatched every morning at one. The mail from Glasgow arrives every morning at one, and is despatched every afternoon at three.

*Note.—*Letters must be put into the office for the London and Carlisle mail before nine at night, and for Glasgow before two in the afternoon.

PLACES OF WORSHIP.

ESTABLISHED CHURCH—Rev. Alex. Johnston, Minister, Manse

UNITED SECESSION CHAPEL—Rev. John Monteith, Minister

PAROCHIAL SCHOOL.

John Stevenson, Master

RESIDENT GENTRY.

Amos Mr. Adam
Craig Mr. Alex. Burn Braes
Henderson Mr. Thomas
Jardine Thos. esq. Granton
Johnston John, esq. Hunter Hack
Johnston Mr. John
Johnston Michael, esq. Arch Bank
Johnston Peter, esq. Old Town
Johnston Walter, esq. Caplegill, Moffat
Johnstone Rev. Alexander, Moffat Manse
Johnstone John Hope, esq. Moffat House
Marjoribanks Lieut. John, R.N.
Monteith Rev. John
Proudfoot Thos. esq. Craigie Burn
Rogerson Dr. John, Physician to the Forces, Dumcrief House
Stevenson Alex. esq. Larch Hill
Tod Mr. Peter
Welsh Mr. George, Brae Foot
Welsh Mr. James
Wilson Mrs. Mary

MERCHANTS, TRADESMEN, &c.

BAKERS.
Brown Joseph
Brown William
Henderson John
Kerr William

BLACKSMITHS.
Aitchison Thomas
Brown William
Dawling William
Little Michael
Muir James

BOOT & SHOE MAKERS.
Coutts William
Ferguson Thomas
Grieve William
Johnston Gilbert
Little John

FIRE OFFICES AND AGENTS.
CALEDONIAN, Samuel Mc Millan
INSURANCE Co. of Scotland, Rd. Johnstone

FLESHERS.
Halliday William
Johnston Alexander
Mc Night Thomas

GROCERS AND SPIRIT DEALERS.
Alexander Jane
Brown Joseph
Carmichael John

Gibson Henry
Grieve William
Johnston Robert
Mc Millan Samuel, (& wine merchant)
Mouncie William
Palmer William
Telford Robert
Walker William
Wilson Henry
Wilson William

INNS.
Beattock Inn, (and posting house, two miles from Moffat) Mr. Thomas Wilson, proprietor
Black Bull, Daniel Kirk
Spur, Thomas Workman
Star, Robert Johnson
Yew and Lamb, Thos. Mc Night

IRONMONGERS.
Johnston Robert
Mc Millan Samuel
Walker Wm. (& stationer)

JOINERS & CARPENTERS.
Aitchison John
Brown John
Carruthers James
Grieve John
Grieve Walter
Sanderson John

LINEN AND WOOLLEN DRAPERS.
Burnie Robert
Tait George
Watt William

LODGINGS.
Alexander Mrs. William
Briggs Joseph
Burnie Robert
Grieve Thomas
Grieve William
Hamilton James
Hyslop Mrs. Andrew
Johnston John
Mc Millan Samuel
Mouncie William
Palmer William
Russell Robert
Scott Mrs. Robert
Smith George
Tait George
Walker William
Wilson Henry

MANUFACTURERS.
Simpson John, (woollen) Burn-brae Mill
Trett James, (cotton)

MASONS & BUILDERS.
Johnston James
Morrison John
Rutherford Andrew

T T

SADDLERS.
Johnston James
Wilson William

SURGEONS & DRUGGISTS
Johnston James
Smith George
Welsh William, M.D.

TAILORS
Brown Peter
Cowen James
Cowen Samuel
Geddies Robert
Moffat Adam
Moffat John
Hill William

TEACHERS.
Beattie John, (English)
Cowen ——, (music)
Johnston Ebenezer, (English)
Robertson ——, (dancing)

WATCH AND CLOCK MAKERS.
Graham John)
Leithead James
Russel Robert
Wightman Alexander

WRITER AND NOTARY.
Johnstone Richd. (& messenger)

Miscellaneous.
Alexander John, land surveyor
Bell Barbara, dress maker
Dickson Adam, dyer
Hamilton & Williamson, millers and millwrights
Kennedy Adam, auctioneer
Mc Dougal Matthew, nail maker
Murray Robert, tallow chandler
Rae James, mail contractor
Sanderson James, turner & wheel maker
Scott M. & A. straw hat makers

STAMP OFFICE.
Samuel Mc Millan, Distributor

COACHES.
EDINBURGH, the Royal Mail, from the Spur Inn, every morning at nine, and returns for Dumfries every day at a quarter before one.
GLASGOW, the Royal Mail, from the Beattock Inn, every afternoon at three, and returns for London and Carlisle every morning at one, thro' Lockerbie, and Ecclefechan.

CARRIERS.
CARLISLE, Welsh, and Hargreaves, every Monday and Thursday.
DUMFRIES, John Kilpatrick, every Tuesday, and returns on Wednesday
EDINBURGH, every week.
GLASGOW John Hargreaves, occasionally.
GLASGOW, Welsh, and Hargreaves, every Tuesday and Friday.

SANQUHAR,

AN ancient town near the Nith, and on the road from Dumfries to Glasgow, is 27 miles from Dumfries, 56 from Glasgow, 32 from Ayr, and 56 from Edinburgh. It was created a Burgh of Barony in 1484, and raised to a Royal Burgh by a charter from King James VI, in 1596. It is governed by a provost, three bailies, a dean of guild, town treasurer, and eleven councillors elected yearly at Michalmas. It has been long noted for its stocking manufacture, of which the coarser kinds are chiefly exported to Newfoundland. There are two breweries, a tan work, and a carpet manufactory, which employs from 60 to 70 hands. Sanquhar is the principal coal mart in the county, of which article large quantities are sent to Dumfries and other parts. Sanquhar joins with Dumfries, Annan, Kirkcudbright, and Lochmaben in electing a representative to serve in parliament. The old castle of Sanquhar stands on an eminence at the S. E. end of the town; it has been a strong square building, with towers at the corners, and surrounded by a ditch. This castle formerly belonged to a branch of the family of Crichton, ancestors to the Earl of Dumfries; his title is Lord Crichton, but now, as well as most of the land in the neighbourhood, it is the property of the Duke of Buccleugh. About a mile from it stands the house of Ellioch, the residence of Colonel Andrew Veitch, which claims the honour of being the birth place of the admirable Crichton. Sanquhar possesses a court of requests, a subscription library, and a free masons lodge. The old church being taken down, the present one was erected on the site in 1823; it is a very handsome building with a square tower, and stands on a rising ground at the west end of the town. There are also two secession chapels, and a baptist meeting house. The town hall was built at the sole expense of the late Duke of Queensberry; it stands at the end of the High street and has a tower and clock. The market, formerly held on Friday, is now discontinued: there are five fairs, four of which are quarterly, and are held on the first Fridays in February, May, August, and November, old style; the 5th which is of the greatest note, is held on the second Friday in July, and is called the wool fair.

POST OFFICE.—Post Master, John Halliday. Mail to Thornhill, on Monday, Wednesday and Friday at half past ten in the morning, and arrives at half past eight at night. Mail to Edinburgh, on Monday, Wednesday and Friday, at half past ten in the morning, and arrives at half past eight at night. Mail to Cumnock, on Tuesday, Thursday and Saturday, at eight in the morning, and arrives at half past eight at night.

PLACES OF WORSHIP.
ESTABLISHED CHURCH.—Rev. Thos. Montgomery, Minister
FIRST SECESSION CHAPEL—Rev. James Reid, Minister
SECOND SECESSION CHAPEL, Rev. Robert Simson, Minister
BAPTIST CHAPEL —Variuos.

MUNICIPAL GOVERNMENT.
Thomas Crichton, esq. Provost
Alexander Harvey ⎫
John Braidwood ⎬ Bailies.
George Thomson ⎭

Thomas Barker, Dean of Guild
J. W. Mc. Queen, Writer, Deputy Fiscal
J. Bramwell, Town Treasurer

INCORPORATED TRADES.
John Hislop, Convener.
John Riggs ⎫   ⎧ Smiths
William Russel ⎪   ⎪ Squaremen
William Gilmour ⎬ Deacon of ⎨ Tailors
John Chisholm ⎪   ⎪ Shoemakers
George Lorimer ⎭   ⎩ Weavers

PAROCHIAL SCHOOL
John Henderson, Teacher

RESIDENT GENTRY. &c.
Crichton John, esq.
Mc Adam Mrs. Mary

Otto Mrs. Sarah
Scott Mrs. Mary

Veitch Col. Andrew, Ellioch
Wigham Mrs. Jane

MERCHANTS, TRADESMEN, &c.

BAKERS
Hamilton William
Morison Joseph, (& earthenware dealer)

Pagan Robert
Todd Daniel

BLACKSMITHS.
Graham John
Hislop John

Thomson Robert

BOOKSELLER AND STATIONER.
Halliday John, (and agent for the Caledonian Fire Office)

BOOT & SHOE MAKERS·
Chisholms John
Fingland John
Fingland Walter
Kerr Andrew
Lawrie John
Mc Cririck William
Murray John
Murray William
Simson Alexander
Simson Hugh

BREWERS.
Broom & Co.
—wson & Co.

CARPET MANUFACTORY
Sanquhar Company, Crawick mill

COOPERS·
Gibson Andrew
Gibson James

DRESS MAKERS
Douglas Jesse
Kerr Elizabeth
Turnbull Isabel

FLESHERS·
Cook James
Mc Adam William
Mc Cron James
Wilson William

GROCERS AND SPIRIT DEALERS.
Ilison John
Dawson Jonathan (&earthenware)
Gilmour David
Halliday John, (and stocking dealer)
Harkness Thomas
Hope James
Russell Robert
Russell William
Wilson William

INN·
Queensberry Arms, Wm. Wilson

JOINERS & CARPENTERS.
Duff William
Hair George
Howat James
Mc Millan Andrew
Paterson George, (and cabinet maker)

Russell & Hunter, (& cabinet makers and glaziers)

LINEN AND WOOLLEN DRAPERS·
Ballantine Jane
Broom William
Kirkpatrick Alexander
Watt Francis

MASONS & BUILDERS·
Blackley William
Hair James
Wilson William

MEAL DEALERS·
Hislop Samuel
Mc Donald Wm. (and grocer)

PUBLICANS.
Blackley Wm. (masons arms)
Braidwood John
Crichton Jas. (black bull)
Duff Wm. (royal oak)
Gilmour John
Mc Adam Wm. (red lion)
Mc Michael Geo. (Abercrombie)
Mc Millan Andrew
Stewart James, (crown)
Wilson William

SPADE AND SHOVEL MANUFACTURER·
Rigg John, Crawick forge

SURGEONS.
Purdie Wm. (and druggist)
Taylor John
Thomson George, (& druggist)

TAILORS:
Broadfoot James
Broadfoot Thomas
Brown Robert
Fingland James
Gilmour William
Mackay William
Wigham James

TALLOW CHANDLERS·
Mc Cron James
Whigham Agnes

WATCH AND CLOCK MAKERS.
Cunningham William
Harvey Alexander
Reid John

WINE AND SPIRIT MERCHANT
Halliday John

WRITERS & NOTARIES·
Mc Queen John Wilson, messenger and clerk of the peace)
Smith Wm. (& town clerk)

Miscellaneous.

Blackwood Jas. currier & leather cutter
Blackwood Wm. tanner
Blair William, turner
Brown Jane, straw hat maker
Brown Thomas, slater
Crichton David, miller
Edgar James, saddler
Hamilton Jas. blanket manufacturer
Howat George, nail maker
Kennedy David, tinsmith
Lorimer George, cloth dresser
Lorimer Josiah, teacher
Mc Coll James, locksmith
Mc Phie Alex. hair dresser
Osborne Janet, druggist & grocer
Sinton James, apothecary
Thomson Andrew, auctioneer and sheriff's officer
Tomson John, spirit dealer

STAMP OFFICE
Francis Watt, Distributor

COACHES·
DUMFRIES, Carlisle, &c. the Independent, from the Queensberry Arms, and the New Times from the Black Bull, every lawful day at one.
GLASGOW, the Independent, from the Queensberry Arms, and the New Times, from the Black Bull, every lawful day at twelve.

CARRIERS.
DUMFRIES, John Walker, and Wm. Mc Dougal on Tuesday and return on Friday.
DUMFRIES, Margaret Anderson, on Tuesday, and returns on Thursday.
EDINBURGH, John Gilmour, arrives on Monday and departs on Friday.
GLASGOW, Robert Porteous, Wm. Black, and Robert Williamson, on Monday, and returns on Friday.
GLASGOW, Wm. Ferguson, every other Wednesday.

THORNHILL,
AND THE PARISH OF MORTON:

A Pleasant village of considerable extent, and in a most delightful part of the country, lies on the great road from Carlisle to Dumfries and Glasgow, to which two stage coaches pass and repass every day. It is in the parish of Morton, and distant from Dumfries 14 miles, from Sanquhar 12, Carlisle 48, Kilmarnock 34, Glasgow 66, Cumnock 30, and Annan 30. There are three places of worship, viz: the parish church, a united secession chapel, and a chapel of relief. The trade of the village is chiefly domestic, and the only establishments are a tannery and a brewery. Fairs are held on the second Tuesday in February, the 25th of March, the second Tuesday in May, the last Friday in June, the second Tuesday in August, the second Tuesday in November, and the first Tuesday in December; all old style.

POST OFFICE, High street.—*Post Mistress,* Elizabeth Hunter. Mail to Dumfries is despatched at half past twelve at noon, and arrives at ten minutes before six at night. A post to Minnihive on Mondays, Wednesdays, and Fridays, at half past six in the morning, and returns at a quarter past twelve at noon. A post to Sanquhar on Mondays, Wednesdays, and Fridays, at half past twelve at noon, and is despatched at a quarter past six at night.

PLACES OF WORSHIP.

Established Church—Rev. Dav. Smith, Minister
Relief Chapel—Rev. Edward Dobie, Minister
United Secession Chapel—Rev. Wm. Rogerson, Minister

RESIDENT GENTRY.

Crichton Thos. esq. Dobton | Douglas Capt. Thomas, Holmhill

MERCHANTS, TRADESMEN, &c.

Brown Wm. High st
Gibson Frances, High st
Mc Morine Samuel, High st

BLACKSMITHS.

Begg John, New st
Kirk William

BOOT & SHOEMAKERS.

Brown Robert, High st
Douglas Robert, High st
Ferguson Wm. High st
Jones Thomas, High st
Jones Robt. High st
Johnston John, Old st
Kerr John, High st
Killoch John, High s
Killock John, jun. High st
Mc Caig Robert, High st
Milliken James, High st

BREWER.

Dickson Wm. Nith bridge

CLOG MAKERS.

Frazer Wm. New st
Kerr James, (& cooper), High st
Walker Wm. High st

FLESHERS.

Biggar Wm. High st
Brown Wm. (and spirit dealer)
Old town
Killock Adam, High st
Kirkpatrick John, High st
Wm. Jones John, High st
Williamson Thos. High st

GROCERS AND SPIRIT DEALERS.

Carson Wm. High st
Davidson Agnes, High st
Hastings Wm. High st
Hepburn James, (& ironmonger)
High st
Kellock Robert, Old st
Kennedy Wm. (and seedsman)
High st
Madison David, Old st
Marchbank John, (& earthenware)
High st
Mathison Joseph, High st

INNS.

George & Dragon, Robt. Mc Kinnell

Queensberry Arms, R. & M. Glendining

JOINERS AND CARTWRIGHTS.

Coulthard John
Hairstones Robt. High st
Mc Caig Wm. painter & glazier
Shankland Jas. Kirk st
Walker James, Old st
Wallace Robt. High st
Wilson John, Old town

LINEN AND WOOLLEN DRAPERS.

Dalziel Jas. High st
Hepburn Jas. High st
Richardson Jas. High st
Webster Ann, High st

MASONS.

Dergival Wm. (& builder) Carronbridge
Hogg Robt. (& builder) High st
Laidlow James, High st
Mc Laughlan Thos. High st
Milligan Robt. High st

NAIL MAKERS.

Charters Wm. High st
Mc Clymont Wm. High st

PUBLICANS.

Fingland John, High st
Hepburn John, (& grocer) High st

STRAW HAT MAKERS.

Brown Janet, High st
Webster Ann, High st

SURGEONS.

Maxwell Robert, (and, druggist)
High st
Milliken John, Old st
Mounsie John

TAILORS.

Fraser Alex. New st
Hairstones John, High st
Hiddleston John, (and clothier)
High st
Kali T. Thos. High st
Kennedy Jas. Dry Gill
Kennedy Jas. jun. Dry Gill
Rogerson Robt. Old town

Shankland James, (and clothier)
High st
Sharp Robert, High st
Williamson Wm. Old st

WRITER & MESSENGER.

Connell Thomas

Miscellaneous.

Adie George, tin smith, High st
Hird Henry, watch & clock maker,
High st
Kerr Robt. currier & leather cutter, High st
Kerr Thomas, tanner, High st
Laidlow Alex. teacher, High st
Lawrie John, glazier, High st
Mc Farlane James, hair dresser,
New st
Milliken Jas. auctioneer, Old st
Milliken Wm. bookseller & stationer, New st
Shankland Maria, dress maker
Wilson Primrose K. saddler, Old st

STAMP OFFICE,
HIGH STREET.

Elizabeth Hunter, distributor

COACHES.

DUMFRIES, the New Times, from the Queensberry Arms, and the Independent, from the George, every lawful afternoon at three.
GLASGOW, the New Times, from the Queensberry Arms, and the Independent, from the George, every lawful morning at ten.

CARRIERS.

DUMFRIES, John Walker, Andrew Watson, and Wm. Mc Dougal, every Wednesday and Saturday, and return the same days.
EDINBURGH, Robt. Mc Caig on Monday, and returns on Fridays.
GLASGOW, Robt. Porteous, William Black, and Robert Williamson, on Monday, and return on Friday.
SANQUHAR, John Walker, and Wm. Mc Dougal, on Tuesdays and Fridays, and return the same day.

KIRKCUDBRIGHTSHIRE.

THIS county, or as it is commonly called, stewartry, forms the eastern, and by far the most extensive portion of Galloway. The latter name was anciently applied to an independent principality, which included the greater part of Ayrshire and Dumfries-shire; but is now limited to the two counties of Wigtown and Kirkcudbright. It is bounded on the north-east and east by Dumfries-shire; on the south by the Solway Frith and the Irish Sea; on the west by Wigtownshire, and on the north-west by the county of Ayr; its surface contains 821 square miles of land, 12½ square miles of lakes, 168,243 acres of cultivated, and 357,517 acres of uncultivated land. Kirkcudbright has no subdivisions, except that four of the most northerly parishes, Carsphairn, Dalry, Kels, and Balmaclellan, are commonly called the district of Glenkens. The aspect of the country, however, forms a very natural division in two parts. If a line be drawn from the centre of Kirkpatrick Iron-Gray parish, to the Gatehouse of Fleet, all to the north west, with little exception, is so mountainous, that it may very properly be termed a highland district; while the south and east exhibit a fine champaign and cultivated country. Like other mountainous countries, this is intersected by numerous streams, which, uniting, form four considerable rivers; the Cree on the west; the Fleet; the Dee, formed by the union of the Ken and Dee, and the Orr, or Urr. These rivers, all of which rise in the north, empty themselves into the Solway Frith or the Irish Sea, abound with salmon, and are ornamented with numerous handsome seats. Of late years agriculture has been much improved; the lands have been subdivided and enclosed; and new roads have been formed. Kirkcudbrightshire contains two royal burghs, Kirkcudbright and New Galloway; the former joins in parliamentary representation with Dumfries, Annan, Sanquhar, and Lochmaben, the latter with Stranraer, Wigtown, and Whithorn; the stewartry also sends a member to parliament. This county wants several of those advantages, to which Dumfries-shire and Ayrshire are indebted for their improvements; it has neither coal nor lime, and but little freestone. Marl is found in great plenty, especially in Carlingwark loch, which contains an inexhaustible fund of shell-marl. Ironstone and lead-ore also abound; but the deficiency of coal is a bar to the working of either. The principal heights are Bencairn 1200, Cairnharro 1100, Cairnsmuir 1728, and Criffel 1831 feet above the level of the sea.

POPULATION OF THE SHIRE OF KIRKCUDBRIGHT.

B. Burgh; P. Parish.

	Houses	Males	Females	Total		Houses	Males	Females	Total
Anworth............p	126	425	420	845	Kirkpatrick Durham........p	271	725	748	1473
Balmaclellan..........p	184	457	455	912	Kirkpatrick Iron-Gray.... p	160	425	455	880
Balmaghie............p	208	681	680	1361	Lochrutton... ....p	109	259	335	594
Borgue.............p	155	463	484	947	Minnigaff..............p	344	903	1020	1923
Buittle.............p	179	486	537	1023	New-abbey.............p	205	506	606	1112
Carsphairn..........p	87	238	236	474	Parton..............p	138	419	426	845
Colvend and Southwick....p	272	611	711	1322	Rerwick..............p	207	671	707	1378
Crossmichael.........p	257	621	678	1299	Terregles.............p	117	321	330	651
Dalry..............p	237	557	594	1151	Tongland.............p	162	416	474	890
Girthon.............p	240	948	947	1895	Troqueer.............p	598	1986	2305	4201
Kells..............p	189	556	548	1104	Twynholm.............p	129	357	426	783
Kelton.............p	440	1151	1265	2416	Urr................p	508	1351	1511	2862
Kirkbean............p	157	361	429	790					
Kirkcudbright........b & p	470	1509	1868	3377	Total..	6688	18506	20397	38903
Kirkgunzion..........p	139	371	405	776					
Kirkmabreck..........p	280	722	797	1519					

CASTLE DOUGLAS,

A Neat thriving town in the parish of Kelton, is situated in a pleasant fertile district, upon the N.W. banks of the lake of Carlinwark, and on the great road from London and Carlisle to Portpatrick; it is 93 miles S.S.W. of Edinburgh, 19 W. by S. of Dumfries, 15 from Gatehouse, and 9 from Kirkcudbright. On the S.W. side of the town stands the ruins of the ancient castle of Threeve, and on the S.E. side, at nearly the same distance, is the modern and elegant mansion of Gelston castle, formerly called Douglas castle, now the residence of William Maitland, esq. Castle Douglas was known by the names of Causey End, and Carlinwark, till 1792, when it was by the proprietor erected into a burgh of baro-ny, by its present name. At present it is governed by a bailie and six councillors, but it is in contemplation to obtain a new charter under a provost and bailies. Forty or fifty years ago, this town contained but a few scattered houses; there are now upwards of 400 houses laid out in regular streets. It has a commodious town-house, possessing a good clock; in it a court is held on the first Saturday in every month, for the recovery of debts under 5l.—Here are a post office, a handsome meeting house, three banks, one brewery, two tanneries, a number of good shops, and three large convenient inns. This town owes much of its present flourishing condition to the munificence and public spirit of its late wealthy proprietor, who, at his own expense, erected it into a burgh of barony, built the town-house, and laid out all the streets. Castle Douglas, and its vicinity, appear to have been the scene of much contest during the feudal system, when the ancient Douglasses dwelt in the castle of Threeve, and were lords of this district, for on the west side of the town, are still visible encampments and breast-works, evidently thrown up against the castle.— Within the borough, on the S. W. banks of the lake, is a place still called the Gallows Lot, or Plot, believed to have been the place of execution in former times. The lake above named is upwards of one mile in length, covering at present 118 acres, but, before it was partially drained by the canal, cut from it to the river Dee, its area was much greater.

It contains a number of small islands, one of which, in the middle of the lake, has been bound round its base with huge frames of oak, but whether the island has been artificially formed upon them, as some think, or they have been placed there with an intent to support some vast superstructure, cannot now be known. The lake is plentifully stored with pike and perch, and contains at its bottom an inexhaustible treasure of the best shell marl. The market, which is very considerable for grain, is held on Monday, it is all sold by sample, and principally exported to England, and the North of Scotland.— There are three fairs at Kelton Hill, viz. the first Monday after the 12th February, the first Tuesday after the 1st of July, and the first Tuesday after the 12th of November.

POST OFFICE, King-street.—*Post Master*, Mr. William Green. The London, Edinburgh, and all the south mails arrive at six in the evening, and are despatched at three in the afternoon. The mails for Kirkcudbright, Gatehouse, Creetown, Newton-Stewart, Glenluce, Stranraer, Portpatrick, & Ireland, arrive at three in the afternoon, and are despatched at six in the evening. A by-post to New Galloway every Sunday, Tuesday, and Friday, at half-past six in the evening, and returns on Monday, Wednesday, and Saturday, at three in the afternoon.

PLACES OF WORSHIP.

KELTON—Rev. John Mc Clellan, Minister
BUITTLE—Rev. Alexander Crosbie, Minister

PAROCHIAL SCHOOLS.

CASTLE DOUGLAS—Rev. James Murray, Master; Robert Mc Kinna, and Thomas Lorimer, Assistants.
KELTON HILL—John Mc Curty, Master
GELSTON—John Gordon, Master
BUITTLE—Alexander Cunningham, Master of the first School; John Tate, Master of the second School

Justices of the Peace for Castle Douglas District.
David Hannay, esq. Castle Douglas

Lockhart Muir, esq. Liviston
Robert Maxwell, esq. Breoch
John Napier, esq. Mollance, Castle Douglas
Rev. Dr. Lamont, Durham Hill

MUNICIPAL GOVERNMENT.

Andrew Kirkpatrick, Bailie
James Barbour, ⎫
John Sinclair, ⎪
John Milligan, ⎬ Councillors
William Green, ⎪
John Graham, ⎪
William Miller, ⎭

Stamp Office, King-street.

Alexander Mc Millan, Distributor

GENTRY.

Bell Allan, esq. Hillowton
Bell John, esq. Dunjop
Black William B. Grove
Campbell Major Jas. Walton park
Coltart Robt. esq. Blue Hill
Culton Major, Nutwood
Cunningham John, esq. Hensol
Ferguson Henry, esq. Orroland
Gordon Sir Alex. Sheriff of the county, Greenlaw
Herries Wm. Young, esq. Spottes
Jones Geo. Chas. esq. Brooklands

Kerr Alex. esq. (of *Serggie Hill*) Buittle
Kerr Robert, esq. Milton Park, Buittle
Lawrie Mrs. Ernspie
Maclaharty James, esq. St. Andrew's st
Mc Dougall Mrs. Dildawn
Mc Kinzie Wm. gent. King st
Mc Knight Robt. esq. Barlochan, Buittle
Maitland Col. Alex. Chipperkyle
Maitland W. esq. Gelston Castle

Martin Mrs. Kilwhanidy
Maxwell Colonel, Orchardton
Maxwell John Herries, esq. Munches, Buittle
Maxwell Robert, esq. Breoch, Buittle
Napier John, esq. Mollance
Neilson Nathl. esq. Springfield
Reid Robert, esq. Kirk kennen
Richardson Saml. gent. Queen st
Skirving Robert, esq. Croyes
Thomson Samuel, esq. Forest
Wight Mrs. Colonel, Largneau

MERCHANTS, TRADESMEN, &c.

AUCTIONEERS.

Gifford John, King st
Sproat Peter, St. Andrew's st

BAKERS.

Mc Pherson Jno. St. Andrew's st
Rankine Bryce, (& spirit dealer) King st

BANKERS.

Barbour James, (private bank) St. Andrew's st
Napier John, draws upon Hankey and Co. London, and Rt. Allan and Son, Edinburgh, King st
Welsh Arthur, (agent to the British Linen Company's Bank), King st

BOOT & SHOEMAKERS.

Blacklock James, King st
Blyth Alexander, King st
Mc Clellan John, St. Andrew's st

DRESS MAKERS

Beattie Jeanett, King st

Mc William Mary, King st
Tait Jane, King st

FIRE, &c. OFFICES AND AGENTS.

FIFE INSURANCE Co. James Barbour
INSURANCE Co. of Scotland, John Sinclair
ROYAL EXCHANGE, Anthony Davidson

GROCERS.

Gordon Chas. (& draper) King st
Johnston William, (& bookseller) King st
Kirkpatrick & Green, (& wine & spirit merchants) King st
Mc Clellan John, King st
Macmillan Thos. St. Andrew's st
Mc Pherson Ellen, King st
Wallace John, King st

INNKEEPERS.

Cochran Elizabeth, King st

Douglas Robert, (Douglas Arms) King st
Sproat Peter, (King's Arms) St. Andrew's st

JOINERS.

Anderson Wm. St. Andrew's st
Gordon John, Queen st
Graham John, (& cabinet maker) St. Andrew's st

LINEN AND WOOLLEN DRAPERS.

Edgar J. D. & Co. King st
Mc Lellan —, (& dealer in china, chrystal, and earthenware) King st

MESSENGERS.

Barbour Thos. St. Andrew's st
Thomson David, King st

PAINTERS & GLAZIERS.

Mac Murray James, King st
Mac Murray Robert, King st

PUBLICANS.
Gordon Hugh, King st
Muncy James, St. Andrew's st
Nish James, King st
Parker Anth. St. Andrew's st
Rae William, St. Andrew's st

STRAW BONNET MAKERS.
Law Janet, King st
Mc Ghie Jane, St. Andrew's st

SURGEONS.
Anderson Patrick, King st
Mc Keur Samuel, King st

TAILORS
Bell James, St. Andrew's st
Muir John, King st
Shaw Wm. (& draper) King st

TALLOW CHANDLERS.
Kissock John, Cotton st
Robertson Elizabeth, King st

TANNERS.
Aitken & Wilson, King st
Milligan & Barbour, Queen st

WINE AND SPIRIT MERCHANTS.
Thomson David, King st

Young William, St. Andrew's st
WRITERS.
Barbour James, St. Andrew's st
Gillespie Wm. St. Andrew's st
Hannay & Lidderdale, King st
Sinclair John, St. Andrew's st
Thomson Maxwell, St. Andrew's st

Miscellaneous.

Aitken Joseph, bookseller & stationer, King st
Anderson Jas. bookbinder, Cotton st
Alexander Wm. cooper, King st
Birnie Robt. smith & bellhanger, Queen st
Davidson Anthony, printer and publisher of the Castle Douglas Miscellany, every Monday, Queen st
Gordon Andrew, hosier, Queen st
Grierson Robert, currier and leather cutter, King st
Hewetson James, brewer
Law Robert, watch & clock maker, King st
Macartney Robert, ironmonger, King st

Mc Bain Robt. clogger, King st
Mc George James, blacksmith, King st
Mc Ken James, nursery & seedsman, Cotton st
Martin Wm. cartwright, King st
Milligan John, saddler, King st
Portens Robert, supervisor of excise, Queen st

COACH.
LONDON & Carlisle, the Royal Mail, from the Douglas Arms, every afternoon at three, through Dumfries, Carlisle, &c and returns at six in the evening, thro' Gatehouse, Newton-Stewart, and Stranraer, to Portpatrick

CARRIERS.
EDINBURGH, George Turner, every Wednesday, & arrives every Thursday.
DUMFRIES, Wm. Anderson & James Nish, every Wednesday, & returns every Thursday.
GLASGOW, Thomas Wallat & David Mc Clure, go and return every other Monday.

CREETOWN,

FORMERLY called Ferry Town of Cree, which is beautifully situated on the east side of Wigton Bay, in the parish of Kirkmabreck, is 117 miles from Edinburgh, 12 from Gatehouse, 6 from Newton-Stewart, and about 3 from Wigton across the ferry. It is a burgh of barony, governed by a bailie and a council of four. The town is the property of John Mc Culloch, esq. whose mansion adjoins, and on account of its situation is a very great ornament.— Creetown contains a small kirk, and a respectable mansion, the residence of Major Campbell. The only business transacted here is the exportation of grain, and the importation of coal and lime, for it has neither market nor fair. The mail road from Portpatrick to Dumfries passes through the town, which circumstance may, at some future period, add to its importance.

POST OFFICE.—*Post Master*, Mr. Samuel Adair. The Edinburgh and Glasgow mails arrive by the London mail at half-past ten at night, and are despatched at eleven in the morning. The Irish mails go by Donaghadee.—The English mails by Dumfries. Office hours from eight in the morning till ten at night.

PLACE OF WORSHIP.
ESTABLISHED CHURCH—Rev. John Sibbald, Minister, Half-mark

MUNICIPAL GOVERNMENT.
Alexander Mc Geoch, Bailie.

John Hannah,
William Hannah,
Peter Irving,
James Young,
} Councillors

GENTRY, &c.

Campbell George, esq.
Campbell Major, magistrate, Cassencarrie

Hannay Ramsay, esq. Kirkdale
Mc Culloch John, esq. Berholm
Mc Culloch James, L.H.P.M.

Mc Lean Alexander, esq. magistrate, Mark

SHOPKEEPERS, TRADERS, &c.

Brait Alex. grocer & draper
Chesney John, publican
Connen Robert, publican
Hannah John, joiner
Hannah Wm. joiner & publican
Harris James, apothecary, &c.
Heron Mary, grocer & spirit dlr

Mc Conchie Wm. grocer
Michael Thomas, grocer
Morrow William, grocer
Nae James, grocer
Sinclair John, grocer
Tate John, grocer
Vernon Euphemia, publican

Young James, innkeeper.
COACH.
LONDON, the Royal Mail, every day, at eleven o'clock, thro' Gatehouse, Castle Douglas, Dumfries, &c. & returns for Portpatrick, every night at ten, through Newton-Stewart, Glenluce, &c.

CROSS MICHAEL,

A Small village in the parish of the same name, is situated on the banks of the river Dee, over which, about a mile and a half distant, is an elegant stone bridge, which is crossed by the high road leading from Lawrieston to Castle Douglas, and from Lawrieston to Cross Michael. It is 91 miles from Edinburgh, 5 from Lawrieston, 3½ from Castle Douglas, 3 from Parton, 9 from New Galloway, and 19 from Dumfries. Cross Michael contains the parish church, which is a neat stone edifice.

PLACE OF WORSHIP
ESTABLISHED CHURCH—Rev. Dav. Walsh, Minister

PAROCHIAL SCHOOL.
John Watson, Master

GENTRY.

Donald James, esq. Dunvate | Gordon James Murray, esq. Balmaghie House

TRADESMEN, &c.

Coupland Alexander, grocer
Couts Andrew, publican
Gall William, grocer
Mc Knight Jos. joiner & publican

Milligan John, publican

COACH.
LONDON & Carlisle mail passes thro' Castle Douglas, from Portpatrick, at three in the afternoon, and returns at six in the evening, through Gatehouse, Newton-Stewart, and Shaurner, to Portpatrick.

DALBEATTIE,
AND ITS ENVIRONS.

DALBEATTIE, the principal village in the parish of Urr, is 87 miles from Edinburgh, 13½ from Kirkcudbright, 13½ from Dumfries, and 6 from Castle Douglas, it is situated in the south of the parish, at the junction of Dalbeattie Burn, and the river Urr, which is here navigable for vessels of 70 or 80 tons; this harbour is called Dub-o'-Hass, and is about five miles from the Solway Firth. The village possesses great advantages, in respect to situation, for trade, having a communication by sea with any of the western ports, and some large falls of water, capable of turning any kind of machinery, so that it wants nothing, but a few spirited individuals, to erect some cotton or woollen mills, to make it one of the most improved places in the south of Scotland. There have already been erected two paper mills, a flax, corn, and waulk, or foular mills, and a smith's shop, in which the water drives the hammers. There are two places of worship in the village, viz. a reformed presbyterian meeting house, and a Roman catholic chapel, and an excellent inn, of which Mr. David Murray is the proprietor.

Letters are taken from Dalbeattie every Monday, Wednesday, and Saturday morning, to Castle Douglas, by John Mc Nish, at one penny each · he returns the same day, bringing letters for Dalbeattie at three half pence each.

PLACES OF WORSHIP.

COLVEND—Rev. Andrew Mc Culloch, Minister
KIRKBEAN—Rev. Thomas Grierson, Minister
KIRKGUNZEON—Rev. John Crocket, Minister
URR parish Church, near Haugh—Rev. John Mc Whirr, Minister
ASSOCIATE SYNOD MEETING-HOUSE, at Haugh—Rev. James Blyth, Minister
REFORMED PRESBYTERIAN MEETING-HOUSE, at Dalbeattie—Rev. John Osborne, Minister, and also at Springholm

ROMAN CATHOLIC CHAPEL, at Dalbeattie—Rev. Andrew Carruthers, Pastor

PAROCHIAL SCHOOLS.

COLVEND PROPER—John Halliday, Master
DALBEATTIE—James Copeland, Master
KIRKBEAN—Rev. William Murray, Master
KIRKGUNZION—Wm. Gillespie, Master
SOUTHWICK—William Palmer, Master
URR, at Haugh—Wm. Allan, Master

GENTRY.

Boyd Wm. esq. Milton, Urr
Cochtrie Wm. esq. Rosebank, Urr
Costin Jno. esq. Glenson, Colvend

Dunlop General, Mains, Colvend
Gordon Lieut. Adam, H.P. R.N. Dalbeattie

Kirk John, esq. Drumstiuchell, Colvend
Lowden J. esq. Clonyard, Colvend

MERCHANTS, TRADESMEN, &c. DALBEATTIE.

PROFESSIONAL GENTLEMEN.
Milligan George, surgeon
Wallace John, surgeon

SHOPKEEPERS, TRADERS, &c.
Armstrong Jasper, wheelwright
Blacklock G. boot & shoe maker
Broadfoot James, miller
Elliott William, blacksmith
Grierson William, flesher
Halliday R. grocer & spirit dealer
Hannah Wm. slater & plasterer

Kerr William, cartwright
Kirkpatrick Samuel, hosier
Lewis John, hosier
Lindsay Hugh, dyer
Mc Clellan Jas. house carpenter
Mc Bane John, clogger
Mc Laurin D. grocer & draper
Milligan John, flax dresser
Murray David, linen and woollen draper & innkeeper
Murray James, draper, grocer and spirit dealer
Nisbet Geo. grocer & spirit dealer
Rankine James, baker

Robertson Janet, publican
Shaw John, blacksmith
Sloan Nathaniel, publican
Temple Robert, excise officer
Thomson James, baker
Wilson Alex. paper maker

COACH.
See Cross Michael.

CARRIERS.
DUMFRIES, Robert Adamson, every Wednesday & Saturday, and returns the same days.
EDINBURGH, William Butter, every second Wednesday.

GATEHOUSE OF FLEET,

IN the parish of Girthon, pleasingly seated on the east banks of the Fleet, is 105 miles from Edinburgh, 33 from Dumfries, 50 east of Portpatrick, and 7 west of Kirkcudbright. It was erected into a burgh of barony in 1795, through the interest of Mr. Murray, who is proprietor of the town and parish. Its municipal government is vested in a provost, two bailies, and four councillors. On account of the favourableness of the situation, and the moderate feu duties, it has, in less than half a century, risen from a single inn, or stage house, to a manufacturing town of considerable note. It is well built, regular, and clean, the houses being generally of the same height, the streets running in straight lines, and crossing each other at right angles. Its situation is in a romantic, fertile vale, embosomed in hills and mountains, which form a spacious and delightful amphitheatre. Some of the hills having their summits crowned, and their sides covered with hanging woods, interspersed with rich pasturage; while the higher and more distant mountains, point their naked blue heads to the sky,

445

and exhibit all the rude grandeur and naked wildness of uncultivated nature. This amphitheatre expands with a wide opening toward the south, and exposes full to the view a fine bay of the sea, which runs so far into the land as to appear from Gatehouse, like a large lake. At the foot of the town rolls the pure stream of the Fleet, which here meets the tide, and becomes navigable for vessels of sixty tons burden; the navigation of the river has been considerably improved within the last season, at the sole expense of the proprietor, Mr. Murray, who, at a cost of 3000l. cut a canal in a straight line, from which vessels trading to the port, have already derived incalculable advantage. The exports of Gatehouse are chiefly grain; and its imports lime and coals; but the chief business and manufacture is cotton spinning, extensively carried on here in the mills, formerly built by Messrs. Birtwhistle and Sons, now repaired and worked with much spirit by Mr. Cliffe. Here is also a brewery, the property of Mr. Mc William; with two considerable tanyards, and an extensive nursery. Many families are employed in the weaving of muslin, which goes to the Carlisle, or Glasgow markets. The parish kirk is a commodious building; it was erected in 1817, and its site is well chosen. Here are also a masonic lodge, a subscription news-room, and library, a parochial school, and others of minor importance. In the vicinity of the town are two mines, one of lead, the other of copper; they are of recent discovery, and both said to be worked with success.—In this neighbourhood, in the parish of Anwoth, are the ancient castles of Ruscoe, and Cardoness; and a mile south of the town stands Colly, the noble residence of the proprietor Mr. Murray; and at the distance of about two miles, are the neat villas of Ardwall, and Cardoness. A burgh court for the recovery of debts not exceeding five pounds, is held every fortnight, and a justice of peace court sits every month for the parishes of Girthon, and Anwoth. That part of Gatehouse which is in Anwoth, has extended itself across the Fleet, over which there is a good stone bridge. Saturday is the market day; a fair is held on the first Monday after the 17th of June old style, and a cattle market on Friday, commencing on the first Friday in November, and continuing eight weeks.

POST OFFICE, Front-street—*Post Master*, Mr. Charles Mc Keane. The Edinburgh and Glasgow mails arrive by the London Mail Coach at fifty-five minutes past eight in the evening, and is despatched at one at noon. Portpatrick and Irish mails at half past eight, and return at one at noon. Office hours from eight in the morning till ten in the evening.

PLACES OF WORSHIP.

GATEHOUSE ESTABLISHED CHURCH—Rev. Robt. Jeffrey, Minister; John Armstrong, Clerk
ANWORTH ESTABLISHED CHURCH—Rev. Thomas Turnbull, Minister; John Bell, Precentor

PAROCHIAL SCHOOLS.

GATEHOUSE—John Armstrong, Master
ANWORTH—John Bell, Master

MUNICIPAL GOVERNMENT.

James Credie, esq. Provost
John Johnston } Bailies
Thomas Campbell }

Councillors—Nelson Rea, James Mc Miken, James Murray, and John Colthart
William Mc Nish, Town Clerk

EXCISE OFFICERS.

Johnston Charles, Front street
Marquis William, Front street

Stamp Office, Front-street.

Mc Nish Robert, Distributor, (and agent for the Beacon fire office)

RESIDENT GENTRY AND CLERGY.

Birtwhistle John, esq. Ardwall, Anworth
Brown Jno. esq. Enrick, Girthon
Craig Alex. esq. Lyllodioch, Girthon
Hannay Ramsay, esq. Kirkdale, Kirkmabreck
Hannay Robt. esq. Ruscoe, Anworth
Maxwell Sir David, Cardoness, Anworth
Maxwell Col. David, Cardoness, Anworth
Mc Culloch Alex. esq. Kirkclawgh, Anworth
Mc Culloch David, esq. Knockbrex, Borgue
Miller Rev. Archibald, Swan st
Murray Alex. esq. Broughton, Girthon
Stewart Alex. Jas. esq. Gatehill, Borgue

MERCHANTS TRADESMEN, &c.

ACADEMY.

Rae Mrs. (ladies') Front st

AGENTS.

Marsden John, (for the Ruscoe Lead Mine Co.) Front st
Mc Nish Wm. (to the Norwich Insurance Co.) Front st

AUCTIONEER.

Callander James, Cross st

BAKERS.

Hanning Hugh, Fleet st
Hanning Isabella, Front st
Hunter Margaret, Front st
Mc Whea John, Front st

BOOT & SHOEMAKERS.

Blyth Wm. & Son, Front st
Dryburgh David, Front st
Mc Lean Wm. Front st
Mc William John, Front st
Murdoch James, Front st

BREWER.

Mc William John, jun. Front st

CABINET MAKERS.

Cairns Alex. Back st

Kirk Andrew, Nelson st
Mc Ewen James, Front st
Mc Nish Geo. Back st
Murray James, Fleet st

COOPERS.

Carmont John, Boat Green
Connell Alex. Front st

COTTON SPINNERS.

Cliffe Wastel, Nelson st

GROCERS.

Carnochan James, Fleet st
Campbell Thos. (& earthenware dealer) Front st
Hanning Isabella, (& spirit dealer) Front st
Keand Charles, Front st
Mc Millan & Son, (& hardware dealers) Fleet st
Mc Millan John, Back st
Mc Whea John, (and spirit dealer) Front st
Murchea Mary, Front st
Roy James, (and spirit dealer) Front st
Wilson Peter, Front st

INN.

Harper Alexander, (Murray Arms; Head Inn, and posting house) Front st

LINEN AND WOOLLEN DRAPERS.

Mc Nish Robt. (& dealer in hardware & stationery) Front st
Menzies Wm. Front st
Moor John, Front st
Kirkpatrick Jas. (& hardwareman and dealer in stationary and fancy goods) Front st

PAINTER & GLAZIER.

Tait John, Front st

NURSERY & SEEDSMAN

Credie James, Front st

SADDLERS AND HARNESS MAKERS

Carson Wm. Front st
Mc Burne James, Front st

SHIP OWNERS.

Bain James, Front st
Credie David

Kilpatrick James, Front st
Mc Clellan Samuel, Front st
Ramage Wm. Celly garden
Stoddart Wm. (& coal merchant)
   Front st

SMITHS, &c.
Bain James, Front st
Bryce Wm. Fleet st
Mc Donald Alex. Back st
Turner James, Front st

STONE MASONS.
Hume Wm. Nelson st
Mc Gau John, Covent Garden
Mc Gau P. & Hugh, Front st
Mc Kinnell Wm. Back st
Mc Winnie & Mc Clive, Fleet st

SURGEONS.
Bennet James, Front st
Kennedy Chas. Front st
Rae Nelson, Front st
Watson Jas. (& druggist) Front st

TAILORS.
Bell Walter, Cotton st
Garroway Robt. Front st
Kelvn David, (& grocer) Fleet st
Taggart Samuel, sen. Front st
Taggart Samuel, jun. Back st
Walker James, Front st

TALLOW CHANDLER.
Mc Master Robert, Front st

TANNERS.
Birkett Thos. Fleet st
Selkirk & Menzies, Front st

TAVERNS AND PUBLIC HOUSES.
Carson Mrs. Margaret, (Black Bull) Front st
Carnochan Mrs. Jane, Back st
Mc Can Thos. Front st
Mc Nish John, (Masons' Arms) Front st
Mc Nish Joseph, (Angel Tavern) Front st
Murray James, (Scotch Crown) Fleet st
Selkirk Jauet, (Bay Horse) East Town end
Shannon Wm. (Ship) Fleet st
Thomson Mary, (Crown & Grapes) Front st

WATCH AND CLOCK MAKERS.
Halliday Robt. Front st
Richmond Joseph, Front st

WHEELWRIGHTS.
Henry Samuel, Nelson st
Mc Lachlan Wm. Nelson st

Mc Minn Alex. Back st

WRITER.
Mc Nish Wm. Front st

Miscellaneous.
Bell Wm. haberdasher and straw hat maker, Front st
Birkett Thos. timber dealer, Fleet st
Walker Robt. musician, Back st
Walker Wm. grain dealer, Fleet st

COACH.
The London and Portpatrick Royal Mail leaves the Head Inn, for London every day at one, and returns for Portpatrick every night at half past eight.

CARRIERS.
DUMFRIES, Mrs. Rorison, on Tuesdays, and returns on Thursdays.
GLASGOW, Thos. Wallet, and David Mc Clure alternately once a fortnight on Friday, and return on Thursday.
KIRKCUDBRIGHT, David Shan on Tuesdays, Thursdays, and Saturdays, and returns the same days.
NEWTOWN-STEWART, Jno. Gilkinson, on Fridays, and returns on Tuesdays.
WIGTOUN, Thos. Hughan, every Friday, and returns on Thursday.

KIRKCUDBRIGHT,

TWYNHOLM, AND NEIGHBOURING PARISHES.

KIRKCUDBRIGHT, is the principal town in the stewartry of the same name, distant 100 miles from Edinburgh, 60 from Portpatrick, and about 28 from Dumfries. It is the seat of the stewart courts, and is situated on the east side of the river Dee, about six miles above its confluence with the Solway Frith. It is said to derive its name from an ancient British fortress, about four miles distant, called Caerbantorigum. Kirkcudbright was anciently a burgh of regality, held of the Douglasses, as lords of Galloway. Upon the forfeiture of that family it was erected into a royal burgh by King James II. on the 26th of October, 1455, and this charter was renewed and confirmed by Charles I. on the 20th of July, 1633. The government is vested in a provost, two bailies, and thirteen common councilmen, with a treasurer, and chamberlain. The harbour is the best in the stewartry; at ordinary spring tides the depth of the water is 30 feet, and at the lowest neap tides 18 feet. It is well calculated for commercial purposes; but there is no communication with any of the manufacturing districts, and the inhabitants of the stewartry are chiefly supported by agriculture. The salmon caught in the Dee is abundant, and peculiarly excellent, and the river is navigable for two miles above the town to the bridge of Tongueland, which is built of one arch of 110 feet span, and gives a pleasing effect to the surrounding landscape. Kirkcudbright has been much improved during the last 30 years, the streets are well paved and lighted, the houses, generally two stories high, have a clean and comfortable appearance, and at once bespeak the taste and easy circumstances of the inhabitants. The ruins of Kirkcudbright castle, built in 1582 by Mc Clellan, ancestor of the present Lord Kirkcudbright, are still pretty entire. Here is an elegant courthouse, with a new jail of the Gothic order, built in n 1816 ; one of its towers is 75 feet high, and, at a distance, has a magnificent appearance. A large and elegant academy has also been erected, containing a spacious room for a public subscription library. The established church is an old building, on whose

site was a monastery for grey friars, built in the 12th century; and in the High-street is a small neat chapel, belonging to the united associate congregation. Here are also the remains of the old county jail, with the news and billiard rooms, a county hall, and freemasons' lodge; and the town is said to have been once surrounded by a deep ditch and wall. There is no bridge over the river Dee ; but passengers and carriages are ferried over in a flat bottomed boat, into which the latter can be driven without much difficulty, and which is impelled along a cable stretched across the river. In stormy weather, however, or when there is an unusual current, this conveyance is not without danger, and the erection of a bridge to admit of vessels to pass through, would be a great improvement.—Nothing can be more delightful than the environs of Kirkcudbright, as the rising grounds, on each side of the river, from Tongueland to the sea, are embellished with thriving plantations. St. Mary's Isle, the family seat of the Earl of Selkirk, is distant about a mile from the town. Kirkcudbright is well supplied with butcher's meat, and provisions are comparatively cheap. The cotton weaving is carried on rather extensively, and it possesses a brewery and tan-yard, and on the opposite side of the Dee is a distillery. The market days are Tuesday and Friday. Fairs are held on the 12th of August, or Friday after, and on the 29th of September, or Friday after.

TWYNHOLM, a village in the parish of the same name, consists of a few straggling houses, on the mail road between Gatehouse and Castle Douglas; it is 6 miles east of the former town, 9 west of the latter, and about 3 miles from Kirkcudbright. It possesses a small neat kirk, and a parochial school, with a comfortable residence for the parish minister. At a short distance from the village is the estate of Barwhinnock, the property of Patrick Mc Millan, esq. and on the road to Kirkudbright, Cumpston castle is passed on the left.

POST OFFICE.—*Post Mistress*, Mrs. Ellison Baird. The Edinburgh, Glasgow, and eastern mails, arrive every evening at a quarter past eight, and are despatched at a quarter past one at noon. The west and Portpatrick mails arrive at four in the afternoon, and are despatched at five to the receiving house at Tarff Bridge. Office hours from eight in the morning till ten at night.

PLACES OF WORSHIP.

KIRKCUDBRIGHT ESTABLISHED CHURCH—Rev. Geo. Hamilton, Minister; John Hope, Precentor

BORGUE ESTABLISHED CHURCH—Rev. Jas. Gordon, Minister

RERRICK ESTABLISHED CHURCH—Rev. Jas. Thomson, Minister

TONGLAND ESTABLISHED CHURCH—Rev. Thomas Brown, Minister

TWYNHOLM ESTABLISHED CHURCH—Rev Jno. Williamson, Minister

PAROCHIAL SCHOOLS.

KIRKCUDBRIGHT PAROCHIAL ACADEMY—Mr. John Hope; commercial Teacher; Rev. William Mc Kenzie, English Teacher; and Mr. Alex. C. Donaldson, Teacher of Languages

BORGUE—Wm. Pool and Wm. Lewis, Teachers

RERRICK—Andrew Carter, Master

TONGLAND—John Kelly, Master

TWYNHOLM—John Adamson, Master

MUNICIPAL GOVERNMENT:

William Mackinnell, Provost

Wm. Campbell Low, } Bailies
William Low, jun.

James Burney, Treasurer

Common Council.—William Mure, John S. Shand, Robert Gordon, David Blair, David Morrison, Anthony Sheoch, James Rankin, Thomas Mc Millan, John Henderson, Ebenezer Drew, William Beck, John Mc Cauchie, and James Nevin.

William Marshall, Chamberlain

David Mc Lellan, Town Clerk

INCORPORATED TRADES,

David Hallie, } { Clothiers
Andrew Wilson, | Hammermen
Thos. Mc Connell, | Shoe-makers
John Mc Intire, >Deacon of<
Convener | Squaremen
Gordon Gourley, | Tailors
John Mc Cauchie, } { Weavers

Custom House, High-street.

David Milligan Jolly, esq. Collector

David Mc Lellan, esq. Comptroller

Buchannan Morrison, esq. Surveyor & Landwaiter

EXCISE.

James Ross, St. Cuthbert-street

Stamp Office, High-street.

Thomas Mac Millan, esq. Distributor

Collectors of Taxes Office, High-street

Alexander Melville, esq. Collector

David Melville, jun. Deputy and Stewart's Clerk

COUNTY GAOL.

Robert Miller, Governor

FREEMASONS' LODGE.

James Mc Cauchie, Grand Master

David Clarke, Deputy Master

Duncan Mc Allister, Senior Warden

David Clarke, Junior Warden

NOBILITY, GENTRY, &c.

Bell —, esq. Dunjop, Tongland
Blair David, esq. Borgue Place, Borgue
Brown And. gent. St. Cuthbert st
Coaltert R. esq. Bluehill, Rerrick
Donaldson Robert, Q. M. G. M. Castle st
Dunn Captain Jno. G.M. Castle st
Fergusson ——, esq. of Orroland, Rerrick
Gordon Sir John, bart. Senwick, Borgue
Gordon Colonel James, Balcarry, Rerrick
Gordon Mrs. William, Dee Bank, Tongland
Gordon Misses, Union st

Halliday David, esq. (of *Chapmanton*) High st
Ireland Wm. esq. sheriff's substitute, High st
Irving Lieut. Colonel, Balmca
Kirkpatrick Miss H. High st
Maitland Adam, esq. Cumpston castle, Twynholm
Maitland David, esq. of Barncap, Tongland
Maitland Miss, Valleyfield, Tongland
Mc Cracken John, P.M. G.M. St. Cuthbert st
Mc Culloch Dav. esq. Knockbrax, Borgue

Mc Millan Patrick L. esq. of Barwhinnock, Twynholm
Melville Alex. esq, (of *Barquhar*) High st
Mure Wm. esq. factor to the Earl of Selkirk, High st
Robertson Misses, St. Cuthbert st
Roxburgh Captain Alexander, St. Cuthbert st
Selkirk, the Right Hon. Earl of, St. Mary's Isle
Smith William, esq. (of *Newton*) High st
Thomson Lieut. James, late 10th R. V. Batt., High st
Thomson Misses, High st

MERCHANTS, TRADESMEN, &c.

ACADEMIES.

Broom Jas. (day) Mill Bourn
Conpland Mrs. (ladies' boarding) High st
Donaldson Alex. Ch. (for languages) St. Cuthbert st
Hope Jno. (commercial) Union st
Mackenzie Rev. Wm. (English) Castle st
Mc Nish Robert, (day) Union st
Miller Wm. (day) High st
Mitchell John, (day) Castle st

AUCTIONEERS.

Atkinson William, High st
Bland John, Castle st
Hannay William, Castle st
Waugh James, Castle st

BAKERS.

Birkmyre Ebenezer, High st
Carter James, Castle st
Douglas James, High st
Hobson Mrs. High st
Sloan Eckles, Castle st

BANKS.

Bank of Scotland; James Nivine, esq. agent; Alexdr. Mc Gillie, accountant; Adam Bell, Teller; draw on Mess. Coutts and Co. London

Private Bank; John Napier, esq. agent; James Mc Pherson, accountant; draw on Hankey, Alers & Co. London; & Allan and Son, Edinburgh

BOOKSELLERS STATIONERS, &c.

Cannon John, (& printer & circulating library) High st
Gordon Alex. (& printer & binder) High st
Mackmillan Thomas, High st
Nicholson John, (& binder, dealer in music, instruments, and genuine teas, and circulating library) High st

BOOT AND SHOE MAKERS

Craith Arch. & Sons, High st
Gray David, High st
Henderson Andrew, Castle st
Hornel & Sons, High st
Mc Connell Thomas, High st
Mc Courty & Angus, Castle st
Mc Donnell Alexander, High st

BREWER.

Mc Millan John, Mill Bourn

BUTTON MAKERS.

Brydson & Mc Ewing, High st
Gourlay John, (pearl) High st

CABINET MAKERS.

Carson Robert, St. Cuthbert st
Cowan Andrew, High st
Robertson Samuel, Castle st
Ferguson Mess. & Co. Castle st
Thomson Robert, Mill Bourn

COOPERS.

Anderson John, High st

Beattie Robert, High st
Mc Dowall John, High st

DISTILLERS

Findlay & Co. Bank of Bishoptown

FIRE AND LIFE OFFICES AND AGENTS.

CALEDONIAN, R. Gordon, High st
HERCULES, Wm. Mure, High st
WEST OF ENGLAND, Wm. C. Low, St. Cuthbert st

GROCERS AND SPIRIT DEALERS.

Armstrong William, High st
Carson Robert, St. Cuthbert st
Caren James, (& ship chandler) High st
Ceirns Robert, Mill Bourn
Christal John, High st
Clarke John, Castle st
Douglas James, (& hardware) Castle st
Gowrley Peter, High st
Gray Jean, High st
Hannay John, High st
Johnston William, (& hardware) High st
Knox John, High st
Mc Cleave John, Castle st
Mc Gowan Jennet, High st
Mc Kinnall Wm. High st
Mc Winnie Jean, High st
Moffat Thos. High st
Mouncey Wm. High st
Sproat Thos. (& hardware) High st
Stevenson John, High st

HOSIERS.

Christal James, jun. (& spirit dealer) St. Cuthbert st.
Hart & Son, High st
Todd Samuel, High st

INNS.

Kissock John, High st
Malcomson Samuel, (King's Arms and Head-Inn) High st

LINEN AND WOOLLEN DRAPERS.

Douglas James, High st
Mc Clune Agnes, High st
Miller Richard & Co. Castle st

MILLINERS.

Bell Miss Agnes, Castle st
Carson Misses, High st
Callie Misses, High st
Erskine Miss Jennet, Castle st
Murdoch Misses, Castle st

PAINTERS & GLAZIERS.

Christal Robert, High st
Erskine Robert, Castle st
Morison Thomas, Union st

PUBLICANS.

Black Peter, High st
Callie David, Union st
Callie John, High st
Carson Robert, St. Cuthbert st
Carter James, Castle st
Gray David, High st
Mc Clune Edward, High st
Mc Intire John, Mill Bourn
Mc Myun William, Castle st

SADDLERS AND HARNESS MAKERS.

Maxwell James, High st

Mc Ewen Samuel, Castle st
Walker John, High st

SHIP BUILDERS AND CARPENTERS.

Alexander George, Castle st
Grant Andrew, High st
Harris William, St. Cuthbert st
Millroy John, High st
Millroy Peter, St. Cuthbert st

SHIP OWNERS.

Caig David, Castle st
Grant John, High st
Johnston William, High st
Mc Burnie & Mc Clure, Castle st
Mc Cleave John, Castle st
Mc Kinnell William, High st
Morrison D. & S. St. Cuthbert st and Union st
Mouncey William, High st
Rae John, Tongueland Bridge
Rankine James, (& timber merchant) St. Cuthbert st
Skelly James, Castle st
Williamson Js. (& corn merchant) Sypeland

SLATERS.

Clarke David, St. Cuthbert st
Clarke Thos. & Son, Mill Bourn
Mc Intire James, High st
Mc Intire John, Mill Bourn

STONE MASONS.

Mc Keachie T. & Son, Mill Bourn
Mc Murray John, sen. Castle st
Mc Murray John, jun. Castle st
Milligan James, Castle st
Sharpe Jas. & Brothers, Union st

SMITHS

Anderson Thomas, High st
Bain Jas. (whitesmith) High st
Siggie William, High st

SURGEONS.

Blair David, (to the Kirkcudbright militia) High st
Dick Crawford, Union st
Mc Dowall Wm. St. Cuthbert st
Shaud J. S. (& physician) High st

TAILORS.

Biglam John, High st
Dixon James, High st
Dixon John, High st
Gibson & Son, St. Mary st
Gourley Gordon, High st
Mc Kinnell John & Son, High st
Nairne Joseph, High st
Thomson David, St. Cuthbert st

TALLOW CHANDLERS.

Brown Elizabeth, Castle st
Mouncey William, High st

TANNER.

Thomson John, Mill Bourn

WATCH AND CLOCK MAKERS.

Halliday Robert, High st
Law William, High st
Miller James, High st
Walker Francis, Castle st

WEAVERS.

Beek James, Mill Bourn
Beck John, Mill Bourn

Beck Samuel, St. Cuthbert st
Beck William, Mill Bourn
Dyson James, High st
Gordon John, Mill Bourn
Gourdly Peter, Mill Bourn
Mc Conchie Robert & Sons, St. Mary st
Mc Kenzie John, Castle st
Martin Adam, High st
Wilson David, Mill Bourn
Wilson John, Mill Bourn

WRITERS.

Burnie & Low, (& notaries) St. Cuthbert st
Brown Thomas, High st
Gordon Robert & William B. I. (& notaries & procurators fiscal for the stewartry) High st
Low William Campbell, (& procurator fiscal for the justices of the peace of the stewartry, and of the commissary court) St. Cuthbert st
Mc Caughie Thos. St. Cuthbert st
Mc Lellan David, (& notary, and town and stewartry clerk) Castle street
Morrison David, St. Cuthbert st
Murray & Thomson, (& notaries) Castle st
Nairne John Gordon, Union st
Nivine James, (& notary & clerk of supply) High st
Skeoch Anthony, (and notary) Castle st

Miscellaneous.

Irving Geo. hair dresser, High st
Mc Dowall Wm. dyer, Boraland
Simpson Ebenezer, clerk to the justices, High st

COACH.

No Coach runs through this Town, but the London and Portpatrick Royal Mail passes through Twynholm, a village about three miles distant, for London, every day at two o'clock, through Dumfries, Carlisle, &c. and for Portpatrick every evening a little before eight, thro' Gatehouse, Newton-Stewart, &c.

CARRIERS.

BORGUE KIRK, Isabella Mitchell three times a week.
DUMFRIES, Andrew Houston, from High-street, every Tuesday morning at five, and returns on Thursday evening.
DUMFRIES, John Knox, from High-street, on the same day.
EDINBURGH, George Turner, from Kissock's Inn, once a fortnight, on Monday's; and George Armstrong, every alternate week.
GATEHOUSE, Alex. Shaw, from the Cross, twice or thrice a week.
GLASGOW, Ths. Wallet, from Kissock's Inn, once a fortnight, on Friday.
GLASGOW, — Mc Clure, from Malcomson's, High-street, on Thursday.

CONVEYANCE By Water.

LIVERPOOL, the Christiana, monthly; apply to A. Mc Clure, Castle st
LIVERPOOL, the Patricia, monthly; apply to J. Caven & Co. High st

KIRKPATRICK-DURHAM AND PARTON.

KIRKPATRICK DURHAM is a small village in the parish of the same name, 85 miles from Edinburgh, 7 from Parton, 6 from Castle-Douglas, 13 from Dumfries, and 14 from New Galloway. It is a place of no great account, and contains only a few shops for the accommodation of the inhabitants. A fair is held here on the first Thursday after the 17th of March, old style.

PARTON parish extends itself along the banks of the river Dee. The church is in a romantic situation. The village contains about a dozen houses; the only one worthy of notice is the manse, the residence of the Rev. James Rae, the present minister, it is delightfully situated, fronting the river, and surrounded by hills and wood.

PLACES OF WORSHIP.

KIRKPATRICK—Rev. Dr. Lamont, Minister, Durham Hill; Rev. Robert Wallace, Curate, Manse
PARTON—Rev. James Rae, Parton Manse

PAROCHIAL SCHOOLS.

KIRKPATRICK—John Ferguson, Master
PARTON—James Johnstone, Master

TRADESMEN, &c. KIRKPATRICK.

Affleck Robt. grocer & draper
Armstrong Geo. innkeeper
Hewetson Wm. surgeon
Mc Gill Thomas, tailor
Mc Neil Mich. grocer & draper
Ross Alex. farmer
Roxburgh Peter, publican
Watson Robert, grocer

COACH.
The London Royal Mail, goes through Castle Douglas, from Portpatrick, through Dumfries, Carlisle, &c. every afternoon at three, and returns at six in the evening.

LAWRIESTON

IS a small village in the parish of Balmaghie, 98 miles from Edinburgh, 10 from Gatehouse, 10 from Kirkcudbright, 10 from New Galloway, 7 from Castle-Douglas, and 23 from Dumfries. On the north west the village is skirted by large mountains, which abound with various kinds of game. On the east the land is more fertile, and in general produces good crops. About a mile west of Lawrieston is the mansion of W. B. Kennedy Laurie, esq. who is laird, and, in part, proprietor of the village. The parish church is situated three miles to the east

PLACE OF WORSHIP.
ESTABLISHED CHURCH—Rev. James, Henderson, Minister

PAROCHIAL SCHOOL.
John Hutchison, Master

GENTRY.

Clarke Alex. gent. Lawrieston
Lawrie W. B. Kennedy, esq.
Woodhall
Mc Conchie Wm. gent. Lawrieston
Mc Kinzie John, gent. Lawrieston
Mc Kinzie Wm. gent. Lawrieston

TRADESMEN, &c.

Beon Samuel, slater
Burnett James, farmer
Campbell David, tailor
Durham James, publican
Durham Jn. joiner & publican
Garroway James, tailor
Henderson Andrew, grocer
Kerr Peter, farmer
Lawrie John, cartwright
Liviston Alex. joiner
Mc Dowell Samuel, miller
Mc Lansborough Saml. grocer
Mc Rae David, publican
Miller Alex. tailor
Strachan Wm. grocer

COACH.
The London and Carlisle Mail, passes through Castle-Douglas, seven miles hence.

NEW ABBEY,

IS a small village and parish, 80 miles from Edinburgh, 12 from Dalbeattie, and 7 from Dumfries. Adjoining to the village are the ruins of a famous cistertian abbey in a high state of preservation, although upwards of five hundred years old. Adjoining these ruins is the parish church, a small but neat stone building; a Roman Catholic chapel is also in a great state of forwardness. A corn and woollen mill employs the principal part of the inhabitants of the village.

PLACES OF WORSHIP.
NEW ABBEY ESTABLISHED CHURCH—Rev. James Hamilton, Minister
ROMAN CATHOLIC CHAPEL—Rev. Thomas Bagnall, Pastor
IRONGRAY ESTABLISHED CHURCH—Rev. Dr. Anthony Dow, Minister
LOCHRUTTON ESTABLISHED CHURCH—Rev. Thomas Inglis, Minister
TERREGLES ESTABLISHED CHURCH—Rev. George Heron, Minister

PAROCHIAL SCHOOLS.
NEW ABBEY—Samuel Mc Kee, Master
IRONGRAY— — Carnochan Master
LOCHRUTTON—John Wilson, Master
TERREGLES—William Bryden, Master

GENTRY.

Maxwell Welwood, esq. Barncleugh, Irongray
Riddle John R. esq. Kinharvey, New Abbey
Stewart Wm. esq. Shambray, New
Abbey
Walker James, esq. Woodlauds, Terregles

TRADESMEN, &c.

Brown John, publican & grocer
Corrie Joseph, publican
Dickson John, publican
Kerr James, grocer
Mc Connochie Alex. publican and flesher
Mc Kennel Robt. publican
Millar Richd. & Walter, grocers
Millar Thomas, miller

CARRIER.
DUMFRIES, James Turner, every Wednesday and Saturday, & returns on the same days.

NEW GALLOWAY,
BALMACLELLAN, DALRY, AND CARSPHAIRN.

NEW GALLOWAY, a royal burgh in the parish of Kells, is 84 miles south west of Edinburgh, 8 from Parton, 14 from Castle-Douglas, 18 from Newton-Stewart, and 25 from Dumfries. The town is pleasantly situated on the west banks of the river Ken, over which, in the year 1822, an elegant stone bridge of five arches was erected, which lying in the valley below the town, has a very pleasing effect. At the completion of this bridge, a dinner was given by Lord Visc. Kenmure, to fourteen of the oldest inhabitants of the town, whose united ages amounted to 1264 years. At a short distance south of the town stands the ancient castle of Kenmure, once a place of considerable strength. Mary Queen of Scots lodged in it one night, on her way from this country to England. On the north side of the town, within the distance of half a mile, is the parish church, a neat stone edifice with a square tower in the centre, built in 1822. In the same year, a Sunday school was established, in which upwards of one hundred children are gratuitously taught by the inhabitants. The municipal government is vested in a provost, two bailies, and fifteen councillors. Loch Ken, which joins the town, is four miles and a half long, and in many places more than a mile broad; it abounds with pike and perch, and some of the former have been caught of the astonishing weight of fifty and sixty pounds.—A justice of peace court is held on the first Monday in every month, for the recovery of debts under five pounds. Attached to the court is a criminal and debtors' gaol, with a steeple and town clock. Fairs are held on the first Wednesday after the 12th of April, the first Wednesday after the 12th of July, the first Wednesday after the 12th of August, and the first Wednesday after the 12th of November.

DALRY, a parish, the south part of which is situated in a beautiful valley along the river Ken, and is considered the richest arable land in the district; the high grounds are chiefly used for grazing cattle and sheep. It contains the village of Dalry, which is surrounded with beautiful scenery.

CARSPHAIRN village, situated near the river Deogh, contains a modern parish church, and the parochial school. The parish, excepting two or three farms, is almost wholly a grazing country. The mountains are here high and beautiful, being green to their tops. Though this parish is the second in extent in the stewartry, it rates lowest in population; but the proprietors, and the graziers are wealthy, and the shepherds are in comfortable circumstances.

At present there is no trade or manufactory carried on in these parishes, but preparations are making at Dalry, by John Kennedy, esq. of Manchester, for a woollen manufactory, which, when completed, will give employment to a considerable number of the inhabitants. The parishes of Carsphairn, Dalry, Kells, and Balmaclellan, are called the district of Glenkens, famed for the true breed of black faced sheep and black cattle, as also for good horses of the Galloway breed.

POST OFFICE, New Galloway; Post Master, Mr. James Murray. The Edinburgh and Castle-Douglas mails are despatched at half-past twelve at noon, on Monday, Wednesday, and Saturday, and arrive at a quarter past nine in the evening, on Sunday, Tuesday, and Friday.

PLACES OF WORSHIP.
KELLS ESTABLISHED CHURCH—Rev. Wm. Gillespie, Minister
BALMACLELLAN ESTABLISHED CHURCH—Rev. James Thomson, Minister
DALRY ESTABLISHED CHURCH—Rev. Alex. Mc Gowan, Minister
CARSPHAIRN ESTABLISHED CHURCH—Rev. Henry Corrie, Minister

PAROCHIAL SCHOOLS.
NEW GALLOWAY—John Moor, Master
BALMACLELLAN—James Mc Kay, Master
DALRY—James Buchanan, Master
CARSPHAIRN—James Sloan, Master

Justices of the Peace.
Carson James, esq. (of Barscobe) Balmaclellan
Kennedy David, esq. Knocknalling, New Galloway
Mc Millan David, esq. (of Dalshangan) [and surveyor of assessed taxes] Viewfield, New Galloway
Mc Millan Thos. esq. (of Lamloch) Carsphairn

NOBILITY AND GENTRY.

Alexander Lieut. John, H. P. Barskaoch, New Galloway
Ashburton Rt. Hon. Lady, Glenlee Park, New Galloway
Barber Wm. esq. Holm, Balmaclellan
Brown Major Saml. Balmaclellan Manse
Hunter Jas. esq. Milmark, Dalry
Kenmure Lord Viscount, Kenmure Castle, New Galloway
Kennedy Alex. esq. Milton Park, Dalry
Mc Kie Capt. Wm. of the East India Company's Service, Kenbank, Dalry
Mc Millan John, esq. (of Holm) Carsphairn
Mc Millan Robt. esq. (of Holm) Carsphairn
Mc Millan James, esq. Dalshangan, Carsphairn
Moffat Jas. esq. (of Drumwhim) Balmaclellan
Moffat Robt. esq. Craig, Balmaclellan
Murray John, esq. New Galloway
Murray Peter, esq. (of Troquhain) Balmaclellan
Shaw John Alex. esq. Mackilston, Dalry

MERCHANTS, TRADESMEN, &c.

NEW GALLOWAY.

Andrew James, miller, Glenlee Mill
Andrew Jn. factor to Lord Glenlee, Glenlee Mill
Cannon James, farmer, Shiel
Crosbie John, boot & shoemaker
Douglas Archibald, surgeon
Hair Jane, grocer & spirit dealer
Halliday James, grocer
Hope Rt. cattle dealer, Glenlee
Johnstone Rt. farmer, Stranfaskat
Kennedy Jas. surveyor of assessed taxes
Lamont James, hosier
Mc Gill James, flesher
Mc Kay John, grocer & draper
Maclaren Mary, publican
Mc Turk Rbt. & Wm. cattle dealers, Bankend
Manson Wm. publican
Muir James, bailie
Murdoch Wm. publican [House]
Sinclair John, farmer, Troghie
Todd Wm. saddler
Watt John, farmer, Burnhead
Wilson Robt. innkeeper.

BALMACLELLAN.

Anderson Geo. farmer, Martinston
Bell Thos. & Robt. grocers and drapers
Black Joseph, grocer & spirit dealer

451

Barber Gordon, farmer, Bogue
Bell Jno. grocer & spirit dealer

Barber Eliz. grocer
Barber James, farmer, Moordrockwood
Campbell Wm. grocer
Chalmers Ths. farmer, Loch-head
Dempster Robt. publican
Gibson Wm. farmer, Moor
Jackson Wm. farmer, Waterhead
Jamieson Robt. farmer, Castlemadie
Mc Rae James, publican

DARLY.

Donaldson Jas. grocer & spirit dealer

CARSPHAIRN.

Mitchell Jas. farmer, Garryhorn
Mitchell Wm. farmer, Woodhead
Wallace John, farmer. Marbreck

COACH.

The London Royal Mail, from Portpatrick, passes through Castle-Douglas, fourteen miles from New Galloway, through Dumfries, Carlisle, &c. every afternoon at three; and returns at six in the evening, passing through

Smith Jas. farmer, Todston
Sproat Ths. farmer, Grennan

Gatehouse, Creetown, Newton-Stewart, Glenluce, and Stranraer, to Portpatrick.

CARRIERS.

DUMFRIES, from New Galloway, Wm. Clement, every Tuesday, and returns every Thursday.

DUMFRIES, from Dalry, Alex. Good, every Tuesday, and returns every Thursday.

452

WIGTONSHIRE.

THE county of Wigton, sometimes called Upper or West Galloway, is of an irregular figure, being about 30 miles at its greatest length, and about 12 at its greatest breadth. It is bounded on the S.E. by the bay of the same name, on the S.W. by the Irish Channel, on the N. by Ayrshire, and on the east by the Stewartry of Kirkcudbright. In this county there are two narrow promontories, called the Mull of Galloway and Burgh Head, and the bays of Luce and Ryan, which extend inland, form by their aproximation a peninsula, called the Rhyns, or Rinos, of Galloway. Wigtonshire contains 4510 square miles of land, and 70 square miles of lakes, 101,136 English acres of cultivated, and 187,824 of uncultivated land. The rivers are the Luce, which falls into the bay of that name, and the Cree, which forms its eastern boundary. It possesses three royal burghs, viz. Wigtown, Stranraer, and Whithorn; the towns of Port Patrick and Newton Stewart, and several considerable villages, and is divided into seventeen parochial districts. The interior or northern parts are barren and hilly, used chiefly for the pasturage of sheep and black cattle. The mountains are Burhullion 814, Knock of Luce 1014, Lang 1758, and Mochrum Fell 1020 feet above the level of the sea.

POPULATION OF THE SHIRE OF WIGTOWN.

T. Town, B. Burgh; P. Parish.

	Houses	Males	Females	Total		Houses	Males	Females	Total
Glasserton................p	198	544	513	1057	Portpatrick................p	269	845	973	1818
Inch.....................p	507	1133	1253	2386	Sorby....................p	210	619	700	1319
Kirkcolm ....p	346	885	936	1821	Stoneykirk...............p	679	1512	1621	3133
Kirkcowan ....p	256	608	675	1283	Stranraer ....b & p	417	1098	1365	2463
Kirkinner ....p	270	738	750	1488	Whithorn...........b & p	421	1081	1280	2361
Kirkmaiden ....p	420	1090	1120	2210	Wigtown......... ..b & p	547	922	1120	2042
Leswalt.................p	414	1138	1194	2332					
Luce, New ....p	121	296	313	609	Total..	6038	15837	17403	33240
Luce, Old, or Glenluce......p	361	981	976	1957					
Mochrum.................p	338	887	984	1871					
Penningham, and Newton-Stewart p t	461	1460	1630	3090					

GARLIESTON, AND SORBY.

GARLIESTON, dignified as being the residence of the Earl of Galloway, is a sea port, delightfully situated on the rivers of Broughton and Pontenburn, over each of these streams are a number of bridges. It is built in the form of a semi-circle, facing the bay, and is a safe commodious harbour, capable of containing a great number of vessels. In spring tides the water here rises eighteen feet. If a break water, which could be done at very little expense, was carried out to a rock they call Allen, vessels belonging to the north English coast, bound for Dublin, when the wind is blowing from south-south west and south-east, might take shelter here at all times of the tide. Galloway house is a splendid mansion, built in 1740; the walks about it for several miles, are extremely picturesque and beautiful.

SORBY is a village, distant 6 miles from Wigton, 13 from Newton-Stewart, 30 from Stranraer, and 39 from Portpatrick. This is a fine country for grain, the land is in a high state of cultivation, the farm houses are handsomely built, and the farmers are generally wealthy. About a mile to the east of the kirk, are the ruins of Sorby tower, formerly belonging to the Hannays. There are also in this parish, the remains of two strong castles on the Headlands of Cruigleton and Eagerness villages.

POST OFFICE.—*Post Master*, Mr. John Marshall. The Mail arrives at eleven in the morning during the months of November, December, January, February, March, and in summer at ten, and is despatched at six every morning during winter, and five during summer.

PLACES OF WORSHIP.
ESTABLISHED CHURCH.—Rev. Elliot Wm. Davidson, Minister. Andrew Mc Clure, Precentor

GARLIESTOWN INDEPENDENT MEETING HOUSE.— Rev. T. Smith, Minister. D. Matthieson, Precentor

PAROCHIAL SCHOOL.
James Pollux, Independent Schoolmaster

NOBILITY, AND GENTRY.
Galloway the Right Honbl. Earl of, Galloway house | Kerly Capt. John, R. N.

TRADESMEN, &c.

Andrews James, publican, Sorby
Baen Jas. locksmith & bell hanger, Garlieston
Broadfoot Jno. grocer, Garlieston
Chambers David, ship carpenter, Garlieston
Coltran Jane, inn & general dealer, Garlieston
Dick Alexander, ship carpenter, Garlieston
Dick William, ship carpenter, Garlieston
Donnan Ebenr. saddler, Sorby
Douglass Elizabeth, grocer &c. Garlieston

Hannay Wm. publican, Garlieston
Hargg Peter, mason, Garlieston
Johnston Francis, publican, Garlieston
Kivend Simon, publican, &c. Sorby
Mc Clure And. cartwright, Sorby
Mc Clure John, grocer, Sorby
Mc Culloch Alex. grocer, Sorby
Mc Gowan Cath. grocer, Sorby
Mc Laland Sarah, grocer, Sorby
Marshall John, grocer & draper, Garlieston
Rankin James, grocer & draper, Garlieston
Riggs James, publican, Garlieston

Robb Alex. boot and shoe maker, Garlieston
Shaw Jno. rope maker, Garlieston
Stewart Eliz. publican, Garlieston
Thompson Maine, publican and smith, Sorby
Walker Jas. damask manufacturer, Sorby
Wilds Wm. miller, Garlieston

CARRIERS
FROM GARLIESTON.
STRANRAER, Wm. Mc Fee, every Tuesday.
WIGTON, William Hannay, every Saturday.

R 4

GLENLUCE,

INCLUDING THE NOBILITY, GENTRY, CLERGY, &c. OF THE PARISHES OF KIRKCOWAN AND NEW LUCE.

GLENLUCE is distant 10 miles from Stranraer, 17 from Wigtown, 16 from Newton-Stewart, and 19 from Portpatrick, beautifully situated on the banks of the river Luce, and is surrounded by an interesting and picturesque country, abounding with game of almost every description. The church is a neat edifice, remarkable only for its simplicity. Here is also a dissenting meeting house. A mile to the northward of the church, are the ruins of an abbey, founded in the year 1190, by Rolland, Lord of Galloway; the walls of several of the apartments are yet standing. These ruins are remarkably interesting, and contain some fine specimens of architecture. Fairs are held here the second Tuesday in May, and the monthly fair, or market, begins on the second Friday in April, and continues till the second Friday in December.

POST OFFICE.—Post Master, Mr. Alexander Mc Crachan. Mails from England, Edinburgh, Dumfries, Castle Douglas, Kircudbright, Gatehouse, Creatown and Newton Stewart, arrive at half-past one every morning, and depart at half-past eight every morning. Mails from Stranraer arrive at half past eight every morning, and depart at half-past one in the morning.

PLACES OF WORSHIP.
GLENLUCE ESTABLISHED CHURCH.—Rev. John Macdowall, Minister
SECESSION.—Rev. Mr. Puller, Minister
KIRKCOWAN PARISH CHURCH.—Rev. Auth. Stewart, Minister
NEW LUCE PARISH CHURCH.—Rev. Wm. Mc Kergo, Minister

PAROCHIAL SCHOOLS.
GLENLUCE.—William Mc Morland and Wm. Main, Masters
KIRKCOWAN.—Alexander Hunter, Master
NEW LUCE.—Andrew Clanochan, Master

GENTRY.
Adair John, esq. Genoch, Balkail
Cathcart John, esq. Genoch
Dalrymple Sir James Hay, bart. Dunragit
Hamilton Capt. Wm. Craichlaw, Kirkcowan

TRADESMEN, &c
Edgar Mrs. G. general dealer
Douglas Peter, grocer
Gibson Jas. tailor, Kirkcowan
Hannay Thomas, tailor
Love Andw. innkeeper, Kirkcowan
Mc Clew D. sadler
Mc Cracken John, surveyor of taxes and grocer
Mc Kie Alex. grocer, &c. Kirkcowan
Mc Master Robert, Kings Arms Inn and Hotel [cowan
Mc Nairn Jas. cartwright, Kirk-
Mc Taldroch James, inn

Mc William Alex. innkeeper, Kirkcowan
Mc William Alex. cartwright, Kirkcowan
Mc William Wm. smith, Kirkcowan
Milligan Jno. grocer, Kirkcowan
Milroy Robert and Co. woollen manufacturers, Kirkcowan
Paul William, ironmonger and hardwareman
Skimming Jas. & Robert, woollen drapers, &c.
Tait Alexander, baker

Templeton James, publican
Wallace Chas. innkeeper & grocer, Kirkcowan
Withers James, tailor & draper
Withers Wm. grocer & draper

COACHES.
DUMFRIES, every morning at half past eight.
PORTPATRICK, every morning at half past one.

CARRIERS.
NEWTONSTEWART, from the Horse every Wednesday & Saturday
WIGTOWN, from the Horse every Thursday.

KIRKMAIDEN AND STONEYKIRK.

KIRKMAIDEN, is distant 20 miles from Stranraer, 30 from Wigton, 36 from Newton-Stewart, and 16 from Portpatrick. The church is a plain edifice, situated near the centre of the parish, six miles to the south-east of which is the Mull of Galloway. At Portnissock, an excellent harbour has been lately erected at the expense of Andrew Mc Douall, esq. its spirited proprietor, who is using every means in his power to improve this place. There is also on the estate of this gentleman, a fish pond well worthy of the observation of the curious. It is hewn out of the solid rock, having communication with the sea by means of iron grating ingeniously contrived. Some of the fish are so tame that they will feed out of the hand. There is also a tolerable harbour at Dromore.

STONEYKIRK is distant 25 miles from Wigtown, 25 from Newton-Stewart, 6 from Stranraer, and 6 from Portpatrick, bounded on the south by Kirkmaiden, on the east and south-east by the bay of Glenluce, and on the north by Inch and Glenluce. On the estate of Captain Maitland, is an artificial mount, supposed to be of Roman origin, and used as a beacon in the time of war. There is also another of a similar kind on the estate of John Mc Taggert, esq. of Ardwell house.

PLACES OF WORSHIP.
KIRKMAIDEN PARISH CHURCH.—Rev. James French, Minister
STONEYKIRK PARISH CHURCH.—Rev. James Anderson, Minister

PAROCHIAL SCHOOLS.
KIRKMAIDEN.—William Todd, Master
STONEYKIRK.—James Crum, Master

GENTRY.
Hawthorn Vance, esq. Garthland castle, Stoneykirk
Mc Douall Andrew, esq. Logan, Kirkmaiden
Mc Taggart John, esq. Ardwell house, Stoneykirk
Maitland Patrick, esq. Bolgregen, Stoneykirk
Paterson John, esq. Kildrochat, Stoneykirk

TRADESMEN, &c.
Hunter Jas. grocer, Stoneykirk
Mc Chlery Thomas, merchant, Dromore, Kirkmaiden
Mc Colm John, grocer, &c. Dromore, Kirkmaiden
Mc Crachen Hugh, innkeeper, Stoneykirk
Mc Douall Alexander, merchant, Dromore, Kirkmaiden
Mc Neely Alex. innkeeper, &c. Dromore, Kirkmaiden
Milwee Alex. innkeeper & grocer, &c. Portnissock
Rhodie Alexander, grocer, &c. Kirkmaiden
Tilley Thomas, innkeeper & grocer, Stoneykirk

MOCHRUM.

MOCHRUM, about 12 miles S. E. from Glenluce, and about 10 S. S. W. from Wigton, is bounded on the east by Kirkinner, on the south by Kirkmaiden, annexed to Glasserton, on the west by the sea, and on the north-west by Glenluce. In this parish is a thriving village, possessing a very good harbour called Port William, and near it is the handsome residence and demesne of Sir William Maxwell, bart. its noble proprietor.

POST OFFICE, Portwilliam.—*Post Master*, Mr. Joseph Hall. Mail arrives between twelve and one, and departs at five every morning.

PLACE OF WORSHIP.
Parish Church.—Rev. John Stean, and Rev. Alex. Young, Ministers

PAROCHIAL SCHOOL.
Alexander Mc Nish, Master

GENTRY.
Maxwell Sir Wm. bart. Monreath | Cumming Jas. esq., Factor, Airlour

TRADESMEN, &c.
Dickson Anthony, grocer, &c.
Mc Garvin John, publican
Mc Master John, publican

Mulhinch Peter, grocer & clothier
Ross James, publican
Sloan John, acting tide waiter

Sloan John, grocer, &c.
Wallace James, grocer, &c.

NEWTON-STEWART,
INCLUDING THE NOBILITY, GENTRY, CLERGY, &c. IN THE PARISH OF MINNIGAFF, KIRKCUDBRIGHTSHIRE.

NEWTON-STEWART, distant 121 miles from Edinburgh, about 82 from Glasgow, 52 from Dumfries, 8 from Wigtown, and 26 from Stranraer, formerly known by the name of Newton-Douglas, is a small thriving town in the parish of Penningham, delightfully situated on the river Cree, over which there is a very handsome stone bridge of five arches, joining Newton-Stewart to the village of Cree bridge, in the parish of Minnigaff. It consists principally of one long street, in the centre of which is the tolbooth, which is the principal ornament of the town. Here is a church of the establishment, one of relief, and one of cameronians; likewise a masonic lodge, reading and coffee room, weaver's society, sabbath school, and the Douglas charity school, for educating twelve poor children out of the parishes of Penningham and Kirkmabrick. There is also an extensive brewery and tanyard, and a branch of the British Linen Bank. The manufacture of cotton is carried on here and in the adjacent country to a considerable extent. The town government is vested in the hands of the magistrates, who meet once a month. To the north of the town, about 1½ miles distant, are the remains of Castle Stewart, formerly belonging to a branch of the Galloway family. There is a weekly market on Wednesday; also cattle markets 1st Friday monthly, except January, February and March, they are generally well attended. Fairs are held the last Wednesday in March, 1st Wednesday after the 15th of June, last Wednesday in July, and last Wednesday in October, all old style.

POST OFFICE.—*Post Master and Stamp Distributor*, Mr. John Paterson. Mail from London, Carlisle, Edinburgh, and Dumfries arrives at half-past eleven every night, and is despatched at half-past ten every day. Mail from Portpatrick arrives at half-past ten every day, and is despatched at half-past eleven every night.

PLACES OF WORSHIP.
Established Kirk.—Rev. J. Black, Minister
Cameronian—Rev. Jas. Reid, Minister

Excise Office.
James Hossac, officer, Campbell's Hotel

NOBILITY AND GENTRY.
Adams J. Smith, esq. Benfield
Boyd Edward, esq. Merton hall
Dill Miss Elizabeth
Douglas Mrs. Minnigaff
Kivan Wm. esq. Bellvue
Mc Caa Mrs.
Mc Caa Wm. esq. Cree bridge, Minnigaff

Mc Clurg Misses
Mackie John, esq. Bargally, Minnigaff
Maitland Rev. J. G. Manse, Minnigaff
Martin J. H. esq. Glencrea
Maxwell Sir Jno. Heron, bart. Keroughtree, Minnigaff

Stewart Honble. Montgomerie, Corsbie
Stewart James, esq. Cairnsmore, Minnigaff
Stewart Lieut. General Sir Wm. Minnigaff

MERCHANTS, TRADESMEN, &c.

PROFESSIONAL GENTLEMEN.
Dill William, writer, notary, and messenger
Douglas John, writer, notary, and auctioneer
Good William, writer, notary, & auctioneer
Hannay Peter, messenger
Mc Millan John, notary
Mc Millan Wm. writer, notary, & justice of peace clerk
Smith Chas. physician & surgeon
Stewart John, writer, messenger, & auctioneer
Thompson James, surgeon and apothecary

ACADEMIES.
Kennedy William

Mc Gill Jas. (parochial) Minnigaff
Martin John, (parochial)
Sloan Miss M. A. (ladies boarding) Minnigaff

BAKERS.
Bilkmyer Thos. Minnigaff
Kelly Alexander
Smith Morrison

BANKERS.
Mc Caa Wm. esq. (agent for British Linen Co.)
Simpson John, (private)

BOOKSELLERS AND STATIONERS.
Mc Nairn Joseph, (& binder and printer)
Paterson John
Thompson John Robert

BOOT & SHOE MAKERS.
Aitken John
Hunter Wm.
Mc Clymont Andrew
Mc Cutchan John
Mc Kie David, Minnigaff
Mc Whey John, jun. (& publican) Minnigaff
Milligan John, Minnigaff
Tod Alex. Minnigaff

BREWERY.
Mc Lauren James

CABINET MAKERS.
Kennedy Wm.
Mc Guffog Alex.

CARPENTERS & JOINERS.
Bell John
Hannah Robert
Mc Kinna Peter

Mc Murray Robert
Smith Walker
Walker John

CARTWRIGHTS.
Bell John
Dewar James
Smith Walker

CORN & FLOUR MERCHTS.
Aird John, (& miller)
Bell James

CURRIERS.
Gibson Hugh
Gibson Thomas

FIRE AND LIFE INSURANCE OFFICES
HERCULES, Wm. Dillon
CALEDONIAN, James Mc Lauren

GLASS & CHINA DEALRS.
Bell James
Glover James & Co.
Mc Nish David
Milligan Andrew
Nelson Jane

GROCERS AND SPIRIT DEALERS.
Aikin Robert, (& seedsman & toy dealer)
Bell James
Brown Wm.
Cannon Wm. Minnigaff
Erskine Wm. (& publican) Minnigaff
Gibson Michael
Glover James & Co.
Hannah John
Mc Clurg Robert
Mc Conochie Samuel
Mc Dowall Alex. Minnigaff
Mc Gaa John
Mc Nish David
Mc Whey John, sen. Minnigaff
Murray Thomas
Scott Ann
Shaw Alexander
Summers Elizabeth
Thompson Wm. (& ironmonger)
Turner John, Minnigaff
Wilson John

HARDWAREMEN.
Gray Thomas
Mc Millan Basil
Mc Nairn Joseph
Thompson Wm.

INNS.
Campbell George
Craik John, (Galloway Arms)
Maconnochie Samuel

IRON MONGERS.
Glover James and Co. (& hardwaremen)
Gray Thomas
Thompson Wm.

MILLERS.
Black John, Minnigaff
Mc Dowall Robt. (mill of Garlies) Minnigaff

NURSERY AND SEEDSMEN.
Aiken Robert, (seedsman only)
Mitchell John
Spark Robert, (nursery only)

PAINTERS & GLAZIERS.
Miler Daniel
Milligan Wm.

SADDLERS.
Hannay John
Murray Wm.

TAILORS
Armstrong Robert
Crawford James
Paterson James
Simpson Alex.

TALLOW CHANDLERS.
Gordon Agnes
Gordon Mrs.
Wilson Mrs.

TANNERS.
Cowan & Sinclair, Minnigaff
Drynan & Wallace

TAVERNS AND PUBLIC HOUSES.
Clannie Johnston
Gibson Thomas
Gordon James, sen.
Gordon James, jun.
Johnston Charles
Kelly Wm.
Mc Clurg Robert
Mc Logan Daniel, Minnigaff
Mc Murray Robert
Macwraith Wm.
Murdoch Agnes

WATCH AND CLOCK MAKERS.
Gourlay James
Jamieson James

WOOLLEN AND LINEN DRAPERS.
Carson James
Dunsmore Andrew
Hughes Peter
Mc Clurg Robert
Mc Millan Basil
Porter James
Tait Andrew, Minnigaff

Miscellaneous.
Adams James, precentor of Established kirk
Aitken Jas. spirit merchant
Bryde Jas. spirit & tea dealer
Donnan John, smith
Girvan Wm. precentor of Relief chapel
Glover Jas & Co. general merchants
Glover John, spirit merchant
Mc Geoch Alex. & Son, wood turners
Mc Nairn Joseph, plumber & tin and coppersmith
Nelson & Andrew, builders, stone masons, and wood & slate merchants
Nicholson Peter, cotton agents
Wells John, dyer, Minnigaff
Wilson Mary, straw bonnet maker

COACHES.
DUMFRIES, Carlisle, and London Royal Mail, from the Galloway Arms, every morning at half past ten, through Gatehouse, Castle-Douglas, Annan, &c.
PORTPATRICK, the Royal Mail, from the Galloway Arms, every night at half past eleven.

CARRIERS.
EDINBURGH, Joseph Bennoch, from Andrew Taits, Cree bridge, twice every three weeks
EDINBURGH, John Candlish, from Samuel Mc Conochie's Inn, every three weeks.
GLASGOW, Michl. and Edw. Gibson, alternately every Monday, through Straiton, Kirkmichael, Ayr, Kilmarnock, leave Glasgow on Thursday, and arrive here again on Saturday.
DUMFRIES, John Gilkison, from his own house, every Monday, leaves Dumfries every Wednesday, and returns here on the following Friday.
DUMFRIES, Wm. Gibson, from his own house, every Monday, leaves Dumfries on Wednesday, and arrives here the following Friday.
KIRKCUDBRIGHT; occasionally
STRANRAER, John Agnew, from his own house, on Tuesday and Friday, and returns the following days
STRANRAER, Alex. Telfer, from Mc Conochie's Inn, every Friday.
WIGTOWN, Michl. and Edw. Gibson, every Monday and Saturday.
WIGTOWN, John Gilkison, and Wm. Gibson, every Saturday, and returns the same day.

CONVEYANCE By Water.
LIVERPOOL, the Rose Packet, from Port Carty, monthly.

PORTPATRICK,

DISTANT 133 miles from Edinburgh, 89 from Glasgow, 6¼ from Stranraer, 35 from Wigtown and 34 from Newton Stewart. This town has long been the great northern thoroughfare for Ireland, and was formerly, with the estate of Dunskey, the property of Lord Mount Alexander, whose residence was the old castle of Dunskey, a place of considerable strength, as appears from the interesting remains. The estate of Dunskey was acquired from the Viscount of Airds by Mr. Blair, the minister of Portpatrick, and is now enjoyed by his descendants. An excellent harbour is now making under the direction of John Rennie, esq. for the convenience of his majesty's packets ; although a difficult undertaking, on completion will be a great national improvement. Steam vessels are now introduced at this place, which will greatly facilitate the communication between this and the sister kingdom.

POST OFFICE.—Post Master, Mr. Thos. Kennedy. The Glasgow Mail arrives at 40 minutes past five every morning, and departs at eleven at night. The English Mail arrives at 40 minutes past four every morning, and departs at six every morning. The Irish Mail arrives and is despatched every day wind and weather permitting.

Custom House.
Robert Hannay, esq. Collector

John Lethwaite, esq. Comptroller
Mr. James Grey, Surveyor, Landwaiter, &c.

GENTRY AND CLERGY.

Blair Forbes Hunter, esq. Dunskey | Henry David, esq. Civil Engineer | Mc Kenzie Rev. Jno. D. D. Manse

TRADESMEN, &c.

Brown James, publican
Cumming Andrew, publican
Gillespie John, dealer in sundries
Knox John, baker
Mc Clew David, dealer in sundries
Mc Cormick John, publican
Mc Crea Mary, dealer in sundries
Mc Lawrin Daniel, grocer
Murdoch John, factor, Dunskey
Taylor Wm. general dealer
Urquhart K. dealer in sundries

INNS.

Gordon William, (Blairs Arms, & Downshire Arms)
Mc Gaa Alex. (King's Arms)

COACH.

DUMFRIES, Carlisle, and London, the Royal Mail, from the Downshire Arms, every morning at six.

CARRIERS.

STRANRAER, daily.

CONVEYANCE

By Water.

DONAGHADEE, the Mail Steam Packet daily, during Summer months, and in Winter a daily sailing packet, wind and weather permitting; John Hannay, agent.

The Liverpool and Glasgow Steam Packets, call at Portpatrick, going and returning.

STRANRAER,

INCLUDING THE NOBILITY, GENTRY, CLERGY, &c. IN THE PARISHES OF INCH, KIRKCOLM AND LESWALT.

STRANRAER, a town of considerable antiquity, 6¼ miles from Port Patrick, is governed by a provost, two bailies, a dean of guild, and fifteen councillors, and joins with Wigton, New Galloway, and Whithorn in sending a member to parliament. It is the seat of a presbytery; and has a custom house, of which all the creeks within the Rhins are members, except Portpatrick and its dependencies; there is also two coast guard establishments under the inspection and command of Captain Campbell. The harbour of Stranraer affords excellent anchorage, and a pier of considerable extent within this last four years has been formed, which has proved a great convenience and benefit to the shipping.— Cairn Ryan also affords good anchorage, and vessels from the West Indies, bound for the Clyde, frequently take shelter at this place, which is quite safe and commodious; so great is the depth of water that a fleet of men of war might anchor here with safety. The exportation trade consists in grain, leather, a considerable quantity of shoes, cheese, &c. Stranraer has a masonic lodge, two news rooms, a subscription and two circulating libraries, a bible society, a saving's bank, dispensary, and sabbath school. Here is also an established church and three dissenting meeting houses. The town-hall is a neat building in George's-street; but the principal feature of this town is the castle, now converted into a jail, which no doubt possesses great claims to antiquity, although the time of its erection cannot be ascertained, it is however mentioned in the town charter granted by King James VI. and is called Port Sallie. Culhorn, the residence of the Earl of Stair, is about 2 miles from this place. Castle Kennedy, about 4 miles distant, is also his property, its scenery is highly picturesque and beautiful, and is much and justly admired. In or near the centre of this charming spot, are the ruins of a castle, formerly an occasional residence of its ancient proprietors, the Earls of Cassiles. A justice peace court is held here on the 1st Monday in every month; also a burgh court every other Saturday. Market day every Friday. Fairs, January horse fair Thursday before New Years Ayr Fair; May, the Friday before Whitsunday; the last Friday in June, at Sandmill; the last Friday in July, at Sandmill; the third and last Fridays in August, St. John's; last Friday in September, at Sandmill; October horse fair, Thursday before Michaelmas Ayr Fair and last Friday, and last Friday in November, at Sandmill.

POST OFFICE.—Post Mistress, Mrs. Dorothy Mc Nish. Mail from Edinburgh arrives at a quarter past five every morning, and is despatched at nine every evening. Mails from London, Dumfries, Castle Douglas, Creetown, Glenluce, Gatehouse, Kircudbright, Newton Stewart, and Wigtown arrives at three every morning, and are despatched at seven in the evening. Mails from Ireland due at a quarter past five every morning, and the bags are made up for dispatch every night at nine.

PLACES OF WORSHIP

STRANRAER PARISH CHURCH—Rev. David Wilson, Minister; John Mc Intyre, Precentor.
CAMERONIAN—Rev. Wm. Symington, Minister
RELIEF—Rev. John Mc Gregor, Minister
UNITED ASSOCIATE SYNOD—Rev. John Robertson, and Rev. Wm. Smilie, Ministers.
INCH PARISH CHURCH—Rev. Peter Ferguson, and Rev. Jas. Ferguson, Ministers.
KIRKCOLM—Rev. Wm. Rose, Minister
LESWALT—Rev. A. Mc Cubbin, Minister

PAROCHIAL SCHOOLS.

STRANRAER—David Mc Murtry, Master
INCH—Alexander Wallace, Master
KIRKHOLM—James Wallace, Master

LESWALT—Alexander Mc Ghee, Master

Magistracy.

The Rt. Hon. the Earl of Stair, Provost
Wm. Black and John Forsyth, Bailies
Charles Morland, esq. Dean of Guild
Mr. James C. Miller, Treasurer
J. H. Ross, Town Clerk

Custom House.

David Gordon, Collector
Alexander Mc Neel, Comptroller
John Semple, Surveyor and Acting Landwaiter

Excise Officers.

John Borthwick, Supervisor
James Grey and David Bryce, Officers

NOBILITY, GENTRY, AND CLERGY.

Agnew Honble. Mrs. Scheuchan house, Leswalt
Agnew Honbl. Mrs. Park house
Agnew Sir Andw. bart. Luchnaw Castle, Leswalt
Agnew Wallace Gen. John Alex Cairn Ryan, Inch
Bennoch Mrs. Hanover st
Campbell Capt. D., R. N.
Crane Lieut. Thomas, R. N. H. P Charlotte street
Frazer Charles, Hanover st
Hannah Samuel, Hill head

Kerr Mrs. Wm. Princes st
Leggatt Wm. Barlockhart
Mc Gregor Rev. John, Church st
Mc Douall Alex. Church st
Mc Douall John, Vaileyfield
Mc Douall Lieut. Col. Robert, C. B. Hanover st
Mc Kenzie John, King st
Mc Nair Major General John, Hanover st
Moore James Carrick, esq. East Corswall house, Kirkcolm
Morrison Allen, King st

Robertson Rev. John, Hanover st
Ross Capt. J, R. N. Observatory
Ross J, esq. Cairnbrock, Kirkcolm
Smillie Rev. Wm. Neptune st
Stair the Rt. Hon. Earl of, Culhorn
Symington Rev. Wm. Stranraer
Taylor Lieut. Jno. H. P. Lewis st
Taylor Lieut. Nathan, H. P. Lewis street
Taylor Lieut. Thomas, H. P, Lewis street
Watt Mrs. King st
Wilson Rev. David

MERCHANTS, TRADESMEN, &c.

ACADEMIES.

Mc Credie Andrew, Castle st
Mc Meicken Mrs. (ladies' boarding and day) Princes st
Mc Meicken Miss, (ladies boarding and day) High st
Moore Miss, High st

BAKERS.

Gartly Simon, Castle st
Lindsay Thos. Georges st
Mc Caig James, Fisher st
Mc Farlane James, Georges st
Mc Nish Uthered, Queen st
Miller Margaret, Hanover st

BANKERS.

British Linen Co. (branch of) Alex. Mc Neel, agent, Georges st
Paisley Banking Co. (branch of) Mc Kie and Morland, agents, King street

BOOKSELLERS, STATIONERS & BINDERS.

Bryce Agnes, Georges st
Dick Robert, Georges st
Mc Credie Wm. (binder) Castle st
Walker Pr. (& binder) Georges st

BOOT & SHOEMAKERS.

Bissett Thos. Castle st
Mc Cubbin James, Georges st
Ross David, Georges st

BREWERS.

Angus Charles, Strand
Thorburn Wm. Princes st

CABINET MAKERS, &c.

Baird John, Queen st
Nibloe John, Castle st
Thorburn Alex. Harbour st

COOPERS.

Gullin James, Fisher st
Mc Tier Wm. Greenvale st

CORN MERCHANTS.

Kerr Wm. Hanover st
Lindsay Thos. Charlotte st
Mc Douall Alex. Church st
Mc Douall James & John
Murray James, Springbank
Ross Andrew, Church st

CURRIERS.

Hill William
Mc Clymont James, Castle st

FIRE OFFICES & AGENTS.

EDINBURGH, Wm. Sprott
HERCULES, C. Morland
PROVIDENT, Alex. Mc Neel

GROCERS AND SPIRIT DEALERS

Buyers James, King st
Campbell Abraham, Georges st
Cowan Mrs. (grocer only) Georges street
Gifford Wm. Georges st
Hunter James, Georges st
Mc Caig Thomas, Queen st
Mc Crea Hugh, Stewartstown, Kirkcolm
Mc Dowell Wm. Cas.. st
Mc Ewing Audrey, Lewis st
Macfarlane Malcolm & Alexander, Georges street
Mc Kenzie Daniel, Leswalt
Mc Lean Andrew, Georges st
Mc Lean James, Hanover st
Mc Master John, Leswalt
Mc Micken Archd. Georges st
Muir John, Bridge st
Robertson Elizabeth, King st
Robertson John, Charlotte st

Robinson Robert, Stewartstown, Kirkcolm
Wallace Matthew, Castle st

HARDWAREMEN AND IRONMONGERS.

Mc Clean Andrew, Georges st
Mc Clean Wm. Georges st
Neilson Charles, Georges st
Paterson John, Charlotte st

INNS.

George Hotel, Elizabeth Paterson
King's Arms, Thos. King

LEATHER CUTTERS AND MERCHANTS.

Black Wm. Georges st
Mc Master Anthony, Georges st
Ross David, Georges st

MESSENGERS.

Adair John, Georges st
Caird James, Georges st
Jolly John, jun. Georges st
Mc Kinnell Wm. Lewis st
Milligan Wm. Lewis st
Sprott Wm. Church st

MILLINERS AND DRESS MAKERS.

Mc Kie Agnes, Hanover st
Mc Nish M. Queen st
Wallace & Ritchie, Lewis st
Warden Miss, Georges st

NURSERY & SEEDSMEN.

Murray James, Hanover st
Murray John, Georges st
Nicol James, Castle st

SADDLERS AND HARNESS MAKERS.

Mc Gouan Anthony, Charlotte st
Mc Kie Alex. Hanover st
Mc Kie Wm. Hanover st
Ronald Thos. Georges st

SURGEONS AND APOTHECARIES.

Agnew Charles, (apothecary only) Georges st
Cargo Wm. Hanover st
Mc Cormick James, Georges st
Wilson Robert, Georges st

TAILORS.

Brown John, Castle st
Gordon James, Georges st
Mc Bride Peter, St. John st
Mc Carlie John, Lewis st
Mc Douall James, King st
Murray Wm. Burnside
Ronald Robert, Sun st
Sprott Thos. Georges st

TANNERS.

Kerr & Shillan, Queen st
Mc Master Thos. Georges st

TAVERNS AND PUBLIC HOUSES.

Angus Elizabeth, Georges st
Biggan Thos. (spirit dealer only) Georges street
Donnon Andrew, Georges st
Drynan John, Bridge st
Kerr John, Clay hole
Mc Caig Thos. Fisher st
Mc Crea Margaret, Stewartstown, Kirkcolm
Mc Clement Janet, Hanover st
Mc Colm Helen, Castle st
Mc Cubbin James, Charlotte st
Mc Douall John, King st
Mc Kenzie Alex. Lewis st
Mc Kie Anthony, Neptune st

Ritchie Wm. Hanover st
Ronald Thos. Georges st
Ross Rt. Stewartstown, Kirkcolm
Shillan Thos. Clay hole
Stewart Jane, Stewartstown, Kirkcolm
Tunnick William, Stewartstown, Kirkcolm

TIMBER MERCHANTS.

Baird John, Georges st
Morland Wm. King st

WATCH MAKERS.

Adair James, Georges st
Adair John, Georges st
Garrick John, Castle st
Mc Credie Thos. Georges st

WOOLLEN AND LINEN DRAPERS

Black Samuel, Georges st
Camlin Nathaniel, Georges st
Douglas John, (and silk mercer) Georges street
Gordon James, Georges st
Kirkpatrick Robert, Georges st
Mc Michan James, Charlotte st
Mc Robert John, Georges st
Thompson James, Georges st
Wither John, Hanover st

WRITERS.

Adair John, Georges st
Caird James, High st
Douglas Wm. Lewis st
Jolly John, Georges st
Mc Kinnell Wm. Lewis st
Mulligan Wm. Lewis st
Nish Gilbert, Georges st
Ross James Hunter, W. S. High st
Sprott Wm. Church st
Young David, Princes st

Miscellaneous.

Bowie Robt. tin plate worker, &c. Georges st
Brown Thomas, agent for packets, Castle street
Carmichael Jno. farrier, Kirrasrae, Kirkcolm
Mc Bride Jane, confectioner, Georges street
Mc Clean Wm. china &c. dealer, Georges street
Mc Culloch David, upholsterer, Church street
Mc Kie Jno. jun. distiller & agent for Lloyds, Hanover st
Miller James, factor, Lewis st
Morland Wm. spirit merchant, Queen street

COACHES.

DUMFRIES, Carlisle, and London, Royal Mail, from the George Hotel, every morning at seven, through Glenluce, Newton Stewart, Gatehouse, and Castle-Douglas.
PORTPATRICK, the Royal Mail, from the George Hotel, every morning at three.

CARRIERS.

AYR, from the George Hotel, every Friday.
GARLIESTOWN, from the Horse, every Thursday.
GLASGOW, from the Horse, every fortnight.
NEWTON-STEWART, from the Kings Arms Hotel, on Wednesday and Saturday.
PORTPATRICK, from the Horse every day.
WIGTOWN, from William Ritchie's, Hanover street, every Thursday.

STEAM BOAT.

GLASGOW, the Dumbarton Castle weekly during Summer.

WHITHORN, &c.

WHITHORN, distant 10 miles from Wigton, 32 from Stranraer; 20 from Newton-Stewart, and 40 from Portpatrick. This town has great claims to antiquity, and was formerly a place of commercial importance; but at present the trade is very inconsiderable. It however retains the privilege of sending a member to parliament, in conjunction with Wigtown, Stranraer, and New Galloway. The church is remarkably neat and spacious, and much superior to most of the parish kirks in this county; it has been finished about a twelvemonth, and is built on part of the venerable ruins of the priory, founded by the pious St. Ninian, who is said to be the first who converted the Picts to the christian faith. These ruins are remarkably grand and imposing; they contain several large vaults, a beautiful Saxon and some Gothic arches, also sculptured royal armorial bearings of Scotland, and the dilapidated arms of the bishops of Galloway. Here are meeting houses for the Cameronians and seceders—they have not however, any settled incumbent to either. Here is also a bible society, a subscription library, and a savings' bank with a capital of 2400l.

THE ISLE OF WHITHORN, is a village pleasantly situated about 2½ miles distant, and is the port to Whithorn. Near it are the remains of an old kirk, said to be the first built in this part of the kingdom, or, as some affirm, the first in Scotland.

POST OFFICE.—Post Mistress, Mrs. Ellen Kindel. The mail from Edinburgh, Newton-Stewart, and Wigtown, arrive at eleven and depart at four in the morning. The office bags are made up every night at eight.

PLACES OF WORSHIP.
CAMERONIAN MEETING HOUSE——No settled Minister
UNITED SECESSION—Rev. John Smith, Minister

GLASSERTON PARISH CHURCH——Rev. Samuel Clanahan, Minister

PAROCHIAL SCHOOLS.
WHITHORN—Samuel Carter, Master
GLASSERTON——, Kennedy, Master

RESIDENT GENTRY.

Hathorn Hugh, Castlewigg
Jefferie Jn. esq. Isle of Whithorn
Milroy Mrs. Janet, Ladycroft
Reid Sir John, Castle, Isle of Whithorn
Stewart Hugh Dun, Touderghie
Stewart Stair, esq. of Physgill & Glasserton house

TRADESMEN, &c.

PROFESSIONAL GENTLEMEN

Broadfoot Robt. surgeon, &c.
Jorie John, writer & town clerk
Kindel Thos. surgeon, &c.
Mc Millan Alex. surgeon, &c.
Mc Millan James, physician

SHOPKEEPERS.
TRADERS, &c.

Aitkin James, watchmaker, plumber, &c.
Anderson Wm. tailor
Black Alex. baker
Broadfoot Dunbar, grocer, Isle of Whithorn
Broadfoot John, grocer
Carr Montgomery, publican, Isle of Whithorn
Carson Robt. Stewart, grocer
Clanahan John, draper & tailor
Cumming Janet, grocer

Dickson Wm. innkeeper & grocer, Isle of Whithorn
Fortray Alex. publican, Isle of Whithorn
Frazer Alex. boot & shoe maker
Gibbs Wm. watch maker
Hannah Alex. grazier
Lawson Alex. spirit dealer
Logan Peter, publican, Isle of Whithorn
Mc Colm James, publican, Isle of Whithorn
Mc Kelvie John, grocer & ironmonger
Mc Kelvie Wm. woollen and linen draper
Mc Kinnell Robt. boot maker
Mc Murray Robt. tailor
Mc Neel Stuart, grocer, draper, &c.
Marquis Agnes, grocer, Isle of Whithorn
Milhinch Peter, linen and woollen draper

Milroy Agnes, linen and woollen draper
Morrison Thos. tallow chandler
Muir Thos. baker
Skimming John, boot maker
Sloan Jane, tanner
Stevenson John, grocer, Isle of Whithorn
Stewart & Mc Neel, tanners
Stewart Andw. saddler
Stewart Janet & Agnes, publicans, Isle of Whithorn
Tremayne Thos. hat maker

INNS & PUBLIC HOUSES.

Chesney John
Connings John
Gordon Alexander
Hathorn Janet
Mc Clumpha Margaret
Milligan Andrew
Stewart Geo. (King's Arms)
Stewart Margaret

WIGTOWN,

A Royal burgh, governed by a provost, two bailies, and sixteen councillors, and joins with Whithorn, New Galloway, and Stranraer, in sending a member to parliament, is distant 105 miles from Edinburgh, 58 from Dumfries, 28 from Stranraer, and 8 from Newton-Stewart. The town is situated on an eminence overlooking the river Cree, near the mouth of the Bladenoch, which at this place jointly fall into the Bay. It is the seat of a presbytery, and port of custom house, comprehending the creeks of Wigtonshire from the Mull of Galloway to the mouth of the river Dee. The principal part of this town, in form, a square, has, in the centre, an enclosed shrubbery tastefully laid out, forming an agreeable promenade for the inhabitants. At the end of this, is a very handsome modern market cross, built of granite, and sculptured in an elegant and tasteful manner. It is in contemplation to build a new Tolbooth; the present building has a tower of considerable height, which adds a degree of dignity to the town. It contains the court house, assembly room, subscription library, and parish school. The justice court is held here monthly, and a sheriff's court occasionally. Here is one established church, and a seceding meeting house.—Also a masonic lodge, and a friendly society established about 30 years, and has a capital of about six hundred pounds. Here is likewise an extensive brewery, and a distillery. Wigtown has a tolerable harbour, allowing ships of moderate burthen to approach the town. The export is principally corn.—The parish is about six miles in length, and four in breadth; at the west end of which are nineteen large granite stones in form of a circle, supposed to have been a druidical temple, and called by some, king Galdus's tomb. The scenery about Wigtown and its neighbourhood is very interesting. The market is chartered for Saturday, but is discontinued. Fairs are held on old candlemas, the first Monday in April, the first Friday in June, and the first Friday in August all old style.

We consider it necessary to warn the public to address letters and parcels, 'Wigtown' and not 'Wigton'; this mistake is often made, causing many packages, &c. to go to Wigton in Cumberland.

KIRKINNER, is about three miles from Wigtown, and is remarkable for its beautiful and picturesque scenery. The principal ornament in this neighbourhood, is the stately mansion of John Vance Agnew, esq. Here is also the remains of the ancient castle of Baldvon, formerly a residence of the Dunbar family; an incident in which family is supposed to have served as the foundation of the 'Bride of Lammermuir," by Sir Walter Scott.

POST OFFICE.—Post Master, Mr. Stewart Gulline. The mails arrive at 20 minutes past seven, and depart at eight.

PLACES OF WORSHIP.

WIGTOWN ESTABLISHED CHURCH—Rev. P. Young, Minister; Wm. Kennedy, Preceutor
SECEDERS'—Rev. Oliver Ogilvie, Minister; George Seambie, Precentor
KIRKINNER PARISH CHURCH—Rev. James Reid, Minister; Alex. Mc Cormick, Precentor

PAROCHIAL SCHOOLS.

WIGTOWN—Thomas Rae, master
KIRKINNER—M. Maxwell, Master

Magistrates.
Lord Garlies, Lord Provost
William Tait } Bailies
David Milligan }

Custom House.

James Tweddale, esq. Collector
John Simpson, esq. Comptroller
Wm. Lindsay, Surveyor and Landwaiter
John Beddie, Clerk
Peter Galloway, Tidewaiter
John Mc Beath, Officer of Excise

GENTRY.

Agnew Geo. esq. (Sheriff's Clerk for the County)
Agnew John Vans, esq. Barnbarroch House, Kirkinner
Douglas James, esq.
Mc Culloch D. Torhousckie
Mc Connell Wm. esq.
Mc Donald Mrs.
Murray John, esq.
Murray Robert, esq.
Thompson Chas. D. esq.

MERCHANTS, TRADESMEN, &c.

ACADEMIES.

Irving Miss, (ladies' boarding and day)
Stewart Duncan

BAKERS.

Mc Candish Elizabeth
Mc Guffie Agnes
Mc Queen Anthony

BANK.

Donnan James

BOOKSELLERS.

Mc Bryde James
Mc Minn William

BREWER.

Frazer James

BOOT & SHOE MAKERS.

Campbell George
Carnochan John
Carnochan Thomas
Daley John
Mc Master John
Mc Master John

CABINET MAKERS.

Bell John
Frazer William
Kelly Thomas
Mc Kie Thomas

CARPENTER.

Cuningham Wm. [ship]

COOPERS.

Furlow John
Milroy Alex. (& lath render)

DISTILLERS.

Mc Clelland John & Thomas

INSURANCE OFFICES AND AGENTS.

UNION, John Black
HERCULES, Stewart Gulline
INSURANCE Co. OF SCOTLAND, Andrew Mc Master

GROCERS AND SPIRIT DEALERS.

Biggan William
Brough Robt. (& spirit dealer and druggist)
Frazer William
Graham Arthur
Mc Coskrie Wm. Kirkinner
Mc Keand Peter

Mc Keand William
Mc Minn Wm. (& druggist)
Mc Quinn Anthony
Milligan David, (& druggist)
Skimming Wm. Kirkinner
Withers Mary

IRONMONGERS.

Dickson Jas. (& iron merchant)
Mc Master Andrew
Milligan David

MESSENGERS.

Marshall John
Mc Kinnell John

MILLERS.

Douglas —, Mill of Airies, Kirkinner
Routledge Wm. Milldreggau, Kirkinner

PHYSICIAN.

Minnoch Alexander, esq.

PUBLICANS.

Bruce John
Couperthwaite Thomas
Dodds John
Donnan William
Hannay Alexander
Law Peter
Mc Guffay James
Mc Laughlan Gavin, Kirkinner
Murray Widow
Murray Catherine
Parker Wm. Kirkinner
Wylie George

SADDLERS.

Kennedy William
Mc Master Andrew

SALT DEALERS.

Frazer William
Owens Michael
Wylie George

SMITHS.

Anderson Peter
Beddie David
Kinghan William
Mc Millan Alexander

SPIRIT MERCHANTS.

Dunn Henry, (& seedsman)
Owens Michael
Wylie George

SURGEONS AND APOTHECARIES.

Dalziel William
Smith John Hawthorn

TAILORS.

Mc Connell John
Mc Taggart William
Smith John
Thompson William
Thornburn John

TALLOW CHANDLERS.

Donnan Catherine
Milligan David
Mc Candlish Mrs.
Richardson Jane

WATCH MAKERS.

Mc Gowan William
Tait William

WRITERS.

Beddie John
Black John
Hawthorn John, (& notary)
Jolly Samuel
Mc Haffie George
Simson John

WOOLLEN AND LINEN DRAPERS.

Mc Bryde James
Mc Guffie James
Morrison Alexander

Miscellaneous.

Anderson Peter, blacksmith
Binnoch Joseph, salesman and grocer
Cowan David, painter
Frazer Geo. & Co. timber merchants & general agents
Kelly Thos. painter
Kevin Alex. tobacco manufacturer
Mc Minn Wm. weavers' agent
Walker Wm. corn marchant

CARRIERS.

DUMFRIES, Wm. Gibson & Jn. Gilkison, every Saturday.
EDINBURGH, Jos. Binnoch & John Mc Candlish, every 3 weeks.
GLASGOW, M. and E. Gibson, from Mrs. Murray's, on Tues. & Sat. and Matth. Sawers, once a fortnight.
STRANRAER, Alex. Mc Tier, weekly
WHITHORN, Alex. Marshall and G Gardner, from W. Donnan's, on Sat

CONVEYANCE By Water.

CREETOWN, daily.
DUBLIN & Glasgow, occasionally.
LIVERPOOL, every month.
WHITEHAVEN, every fortnight.

Pigot & Co.'s Directory
1837–38

DUMFRIES-SHIRE.

THIS is a large and important shire, in the south of Scotland; bounded on the east by the counties of Roxburgh, Selkirk, and part of Cumberland; on the north-west by Ayrshire; on the south-west by the stewartry (or county) of Kirkcudbright; on the north by the counties of Lanark, Peebles, and part of Selkirk; and its south and south-eastern boundary is washed by the Solway Frith. The length of the county, from north-west to south-east, is nearly fifty-five miles; and its extreme breadth, from the south to where it touches Peebles-shire on the north, is nearly thirty miles. According to the latest and best surveys, it embraces an area of 1,228 square miles; or 785,920 statute acres of land, and about ten square miles of lakes. At the epoch of the Roman invasion under Agricola, in the year 80, this part of Scotland was inhabited by a race called the *Selgovæ*, who spread themselves as far as the banks of the Dee, in Galloway: these people continued independent till the year 875, when they were overpowered by the Northumbrian Saxons, who retained the ascendancy for two centuries; during the lapse of this time, however, immense swarms of adventurers from Ireland and Cantyre effected a settlement; and from these intermixtures sprung the Picts, who progressively acquired the paramount sway. At this period Dumfries-shire is understood to have formed part of Cumbria, which district Edgar bequeathed to his youngest brother David, who encouraged the cupidity of many opulent Anglo-Norman barons, and the country was then divided into extensive baronies. The almost interminable border warfare was a frightful calamity to the inhabitants of Dumfries-shire and Cumberland, who for centuries were subjected to all the horrors attendant upon barbarous incursion and reckless feudal hostility. The whole county is now popularly apportioned into three districts, namely—ESKDALE on the east, ANNANDALE in the middle, and NITHSDALE on the west.

SOIL, PRODUCE, MANUFACTURES, &c.—The lower parts of Dumfries-shire are based with brown, red, yellow or white sandstone, which dips generally to the Solway; a considerable body of limestone also lies in this quarter, and beds of ironstone are occasionally found to accompany the other strata. Coal prevails in great plenty in the upper portions of Nithsdale and lower parts of Eskdale, the two extreme points of the county. The limestone of the shire has been of great value in improving the lands: marl likewise abounds in various tracts, and of freestone and whinstone there is a sufficiency in all directions: marble is also procured for different useful and ornamental purposes; and near the northern confines of the county, at Wanloch-head, there are inexhaustible mines of lead. As in most districts of the south of Scotland, there is a very general mixture of arable and pasture land. The upper part of the shire, or Annandale, Eskdale and Ewesdale, is principally devoted to sheep-feeding; in the lower portion the farms are larger, and more adapted to agriculture; the plantations and pleasure-grounds are consequently more numerous, and are remarkable for their beauty and richness. In Annandale the improvement of the breed of cattle has been most apparent; in 1829, at the Highland Society's meeting, some of the choicest specimens of the pure breed of Galloway cows, heifers, and bullocks, that were ever reared in the country, were exhibited by J. J. Hope Johnstone, Esq. The number of oxen, sheep and pigs nurtured in this county are invariably more than adequate to the demands of its population; an exportation, therefore, of the excess product takes place—and the same may be observed of corn, wool, hides and skins. The condition of the county is represented as having been greatly improved within the last thirty years, and at present its affairs may be considered in as prosperous a state as those of any other district in Scotland. Dumfries-shire cannot be ranked as a manufacturing county: the principal branches under this head of commercial industry are the manufacture of hosiery goods and cotton-spinning; the chief seat of the former is limited to the capital of the county—the latter to the town of Annan.

RIVERS, &c.—The chief, indeed the only rivers of consequence, are the NITH, the ANNAN, and the ESK: from these streams the principal divisions of the county obtain their names; from each of these greater divisions diverge vales, which likewise have denominations taken from the waters that are poured through them, such as Moffatdale, Dryfesdale, and Ewesdale. The Nith rises in the eastern hills of Ayrshire, enters Nithsdale by the foot of Carsoncone hill, in the parish of Kirkconnel, and descends into the valley of Sanquhar; having forced its way through the hills which surround this valley, it receives the Crawick water from the north, and the Euchan from the south. The river Cairn, which forms the western boundary of the county, unites its stream with the Nith a little above Dumfries, a short distance southward from which the latter river empties itself into the Solway Frith. Near to Jarborough castle, on the banks of the river Cairn, are to be seen those earthen mounds, called 'Bow-butts,' where the barons of Glencairn, with their vassals, used to practise archery. The river Annan (as well as the Tweed and Clyde), takes its rise in the mountains above Moffat, and runs through the flat part of Annandale for upwards of twenty-three miles; in this course it receives the Evan and Moffat waters, and the Wamphray stream, which irrigates a pleasant valley of that name: passing Johnstone, some other tributary rivulets increase its volume; at Loch Maven it is enlarged by the Ae, and a little lower by the Dryfe, which courses through the vale of Dryfesdale, or Drysdale: at length, approaching the kirk of St. Mungo, it flows over a rocky bed, which may be considered the termination of the vale of Annan. The higher part of Eskdale, for nearly twenty miles, is mountainous: the Esk, in its progress through this district, is joined by the Black Esk, the Meggot, the Ewes, and the Wauchope—(almost the whole of this division belongs to the noble family of Buccleugh): after reaching Broomholm, the river traverses a flat country, and a part of Cumberland, before it reaches the Solway Frith; during this portion of its course it receives the Liddal from Roxburghshire, and the Line water from the county of Cumberland: the entire length of its race is about thirty-eight miles, thirty of which are in the shire of Dumfries. The Solway differs very materially from other estuaries receiving in Scotland the appellation of 'Firths:' its waters are shallow, and have long sandy reaches at the ebbing of the tide. The ebbs and flows of the Solway are proverbial for the rapidity of their action, and this is particularly the case during spring tides and the prevalence of gales from the south-west: the borderers, though well mounted, have, in numerous melancholy instances, been overwhelmed and drowned, when returning from the Cumberland fairs, in crossing the bed of this estuary; even the most experienced persons are liable to be overtaken by the tides, when they have the best expectation of fording it in safety: on one occasion, within these few years, a gentleman who had been thus engulphed was preserved by the sagacity and courage of his horse, which swam with him right across the Firth.

It is ascertained that Dumfries-shire was placed under the government of a sheriff in the thirteenth century, at which period it included the stewartry of Kirkcudbright; the district of Annandale, however, continued to be a stewartry from the period when it merged in the crown, by the accession of Bruce, till the abolition of the heritable jurisdictions. Up to the era of the reformation, Dumfries-shire formed part of the extensive diocese of Glasgow, and was divided into the two deaneries of Nithsdale and Annandale; it now possesses forty-three parishes, which are divided into five presbyteries and one synod. There are four Royal Burghs in the county, viz., DUMFRIES, ANNAN, SANQUHAR, and LOCHMABEN; and six burghs of barony—Moffat, Lockerby, Langholm, Ecclefechan, Thornhill, and Minniehive. The SHIRE sends one member to parliament, and the Royal Burghs before named join with KIRKCUDBRIGHT in returning another representative.

Eminences in Dumfries-shire, with their altitude above the level of the sea.

IN NITHSDALE DISTRICT.		IN ANNANDALE DISTRICT.		IN ESKDALE DISTRICT.	
Wardlaw (in Caerlaverock)	826	Annan Hill	256	Moss Paul (Inn and stage, Vale of Ewes)	820
Auchinleck	1500	Repentance Tower	350		
Wanlockhead (village)	1564	Brunswark Hill (Tundergarth parish)	740	Langholm Hill	1204
Cairn-Kennow (nr. Drumlanrig)	2080			Tinnis Hill	1366
Queensberry Hill	2250	Erickstane Brae	1118	Wisp, in Ewes	1940
Black Larg (border Ayrshr.)	2890	Loch-skene	1300	Etterick, or Phawhope Penn	2220
Lowthers (nr. Wanlockhead)	3150	Hartfell, near Moffat	2629		

---o---

POPULATION OF DUMFRIES-SHIRE,

IN THE YEARS 1801, 1811, 1821, AND 1831, EXHIBITING THE INCREASE OR DECREASE IN THIRTY YEARS.

The Italic letters b. p. and t. respectively signify Burgh, Parish, and Township—dec. means Decrease.

	1801.	1811.	1821.	1831.	Increase in 30 Years.		1801.	1811.	1821.	1831.	Increase in 30 Years.
Annan ....b. & p.	2570	3341	4486	5033	2463	Kirkmahoe ....p.	1315	1464	1608	1601	286
Applegarth ....p.	795	858	943	999	204	Kirkmichael ....p.	904	1035	1202	1226	322
Canonbie ....p.	2580	2749	3084	2997	417	Kirkpatrick—Fleming ..p.	1544	1664	1696	1666	122
Caerlaverock ....p.	1014	1170	1206	1271	257	Kirkpatrick—Juxta ...p.	596	821	912	981	385
Closeburn ....p.	1679	1762	1682	1680	1	Langholm ....p.	2039	2636	2404	2676	637
Cummertrees ....p.	1309	1633	1561	1407	98	Lochmaben ....b. & p.	2053	2392	2651	2795	742
Dalton ....p.	595	691	767	730	135	Middlebie ....p.	1507	1683	1874	2107	600
Dornock ....p.	691	788	743	752	61	Moffat ....p.	1619	1824	2218	2221	602
Dryfesdale ....p.	1607	1893	2251	2283	676	Morton ....p.	1255	1570	1606	2140	885
Dumfries ....b. & p.	7288	9262	11052	11606	4318	Mouswald ....p.	705	769	795	786	81
Dunscore ....p.	1174	1325	1491	1488	314	Mungo, St. ....p.	614	727	709	791	147
Durisdeer ....p.	1148	1429	1601	1488	340	Penpoint ....p.	966	987	1082	1232	266
Eskdalemuir ....p.	537	581	651	650	113	Ruthwell ....p.	996	1184	1285	1216	220
Ewes ....p.	358	338	314	335	dec. 23	Sanquhar ....b. & p.	2350	2709	1357	1527	
Glencairn ....p.	1403	1668	1881	2068	665	Sanquhar ....p.			963	1066	918
Graitney ....p.	1765	1749	1915	1909	144	Wanlockhead ....t.	....	....	706	675	
Halfmorton ....p.	497	....	553	646	149	Tindwall ....p.	980	1204	1248	1220	240
Hoddam ....p.	1250	1428	1640	1582	332	Torthorwald ....p.	703	932	1205	1320	617
Holywood ....p.	809	830	1004	1066	257	Tundergarth ....p.	484	522	518	530	46
Hutton and Corrie....p.	646	677	804	860	214	Tinron ....p.	563	574	513	493	dec. 70
Johnstone ....p.	740	904	1179	1234	494	Wamphray ....p.	423	431	554	580	157
Keir ....p.	771	993	987	1084	313	Westerkirk ....p.	638	698	672	642	4
Kirkconnel ....p.	1096	1017	1075	1111	15						
						TOTAL POPULATION OF DUMFRIES-SHIRE.......	54606	62960	70878	73770	19164

The total annual value of Real Property in this county, as assessed in April, 1815, amounted to £295,621.

ANNAN AND BRIDE-KIRK.

ANNAN is a royal burgh, the capital of the parish of its name, and of the district of Annandale, 79 miles s. of Edinburgh, 87 s.e. of Glasgow, 43 n.e. of Kirkcudbright, 27 s. of Moffat, 16 s. e. of Dumfries, 11 s. of Lockerbie, and 6 from Ecclefechan; situate on the east or left bank of the river Annan, rather more than a mile above its influx into the Solway Firth. The name is derived from that of the river, whose appellation is traced to the Celtic *An*, signifying simply water. It is a town of considerable antiquity, and is one of the most ancient burghs in Scotland. Annan was a Roman station, and the *Veromum* of the geography of Ravenna. It seems to have been held by the Britons after the departure of the Romans, till they were subdued by the Saxons of the Northumbrian kingdom, when it came to the Scotch. It afterwards became a principal port, and was granted, with the territory of Annandale and the port of Lochmaben, to the ancestors of Robert Bruce, by some of whom a castle was erected, which was once occupied as a church, but afterwards went to ruins, and the original wall now forms part of the gaol and town hall. Upon the death of David II, in 1371, this castle, Lochmaben, and the lordship of Annandale, came to Thomas Randolph, Earl of Murray, and went, with his sister Agnes, to the Dunbars, Earls of March; after their forfeiture it went to the Douglasses, who also lost it by similar conduct, and then, having come to Alexander, Duke of Alban,

he, for rebelling against his brother, King James III, and plundering the fair of Lochmaben, in 1484, also forfeited it. Since that period it continued in the hands of the king, and became the great key of the western border. By the accession of the Bruce family to the throne, it became a royal burgh. The existing charter was granted by James VI of Scotland, and is dated July 10th, 1612; it confirms previous charters, and particularly recites one conferred by James V, dated 1st March, 1538, which had with others been burned and destroyed by sieges and the inroads of the English, particularly in 1298, when they entered Annandale, and burnt the town with its church. The burgh is governed by a provost, three bailies, fifteen councillors, a treasurer, dean of guild, and town clerk: it unites with Dumfries, Sanquhar, and Lochmaben, in returning one member to parliament.

The port or harbour of Annan is free, and vessels of 250 tons can come within half a mile of the town, but vessels of much larger burden can enter the river at its confluence with the Solway, distant little more than a mile from the town, at which place two new wooden wharfs or jetties have recently been erected by rival steam boat companies, whose vessels generally make the passage between Annan and Liverpool in twelve hours or less, that is, in one tide only, from harbour to harbour; and a vessel belonging to each company makes, at least, one trip to and from weekly. The convenience afforded by this rapidity of communication with Liverpool, has greatly increased the trade, and a considerable quantity of bacon, grain, live stock, and other commodities, are thus weekly conveyed to the Liverpool market; while, by return of these steam vessels, the principal supply of general merchandize is imported for the consumption of the town, and adjoining country to a very considerable distance, as the harbour of Annan is, in many respects, preferable to that of Dumfries.

A manufactory for spinning cotton has been, for some years, successfully in operation here, by a company whose parent establishment is at Manchester. Among the other branches of trade are those of ship-building, tanning, brewing, and malting; and a company has completed arrangements for erecting a distillery upon an extensive scale, a short distance from the town, up the river. Branches of the 'Commercial Bank of Scotland' and of the ' British Linen Company' are settled here; there is also a bank for savings. Limestone and freestone is abundant in many parts of the parish, which has been long famed for the superior quality of potatoes cultivated within it. Annan, of late years, has been much improved by new streets and buildings. The old bridge, which consisted of five arches, has been removed, and a new one erected on its site, towards which a grant of £3,000. was obtained from government, and the remainder supplied by the county. On the west are the town-house and market-

place, and at the east end of the town is a fine new church, built of stone, with a tower and spire: there are also burgher and relief chapels, parochial and infants' schools, several benevolent societies, and a subscription library: but the principal educational establishment is a classical academy, a very handsome building, erected in 1820, in which are taught most of the elegant and all the useful branches of education: it is governed by the magistrates and a committee of heritors, and the preceptors consist of a rector, and teachers in the several branches.

The market is held on Thursday, at which, during the season, large quantities of pork are sold. There are fairs on the first Thursday in February, the first Thursday in May, the third Thursday in August, first Tuesday after the 29th of September, third Thursday in October, and the first Tuesday after the 11th of Nov.

BRIDE-KIRK is a modern village, 3 miles north of Annan, situate on the west bank of the Annan river. The extent of the parish is about five miles long by three broad, the whole of which is cultivated. It is a new formed parish, and originally consisted of a part of Annan, a part of Hoddam, and a part of Cummertrees. The principal land proprietor is Mrs. General Dirom, through whose interest it was erected into parish in May, 1836; and the same lady built the kirk in 1835; she is looked upon as the responsible supporter of the minister. The remains of Bride-kirk Tower are in this parish. Annan is the post town.

POST OFFICE, High-street, ANNAN, George Pool, *Post Master*.—The LONDON mail, with letters from the South, arrives every morning at seven, and is despatched every afternoon at half-past three.—The DUMFRIES mail, with letters from all parts of Scotland and Ireland, arrives every afternoon at half-past three, and is despatched every morning at seven.

NOBILITY, GENTRY AND CLERGY.

Brown Rev. Hugh M'Bride, Bride-kirk   [bie
Carruthers Alex. esq. of Warman-Carruthers the Misses Cicely and Eliza, North field   [High st
Dalgleish Mr. John (of Prestonfield)
Dirom Capt. Alexander, Cleugh head
Dirom Mrs. General, Mount Annan
Dobbie Rev. James, Ednam st
Douglas Mrs. Colonel, of Greencroft
Ewer James, esq. Watch hall
Forrest John, esq. Oaklands
Hannah Miss Jane, Solway cottage
Irving Lieut. Robert, Plumdon
Johnston Wm. esq. of Summer hill
Laurie Mrs. Frances, High st
Little Mrs. Margaret, Ednam st
Lowther Miss, Wellington st
Monilaws Rev. James, the Manse
Nelson Senhouse, esq. High st
Nicholson Mrs. Jane, Ednam st
Rutherford James, esq. Violet bank
Sandas Mr. James, Scotch road
Smith Mrs. Mary, High st
Tudhope Rev. Archbd. Wellington st
Weall Mr. James, High st

ACADEMIES & SCHOOLS.

ACADEMY, Ednam st—Charles Maxwell, rector; John Dickson, mathematical teacher; Robert Daniel, English teacher
Beattie Jane, George st
Herbertson John, High st
INFANTS' SCHOOL, Solway st—Jesse Williamson, mistress
Lorimer Matthew, Butt st
M'Lellan Franci. Bride-kirk
PAROCHIAL SCHOOL, Annan—George Herbertson, master
PAROCHIAL SCHOOL, Bride-kirk—John Ross, master

BACON CURERS.
(Marked thus * are also Cattle Dealers.)
Barton James, Butt st
*Blacklock Thomas, High st
Forrest William (& factor) High st
*Irving John & George, Butt st
*Jardine John, Scotch road

*Roxburgh John, High st
*Steel David, Butt st
*Turnbull George, Scotch road
Wilkin John, Butt st

BAKERS & FLOUR DEALERS.
Bell John, Bride-kirk
Bryson Alexander, High st
Hay David, High st
Irving William, High st
Reidford John & William, Lady st
Strong Joseph, High st
Weild William, High st
Wright George, High st

BANKERS.
BRITISH LINEN COMPANY (Branch of)—(draw on the Parent Establishment, Edinburgh, and on Smith, Payne & Smith, London) — George Dalgliesh, agent
COMMERCIAL BANK OF SCOTLAND, (Branch of)—draw on the Parent Establishment, Edinburgh, and on Jones, Loyd & Co. London)—James Scott, agent
SAVINGS' BANK, High st—James Saunders, treasurer; Jas. Simpson, secretary

BLACKSMITHS.
Beattie James, Port st
Cock James, George st
Dalgliesh James, Butt st
Jamieson Ebenezer, Bride-kirk
Johnston Thomas, Port st
Johnstone Thomas, Downie's wynd
Moffat William, High st
Rae William, Downie's wynd
Rutherford John, Bride-kirk

BOOKSELLERS & STATIONRS.
Cuthbertson William, High st
Richardson Wellwood (and circulating library), High st

BOOT & SHOE MAKERS.
Beard John, High st
Bell John, Bride-kirk
Burnie William, Downie's wynd
M'Neish William, Murray st
Martin William, Bride-kirk
Morton Thomas, High st
Moussey Robert, High st
Murdoch James, High st
Rae John, Port st

Rae Thomas, High st
Reid William, Downie's wynd
Scott John, Bride-kirk
Shennan William, High st
Thomson George, High st
Thomson James, Thorns, Bridekirk
Thomson John, Johnston st
Waugh George, Carlyle place

BREWERS & MALTSTERS.
Gass and Hope, Annan Brewery, Port st

CHYMISTS & DRUGGISTS.
Duncan & M'Kinnell, High st
Potts John, High st
Rome Robert, High st

CLOG MAKERS.
Beattie Agnes, Scotch road
Bell Thomas, Bride-kirk
Burnie William, Downie's wynd
Irving John, Lady st
Ross Thomas, Bride-kirk

CLOTHES BROKERS AND DRAPERS.
Johnston William, Butt st
Lewis Abraham, Fish cross
Lewis Henry, High st

COAL DEALERS.
Baxter David, Port st
Richardson Robert, High st
Scott John, Port st
Wightman Robert, Port st

CONFECTIONERS.
Norval Isabella, High st
Strong Joseph, High st
Thompson Elizabeth, High.

COOPERS.
Beattie James, Ednam st
Boyes James, Bride-kirk
Crawford David, Johnston's place
Edgar Robert, High st   [Port st
Johnstone Wilson (and fish curer), M'Connochie Thos. Downie's wynd

COTTON SPINNERS.
Douglas William & Co. Annan Cotton Factory, Port st—John Sawyer, manager

CURRIERS.
Baxter William, Butt st
Nicholson William, Ednam st

DRESS MAKERS AND MILLINERS.
Anderson Eliz. & Christiana, High st
Anderson Mary, High st
Cuthbertson Mary, High st
Holmes Ann, Butt st
Irving Jesse, Ednam st
Johnstone Janet, Murray st
Little Jane, High st
M'Neish Jane, Murray st
Marshall Jane, High st
Mundell Betsy, High st
Nelson Maria, High st
Nicholson Ann, High st

FIRE, &c. OFFICE AGENTS.
CALEDONIAN, Nathaniel Weild, High street [High st
NORTH BRITISH, James Simpson,

FLESHERS.
Armstrong Joseph, High st
Douglas Robert, North st
Hill Francis, Pool's wynd
Irving John, Butt st
Johnstone Thomas, Murray st
Lindsay John, Battery
Moffat William, High st
Patterson Daniel, High st
Robinson Robert, High st

GROCERS & SPIRIT DEALRS.
Beattie James, High st
Cartner Thomas (& flour) Murray st
Ewart James, High st [High st
Ferguson Wm. Ross (& seedsman)
Forsythe John, Bride-kirk
Foster David, High st
Fryer Mary, Lady st
Geddes Janet, High st
Glover Mary, High st
Graham Sarah, Bride-kirk
Irving Benjamin, High st
Irving Jane, Bride-kirk
Irving Janet, Port st
Johnstone Joseph G. High st
Little John, High st
M'Lean James, Bridge end
M'Lean Thomas, High st
Miller John, High st
Muir John, Scotch road
Patterson John, High st
Pool David, High st
Pool George, High st
Pool William, High st
Quin Robert, High st
Richardson Robert, High st
Rogerson William, Port st
Rule Mary Ann, High st
Scott James, High st
Shankland Jno. High st [High st
Williamson Ann (& dealer in drugs)
Wilson Adam, High st
Wright George, High st

HAIR DRESSERS.
Blaylock John, High st
Hind Simon, High st

INNS.
Blue Bell, Isaac Hope, High st
Commercial, Ann Hetherington, Fish cross
Queensberry Arms (and posting house), James Benson, High st
Union Hotel, Joseph Madely, High st

IRON MERCHANTS.
Forrest William, High st
Gunning John, High st

IRONMONGERS.
Carruthers David, High st
Gunning John, High st
Halliday James, High st

JOINERS & CARPENTERS.
Aitcheson James, High st
Blacklock John, Downie's wynd
Copeland William, High st
Cuthbertson Richard (and cartwright) Bride-kirk [Bride-kirk
Ewart William (and cartwright),

Gass James, Port st
Graham George, Ednam st [st
Green Geo. (& cabinet makr) Ednam
Harkness Robert, Bride-kirk
Irving William, Downie's wynd
Irving William, Butt st
Johnston Douglas, Scotch road
Little Andrew, Johnston st
Oliver George, Ednam st
Rome William, High st
Williamson James, Port st

LIME BURNERS.
Barker John, Kelhead
Crichton Mrs. Donkins
Little John, Blackwoodridge
Rome Andrew, Burnhead

LINEN & WOOLLEN DRAPRS.
Little John, High st
Montgomery John, High st
Owen James, High st
Thomson John, High st
Waugh William, High st
Weild David, High st

MASONS & BUILDERS.
Beattie James, Bride-kirk
Black James, Bride-kirk
Brown Robert, Port st
Easton William, Bride-kirk
Guillon John, Bride-kirk
Irving John, High st
Johnston John, Johnston st
Laidlaw Andrew, Murray st
Laidlaw William, High st
M'Dowie John, Murray st

MESSENGER AT ARMS.
M'Lellan John, High st

MILLERS.
Brown Robert, Bride-kirk
Clark John, Windmill

NAIL MAKERS.
Baxter William, Port st
Forrest William, High st
Irving James, George st
Ker John, High st

NURSERY & SEEDSMEN.
Boggie William, Stapleton road
Dickson Robert, High st
Duncan William, Johnston st
Palmer John, Lady st

PAINTERS, GLAZIERS AND GILDERS.
Cleminson John, High st
Gunning John, High st
Moyes David, Downie's wynd
Wadeson Robert, Murray st

PLUMBERS.
Roxburgh William (& zinc worker) High street
Smith John, George st

PRINTER—LETTER-PRESS.
Cuthbertson William, High st

ROPE MAKERS.
Irving John, High st
Lawson John, Scotch road
Wilkin John, Butt st

SADDLERS.
Bell William, High st
Hill James, High st
Johnstone William, High st

SHERIFF'S OFFICERS.
Hill Thomas, Murray st
Smith John, High st

SHIP BUILDERS.
Mundle George, Port st
Neilson Walter, Port st
Rogerson James, Port st

SHIP OWNERS.
Carlyle Mrs.
Duff James
Ewart James
Faulds George
Forrest William
Gillard John
Hudson John
Irving David
Irving John
Irving Matthew
Irving Mrs.
Jackson Christr.
Johnson John
Lawson William

Logan John
Nicholson John
Rae Robert
Richardson Robt.
Rome John
Scott John
Scott John, jun.
Scott, Scott and Nelson
Thomson Mrs.
Thomson Thos.
Vivers John

STRAW HAT MAKERS.
Anderson Elizabeth and Christiana, High street
Armstrong Nicholas, High st
Carruthers Jane, Murray st
Little Margaret, High st
Lottimer Ann, High st

SURGEONS.
Edgar William, Port st
Irving & Johnstone, Moat
Thom William, Port st
Waugh John, High st
Williamson Thomas, High st

TAILORS.
Anderson John, High st
Anderson William, Port st
Drummond Thomas, Port st
Ferguson Alexander, High st
Farish John, Carlisle place
Henderson John, Fish cross
Hill James, High st
Irving George, Rutherford's wynd
Irving John, Port st
Jardine James, Murray st
Jeffery Adam, High st
Rae William, Bride-kirk
Richardson James, Scotch road
Seaton Thomas, Downie's wynd

TANNER.
Baxter William, Butt st

TIMBER & SLATE MERCHNTS
Nelson Benjamin, Ednam st
Nicholson John (and corn factor) Port street
Weild David, High st

TIN-PLATE WORKERS.
Roxburgh William (& coppersmith) High street
Smith John, George st

VINTNERS.
Bell Wm. (King's Arms) High st
Breeze Saml. (King's Arms) High st
Broatch Robert (Grapes) High st
Creighton James, Bride-kirk
Dalrymple George, High st
Farries William (Bush) High st
Graham William (Coach & Horses) High street
Greaves Mary (Ship) Port st
Hestie James, Wellington st
Holliday Jno. (Turk's Head) Fish cross
Hudson John (Steam Packet) Port st
Irving Geo. Martindale (Old Bush) High street
Irving William (Globe) Fish cross
Lockerbie David (Annandale Arms) Thomas street
Moffat William, High st
Robinson George (Buck) High st
Robinson John, Downie's wynd
Rogerson James (Plough) High st
Roxburgh Mary (Queen's Head) High street
Scott John, High st
Thomson John (Drove) High st
Torbron Ann (Scotch Arms) High st

WATCH & CLOCK MAKERS.
Hodgson John, High st
Little John, High st

WRIGHTS.
See Joiners and Carpenters.

WRITERS.
Carruthers William, Bridge end
Farish & Dalgliesh (and notaries) High street
Little James (& notary) High st
M'Lellan John, High st
Thomson George, High st

Miscellaneous.

Adamson Jno.boro' officer,Downie's wynd
Baxter James, tallow chandler, High st
Bell William, sheep dealer, Scotch road
Blalock Wm.cotton check weavr.Murray st
Carlisle Adam, check weaver, Murray st
Clemenson John, dyer & scourer, Port st
Cowan Jane, shopkeeper, Scotch road
CUSTOM HOUSE,Port st—Robt. Chalmers, principal coast officer & landing waiter
Dockray John B. hat manufr. Gullilands
Edgar Richard, agent for American emigrants, Port st   [st
Ferguson William Ross, auctioneer, High
Geddis Wm. master mariner, Scotch street
Holmes John, block maker, &c. Port st
Little William, shopkeeper, High st
Lorimer John, engraver, High st
M'Kay Joseph, flax dresser, Bride-kirk
Marshall Thos. road surveyor, Ednam st
Matthews Wm.boro' officer,Downie's wynd
Muir Matthew, carter, Scotch road
Park Walter, plasterer, Johnston st
Patterson Robt. general agent, Ednam st
Rome Wm. cabinet maker, &c. High st
Smith Andrew, tea dealer, Thomas st
STAMP OFFICE, High st—George Thomson, distributer
Thomson John, cattle dealer, Beckfoot
Vickers John, gardener, Murray st
Watt David, bookbinder, Murray st

PLACES OF WORSHIP.

ESTABLISHED CHURCH, Rev. James Monilaws
ESTABLISHED CHURCH, Bride-kirk —Rev. Hugh M'Bride Brown
BURGHER CHAPEL, Rev. Jas. Dobie
RELIEF CHAPEL, Rev. Archibald Tudhope

COACHES.

To CARLISLE, the *Royal Mail* (from Dumfries), calls at the Queensberry Arms, every afternoon at half-past three, and the *Independent* (from Glasgow), every evening at seven—and the *Marquess* (from Dumfries), calls at the Blue Bell, every Monday, Wednesday, and Friday afternoon at one.

To DUMFRIES, the *Royal Mail* (from London), calls at the Queensberry Arms, every morning at seven, and the *Independent* (from Carlisle), every morning at six—the *Marquess* (from Carlisle,) and the *Royal William* (from Langholm), call at the Blue Bell Inn, every Tuesday, Thursday & Saturday evening at seven.

To GLASGOW, the *Independent* (from Carlisle), calls at the Queensberry Arms, every morning at six; goes thro' Dumfries, Thornhill, Sanquhar, Cumnock, Mauchline, Kilmarnock & Kingswell.

To LANGHOLM, the *Royal William* (from Dumfries), calls at the Blue Bell, every Monday, Wednesday & Friday at one; goes thro' Ecclefechan and Waterbeck.

To LONDON, MANCHESTER, and LIVERPOOL, the *Royal Mail* (from Dumfries), calls at the Queensberry Arms, every afternoon at half-past three, and the *Independent* (from Glasgow) every evening at seven; both go thro' Carlisle, &c.

CARRIERS.

To CARLISLE, James Ferguson, from Lady street, every Mon. Tues. & Sat.— Peter Johnston,from Carlisle place,every Mon.& Sat.—and Thomas Baxter, from the Buck Inn, every Friday.
To DUMFRIES, Thomas Baxter, from the Buck Inn, every Tuesday—Peter Johnston, from Carlisle place, William Hutchinson,from Port street,and James Patterson, from the Bush Inn, every Wednesday—and James Richardson, from the same Inn, every Thursday.

To EDINBURGH, Gavin Johnston, from the Buck Inn, every Monday, and Jacob Richardson, from Scotch street, once a fortnight.
To GLASGOW, Robert Crighton, from the Buck Inn, every Saturday, and Thomas Richardson, from the Bush Inn, every alternate Monday.
To LANGHOLM & ECCLEFECHAN, John Jardine, from the Bush Inn, every Thursday.
To LOCKERBIE, John Shaw, from the Bush Inn, every day (Thurs. excepted), and Gavin Johnston, from the Buck Inn, every Monday.
To NEWCASTLE, John Moffat, from Johnston st, every Monday, and Thos. Baxter, from the Buck, every Friday.
To MOFFAT, Gavin Johnston, from the Buck Inn, every Monday, and Jacob Richardson, from Scotch street, once a fortnight.
To RIGG, William Adamson, from the Grapes, High street, every Thursday.
To RUTHWELL, the Postman, from the Bush Inn, every Tues. Thurs. and Sat.
To SPRINGFIELD, James Davidson, from the Grapes, High st. every Thurs.

CONVEYANCE BY WATER.

STEAM PACKETS.

To CARLISLE and LIVERPOOL, the *City of Carlisle*, three times a fortnight— John Nicholson, merchant and agent; and the *Newcastle*, three times a fortnight—David Baxter, agent
*** For the convenience of passengers coaches await the arrival of the steam packets at Annan Water foot.*

FERRY BOAT.
The SKINBURNESS ferry boat arrives at the Scotch Arms, High street, every day, an hour before high water, and returns the same tides.

CAERLAVEROCK PARISH,

INCLUDING THE VILLAGES OF BANK-END, BRIDGE-END, OLD QUAY & NEIGHBOURHOODS.

THE parish of CAERLAVEROCK occupies a sort of Peninsula, formed by the Solway Firth, the River Nith, and Lochan water. The only object of curiosity is the magnificent ruin of Caerlaverock castle, situate on a level plain, between 8 and 9 miles from Dumfries. It is an ancient possession of the Maxwells, once a powerful family in this part of Scotland, and wardens of the western marches. It was besieged and captured by Edward I, in 1300, and by Cromwell in 1651. After this it ceased to be a tenable fortress, and fell into decay: it now presents a ruin massive and picturesque, eminently worthy the notice of the tourist. This ancient fortalice was the scene of a foul and remarkable murder, about the middle of the fourteenth century, which has furnished the theme of a very beautiful ballad by K. Sharpe, Esq. published in the 'minstrelsy of the Scottish border.' The tragical event was connected with the assassination of the Red Cumine (a powerful chieftain, who formerly held the regency of Scotland), by Robert Bruce, attended by Kirkpatrick and Lindsay, two of his adherents.

BANK-END is a clean, pleasant, and small village, about 6 miles from Dumfries, containing the parochial and grammar school, which is also a boarding academy: there are two others in the parish—Highmains (English), and the village school. The manse and kirk are at BRIDGE-END, a small village about a mile from Bank-End. The old quay wharf, on the banks of the Nith, in this parish, is where numbers of coasting traders discharge and take in their cargoes, for various parts of the united kingdom; and when the tide serves, the steamers from Liverpool, &c. land their passengers here, from whence they are conveyed to Dumfries in omnibusses.

GENTRY & CLERGY.
Connell James, esq. of Conheath
Gillies Rev.Robt.Caerlaverock manse

ACADEMY AND SCHOOLS.
Beattie John, Highmains school
Hill John (parochial school & boarding academy) Bank-End
M'William John, Blackshaw

INN-KEEPERS & VINTNERS, AT OLD QUAY.
Dick Ann
Edgar John (Crown & Anchor)

Ferguson David (Britannia)
M'Kinnel John (Ship)
Thomson William
Wilson Janet (Anchor)

SHOPKEEPERS & TRADERS.
Anderson John, shoe maker, Bank-End   [Bank-End
Anderson William, shoe maker,
Boyd Thos. cartwright, Bank-End
Boyd William, tailor, Bank-End
Brisbane Thomas, miller, Bank-End
Brown Wm. shoe maker, Bank-End

Davidson Thomas, grocer, Old Quay
Finley James, ship builder, Kelton
Fleming Ths. blacksmith, Bank-End
Geddes David, tailor, Bank-End
Hunter George, joiner, Old Quay
Jackson Mary,tobacconist, Old Quay
Jamieson Wm. meal dealer, Old Quay
M'Lean Wm. shopkeeper, Bank-End
Muir Thos. blacksmith, Bank-End
Reid John, shopkeeper, Bank-End
Thomson Wm.coffee house, Old Quay
Thomson Wm.ship builder, Old Quay

CLOSEBURN, GLENCAIRN, DUNBREGGAN,

MINNIEHIVE, KEIR, KIRKMICHAEL, AND TYNRON.

CLOSEBURN is an inland parish in the district of Nithsdale; it has incorporated with it the parish of Dalgarno, and is about ten miles in length, by about seven and a half in breadth. The annual produce of the parish amounts to £40,300, of which £3,500 arises from the sale of lime only. The ruins of the ancient Castle of Closeburn, the property of C. G. S. Menteath, Esq. forms an interesting object in the scenery here, which derives additional beauty from some romantic waterfalls, within two miles of the castle, and some caverns, in one of which latter the hunted covenanters used to take up their abode, to evade pursuit: it is considered to be the place alluded to by the author of Waverley, in his description of the cave occupied by

Balfour, of Burley. A free school was most amply endowed in 1723, by one John Wallace, a native of the parish; it is placed under the government of the presbytery of Penpont, and in it all the children of the parish are taught the elements of education, free of expense.

The parish of GLENCAIRN is also in Nithsdale, and extends eleven miles in length, by from three to five in breadth. Several small rivulets meander beautifully through it, enriching the scenery, to which the elegant mansion and grounds of H. Ferguson, Esq. contribute much. On the south-west verge of the parish is Loch Urr, from which issues the river of that name. A new church is in progress of erection (1836), a short distance from the site of the old edifice.

DUNBREGGAN is a small well-built village, in the parish of Glencairn, five miles and a half south-east of Penpont, situate on the north bank of the Dalwhat water, where it is crossed by a bridge to MINNIEHIVE, a small but pleasant village, in the same parish as Dunbreggan, half a mile therefrom, and sixteen from Dumfries. This is a place of some antiquity, and formerly of more consequence than it now is, having been a burgh of barony, chartered in the reign of Charles I.

KEIR is a small parish, possessing a considerable quantity of plantation and limestone; it is bounded on the east by Closeburn, on the north-west and north by Tynron and Penpont, and on the south by Dunscore; is about two miles and a half in breadth, and seven and a half in length.

KIRKMICHAEL, united with Garren, in the district of Nithsdale, is about ten miles long, and four broad. The parish of Kirkpatrick-juxta bounds it on the north-west, Johnstone on the north-east, Lochmaben on the south-east, Tinwald and Kirkmanse on the south, and Closeburn on the west. Many remains of ancient fortifications and Roman roads are visible in this district. The parish kirk is near the Ae river, which bounds the parish on the west.

TYNRON parish lies between Penpont on the north and north-east, and Glencairn on the south, and extends nine miles in length, by a breadth of from two to three. It is watered partially by the Shinnel rivulet, along the banks of which there is some pleasing scenery. Near the eastern extremity of the parish rises the Doon of Tynron, a conspicuous pyramidical hill, near the summit of which is an ancient Castle. A new church is erecting in the parish, on the site of the old one.

POST OFFICE, MINNIEHIVE, Margaret Collow, *Post Mistress.*—Letters from THORNHILL arrive every afternoon at three, and are despatched every afternoon at four.

GENTRY AND CLERGY.

Arundel Godolphin, esq. (of Barjarg), Keir   [manse
Bennet Rev. Andrew, Closeburn
Brown Rev. Alexander, Minniehive
Brown Rev. John, Glencairn manse
Collow Gilbert, esq. of Upper Kirkcudbright
Collow Miss, Auchenchain [Keir
Copland Wm. esq. (of Blackwood),
Corson Mrs. Mary, of Hill
Dobie Rev. Hugh, Kirkmichael manse
Fergusson Sir Adam, Kirkmichael
Fergusson Robert C. esq. M.P. (of Craigdarroch), Glencairn
Graham Colonel Nicholas Graham, Jarbruck   [Keir
Hoggan James, esq. (of Belleview),
Hunter Mr. Thomas, M.D. Minniehive   [Tynron
Kennedy John, esq. (of Kirkland),
Kennedy Robert, esq. of Dalwhat
Kennedy William, esq. (of Dalmakerran), Tynron
Kirkpatrick Sir Thomas, bart. (of Capenoch) Keir
Lawrie Sir Robert, K.C.B. of Maxwelltown house   [niehive
Lenox Charles Adam, esq. R.N. Minnie
M'Call Samuel, esq. of Caithlock
M'Geoch Rev. James, Minniehive
M'Turk Robt. esq. of Hastings hall
Menzies Rev. William, Keir manse
Moffat Alexander, esq. of Barbuie
Moffat Samuel, esq. (of Auchenhaistinne), Tynron
Monteath Charles Grenville Stuart, esq. of Closeburn hall
Pringle Andrew, esq. (of Land), Tynron   [Closeburn
Smith Mr. John, Camphie green,
Smith Mrs. Margaret, Ingliston
Smith Mr. Thomas, Penfillan
Stewart Walter, esq. of Youngston

Wilson Rev. Robert, Tynron manse
Young Mr. Alexander Goldea, M.D. Minniehive

ACADEMIES AND PUBLIC SCHOOLS.

Austine William, Minniehive
Dalziel Sarah & Justina, Minniehive
Drummond William, Minniehive
GRAMMAR SCHOOL, Closeburn—Robert Mundell, master
PAROCHIAL SCHOOLS :—
Glencairn—George Hunter and David Morine, masters
Keir—John Crosbie and James M'Kinnel, masters   [ter
Kirkmichael—John Burnet, mas-
Tynron—Rober Newall & James Hunter, masters

INNS.

Brown Hill Inn, Archibald Fisher, Closeburn
Craig Darroch Arms, John Donaldson, Minniehive
George Inn, Janet Todd, Minniehive

SHOPKEEPERS & TRADERS.

Black Robert, blacksmith, Tynron
Brown John, miller, Craigdarrock
Brown Wm. blacksmith, Glencairn
Chambers John, smith, Minniehive
Collow William, joiner, Minniehive
Coltart John, shopkeeper, Closeburn
Coltart William, joiner, Closeburn
Dalziel Jno. blacksmith, Minniehive
Dalziel Samuel, grocer, Minniehive
Douglas Walter, shoe mkr. Minniehive
Fergusson Wm. tailor, Minniehive
Gordon Wm. joiner, Minniehive
Harper Jas. shoe maker, Minniehive
Harper Wm. shoe maker, Minniehive
Henderson James, shopkeeper, Minniehive   [cairn
Henderson John, shopkeeper, Glen-
Hiddleston Jas. joiner, Minniehive
Kennedy Adam, miller, Gapes mill

Kirkpatrick and Dalziel, saddlers, Minniehive
M'Call Jane, shopkeeper, Glencairn
M'Call Wm. blacksmith, Minniehive
M'Chain Wm. shoe makr. Minniehive
M'Kay James, baker, Minniehive
M'Naught David, shoe maker, Minniehive   [niehive
M'Turk James, shopkeeper, Min-
Melross Jno. shopkeeper, Minniehive
Muirhead Wm. tailor, Minniehive
Newland David, shopkeeper, Closeburn   [Closeburn
Proudfoot George, shoe maker,
Proudfoot John and George, dyers, Waulk mill, Minniehive
Proudfoot James, joiner, Glencairn
Siton James, joiner, Tynron
Smith Thomas, joiner, Tynron
Smith Wm. shopkeeper, Minniehive
Smith William and Peter, tailors, Minniehive
Todd Alexander, tailor, Minniehive
Wallace Thomas, grocer & draper, Minniehive   [Tynron
Williamson James, shopkeeper,
Wilson Peter, nailer, Minniehive
Wilson Alex. wheelwright, Tynron

PARISH CHURCHES.

CLOSEBURN, Rev. Andrew Bennet
GLENCAIRN, Rev. John Brown
KEIR, Rev. William Menzies
KIRKMICHEL, Rev. Hugh Dobie

UNITED SECESSION CHURCH, Glencairn—Rev. James M'Geoch

COACH.

To DUMFRIES, the *Craigingillan Castle* (from Glasgow), calls at the Craig Darroch Arms, every Tuesday, Thursday, and Saturday evening at six.
To GLASGOW, the *Craigingillan Castle* (from Dumfries), calls at the Craig Darroch Arms, every Monday, Wednesday, and Friday morning at half-past eight.

CUMMERTREES, DALTON, MOUSWALD, RUTHWELL,
POWFOOT AND NEIGHBOURHOODS.

CUMMERTREES is a particularly clean and neat village, 84 miles s. of Edinburgh, the like distance s. E. of Glasgow, 22 N. w. of Carlisle, 13 s. E. of Dumfries, 10 s. E. of Lochmaben, the like distance s. from Lockerbie, 6 from Ecclefechan, and 4 from Annan. The parish, which is about four miles in length by three in breadth, is bounded on the north-east by the river Annan, and on the south by the Solway Frith. It is a flat, fertile, and well cultivated district, and is now well enclosed. The name is derived from the British words *Cum-ber-tree*, signifying the hamlet at the short valley, and is sufficiently descriptive of the local situation of the village.—About a mile south-east of Cummertrees is POWFOOT, a very pretty watering place, and a branch station of an extensive fishery.

DALTON is a small village between three and four

miles from Cummertrees. The parish, which now comprehends the two ancient ones of Meikle Dalton and Little Dalton, is four miles in length by three in breadth. Its general appearance is that of high cultivation, which has been extended over once unprofitable moors and commons. The village contains the kirk and parochial school, together with a female day and Sunday school.

Mouswald village is situate six miles from Dumfries, lying between that town and Annan. The kirk, which is about a quarter of a mile from the village, on an elevated site, contains a dilapidated effigy of Sir Simon Carruthers, once laird of Mouswald. Sir Robert Grierson, Baronet, of Lagg, has a noble mansion here.

Ruthwell village is about three miles from Cummertrees; this place is a barony, and is privileged to hold markets and fairs, but it is long since the inhabitants availed themselves of these rights. It was in early days celebrated for the manufacture of salt by a peculiar process; but the art has not been practised for a length of time. The shore of this parish is graced by the little sea-bathing village of Brow, where Burns spent several of the last weeks of his existence. The kirk and manse of Ruthwell stand about a quarter of a mile from that village. The gardens of the manse, which are extensive and laid out with great taste, contain a very ancient Runic monument, in a good state of preservation. The parochial school is at Clarencefield.

POST, Cummertrees.—Letters arrive from and are despatched to Annan three days a week.

POST, Dalton.—Letters arrive from and are despatched to Ecclefechan daily.

POST, Mouswald & Ruthwell.—Letters arrive from and are despatched to Dumfries three days a week.

NOBILITY, GENTRY AND CLERGY.

Bell Wm. esq. of Rammerscales), Dalton   [Dalton
Carruthers Thomas (of Dormont), Dickson Wm. Clark, esq. (of Locharwoods), Ruthwell   [manse
Duncan Rev. Henry, D. D. Ruthwell
Gillespie Rev. George, Cummertrees manse
Grierson Alex. esq. Rockhall cottage, Mouswald
Grierson Sir Robt. bart. (of Lagg), Rock hall, Mouswald
Macrae Jas. Charles, esq. (of Holmains), Dalton
Mansfield the Earl of, Commlongan castle, Ruthwell
Murray Rev. Andrew Beveridge, Mouswald manse
Murray John Dalrymple (of Murraythwaite house), Cummertrees
Philips Walter, esq. Commlongan castle, Ruthwell
Queensberry the Marquess of, Kinmount house, Cummertrees
Sharp General Matthew, M.P. Hoddom castle, Cummertrees
Somerville Samuel Henderson, esq. (of Whitecroft house), Dalton
Thomson Rev. Thomas Hunter, Dalton manse

SCHOOLS.

Dickson John, Mouswald
M'Caa Wilhelmina, Hetland, Dalton
M'Lean Agnes, Ruthwell
PAROCHIAL SCHOOLS: --
Mouswald——Francis Halliday, master   [master
Clarencefield——Thos. Ferguson,
Cummertrees——Jno. Owen, mastr
Dalton——John Rae, master
Smith Janet, Cummertrees
INN-KEEPERS & VINTNERS.
Dalgleish Robt. (Queensberry Arms) Cummertrees   [Mouswald
Dickson Margaret (Coach & Horses)
Hetherington Thomas, Clarencefield
Kennedy Walter (Royal Oak) Dalton
Lorimer Ths. (Black Bull) Mouswald
SHOPKEEPERS & TRADERS.
The names without address are in CUMMERTREES.
Anderson Margaret, shopkeeper
Broatch John, surgeon, Mouswald
Carruthers James, joiner
Clark Janet, shopkeeper, Mouswald
Dick Wm. joiner & shopkpr. Dalton
Dickson James, clogger, Mouswald
Dickson Jno. blacksmith, Mouswald
Dickson Wm. joiner, Ruthwell
Dunbar Wm. cooper, Ruthwell
Farish Alexander, shoe maker
Fisher Thos. baker, Carrutherstown
Graham John, cartwright, Hetland

Graham Robert, bacon curer
Grierson Wm. slater, Ruthwell
Hyslop Thos. shopkeeper, Ruthwell
Irving Thomas, tailor
Johnstone John, blacksmith
Johnstone John, joiner, Ruthwell
Johnstone Mary, shopkeepr. Ruthwll
Kennedy Walter, blacksmith, Dalton
Kerr Joseph, blacksmith, Mouswald
M'Dougall Ths. blacksmith, Ruthwll
M'Kay Janet, shopkeeper, Mouswald
M'Lean David, joiner, Ruthwell
M'Lean William, tailor, Ruthwell
Marshall Francis, blacksmith
Mawell Wm. cartwright, Mouswald
Mundell Agnes, shopkpr. Mouswald
Mundell Edwd. shoe makr. Ruthwell
Porteous Thomas, shoe maker
Roddick John, tailor
Rodgerson William, tailor
Scott John, shoe maker
Smith John, surgeon, Ruthwell
Tweddie Walter, joiner, Mouswald
Willis Wm. miller, Brocklehirst, Mouswald

COACHES.

To & from DUMFRIES & CARLISLE, pass through the parishes of Cummertrees and Ruthwell two or three times a day.

CARRIER.

To DUMFRIES, John M'Gragh, from Mouswald, every Wed. and Saturday.

DORNOCK, GRAITNEY (OR GRETNA),
WITH SPRINGFIELD, KIRKPATRICK-FLEMING AND NEIGHBOURHOODS.

Dornock is a small village, 84 miles s. of Edinburgh, 18 s. of Langholm, 17 s. E. of Dumfries, 12 s. E. of Lockerbie, 7 s. of Ecclefechan, and 2 E. of Annan; situate on the high road from the latter town to Carlisle, and about a quarter of a mile from the shore of the Solway Frith, where there is good sea-bathing. The parish, which is about two miles and a half square, is washed on its southern part by the Solway. An ancient erection, called Stapleton tower, stands on the estate of Stapleton, in this parish; as is Robgill tower, formerly belonging to the Irvings, of Robgill. The Duke of Buccleugh and the Earl of Mansfield are the principal owners of the land, which for the most part is in a high state of cultivation. The kirk and the parochial school are in the village.

Graitney (more popularly called Gretna) is a parish in the south part of the county, lying on the west side of the small river Sark. The present parish comprehends the old parishes of Gretna and Redpatrick, or Redkirk, which were united in 1609. The village of Gretna, or Gretna-green, is situate on the road from Annan to Carlisle—eight miles and a half from the former, nine miles and a half north from the latter town; and is the first stage on entering Scotland from England. This village has been long noted for the celebration of clandestine marriages: any person can perform the ceremony, which merely amounts to a confession before witnesses that certain persons are man and wife—such an acknowledgment being sufficient to constitute a valid marriage in Scotland; by a certificate being subscribed by the officiating priest and witnesses, the union becomes quite indissoluble. Upon

the average, three hundred couples are thus married in the year; and the fee charged varies, according to circumstances and the means of the party, from half a guinea to £40. and even £50. An attempt was made in the general assembly of the kirk of Scotland, in 1826, to suppress this system of fraud and profanity, but without success. It is now upwards of seventy-five years since this traffic was commenced by a person of the name of Joseph Paisley, a tobacconist by trade, and not a blacksmith, as is usually supposed; after a long life of desecration and drunkenness, he died so lately as 1814. At present there are five rivals here for the hymeneal office; perhaps the most respectable of these is a Mr. Linton, of Graitney-hall—a large house recently converted into an inn, where visiters receive every attention and accommodation. About a quarter of a mile from Gretna is the village of Springfield, which participates in this matrimonial trade; this village is the property of Sir Patrick Maxwell, and that of Gretna belongs to Colonel Wm. Maxwell. At Sarkfoot, about a mile from the latter village, every convenience is found for sea-bathing. About the same distance, in another direction, is the small village of Rigg, where there is a dissenting chapel.

The parish of Kirkpatrick-Fleming, highly interesting in Scottish legend and song, is bounded on the east by Graitney; the kirk and parochial school, which stand at the southern end of the parish, are about three miles from Gretna. Lime and freestone abound in this district, in which are likewise several mineral springs, possessing medicinal properties similar to those of Hartfield spa, near Moffat.

POST, GRAITNEY.—Letters arrive from CARLISLE for GRAITNEY, SPRINGFIELD and their neighbourhoods (by the Port Patrick mail) every morning at eight in winter and seven in summer, and are despatched every afternoon at half-past four.

GENTRY AND CLERGY.

Barker Mrs. Anna Maria, (of Langshaw), Kirkpatrick-Fleming
Graham Colonel William (of Moss know), Kirkpatrick-Fleming
Hastie Rev. George, Manse, Kirkpatrick-Fleming
M'Gill Rev. Matthew, Rigg, Graitney
Mair Mrs. Ann (of Wiseby), Kirkpatrick-Fleming
Maxwell Sir Patrick (of Springkell), Kirkpatrick-Fleming
Ogilvie George, esq. (of Cove) Kirkpatrick-Fleming
Rae Matthew, esq. (of Newton), Kirkpatrick-Fleming
Roddick Rev. Jas. Manse, Graitney
Sloan Rev. Nicholas, Manse, Dornock
Smail William Archibald, esq. (of Rohgill), Dornock

SCHOOLS—PAROCHIAL, &c.

DORNOCK (& gentlemen's boarding), William Purdie, master
GRAITNEY, Robert Roddick and James Barclay, masters
KIRKPATRICK-FLEMING, Saml. Kerr & John Irving Roddick, masters

INN-KEEPERS & VINTNERS.

Beattie Simon, Graitney
Bell John (Cross Keys), Dornock

Bell William, Dornock
Clashan James, Dornock
Davidson John, Dornock
Dickson John (Coach & Horses), Dornock
Haugh Joseph, Graitney
Johnston Robert, Rigg
Johnston Thomas, Springfield
Linton John (Graitney Hall Inn, & keeper of post horses), Graitney
Little Thomas (Wedding-house), Springfield

SHOPKEEPERS, TRADERS, &c.

Bell Andrew, miller, Dornock
Bell John, shopkeeper, Dornock
Birnie Walter, shopkeeper, Dornock
Blythe Mary, shopkeeper, Springfield
Blythe Wm. shopkeeper, Springfield
Clark George, blacksmith, Dornock
Dally Wm. tailor, Dornock [field
Davidson James, shopkeeper, Springfield
Davidson Jno. shopkeeper, Dornock
Edgar David, joiner & cartwright, Dornock
Graham John, grocer & spirit dealer, Springfield
Graham Wilhelmina, straw hat maker, Springfield
Graham William, clogger, Springfield
Harkness Jas. blacksmith, Graitney

Harkness John, grocer and draper, Springfield
Irving John, shoemaker, Springfield
Johnston Christopher, cartwright and joiner, Graitney
Johnston John, shopkeeper & shoemaker, Springfield
Johnston Wm. draper, Springfield
Lattimer William, joiner and cartwright, Dornock [nock
M'Crackan James, blacksmith, Dornock
Nicholson Dav. shoemaker, Dornock
Nicholson Maxwell, tailor, Dornock
Rome Andrew, teacher, Lowtherfield, Dornock
Steel James, blacksmith, Springfield
Steel William, clogger, Dornock
Wallace John, shopkeeper, Rigg

COACHES.

To CARLISLE, the *Royal Mail* (from Portpatrick), passes thro' Gretna, every afternoon at half-past four.
To GLASGOW & PORTPATRICK, the *Royal Mail* (from Carlisle), passes thro' Gretna every morning at eight in winter and seven in summer.

CARRIERS.

To EDINBURGH, GLASGOW & CARLISLE, Carriers pass through Kirkpatrick-Fleming twice a week.

DUMFRIES, MAXWELLTOWN & NEIGHBOURHOODS.

DUMFRIES, the capital of its county and parish, a royal burgh, the seat of the synod and presbytery of Dumfries, is 338 miles from London (by the route of Manchester), 71 s. of Edinburgh, 72 s. e. of Glasgow, 180 s. by w. of Aberdeen, 60 s. e. of Ayr, 56 s. e. of Kilmarnock, 55 n. e. of Wigtown, 33 n.w. of Carlisle, 34 s. e. of Cumnock, 30 w. by s. of Langholm, 28 n.e. of Kirkcudbright, 26 s. e. of Sanquhar, 18 n. e. of Castle-Douglas, 15 n.n.w. of Annan, 16 w. of Ecclefechan, 14 s. e. of Thornhill, 12 s. w. of Lockerbie, and 8 s. w. of Lockmaben. This town, which may be considered as the metropolis of the south-west quarter of Scotland, is seated on the left bank of the river Nith, about nine miles above its confluence with the Solway Frith. Of the precise period at which it was founded no record has been preserved. Antiquarians, without recurring to the Celtic, have bewildered themselves in endeavouring to settle the etymology of its name, which, in fact, has undergone but one trifling change from what it was originally, viz. *Drium-a-Phrish*—afterwards altered to 'Drumfries,' and, within the last sixty or seventy years, changed to Dumfries for the sake of euphony: *Druim-a-Phrish,* or 'Drum-fries,' signifying in the Celtic 'the back or ridge of a woody or shrubby eminence;' is truly descriptive of the situation of the town—rising, as it does, gradually from the river side, and embosomed in one of the finest and best sheets of dale country in Scotland: the prospect, which is terminated at the distance of a few miles by a continued chain of hills, covered with wood, or cultivated to their summits, is altogether one of the grandest scenes in Britain. Serving as a kind of capital, not only to its own shire, but also a portion of Galloway—and possessing an easy and frequent intercourse with London, Edinburgh, and Glasgow—it is a place of great resort for the nobility and gentry of the neighbouring counties: independently of those who have amusement only in view, many families are attracted hither by the cheapness of living, the salubrity of the air, and, above all, by its excellent seminaries of education; society, therefore, possesses a greater share of elegance and gaiety here, than can be found, probably, in any other town of its size in Scotland. The circuit court of justiciary, which is held twice a year (in spring and autumn), induces many to repair to Dumfries; and the time has been when the judges were attended to court by a whole body-guard

of country gentlemen; but this, like many other former customs, has progressively sunk into disuetude. In a work published in 1832, entitled the 'Picture of Dumfries,' published by John Gallatly, of Edinburgh, we find the following passage :—'The late Sir Thomas Reid Burnet, the late Alexander Maxwell, Esq., of Terraughty, A. Kay, Esq., and others, themselves Dumfriesians, and gentlemen of great influence in London, exerted themselves in favour of the natives of this town; and through their patronage numbers of young gentlemen, of good family and education, entered the service of the East India Company, and, as soldiers, sailors, and civilians, acquired both fame and fortune: a few of these died in middle life, after bettering in various ways the circumstances of friends and relatives at home; but the majority returned to their native district—purchased land, planned, built, planted and improved—happy themselves, and diffusing the means of happiness within their respective localities. Others, again, have been equally fortunate in the West Indies, America, Liverpool and London; and, drawing rather a narrow circle around Dumfries,' (the writer speaks with the fact when he says) 'there are individuals who possess among them tangible property closely verging on one million sterling.'

A spirit of improvement has been shewn by the inhabitants, assisted by the commissioners of police, in numerous alterations, public structures &c., amongst which may be named the erection of a new suite of assembly-rooms, new market-places, the widening of Bank-street, and lighting the town with gas; a spacious quay has been constructed along the side of the town; and a fine Doric column, raised by the county of Dumfries to the memory of the late Duke of Queensberry, adorns the centre of the burgh. The Court-House is a large elegant edifice, comprising a very capacious court-room and other offices; nearly opposite stands the gaol, whence the prisoners are conveyed for trial through a subterraneous passage which communicates with the court-room. Courts are held in April and September for Dumfries-shire and the stewartry of Kirkcudbright; there are also a small debt, sheriff and borough courts. The *Theatre* is rather a handsome building of stone, with a projecting portion; the interior, which is tastefully decorated, is lighted with gas: it is generally open a few weeks in the winter. It was here that Kean first evinced his dawning talents; to the last, that great actor never forgot the attention paid to him in early life in Dumfries. There are three subscription reading and news rooms, supplied with London and provincial papers, magazines, &c. (the principal one has an excellent billiard table); one library supported by subscription, and also a law library. A coursing club has two meetings during the summer; races are held in October, and the Caledonian Hunt once in five years. As already observed, a variety of ancient customs, formerly upheld in Dumfries, are now relinquished; but one, called 'shooting for the silver gun,' still exists, and is celebrated with great enthusiasm. The silver gun, which is still preserved, derives great importance from being the gift of James VI, of Scotland, who ordained it as a prize to the best marksman among the incorporations of Dumfries: the contest was by royal authority to take place every year; but, from the great trouble and expense, it has become a 'once in seven years' jubilee . . . e birth-day of the reigning monarch is the . . . ariably chosen for the celebration: the last festival occurred a few years ago; and, considering the changes that have operated within the ranks of the ancient corporations, it is a matter of considerable doubt whether this usage of the olden time will ever be revived.

The commercial advantages of Dumfries have been much increased by obtaining an act of parliament empowering a certain number of commissioners to be annually appointed to conduct the shipping business of the river, since which period great and important improvements have been effected: the dangerous sandbank, in the Solway Frith have been rendered comparatively safe, by judiciously placing buoys in the Scotch and English channels; many permanent obstructions have been removed; the river Nith has been confined by solid embankments and stone jetties; new cuts have been made, where necessary; and at present most of the vessels, which were formerly obliged to unload at a considerable distance down the river, may discharge their cargoes close to the town. The principal imports are timber, hemp, tallow, coals, slate, iron, and wine; the exports consist of wheat, barley, oats, potatoes, wool, and freestone. Considerable business is done in the manufacture of hosiery (lamb's wool to a very great extent), hat-making, breweries, tan-yards, and the glue manufactory; the amount is not under £100,000. sterling. Dumfries was for many years the leading market for hare-skins in Scotland, and even regulated the price of home fur in England; and it is still looked to as the arbiter of prices. The trade of the town and district is assisted by branches of the 'Bank of Scotland,' the 'National Bank of Scotland,' the 'Commercial Bank of Scotland,' and the 'British Linen Company.' The principal inns are the 'King's Arms,' the 'George,' and the 'Commercial:' they are all highly respectable establishments; the latter attracts notice from the circumstance of its having been the temporary head-quarters of the Pretender, in 1745. Three weekly newspapers are published, two of which are issued on Tuesday, and the third on Friday; their names are, the 'Dumfries Courier,' the 'Dumfries Times,' and the 'Dumfries Herald:' the 'Courier' has existed twenty-seven years, the 'Times' upwards of three, and the 'Herald' more than one year.

The municipal government is vested in a provost, three bailies, a dean of guild, a treasurer, two town clerks, and twelve councillors, to whom the entire jurisdiction of the burgh is confided. Until a recent period, the craftsmen were divided into seven corporations, with each a deacon chosen from their respective trades, who elected one of their own number to be convener, and another to be general box-master; all of whom formed what was termed a grand committee of the seven trades: these distinctions, however (for distinctions of considerable importance they were in former times), were virtually abolished by the reform bill; some of the trades possessed considerable property, which has since been publicly sold, and the proceeds equitably divided among the respective parties. Dumfries unites with Annan, Lockmaben, and Sanquhar, in returning one member to parliament.

The PLACES OF WORSHIP consist of two churches of the establishment; a relief chapel, two united secessional, an episcopal, a Roman catholic, and a methodist; and a reformed presbyterian, or Cameronian

meeting-house, opened in 1832: it was erected at an expense of £750; its site is well chosen, in an agreeable part of the town. Opposite to this edifice is the congregational chapel, opened in August 1834, and built at the cost of £700.; it is the property of a respectable body of individuals, who, in common with their brethren in England and Scotland, formerly assumed the name of independents. St. Michael's, or the parish church, claims peculiar notice, on account of its cemetery, which contains numerous elegant and curious monuments, many of them very ancient; but the most attractive is the fine mausoleum raised to the memory of the Scottish bard, Burns. By the erection of this monument it may be said that Scotland has repaid the debt so long due to the memory of him of whose natural genius his countrymen may well be proud; but while as Scotsmen they justly exult that it was reserved for their country to give birth to such a poet, the hard fate of Burns while living, and the comparative obscurity in which he closed his days, prove also that he was not sufficiently valued in life. Burns died at Dumfries on the 21st July, 1796, aged 37 years, and his remains were deposited in the church-yard of St. Michael's; but it was some time before even a stone was placed over the sod that covered the ashes of departed genius—and this was but a plain memento, reared by a widow's affections, and bedewed with a widow's tears. It was not until 1813 that any worthy or decisive plan was adopted; and it was then chiefly owing to the indefatigable perseverance of William Grierson, Esq., of this town, that a public meeting was convened, on the 6th of January, 1814, at which General Dunlop, M.P., presided. A public subscription was immediately commenced, the amount of which soon proved that it only wanted a spark to kindle into a flame the generous sentiment of paying due honour to the inspired talent of their immortal countryman; his late Majesty, then Prince Regent, graciously sent a donation of fifty guineas. The design of the mausoleum was furnished by Thos. F. Hunt, Esq., of London; and a model by Peter Turnerelli, Esq., was chosen for the marble sculpture to be placed in the interior. The subject is happily taken from words which occur in the dedication of an early edition of the bard's own poems to the noblemen and gentlemen of the Caledonian Hunt :—' The poetic genius of my country found me, as the prophetic bard Elijah did Elisha, at the plough, and threw her inspiring mantle over me.' The foundation-stone was laid 5th June, 1815, and the body removed from the place in which it was originally interred on the 19th September following. It is surrounded with handsome iron palisades and evergreens, which add highly to the melancholy beauty of its appearance. The whole expense amounted to about £1,500., and it certainly is a cemetery worthy of Caledonia's inimitable bard—

' Where still that fresh, that unforgotten name
Shall pay the arrear of monumental fame,
As oft the traveller, oft the poet, turns
To muse, and linger o'er the grave of Burns.'

With a desire to do further honour to the memory of Burns, a number of gentlemen have formed themselves into a club, and meet annually to celebrate his natal day. Of the family of the poet, three sons still survive :—Robert, the eldest, aged 50, who served twenty years in the legacy-duty department of the stamp-office, Somerset-house, London, and who now resides in his native town on a retired allowance; William, the second, stationed at Madras, is captain and assistant commissary-general in the East India Company's service; and James Glencairn Burns, also a captain in the same service, and lately appointed superintendent of Upper and Lower Cocher.

CHARITABLE, EDUCATIONAL AND SCIENTIFIC INSTITUTIONS.—The *Infirmary* was founded in 1776, at a period when very few charities, of a similar nature, were in Britain; and this is still the only one in the South of Scotland. Medical advice and medicines are gratuitously afforded to every applicant who is an object of charity. It is supported by annual subscriptions, legacies, donations, benefactions, &c. and is under the management of governors. There is also a *Lunatic Asylum* connected with it.—The *Poors' Hospital* is for the purpose of supporting aged and indigent poor, and destitute children, who are taught to read and write. It is governed by the magistrates, town council, &c. and it is supported by a part of the collections from the church doors, numerous benefactions, donations and annual subscriptions. The health, morals, and comfort of its poor inmates are studied with the greatest care. It was founded, in 1753, by Messrs. J. and W. Moorhead, merchants. Dumfries also contains a society for promoting education in the Highlands, a missionary society, a society for promoting Christianity amongst the Jews, a Bible society, a local Sabbath school society, an infants' school, a ladies' free school, a juvenile society, a branch of the Scottish missionary society, and a penny a week Bible and missionary society.—The *Acad my.* This elegant and useful seminary was founded in 1802, on one of the most delightful and healthy situations to be found in the town or neighbourhood. The expenses of the ground, and of building and finishing the fabric, were entirely defrayed by voluntary subscription. A committee of management having been chosen by a general meeting of the subscribers, the whole operations were carried into execution under their superintendence, and, in October, 1814, the structure was formally delivered over to the magistrates, as patrons and guardians of the institution, who, along with other members of the town council, have the exclusive privilege of appointing the masters.

Dumfries and Maxwelltown Astronomical Society. —This society, which is of recent formation, have erected, on Corbelly hill, on the Maxwelltown side of the river, an observatory, which is regarded as a highly ornamental feature in one of the most unique half-city, half-sylvan landscapes: it commands an extensive view of beautiful and varied scenery: the cost exceeded 1,000 guineas, which was raised in £5. shares. The plans were by Mr. Newall, architect, and the building was completed in little more than twelve months. It contains four stories,—the lower one for the use of the keeper; three others for the accommodation of the subscribers and strangers, which are furnished with globes, mathematical instruments, newspapers, and periodicals; the upper story is set apart for a camera obscura and prism. The observatory is seen from a great distance: the grounds, which consist of more than half an acre, are laid out with much taste, containing flowers and shrubs of various kinds. The management consists of Mr. R. Thomson, treasurer, and Mr. John Jackson, secretary.

MARKETS AND FAIRS.—The market days are Wednesdays. The two principal half yearly markets take the name of the Candlemas and rood fairs. Until very lately about 30,000 head of black cattle were sold for the markets of the south alone, independently of much inferior stock, which merely passed from the keeping of one farmer to another; of the heavy stock in good years the value was nearly £300,000. sterling; but the trade has declined, and must still decline, as regards the Norwich and other markets. The facilities afforded by steam navigation, and the spread of turnip husbandry, induce farmers to feed a portion of their stock fat, which was formerly sent to Norfolk, and there fattened for the London markets: independently of this, great numbers of sheep are fattened on turnips from November till April, a practice very little known previous to 1822. Vast quantities of pork are sold in Dumfries from the beginning of December to the end of February; the trade is strictly a ready money one, and repeatedly four, five, and six thousand pounds have been paid and received for this commodity before breakfast on a Wednesday morning. The fairs are the first Wednesday in February, the third Wednesday in March, the third Wednesday in April, 26th May or Wednesday afterwards, third Wednesday in June, the third Wednesday in July, third Wednesday in August, third Wednesday in October, 22d or Wednesday afterwards in November, and third Wednesday in November, for cattle (all old style).

MAXWELLTOWN, formerly a village, is now a burgh of barony, in the stewartry of Kirkcudbright, and connected with Dumfries by two bridges across the Nith. In no instance have the good effects of erecting a village into a burgh of barony been more conspicuous than in Maxwelltown. The charter was obtained from the crown in 1810, and since that time, from being a poor village, notorious for disorderly conduct,—(for it was a remark of the late Sir John Fielding, that he could trace a rogue over the whole kingdom, but always lost him at the bridge-end of Dumfries, now Maxwelltown, or in the Gorbals of Glasgow),—it has improved in value and extent of houses, and increased considerably in the number and respectability of its inhabitants: it is governed by a provost, two bailies, and councillors. A new church was erected here in 1829 by subscription; it is a neat edifice, and its site well chosen. Maxwelltown also possesses warm and cold baths, as well as two breweries and two iron foundries.

POST OFFICE, Castle-street, DUMFRIES, Robert Threshie, *Post Master.*—The LONDON mail, with letters from the whole of ENGLAND, arrives every morning at nine, and is despatched every afternoon at half-past one.—The EDINBURGH, GLASGOW, MOFFAT, &c. mail arrives every morning at half-past six, and is despatched every morning at six.—The IRISH, PORTPATRICK, and the whole of GALLOWAY letters arrive every morning at half-past five, and are despatched every morning at nine.—Letters from THORNHILL, SANQUHAR and MINNIEHIVE arrive every night at half-past eleven, and are despatched every morning at nine.—Letters from LOCHMABEN and TORTHORWALD arrive (by foot post) every morning at six, and are despatched every morning at nine.—Letters from NEW ABBEY and KIRKBEAN arrive (by foot post) every evening at seven, and are despatched every morning at nine.

Office hours—from seven in the morning during summer, and eight in the winter, until eight at night.

NOBILITY, GENTRY AND CLERGY.

Adair Major Jas. Nunfield cottage
Allan Mrs. Sophia, Mill bank, Maxwelltown
Allen John, esq. of Fountainbleau
Anderson Mr. Allen, Allen bank
Babington Rev. Charles Maitland, Stakford cottage, Terregles
...ington John, esq. Summerville
Baillie William, esq. (sub-sheriff), Nunholm
Barclay Major Peter, Newton lodge,
Bell Mrs. Jane, 2 Portland place
Bell Mrs. Jesse, George st
Bevan Mr. Robert, Nith place
Biggar James, esq. (of Maryholm), Terregles
Blair Miss Janet, 10 Glasgow street,
Brown Mrs. Agnes, of Brown hal
Brown Miss Mary, of Maryfield
Brown John, esq. (of Nunwood), Terregles
Burns Mr. Robert, Burn st
Burnside Mrs. Ann, 12 Buccleugh st
Campbell Jno. M'Candie, esq. Craigs

Carruthers Miss Elizabeth, Castle st
Cavan Mr. Douglas, Nith bank
Clark Miss Christiana, High st
Clark Mrs. Isabella, 26 Castle st
Clark Miss Jane, 13 Buccleugh st
Clark Mr. John, Laurie Know, Troqueer
Clyde Rev. James, Loreburn st
Colton Miss Mary, Irish st
Comrie Mrs. Janet, George st
Cowans Rev. Geo. Nith bank [st
Crawford Mr. Jno. Innis, Buccleugh
Creighton Mrs. Ann, Castle st
Cririe Mrs. Janet, Kerfield
Dalrymple Rev. James, Drungan's lodge, Troqueer
Dalzell Captain, Castle st
Dalzell James, esq. Castle st
Dalzell James Allen, esq. Cargen
Davis Major W. St. Michael st
Dawson Rev. Æneas, Shakspeare st
Dickson Mrs. Hannah, 4 Portland place, Maxwelltown
Dow Rev. David, 21 Irish st
Drummond Mrs. Mary, Castle st
Dugeon Mr. Henry, of Woodhead

Duncan Rev. Thos. M.D. Moat house
Dunlop Miss Keith, Albany place
Dunlop Rev. Walter, 26 Buccleugh st
Ferguson Mrs. Nicholas, 10 Buccleugh street [Troqueer
Ferguson Mrs. William, Rotchell,
Forsyth Mrs. Joseph, of Spittlefield
Forsyth Philip, Nithside, Troqueer
Fyfe Rev. Andrew, Loreburn st
Gilchrist Miss, Irish st
Gillespie Mrs. Castle st
Gillett Captain Aurelius, Greenhead, Troqueer [Troqueer
Goldie Miss Jane, Summer hill,
Goldie Miss Margaret, Castle st
Goldie Mrs. Nairn, 15 Buccleugh st
Gordon Miss, 21 Buccleugh st
Gracie Miss Jane, George st
Grove Major Henry, Shakspeare st
Hairstens Mrs. Jane, 15 Galloway street, Maxwelltown
Hamilton Miss Eliza, Bank st
Hannah John, esq. of Hannafield
Harkness Mrs. Elizabeth, George st
Harley Miss Agnes, George st
Howat Mrs. Helen, Castle st

GENTRY, &c.—Continued.

Howat Robert Kirkpatrick, esq. (of Mabie), Troqueer [Irish st
Hysslop the Misses Helen and Eliza, Irving Sir Paul, bart. Lochvale
Irving William, esq. St. Michael st
Jardine Robert, esq. of Creswell
Johnston Mr. Mark, Stone house croft, Maxwelltown
Johnstone Peter, esq. of Carnsalloch
Kennedy Mrs. Elizabeth, Denholm, Academy street [place
Kirkpatrick Miss Isabella, Albany
Lennock Capt.George Gustavus,R.N. Woodlands, Terregles
Lennox Jas.esq.Dalskairth,Troqueer
M'Adam John, esq. of Castle dykes
M'Culloch Alex. esq. St. Michael st
M'Dermid Rev. John, Albany place
M'Dowall Capt. Robert, Castle st
M'Ghie Miss Agnes, Corbelly sq. Troqueer [Friars' vennel
M'Ghie Mrs. Cicely Nicholson, 48
M'Ghie Mrs. Jane, Castle hill, Troqueer [Maxwelltown
Machray Rev. Robert, Galloway st,
M'Morrine Miss Elizbth. Castle st
M'Murdo Col. Bryce, of Mavis grove
M'Murdo Mrs. Catherine, Castle st
Macourtie Mrs. Mary, Castle st
M'Vicar John, esq. Castle st
M'Whir Mrs. Jane, 3 Portland place, Maxwltwn [Albany pl
Manuel Miss Elizabeth Hamilton,
Maxwell Miss Catherine, Castle st
Maxwell Miss Isabella, 11 Buccleugh street
Maxwell Miss Margaret, Castle st
Maxwell Mrs. Marion (of Terraughty) Torqueer
Maxwell Marmaduke Constable,esq. of Terregles
Maxwell Miss —, of Kirkconnel
Maxwell Col.Wm. Neivall (of Goldie Lea), Troqueer [Troqueer
Maxwell Wm. esq. (of Carruchan),
Melville Alex. esq. M.D. Castle st
Mitchelson Miss Susan, Loreburn st
Moffat Mrs. A. 13 Buccleugh st
Monielaws Mrs.Catherine, Cottage, English road
Monies William,esq. of Netherwood
Murray Peter, esq. 1 Portland place, Maxwelltown
Pagan Wm. esq. of Carriestanes
Paterson Robert, esq. of Nunfield
Pew Mrs. Harriet Syme, Castle st
Phillips Mr. Charles Hutchinson, Bank house, Troqueer
Ranken Rev. James, Lawrie Know cottage, Maxwelltown
Reid Rev. William, Shakspeare st
Rimmer Richd. esq. of Marchmount
Robinson Mrs. Margaret, of Pear mount, Troqueer [Troqueer
Ross Mrs. Mary Eliz.of Cargenholm,
Samson Mrs. Janet, 19 Galloway st, Maxwelltown [tonhead
Shortridge Saml. esq. M. D. of Kel-
Smith Mrs. Lorimer,3 David street, Maxwelltown
Smith Mrs. Mary, 12 Academy st
Staig Miss Ann, Castle st
Staig John, esq. Castle st
Swanson Captain Francis,Millbank, Maxwelltown
Taylor Mrs. Captain, Cesseylauds cottage, Maxwelltown
Taylor Robert, esq. of Broomland
Taylor Mrs. Wm. of Troqueer holm
Thompson Mr. John, Ramsay cottage, Troqueer
Thorburn Rev.Wm. Troqueer manse
Turner Miss Jane,4 David st,Mxwltn
Walker John, esq. of Kelton mains

Wallace Lady, Millbank, Maxwltwn
Wallace Rev. Robert, St. Michael's manse [Troqueer
Whaley Rev. Arthur, Corbelly sq.
Whigham George, esq. Allanton, Dunscore
Wightman Mrs. Nicholas, Irving st
Wood Mrs. Elizabeth, George st
Woodburn Wm.esq.Terregles banks
Young Hon. Mrs. Patricia (of Lincluden), Terregles [Broomrig
Young Samuel Denholm, esq. of

ACADEMIES AND PRIVATE TEACHERS.

Affleck Alexander, Loreburn st
Attwood Phœbe (music), Queensberry square
Balieff Elizbth. & Rebecca, High st
Brown John, Queensberry square
Bushby Elizabeth, Castle st
Campbell Walter, Loreburn st
DUMFRIES ACADEMY, Academy st— John Macmillan, rector; Wm. Armstrong,mathematical teacher; Jas. M'Robert,English & French; John Craik, writing
DUMFRIES & MAXWELLTOWN BENEVOLENT SOCIETY'S SCHOOL, Green sands—Wm. Keay,master; Jane Cunningham, mistress
Gemmill William, Queensberry st
Gordon James, Shakspeare st
Guillemette Louis (French and Italian), Academy st [welltown
Halliday John, 2 Howgate st, Max-
INFANTS' SCHOOL, Academy street —Barbara Cruickshank, teacher
Melville Ann Isabella, Buccleugh st
Oliver Samuel (English & commercial day and boarding establishment), High st [herry st
Riddick Euphemia& Phillis,Queens-
Roberts Mary (music), 44 High st
Shaw Mrs. Jas. (music), English st
Smith James, Irish st
Stampa Joanna (music) 145 High st
White Jane, St. Andrew st

APOTHECARIES & CHYMISTS

Clanahan Mark, 167 High st
Duncan Walter, 82 High st
Fraser James, 112 High st
Watson George William, 87 High st

ARCHITECT.

Newall Walter, 1 Bank st

AUCTIONEERS.

Dawson John, Queensberry square
Dawson John Charters, English st
Dixon William, High st
Dunbar George, Church place
Gowanlock Thomas, English st
Watson John, Queensberry st

BAKERS & FLOUR DEALERS.

Armstrong William, 103 High st
Beveridge David, 59 Galloway st, Maxwelltown [street
Corson Adam (army baker),72 High
Edgar John, High st
Hair Ninian, 144 High st
Hill Edward, 18 English st
M'Lellan George, High st
Montgomery William, 103 High st
Murray Francis, 79 High st
Rain Robert & Son, 15 English st
Sharp John, 120 High st [town
Shortridge Jas.61 Galloway st,Mxwl-
Smith Agnes, 60 High st
Thomson James, 2 Friars' vennel

BANKERS.

BANK OF SCOTLAND (Branch), Irish st—(draws on the Parent Establishment.Edinburgh, & Coutts& Co.London)—John Barker, agent
BRITISH LINEN COMPANY (Branch), Irish street —(draw on the Parent Establishment, Edinburgh, & on

Smith, Payne & Smiths, London) —Robert Adamson, agent
COMMERCIAL BANK OF SCOTLAND (Branch), Irish street—(draws on the Parent Establishment, Edinburgh, and on Jones, Loyd & Co. London)—William Goldie, agent
NATIONAL BANK OF SCOTLAND (Branch), Bank street—(draws on the Parent Establishment, Edinburgh, and Glyn, Halifax and Co. London)—Alex. Hannay, agent
SAVINGS' BANK, Chapel st—Rev Thomas Duncan, secretary; John Gibson, treasurer

BLACKSMITHS.

Daling John, Old Bridge st,Maxwltn
Gillespie John, White sands
Haining Wm. Turner's close,High st
Haugh George, 50 High st [st
Huddleston Robt. New Fleshmarke
Kerr John, Mill-dam head
M'Nae Alex.12 Galloway st,Mxwltn
Moffat Brice, 147 High st
Muir John, Shakspeare st
Nicholson Robert, Shakspeare st
Shanks John, Brewery st
Smart William, Irish st
Weild James, Loreburn st
Wilson David, Wall green

BLEACHERS.

Cruickshank William, Trailflat— Joseph Welsh, agent, Galloway street, Maxwelltown
Henry John,Sandbed—James Beck, agent, Howgate st, Maxwelltown

BOOKBINDERS.

Henry James, 35 Irish st
Johnstone Wm. Francis,50 Glasgow street, Maxwelltown

BOOKSELLERS, STATIONER'S AND BINDERS.
(See also the preceding Head.)
Marked thus * keep Circulating Libraries
*Anderson Allan, 70 High st
*Anderson John, 74 & 75 High st
Fraser Janet, 94 High st
Halliday David, 113 High st
Johnston John, High st
*M'Kie John (& agent for London newspapers), Midsteeple, High st
M'Kinnell John (& music dealer), 104 High street
Norval John, 21 English st
Sinclair John (& agent for London newspapers), 22 High st

BOOT & SHOE MAKERS.

Affleck James, Bank st [st
Anderson Geo. & Samuel,108 High
Beck Alexander, Chapel place
Brown James, Queensberry st
Ferguson James. St. Michael st
Gordon John, 60 Friars' vennel
Harkness Jas.Market st.Maxwltwn
Henderson James, 25 Irish st
Henderson Peter, 6 English st
Hunter Rbt. 8 Galloway st, Maxltw
Hutton Andrew, 31 Friars' vennel
Irving John, 4 Friars' vennel
Irving Peter, 90 Friars' vennel
Irving Waltr.Market st,Maxwlltwn
Irving William, 63 High st [town
Johnston Jas.1 Market st,Maxwell-
M'Cormick John, 50 High st
M'Lellan James. 17 High st
M'Lellan John, 14 Friars' vennel
Mitchell Robert, 168 High st
Mouncey William, 22 Friars' vennel
Mundell Dav.35 Glasgow st,Mxwltn
Nibloe James, 26 Friars' vennel
Reid Jas.6 Old Bridge st, Mxwlltwn
Richardson John, 24 Friars' vennel
Richardson William, 33 Irish st
Scott William, 60 English st

Shanks Walter, 48 Friars' vennel
Shaw John, Queensberry st
Shortridge Jas.Galloway st,Mxwltn
Shortridge Jno.Redlion st,Mxwltwn
Smith Jas.35 Market st,Maxwlltwn
Todd John,20 Glasgow st,Mxwltwn
Underwood James, 12 High st
Wells Andw. Market st, Mxwlltwn
Wilson John, 95 Friars' vennel

BRASS FOUNDERS.
(See also Iron Founders.)
Aitken William, 56 High st
Stafford John, High st

BREWERS & MALTSTERS.
Corson George, Irish st
M'BurneyThs.Galloway st, Mxwltn
Morrison James, Irish st
Murray Robert, Old Brewery, Buccleugh st   [Maxwelltown
Shortridge James, 61 Galloway st,
Whaley Richard, White sands

BUILDERS.
See Masons and Builders.

CABINET MAKERS.
Marked thus * are also Upholsterers.
*Aitchison William& Thos.Castle st
*Bell Irving, 79 English st   [sq
*Burnside Wm.& Son, Queensberry
Donaldson Charles, Queensberry st
Donaldson George, Queensberry st
*Dunbar George, Church place
*Gibson John, Church place
*Gregan William, High st
Halliday John & William, 63 College st, Maxwelltown   [town
Howat Jas. 57 College st, Maxwell-
*Kerr George, Queensberry st
*Robb Charles, jun. 4 Church place

CARPET & MOREEN WAREHOUSE.
Berwick John, 59 High st

CARVERS & GILDERS.
Barry Alexander, St. Michael st
Crackstone Gilbert (& looking glass manufctr. & optician),6 Church pl
M'Kay John, 27 Buccleugh st
M'Pherson Robert, 15 Bank st
Roberts Thomas, Church place
Spence William, Queensberry st

CHAIR MAKERS.
Black Saml.Market st,Maxwelltwn
Nicholson William,Queensberry st

CLOG & PATTEN MAKERS.
Cunningham Janet, Academy st
Davidson John, 60 Galloway st, Maxwelltown   [welltown
Graham Robert,17 Market st,Max-
Hammond Joseph, 8 St. David st
Moffat Thomas, 76 High st
Richardson John, 24 Friars' vennel
Richardson William, 33 Irish st

CLOTHES DEALERS AND BROKERS.
Docherty James, 28 Buccleugh st
Hay Mary, 27 Friars' vennel
M'Cluskay Peter, 32 Friars' vennel
Richardson Burnside, 2 Church pl
Wallace James, 63 Friars' vennel
Weemys Jane, 27 Bucclengh st

COACH MAKERS.
Beck Joseph, 31 English st
Inglis James, Irish st

CONFECTIONERS.
Bell Euphemia, 134 High st
Dick William, 14 English st
M'Gregor Hugh, 65 High st
M'Lellan George, 1 Church place
Taylor William, 99 High st

COOPERS.
Affleck Samuel, Bank st
Beattie Robert, Long close. High st
M'Burnie Jno. Galloway st,Mxwltn

Moffat William, Irish st
Scott Robert, Queensberry st

CORK CUTTERS.
Leighton Miles, Assembly st
Matthews James, 55 Friars' vennel

CORN MERCHANTS AND DEALERS.
Bairden Thomas, Queensberry sq
Gillespie John (and general agent), New quay   [quee
Smith James, Nether town, Tro-
Taite Joseph, 82 Friars' vennel
Thompson William, Queensberry st

CURRIERS AND LEATHER CUTTERS.
Bailey Charles, White sands
Nicholson John, 136 High st   [nel
Primrose James& Sons, Friars' ven-

CUTLERS.
Hinchsliffe Jos. Walker, 126 High st
Hinchsliffe Mark, 81 English st
Love Robert, 60 Friars' vennel

DRESS MAKERS & MILLINRS.
Baxter Janet, 49 High st   [Bank st
Brown Mary, Elizabeth and Anna,
Bruce Mary & Isabella, 10 High st
Brydone Ann and Catherine, 4 Buccleugh street
Caird Helen, 4 New Bridge st
Crawford Isabella and Janet, Galloway street, Maxwelltown
Dixon Ann, 24 Buccleugh st
Duff Margaret, English st
Dunn Mary and Ellen, High st
Fraser Agnes, High st   [wlltwn
Grierson Sarah,59 Glasgow st,Max-
Halliday Sisters, 59 High st
Henchan Margaret, 1 Bank st
Howston Agnes, David st, Maxltwn
Hunter Jane& Euphemia,85 High st
Hyslop Jane,135 High st
Ireland Sarah, 50 Glasgow street, Maxwelltown
Lawson Ellen, Queensberry square
M'Kinnell Janet and Margaret, Church place
M'Lellan Janet, 41 High st
M'Leod Janet, Buccleugh st
M'Morrine Jane, 82 Chapel st
Penny Jane, 4 New Bridge st
Ramsay Mary, 50 High st
Riddick Bethen, Mary and Jesse, Church place   [berry st
Sandelands Mary & Sister, Queens-
Simpson Mary, 18 Castle st
Stampa Ann Maria, 145 High st
Stewart Betsy. High st   [High st
Underwood Isabella and Sophia, 97

DYERS.
Armstrong & Brown, Waulk mill
Armstrong William, 3 White sands
Brown James, Market st, Maxltwn
Miller Jane ,44 Glasgow st,Maxltwn
Shaw Eliz. 27 Glasgow st,Maxltwn
Thomson Andrew, St. Michael st

EARTHENWARE AND CHINA DEALERS.
Crosbie Janet, 122 High st
Dougherty Peter, 64 Friars' vennel
Gallaugher John (and provision dealer), 5 Queensberry square
Grainger Robert, 45 High st
Henderson Joseph, 145 High st
Hepburn Jemima, 4 St. Andrew st
Hume Mary, St. David st
Smith John, 12 St. David st
Wallace Hugh (& glass) 149 High st
Whiteright John, 9 Galloway st, Maxwelltown

ENGINEER & SURVEYOR.
Bertram Thomas Hardy, Bank st

FIRE, &c. OFFICE AGENTS.
ALLIANCE, James Broom, High st
ATLAS, John M'Kie, 43 High st
EUROPEAN, William Broun, Bank st

HERCULES, James Caldon, Bank of Scotland, Irish st   [st
IMPERIAL, David Johnstone. Castle
INSURANCE OF SCOTLAND, William M'Gowan, 10 English st
MANCHESTER, Robert Wallace, Long close, High st
NORTH BRITISH, Alexander Hannay, Bank st
NORWICH UNION, John M'Diarmid, 117 High st
PHOENIX, George Reid, Commercial Bank, Irish st
SCOTTISH EQUITABLE, Threshie & Crichton, 1 Buccleugh st
SCOTTISH UNION, John Barker, Bank of Scotland, Irish st   [st
SUFFOLK. Thos. Harkness,150 High
SUN, Charles M'George, Queen st
UNITED KINGDOM, Christopher Harkness, 150 High st
WEST OF ENGLAND, Archibald Hamilton, Assembly st   [High st
WEST OF SCOTLAND, John Brand,

FISHING ROD AND TACKLE MAKERS.
Charters J. M. 25 Buccleugh st
Watson William, Queensberry st

FLAX DRESSERS.
Burns James, 76 Friars' vennel
Hepburn Jemima, 4 St. Andrew st
Little William, 70 Friars' vennel

FLESHERS.
Dalrymple Catherine, Market st, Maxwelltown
Douglas John, Bridge st   [town
Foster Alex. 3Galloway st,Maxwell-
Howat Charles, 86 English st
Kerr James, Friars' vennel foot
Kerr Janet, 74 Friars' vennel
M'Kune Joseph, Market st,Maxltwn
Morine James, Queensberry st
Palmer Joseph, 65 Friars' vennel
Payne John & Jas. 83 Friars' vennel
Selkirk Alexander, 71 English st
Selkirk Robert, High st
Selkirk Robert, jun. High st
Selkirk William, jun. Queensberry st
Thomson Benjamin, 22 Market st, Maxwelltown   [Maxwelltown
Thomson Henrietta, 16 Market st,
Thomson William, 15 Market st, Maxwelltown

GLUE MANUFACTURERS.
Lookup Alexander, Shakspeare st and Mill street
Watt William, Mill st

GROCERS & TEA DEALERS.
Marked thus * are also Spirit Dealers.
(See also Shopkeepers, and also Spirit Dealers.)
*Armstrong James, High st
*Bairden Thomas, 6 Queensberry st
*Begg William, 13 New Bridge st
Bell Jno.(& grain dealer) Church st, Maxwelltown   [welltown
*Bell John, 35 Galloway st, Max-
*Bell Rachael, 80 Friars' vennel
*Bell Thomas, 11 English st
*Bendall James, 68 Friars' vennel
*Black John, 73 English st
Boyd Wm. Market st, Maxwelltown
*Byers James, 72 English st   [town
*Cameron Richd.Market st, Mxwell-
Caven Robt Galloway st,Maxwlltwn
*Crosbie David, 125 High st
*Crosbie John, 17 English st
Dickson William, 80 High st
*Dobbie Thos. Queensberry square
*Dobie Robert. Queensberry st
*Edgar John, 29 Friars' vennel
Farrish Hugh (and flour and grain dealer) Academy street
Ferguson David, 35 High st
Ferguson Joseph and Son, High

3

GROCERS, &c.—Continued.

*Fleming Andrew, 38 Galloway st, Maxwlltwn   [Maxwlltwn
Glendinning Andrew,17 Glasgow st,
*Henderson James, Queensberry st
Hepburn Jas.50 Glasgow st,Mxwltn
Hume John, Nith place
*Irving Henrietta, Queensberry st
Jardine Margaret, 46 High st
*Kirk David, 137 High st
Leighton Miles (and drysalter) Assembly street
*Lindsey David, 148 High st
*M'Burnie David, Queensberry st
M'Dougall Dugald (& oil & Italian warehouse) 5 Castle st
*M'Kaig John, 81 High st
M'Robert James, St. Michael st
*M'Turk Maxwell, 47 College st, Maxwelltown
*Millar John, St. Michael st
*Mi ligan Samuel, 38 Friars' vennel
Moffat Hanh.48 Glasgow st,Mxwltn
*Mundell William, 158 High st
Nicholson Francis, Queensberry st
*Parkins Joseph, St. Michael st
*Paterson Joseph, Queensberry st
Paterson William, Galloway street, Maxwelltown   [square
*Redmond&Wallace,1 Queensberry
Richardson John, 61 High st
*Robertson George, 41 High st
Sloan Robert, 2 Queensberry square
*Smith James, 3 Friars' vennel
*Sutherland Gilbert, 42 Glasgow st, Maxwelltown
*Swan William, Queenberry st
Thomson John, 12 Friars' vennel
Thomson Robert, jun. (and seedsman) 57 High street

GUNSMITHS.

Hinchsliffe Mark, 81 English st
Keir John, Irish st   [wlltwn
M'Burnie Ths.17 Galloway st,Max-
Newton Thomas, 1 English st

HAIR DRESSERS.

Dunlop John, Market st, Maxwelltn
King Peter, Queensberry st
M'Caskie John, 86 Friars' vennel
M'Caskie Robert, 17 Friars' vennel
M'Kay John,7 Galloway st,Mxwlltn
M'Knight Edward, 26 Bucclengh st
Porteous Robert, 11 English st
Simpson James, Chapel st
Smith Wm.(& perfumer)2 English st
Wilkinson Andrew, 26 English st

HAT MANUFACTURERS AND DEALERS.

Balieff Samuel and John, High st
Balieff William & Son, St. David st
Hunter David & Co. 11 Church st
Thomson Elizabeth, High st

HAY DEALERS.

Bryden William, English st
Hollis Edmund, St. Michael st
Powell John, Irish st
Waugh John, English st

HOSIERY MANUFACTURERS.

Dinwiddie James & Jas. Academy st
Dinwiddie William, 38 High st
Gibson James, Queensberry st
M'Noah Thomas, Queensberry st
Milligan & Tait, Buccleugh st
Pagan John, Irish st
Scott Robert & Son. 37 English st

INNS & POSTING HOUSES.

Commercial (and hotel), William Wilson, High street
George, Ambrose Clerke, High st
King's Arms, John Fraser, High st

IRON FOUNDERS.

Affleck Sarah, King st, Maxwelltown
Scott Alexander, Stakford foundry, College street, Maxwelltown

IRON MERCHANTS.

Armstrong Adam Rankine,37 High st
M'Burnie David, Queensberry st
Sloan Robert, 2 Queensberry square
Watt Robert, 38 High st

IRONMONGERS.

Armstrong Adam Rankine,37 High st
Bell John, 109 High st
Bell Robert (and smith and bell-hanger) High st   [town
Clark John, 1 Glasgow st,Maxwell-
Frazer Wm. 63 High st   [place
Halliday James (& smith) 10 Church
Hyslop John, 86 High st   [vennel
Smith Wm. (& jeweller) 49 Friars'
Watt Robert (& smith, & manufacturer of grates & jacks) 38 High st

JEWELLERS AND SILVER-SMITHS.

Gray David, 83 High st
Halliday James, 10 Church place
Hinchsliffe Jos. Walker, 126 High st
Hinchsliffe Mark, 81 English st

JOINERS & CARPENTERS.

Affleck David, Howgate, Maxwlltwn
Bell John, Burn st   [welltown
Dickson Adam, Galloway st, Max-
Donaldson Charles, Queensberry st
Ferguson Thomas, Queensberry st
Forsyth Jn. 38 Glasgow st,Mxwlltn
Gillies Wm. King st, Maxwelltown
Gregan John, Clerk hill
Grierson Edward, White sands
Hair George, Hale steps, Troqueer
Herries Robert, 83 Friars' vennel
Kerr James, Friars' vennel
M'Cubbin & Geddes, Palmerstone, Maxwelltown   [Queensberry st
M'Knight Ellen B.Robinson's close
Milroy Thomas, 59 High st   [st
Thomson James, New Fleshmarket
Thomson John, 12 Friars' vennel
Walker John, White sands
Weild David, 24 Buccleugh st

LIBRARIES.

(See also Booksellers, & Stationers, and also Reading Rooms.)
DUMFRIES LIBRARY, High street—James M'Robert, secretary
LAW LIBRARY,Court house—Robert M'Lellan, secretary

LINEN & WOOLLEN DRAPRS.

Anderson Andrew, 101 High st
Baxter Thomas & John, 49 High st
Blaind Samuel, 92 High st
Brown James, 52 High st
Corrie John & Robert, 36 High st
Corrie Samuel, 48 Friars' vennel
Creighton David, 105 High st
Hairstens James, 118 High st
Hogg Ann S. 53 High st
Howat William, High st
Jameson Thomas, 37 High st
Kissock Alexander & Robert (and furriers), 59 High st
M'Kay James, 41 High st
M'Kay Wm. Glasgow st,Mxwlltwn
M'Robert Samuel, 55 High st
Montgomery George, 100 High st
Roan William, 51 High st
Thomson James, 40 High st
Wylie Ann Craig (muslin, &c.), 152 High street

LIVERY-STABLE KEEPERS.

Connell Walter, 14 Shakspeare st
Kirkpatrick Thomas, White sands
Pagan Robt.1 Market st,Maxwlltwn

MALTSTERS.

See Brewers & Maltsters.

MASONS & BUILDERS.

Affleck Robert, Chapel st
Aitken John, Queensberry st

Crombie Andrew, St. Michael st
Dobie Wm. King st, Maxwelltown
Edgar Ths.Glasgow st,Maxwelltwn
M'Gowan William, Irving st
M'Kaig Thomas, Castle st
Montgomery & Robertson, David st,Maxwelltown, & Friars' vennel
Ramsay Alexander, Nith bank

MEAL DEALERS.

(See also Grocers & also Shopkeeprs.)
Crosbie Jos.20 Glasgow st,Maxwltn
Hewatson Joseph,11 Old Bridge st, Maxwelltown   [street
Kelly John (& grain), New Bridge
M'Turk Maxwell (and provision), Galloway st, Maxwelltown

MESSENGERS AT ARMS.

Baird Charles, County buildings, Buccleugh st
Dickson David, High st
Hainning Thomas, 42 High st
Hamilton Archibald, Assembly st
Kemp Robert, High st
M'George Charles, Queen st
M'Lellan Robert, High st
M'Minn Charles, 14 Academy st

MILLERS.

Beveridge David (steam mill), 59-Galloway st, Maxwelltown
Hannay Alexander (barley mill), Maxwelltown
Welsh Joseph (malt & oats), Max-welltown   [welltown
Wright Robert (wheat mill), Max-

MILLINERS.

See Dress Makers & Milliners.

NAIL MAKERS.

Boyd Wm. Market st, Maxwelltown
Graham John, New Fleshmarket st
Lewis Geo. Glasgow st,Maxwlltwn
M'Kinnell Jno. & Jos.Queensberry st
M'Kinnell William, King st
Russell Joseph, Queensberry st
Russell Thomas, Queensberry st
Wood William, Townhead st

NEWSPAPERS.

DUMFRIES COURIER (Tuesday),Jno. M'Diarmid & Co. 117 High st
DUMFRIES TIMES (Tuesday), Robt. Wallace & Co. proprietors, Long close, High street
DUMFRIESSHIRE AND GALLOWAY HERALD & ADVERTISER (Friday), Thomas Aird, editor; William Curfrae Craw, publisher, High st

NURSERY & SEEDSMEN.

Irving Thomas & John, 8 Galloway street, Maxwelltown
Kennedy Thomas, 110 High st
Learmont John, 49 English st
Learmont John, Townhead st
Richardson & Pringle, 1 Galloway street, Maxwelltown

PAINTERS & GLAZIERS.

Aitken John, English st
Anderson James, 17 St. David st
Dinwiddie James, 42 Friars' vennel
Irving Peter (and paper hanger), 17 Bridge st   [High st
M'Diarmid James Kirkpatrick, 121
M'Kay John, 21 Castle st
M'Morine Andrew, 16 Castle st
M'Pherson Thomas, 135 High st
Neilson Robt.5 Galloway st,Mxwltn
Wightman William, Chapel st

PHYSICIANS.

Grieve James, 20 Castle st
M'Culloch Jas. Murray, 16 Irish st
Symons John, Irish st
Thorburn David, George st

PLASTERERS.

Crocket Thomas, Friars' vennel
Dixon William, English st

Kerr James, Academy st
M'Kendrick Matthew, High st
Parke William, 58 Friars' vennel

PLUMBERS.
Clark Jane, 101 High st
Marshall & Son, St. David st
Milligan Thomas (& copper and tin smith), 91 High st

PORTRAIT PAINTERS.
Allan John, Buccleugh st
Dacre James Murray, 14 Academy st

PRINTERS—LETTER PRESS.
Halliday David, 113 High st
M'Diarmid John & Co. 117 High st
Wallace Rt.& Co.Long close,High st

READING ROOMS.
COMMERCIAL, 113 High st——John Stevenson, keeper
SUBSCRIPTION, 131 High st—Thos. Glendinning, keeper
UNION, Church crescent——John M'Kie, treasurer

ROPE & TWINE MAKERS.
Armstrong George, English st
Knight Edward, Dock ropery
Little William, 70 Friars' vennel

SADDLERS.
Lancaster Joseph, 58 Friars' vennel
Weir John, 78 English st

SHERIFFS' OFFICERS.
Dickson William, 89 High st
Nelson Robert, Nith place
Richardson William (and for the stewartry), Chapel st

SHIP OWNERS.

Affleck Samuel	Irving Peter, sen.
Anderson James	Johnstone Mark
Barker John	Leighton Miles
Beattie Robert	M'Gill David
Bendall James	M'Harg —
Blaind Samuel	Martin John
Broom James	Riddick John
Crombie Andrw	Robinson James
Croshie Daniel	Sinclair John
Dinwiddie Jas.	Smart William
Dudson James	Thomson Robert,
Edgar John	jun.
Gillespie John	Thomson Wm.
Hair George	Turner Wm & Son
Hutton John	Walker Jno & Son

SHOPKEEPERS & DEALERS IN SUNDRIES.
Croshie Robert, 41 Queensberry st
Dalling John, 24 Market st,Mxwltn
Gibson Jno. 6 Old Bridge st,Mxwltn
Glover Ann, 6 St. Andrew st
Lookup Janet,13Redlion st,Mxwltn
M'Dougall Agnes, St. Michael st
M'Quhae William, Chapel st
Marchbank Walter,NewFleshmkt st
Mariner Peter, St. Michael st
Martin Hugh, Market st,Maxwltwn
Millar Christian, Loreburn st
Neilson Sarah, St. Michael st
Palmer Margaret, Brewery st
Rae Catherine, St. Michael st
Rae Julia, St. Michael st [town
Smith Eliz. 39 Market st,Maxwly-
Stevenson Robt. New Fleshmarkt st
Thomson Ann, St. Michael st
Turner Agnes, Church st,Mxwltwn

SKINNERS.
Lookup Alexander, Mill st
Watt William, Mill st

SLATERS.
Briggs John, Townhead st
Hanline John, Wallace close,High st
Irving Newall, 50 High st
M'Quhae Alex. 20 Friars' vennel
M'Quhae James, English st
Mysie & Elder, Market st, Maxwln

SMALLWARE DEALERS.
Carson William, 1 Church place
Moffat Thomas, 3 Buccleugh st
Moffat William, 90 High st

SPIRIT DEALERS.
Marked thus * are also Provision Dealers.
(See also Wine & Spirit Merchants.)
*Affleck Robert, Friars' vennel
Aitken John, Queensberry st
Anderson John, 27 English st
Bell Samuel, Queensberry st
*Bell William, 64 English st
Carmont Robert, 165 High st
Carson William, 31 High st
Carson William, 95 High st
Currie Robert, 143 High st
Dalrymple Thomas, 139 High st
Dickie William, 67 English st
Dowling John,14Market st,Mxwltn
Duffie Felix, 59 English st
Edwards Agnes, Queensberry st [st
Ferguson Jane (& flour) Queensberry
Grierson James, Bank st
Grierson Janet, 76 English st
M'George Margaret, 101 High st
*M'Lean Elizbth. 59 Friars' vennel
M'Naught Wm. (& wine) Friars' venl
Mason William (& tea), Galloway street, Maxwelltown
Neilson Robert, St. Michael st
Nicholson Hugh, 56 Friars' vennel
Nicholson Joseph, Church st
Rogerson John, Turnpike close
Thomson John, 52 Friars' vennel
Tweedie Geo. 3 Glasgow st,Mxwltn
Watson Mary, 27 Irish st [town
Wilson Robt. 31 Galloway st,Mxwl-

STAY MAKERS.
Barnes John, Irish st [cleugh st
Brydone Ann & Catherine, 4 Buc-
Haining Alice, 50 Friars' vennel
M'Dowall John, 21 English st
Moore Alice, 62 Friars' vennel

STRAW HAT MAKERS.
Birrell Catherine, 88 High st
Campbell Martha, 5 Church place
Craw Mrs. Academy st
Dinwiddie Mary Ann, 54 High st
Hannay Margt. Galloway st,Mxwltn
Irving Janet, 37 Friars' vennel
Mitchell Betsy, 63 Friars' vennel
Palmer Marion, Brewery st
Thompson Mary, 1 Bank street and 107 High street
Watson Mary Ann, 85 High st

SURGEONS.
Blacklock Archibald, Castle st
Burnside John,5Glasgow st,Mxwltn
Bushnam John Stevenson, Saint Michael street
Clanahan Mark, 167 High st
Fraser James, 112 High st
Fyfe James Corson, 25 Buccleugh st
M'Culloch Jas. Murray, 16 Irish st
M'Kenzie Jas. New Fleshmarket st
M'Lauchlan James, Assembly st
Robson Alexander, 25 Castle st
Spalding James, jun.14 Buccleugh st
Wilkin Thomas, Castle st

TAILORS.
Marked thus * are also Clothiers.
(See also Woollen Drapers and Clothiers.)
Anderson John & Sons,60 College st, Maxwelltown
Beck Joseph, 81 English st
Bothwick James, Queensberry st
Costin Robt.13 Galloway st,Mxwltn
Dixou Andrew, Brewery st [st
*Douglas Hugh Richardson,132High
Haining Edward, St. Andrew st
Haining James, Irish st
*Hellon & Jackson, 130 High st
Johnson Alexander, 16 English st
Kerr John, 57 Queensberry st
Little Thomas, 39 High st [town
M'Connell Robt.2 Market st,Mxwl-
*M'Kie David, 12 Church place
M'Lachlan David, 44 High st

*Oney Benjamin, 82 English st
*Richardson Burnside, Church pl
Riddick John, 116 High st
*Roan William, 51 High st
Robson Alexander, 44 High st
Thomson George, 92 High st
Threshie Mungo, 68 High st
Tweedie Geo. 3 Glasgow st,Maxltwn
Wells Richard, Friars' vennel

TALLOW CHANDLERS.
Nicholson Francis, Queensberry st
Riddick Samuel, 75 Friars' vennel
Smith William, Queen st

TANNERS.
Crosbie Archibald, Shakspeare st
Hairstens John, Redlion st, Max-
welltown [Maxwelltown
Hairstens Thomas, Galloway st,
Kennedy and Kerr, St. Michael st
Lookup Alexander, Shakspeare st,
and Mill street [town
Primrose James & Sons, Maxwell-
Thorburn Thomas & James, Mill st
Watt William, Mill st

TIMBER MERCHANTS.
Robertson James, New quay
Thomson & Son (& slate) Whitesands
Walker John and Son, Bank st

TIN-PLATE WORKERS AND BRAZIERS.
Clark Jane, 101 High st [town
Dyer James,56 Glasgow st,Maxwell-
Milligan Thomas, 91 High st
Wilson Mary, 37 Friars' vennel

TOBACCONISTS.
Fraser William (and manufacturer,
& dealer in tea & coffee) 17 Irish st
Mundell Peter, High st

TURNERS.
Bell William, 87 English st
Charters James, Mill st
Strong Oliver, 67 High st

UMBRELLA MAKERS.
Blaind Adam, 92 High st }
Clark Daniel, 59 High st
M'Clellan Hugh, 54 Friars' vennel

UPHOLSTERERS.
See Cabinet Makers.

VINTNERS.
Admiral Duncan, John Grierson, Queens-
berry street
Anchor, Marion Smith, 81 English st
Barley Sheaf, John Mitchell, Galloway st, Maxwelltown
Bay Horse, Thos. Kirkpatrick, White sands
Bay Horse, Jno. Muirhead,97 Friar's vennel
Black Bull, Robert Pupple, Brewery st
Black Horse,Robt.Campbell,NewBridge st
Black Horse, Daniel Clark, 59 High st
Blue Bell, Jas. Munsie, 92 Friars' vennel
Buck, John M'Murdo, 4 White sands
Bunch of Grapes,John Irving,White sands
Caerlaverock Castle, James Twynham,
Watts' close, High st [High st
Coach & Horses, John Fraser Gracie, 156
Coach & Horses, William M'Lachlan, 72
English st [st
Coffee House, John Stevenson, 113 High
Coffee Room, Isabella Dunkell, High st
Compasses&Square,Wm.Laurie,50High st
Cross Keys, Robt. Burgess,Queensberry st
Crown, David Thomson, Queensberry st
Crown & Anchor,Margt.Ralton,117High st
Crown Inn, Edward Dove, 74 High st
Deer, John Nelson, Friars' vennel
Earl Grey, Thomas Thomson, 73 High st
Ewe&Lamb,Adam Johnson,Queensberry st
Farmers' Arms, Jas. Hyslop,9 White sands
Globe, Mary Graham, 138 High st
Golden Bull, John Grierson, High st
Golden Fleece, Reuben Fildes, Queens-
berry square [st
Hammerman's Arms, Jas. Fallas, 64 High
Highland Drove, Wm. Corrie,White sands
Hole in the Wall,Jane Grierson,93 High st
Hope & Anchor, Geo. Mollins, New quay
Horse & Plough, Jas. Paton, Queensberry st
King's Arms, Joseph Pagan, 59 Glasgow
street, Maxwelltown
King's Arms, Jno. Sloan,14 New Bridge st
King's Head, Thomas Dickie, 68 High st

VINTNERS—Continued.

Lion & Lamb, Thos. Wells, Queensberry st
Lord Russell, William Glendining, Queensberry street [street
New Bridge, David M'Gill, New Bridge
Pack Horse, Mary Houston, 119 High st
Plough, Mary Clark, Bridge st [High st
Plume of Feathers, Ann Hodgson, 136
Rainbow, Thomas Baxter, 108 High st
Red Lion, Alexander Robson, Chapel st
Royal Oak, John Brown, 42 Brewery st
Royal Oak, James Farres, 62 High st
Salutation Inn, Robert Pagan, Market st, Maxwelltown
Ship, Janet Copland, New Quay
Sod Tavern, William Edgar, New quay
Spread Eagle, Jas. Murray, Queensberry st
Spur, John Rae, 2 White sands
Swan Inn, Robt. Osburn, Queensberry st
Thistle and Crown, James Mundell, Queensberry street [berry st
Three Crowns, Saml. Patterson, Queens-
Two Sheafs, Elizbth. Buttler, 40 High st

Vintners,
Whose Houses have no Sign.

Bell Robert, High st
Buchanan Janet, King st [town
Carmont Robert, 1 Church st, Maxwell-
Johnson James, Bank st
Little William, Long close, High st
Meers Mary, Shakspeare st
Tait James, White sands
Wyle Mary, King street

WATCH & CLOCK MAKERS.

Black Thomas, 17 Castle st
Charters William, 68 High st
Ingram Richard, 16 English st
M'Adam Robert, 105 High st
Sharpe Francis, 3 Church place
Todd John, 5 St. Andrew st

WHITESMITHS AND BELL-HANGERS.

Fallas James, 64 High st
Haugh James, 50 High st
Milligan John, 136 High st

WINE & SPIRIT MERCHANTS.

Bryden Elizabeth, 25 English st
Dickson John (and tea dealer) 1 Bank street

Rankine Adam, Nith place, & New Bridge st
Walker John and Son, Bank st

WOOLLEN DRAPERS AND CLOTHIERS.

Douglas Hugh Richardson, 132 High street
Hellon and Jackson, 130 High st
M'Kie David, 12 Church place
Oney Benjamin, 82 English st
Roan William, 51 High st

WRIGHTS.
See Joiners and Carpenters.

WRITERS.
Marked thus * are also Notaries.

*Adamson Robert, Irish st
*Armstrong David, High st
*Brand John, High st
*Broom James, High st [Bank st
*Broun Wm. (& presbytery clerk) 4
Brydone John, Friars' vennel
Comrie Robert, George st [place
Crichton James M'Millan, Church
Dawson John Charles, Pleasance
Dinwiddie William, Bank st
Ferguson John, Buccleuch st
Forsyth Philip (and town clerk of Maxwelltown), 5 Buccleugh st
*Gordon William, Bank st
Halliday William, 18 Castle st
*Hamilton Archibald, Assembly st
*Hannay Alexander, Bank st
Harkness Christopher, 150 High st
Harkness Thomas, 150 High st
Hunter Thomas (& fiscal of Max-welltown), Galloway st
*Kemp Robert, High st
M'George Charles, Queen st
M'Gowan William, 10 English st
M'Lellan Robert, High st
Moyses James William, Irish st
*Primrose & Gordon, Buccleugh st
Sanders John, Queen st
*Shortt & Johnstone, Castle st

*Smyth Christopher and Thomas Robinson, English st
*Spalding James, (and clerk of the peace), 14 Buccleuch st
*Thomson James, Castle st
*Thomsons & Jackson, High st
*Thorburn James, Mill st
Thorburn John, Assembly st
*Threshie & Crichton, Buccleuch st
Threshie Robert, sen. (and county clerk and commissary clerk, and treasurer to the trustees of the roads), Buccleugh st
*Wallace Robert, Castle dykes
Wright James, 72 English st
*Young Alexander (and fiscal of Dumfries-shire), Castle st

Miscellaneous.

Bell David, coal dealer, 63 English st
Beveridge David, hot and cold baths, 62 College st, Maxwelltown
Brodie John, game dealer, Town Head st
Feren & Co. clock makers, 27 Irish st
Fletcher Thomas, last maker, 55 Glasgow street, Maxwelltown [st
Gillies Bryce, copper-plate printer, 89 High
Gillies Wm. cartwright, King st, Maxwelltn
Goold John, frame smith, St. Michael st
Graham Mary, keeper of horses and gigs for hire, 138 High st [Maxwelltown
Hair George, coal merchant, Galloway st,
Hammond Jos. basket mkr. 8 St. David st
Howat John, fish-hook dresser, Market st, Maxwelltown [Andrew st
Kirkpatrick Robt. stocking frame mkr. St.
Lauder Thomas, veterinary surgeon and shoeing smith, White sands
M'Harg Robt. bacon factor, Loreburn st
M'Kay John, cotton manufacturer, 6 David street, Maxwelltown [welltown
Morrison John, weaver, 13 David st, Max-
Norris James, fruiterer, High st
Pearson George, hygeist, High st [town
Raffle Jno. pavier, 52 Glasgow st, Maxwell-
Reid James, furrier, High st
Scott Wm. fishery lessee, 60 English st
Threshie Robert, jun. clerk to the road trustees, Town hall, Buccleugh st
Woodmass John, glover, 166 High st

Public Buildings, Institutions, and Offices.

PLACES OF WORSHIP.

ST. MICHAEL'S CHURCH—Rev. Robert Wallace.
NEW CHURCH—Rev. Dr. Thomas Duncan.
MAXWELLTOWN CHURCH—Rev. James Ranken.
TROQUEER CHURCH—Rev. William Thorburn. [Dunlop.
UNITED SECESSION CHAPELS—Rev. Jas. Clyde & Rev. Walter
CAMERONIAN CHAPEL—Rev. John M'Dermid.
CONGREGATIONAL CHAPEL—Rev. Robert Machray.
RELIEF CHAPEL—(Various Ministers.)
SCOTCH EPISCOPAL CHAPEL—Rev. Chas. Maitland Babington.
METHODIST—(Various Ministers.)
ROMAN CATHOLIC—Rev. Wm. Reid & Rev. Æneas Dawson.
JAIL AND INFIRMARY CHAPEL—Rev. George Cowans.

DUMFRIES & GALLOWAY ROYAL INFIRMARY, ST. MICHAEL-STREET.

House Surgeon—George Smith. *Matron*—Grace Grierson.

DUMFRIES & MAXWELLTOWN ASTRONO-MICAL SOCIETY, MAXWELLTOWN.

Treasurer—R. Thomson. *Secretary*—John Jackson.

CUSTOM HOUSE, BANK-STREET.

Collector—John Staig.
Collector's Clerk—George Kirkland.
Comptroller—Michael Doyle.
Searcher and Landing Waiter—James Lock.
Principal Coast Officer—Robert Chalmers, Annan.
Coast Waiter—David Clark Pagan, Carsethorn.
Tide Waiter—Robert Millar, Glencaple.

NOTE.—Kirkcudbright and Wigtown are sub-ports under this collection. Vessels are invoiced and cleared coastwise at Annan: they are also cleared coastwise at Gatehouse, Barlochan, Creetown, Garliestown, Port William, and Whithorn.

EXCISE OFFICE, NITH-PLACE.

Collector—Joseph Longrigg.
Collector's Clerk—Charles Dalrymple Porteous.
Supervisor—Alexander Myles.

ASSEMBLY ROOMS (New), George street.
ASSEMBLY ROOMS (Old), Assembly street.
BATHS (hot and cold), College street, Maxwelltown.
BENEVOLENT SOCIETY'S SCHOOL HOUSE, Green sands.
COUNCIL CHAMBER, High street—Francis Shortt and James Broom, town clerks.
COUNTY PRISON, Buccleugh street—Thomas Hunter, keeper.
COUNTY TAX OFFICE, Irish st—Roger Kirkpatrick, collector.
COURT HOUSE, Buccleugh st—Wm. Thomson, sheriff's clerk.
DISPENSARY, 25 Buccleugh street.
FLOUR, MEAL, AND GRAIN MARKET, Queensberry square.
GAS WORKS, Shakspeare street—William Colhart, manager.
HORTICULTURAL SOCIETY—Major Adair, secretary; D. Johnsione, treasurer.
MECHANICS' INSTITUTE, at the Academy—Thomas Roberts, librarian; John M'Kie, secretary.
NEW MARKET HOUSE, Fleshmarket street.
NEW QUAY STORES, New quay.
POLICE OFFICE, Midsteeple.
POOR'S HOSPITAL, St. Michael st—Robert Garmery, master; Mary Garmery, matron.
STAMP OFFICE, Irish st—William Ireland Syme, distributer.
THEATRE, Shakspeare street.
TOLBOOTH, Maxwelltown—Daniel Montague, keeper.
TRADES' HALL, Queensberry square.
WIDOWS' FUND SOCIETY, Coffee House, High street—David Johnson, secretary and treasurer.

COACHES.

To CARLISLE, the *Independent*, from the King's Arms, every evening (Sunday excepted) at twenty-five minutes past five, and the *Marquess*, from the George Inn, every Monday, Wednesday, and Friday forenoon at a quarter before eleven; both go through Annan, Springfield and Longtown.

To EDINBURGH, the *Royal Mail*, from the King's Arms, every morning at ten minutes past six; goes through Moffat and Noblehouse—the *Red Rover*, from the George Inn, every Monday, Wednesday, and Friday morning at seven, and the *Despatch*, from the Commercial Inn, the same mornings at eight; both go through Thornhill, Crawford, Chesterhall, and Biggar.

To GLASGOW, the *Independent*, from the King's Arms, every morning (Sunday excepted) at half-past eight; goes thro' Thornhill, Sanquhar, Cumnock & Kilmarnock—and the *Craigingillan Castle*, from the George Inn, every Monday, Wednesday, and Friday morning at a quarter before six; goes thro' Minniehive, Carsfearn, Dalmillington, Ayr, and Kilmarnock.

To KILMARNOCK, see GLASGOW.

To KIRKCUDBRIGHT, the *Morning and Evening Star,* from the George Inn, every morning (Sunday excepted) at nine; goes through Dalbeattie, Haugh, and Castle Douglas.

To LANGHOLM, the *Royal William,* from the George Inn, every Monday, Wednesday, and Friday forenoon at a quarter before eleven; goes thro' Annan and Ecclefechan.

To LONDON, MANCHESTER, and LIVERPOOL, the *Royal Mail,* from the King's Arms, every afternoon at half-past one; goes through Carlisle and Penrith—and the *Independent,* from the same Inn, every evening (Sunday excepted) at twenty-five minutes past five; goes through Annan and Carlisle.

To PORTPATRICK, the *Royal Mail,* from the King's Arms, every morning at a quarter-past nine; goes through Castle Douglas, Gatehouse, Newton-Stewart, Glenluce, and Stranraer.

CARRIERS.

To ANNAN, John Baxter, from the Globe Inn, every Wednesday.

To ANNAN and MOUSWALD, John M'Craw, from the Ewe & Lamb, every Wednesday and Saturday.

To ANNAN and RUTHWELL, James Richardson, from opposite Mr. Balieff's, High street, every Wed. & Saturday.

To ANNAN, BRIDEKIRK & WATERBECK, John Jardine, from opposite the Golden Bull, every Wednesday.

To APPLEGARTH, William M'George, from Wells's, King st. every Wednesday.

To AULDGIRTH BRIDGE, Jas. Hiddlestone, from John Neilson's, Friars' vennel, and Thomas Wilson, from Chapel street, every Wednesday.

To BANK END, Jno. Reid, from opposite Mr. Mundell's, grocer, High st. every Wednesday.

To BERESCARR, John Scott, from the Three Crowns, every Wednesday.

To BORELAND, J. Hay, from — Grierson's, High street, every Wednesday.

To CARLISLE, Peter Johnstone and T. Baxter, from opposite Mr. Balieff's, and William Aitchison, from the Globe Inn, every Wednesday; go through Annan.

To CASTLE DOUGLAS, James Nish, from opposite Mr. Hairsten's, Samuel Mounsie, from the Thistle and Crown, and James Robertson, from opposite Mr. Johnston's, High street, every Wednesday—Alexander Johnstone, from opposite Mr. Ferguson's, High street, and James Palmer, from the head of Bank street, every Wednesday and Saturday.

To CARSETHORN, William Miller, from the Deer Inn, every Wed. & Saturday.

To CLOSEBURN, James Hiddlestone, from John Neilson's, Friars' vennel, and K. D. Smith, from opposite the New Church, every Wednesday.

To COLVEND and AUCHENCAIRN, Robert Adamson, from the Deer Inn, every Wednesday.

To COLVEND and SOUTHWICK, — Paine, from opposite — M'Murdo's, Sands, every Wednesday.

To CUMNOCK, J. & W. Robb, from opposite Mr. Hairsten's, High street, and

T. & W. Ferguson, from opposite Mr. M'Diarmid's, every Wed. and Friday.

To DALBEATTIE, Robert Adamson and Mrs. Porter, from the Deer Inn, and Jane Thomson and James Watson, from opposite the New Church, every Wed.

To DALRY, James Watson, from opposite the New Church, and Geo. Nelson, from Mrs. Ferguson's, Queensberry st. every Wednesday.

To DALSWINTON & KIRKMAHOE, Robert Sharp, from Mr. Ferguson's, Queensberry street, every Wednesday.

To DUNCOW, John Menzies, from Mrs. Ferguson's, Queensberry st. every Wed.

To DUNSCORE, James Hiddlestone and J. Hunter, from the Deer Inn, every Wednesday and Saturday.

To ECCLEFECHAN, J. Johnson, from opposite the Commercial Inn, every Wed.

To EDINBURGH, T. & H. Pennycuick, from opposite the Church, and Samuel Mounsie, from the Thistle and Crown, every Wednesday—James Robert Dickson, from Queensberry square, every Thursday—and J. Glencross, from Mr. Pagan's, every Friday.

To GATEHOUSE, James Robertson, from opposite Mr. Johnston's, High st. every Wednesday.

To GELSTONE CASTLE & CROSS-MICHAEL, Alexander Johnston, from opposite Mr. Ferguson's, High street, every Wednesday and Saturday.

To GLASGOW, J. & W. Robb, from opposite Mr. Hairsten's, High street, and T. & W. Ferguson, from opposite Mr. M'Diarmid's, every Wed. & Fri.—and D. Wells, from T. Wells's, King street, once a fortnight.

To GLENCAPLE, William Millar, from opposite the George Inn, every Wednesday and Saturday.

To HAUGH & BUITTLE, James Tait, from the Deer Inn, every Wednesday.

To HAUGH OF URR, William Craig, from the Black Horse, High st. every Wednesday.

To HAWICK, — Patterson, from opposite Mr. Grierson's, High st. every Wed.

To HIGHTAE, — Wright, from Queen street, every Wednesday.

To KER & PENPONT, Thos. M'Kune, from the Deer Inn, and T. M'Queen, from opposite the New Church, every Wednesday—— and Charles Hairstens, from the same place, every Wed. & Sat.

To KILMARNOCK, J. & W. Robb, from opposite Mr. Hairsten's, High street, and T. & W. Ferguson, from opposite Mr. M'Diarmid's, every Wed. and Fri.

To KIRKBEAN, PRESTON MILL and NEW ABBEY, James Brown, from the Meal market, and Robert Boyle, from the Royal Oak, every Wednesday.

To KIRKCUDBRIGHT, KELTON-HILL, BOGUE and DUNDRENNAN ABBEY, John M'Night, from opposite Mr. Lonsdale's, every Wednesday.

To KIRKPATRICK, — Corrie, from the Black Bull, and — Barclay, from opposite Mr. M'Murdo's, White sands, every Wednesday.

To LANGHOLM, John Jardine, from opposite the Golden Ball, and J. Johnston, from opposite the Commercial Inn, every Wednesday.

To LOCHMABEN, Gabriel Brown, Geo. Allison, and James Hall, from Queen street, every Wednesday.

To LOCKERBIE, John Graham, from — Grierson's, Queensberry street, and John M'Kie, every Wednesday.

To MINNIEHIVE, James Hunter, from the Deer Inn, and James Rigg, from the Bay Horse, every Wed. and Saturday.

To MOFFAT, Jas. Johnston, from Loreburn street, J. Kirkpatrick, from opposite Mr. Mundell's, tobacconist, High street, and Samuel Mounsie and John Johnston, from the Thistle and Crown, every Wednesday—and James Robert Dickson, from Queensberry st. every Thursday.

To NEW ABBEY, J. Thompson, from the Meal market, every Wed. & Sat.—and James Brown, from the same place, and Robert Boyle, from the Royal Oak, every Wednesday.

To NEW GALLOWAY, James Watson, from opposite the New Church, and — M'William and — M'Cutchin, from the Royal Oak, every Wednesday.

To NEWTON STEWART, W. Raeside, from Mr. Pagan's, Maxwelltown, every Wednesday.

To OLD QUAY, William Miller, from opposite Mr. Miller's, baker, High st. every Wednesday.

To SANQUHAR & THORNHILL, J. and W. Robb, from opposite Mr. Hairsten's, High street, every Friday—and — M'Dougall, from Queensberry square, every Wednesday.

To SOUTHERNESS & KIRKBEAN, James Hunter, from opposite Mr. Balieff's, High street, every Wednesday.

To THORNHILL, Andrew Watson, from Queensberry square, every Wed. & Sat. —and J. Glencross, from Mr. Pagan's, Maxwelltown, every Friday.

To TYNRON and PENPONT, James Hairstens, from the Deer Inn, every Wednesday and Saturday.

To WAMPHRAY, J. Charters, from — Wells's, King street, every Wednesday.

To WIGTON & CREETOWN, W. Raeside, from Mr. Pagan's, Maxwelltown, every Wednesday.

CONVEYANCE BY WATER.

STEAM PACKET.

To LIVERPOOL, the *Nithsdale* (Capt. Lockup), every Wednesday & Saturday during summer, and every Friday in winter.—James Walker, Dumfries, and Robert Sproat, 20 Water street, Liverpool, agents.

COASTING VESSELS.

To GLASGOW, the *Prosperity* and the *Henrietta* (John Edgar, agent), the *Solway* (James Rigg, agent), and the *Lord Nelson* (William Turner, agent, Maxwelltown), sail once a month.

To LIVERPOOL, the *Queensberry* and the *Stuart Monteith* sail every ten days. —Robert Thomson, jun. owner, Dumfries; J. D. Thomson, agent, 13 Water street, Liverpool.

To WHITEHAVEN, the *Plywell* (John Gibson, master), sails every ten days; Samuel Blaind, agent—and the *Active,* once in ten days; Jas. Bendall, agent.

DUNSCORE, HOLYWOOD AND KIRKMAHOE.

DUNSCORE, a parish in the district of Nithsdale, is bounded by Glencairn and Keir on the north, and Holywood and Kirkcudbrightshire on the south. It is twelve miles in length, and its breadth varies from one to four miles: the land is arable on the banks of the Nith, which irrigates its eastern part; it is also intersected by the Cairn. Sheep and black cattle are reared off these lands, for the southern markets; and oats, barley, wheat, potatoes, and turnips, are produced in great quantities. The kirk of the parish is about nine miles from Dumfries, and seven from Minniehive. Robert Burns, at one time, held a farm in this parish, near the Nith, named Friars' carse; and it was while here that he had an opportunity of eulogizing the Cluden river, which is a continuation of the Cairn water. At this period he took charge of a village li-

brary, instituted by his landlord, Robert Riddel, Esq.

HOLYWOOD parish, which is bounded by Dunscore on the north and west, extends for ten miles along the right bank of the Nith, its breadth being from two to three miles. The church, an exceedingly neat erection, and much admired, stands in a most delightful part of the country, about three miles from Dumfries. In the church-yard are vestiges of an old abbey, supposed to have been built in the twelfth century.

KIRKMAHOE is a small modern village in the parish of its name, and district of Nithsdale, five miles from Dumfries, situate on a rivulet, tributary to the Nith, near the southern extremity of the parish. The church is a handsome gothic edifice of recent erection. The lands of the parish are well cultivated, and there are several plantations.

GENTRY & CLERGY.

Anderson John, esq. (of Farthingrush), Dunscore   [Dunscore
Beattie Rev. Matthew (of Newton),
Brydon Rev. Robt. Dunscore manse
Crichton Mrs. Elizabeth (of Friars' carse), Dunscore   [Dunscore
Grierson James, esq. (of Dalgoner),
Johnstone Capt. James Charles, R.N. (of Cowhill), Holywood
Johnstone Peter, esq. (of Carnsalloch) Kirkmahoe   [manse
Kirkwood Rev. Robert, Holywood
Lawrie Jas. esq. (of Milliganton), Dunscore
Macalpineleny James, esq. (of Dalswinton), Kirkmahoe
M'Kinnel John, esq. (of M'Murdoston), Dunscore
Maxwell Francis, esq. (of Gribton), Holywood   [Kirkmahoe
Maxwell Henry, esq. (of Millhead), Morin John, esq. (of Carzield), Kirkmahoe   [Kirkmahoe
Morin John, jun. esq. (of Elderslee),
Robinson Wm. esq. (of Kemyss hall), Kirkmahoe   [Dunscore
Whigham George, esq. Allanton,

Wightman Rev. John, Kirkmahoe manse   [han], Dunscore
Wilson Johnston, esq. (of Stroquhan), Dunscore
Young Samuel Denholm, esq. (of Guilly hill), Dunscore

SHOPKEEPERS, TRADERS, &c.

The names without address are in DUNSCORE.

Bell Kenneth, blacksmith, Duncow bridge   [vintner (George)
Broatch William, blacksmith and
Bryden John, tailor
Campbell Walter, joiner
Copland James, shopkeeper
Crosbie Jas. vintner (King's Arms)
Dalziel Robert, shopkeeper
Dickson Robt. surgeon & apothecary
Dobie Robert, shoe maker
Farish Peter, joiner
Fisher James, joiner, Kirkmahoe
Kirk James, joiner
Maxwell Thomas, shopkeeper

PLACES OF WORSHIP.

ESTABLISHED CHURCH, Dunscore—Rev. Robert Brydon
ESTABLISHED CHURCH, Holywood—Rev. Robert Kirkwood

ESTABLISHED CHURCH, Kirkmahoe—Rev. John Wightman
RELIEF CHAPEL, Dunscore—Matthew Beattie

PAROCHIAL SCHOOLS.

DUNSCORE:—David Biggar, Dunscore; James Lawrie, Burnheud; John Craig, Glenestin
HOLYWOOD, James Scott, William Hamilton, and John Milligan, masters
KIRKMAHOE:—Adam Robson, Duncow; James M'Lellan, Dalswinton; John Bell, Glendingholm; John Maxwell (endowed), Kirkton

COACHES.

To DUMFRIES, the Craigengillan Castle (from Glasgow), calls at the George Inn, Dunscore, every Tuesday, Thursday, and Saturday evening at seven.
To GLASGOW, the Craigengillan Castle (from Dumfries), calls at the King's Arms, Dunscore, every Monday, Wednesday, and Friday morning at half-past seven; goes through Minniehive, Carsfearn, Dalmellington, Ayr & Kilmarnock.

CARRIERS.

To DUMFRIES, James Hiddlestone and J. Hunter, every Wed. and Saturday.

ECCLEFECHAN,

WITH THE VILLAGE OF WATERBECK IN MIDDLEBIE AND NEIGHBOURHOODS.

ECCLEFECHAN is a considerable and thriving village, in the parish of Hoddam, 71 miles s. of Edinburgh, 76 s. e. of Glasgow, 13 n. w. of Carlisle, 16 e. of Dumfries, and 6 n. of Annan; lying in a fine situation, near the foot of Annandale, and on the mail road from Glasgow to Carlisle; which great line of thoroughfare has undergone vast improvement within the last few years, particularly in the vicinity of this village. The land of Hoddam parish is of the very best quality, under a superior system of cultivation, and the district is perhaps one of the most healthy and pleasant in the south of Scotland. The principal employment of the inhabitants is weaving cotton goods for the Carlisle manufacturers, who have constantly a demand for the labours of the loom, and which enables the operatives to enjoy many comforts which they would otherwise be deprived of. Ecclefechan contains many respectable shops, in which a variety of trades is carried on, the prosperity of which is mainly sustained by the extensive cattle markets, for which this village has been so long noted. These great marts are held on the first Fridays after the 11th in the months of January, February, March, April, and

July; the Friday before the 26th of August, the 18th of September (or the Friday before), the 26th of October, the Friday after the 11th of November, and the Friday after the 11th of December. The first Friday after the 11th of May and the 26th of October are hiring days for servants, the latter being also a cattle market; and the first Tuesday after the 11th of June is a fair for cattle and general merchandise. On the two fair days in June and October, the Duke of Buccleugh, as superior, claims certain customs for all standings, and for all cattle exposed for sale.

MIDDLEBIE is a village in the parish of its name, situate on the road between Langholm & Ecclefechan, twelve miles from the former, and two from the latter place. The parish, which is about seven miles in length by four in breadth, abounds in red freestone, and is valuable for its lime quarries; but much of the land is of rather poor quality.

WATERBECK village, in the above parish, is two miles from Middlebie, on the road to Langholm, is a pretty little rural place, and has been greatly improved and almost the whole of it re-built by Mr. Robert Carlyle, the proprietor.

POST OFFICE, ECCLEFECHAN, William Johnstone, Post Master.—Letters from the South arrive every morning at a quarter before seven, and are despatched every afternoon at half-past three.—Letters from the North arrive every afternoon at half-past three, and are despatched every morning at a quarter past seven.

GENTRY & CLERGY.

Arnot Mr. Archibald, M.D. Hall of Kirkconnel
Bell Mr. George, of Langlands
Bell John, esq. of Torbeck hill
Black John, esq. (of Abbie), Middlebie
Curr Alexander, esq. of Newfield
Harkness Rev. James, Ecclefechan
Hart Major Thomas, of Castle-milk
Holliday Jno. esq. (of Nether Abbie) Middlebie   [Middlebie
Irving John, esq. (of Burnfoot)
Irving John, esq. Middlebie
Little William, esq. of Cressfield
Menzies Rev. Robert, Luce manse
Murray John, esq. (of Haregills) Middlebie
Murray William, esq. (of Kirtleton) Middlebie
Nivison Rev. Rchd. Manse, Middlebie
Scott Alexander, esq. of Knockhill
Sharp General Matthew, M.P. Hoddam castle
Watson Rev. James, Waterbeck

BACON CURERS.

Morrow John, Ecclefechan
Paterson & Rome, Ecclefechan

BAKERS & MEAL DEALERS.

Johnston Andrew, Waterbeck
Park James, Ecclefechan
Short Matthew, Ecclefechan

BLACKSMITHS.

Barton James, Middlebie
Irving John, Chapple Middlebie
Johnston James, Middlebie
Kinsley William, Ecclefechan
Miller James, Waterbeck
Scott Robert, Ecclefechan
Tait William, Ecclefechan

BOOT & SHOE MAKERS.

Irving Peter, Ecclefechan
Johnston George, Ecclefechan
Johnston John, Ecclefechan
Moffat William Hall, Ecclefechan
Wells Thomas, Waterbeck

CARTWRIGHTS.

Bell Thomas, Waterbeck
Dixon John, Middlebie
Graham Thomas, Ecclefechan

CLOG MAKERS.

Bell George, Chapple Middlebie
Johnston John, Ecclefechan
Little James, Waterbeck
Moffat John, Waterbeck
Moffat William Hall, Ecclefechan
Steel James, Ecclefechan

CORN FACTOR.

Paterson John, Townfoot

DRESS MAKERS.

Moffat Barbara, Ecclefechan
Rae Barbara, Ecclefechan

FLESHERS.

Kennedy David, Ecclefechan
Moffat John, Ecclefechan
Smith John, Chapple Middlebie.

GROCERS & SPIRIT DEALERS.

Carlyle Robert (& druggist, woolstapler & ironmonger) Waterbeck
Currie Alexander, Ecclefechan
Johnston Wm. (& wine) Ecclefechan
Little James, Waterbeck
Thomson Janet, Ecclefechan

JOINERS.
Bell Thomas, Waterbeck
Dixon John, Middlebie
Graham Thomas, Ecclefechan
Laidlow James, Ecclefechan
Rome Robert, Ecclefechan
Scott John, Ecclefechan
Scott Thomas, Ecclefechan
Scott Thomas, jun. Ecclefechan

LINEN & WOOLLEN DRAPRS.
Carlile Robert, Waterbeck
Graham John, Ecclefechan
Johnston Margaret, Ecclefechan

MASONS.
Carruthers Andrew, Ecclefechan
Easton George, Ecclefechan
Easton Peter, Ecclefechan
Easton Peter, jun. Ecclefechan
Ferguson William, Ecclefechan

NAIL MAKERS.
Fletcher Isaac, Ecclefechan
Lockie John, Ecclefechan

SADDLERS.
Bell George, Chapple Middlebie
Manderson George, Ecclefechan

SHOPKEEPERS & DEALERS IN SUNDRIES.
Bell John, Ecclefechan
Kennedy David, Ecclefechan
Lockie John, Ecclefechan
Murray Samuel, Ecclefechan
Rae Mrs. John, Ecclefechan
Robinson William, Ecclefechan
Short Matthew, Ecclefechan

SURGEONS.
Bell William, R. N. of Sinclairburn
Kerr John, Ecclefechan

Little George, Ecclefechan
Simpson John, Ecclefechan

TAILORS.
Bell Archibald, Ecclefechan
Garthwaite John, Ecclefechan
Garthwaite Thomas, Ecclefechan
Wells John, Waterbeck
White Robert, Ecclefechan
Wright Andrew, Ecclefechan
Wright John, Ecclefechan

VINTNERS.
Bell Andrew (Peacocks) Waterbeck
Bell Ann (Bush Inn) Ecclefechan
Bell Thomas (Crown) Waterbeck
Farries Margt. (Globe Inn) Ecclefechan
Johnston Edward, Ecclefechan
Moffat Jno. (Ewe & Lamb) Ecclefechau
Sharp Robt. (Blue Bell) Ecclefechan

Miscellaneous.
Charters Wm. teacher, Ecclefechan
Farries Joseph, road surveyor, Ecclefechan
Hill Margaret, straw hat maker, Ecclefechan
Jamieson David, earthenware dealer, Ecclefechan
Phillip James, plough maker, Middlebie
Russell James, overseer and contractor for roads, Ecclefechau
Smith William, school, Ecclefechan
White Robert, cooper, Ecclefechan
Wright Walter, watch and clock maker, Ecclefechan

PLACES OF WORSHIP.
ESTABLISHED CHURCH, Luce—Rev. Robert Menzies

ESTABLISHED CHURCH, Middlebie—Rev. Richard Nivison
RELIEF CHAPEL, Waterbeck—Rev. James Watson
UNITED SECESSION CHAPEL, Rev. James Harkness

PAROCHIAL SCHOOLS.
ECCLEFECHAN, Rev. William Gullen, master
MIDDLEBIE, John Lorrain, master
WATERBECK, John Struthers, mastr

COACHES.
To CARLISLE, the *Royal Mail* (from Glasgow) every afternoon at half-past 3.
To DUMFRIES, the *Royal William* (from Langholm), every Tues. Thurs. & Sat. evening at six; goes through Annan.
To GLASGOW, the *Royal Mail* (from Carlisle), every morning at a quarter before seven.
To LANGHOLM, the *Royal William* (from Dumfries), every Monday, Wednesday, and Friday afternoon at two; goes through Middlebie and Waterbeck.

CARRIERS.
To ANNAN, John Jardine, every Thurs.
To CARLISLE, William Johnston and James Rae, every Friday.
To DUMFRIES, John Jardine & James Johnston, every Wednesday morning.
To EDINBURGH, Andrew Smith, every alternate Monday morning.
To GLASGOW, Robert Creighton, every alternate Monday morning.
To LANGHOLM, James Johnston, every Monday morning, and John Jardine, every Friday morning.
To LOCKERBIE, James Rae, every Monday morning.

LANGHOLM,

AND THE PARISHES OF CANONBIE, ESKDALEMUIR, EWES, WESTERKIRK & NEIGHBOURHOODS.

LANGHOLM is a thriving market town and burgh of barony, in the parish of its name; 70 miles s. of Edinburgh, 80 s. w. of Glasgow, 30 E. by N. of Dumfries, the like distance s. E. of Moffat, 21 N. of Carlisle, 18 N. N. E. of Annan, and 12 N. of Longtown (in Cumberland); delightfully situate on the left or east bank of the Esk, over which there is a stone bridge of three arches. The town owes its origin to a border house or tower, which was formerly the property of the all-powerful Armstrongs, but is now only seen in a state of ruin. The curious stranger may also direct his observation here to a spot where several witches suffered in the century before last: the witches of Eskdale are said to have played pranks beyond all example in the annals of female necromancy; some of them occupied themselves in the obstetric art, and upon those occasions transferred the pains of parturition from the 'gude-wife' to her husband. Langholm was long famed for an ingeniously formed iron instrument, called the 'branks,' which fitted upon the head of a shrewish female, and, projecting a sharp spike into her mouth, fairly subdued the more annoying weapon within; this instrument was deemed more effectual than the ducking (or cucking) stool, used in some parts of England, as the latter permitted liberty to the unruly member between every dip. The author of the 'Picture of Scotland' says—'Eskdale derives more than common charm from the memory of Johnnie Armstrong, whose name is associated with many of its localities.' His tower of Gilnockie still stands, though converted into a cow-house, a few miles below Langholm, on the left bank of the Esk. It was on 'Lanty-holm Holm' that, when going to meet the king, he and his 'gallant companie' of thirty-six men 'ran their horse and brak' their spears.' Johnie terminated his mortal career at Carlenrig, a place not far distant from Mosspaul, on the road between Langholm and Hawick. The story of the judicial execution of this border-thief and his companions, by James V, is well-known; the graves of the whole of the marauding band are to be seen in a deserted church-yard at Carlenrig. In the [...] day Langholm does not [...] seem to partake of [...] the peculiarities which distinguish [...] ished the com [...]

ages of superstition, being now one of the most thriving towns of its size in Scotland. It is built in the bosom of a lovely woodland scene, along the Edinburgh and Carlisle road; and is composed generally of good stone houses, roofed with blue slate. The bridge connects the ancient town with a more modern suburb on the opposite side of the river, called New Langholm, or New Town. In the market-place of the old town stands the town-hall and jail, ornamented with a neat spire and clock; the burgh is about to be lighted with gas, for which purpose works are now being erected in the old town. The chief trade in Langholm is the manufacture of cotton and woollen goods, as checks, stockings, &c.: it likewise possesses a number of respectable shops, branches of the 'National Bank of Scotland' and of the 'British Linen Company,' a distillery, dyehouses, tanneries, and some excellent inns. The government of the town is vested in a Baron bailie, appointed by the Duke of Buccleugh, who is the superior. A court for recovery of debts not exceeding £5. is held every alternate Monday by county justices. The places of worship are the parish church, and relief and united secession chapels. A good parochial school, and one endowed by the late Captain George Maxwell, of Broomholm, are the institutions for instruction; and there are two extensive well supported libraries. The market day is Wednesday; the fairs are held on the 16th April, the last Tuesday in May (old style), 25th July, 18th September, and in November; there are also two hiring days — one in May, the other in November; the July fair is noted as great one for lambs.

CANONBIE (or *Canonby*) is a village most delightfully situate on the banks of the Esk, half way between Longtown and Langholm, and on the southern border of the county; it is separated from England by the river Liddal, whose romantic banks present some pleasing scenery. This parish is about nine miles long and six broad; the high road from Edinburgh to London runs through the village. The kirk is a very large stone building, calculated to accommodate 1,400 persons. There are inexhaustible mines of coal, and lime-quarries of excellent quality, in the parish, but only a small portion of them worked. The scenery along the Esk is considered to be the finest in the south of Scotland. The HOLLOWS is a small village, about a mile and a half from Canonbie; near to which, on the east, is Gilkavekil tower, and on the west is Hollows tower. The Duke of Buccleugh is sole proprietor of this parish.

ESKDALEMUIR is a mountainous pastoral parish, on the north-eastern border of the county, and in the district of Eskdale; the manse, which is about the centre of the parish, is fourteen miles from Langholm. A very small portion of Eskdalemuir is under cultivation; the principal land proprietor is the Duke of Buccleugh.

The parish of EWES, situate on the eastern extremity of the county, is remarkable for its beautiful

ranges of green hills, covered with verdure to their summits, and the clearness of the river, which affords excellent trouting. Numerous plantations, on the properties of the Duke of Buccleugh and Mr. Beattie (of Meikledale), add additional beauty to the lovely appearance of the sweet dale of the Ewes.

WESTERKIRK parish is also situate near the eastern boundary of the county, about six miles from Langholm. Nearly the whole of this portion of the district is devoted to pasture for sheep and black cattle; but there are several elegant villas, which in some degree relieve its otherwise monotonous appearance. The church stands on the left bank of the river Esk. Sir Robert Walpole was a native of this parish.

POST OFFICE, LANGHOLM, John Nicol, *Post Master.*—The LONDON mail, with letters from all parts of the South, arrives every morning at half-past seven, and is despatched every afternoon at half-past three.—The EDINBURGH mail, with letters from the North, arrives every afternoon at half-past three, and is despatched every morning at half-past seven.—Letters from NEWCASTLETON arrive (by penny post) every afternoon at three.

NOBILILY, GENTRY & CLERGY
Bell George Graham (of Crurie and Castle o'er), Eskdalemuir
Bogie Mrs. Jane, High st
Borthwick Miss Jane, High st
Buccleugh his Grace the Duke of, Langholm lodge
Cross Rev. James, Langholm
Cunningham Rev. Adam, Manse, Eskdalemuir
Dobie Rev. John, Townhead [bie
Donaldson Rev. Jas. Manse, Canon-
Douglas Lieut. John, Market place
Elliot George Scott, Woodslie, Canonbie [kirk
Green Rev. James, Manse, Wester-
Hurdie Miss Ellen, Buccleugh sq.
Irving Miss Janet, Langholm
Jardine Mrs. Patterson, Francis st
Johnstone Sir Frederick, bart. (of Wester hall), Westerkirk
Little Mrs. Isabella, Charles street
Little Mrs. Janet, Elizabeth st
M'Kinley Mr. Archibald, Rose vale
Malcolm Sir James, Clinthead
Malcolm Sir Pulteney (of Douglen, Burnfoot), Westerkirk
Maxwell Mr. Alex. Harley, Irving
Maxwell Miss 'en, Langholm
Maxwell George. esq. of Broomholm
Mein Lieut.-Col. Nicol Alexander, (of Marsh house), Canonbie
Mein Pulteney, esq. (of Forge), Canonbie
Shaw Rev. Robert, Manse, Ewes
Shaw Rev. William Barry, Manse
Thomson Mrs. Jane, Cottage
Wright Rev. Jacob, Manse

BAKERS.
Armstrong Andrew, High st
Armstrong Francis, Langholm
Grieve Charles, Langholm
Hogg David, Langholm
Hyslop William, Langholm
Laidlow William, Charles street
Reay William, Langholm

BANKS.
BRITISH LINEN BANK (Branch) —draws upon the Parent Establishment, Edinburgh, and on Smith, Payne & Smiths, London) —Alexander Stevenson, agent
NATIONAL BANK OF SCOTLAND (Branch)—draws upon the Parent Establishment, Edinburgh, and on Glyn, Halifax, Mills and Co. London)—John Nicol, agent; Patrick Borthwick, manager

BLACKSMITHS.
Anderson William, Elizabeth st
Dalgliesh Michael, Langholm
Johnston Richard, Langholm
Scoon Walter, Langholm
Scott George, Hollows, Canonbie

BOOT & SHOE MAKERS.
Anderson Walter, Charles st
Atchison Thomas, Charles st

Brown Thomas, Market place
Grieve Thomas, Langholm
Hairstanes Charles, Langholm
Jardine John, Elizabeth st, New L.
Kershaw John, Langholm
Lockart John, Langholm
Murray James, George st
Murray Thomas, Canonbie
Reid Robert, Brae
Watt Joseph, Canonbie
Whillans Robert, Langholm
Wilson John, Langholm

BREWER AND MALTSTER.
Chalmers Walter, Langholm

CLOG MAKERS.
Atchison Thomas, Charles st
Grieve James, Langholm
Hownam Thomas, Charles st
Platoff William, Henry street
Scott Francis, Langholm
Turnbull Thomas, Church wynd
Watt Joseph, Canonbie

CONFECTIONERS.
Nelson Isabella, High st
Pasley Robert, Langholm

DISTILLERS.
LANGHOLM DISTILLERY COMPY.— James Kennedy, acting manager

DRESS MAKERS AND MILLINERS.
Armstrong Elizabeth, Langholm
Brown and Park, Langholm
Brown Janet, High st
Carruthers Mary & Janet, Meikleholm, New Langholm
Esplin Grace, Margaret and Elizabeth, Langholm
Yeoman Miss Jane (& girls' school) Henry st, New Langholm

FIRE, &c. OFFICE AGENTS.
CALEDONIAN, Andrew, Irving, Langholm [holm
COUNTY, George Scott, jun. Lang-
NORTH BRITISH, Alexander Stevenson, Langholm

FLESHERS.
Anderson Walter, Buccleugh square
Bell Andrew, Toll bar
Scott George, Langholm
Sword John, Parliament sq

GLAZIERS.
Collister John, Langholm
Foster Walter, Langholm [st
Johnston William (& painter) High

GROCERS.
Marked thus are also Spirit Dealers.
Armstrong Andrew, High st
*Armstrong Francis, Langholm
Barclay Fras. Overtown, Canonbie
Bell George, Canonbie
Broadie Gilbert, Langholm
*Burrell John, Langholm
*Elsdon William & Co. Langholm
Forsythe Mary, Martin st, New L.
*Goodfellow John, Langholm
Grieve James, Langholm
Halliday William, Canonbie

Hope Walter, High st
Hyslop William, Langholm
Irving Andrew, High st
*Irving Mary, Market place
Leishman David, Canonbie
Little William, Langholm
Pasley Robert, Langholm
Reay William, Langholm [holm
Reid Thomas, Henry st, New Lang-
*Scott George, jun. Langholm
*Scott James, Canonbie
Young Mary, Langholm

FRAME DRESSERS.
Cairns Andrew, Langholm
Scott Robert, Henry st

INNS.
Black Robert Tedcastle, High st
Commercial, Jno. Thomson, High st
Cross Keys (and livery stables), Fergus Armstrong, Canonbie
Crown (and posting house), Andrew Dow, High st
Salutation, John Young, High st

JOINERS.
Armstrong Thomas (and cabinet maker), Langholm
Collister John, Langholm
Foster Walter, Langholm
Foster Walter, jun. Langholm
Irving William, Hollows, Canonbie
Johnstone William, Martin st
Knox John (& cartwright) Martin st
M'Vittie Thomas, Henry st
Nicol Robert, Montague st [st
Wilson Ninian (& cartwright) Lang
Wilson Thomas, Montague st

LIBRARIES.
NEW LIBRARY, Parochial school, New Langholm—John Brown, treasurer [librarian
SUBSCRIPTION, High st—Jno. Nichol.

LINEN AND WOOLLEN DRAPERS.
Armstrong Elizabeth, Langholm
Bell George, Canonbie
Broadie Gilbert, Langholm
Irving Andrew, High st
Irving Mary, Market place
Little William, Langholm
Roberts Elizabeth, High st
Scott George, jun. Langholm
Scott James, Canonbie

MANUFACTURERS.
Bowman James (patent thread), Henry street
Byers Andrew (hosiery), Charles st
Chambers Geo. (hosiery), Langholm
Reid David (woollen and cotton goods), Henry st
Renwick Thomas and Alexander (hosiery, and worsted spinners), New Langholm, and Ewes mills, near Langholm [Henry st
Thorburn Thomas (cotton checks),

MASONS & BUILDERS.
Borthwick Alexander, Langholm
Byers Langholm

Byers Robert, Charles st
Hotson Alexander, George st
Hotson John, Buccleuch square
Scott John & George, Langholm
Scott Robert, Langholm
Scott William, Langholm

MEAL DEALERS.
Armstrong Andrew, High st
Armstrong Francis, Langholm
Armstrong James, Charles st
Atchison John, Langholm
Grieve Charles, Langholm
Halliday William, Canonbie
Hogg David, Langholm
Hyslop Jane, Langholm
Jardine James, Henry st
Leishman David, Canonbie
Little John, Martin st
Thorburn Thomas, Henry st

MILLERS.
Graham John, Hollows, Canonbie
Irving John, Langholm Corn mills
Millar Geo. Meikleholm Water mills

NAIL MAKERS.
Glendining Walter, High st
Lightbody William, Langholm
Thwaites John, Langholm

SADDLERS.
Clark John (and trunk maker), Langholm
Elliot John, Parliament square

SHOPKEEPERS & DEALERS IN SUNDRIES.
Anderson Elizabeth, New Langholm
Armstrong Mary, New Langholm
Clarke David, New Langholm
Dalgleish Michael, Langholm
Hotson Jane, New Langholm
Johnstone Euphemia, New Langhlm
Little Jane, Hollows, Canonbie
Murray Elizabeth, Langholm
Nichol Jane, New Langholm
Scott George, Langholm
Thomson James, Langholm
Wilson Margt. Hollows, Canonbie

STRAW HAT MAKERS.
Armstrong Elizabeth, Langholm
Brown & Park, Langholm
Brown Janet, High st
Grieve Janet, Langholm

SURGEONS.
Little Peter, Clint head
Maxwell William, Buccleugh square

TAILORS.
Anderson Robert, Charles st
Beattie James, Church wynd
Bell Francis, Canonbie
Dalzell William, Langholm
Ferguson Francis, Langholm
Foster Thomas, Church wynd
Foster Thomas, jun. George st

Harkness George, Langholm
Oliver Peter, Church wynd
Rickarby Alexander, Langholm

TANNERS.
Johnstone James (and skinner), Elizabeth street
Park James, Henry st

TEA DEALERS.
Beattie William, Charles st
Rickerby John, Langholm

TURNERS.
Armstrong Walter, Langholm
Jackson Henry, Ewes mills

VINTNERS.
Foster Thomas (Ewe and Lamb), Church wynd [Hollows
Greenwell Wm. (Gilknockie Inn),
Johnson William (Old Royal Oak), Langholm [Charles st
Laidlow William (Wheat Sheaf),
Little Dav. (Masons' Arms) Charles st
Lorrain John (Royal Oak) Langholm
Oliphant John (Shoulder of Mutton), Langholm
Scott William, Langholm [holm
Tedcastle Janet (King's Arms), Laug-
Telford Peter, High st
Thorburn John (Swan), Henry st
Yeoman James, New Langholm

WATCH & CLOCK MAKERS.
Carruthers George, Langholm
Graham John, Church wynd
Johnston Samuel, Langholm

WRIGHTS—See Joiners.

WRITERS & NOTARIES.
Henderson George (& surveyor of taxes), Clint head
Nichol John, High st
Stevenson Alexander, Baron bailie

Miscellaneous.
The names without address are in Langholm
Ballantyne John, wood forester to the Duke of Buccleugh, Canonbie
Bowman William, dyer, Charles st
Brown John, agent for the sale of Glasgow and Carlisle goods, Brae
Duncan David, tin-plate worker
Esplin James, needle maker
EXCISE OFFICE—Andw. Vair, supervisor
Fenwick John, bookseller, &c. High st
GAS WORKS— Andrew Irving, collector and treasurer; Alex. Stevenson, clerk
Glendining Walter, ironmonger and spirit dealer, High st
Greenville John, chair maker
Hanney Alexander, collector of poors' rates and session clerk, Buccleugh sq
Hogg David, spirit dealer
Hope James, tallow chandler
Irving Walter, sawyer, Buccleugh square
Jamieson Matthew, overseer for the Duke of Buccleugh, Charles st
Kennedy David, earthenware dealer
Murray John, schoolmaster, Church wynd

SMALL DEBT COURT—John Nicol, district clerk
STAMP OFFICE—George Scott, jun. distributer
Telford Peter, cooper, High st
Thorburn Thomas, agent for the sale of Glasgow checks, Henry st
Todd George Johnson, schoolmaster

PLACES OF WORSHIP.
ESTABLISHED CHURCH, Church wynd—Rev. William Barry Shaw
RELIEF CHAPEL, Town Foot—Rev. James Cross
UNITED SECESSION CHAPEL, Town head—Rev. John Dobie

PAROCHIAL SCHOOLS.
LANGHOLM, Buccleugh square— Alexander Hanney, head master
LANGHOLM ENDOWED, Geo. Johnson Todd, master
ESKDALEMUIR, James Yooll, master
EWES, James Little, master
WESTERKIRK, James Bryce, master

COACHES.
To DUMFRIES, the *Royal William*, from the Salutation Inn, every Tues. Thurs. & Sat. afternoon at half-past three; goes thro' Waterbeck, Ecclefechan & Annan.
To EDINBURGH, the *Royal Mail* (from London), calls at the Crown Inn, every morning at half-past seven, and the *Standard*, at half-past nine; both go thro' Hawick, Selkirk, and Galashiels.
To LONDON, the *Royal Mail* (from Edinburgh), calls at the Crown Inn, every afternoon at three, and the *Standard*, every morning at two; both go through Carlisle, &c.

CARRIERS.
To ANNAN, James Johnstone, from the Commercial Inn, three times a week.
To CARLISLE, James Machell (William Goodfellow, agent) & John Hargreaves (Jas. Irving, agent), every Tues. & Fri.—James Armstrong, from the Buck Inn, every Monday & Thursday—and John Coltart, every Wednesday.
To DUMFRIES, James Patterson and James Johnstone, from the Buck Inn, every Monday, and James Jardine, every alternate Friday.
To ECCLEFECHAN, James Johnstone, from the Buck Inn, every Wednesday, and Jas. Jardine, every alternate Friday.
To EDINBURGH, John Hargreaves and James Machell, every Monday & Thursday, and David Murray, every alternate Monday.
To HAWICK, John Dixon, from the Commercial Inn, every Monday & Friday—Thomas Whintrop, from the Buck Inn, every Wednesday & Saturday, and James Patterson, every Thursday.
To NEWCASTLE, George Vevirs, from John Oliphant's, every Monday.
To NEWCASTLETON, Walter Borthwick, from the Commercial Inn, Friday.

LOCHMABEN,

WITH THE PARISHES OF TINWALD AND TORTHORWOLD, AND THE VILLAGES OF COLLIN, ROUCAN AND NEIGHBOURHOODS.

LOCHMABEN is a town of considerable antiquity, a royal burgh, the seat of presbytery, and capital of the parish of its name, 65 miles s. of Edinburgh, 70 s. e. of Glasgow, 33 s. e. of Sanquhar, 30 n. w. of Carlisle, 21 s. e. of Thornhill, the like distance w. of Langholm, 15 s. of Moffat, 13 n. w. of Annan, 10 w. n. w. of Ecclefechan, 8 n. by e. of Dumfries, and 4 w. of Lockerbie; situate in a level country, surrounded by a beautiful amphitheatre of hills, and by all the charms which wood and water can bestow. It traces its origin to a very early age, and derives its name from the loch on which it is so delightfully placed, the word *Lochmaben* signifying, in the Scoto-Irish, the lake on the white plain. The loch, which is about three miles in circumference, abounds with several sorts of fish—among others the vendace (or vendise), which is peculiar to these waters, and is said not to be met with any where else in Britain. The town owes its rise to the protection of a castle of vast strength, which was built by Robert Bruce, lord of Annandale, and was the chief residence of the Bruces till the end of the thirteenth century. It stood on the north-west of the lake, which was called the Castle Loch, and the castle was surrounded by a deep moat. This ancient castle was succeeded by a much larger fortress, built on a peninsula on the south-east side of the loch. This edifice, with its ontworks, covered about 16 acres; after different grants to various relations of the Bruces, it was annexed, by parliament, in 1487, to the crown. Some of the walls still exist; they are of great thickness, and, with the melancholy firs which mingle with them, present a gloomy yet interesting mass of ruins. The period of the first erection of Lochmaben into a royal burgh is of too remote a date for conjecture; its present charter was granted by James VI, and bears date 16th of July, 1612, from which it appears that the town was more than once destroyed and burnt during the civil wars, its public edifices plundered; and its ancient records, &c. totally lost; but although the whole of the former privileges have been regained, the place itself has never recovered its former consequence. The municipal government is vested in a provost, three bailies, a dean of guild, and treasurer, all of whom are chosen out of fifteen councillors. The burgh unites with Dumfries, Annan, and Sanquhar, in returning one member to parliament. The town-house, with its tower and clock, stands at the end of the principal street. A subscription library affords literary and other information to the gentlemen by whom it is supported, and there are free masons lodges and a savings' bank; but it is a place of narrow trade, and, with the exception of a few stockings that are made, is unconnected with manufactures; it is, in fact, a rural town, solely dependant upon its own resources.

The parish church is a handsome and convenient building in the pointed style, with a bold square tower, in which are two well-toned bells. The first stone was laid on the 10th of April, 1818, and the church was opened for divine worship in July, 1820. The expense of its erection amounted to about £3,000: it contains sittings for 1,200 persons, but is capable of holding 1,400. There is also a chapel for the united secession congregation and one for the Cameronians. The market is, during the winter months, every fortnight, for the sale of pork, &c. but fairs are held on the first Tuesdays of January, April, July, and October, all old style.

The small village of TINWALD, which is situate about six miles from Lochmaben, was the birth-place of Paterson, the projector of the Bank of England, and the planner of the disastrous Darien expedition. The parish is of a triangular figure, each side of which is about four miles and a half in length; its northern boundary is watered by the pleasant river Ae. The greater part of the parish is arable: within its precincts, five miles from Dumfries, is Amisfield Castle, the seat of the ancient family of Charteris.

The parish of TORTHORWOLD lies near the foot of Nithsdale, and is bounded by Tinwald on the north, by Lochmaben and Mouswald on the east, and separated on the west from Dumfries parish by the Lochar water. It extends six miles in length from north to south, by a breadth, at the northern extremity, of about two miles and a half, tapering to a point on the south. The village, which is situate in the north of the parish, is about four miles from Lochmaben, and the like distance from Dumfries. In the vicinity of the village are the ruins of the ancient castle of Torthorwold, supposed to have existed since the thirteenth century. On the road between Dumfries and Annan is COLLIN, and near the parish church is ROUCAN, both villages belonging to this parish.

POST OFFICE, LOCHMABEN, Robert Henderson, *Post Master.*—Letters from DUMFRIES and all parts of the North arrive every afternoon at one, and are despatched every morning at half-past four.—Letters from LOCKERBIE and all parts of the South arrive every evening at eight, and are despatched every afternoon at one.

GENTRY & CLERGY.
Bell William, esq. of Rammerscales
Brown Sir Jas. of Mayfield [chapel
Brown Lawrence, esq. of Broad
Carruthers Miss Eliz. Lochmaben
Carruthers Miss Janet, Lochmaben
Carruthers Miss Mary, Lochmaben
Cruickshank George, esq. Trailflat
Cruickshank Richd. esq. of Broomhill
Cruickshank William, esq. Trailflat
Dalziel Major, Glencœ [shields
Dickson John Edgar, esq. of Elshie-
Farish David, esq. of Todhillmuir
Ferguson Mr. John, Lochmaben
Glover Mrs. Janet, Lochmaben
Graham Peter, esq. of Smallrig
Graham William Jardine, esq. of Priesthead
Greig Rev. George, Tinwald manse
Greig Rev. Geo. jun. Tinwald manse
Greirson Sir Robert, of Rock hall
Halliday John, esq. of Dam
Hoggan Miss Eliza, Lochmaben
Hoggan Mrs. Elizabeth, Lochmaben
Hoggan Miss Margaret, Lochmaben
Irving John, esq. of Amisfield
Jardine Sir William, bart. of Jardine hall, Applegarth
Johnstone Andrew, esq. of Halleaths
Lorimer Thomas, esq. of Ladyward
M'Gill Rev. James, Hightae
Marjoribanks Rev. Thomas, Manse, Lochmaben
Martin Rev. Andrew, Lochmaben
Murray William, esq. of Castlemains
Rogerson David, esq. of Maryfield
Thomson William, esq. of Parkend
Wright John, esq. of Smallholmburn
Yorstoun Rev. John, Torthorwold manse

ACADEMIES & SCHOOLS.
Brown William, Lochmaben moor
Graham John, Lochmaben
Kirkpatrick Joseph, Collin
PAROCHIAL, Lochmaben —— John Cairns & Robt. Hannah, masters
PAROCHIAL, Tinwald—Theodore Edgar & James Smith, masters
PAROCHIAL. Torthorwold—William Stewart Smith, master
Wilson James, Lochmaben

BLACKSMITHS.
Dalziel William, Kirkland, Tinwald
Glendinning Jas. Amisfield, Tinwald
Hamilton John, Torthorwold
Irving David, Barras
Lockerby William, Collin
Richardson David, Lochmaben
Rogerson James, Trailflat, Tinwald
Smail James, Lochmaben
Thomson James, Parkburn, Tinwald
Thomson John, Lochmaben
Wells William, Lochmaben

BOOT & SHOE MAKERS.
Bell David, Barras
Coupland James, Roucan
Halliday Robert, Collin
Harkness Joseph, Lochmaben
Henderson Thomas, Lochmaben
Millar William, Lochmaben
Patterson John, Roucan
Reid James, Torthorwold
Smith Thomas, Collin
Thomson James, Roucan
Thorburn John, Lochmaben
Wells William, Lochmaben
Wright David, Torthorwold

CARTWRIGHTS.
Brown David, Kirkland, Tinwald
Henderson John, Lochmaben
Jardine George, Lochmaben
Johnstone David, Lochmaben
Johnstone David, Torthorwold
Pagan Thomas, Parkburn, Tinwald
Swan John, Roucan
Wright John, Torthorwold

CLOG MAKERS.
Halliday William, Lochmaben
Jardine James, Lochmaben

COOPERS.
Wells John, Barras
Wells William, Lochmaben

DRESS MAKERS.
Richardson Margaret, Lochmaben
Robertson Jane, Lochmaben
Wilson Margaret, Lochmaben
Wright Isabella, Lochmaben

GROCERS & SPIRIT DEALRS.
Austin James, Lochmaben
Graham William, Lochmaben
Hetherton John (& flesher), Lochmaben
Kinghorn Adam, Lochmaben
Lotimer Janet, Lochmaben
M'Courty John (& ironmonger and stamp distributer), Lochmaben
Paterson Adam, Lochmaben
Robertson George, Lochmaben
Wright James, Lochmaben

INNKEEPERS & VINTNERS.
Farish David (King's Arms), Lochmaben [Lochmaben
Harkness William (Mason's Arms), Little John, Torthorwold
Mitchell Wm. (Crown), Lochmaben

JOINERS.
Henderson John, Lochmaben
Johnstone David, Lochmaben
Johnstone James, Beerflat
Rule Thomas, Collin
Smith William, Collin

LINEN DRAPERS.
Craig James, Lochmaben
Crinean Robert, Lochmaben
Housten James, Lochmaben
Watt John, Lochmaben

MILLERS.
Beattie William, Trailflat mill
M'Kitterick William, Torthorwold
Nicholson Christphr. Tinwald mill

MILLWRIGHTS.
Cowen Adam, Amisfield, Tinwald
Johnstone James, Beerflat
Johnstone Robt. Amisfield, Tinwald

PLASTERERS.
Beattie William, Lochmaben
Wells John, Lochmaben

SHOPKEEPERS.
Esdale John, Collin
Henderson Robert, Roucan
Little William, Roucan
Wells Janet, Collin

STOCKING MAKERS.
Aitkin James, Side Tinwald
Hume John, Lochmaben
Lindsay John, Lochmaben
Lindsay William, Lochmaben
Paton James, Torthorwold
Rae James, Roucan
Scott James, Lochmaben
Tweedie William, Torthorwold

STONE MASONS.
Burgess James, Lochmaben
Lauder John, Lochmaben
Palmer George, Lochmaben

SURGEONS.
Allan Andrew, Lochmaben
Brown Thomas, Lochmaben
Cunningham John, Collin

TAILORS.
Creighton David, Roucan
Graham Thomas, Lochmaben
Johnstone James, Lochmaben
Lockerby James, Barras

Morrison George, Roucan
Rogerson James, Lochmaben
Thorburn Robert, Lochmaben
Watt John, Lochmaben

TURNERS.

Smail Archibald, Lochmaben
Smith Archibald, Lochmaben

WHEELWRIGHTS.

Bell David, Amisfield
Newall Robert, Roucan
Smith Archibald, Lochmaben

Miscellaneous.

Cruickshank William, bleacher, Trailflat, Tinwald
Fraser John, painter, Lochmaben
Gibson Wm. jun. slater, Lochmaben
Jardine James, writer, Lochmaben
Smith Thos. auctioneer, Lochmaben

PLACES OF WORSHIP.

ESTABLISHED CHURCH, Lochmaben—Rev. Thomas Marjoribanks
ESTABLISHED CHURCH, Tinwald—Rev. George Greig, jun.

ESTABLISHED CHURCH, Torthorwold—Rev. John Yorstoun
CAMERONIAN CHAPEL, Rev. James M'Gill
UNITED SECESSION CHAPEL, Lochmaben—Rev. Andrew Martin

CARRIERS.

To DUMFRIES, George Allison & James Hall, every Wednesday & Saturday, and Gabriel Brown, every Wednesday.
To GLASGOW, Thomas Wright, every alternate Saturday.

LOCKERBIE,

AND THE PARISHES OF DRYFESDALE, ST. MUNGO, TUNDERGARTH AND APPLEGARTH.

LOCKERBIE is a neat small market town, in the parish of Dryfesdale, 65 miles s. of Edinburgh, 12 N.E. of Dumfries, 11 N.W. of Annan, 6 N.W. of Ecclefechan, and 4 E. of Lochmaben; situate on the great mail road betwixt Glasgow and Carlisle, 72 miles s. E. of the former, and 26 N. W. of the latter city. The town occupies a considerable space of ground; the buildings have a regular and clean appearance, and the surrounding country presents some fine scenery. The origin of this place is remote, and probably, for a long period, its character was only that of a small hamlet, attached to and protected by the residence or strong-hold of a family of some power. It is within the last century that improvements have manifested themselves to some extent, which may be mainly ascribed to the liberality of the proprietors, who have granted long terms to the tenants on their estates. Manufactures have not made their appearance in Lockerbie, but the trade in articles of general and domestic consumption is good, and progressively augmenting with the increasing prosperity of its fairs and public markets. A branch of the Western Bank of Scotland is settled here; and there are two good inns: a bank for savings, established in 1824, has been eminently successful.

The parish church stands about thirty yards off the High-street, and is centrically placed in relation to the parish generally, the extreme points not being at a greater distance than three miles and a half. It has lately undergone repair and received considerable addition, which renders it a neat and commodious edifice. The chapel, belonging to the united associate congregation, is also a convenient building. There is a female society for the relief of the occasional poor, a masonic lodge, and two libraries—one parochial, the other circulating.

The market is held on Thursday, and from the commencement of October till the end of April it is extensively supplied with pork, at which there is sometimes sold, in a single day, from £1,000. to £2,000. worth; there is also a market for hiring of servants on the second Thursday of October, old style. Fairs are held on the second Thursdays in January, February, March, April, and May, the third Thursday in June, and the second Thursday in August, all old style; the last fair, which is for lambs, is the largest and last lamb fair in Scotland: the number of lambs on the

ground being, in some years, from 30 to 40,000; a new one (established for the sale of cattle) in September, the second Thursday in October for cattle and horses, the second Thursday in November, and the Thursday before Christmas, all old style. These fairs add much to the prosperity of the town, being well attended; the new one in September takes place the Thursday before the large fair on Brough Hill, and is likely to become considerable. Lockerbie contains 264 houses, and about 1,500 inhabitants.

DRYFESDALE parish is in the district of Annandale, the extreme length from north-east to south-west is about seven miles; the average breadth of the upper part is about three miles, and of the lower half about one and a half; about two-thirds of the parish is low land, and the rest is hilly. There is also a considerable extent of holm land towards the junction of the Annan and the Dryfe. Of the whole extent of 10,000 acres in this parish, about 8,000 are either cultivated or have occasionally been in tillage, the remainder remaining in moor and pasturage. The point which assumes the greatest height is Whitewoolen hill, the elevation of which is 650 feet above the level of the sea.

ST. MUNGO is in the district of Annandale, through which the road to Glasgow and Carlisle passes, and at a short distance from the villages of Ecclefechan and Lockerbie. Castlemilk, the residence of Major Hart, is one of the most beautiful mansions in this part of Scotland, being romantically situated in the midst of pleasure grounds, and in the bosom of a fine valley.

TUNDERGARTH is a parish in which a great number of sheep are pastured, and is separated from that of St. Mungo's on the west, is nearly 13 miles in length, by a breadth of only about two miles at its widest part. The old castle, now in ruins, is deserving of notice, as it was formerly the residence of the Marquesses of Annandale. The conspicuous hill, called Brunswark, overlooks the district from the south.

APPLEGARTH (or Applegirth) is a parish in the presbytery of Lochmaben; in length northwards it extends nearly five miles and a half, and its breadth eastward is nearly the same. It is bounded by Wamphray on the north-east, by Hutton on the east, by Johnstone and Lochmaben on the west, and by Dryfesdale on the south. The village lies on the banks of the Annan, about eleven miles from Dumfries.

POST OFFICE, High-street, LOCKERBIE, Margaret Johnstone, Post Mistress.—The Mail from the South, with letters from ANNAN and all parts of ENGLAND, arrives every morning at a quarter past seven, and is despatched every afternoon at three.—Letters from EDINBURGH, GLASGOW and MOFFAT arrive every afternoon at three, and are despatched every morning at a quarter past seven.—Letters from DUMFRIES and LOCHMABEN arrive (by foot post) every afternoon at half-past two, and are despatched every night at seven.

NOBILITY, GENTRY & CLERGY

Douglas Rev. Hugh, High st
Douglas Jno. esq. of Lockerbie house
Douie Rev. David Buchan, Dryfesdale manse
Dunbar Rev. William, Applegarth
Graham George, esq. of Shaw
Hart Major Thomas, Castlemilk
Jamieson Rev. Andrew, St. Mungo
Jardine James, esq. of Bishopcleugh
Jardine Sir William, bart. (of Jardine hall), Applegarth
Johnstone Mrs. Captain Charles Hope, Hewk, Applegarth
Johnstone Thos. esq. of Underwood
Little Rev. Thomas, Tundergarth
Rogerson William, esq. Gillesbie

Roy William, esq. (of Milkbank) St. Mungo [Hillside
Stewart Chas. esq. (of St. Michael's)
Stewart James Hope, esq. (of Hillhead) Gillinbie
Wright Rev. Jacob, Hutton

ACADEMIES & SCHOOLS.

Blackstock Simeon, High st
Dunbar Rev. Wm. (bridng.) Applegarth
Gillespie Agnes (ladies') High st
Hawkins James, High st
PAROCHIAL SCHOOL, Top of Bridge st—Alexndr. Ferguson, A.M. master

AUCTIONEERS & SHERIFF'S OFFICERS.

Jamieson John, Bridge st
Thomson Robert, Bridge st

BACON CURERS.

Anderson John, Whitewoollen hass
Armstrong John (& cattle dealer) Townhead
Johnstone William, High st
Wright John, High st

BAKERS.

Johnstone Archibald, High st
Messenger John, Bridge st
Mundell James, High st
Shankland Thomas, High st [st
Shaw John (& confectioner) Bridge
Wright John, High st

BANKERS.

WESTERN BANK OF SCOTLAND (Branch)—(draw on the Establishments, Edinburgh & Glasgow,

BANKERS.—Continued.
and on Jones, Loyd & Co. London)
—William Richardson, agent
SAVINGS' BANK, Parochial School-
house—Alex. Ferguson, treasurer
and secretary

BLACKSMITHS.
Black William, High st
Hawkins Robert, High st
Johnston Robert (& farrier) Bridge st
Robertson Ridford, High st
Smith John, High st
Steel John, Bridge st

BOOKSELLER & STATIONER.
Walker Thomas (and circulating
library), High st

BOOT & SHOE MAKERS.
Blacklock Alexander, High st
Clemieson William, High st
Dinwoodie William, Bridge st
Gladstanes William, High st
Johnstone William, High st

CARPENTERS AND JOINERS.
Donaldson Robert, Bridge st
Patterson John & George, Bridge st
Portous Wm. (& millwright) High st
Williamson Robert & Peter, High st

CLOG MAKERS.
Johnston Robert, High st
Rae George, High st
Wright Alexander, High st
Wyper Joseph, High st

DRESS MAKERS.
Davison Mary, High st
Linton Georgiana, High st
Mundell Betsy, High st
White Sally, High st

FLESHERS.
Crichton James, High st
Elliot John, High st
Smith James, Bridge st

GROCERS & SPIRIT DEALRS.
Beattie William, High st
Brand Ann, High st
Dohie Jane, High st
Duncan Agnes, High st
Hornal Peter, Bridge st
Irving James, High st
Jardine Mary, High st
Jardine Mrs. Richard Bell, High st
Johnston James, High street
Johnstone Archibald, High st
Johnstone William, High st
M'Cullam Major, High st
Sanders Jane, Bridge st
Wallace Alexander, High st
Wright David, High st

INNS.
Blue Bell, Elizabeth Watters. High st
King's Arms (posting) Thomas
Lawrence, High street

IRONMONGERS.
Little John, High st
Wright James, High st

LINEN & WOOLLEN DRAPRS.
Dobie William, High st
Edgar John, High st
Johnstone John, High st
Pagan John, High st

MASONS AND BUILDERS.
Gladstanes James, High st
Lockerbie John, Bridge st
Murray Walter, Townhead

MESSENGERS.
Martin William, High st
Richardson William, High st

NAIL MAKERS.
Johnston John, High st
M'Intosh John, High st
Scott James, Bridge st

SADDLERS.
Lancaster Robert, High st
Nicholson James, High st
Turner William, Bridge st

SURGEONS.
Imrie John, High st
Johnstone David, High st
Newbiggin Robert, High st
Wilson James Thomson, High st

TAILORS.
Bell George, High st
Carruthers William, High st
Henderson James, High st
M'Nay James, High st
Murray James, High st
Richardson Johnston, High st
Thomson Samuel, High st

TURNERS & WHEEL MAKRS.
Jardine Alexander (& pump) High st
Linton Alexander (& rake) High st

VINTNERS.
Brand Ann, High st
Bredick James (Buck) High st
Cowan Geo. (Cross Keys) Bridge st
Dinwoodie John (Ewe and Lamb)
High street
Ferguson John (Globe) High st
Jamieson John, Bridge st
Johnston Francis, High st
Johnston Margaret, Townhead
Lawson Adam (Star) High st
Pool John (Coach & Horses) High st
Richardson John (George) High st
Richardson Thos. (Plough) High st
Shankland Rbt. (Commercial) High st
Shaw John (Crown) Bridge st
Smith William (Black Bull) Bridge st
Steel Robert, Bridge st
Williamson Peter (Eagle) High st

WRIGHTS.
See Carpenters and Joiners

WRITERS.
Baird John (& notary) High st
Richardson William (& notary, and
agent to the Caledonian Assurance
Company) High street
Wright Andrew, High st
Wright William (& notary) High st

Miscellaneous.
Bell Francis, sheriff's officer, High st
Cairns Rbt. nurseryman, Broom bush
Dickson James, cooper, High st
Graham Miss, straw hat manufac-
turer, Bridge street
Irving John, brewer, Bridge st [st
Johnston Jas. tallow chandler, High
Johnston Thomas, tin-plate worker
and brazier, High st [mill
Johnstone Jas. miller, Johnstone's
Johnstone Margaret, stamp distri-
buter, High st
Kerr John, cartwright, Bridge st
M'Naught Thomas, stocking maker,
Townhead
Rae Andrew, tanner and leather
dealer, High st

ESTABLISHED CHURCHES.
APPLEGARTH, Rev. William Dunbar
DRYFESDALE, Rev. David Buchan
Donie
ST. MUNGO, Rev. John Jamieson
TUNDERGARTH, Rev. Thomas Little

UNITED SECESSION CHAPEL, Rev.
Hugh Douglas, Lockerbie

COACHES.
To CARLISLE, the *Royal Mail* (from
Glasgow), passes thro' Lockerbie every
afternoon at half-past three; goes thro'
Ecclefechan and Gretna.
To GLASGOW, the *Royal Mail* (from
Carlisle), passes thro' Lockerbie every
morning at a quarter-past seven; goes
thro' Battick Bridge, Crawford, Douglas
Mill, and Hamilton.

CARRIERS.
To ANNAN, John Shaw, daily—John
Hargreaves & Son, every Tuesday and
Friday—Gavin Johnston & Jacob Rich-
ardson, every Friday—and Simeon Bell,
every Saturday.
To CARLISLE, John Hargreaves & Son,
every Tuesday & Friday—and Simeon
Bell, every Saturday.
To DUMFRIES, John Graham & John
M'Kie, every Wednesday.
To EDINBURGH & MOFFAT, William
Smith and Gavin Johnston, every Mon-
day——Andrew Smith, every alternate
Monday—and Jacob Richardson, once
a fortnight.
To GLASGOW, John Hargreaves and
Son, every Monday and Thursday.

MOFFAT,

WITH THE PARISHES OF JOHNSTONE, KIRKPATRICK JUXTA AND WAMPHRAY.

MOFFAT is an interesting and genteel small town, in the parish of its name, and district of Annandale; 51 miles s. of Edinburgh, 21 N. of Dumfries, and 16 N.N.W. of Lockerbie; pleasantly situate upon rising ground gently declining towards the south, immediately at the foot of a chain of mountains, which form the northern boundaries of Dumfries-shire with the adjacent counties of Lanark, Peebles, and Selkirk, and which completely environ it on the west, north, and east: the huge summits of this elevated region reach to various altitudes; some covered with wood—others beautifully chequered and skirted with planta- tions of unequal size, and natural clumps of birch, oak, and mountain ash, affording shelter and inclosure to the intervening grounds, which are partly cultivated and partly in pasture. The principal street of the town (High-street) is wide and spacious, and laid down upon the principle recommended by the late Mr. M'Adam—exceedingly smooth, clean and dry, even within a few minutes after the heaviest fall of rain; it commands an extensive and fine prospect of a de-

lightful valley, stretching towards the south, inter- spersed with hedge-rows, meadows and corn-fields, and pleasingly diversified by the windings of the river Annan, which first makes its appearance in an extra- ordinary ravine in this district, and runs at the distance of about two hundred yards from the town; the sur- rounding plantations, every year increasing in extent and beauty, are within view from the street. The houses are modern and commodious, admirably suited to accommodate visitors; there are several excellent inns, and an eminent and well supported academy and boarding-school Moffat has long and justly been celebrated as a fashionable summer resort, and for the medicinal virtues of its mineral waters. The springs are three in number, one sulphureous and two chaly- beate; the sulphureous spring is distinguished by the name of 'Moffat well,' and is about a mile from the town, a very good carriage-road leading to it, and a room with other conveniences upon the spot, for the use of the company while drinking the waters; there are likewise well-frequented bath-rooms in the town, to which the water is conveyed in leaden pipes. It is now upwards of two hundred years since the discovery of the valuable qualities of this spring, during which time it has been much frequented from all parts of Scotland, the northern counties of England, and in some instances from Ireland. In all scrofulous and scorbutic cases it is a powerful remedy, being seldom known to prove ineffectual when the lungs were not diseased; in the removal of bilious complaints, also, it is eminently successful, as well as in creating appetite and promoting digestion; and it is an excellent specific for gravel and rheumatism: it sparkles in the glass like champagne, but is so volatile that it can be drunk in perfection only at the fountain. Hartfell spa was first discovered in the year 1748, by a man named John Williamson: it issues from a rock of alum slate, in the side of Hartfell mountain, near Moffat; it may be carried to any distance, and will keep for years; it is a potent restorative, highly beneficial in all complaints peculiar to the fair sex, and may be advantageously used as a wash in the healing of obstinate cutaneous eruptions. The other chalybeate is of a peculiar nature, and obtained in a very curious manner, viz. by pouring water upon a rock in the side of a savage dell, called 'Gartpool Linn,' in the vicinity of the town: the surface of this rock is strongly impregnated with sulphat of allumina and iron; the water is much stronger than that of Hartfell, and consequently is taken in smaller portions—not more than a wineglass full at a time. About four miles north-west from hence there is a petrifying spring, and there are others that do not attract so much notice. To the antiquary the neighbourhood of Moffat presents many objects of gratification, and to these are attached traditions worthy of attention, but too numerous and prolix for detail in a work like the present. The celebrated road-maker, John Loudon M'Adam, died in this town on the 26th November, 1836, in his eighty-first year: he was a native of Ayrshire, but was much attached to the locality of Moffat, where he spent a great portion of his early life; he has left a widow, and two or more sons by his first marriage, upon one of whom was conferred the honour of knighthood, which his father had declined on account of his age and growing infirmities. Mr. M'Adam received from government £10,000. in two separate instalments; to his credit it is recorded that, during the whole career of his honourable independent service, he never contracted for works, deeming such a method of acquiring wealth incompatible with the duties of an engineer.

The parish and town of Moffat derive their name from the principal stream, the vale of which is deep, and of a very romantic and pastoral character; it was formerly densely wooded, and must, therefore, have well accorded with the appellation it received—Moffat being a corruption of *Oud-vat*, which signifies, translated from the Gaelic, 'the long deep mountain hollow.' The parish is the highest in the entire district of Annandale; its greatest length is about fifteen miles, and its breadth from eight to nine. The different rivers supply abundance of amusement to the trout-angler; and the celebrated alpine lake, Lochakeen (whose elevation is upwards of one thousand feet above the level of the sea), contains the finest species of that fish in the south of Scotland. The outlet of the waters of this lake is by the lofty and magnificent cascade called the 'Grey Mare's Tail,' tumbling over precipitous rocks,

computed to be about four hundred feet above the level of the vale, and which appears, from the opposite side of the glen, to be one unbroken fall. The population of the parish, in 1836, was 2,265; and the village contained 1,400 of that number.

The parish of KIRKPATRICK JUXTA derives its name from its vicinity to a chapel formerly dedicated to the famous missionary, meaning 'the lands nigh to the kirk of St. Patrick;' it is situate in the upper district of Annandale—bounded on the north by Moffat, and on the east by Wamphray. The celebrated Gartfel Linn is in this parish; likewise the castle of Auchincass, the ruins of which cover a considerable extent of ground: it was erected by Randolph, Earl of Murray, during the minority of David 'the Bruce;' and subsequently was in the possession of Douglas of Morton: its antiquity, therefore, is unquestionable; the old tower of Lochhouse is supposed to have been rebuilt by James Johnstone, of Corehead, chamberlain to Bishop Whiteford, of Brechin, whose daughter the chamberlain married, and with her obtained possession of the extensive lands belonging to the bishop in Kirkpatrick Juxta and Moffat. There are other ruins of ancient edifices, which excite some interest and are worthy of survey. The summer residence of William Younger, Esq., Craigland, is the only modern mansion of any note in the parish, with the exception of the Beatock Inn, about a mile and three quarters from Moffat. About one-third of the land is under tillage; the larger portion is unimproved and pasture.

JOHNSTONE parish is in the district of Annandale, adjoining Kirkpatrick Juxta; it is six miles in length and three in breadth. The remains of Lochwood tower, situate at the northern end of the parish, in the centre of a venerable and picturesque wood, and surrounded by impassable bogs, are the only vestiges of antiquity, sufficiently interesting to attract attention, in the parish: regarding the (now unknown) personage by whose order it was originally erected, James VI is recorded to have remarked, that, 'however honest he might have been in outward appearance, he must have been a rogue at heart;' Robert, natural brother to the chieftain Lord John Maxwell, of Nithsdale, burnt it down with savage glee in the sixteenth century. John Hope Johnston, Esq., of Raehills, M.P. for the county, is proprietor, and occupies an elegant mansion, the only notable residence in the parish. There is nothing peculiar to be observed respecting this local portion of the district, further than that (on the authority of the present reverend minister,) 'in this populous rural parish there is neither public-house nor meeting-house, nor resident surgeon nor village, nor post-office nor prison, nor lawyer nor beggar.'

The parish of WAMPHRAY received its name from its situation, emphatically expressed by the Gaelic word *Uamh-fri*, signifying 'the den in the forest.' Agreeably to this etymology, the church stands in a deep woody recess, by the side of Wamphray water, which brawls and thunders its way through a most romantic and picturesque glen, formed on both sides either by high steep banks, clad with thriving plantations—or by lofty basaltic columns, mantled with ivy, and sportively adorned by saplings of ash rising from their interstices. This parish adjoins Kirkpatrick and Johnstone; it is of an oblong figure, six miles and a half in length by three in breadth. There are but four resident proprietors.

POST OFFICE, MOFFAT, Thomas Grieve, *Post Master.*—Letters from LONDON arrive every morning at ten, and are despatched every day at noon.—Letters from EDINBURGH arrive every morning at four, and are despatched every morning at half-past eight.—Letters from DUMFRIES arrive every morning at half-past eight, and are despatched every morning at four.—Letters from GLASGOW arrive every afternoon at two, and are despatched every morning at a quarter before eight.

⁎⁎ *The names without address are in* MOFFAT.

GENTRY & CLERGY.

Barrie Mr. Thos. Poldean, Wamphray	Jardine Thomas, esq. Craigeburn	Johnstone Captain William Hope, R.N. Moffat house
Carruthers Samuel, esq. (of Mill) Wamphray	Jardine Thomas, esq. of Granton	
	Johnston Mr. John, Hunterheck	Marjoribanks Mrs. Mary,
Carruthers William, esq. (of Senerish hill), Wamphray	Johnston Mr. Michael, Archbank	Moffat Mr. Wm. Craigbeck
	Johnston Peter, esq. of Harthope	Monteath Rev. John, Moffat
Colvin Rev. Dr. Robert, Johnstone	Johnston Walter, esq. (of Bodesbeck) Capplegill	Patterson Rev. Henry, Gateside, Wamphray
Corrie Mr. Hope, Pumplawburn, Wamphray	Johnstone Rev. Alexander, Mause	Proudfoot Mrs. Thomas, of Craigeburn
	Johnstone Major Jno. Langshawbush	
Dickson Rev. Charles, Wamphray	Johnstone John James Hope, esq. M.P. (of Annandale) Raehills	Rogerson David, esq. (of Leithenhall), Wamphray
Hope Capt. Charles, R.N. Larchhill		

GENTRY, &c.—Continued.

Rogerson John, esq. M.D. (of Wamphray) Dumcrieff [Wamphray]
Rogerson John, esq. (of Girthhead)
Singers Rev. Dr. William, Kirkpatrick Juxta
Tod Mr. Raecleuch
Tod Mr. Peter, Meikleholmside
Tod Mrs. Robert, Heathery haugh
Welsh James, esq. (of Earlhaugh)
Braefoot [lands
Younger William, esq. of Craigie-

ACADEMIES & SCHOOLS.

ACADEMY (and boarding establishment for gentlemen)—Alexander Steele, *rector*; Jno. Gordon, *usher*
INFANTS' SCHOOL, Miss Thomson, mistress
Johnston Ebenezer
Mitchell William

BAKERS.

Brown William
Carmichael Mary
Moffat John
Steele William

BANKERS.

GLASGOW UNION BANKING COMPY. (Branch)—(draw on the Parent Establishment, Edinburgh, and on Jones, Loyd and Co. London)
—David Jardine, agent

BLACKSMITHS.

Brown William | Little Michael
Dalling George | Porteous John
Halliday George | Thomson Andw.

BOOT & SHOE MAKERS.

Coutts William | Halliday John
Davidson Thos. | Henderson Jas.
Grieve George | Little John
Grieve William | Neilson John

DRESS MAKERS & MILLINRS.

Johnston Agnes Jane
Johnston Janet
Lunham Agnes
M'Night Margaret
Mitchell M.
Wilson Jane

FIRE, &c. OFFICE AGENTS.

ALLIANCE, Alexander Johnston
CALEDONIAN, James M'Millan
INSURANCE COMPANY OF SCOTLAND, William Tait

FLESHERS.

Cartmer John
Halliday William
Johnston Alexander
Rogerson William (& spirit dealer)

GROCERS & SPIRIT DEALERS.

Kerr Jane [buter]
M'Millan James (and stamp distri-
Moffat Francis
Russell John
Stewart William

Tait Alleson
Wilson Helen

INNS.

Beatock Inn (posting) Thos. Wilson
Black Bull, Robert Anderson
Spur (posting) Jane Cranstoun
Star, Robert Charters

IRONMONGER.

M'Millan James (& iron merchant)

JOINERS AND CARPENTERS.

Aitchison John and Son
Brown John
Carruthers James
Grieve John
Hamilton & Williamson (and millwrights, and millers)
Henderson & Grieve
Sanderson James
Thompson John

LINEN & WOOLLEN DRAPERS.

Anderson James
Burnie Robert
Montgomery Joseph and Co.
Tait William

LODGING HOUSES.

Beattie John | M'Millan Saml.
Bowes Henry (& | Mathieson Adam
boarding) | Morrison Alex.
Craig Alexander | Mouncie Wm.
Dickson James | Patterson Mrs.
Dickson William | Proudfoot Mrs.
Goldie Marion | Thomas
Grieve Thomas | Rae Mrs. James
Grieve Walter | Russell John
Grieve William | Smith George
Hamilton James | Tait William
Johnston Alex. | Williamson Jas.
Johnston John | Wilson Helen

MASONS & BUILDERS.

Johnston James
Morrison Alexander

MEAL DEALERS.

Bell John (and grain)
Burgess William (and barley)
Carmichael Mary (and barley)

SADDLERS.

Johnston James
Wilson John

STRAW HAT MAKERS.

Johnson Mary
Johnston Elspeth
Lindsay and Craig
Scott Janet

SURGEONS AND DRUGGISTS.

Dalgliesh James
Johnston James
Smith George, R. N. (and dealer in stationery and perfumery)

TAILORS.

Brown John | Cowan John
Carruthers Sa- | Cowan Samuel
muel | Geddes David
Cowan James | Amos

Grieve Archibald | Moffat Adam
Hastie John | Riddle William

WATCH & CLOCK MAKERS.

Graham John
Leithead James
Russell Hugh (and jeweller)
Wightman Alexander

Miscellaneous.

Dickson James, woollen manufacturer and dyer
Dinwoodie Peter, vintner
Easton John, clogger
Finis John, plasterer
Grieve Wm. stocking manufacturer
Jardine Matthew, nailer
Kennedy Adam, sheriff's officer
Mathieson Adam, brewer, Amos pl
Robertson Jos. professor of dancing
Sanderson James, cooper
SUBSCRIPTION LIBRARY, James Millan, secretary

PLACES OF WORSHIP.

ESTABLISHED CHURCH, Kirkpatrick Juxta—Rev. Dr. William Singers
ESTABLISHED CHURCH, Moffat—Rev. Alexander Johnstone
ESTABLISHED CHURCH, Gateside, Wamphray—Rev. Henry Patterson
ESTABLISHED CHURCH, Wamphray—Rev. Charles Dickson
UNITED SECESSION CHAPEL, Moffat—Rev. John Monteath

COACHES.

To EDINBURGH, the *Royal Mail* (from Dumfries), calls at the Spur Inn, every morning at nine; and returns for DUMFRIES at four in the morning.
To GLASGOW, the *Royal Mail* (from Carlisle), calls at the Beatock Bridge Inn, (two miles distant from Moffat, on the high road from Carlisle to Glasgow,) every morning at a quarter before nine; and returns for CARLISE at a quarterpast one; going through Lockerbie and by Ecclefechan.

CARRIERS.

To ANNAN, Gavin Johnson and Jacob Richardson, every Friday.
To CARLISLE, Hargreaves & Son, twice a week. [Tuesday
To CASTLE DOUGLAS, Saml. Mounsie,
To DUMFRIES, James Johnston, James Robert Dickson, Samuel Mounsie, John Kilpatrick, & John Johnston, Tuesday.
To EDINBURGH, William Smith, John Proudfoot & Robert Baird, every Monday—James Johnston, Samuel Mounsie and James Robt. Dickson, every Thursday—and Andrew Smith, Gavin Johnston, and Jacob Richardson, weekly.
To GLASGOW, Hargreaves & Son, twice a week—and Samuel Scott & William Denham, once a fortnight.
To LOCKERBIE, Hargreaves and Son, twice a week, and Wm. Smith, Friday.

SANQUHAR,

WITH THE VILLAGE OF KIRKCONNEL AND NEIGHBOURHOODS.

SANQUHAR is an ancient town and burgh of barony, in the parish of its name, and district of Nithsdale, 56 miles s. s. w. of Edinburgh, the like distance N. by E. of Glasgow, 32 E.S.E. of Ayr, and rather more than 26 N.W. of Dumfries; situate on the line of road, up the left bank of the Nith, passing from this county into that of Ayr. The town, it is supposed, owes its origin to a castle of considerable importance, the ruins of which are now to be seen at a short distance to the south-east, on a high bank overlooking the river Nith. It must have been a building of great strength, having towers at the angles, and was surrounded by a ditch. It formerly belonged to a branch of the family of Creighton (or Crichton), ancestors to the Earl of Dumfries. The castle, as well as greater part of the land in the neighbourhood, is now the property of the Duke of Buccleuch. About a mile from it stands the house of Eliock, the residence of the family of Veitch, which gave a senator to the college of justice in the last cen-

tury; this mansion lays claim (which is disputed by some authorities) to the honour of being the birthplace of the 'admirable Crichton.' Sanquhar consists chiefly of one main street. The family of Queensberry has been great patrons of this town, particularly in improvements on the roads which pass through or approach to it. The late duke also erected the townhall, at his sole expense; it stands at the end of Highstreet, and has a tower, with a clock. Sanquhar is the principal coal mart in the county, and large quantities are supplied to Dumfries and other parts. In this parish, as well as that of Kirkconnel, the seams of this article of fuel are most valuable; the field extends seven miles in length and two and a half in breadth, and the veins are from three feet eight inches to four feet six inches in depth. The Duke of Buccleugh is the chief proprietor. At the eastern extremity of the parish, about nine miles from the town, are the valuable lead mines of WANLOCKHEAD, belonging likewise to the nobleman before mentioned. They are said to have been discovered, in the minority of James VI, by some Germans, who were employed in searching for gold about this spot. At the present period employment, by these works, is furnished to upwards of 200 miners, artisans and others. At the village of CRAWICK MILL, half a mile north-west of the town, on the banks of the Crawick stream, is a considerable manufactory for carpets, in which upwards of sixty men, forty women, and a number of children of both sexes are employed; and from the looms in the town about 20,000 yards of tartan cloth are produced annually for the Carpet Company. There are also about 100 cotton weavers employed by the Glasgow manufacturers, and upwards of 300 females of the neighbourhood are occupied in embroidering muslins for the same market. In the town is a large manufactory for spades, shovels, and other agricultural implements. A branch of the British Linen Company's bank is settled here, and there is one for savings.

Sanquhar was erected into a burgh of barony in 1484, and advanced to the dignity of a royal burgh, by charter from James VI, in 1596. It is governed by a provost, three bailies, a dean of guild, and eleven councillors, and, in connexion with Dumfries, Annan, and Lochmaben, it sends one member to parliament. The places of worship, in the town, are the parish church and two secession chapels. The present church, which was erected in 1823, on the site of the old one, is a very handsome edifice, with a square tower, and stands on elevated ground at the west end of the town. At Wanlockhead is a chapel, in connexion with the establishment, for the accommodation of the miners and others employed in the lead works. The executors of the late James Crichton, of Friars' carse, in this county, and a native of Sanquhar, have appropriated £2,000. for the purpose of erecting and endowing a free school in Sanquhar: the interest of the money, since it was set apart for this design, has been laid out in purchasing a site for the school, and the surplus, after the building is completed, will be invested for its endowment.

The market, formerly held on Friday, is now discontinued: there are five fairs, four of which are quarterly, and are held on the first Fridays in February, May, August, and November, old style; the fifth, which is of the greatest note, is held on the 17th July, or the first Friday after, and is called the sheep, lamb, and wool fair.

KIRKCONNEL village is four miles from Sanquhar, and eight from New Cumnock; situate on the high road between Dumfries and Glasgow. It contains the parish church and parochial school. The parish, which is bounded by that of Sanquhar on the south and east, is fifteen miles in length and eight in breadth. In it are two mineral springs, one possessing medicinal properties similar in effect to those of Hartfield spa, near Moffat; the other similar to the Kirkland spa, in Galloway. The Duke of Buccleugh is proprietor of nearly the whole of this parish.

POST OFFICE, Sanquhar, John Halliday, *Post Master.*—Letters from LONDON and the SOUTH arrive (from THORNHILL) every afternoon at four, and are despatched every afternoon at five.—Letters from GLASGOW and the NORTH arrive every afternoon at three, and are despatched every morning at three.

POST OFFICE, Kirkconnel, Robert Ritchie, *Post Master.*—Letters from all parts arrive (from SANQUHAR) every morning at half-past six, and are despatched to CUMNOCK immediately after the arrival.

GENTRY AND CLERGY.
Bramwell Mr. John, Blackeddie
Broom Mr. William, Sanquhar
Hutchinson Miss Margaret, Killoside, Kirkconnel [har manse
Montgomery Rev. Thomas, Sanquhar
Otto Mr. James, Newawrk
Reid Rev. James, Sanquhar
Richardson Rev. James, Kirkconnel manse
Simpson Rev. Robert, Sanquhar
Thomson Mr. George (surgeon), Sanquhar
Veitch Col. Henry, of Eliock

ACADEMIES & SCHOOLS.
Kennedy James, Sanquhar
Lorimer Josiah, Sanquhar
PAROCHIAL SCHOOL, Sanquhar—John Henderson, master
PAROCHIAL SCHOOL, Kirkconnel—William Hastings, master

AGENTS FOR MANUFCTRERS.
AT SANQUHAR.
Brown Alxandr. | Osburne George
Hyslop Thomas | Russell William
Kerkhope Wm. | Whigham Saml.

BAKERS.
Hyslop Robert, Sanquhar
Stoddart Robert, Sanquhar
Todd Daniel, Sanquhar

BANKS.
BRITISH LINEN COMPANY (Branch) —draw on the Parent Establishment, Edinburgh and Glasgow, and on Smith, Payne and Smiths, London)—John Wilson Macqueen, agent
SAVINGS' BANK, John Halliday, treasurer

BLACKSMITHS.
Black Peter, Kirkconnel
Graham Thomas, Sanquhar
Hyslop John, Sanquhar
Thomson Robert, Sanquhar
Turnbull William, Sanquhar
Williamson Robert, Kirkconnel

BOOT & SHOE MAKERS.
Corson John, Kirkconnel
Davidson James, Kirkconnel
Fingland Walter, Sanquhar
Henderson John, Kirkconnel

Kerr Andrew, Sanquhar
Laughlason William, Sanquhar
Lawrie James, Sanquhar
M'Cririck William, Sanquhar
Merrie William, Sanquhar
Simpson Alexander, Sauquhar
Thomson William, Sanquhar

CARPET MANUFACTURERS.
SANQUHAR CARPET COMPANY, Crawick mill—John Halliday, managing partner

CLOG MAKERS.
Irving James, Sanquhar
Kerr Andrew, Sanquhar
Oliver David, Sanquhar

COAL AGENTS.
Anderson Christopher, to George Whigham, esq. of Allanton, near Dumfries
Morrison James; to C. G. S. Monteath, esq. of Closeburn

DRESS AND STRAW HAT MAKERS.
Anderson Sarah, Kirkconnel
Bell Helen, Sanquhar
Brown Jane (straw hat) Sanquhar
Corson Mary, Kirkconnel
Currie Agnes, Sanquhar
Edgar Janet, Sanquhar
Hodson Margaret, Kirkconnel
Kerr Jane, Sanquhar
Shaw Mary, Kirkconnel
Thomson Agnes. Sanquhar
Weir Margaret, Sanquhar

GROCERS & SPIRIT DEALERS.
Braidwood Alexander, Sanquhar
Brown Alexander, Sanquhar
Dalziel James, Sanquhar
Dickson John, Crawick mill
Hair Aaron, Sanquhar
Halliday John (& wine merchant, woolstapler,&stationer)Sanquhar
Harkness Thomas, Sanquhar
Hill Hugh, Sanquhar
Hyslop Thomas, Sanquhar
Kerkhope William, Sanquhar
Lairder Margaret, Sanquhar
Osburne George, Sanquhar
Ritchie Gilbert, Kirkconnel
Taylor James, Sanquhar
Turnbull Archibald, Sanquhar
Weir Margaret, Sanquhar

Wigham Edward, Sanquhar
Wilson Mary, Sanquhar
Wilson Mungo, Sanquhar

INN.
Queensberry Arms (and posting house),Jane M'Glashan,Sanquhar

JOINERS & CARPENTERS.
Duff William, Sanquhar
Hair Alexander, James and John, (and builders), Sanquhar
Howat James, Sanquhar [connel
Kerr John L. (& cartwright) Kirk-
M'Millan Andrew, Sanquhar
Paterson George (& cabinet maker) Sanquhar [Sanquhar
Weir Alexander (& cabinet maker)

LINEN & WOOLLEN DRAPRS.
Anderson Robert Beattie, Sanquhar
Ballantine Jane, Sanquhar
M'Nae James, Sanquhar
Telfer Jane, Sanquhar
Wigham Edward, Sanquhar

MASONS AND BUILDERS.
Blackley William, Sanquhar
Hair Alex. James & John, Sanquhar
Weir David, Kirkconnel

SHOPKEEPERS & DEALERS IN SUNDRIES.
Black Peter, Kirkconnel
Carmichael John, Kirkconnel
Dawson Alexander, Kirkconnel
Samson William, Kirkconnel
Shaw Robert, Kirkconnel
Weir Jane, Kirkconnel
Wilson Ellen, Kirkconnel

SPADE AND SHOVEL MANUFACTURERS.
Rigg Charles & James (and scrap iron & agricultural implement), Crawick forge

TAILORS.
Black John, Kirkconnel
Broadfoot James, Sanquhar
Broadfoot William, Sanquhar
Brown Robert, Sanquhar
Carruthers Robert, Kirkconnel
Fingland William, Sanquhar
Gilmour William, Sanquhar
Hyslop John, Kirkconnel
Kirk James, Sanquhar
M'Kay William, Sanquhar
Samson William, Kirkconnel

TAILORS.—Continued.
Walker Andrew, Sanquhar
Wigham James, Sanquhar

TALLOW CHANDLERS.
M'Cron Jas. (& flesher) Sanquhar
Wigham Agnes, Sanquhar

VINTNERS.
Bell Robert, Sanquhar
Borthwick William, Sanquhar
Braidwood John, Sanquhar
Carmichael William, Kirkconnel
Crichton James, Sanquhar
Duff William, Sanquhar
Gibson John, Sanquhar
Gilmour John, Sanquhar
Inglis Thomas, Sanquhar
Kay John, Kirkconnel
Laidlaw Thomas, Kirkconnel
Lamont Andrew, Sanquhar
M'Michael George, Sanquhar
Sommerville John, Kirkconnel
Thomson John, Sanquhar

WATCH & CLOCK MAKERS.
Cunningham William, Sanquhar
Reid John, Sanquhar

WRIGHTS.
See Joiners and Carpenters.

WRITERS & NOTARIES.
Macqueen John Wilson (and town clerk, sub-distributer of stamps, and agent for the Caledonian Assurance Company), Bank
Smith William, Sanquhar

Miscellaneous.
IN SANQUHAR.
Blair William, woollen yarn spinner
Borthwick William, flesher
Brown Thomas, slater
Edgar James, saddler
Gibson Daniel, tinsmith
Howat George, nail maker
M'Kivers John, cooper
Sinton Maria, earthenware dealer
SOCIETIES VICTUALLING STORE
SUBSCRIPTION LIBRARY, George Paterson, librarian

PLACES OF WORSHIP.
AT SANQUHAR.
ESTABLISHED CHURCH, Rev. Thomas Montgomery

FIRST SECESSION CHAPEL, Rev. James Reid [Robert Simpson
SECOND SECESSION CHAPEL, Rev.

COACH.
To DUMFRIES & CARLISLE, the *Independent* (from Glasgow), calls at the Queensberry Arms, every afternoon at half-past one; goes through Thornhill, Annan, and Gretna.
To GLASGOW, the *Independent* (from Carlisle), calls at the Queensberry Arms, every forenoon at half-past eleven; goes through New and Old Cumnock, Kilmarnock, and Kingswell.

CARRIERS,
FROM SANQUHAR.
To DUMFRIES, Thomas Ferguson, every Tuesday & Thursday—John & William Robb, every Tuesday and Friday—and John Glencross, every Thursday.
To EDINBURGH, John Gilmour & John Glencross, every Monday.
To GLASGOW, William Coke & Robert Slimmon, every Monday—Thomas Ferguson, every Tuesday—John & William Robb, every Thurs.—and James Campbell and John Campbell, every Friday.

THORNHILL,
AND THE PARISHES OF MORTON, DURISDEER, AND PENPONT, THE VILLAGE OF CARRON-BRIDGE, AND NEIGHBOURHOODS.

THORNHILL is a highly respectable and considerable village, in the parish of Morton, 66 miles s. by E. of Glasgow, 48 N.W. of Carlisle, 40 N.E. of Newton Stewart, 34 S.E. of Kilmarnock, 30 N.W. of Annan, the like distance S.E. of Cumnock, 22 N.E. of New Galloway, 14 N.W. of Dumfries, 12 S.E. of Sanquhar, and 7½ N.E. of Minniehive, most delightfully situated upon an eminence on the banks of the Nith, and on the great road from Carlisle to Dumfries and Glasgow. The country around Thornhill is extremely beautiful, the hills bounding in the scene as with an immense wall. The vale of the Nith is here very spacious, and the hills spring suddenly up from the plain, at such a distance, as to suggest no idea of sterility. From the rising grounds, a little way up the hills to the west of the village, the noble massive castle of Drumlanrig, the property of the Duke of Buccleugh, looks down upon the plain. The scenery is also ornamented by Capenoch, the property and residence of Thos. Kirkpatrick, Esq.; Eccles House, that of Lauderdale Maitland, Esq.; Waterside, belonging to the heirs of the late James Hoggan, Esq.; Barjarg Tower, W. F. Arundel, Esq.; Closeburn Hall, C.G.S. Menteath, Esq.; Dabton, Thomas Crichton, Esq.; Holm Hill, Miss Douglas; Nith Bank, the Misses Gorstoun, and Baitford, Wm. Grierson, Esq. The Duke of Buccleugh is sole superior of this thriving village, and since his majority has expended very considerable sums in its improvement. Thornhill formerly ranked as a burgh of barony, and within the last 35 years the ruins of the old gaol were to be seen: the site is now covered by a handsome house, the property of Mr. James Dalziel. The streets are wide and airy: in the centre of the village is a handsome monument or cross (erected by the late Duke of Queensberry), surmounted by the figure of a winged Pegassus, associated with the arms of that noble family. The trade of the village is chiefly of a domestic nature: there are, however, a tannery and a brewery, and it can boast of two of the most respectable and comfortable inns (the George, and Queensberry Arms) that can be met with in the south of Scotland. Thornhill possesses a subscription library, consisting of 400 volumes; a literary and philosophical society; an elegant freemasons' hall, erected in 1834, and two benevolent societies; and, for a place of recreation, a spacious bowling-green and an extensive quoiting ground.

The parish church, which was erected in 1781, is inconveniently situated, as regards the accommodation of the majority of the inhabitants; a new one is, therefore, about to be erected, in a handsome style, contiguous to the village. Fairs are held on the second Tuesdays in the months of February, May, August, and November (old style); and on the last Friday in June; the latter chiefly for hiring reapers and agricultural labourers.

About two miles to the north of Thornhill, on the road to Sanquhar, and seated on the banks of the rivulet from which it derives its first appellative, is the small romantic village of CARRON-BRIDGE: it stands partly in the parish of Morton, and partly in that of Durisdeer, and contains about 160 inhabitants.

The parish of MORTON extends from the left bank of the Nith north-eastward to the borders of Lanarkshire, a distance of between six and seven miles by a breadth of about four; it is bounded on the north and north-west by Penpont and Durisdeer, and on the east and south by Closeburn: it is both pastoral and arable, and, where cultivated, is well enclosed and fertile. In addition to the Nith, the Carron and Cample streams let pass through the parish, nearly the whole of which is the property of the Duke of Buccleugh. Within the district is the large ruin of Morton Castle, the ancient residence of the Earl of that title.

PENPONT parish, which gives name to a presbytery, is an extensive agricultural district, of irregular form and uneven surface, having comparatively little flat or low grounds; the latter description of land lies chiefly upon the verge of the rivers which flow through it. The village is about two miles from Thornhill; the church, which is contiguous to the village, was built in 1782; it underwent a thorough repair in 1834, when a session-house was annexed to it. There are two other places of worship in the parish: one for the relief congregation (erected in 1800), of which the Rev. John Smith is the minister; the other belonging to the reformed presbytery. The stupendous Glenquhargen Craig, rising perpendicularly one thousand feet, and one of the greatest natural wonders in Scotland, is in this parish; there are likewise the remains of Roman encampments, causeways, and a castle. The Duke of Buccleugh is nearly the sole proprietor of this parish. Three hiring markets are annually held here, viz., on the third Tuesdays of March, June, and October.

The parish of DURISDEER is bounded on the south and south-east by Morton, on the north and north-east by the parish of Crawford, on the south and south-west by Penpont, and on the north-west by Sanquhar; it is eight miles in length, and six in breadth. In this parish is Drumlanrig Castle, the splendid and noble residence of the Duke of Buccleugh; it was erected towards the close of the seventeenth century. About a mile above the church the traces of a Roman encampment are obvious. Exclusive of three small properties, the entire parish belongs to His Grace the Duke of Buccleugh.

POST OFFICE, THORNHILL, Elizabeth Hunter, *Post Mistress.*—Letters from the SOUTH and EDINBURGH arrive every day at twelve, and are despatched every night at a quarter before ten.—Letters from SANQUHAR and MINNIEHIVE are despatched every day at half-past twelve, and arrive five minutes previously.

NOBILITY, GENTRY, AND CLERGY.

Buccleuch His Grace the Duke of, Drumlanrig castle
Carmichael Rev. Peter, Penpont
Crichton Thomas, esq. (of Auchenskeoch) Dabton
Dobbie Rev. Edward, High st
Douglas the Misses, Holm hill
Ewart Mrs. Alison, Nith bank
Grierson Mr. William, of Baitford
Hewitson John, esq. (of Grennan) Penpont
Kirkpatrick Sir Thomas (sheriff of Dumfries-shire, of Capenoch) Keir
Lawson Mrs. Agnes, Nith bank
Milligan Mrs. Knowe, Penpont
Moffat Samuel, esq. (of Auchenhastenine) Penpont
Richardson James, esq. (of Slongabar) Chapel street
Rogerson Rev. William, Chapel st
Smith Rev. David, Morton manse
Smith Rev. George, Penpont manse
Smith Rev. John, Burnhead, Penpont
Wallace Rev. Geo. Durisdeer manse
Wilson Mrs. Carronfoot, Durisdeer
Yorstoun the Misses Catherine and Edgar, Nith bank

ACADEMIES AND SCHOOLS.

Baxter Mary, Grass yards
Crosbie John, Drumlanrig st
Mathieson Daniel, Academy place
Milligan Archibald, Drumlanrig st
Pagan Alexander, Penpont
PAROCHIAL SCHOOL, Church street, Thornhill—John Hamilton, mastr
PAROCHIAL SCHOOL, Durisdeer—Wm. Munsie & John Hunter, mstrs
PAROCHIAL SCHOOL, Penpont—Robt. Kellock & Jas. Wright, mastrs
Williamson William, Carron-bridge

BAKERS.

Henderson William, Drumlanrig st
M'Morine Samuel, High st
Melross James, Drumlanrig st

BLACKSMITHS.

Brown John, Penpont
Dalziel John, Carron-bridge
Kirk William, Church st
M'Millan James, Penpont
M'Millan Walter, New st
Maxwell Walter, Burnhead, Penpont
Shankland John, Church st
Wilson Robert, Chapel st

BOOT & SHOE MAKERS.

Ferguson Samuel, Penpont
Gibson William, Drumlanrig st
Hunter Thomas, Drumlanrig st
Kellock John, Penpont
M'Caig Joseph, Drumlanrig st
M'Lean John, Drumlanrig st
Milligan James, Grass yards
Mitchell William, Penpont

CLOG MAKERS.

Easdale Thomas, High st
Kerr James, Drumlanrig st
Moffat Joseph, Penpont
Walker William (& cooper) Drumlanrig street

FARMERS.

Blackley John, Drumcruil, Durisdeer
acie Robert, East Morton
ainger Andrew, Morton mains
ewitson Robert, Auchenkenzie, Penpont
Hunter John, Morton mill
Hyslop Wm. Cosshogle, Durisdeer
Kennedy Thos. Muiryhill, Durisdeer
Lorimer George, Drumcork, Morton
Milligan James, Hayfield, Morton
Nivison Alexander, Burn, Morton
Rae William, Gateslack, Durisdeer
Smith Thomas, Pempillan
Smith William, Cample green, Closeburn
Wilson John, Dalvin, Durisdeer

FLESHERS.

Brown William, Church st
Hamilton William, Penpont
Killock Robert, Chapel st
Kirkpatrick John, Chapel st
Laidlow Robt. & Wm. Drumlanrig st
Pearson John, Carron-bridge

GROCERS & SPIRIT DEALERS

Armstrong James (& draper) High st
Armstrong William (and wine merchant) Penpont
Beck George (and dealer in china) Carron-bridge
Carson William, Chapel st
Davidson William (and wine merchant) Drumlanrig street
Hastings William, Drumlanrig st
Horn Robert, Drumlanrig st
Laidlaw Robt. & Wm. Drumlanrig st
Lawrie James, Penpont
Mathison Joseph (and stamp distributer) High street [bridge
Meggat Alex. (and draper) Carron-
Melross James, Drumlanrig st
Pearson Peter, Penpont
Robertson Alexander, Penpont
Waugh Robert, Chapel st

INNS & POSTING HOUSES.

George, Mrs. M'Kinnell, High st
Queensberry Arms, Robert Glendinning, High street

IRONMONGERS.

Hepburn James, jun. Drumlanrig st
Kellock James, Drumlanrig st

JOINERS & CARTWRIGHTS.

Coltart John, Carron-bridge
Harkness John, Penpont
Hastings Robert, Grass yards
Lotimer William, Penpont
M'Caig William, Drumlanrig st
M'Millan Wm. Burnhead, Penpont
Shankland James, Church st

LINEN & WOOLLEN DRAPERS.

Dalziel James, High st
Farish William, High st
Hastings William, Drumlanrig st
Sloane Robert, Penpont
Thomson John, Drumlanrig st
Webster John, Drumlanrig st

MASONS.

Dergival William, Carron-bridge
Laidlaw James, jun. Chapel st
M'Cubbin George, Penpont
M'Laughlan Thomas, Chapel st
Milligan Robert, Drumlanrig st

NAIL MAKERS.

Allan James, Church st
Russell John, Drumlanrig st

PAINTERS AND GLAZIERS.

Laurie John (& dealer in china and glass) High street
Wood Alexander, High st

SADDLERS.

Dalziel & Kirkpatrick, Drumlanrig st
Lorimer Andrew, Drumlanrig st
Wilson William, Penpont

STRAW HAT MAKERS.

Armstrong Janet, Drumlanrig st
Brown J. Drumlanrig st
Lorimer Lydia, Drumlanrig st
M'Lellan Sarah, Carron-bridge
Webster Agnes, Drumlanrig st

SURGEONS.

Dickson James, Chapel st
Douglas John, Penpont
Munsie John (and stationer) Drumlanrig street
Russell Jas. Lockhart, M. D. High st

TAILORS.

Hastings James, Chapel st
Hastings John, Chapel st [st
Hidleston John (& clothier) Chapel
Kennedy James, Church st
Killock Thomas, Chapel st
M'Kie Peter, Penpont

Martin Robert and Thomas (and clothiers) Penpont
Morrison George, Penpont
Rogerson Robert, Old town
Shankland James & Son (& clothiers) Drumlanrig street
Sharp Robert, Drumlanrig st
Williamson William, Chapel st

VINTNERS.

Clark Samuel, Penpont
Coltart John, Carron-bridge
Farish Mary, Drumlanrig st
Fingland John, High st
Kellock George, Drumlanrig st
Pearson John, Carron-bridge
Pearson Walter, Penpont
Reid John, Drumlanrig st

WATCH MAKERS.

Bennoch James, Penpont
Hird Henry, Drumlanrig st

WINE MERCHANTS.

Armstrong William, Penpont
Davidson William, Drumlanrig st
Kennedy Alexandar & William (& nursery & seedsmen) Drumlanrig st

WRITER AND MESSENGER.

Connell Thomas (& notary public) High street

Miscellaneous.

Baxter John, stocking maker, Drumlanrig street [bridge
Carse and M'Caig, brewers, Nith
Dalziel Christiana, dress maker, High street
Ferguson John, plumber, and tin and coppersmith, Drumlanrig st
Gibson Daniel, tinsmith, Penpont
Gilchrist James, sheriff's officer, Chapel street [High st
Kerr Robert, tanner and currier,
M'Caig William, cabinet maker and upholsterer, Drumlanrig st
M'Farlane James, hair dresser, Drumlanrig street
M'Kinnell Robert, coach proprietor, High st [Chapel st
Smith John, bookseller & stationer,

PLACES OF WORSHIP.

ESTABLISHED CHURCH, Durisdeer—Rev. George Wallace
ESTABLISHED CHURCH, Morton—Rev. David Smith
ESTABLISHED CHURCH, Penpont—Rev. George Smith
RELIEF CHAPEL, Penpont—Rev. John Smith
UNITED SECESSION CHAPEL, Thornhill—Rev. William Rogerson
REFORMED PRESBYTERIAN, Scarrbridge—Rev. Peter Carmichael

COACHES.

To DUMFRIES, the Red Rover (from Edinburgh), calls at the Queensberry Arms, every Tuesday, Thursday, and Saturday afternoon at four.
To DUMFRIES & CARLISLE, the Independent (from Glasgow), calls at the George and Dragon, every afternoon at three; goes thro' Annan & Gretna Green.
To EDINBURGH, the Red Rover (from Dumfries), calls at the Queensberry Arms, every Monday, Wednesday, and Friday morning at half-past nine; goes thro' Crawford, Chesterhall & Biggar.
To GLASGOW, the Independent (from Dumfries), calls at the George & Dragon, every morning at ten; goes thro' Sanquhar, New & Old Cumnock, Mauchline, Kilmarnock, and Kingswell.

CARRIERS.

To DUMFRIES, Andrew Watson, Wm. M'Dougall, James Hasting, & Thomas M'Queen, every Wed. and Saturday.
To EDINBURGH, Robert M'Caig, from his house, every Monday.
To GLASGOW, Robert Porteous & John Baird, every Monday.
To SANQUHAR, William M'Dougal, every Monday and Thursday.

KIRKCUDBRIGHTSHIRE,

COMMONLY called a STEWARTRY, but in reality and to all intents and purposes a sheriffdom or shire, lies in the south of Scotland, and forms the eastern and by far the most extensive portion of the ancient district of Galloway. It is bounded by Dumfries-shire on the east and north-east, on the south by the Solway Frith and the Irish Sea, by the county of Ayr on the north and north-west, and by Wigtonshire (or Western Galloway) on the west. In extent it measures, from south-east to north-west, about forty-four miles, by a breadth varying from twenty to thirty miles, the narrowest part being towards its north-western limits: it comprises a superfices of 855 square miles, or 547,200 statute acres, including twelve square miles of lakes: about one-third of the whole surface may be said to be brought into cultivation. It appears that the denomination of 'stewartry' originated at the period when, by the forfeiture of the possessions of the Baliols, the Cummins, and their various vassals, this district became the property of the crown, when it is understood to have been first put under the authority of a royal STEWART; in subsequent times the office of stewart, in the appointment of the king, was one of much honour, and was often the subject of contest. For a considerable lapse of time, however, after the establishment of a separate stewartship, the district was still in some measure esteemed to be politically attached to Dumfries-shire, but this nominal connexion was formally dissolved before the civil wars in the reign of Charles I. From the force of ancient usage, the appellation of stewart, instead of that of sheriff, has, down to the present day, been popularly continued, although by the civil arrangements of modern times there is not the least difference in the two offices.

SOIL, PRODUCE, MANUFACTURES, &c.—The soil of the county is principally composed of a thin mould, or a brownish loam mixed with sand—and is incumbent sometimes on gravel, and in many places on rock; the whole surface is interspersed with meadows, and mingled with moss. The shire has no statistical subdivisions, except that four of the most northerly parishes—Carsphairn, Dalry, Kells, and Balmaclellan—are commonly designated the district of 'Glenkins.' The aspect of the country, however, forms a very natural distinction into two divisions: if a line be drawn from the centre of Kirkpatrick-Iron-Gray parish to the Gatehouse of Fleet, all to the north-west, with little exception, is so mountainous, that it may with propriety be termed a Highland district; while the south and east parts exhibit a fine champagne and cultivated country—a contrast strikingly obvious. Anciently the greater proportion of the land was covered with a forest, which is now eradicated, or to be traced only in trifling remnants on the banks of the streams. It appears that, so early as the twelfth and thirteenth centuries, this hilly territory was under a productive process of agriculture, originated and improved by the assiduity of the monks of the different abbeys in the district; and it is upon record that in the memorable year 1300, when Edward I subdued Galloway, he caused considerable quantities of wheat to be exported from the harbour of Kirkcudbright to Cumberland, and even to Dublin, to be manufactured into flour, in which state it was brought back to victual the various strong holds and castles held by that monarch. In these times the staple products were wheat and oats—the culture of barley, pease and beans being very limited. This age of agricultural prosperity was succeeded by destructive intestine wars, fanaticism, improvidence, and consequent misery, which lasted four hundred years, and reduced the country to a desert. It was not until the beginning of the eighteenth century that any measures were adopted to effect a resuscitation of its agricultural capabilities, which for so long a period had lain dormant. The inclosure of the lands with fences was the first attempt at a series of improvements; but this judicious preliminary was encountered by a riotous opposition from the rural population, who rose in considerable numbers, under the title of 'levellers,' and proceeded to demolish the newly-formed boundaries, under the influence of some extravagantly wild notions as to a natural general right in property; and they were not subdued until the most energetic measures were employed for that purpose: this mischievous result of ignorance having been overcome, however, and the 'levelling' delusion dissipated, the county steadily advanced in an accelerated progress of improvement; and towards the close of the same century the district could compete with Dumfries and other adjacent shires in agricultural prosperity. Planting has been introduced by several noblemen and gentlemen of the stewartry, and much has been accomplished in reclaiming moss-lands. The number of horses, cattle and sheep reared in the county is sufficiently large to evince the possession of much practical knowledge, and consequent success, in this branch of productive economy; and the breed of swine has increased to a prodigious extent, these animals being now a staple commodity both for home consumption and exportation. The district is very nearly destitute of coal, which, as well as the greater part of the lime used, is brought from Cumberland; and there is very little freestone. Marl is found in great plenty, especially in the loch of Carlinwark, which contains an inexhaustible store of the best shell-marl; ironstone and lead ore also abound, but the deficiency of coal presents an obstruction to either being made available for the smelting process. Besides the salmon fishings at the mouths of the rivers, the Solway Frith affords every opportunity for the capture of the inhabitants of the deep. The manufacture of linen, woollen and cotton goods engages a considerable number of hands in the towns and villages.

RIVERS, &c.—Like other mountainous countries, this is intersected by numerous streams, which, uniting, form four considerable rivers; these are—the DEE, the KEN, the CREE, and the URR. The Ken is considered the largest, receiving in its course numerous rivulets which drain the neighbouring hills, and even affording an asylum to the waters of the Dee, although the latter assumes the appellative privilege after entering the Ken. All these rivers rise in the north, and empty themselves into the Solway Frith or the Irish Sea. The smaller streams are the Fleet, the Tarf, the Deogh, and the Cluden. The Solway Frith, in a circular form, washes the coast of the stewartry from the Nith to the Cree, a space of forty-five miles; and along the shore of this beneficial estuary the coast is bold and rocky, the cliffs in some instances rising to a great height.

The shire, or stewartry, comprises twenty-eight parishes, and contains two royal burghs—KIRKCUDBRIGHT and NEW GALLOWAY; the latter, in conjunction with Wigtown, Stranraer and Whithorn (in Wigtownshire), sends a member to parliament; and the STEWARTRY, like the other counties of Scotland, returns another representative to the senate. The principal eminences in this district, above the level of the sea, are—Criffel (or Crawfell), 1,831 feet; Cairnsmuir, 1,728; Bencairn, 1,200; and Cairnharro, 1,100.

[POPULATION, see over.

511

POPULATION OF KIRKCUDBRIGHTSHIRE,

IN THE YEARS 1801, 1811, 1821, AND 1831, EXHIBITING THE INCREASE IN THIRTY YEARS.

The Italic letters p. and b. respectively signify Parish and Burgh.

	1801.	1811.	1821.	1831.	Increase in 30 Years.		1801	1811.	1821.	1831.	Increase in 30 Years.
Anworth ....*p.*	637	740	845	830	193	Kirkgunzion ....*p.*	545	659	776	652	107
Balmaclellan ....*p.*	554	734	912	1013	459	Kirkmabreck ....*p.*	1212	1264	1519	1779	567
Balmaghie ....*p.*	969	1110	1361	1416	447	Kirkpatrick-Durham...*p.*	1007	1156	1473	1487	480
Borgue ....*p.*	820	858	947	894	74	Kirkpatrick-Iron-Gray..*p.*	730	841	890	912	182
Buittle ....*p.*	863	932	1023	1000	137	Lochrutton ....*p.*	514	563	594	650	136
Carsphairn ....*p.*	496	459	474	542	46	Minnigaff ....*p.*	1609	1580	1923	1855	246
Colvend & Southwick ..*p.*	1106	1298	1322	1358	252	Newabbey ....*p.*	832	1045	1112	1060	228
Crossmichael ....*p.*	1084	1227	1299	1325	241	Parton ....*p.*	426	569	845	827	401
Dalry................*p.*	832	1061	1151	1246	414	Rerwick ....*p.*	1166	1224	1378	1635	469
Girthon..............*p.*	1727	1780	1895	1751	24	Terregles ....*p.*	510	534	651	606	96
Kells ....*p.*	778	941	1104	1128	350	Tungland ....*p.*	636	802	890	800	164
Kelton ....*p.*	1905	2263	2416	2877	972	Troqueer ....*p.*	2774	3409	4301	4665	1891
Kirkbean.............*p.*	696	800	790	802	106	Twynholme ....*p.*	683	740	783	871	188
Kirkcudbright......*b.&p.*	2380	2763	3377	3511	1131	Urr..................*p.*	1719	2329	2862	3098	1379

TOTAL POPULATION OF KIRKCUDBRIGHTSHIRE........ | 29210 | 33681 | 38903 | 40590 | 11380

The total annual value of Real property in this county, as assessed in April, 1815, amounted to £213,308.

AUCHENCAIRN, AND DUNDRENNAN IN RERWICK.

AUCHENCAIRN, the principal village in the parish of Rerwick (or Rerrick), is 8 miles s. of Castle Douglas, 14 E. of Kirkcudbright, and 22 s. w. of Dumfries; situate on the main road between the two last named towns. The inhabitants are principally employed in frame-work knitting. In the mouth of Auchencairn bay lies the small island of Heston, which stands high out of the water, and affords excellent pasture for sheep. A fair is held on the 16th of August.

DUNDRENNAN is a small village in the same parish as Auchencairn, four miles from that village, deriving its chief, indeed only importance from having in its vicinity the ruined abbey of Dundrennan, the greatest attraction in this part of the country. This abbey, the venerable remains of which stand about a mile and a half from the sea, was founded by Fergus, Lord of Galloway, in the year 1142. The church was built, as usual, in the form of a cross, with the spire rising two hundred feet from the centre. The body was one hundred and twenty feet in length; and on the south side of the church were the cloisters, with a grass-plot in the centre. From what remains of the edifice, the whole must have been built in a style of great taste and architectural beauty. The buildings are now greatly dilapidated, and are almost entirely covered with a pale gray-coloured moss, which gives a character of peculiar and almost airy lightness to the lofty columns and gothic arches, many of which are entire. This sacred edifice afforded a temporary shelter to Mary Stuart during the last hours she spent in Scotland. Tradition has traced with accuracy her course from Langside to the scene of her embarkation for England. She arrived at this spot in the evening, and spent her last night within the walls of the monastery, then a magnificent and extensive building. The spot where she took boat next morning for the English side of the Solway is at the nearest point of the coast; the road from the religious establishment thither runs through a secluded valley of surpassing beauty, and leads directly to the shore, where the rock is still pointed out by the peasantry from which the hapless queen embarked on her death-destined voyage; it is situated in a little creek, surrounded by vast and precipitous rocks, and called 'Port Mary,' in commemoration of the unfortunate monarch's departure from it. The scene is analogously wild and sublime; and besides being inspirative of melancholy associations in the mind of the poet or romantic tourist, the coast here and in the neighbourhood merits the attention of the painter and the investigation of the mineralogist.

POST OFFICE, AUCHENCAIRN, Mary Kissock, Post Mistress—Letters arrive (by mail gig) from CASTLE DOUGLAS every afternoon at two, and are despatched at seven in the evening.

⁎⁎ *The names without address are in* AUCHENCAIRN.

GENTRY AND CLERGY.

Coltart Robert, esq. of Blue hill
Colton Jno. esq.of Auchternaburney
Gordon Colonel, of Balcarrie
Henry James, esq. of Auchenlech
Maxwell Colonel, of Orchardton
Thompson Rev. Jas. Rerwick manse
Welsh David, esq. of Collin

SCHOOLS.

M'Nally Andrew, Auchencairn
PAROCHIAL, Dundrennan—Andrew Carter, master
PAROCHIAL, Robert Scott, master

VINTNERS.

Anchor, Mary M'Bride, Dundrennan
Cross Keys, Mary Kissock
Cross Keys, Samuel M'Craith, Dundrennan
King's Arms, James Wilson
Plough, Samuel Kirkpatrick, Dundrennan
Ship, Anthony Milroy

SHOPKEEPERS & TRADERS.

Bennett John, miller, Fargra mill
Brown John, joiner, Dundrennan
Bunn James, joiner
Caig James, stone mason
Caig John, joiner
Callan James, cartwright
Carter James, tailor, Dundrennan
Craig Peter, shoe maker   [nan
Crosby Jas. shoe maker, Dundrennan
Geddes Robert, stone mason
Ghirr Maxwell, stone mason
Glover William, blacksmith, Dundrennan   [drennan
Gordon Andrew, shopkeeper, Dundrennan
Graham John & Geo. stone masons
Gunning Jane, baker and grocer
Hannay John, miller and joiner
Heuchan John, blacksmith
Keaddie Andrew, shopkeeper
Kissock Mary, shopkeeper   [mill
Kissock Thomas, miller, Balmangan
Lock James and Samuel, tailors

M'Clune Mary, dress maker
M'Clure William, stocking maker
M'Knight Andrew, meal seller
M'Knight William, shoe maker
M'Vittie David, cartwright
Milroy Anthony, joiner
Murray Robert, tailor
Nairn James, nailor
Robertson J. shoe maker
Shannon Janet, milliner and draper
Sharp William, stone mason
Shaw Robert, tailor
Trotter Robert, surgeon
Wilson James, grocer & ironmonger
Woodrow James, boot and shoe maker, Dundrennan

CARRIERS.

To CASTLE DOUGLAS, Nathan Copland, from Auchencairn, every Monday, Thursday and Saturday.
To DALBEATTIE, Robert Adamson, from the King's Arms, every Thursday.

CASTLE·DOUGLAS,
WITH THE VILLAGE OF KELTON-HILL, AND NEIGHBOURHOODS.

CASTLE DOUGLAS is a modern, neat, thriving town and burgh of barony, in the parish of Kelton; 90 miles s.s.w. of Edinburgh, 18 w. by s. of Dumfries, 15 N.E. of Gatehouse, and 10 N.N.E. of Kirkcudbright; situate on the road between the two latter towns, and on that from Portpatrick to Carlisle, in a pleasant fertile district, on the banks of the Carlinwark water, from which lake the original name of the place was derived. In 1792 it was erected by the proprietor into a burgh of barony by its present appellation, and its government vested in a provost, two bailies, and seven councillors. Fifty or sixty years ago it was composed of but a few detached houses; it has now upwards of four hundred and fifty respectable dwellings, laid out in regular streets, the principal one lining the public road. In the town-house, which is a modern commodious edifice, with a good clock, a court is held on the first Monday monthly for the recovery of debts under £5. There are three principal inns, and several others of a respectable character, but less elevated pretensions; among the latter is a comfortable tavern, called the 'Threeve Castle,' the occupier of which, Mr. Saml. Murphy, is in possession of the chair in which Mary Queen of Scots sat at dinner previous to her embarking at Port Mary, as noticed under the head of the foregoing parish. There are established in this town three banking houses—one a native firm, and two branches; three or four tanneries, a brewery, and a number of handsome shops—those particularly in King-street, for the sale of drapery goods, are furnished with extensive stocks of fashionable articles in that line of business. Altogether Castle Douglas may be considered one of the most respectable and prosperous little towns, although not of remote origin, in the south of Scotland.

On the south-west side of the town are the ruins of the ancient Castle of Threeve; and on its south-eastern quarter stands the modern and elegant mansion of Gelston Castle (formerly called Douglas Castle), now the residence of William Maitland, Esq. Carlinwark

lake, before mentioned, is upwards of a mile in length, and occupies one hundred and eighteen acres; before it was partially drained, however, by the canal cut from it to the river Dee, its area was much greater. It contains a number of small islands, one of which, in the middle of the lake, has been bound round its base with huge frames of oak; but whether the island has been artificially formed upon them, as some think, or they have been placed there with intent to support some vast superstructure, cannot now be decided. The lake is plentifully stored with pike and perch, and at its bottom is an inexhaustible treasure of the best shell marl. Castle Douglas and its vicinity appear to have been the arena of much contest during the feudal system, when the ancient Douglases dwelt in the castle of Threeve and were lords of this district; for on the west side of the town are still visible encampments and breastworks, evidently thrown up against the castle; and on the south-west bank of the lake is a spot still termed the 'gallows lot' or 'plot,' said to have been the place of execution in former times. The market, which is very considerable for grain in winter and cattle in summer, is held on Monday; the grain, which is sold by sample, is principally exported to England and the north of Scotland. Fairs are held on the 11th February, or the following Monday, for horses; on the last Monday in March, for hiring servants; on the 23d September, or following Monday, for the latter purposes and also for horses; and on the 13th November, or the following Monday, for horses.

KELTON-HILL (or Roanhouse) is a small village, in the same parish as Castle Douglas, about two miles and a half from that town. It was once noted for its extensive horse-fairs, now (with the exception of one) transferred to Castle Douglas—an alteration of considerable advantage to that town, but of a very contrary result to this place. The fair it still retains is held on the 17th June, old style, or following Tuesday; and is a large one for horses, and for hiring harvest servants.

POST OFFICE, King-street, CASTLE DOUGLAS, William Green, *Post Master.*—Letters from LONDON arrive (by way of DUMFRIES) every forenoon at half-past eleven, and are despatched every morning at three.—Letters from PORTPATRICK, &c. arrive every morning at three, and are despatched every forenoon at half-past eleven.

Letters are despatched (by cross posts) to NEW GALLOWAY, AUCHENCAIRN, DALBEATTIE, KIRKPATRICK, LAWRIESTON, and KELTON-HILL every day at twelve.

GENTRY & CLERGY.
Barbour James, esq. of Dunmuir
Bell Allan, esq. of Hillowton
Blackie John, esq. Greenlaw house
Cunningham John, esq. of Duchrae
Gordon —, esq. of Dee bank
Herries Wm. Young, esq. of Spottes
Lawrie Mrs. Barbara, of Ernaspie
M'Dougal Mrs. Frances, of Dildawn
M'Kenzie Mr. William, King st
M'Lachlan Rev. Malcolm, Queen st
Maitland Wm. esq. (of Auchlane), Gelston castle
Maxwell Robert, esq. of Breoch
Napier John, esq. of Mollance
Welch Mrs. Margaret, King st

ACADEMIES & SCHOOLS.
Graham Margaret, St. Andrew st
Halliday Mary Ann, King st
PAROCHIAL, Kelton-Hill (top of Queen st)—John Sturgeon, master; Alexander Gibson, assistant
PAROCHIAL, King st—Jno. Sturgeon
M'Phail Thomas (& land surveyor), King st
Trotter Isabella, King st

AUCTIONEERS.
Kissock John, King st
Sproat Peter, St. Andrew st

BAKERS.
Blair John, King st
Geddes John, King st
Green William & Samuel, King st
Patterson James, St Andrew st
Thomson James, King st

BANKERS.
Barbour William, St. Andrew st
BRITISH LINEN COMPANY, King st—(draw on Smith, Payne & Smiths, London)—John Sinclair, agent
NATIONAL BANK OF SCOTLAND, King st—(draws on Glyn & Co. London)—James Lidderdale, agent

BOOKSELLRS & STATIONERS
Aitken Joseph, King st
M'Millan Samuel, King st

BOOT & SHOE MAKERS.
Blacklock James, King st
Blacklock Matthew, Kelton-Hill
Blyth Alexander (and leather merchant), King st
Blyth Samuel, King st
Broadfoot William, Kelton-Hill
M'Clellan John, St. Andrew st
Palmer David, Kelton-Hill

BREWER.
Hewetson James, Queen st

CABINET MAKERS AND UPHOLSTERERS.
Fergusson Fergus (& undertaker), King st
Wilson & Nitters, King st

CHINA, GLASS, &c. DEALERS.
Galloway George, St. Andrew st
M'Clellan John, King st

COACH BUILDERS.
Brown James, King st
Iugles James, King st

DRESS MAKERS.
Beattie Janet, King st
Black Janet, St. Andrew st
M'William Mary, King st

Parker Elizabeth, St. Andrew st
Rain Grace, King st
Shannon Margaret, King st
Thomson Jane, King st

FIRE, &c. OFFICE AGENTS.
CALEDONIAN, James Kissock, Cotton street   [King st
EDINBURGH (life) James Lidderdale,
STANDARD, John Sinclair, King st

FLESHERS.
Barber William, St. Andrew st
Barber William, jun. Queen st
M'Adam Adam, King st
M'William Alexander, King st

GROCERS.
(*See also Shopkeepers, &c.*)
Carson Andrew, King st
Green William & Samuel (& spirit dealers), King st   [King st
Nicholson John (& spirit dealer), King st

INNS.
Commercial, Sml. Macqueen, King st
Douglas Arms, Marion Douglas, King st   [drew st
King's Arms, Peter Sproat, St. Andrew st

IRONMONGERS.
Carson Andrew, King st
Dobie Andrew & Co. King st

JOINERS.
Gibson Henry, Loch Isle
M'Lellan Charles, King st
M'Taggart John, Kelton-Hill
Martin John, Queen st
Martin William, George st

LIBRARIES, &c.
NEWS and READING ROOM, St. Andrew st—Jas. Lidderdale, treasr.

LIBRARIES, &c.—Continued.
OPERATIVE MECHANICS, Queen st
SUBSCRIPTION, Queen st—John
M'Clellan, librarian

LINEN & WOOLLEN DRAPERS
Anderson Andrew & Co. King st
Black James & Co. King st
Edgar Jacob Dixon, King st
Gordon Samuel, King st
Green Joseph George, King st

MESSENGERS.
Mure James. Queen st
Nairne John Gordon, Cotton st

PAINTERS & GLAZIERS.
Borland John, King st
M'Murray Isabella, King st
M'Murray Robert, Castle st

SADDLERS AND HARNESS MAKERS.
Milligan John, King st
Parker Arthur, St. Andrew st
Robertson Gordon, King st

SHOPKEEPERS & DEALRS IN GROCERIES & SUNDRIES.
Blair John, King st
Carson John, St. Andrew st
Carson Mary, King st
Casteen Thomas, St. Andrew st
Connal Robert, Kelton-Hill
Craig Joseph, King st
Gibson Thomas, King st
Gordon Charles, King st
Halliday Jane, King st
Harper William, King st
Johnston William, King st
M'Ghie William, King st
M'Vane John, King st
Morrison Nathaniel, Kelton-Hill
Rae Janet, King st
Robertson Eliza, New st
Tracey Edward, King st

SILVERSMITH.
Burgess Adam (& jeweller), King st

SMITHS.
Burgess James, Kelton-Hill
M'George James, Cotton st
Payne John, Queen st
Shaw Thomas, Kelton-Hill
Smith Robert, King st

STONE MASONS.
Connal Adam, Kelton-Hill
Cowan Samuel (& stone cutter), Cotton street
Darley James, Queen st
Geddes David, Kelton-Hill
Geddes Samuel, Kelton-Hill

Gordon John, King st
M'Knight Robert
M'Knight Thomas, St. Andrew st
Tait Robert, King st

STRAW HAT MAKERS.
Gordon Margt. & Eliza, St. Andrew st
Law Margaret, King st
M'Farlane Janet, King st
M'Genr Nicholas, King st
Payne Agnes, King st
Robertson Isabella, King st

SURGEONS.
Anderson Patrick, St. Andrew st
Inglis James, M. D. King st
M'Keur Samuel, King st
Thomson John, King st

TAILORS.
Bell James, King st
Blair William, St. Andrew st
Glen James, King st
Kirk R. Cotton st
M'William John, King st
Morrison Thomas, Kelton-Hill
Shaw William, King st

TANNERS AND SKINNERS.
Grierson Robert, King st
Milligan Andrew, Queen st
Robertson Robert, Queen st
Robertson Samuel, Queen st

VINTNERS.
Black Bull, Jean Riddick, St. Andrew st
Blue Bell, David Palmer, Kelton-Hill
Boar's Head, John Gordon, King st
Bush, Robert Tait, King st [drew st
Coach & Horses, Anthony Parker, St. Au-
Cross Keys, Grace Murdoch, King st
Crown, George Hutton, Kelton-Hill
Crown, Nathaniel Heron, King st
George, Samuel Carson, King st
George, William Milroy, King st
Globe, Robert Campbell, King st
Golden Bell, Hugh Garmory, King st
Grapes, Eliza Robertson, New st
Gray Horse, Edward Tracey, King st
M'Quinne James, St. Andrew st
Plough, Jane Douglas, King st
Ram, John Wilson, King st
Rodney's Head, James Moore, Kelton-Hill
Royal Oak, John Gordon, King st
Salutation, Thos. M'Millan, St. Andrew st
Ship, James Culton, King st
Square & Compass, James Nisb, King st
Swan, Hugh Gordon, King st
Thistle, James Hunter, King st
Thomson Margaret, King st [bank
Threeve Castle, Samuel Murphy, Threeve
Wheat Sheaf, John Geddes, King st

WATCH & CLOCK MAKERS.
Law James, King st
M'George David, St. Andrew st
Yuil Thomas, Queen st
Yule James, King st

WINE & SPIRIT MERCHNTS.
M'Taggart Peter, King st
Young William, St. Andrew st

WRITERS AND NOTARIES.
Barbour William, St. Andrew st
Kissock James, Cotton st
Lidderdale, James, King st
Mure James (writer), King st
Sinclair John, King st

Miscellaneous.
Anderson James, bookbinder, Market hill
Apedale Thos. supervisor of excise, King st
Bannatyne Jno. tin-plate wrkr. St. Andrew st
Blakeley Robert, road surveyor, Queen st
Davidson Anthony, letter-press printer, Cotton street
Halliday Hugh, nail maker, King st
Johnston Alexander, carrier, St. Andrew st
M'Bain John, clog maker, King st
M'Clure David, carrier, Queen st
Milroy James, miller, Kelton-Hill
Palmer John, carrier, King st [st
Robertson Isabella, tallow chandler, King
Shaw John, town clerk, Cotton st
Stuart John, hair cutter, King st
Sturgeon John, session clerk, King st

COACHES.
To DUMFRIES, the *Royal Mail* (from Portpatrick), calls at the Douglas Arms, every morning at three—and a Coach (from Kirkcudbright), calls at the King's Arms, every afternoon (Sunday excepted) at half-past five.
To KIRKCUDBRIGHT, a Coach (from Dumfries), calls at the King's Arms, every day (Sunday excepted) at twelve.
To PORTPATRICK, the *Royal Mail* (from Dumfries), calls at the Douglas Arms, every forenoon at half-past eleven; goes through Gatehouse, Creetown, Newton Stewart, &c.

CARRIERS.
To DALBEATTIE and PALNACKIE, David M'Clure, once a fortnight.
To DUMFRIES, Samuel Mouncy, every Wednesday—and Alexander Johnston, every Wednesday and Saturday.
To EDINBURGH, Samuel Mouncy, from his house, every Wednes. morning.
To GATEHOUSE, Samuel Mouncy, every Saturday, and David M'Clure and Thomas Wallett, alternately on Thursday
To GLASGOW, David M'Clure and Thomas Wallett, alternately on Monday.
To KIRKCUDBRIGHT, D. M'Clure, Samuel Mouncy, and T. Wallett, every Friday.

CREETOWN

IS a small town and burgh of barony, in the parish of Kirkmabreck, 117 miles s. w. of Edinburgh, twelve w. of Gatehouse, about seven s. e. of Newton-Stewart, and three from Wigton, across the ferry. It was formerly called *Ferry Town of Cree*, and derived that appellation, doubtless, from its situation—the town being seated on the east side of the creek of the river Cree, at the head of Wigton bay, and opposite the peninsula, on which stands the town of Wigton. It is a place of but trifling commercial consequence, the only trade it possesses being almost confined to the importation of coal and lime, and the exportation of grain and granite; the latter, of which there is a fine quarry in the vicinity, is wrought by the trustees of the Liverpool docks. The mail road from Portpatrick to Dumfries passes through the town, which circumstance conduces, in some degree, to its importance. This place is the property of John M'Culloch, Esq. whose mansion is a great ornament to it; and there are some few other handsome residences in the neighbourhood. The church, which is a modern edifice, having been erected in 1834, is a neat building.

POST OFFICE, John Hannah, *Post Master.*—Letters from DUMFRIES arrive every afternoon at three, and are despatched every night at half-past eleven.—Letters from PORTPATRICK arrive every night at half-past eleven, and are despatched every afternoon at three.

GENTRY AND CLERGY.
Anderson John, esq. of St. Germains and Mark [Creetown
Denniston Captain James Murray,
Hannay Miss, of Kirkdale
Hannay Sir Samuel, of Mochrum
Hughan Thomas, eesq. of Airds
M'Culloch John, esq. of Barholm
M'Kenz Sir John William Pitt Muir, Cassencarrie
Muir Rev. John, Creetown

ACADEMIES & SCHOOLS.
M'Nay Mary, Mill lane
Mein David, Creetown

PAROCHIAL, David Mein, master
Scott Mary, Creetown

BAKERS.
M'Coschrie Janet, Harbour st
Tait John, St. John st

BLACKSMITHS.
M'Nish Samuel, Church st
Sproat Andrew, Church st

BOOT & SHOE MAKERS.
Hunter William
Kelly Peter, Harbour st
M'Kean Thomas, Silver st
M'Kie Peter
Murdoch William, Harbour st

Rodgers Daniel, Harbour st
Rogan Edward, St. John st

CARPET MANUFACTURERS.
Blair and Dunlop

GROCERS.
See Shopkeepers, &c.

JOINERS.
Aiken David (& builder) St. John st
Caldow Robert
M'Credie Hugh, Silver st

INN-KEEPERS & VINTNERS.
Barber James (M'Culloch's Arms) Silver street

Brown Catherine, St. John st
Conning Robert, Silver st
Hughan Thomas, St. John st
Johnston John, St. John st
Kevand John, Silver st
Young James (Inn) Harbour st

LINEN DRAPERS.

Cowan Robert, St. John st
Crawford Hugh, St. John st

MILLERS.

Henderson Ann & Alex. Mill lane

MILLINERS AND DRESS MAKERS.

Carson Barbara, St. John st
Johnston Margaret, Harbour st

SHOPKEEPERS & DEALRS IN GROCERIES & SUNDRIES.

Blaen John, St. John st
Carson Robert, St. John st
Heron John, Harbour st
M'Coschrie Janet, Harbour st
M'Kean Alexander, St. John st
M'Kiterick Jean, St. John st
Michael Thomas, St. John st
Shennan Janet, St. John st
Tait John (& flesher) St. John st
Vernon Euphemia, St. John st

TAILORS.

Lennox James & Son, St. John st
M'Nish Andrew, Church st
M'Nish George, St. John st

WRIGHTS—See Joiners.

Miscellaneous.

Cameron David, nail maker
Crichton Alex. surgeon, St. John st
Crosty Thos. hair cutter, St. John st
Gilchrist Robert, messenger
Irving Peter & Sons, fishmongers, Harbour street [Burnfoot
Templeton William, stone mason,
Welch William, agent to Liverpool dock trustees, Kilmabreck

COACHES.

To DUMFRIES, the Mail (from Portpatrick) passes through every night at half-past eleven; goes through Gatehouse and Castle Douglas
To PORTPATRICK, the Mail (from Dumfries) passes through every afternoon at three; goes through Newton Stewart.

CROSSMICHAEL AND PARTON.

CROSSMICHAEL is a small village in the parish of its name, 91 miles s.s.w. of Edinburgh, 19 s.w. of Dumfries, and 9 s.s.E. of New Galloway, pleasantly situate on the banks of the Dee, which river is crossed, about a mile and a half from the village, by an elegant stone bridge, over which the high road passes leading to Lawrieston and Castle Douglas; Crossmichael being distant five miles from the former, and three and a half from the latter town. In the village is the parish church, the patron saint of which, prior to the reformation, was Saint Michael, and hence the name, though of the cross there are neither remains or traditions preserved. The parish lies nearly in the centre of the Stewartry, having the Urr water on the east, and the Dee or Loch Ken on the west. Two small lakes which have an outlet to the Dee water furnish good perch and pike fishing.

PARTON parish lies along the banks of the Dee, that water and the Urr being its western boundary; it extends from six to seven miles in length, its breadth varying from four to six. A large portion of the parish is hilly, heathy, and pastoral, especially in the northern quarter—towards the Dee the land is flat and arable, and under cultivation. What may be called the village, which contains but a few houses, the church (a neat building erected in 1834), and the manse, is about three miles from Crossmichael. The manse occupies a very pleasant situation fronting the river, and is surrounded by hills and wood. In the vicinity is an excellent slate quarry.

POST OFFICE, PARTON, William Landsburgh, Post Master.—Letters from CASTLE DOUGLAS arrive (by horse post) every afternoon at half-past one, and are despatched every night at eight.

GENTRY AND CLERGY.

Crosby Mr. James (factor to Edward Fletcher, esq.), Parton
Crosby Mr. Robt. Markland, Parton
Crosby Rev. Wm. G. Parton manse
Fletcher Capt. Edward, of Corsock, Parton
Glendinning Miss Xeveria, of Parton
Glover Rev. William, Crossmichael manse
Lawrence G. W. esq. of Largnane, Crossmichael
Maxwell Clark, esq. of Nether Corsock, Parton
Shaw Ebenezer esq. of Drumrash, Parton

SCHOOLS.

Johnston James, Crossmichael
PAROCHIAL, Crossmichael—John M'George, master
PAROCHIAL, Partou—James Johnstone, master

SHOPKEEPERS & TRADERS.

The names without address are in CROSSMICHAEL.

Anderson Joseph, shoemakr. Parton
Austin John, miller
Bell Alexander, tailor, Parton
Bell John, shopkeeper, Parton
Bryson William, shoemaker
Clark Eleazer, stone mason, Parton
Copland Alexander, shopkeeper
Dickson Abraham, clogger

Donaldson John, blacksmith, Parton
Gall William, shopkeeper
Green William, shopkeeper, Parton
Heslop James, blacksmith
Hornel J. shoemaker
Lawrie Walter, joiner
Lawrie William, joiner
Middleton Christopher, well sinker
Milligan John, vintner
Mountree John, letter cutter
Muirhead Robert, tailor
Richardson William, miller, Parton
Sturgeon John, joiner
Thompson James, joiner, Parton
Walker Samuel, shopkeeper
Walker Samuel, vintner

DALBEATTIE AND NEIGHBOURHOOD.

DALBEATTIE, the principal village in the parish of Urr, is 87 miles s.s.w. of Edinburgh, 13¾ N. by E. of Kirkcudbright, the like distance s.w. of Dumfries, and 6 from Castle Douglas; most eligibly situate on the Dalbeattie burn, a rivulet which falls into the water of Urr; which latter is here navigable for vessels of seventy or eighty tons. This harbour, which is called Dub-o'-Hass, is about five miles from the Solway Firth. The village possesses great advantages, in respect to situation, for a maritime trade, having a communication by sea with the western ports, and it possesses some large falls of water, capable of turning any kind of machinery, so that it requires nothing but some spirited individuals to render it one of the most improved places in the south of Scotland. The mills now in operation are a paper, a flax, a corn and a waulk mill, and two for sawing timber, the whole propelled by water; there is also an extensive smithy, the hammers of which are also worked by the same power. In the village are places of worship for presbyterians and Roman catholics, and a comfortable inn. Within the parish, and situate on the banks of the river, about a mile below Urr church, is the celebrated Mote of Urr, an artificial mount rising from the centre of elevated circles, and used in primitive times as a seat for courts of judicature by the petty chiefs of this district of Galloway. The surface of the country around here is pretty level, and the soil is light.

POST OFFICE, DALBEATTIE, David Murray, Post Master.—Letters arrive from CASTLE DOUGLAS every afternoon at three, and are despatched every evening at six.

GENTRY AND CLERGY.

Cochtrie Mr. William, Dalbeattie
Costin Jno. esq. (of Glenson) Colvend
Craik Hamilton, esq. (of Arbigland) Kirkbean [manse
Crocket Rev. John, Kirkgunzeon
Grierson Rev. Thos. Kirkbean manse
Herries William Young, esq. (of Spottes) Urr [Colvend
Kirk John, esq. (of Drumstinchell)
Lowden John, esq. (of Clonyard) Colvend [manse
M'Culloch Rev. Andrew, Colvend

M'Knight Robert, esq. (of Barlochan), Urr
M'Lauchlan Mr. James, Dalbeattie
M'Michan John, esq. of Faith Head
M'William Miss Elizabeth, Dalbeattie
Maxwell Mr. Francis, Dalbeattie
Maxwell John Herries, esq. of Munches
Murray Rev. William, Kirkbean
Rosemond Rev. —, Dalbeattie
Simpson Saml. esq. of King's grange
Stewart Mark, esq. (of Mains) Colvend
Strain Rev. John, Dalbeattie

BAKERS.

Patterson David
Thomson James

BLACKSMITHS.

Elliott William, sen.
Shaw John
Tait Andrew

BOOT & SHOE MAKERS.

Blacklock James
Dornan William

CARTWRIGHTS & JOINERS.

Adamson James | Kerr William
Henchan James | M'Lellan James

GROCERS.
See Shopkeepers, &c.

INN-KEEPERS & VINTNERS.
Brown Cow, John Carmont
Commercial, John M. Lowden
Copeland Arms, Dougald M'Laurin
King's Arms, John Patterson
Maxwell's Arms, David Murray
Plough, John Heslop
Thistle, Agnes Nisbett

LINEN DRAPERS.
Lowden Samuel   [hosier, &c.]
Rawline Thomas (& woollen draper,

NAIL MAKERS.
Halliday James
Milligan John

REAPING-HOOK MAKERS.
Elliott John and William

SHOPKEEPERS & DEALRS IN GROCERIES & SUNDRIES.
Couden Hugh
Irvine William
Kirkpatrick Margaret   [maker]
Kirkpatrick Samuel (and stocking
Lowden John
M'Laurin Dougald
Murray David

Nisbett Agnes
Patterson Isabella
Telfer Jean

STONE MASONS.
Copeland James
Newall Andrew
Nish John

STRAW HAT MAKERS.
Aiken Mary
Maxwell Mary

TAILORS.
Lockerby William
Porter Eleazer
Smith William

WOOL CARDERS AND MANUFACTURERS.
Milligan William and Alexander

WRIGHTS.
See Cartwrights and Joiners.

Miscellaneous.
Broadfoot Anthony, miller
Brookbank Thos. wood merchant
Carmont John, flesher
Carrie James, surgeon   [bank
Hunter Andrew, agent to T. Brook-
Kerr James, clog maker
Lewis William, paper maker

Lindsay Hugh, dyer
Maxwell Thomas, school master
Rigg Anthony, farmer, Torkatrine
Strachan Rbt. slate merchant&slater
Welch Edward, meal seller

PAROCHIAL SCHOOLS.
COLVEND, John Halliday
DALBEATTIE, James Copland
HAUGH OF URR, William Allan
KIRKBEAN, Rev. William Murray
KIRKGUNZEON, William Gillespie
SOUTHWICK, — Palmer

COACHES.
To DUMFRIES, a Coach (from Kirk-cudbright), calls at the Maxwell Arms, every evening (Sunday ex.) at seven.
To KIRKCUDBRIGHT, a Coach (from Dumfries), calls at the Maxwell Arms, every forenoon (Sunday excepted) at eleven; goes through Castle Douglas.

CARRIERS.
To AUCHENCAIRN, Hugh Milligan, every Thursday.
To COLVEND, Hugh Milligan, every Tuesday and Thursday.
To DUMFRIES, Hugh Milligan and James Watson, every Wed. and Sat.

GATEHOUSE-OF-FLEET

IS a neat modern town partly in the parish of Anwoth, but chiefly in that of Girthon, 105 miles s. s w. of Edinburgh, 50 E. of Portpatrick, 33 s. w. of Dumfries, and 7 w. of Kircudbright, lying chiefly on the east bank of the Fleet, at the entrance of that river into Fleet Bay. On account of the favourableness of the situation, and the moderate feu duties, Gatehouse has, in less than half a century, risen from a single inn, or stage house, to a manufacturing town of considerable note. It is well built, regular, and clean, the houses being generally of the same height, the streets running in straight lines, and crossing each other at right angles. A good stone bridge crosses the Fleet, connecting the principal part of the town with that in Anwoth parish. The situation of Gatehouse is truly beautiful, being seated in a romantic, fertile vale, embosomed in hills and mountains, which form a spacious and delightful amphitheatre. Some of the hills having their summits crowned, and their sides covered with hanging woods, interspersed with rich pasturage; while the higher and more distant mountains, point their naked blue heads to the sky, and exhibit all the rude grandeur and naked wildness of uncultivated nature.. This amphitheatre expands with a wide opening towards the south, and exposes full to the view a fine bay of the sea, which runs so far into the land as to appear from Gatehouse, like a large lake. At the foot of the town rolls the pure stream of the Fleet, which here meets the tide, and becomes navigable for vessels of sixty tons burden; and the navigation of the river has been considerably improved, at the sole expense of the proprietor, Mr. Murray, who, at a cost of 3000l. cut a canal in a straight line, from which vessels trading to the port have already derived incalculable advantage.

The exports of Gatehouse are principally grain; and its imports lime and coals; but the chief business is the spinning and manufacture of cotton goods, extensively carried on here, in the mills formerly built by Messrs. Birtwhistle and Sons, now repaired and worked with much spirit by Messrs. Davidson and Co., who have much enlarged the premises. Many families are employed in the weaving of muslin, which goes to the Carlisle or Glasgow markets. There are two extensive tan yards, and in the vicinity a large and well laid out nursery. Mines of lead and copper have been discovered in the neighbourhood, which have been wrought to some advantage. Gatehouse was erected into a burgh of barony in 1795, through the interest of Mr. Murray, who is proprietor of the town and parish. Its municipal government is vested in a provost, two bailies, and four councillors. A burgh court for the recovery of small debts not exceeding five pounds, is held every fortnight, and a justice of peace court sits every month for the parishes of Girthon and Anwoth.

The parish kirk, which is a commodious building, was erected in 1817, and its site is well chosen. Here are also a masonic lodge, a subscription news-room and library, and a parochial school. In this neighbourhood, in the parish of Anwoth, are the ancient castles of Ruscoe and Cardoness; a mile south of the town stands Cally, the noble residence of the proprietor, Mr. Murray; and at the distance of about two miles, are the neat villas of Ardwall and Cardoness. Saturday is the market day; a fair is held on the first Monday after the 17th of June, old style, and a cattle market on Friday, commencing on the third Saturday in September, continuing on that day for eight weeks.

POST OFFICE, Front-street, Janet M'Keand, *Post Mistress.*—Letters from DUMFRIES arrive every afternoon at half-past one, and are despatched every morning at one.—Letters from PORTPATRICK arrive every morning at one, and are despatched every afternoon at half-past one.

GENTRY AND CLERGY.
Brown Mr. John (agent to Alexander Murray, esq.), of Broughton
Campbell Mr. William. Roseville
Colomb Major George, Knockbrex
Gordon Mrs. Mary, Gatehouse
Hannay Miss, of Kirkdale
Hannay Robert, esq. of Rusko
Jeffrey Rev. Robert, Girthon manse
M'Cartney Mrs. Jean, Gatehouse
M'Culloch Alex. esq. Kirkclaugh
M'Culloch James Murray, esq. of Ardwall
Maxwell Sir David, of Cardoness
Murray Alex. esq. (of Broughton), Cally   [st
Smith the Misses Jean & Janet, Front
Stewart Alexander, J. P. Barharrow
Thomson Mrs. Dorothea, Front st

Turnbull Rev. Thos. Anwoth manse
Yorstoun Mrs. Castramount

ACADEMIES AND SCHOOLS.
Armstrong William, Old lodge
M'Adam Alexander, Croft st
PAROCHIAL, George Dunn, master, Front street
Wilson Eliza, Front st

AGENTS.
Long Henry (to manufacturers), Swan st
M'Adam David (shipping)
M'Taggart John (to manufacturers), Back street   [Swan st
Miller James (to manufacturers)
Williams Richard (mining) Front st

BAKERS.
Hunter Margaret, Front st
M'Minn Margaret, Front st

M'Robert Jean, Back st
Millar John, Front st
Parker Jean, Front st
Porter Janet, Front st

BANK.
COMMERCIAL BANK OF SCOTLAND (Branch)—(draws on Jones, Loyd & Co. London)—Richard Mundell, agent

BOOT AND SHOE MAKERS.
Blyth Mary, Front st
Dryburgh John, Front st
M'Lean William, Cross st
M'Taggart James, Front st
Murdoch Robert, Front st
Telford Samuel, Back st

CARTWRIGHTS.
Henry Samuel, Fleet st
M'Minn Alexander, Back st

516

COTTON SPINNERS.
Davidson James & Co. (and manufacturers)

FARMERS.
Black William, Goat end
Brown William, Enrick
Gardner John, Murray town
Rain James and John, Cully mains
Ramage William, Boreland

FIRE, &c. OFFICE AGENTS.
GLOBE, Richard Mundell, Fleet st
NORWICH UNION, James M'Nish

FLESHERS.
Forsyth James, Cross st
Muir John
Wilson James, Front st
Wilson Peter, Front st

GROCERS.
(See also Shopkeepers, &c.)
Bain Jas. (& ironmonger), Front st
Campbell James, Front st
Campbell Thomas, Front st
Cultart Robert (& tallow chandler), Front st

INN-KEEPERS & VINTNERS.
Anchor, Anthony Hewetson, Fleet st
Angel, Peter Wilson, Front st
Bay Horse, John Biers
Black Swan, James Roy, Front st
Blue Bell, William Munro, Back st
Commercial, David Sproat, Front st
Crown, Thomas Fowler, Front st
Crown and Thistle, James Murray, Fleet st
Earl Grey, David Kelvie, Cross st
Mason's Arms, John Finlay
Murray Arms Inn, John Nish [st
Robert Burns, James Robison, Cross
Royal Oak, Alex. Purdie, Cross st
Ship, James Cowan, Fleet st
Shoulder of Mutton, David Wilson
Thistle, John Denniston, Front st

JOINERS & CABINET MAKRS.
Cowan Alexander, Front st
Cunningham John, Fleet st
Gordon James, Back st
Grierson James, Back st
Kirk Andrew
M'Lachlan William
Snodgrass Peter, Front st

LINEN & WOOLLEN DRAPERS
Campbell James, Front st
Kirkpatrick James (& merchant), Front street
Menzies William, Front st

MILLINERS & DRESS MAKRS
Bell Jean, Front st
Carmont Elizabeth, Front st
Carson Janet, Front st
Jackson & Duncan, Front st [st
M'Geoch Catherine & Sisters, Front

NURSERY AND SEEDSMAN.
Credie David

PAINTERS & GLAZIERS.
Payne Andrew, Front st
Tait Joseph, Front st

SADDLER AND HARNESS MAKER.
Hannah John, Front street

SHIP OWNERS.
Kirkpatrick James, Front st
M'Master Robert, Fleet st

SHOPKEEPERS & DEALRS IN GROCERIES & SUNDRIES.
Dalzell Agnes, Front st
Denniston John, Front st
Donaldson John, Front st
Forsyth James, Cross st
Fowler Thomas, Front st
Hauning Alexander, Cross st
Kelvie David, Cross st
M'Millan John, Back st
M'Minn Margaret, Front st
Miller James, Swan st
Milligan Hugh, Front st
Murdoch Robert, Fleet st
Parker Jean, Front st
Pollock Martha, Fleet st
Porter James
Shannon Peter, Fleet st

SMITHS, &c.
Bain James, Front st
Bryce William, Fleet st [Back st
Halliday Archibald (& nail maker),
M'Donald Alexander, Cross st
Turner James, Front st

STONE MASONS.
Hume William and Sons
M'Clive John, Fleet st
M'Gae Charles & Brothers, Front st
M'Kie William, Fleet st
Stewart John & Son, Fleet st
Thomson James, Front st

SURGEONS.
Bennett James, Front st
Kennedy Charles, Front st
Watson James, Front st

TAILORS.
Clinton John, Front st
Garraway William, Front st

Graham William, Cross st
Kennedy John, Front st
Walker David, Fleet st
Walker James, Front st

TANNERS.
Blyth Samuel, Fleet Vale Cottage
Menzies Samuel

WRIGHTS.
See Joiners & Cabinet Makers, and also Cartwrights.

Miscellaneous.
Bell James, hoop maker
Finlay Andrew, watch maker, Front st
Gordon William, auctioneer, Front st
Halliday & Spiers, sawyers, Cally Saw mills
Hopkins Hugh, musician, Front st
Hyslop Mary, straw hat maker, Front st
Johnston John, linen weaver, Back st
Kirkpatrick James, stamp distributer and collector of taxes, Front st
M'Adam James, wool carder, Front st
M'Connell Alexander, cooper, Back st
M'Millan William Douglas, bookseller, stationer and binder, Fleet st
M'Nish James, writer, Front st
Morison James, maltster
Murray Peter, skinner, Front st
Pollock Hugh, tin-plate worker, Front st
Rae Margaret, druggist, Front st

COACHES.
To DUMFRIES, the *Royal Mail* (from Portpatrick), calls at the Murray Arms Inn, every morning at one; goes thro' Castle Douglas.
To PORTPATRICK, the *Royal Mail* (from Dumfries), calls at the Murray Arms Inn, every afternoon at half-past one; goes through Creetown, Newton Stewart, &c.

CARRIERS.
To CASTLE DOUGLAS, James Robinson, from his house, Cross street, and — Reside (from Wigton), every Tuesday.
To CREETOWN, Peter Walker, every Tuesday and Thursday—and Alexander M'Quaker & — Reside, every Thursday
To DUMFRIES, James Robinson and — Reside, every Tuesday.
To EDINBURGH, Samuel Mounsey, every Saturday—and — Pennycuick, once a fortnight.
To GLASGOW, Thomas Wallett and David M'Lure every Thurs. alternately
To KIRKCUDBRIGHT, James Lees, every alternate Friday.
To NEWTON STEWART and WIGTOWN — Reside, every Thursday.

KIRKCUDBRIGHT, TWYNHOLME & NEIGHBOURHOODS.

KIRKCUDBRIGHT is a royal burgh, the seat of a presbytery, and capital of the stewartry and parish of its name; 100 miles s.s.w. of Edinburgh, 55 E. of Portpatrick, and 28 s.w. of Dumfries; occupying a peninsular situation on the east or left side of the Dee, about six miles from the confluence of that river with the Solway Frith. Kirkcudbright is a town of considerable antiquity, but of its origin there is no authentic or even traditionary record; it is merely a matter of conjecture that it is as old as the church of St. Cuthbert, which was erected as early as the eighth century. The establishment of St. Cuthbert's church was followed by the construction of a small fort by the lords of Galloway, which in after-times was superseded by a castle in the proprietary of the crown, by whose authority the place was put under the government of a constable. During the domination of the Douglasses in Galloway, Kirkcudbright became a burgh of regality under their influence: on their forfeiture, James II erected the town into a royal burgh, by charter dated at Perth, 26th October, 1455; this grant was renewed and confirmed by Charles I, on the 20th July, 1633; and the burgh has since been under the government of a provost, two bailies, and thirteen councillors, with a treasurer and chamberlain; it joins with Dumfries, Annan, Sanquhar and Lochmaben in returning a member to parliament. The revenue of the corporation is considerably increased by the salmon fishings in the Dee; and the town derives a certain degree of consequence and advantage from being the seat of the stewartry courts.

Kirkcudbright, which has been materially improved within the last forty years, at the present day presents an aspect remarkably pleasing: within, it is regular, clean and neat; and externally it appears embosomed in the bountiful foliage of a fine sylvan country. It is composed of six or seven distinct streets, built at right angles with each other, and well paved; the houses, which are for the most part two stories high, have a respectable and comfortable appearance, and at once bespeak the taste and easy circumstances of the inhabitants. The stewartry buildings and gaol, erected in 1816, exhibit a highly imposing appearance; and from one of the lofty towers which surmount the latter an extensive view may be obtained of the beautiful environs of the town, including the ruins of the ancient castle of Kirkcudbright, built in 1582, by M'Clellan, ancestor of the present Lord Kirkcudbright. The former gaol and court-house is a very curious old edifice (with the market cross stuck up against it), supposed to have been erected about the middle of the sixteenth century. The burgh possesses but little trade besides that which is the off-spring of its own resources, and dependent upon its own consumption, essentially promoted by its resort as the county town and the residence of many opulent families. The manufacture of cotton goods and hosiery exists here to a limited extent, and the shops and inns are of the most respectable order; of the latter there are four of a superior grade, two in St. Cuthbert-street, and the other two in High-street; the 'Commercial Inn' is the principal posting house. The harbour is the best in the stewartry; at ordinary spring-tides the depth of water is thirty feet, and at the lowest neap-tides eighteen feet: it is well calculated for commercial purposes, but the place has no organized communication with any of the manufacturing districts. The river is navigable for two miles above the town, to the bridge of Tongland, which is constructed of one arch of one hundred and ten feet span, and picturesquely blends with the surrounding landscape. As yet there is no bridge across the Dee at Kirkcudbright, and passengers and carriages have to be ferried over in a flat-bottomed boat, or sort of floating bridge of peculiar formation; in stormy weather, however, or when there is an excessive current, this mode of conveyance is not without danger; and the construction of a drawbridge, to admit of vessels passing through, would be esteemed a great improvement as well as advantage to the district. There is a regular communication kept up between this place and Liverpool, by means of a steam-vessel, at least once a week. The established church, an old building, stands near the harbour, on the site of the Franciscan monastery, founded in the twelfth century; a new church is now in progress of erection: in High-street is a neat chapel belonging to the united associate congregation. The Kirkcudbright academy, or grammar-school, is a large and elegant edifice, comprising a spacious room for a public subscription library: there are likewise in the town news and billiard rooms, and a free-masons' lodge. The environs of Kirkcudbright are most delightful: the rising grounds on each side of the river, from Tongland to the sea, are embellished with thriving plantations; and the general prospect, both marine and inland, is truly lovely. St. Mary's Isle, a beautiful spot, the seat of the Earl of Selkirk, is about a mile from the town. The burgh is amply supplied with all domestic necessaries, and provisions are comparatively cheap. The market day is Friday, and there are two annual fairs, namely, on the 12th of August or following Friday, and the 29th September or Friday after.

The small village of TWYNHOLME, in the parish of its name, is situate three miles from Kirkcudbright, on the main road from Gatehouse to Castle Douglas. The soil is fertile, and the surface of the district rises into many small hills, partly arable. Of the extensive woods with which this part of Galloway was formerly covered, the only remains now existing are around the old castle of Campstone, a building pleasantly situated on an eminence nigh the junction of the rivers Dee and Tarf. The village contains a small neat parish kirk; and at a short distance from it is Barwhinnock, the seat and estate of P. L. M'Millan, Esq.

POST OFFICE, Castle-street, KIRKCUDBRIGHT, Charles James Finlayson, *Post Master.*—Letters from LONDON and EDINBURGH arrive every afternoon at two, and are despatched every night at ten.—Letters from PORTPATRICK arrive every morning at nine, and are despatched every forenoon at eleven.

NOBILITY, GENTRY AND CLERGY.

Brown Mr. Andrew, St. Cuthbert st
Caig Mr. David, Castle st
Carson Mrs. Elizabeth, High st
Carson the Misses, High street
Cochran Mrs. Elizabeth, St. Cuthbert street [High st
Drew the Misses Sarah & Margaret,
Dun Capt. John, G. M. Castle st
Edie Mrs. Penelope, Castle st
Gordon Alexander, esq. of Deebank and Campbellton
Gordon Col. James, of Balcarrie
Gordon Sir John, bart. of Earlston
Gordon Rev. Jno. Twynholme manse
Gordon the Misses, St. Cuthbert st
Hamilton Rev. George, High st
Hannay Mrs. John, Castle st
Henderson Mr. John, High st
Ireland William, esq. (of Barbey), sheriff substitute, High street
Irving Colonel, of Balmca
Ker Rev. David, Castle st
M'Call Miss Janet, Quay st
M'Caul Mrs. Grace, Castle st
M'Lellan Mrs. David, Castle st
M'Millan Patrick Lawrence, of Barwhinnock
M'Minn the Misses, St. Cuthbert st
M'Taggart Mrs. Jean, Castle st
Maitland Adam, esq. of Campstone
Maitland David, esq. of Barcaple
Melville Miss Jean, High st
Morrison Mrs. Catherine, Castle st
Muir Mrs. Jean, St. Cuthbert st
Mure Mr. William (factor to the Earl of Selkirk), High st
Napier Mr. John, High st
Paul Mr. John, High st
Roy Thomas, esq. Janefield
Selkirk the Right Hon. the Earl of, St. Mary's Isle
Sims Mrs. Elizabeth, Castle st
Smith Rev. Samuel, Borgue manse
Welch Mrs. Jean, Union st
Williamson Rev. Dougald Stewart, Tongland manse
Wood Rev. George, St. Cuthbert st

ACADEMIES & SCHOOLS.

Broom James, St. Mary's st
Coupland Margaret, High st
GRAMMAR SCHOOL, Kirkcudbright—Thomas M. Hope, *rector;* John Hope, *commercial & mathematical teacher;* Rev. William Mackenzie, *English teacher*
M'Millan Jane & Mary, Castle st
Mitchell John, Castle st
PAROCHIAL, Borgue—Wm. Poole, master; — Currie, assistant
PAROCHIAL, Twynholme — John Adamson, master [master
PAROCHIAL, Tongland—John Kelly,

AGENTS TO MANUFACTURERS.

Cairns Elizabeth, High mill burn
Gordon John, St. Mary st

BAKERS.

Bain William, High st
Douglas Ellen, High st
Greive John, High st
Hobson Margaret, High st
M'Cleave James, High st
M'Lennan John, High st

BANK.

BANK OF SCOTLAND (Branch)—(draws on the Bank of England, Coutts and Co. and Smith, Payne and Smiths, London)—William Hannay M'Lellan, agent; Adam Bell, agent

BOOKSELLERS, STATIONERS, AND PRINTERS.

Cannon John (& stamp office) High st
Gordon Alexander, High st [st
Nicholson John (& tea dealer) Castle

BOOT & SHOE MAKERS.

Angus John, Union st
Caird George, High st
Gray David, High st
Hornel John and James, High st
Hornel William, High st
Jamieson William, Castle st

COOPERS.

Anderson John, High st
Beattie Robert, High st
M'Dowall John, High st

EARTHENWARE DEALERS.

Cannon John, Kirkcudbright
Stevenson Jane, High st

FLESHERS.

Gourlay Henry, Castle st
Johnston David, High st
M'Ewen Thomas, High st
Noble William, High st
Rain William, High st
Stewart John, High st

GROCERS & SPIRIT DEALERS.

(*See also Shopkeepers, &c.*)
Casteen John, High st [st
Caran James (& shipping agent) High
Hornel James, jun. High st
Johnston William, High st
M'Kinnell William, High st [st
M'Myn William (tea dealer) St. Mary
M'Whinnie Jane, High st [st
Sproat Thomas (& ironmonger) High

INNS.

Commercial, Robert Carson (& posting house) St. Cuthbert st
Galloway Arms, David Kissock, St. Cuthbert street [High st
King's Arms, Janet Malcomson,
Selkirk Arms, Margt. Kissock, High st

JOINERS & CABINET MAKRS.

Blaind John, Twynholme
Fergusson Peter, High st
M'Ewen James, St. Cuthbert st
M'Kay William, High miln burn
M'Nish James, Twynholme
Murray John, Bank of Bishoptown
Robertson Samuel, Castle dykes
Thomson John (and cartwright), Twynholme

LINEN & WOOLLEN DRAPRS.

Beattie Jonathan, Castle st
Black John, St. Cuthbert st
M'Clune Agnes, High st

MILLER.

Birkmire James, Mill burn

MILLINERS AND DRESS MAKERS.

Callie Jean and Margaret, Union st
Erskine Janet and Ann, Castle st
Gourlay Ellen and Grace, Highmiln burn
Kissock Margaret, Wynd

NAIL MAKERS.

Gordon William, High st
Gourlay James, High st
Halliday John, High st
M'Knight Alexander, Castle st
Price John, High st
Wilson Andrew, High st

PAINTERS & GLAZIERS.

Chrystal Robert, Castle st
Erskine Robert, Castle st
Fergusson Robert, Castle st
M'Murray James, Castle st
M'Murray William, Castle st
Morrison Thomas, Union st

SHIP BUILDERS.

Campbell James, Old yard, Quay
M'Ewen & Jenkinson, New yard, Quay

SHIP OWNERS.

Bee Robert, St. Cuthbert st
Caig David, Castle st
Cavan James, High st
Christal James, Castle st
Conning John, St. Cuthbert st
Dickson James, St. Cuthbert st
GALLOWAY STEAM NAVIGATION
  Compy, Jas. Cavan, agent, High st
Grant John, High st
Johnston William, High st
M'Cleave James, High st
M'Clure John, High st
M'Keachie James, High st
M'Kinnell William, High st
M'Murray Robert, Castle st
Mitchell John, Tongland bar
Pain William, Sandside
Rankine James, St. Cuthbert st
Sproat Thomas, High st
Sproat William, Tongland
Wishart George, Twynholme

SHOPKEEPERS & DEALERS IN SUNDRIES.

Marked thus * are also Spirit Dealers.

Brown Elizabeth, Castle st
Cairns Agnes, Union st
Cairns Elizabeth, Highmiln burn
Cavan Samuel, High st
*Cavan William, St. Mary st
Davies Robert, Twynholme
Gourlay Peter, High st
Grant John, High st.
*Gray Jean, High st
*Grieve John, High st
Guthrie Hugh, High st
Kinean Janet & Margaret, Union st
M'Cleave James, High st
*M'Ewen Mary, High st
M'Whinnie Thomas, High st
M'Whinnie William, St. Cuthbert st
Peat Elizabeth, Castle st
Rae Samuel, Castle st
Rain John, Twynholme
Telfer Catherine, Castle st

SLATERS.

Clark David, St. Cuthbert st
Clark David, jun. St. Mary st
Clark Thomas, St. Mary st

SMITHS.

Anderson Thomas, High st
Mitchell James, Twynholme
Puries Thomas, Twynholme
Seggie William, High st

Stivenson Samuel, High st
Wasson Wm. Bank of Bishopton

STONE MASONS.

M'Keachie James, High st
M'Murray Robert, High st
Milligan James, St. Mary st
Sharpe Brothers, Union st

SURGEONS.

Blair David, High st
Hamilton Gavin, Castle st
Hewitson John, Castle st
Shand John S. M.D. High st

TAILORS.

Carter James, High st
Dixon John, High st
Gibson James & Sons, St. Mary st
M'Kinnell Alexander, High st
Nairn Joseph, High st

TALLOW CHANDLERS.

Brown Elizabeth, Castle st
Christal Robert, Castle st

TINSMITHS.

Finlayson Charles James (& ironmonger), Castle st
M'Murray James, Castle st

VINTNERS.

Armstrong Isabella (Ship), Shore
Black Nicholas (Farmers' Arms),
  top of High street
Clarke John, High st
Gordon Jno.(Cross Keys),St.Mary st
Houston John, Castle sod
Knox John (Masons' Arms), High st
Leiter John (Rose), St. Cuthbert st
M'Intyre John (Crown & Anchor),
  Waterloo street   [Castle st
M'Intyre Jno.(St. Cuthbert's Lodge)
M'Whan David (Royal Oak), Quay
Mitchell John, Tongland bridge
Postlethwaite Ellen, High st
Rae Alx.(SteamBoat)St.Cuthbert st

WATCH & CLOCK MAKERS.

Halliday Robert, Union st
Law William, High st
M'George John, High st

WINE & SPIRIT MERCHANTS.

Finlayson Charles James, Castle st
M'Knight Samuel, High st

WRITERS & NOTARIES.

Burnie James, St. Cuthbert st
Gordon William J. B. (& procurator
  fiscal for the county), High st
Johnston Bryce, St. Cuthbert st
Low William Campbell (& procura-
  tor fiscal), St. Cuthbert st

Macbean William, Castle st
Melville David (steward and com-
  missary clerk), High st   [st
Morrison David (writer) St. Cuthbert
More and Mackenzie, High st
Murray Andrew (writer) St. Cuth-
  bert street   [st
Niven David (&clerk of supply) High
Skeoch Alexander, St. Cuthbert st

Miscellaneous.

Brydson John, general dealer, High st
Callie John, harbour master, St. Mary st
Clark John, session clerk, High st
COUNTY GAOL, High street—Alexander
  Munro, gaoler   [Jolly, collector
CUSTOM HOUSE, High street—David M.
Findlay John, distiller, Bank of Bishopton
Gillone John, land surveyor, Twynholme
Hay Peter, plumber, High st
Kelly Daniel, dyer, Back High st
Law Isabella, straw hat maker, High st
M'Ewen John, button maker, High st
M'Millan Jno. & Wm. sawyers, Boreland
Murray William, saddler, High st
NEWS ROOM, High st—John C. Mac-
  kenzie, secretary   [bert st
Rankine James, timbermerchant, St. Cuth-
Seggie Ann, meal seller, High st   [st
Smith Wm. clogger & leather cuttr, St. Mary
STAMP OFFICE, High st—James Cannon,
  distributer
Thomson James, hair cutter, High st
Waugh James, auctioneer, Castle yard

COACH.

To DUMFRIES, a Coach, from the Commercial Inn, every afternoon at four;
goes thro' Castle Douglas & Dalbeattie.

CARRIERS.

To CASTLE DOUGLAS, Saml. Mouncey, David M'Clure and Thos. Wallett,
from the Commercial Inn, every Friday.
To DUMFRIES, William M'Knight,
from High street, every Tuesday.
To EDINBURGH, Samuel Mouncey,
from the Commercial Inn, every Friday
—and Hugh Pennycuick, from the Selkirk Arms, once a fortnight.
To GATEHOUSE, James Lees, from
his house, and Hugh Pennycuick, from
the Selkirk Arms, once a fortnight.
To GLASGOW, Thomas Wallett and
David M'Lure alternately, from the
Commercial Inn, every Friday.
To NEW GALLOWAY, — M'Cutcheon,
from the Commercial Inn, every Friday.

CONVEYANCE BY WATER.

To LIVERPOOL, the *Countess of Galloway*, steam packet.

KIRKPATRICK-DURHAM AND OLD BRIDGE OF URR.

KIRKPATRICK-DURHAM is a small village in the parish of its name, 85 miles s.s.w. of Edinburgh, 14 s.e. of New Galloway, 13 w. of Dumfries, 7 e. of Parton, and 6 n. of Castle Douglas; situate on a streamlet that falls into the Urr. The parish, which is skirted by the Urr water on its western side, derives its name from the old church dedicated to St. Patrick, and Durham, a hamlet where it stood—the latter appellation signifying the 'hamlet on the water.' Formerly, a woollen mill furnished employment to many inhabitants of the village, but it is now undistinguished by manufactures of any kind, and is a place of no trade but that which belongs to a few shops for the reciprocal accommodation of the inhabitants. The parish, which is between nine and ten miles in length, and about four miles in breadth, is partly pastoral and partly arable; the former character prevailing in the north, the latter in the south of the district. One annual fair is held on the first Thursday after the 17th of March, old style.

OLD BRIDGE of URR is a small village in the parish of Kirkpatrick-Durham, two miles therefrom, seated on the banks of Urr Water; it contains only a few houses, and a small dying establishment.

POST OFFICE, KIRKPATRICK-DURHAM, Joseph Leslie, *Post Master.*—Letters from DUMFRIES arrive every forenoon at eleven, and from CASTLE DOUGLAS every afternoon at half-past three, and are despatched (by foot post) every afternoon at five.

GENTRY AND CLERGY.

Campbell Major Jas. Walton park
Duncan Rev. George John, Walton
  cottage
Ireland William, esq. (sheriff sub.)
  of Dunpark
Jones Mrs. of Brooklands   [hill
Lamont Rev. David, D.D. Durham
Maitland Mrs. of Chippercail
Martin Mrs. Mary, of Kilwhannity
Skirving Robert, esq. of Croys

INNKEEPERS & VINTNERS.

Barkley John
Boar's Head, Patrick Roxburgh
  vias. Elizabeth Armstrong
Royal Oak, John Oliver
Swan, Mary M'Neill

SHOPKEEPERS, TRADERS, &c.

*** The names without address are in
KIRKPATRICK-DURHAM.

Affleck Robert, shopkeeper   [Urr
Affleck Wm. shopkeeper, Bridge of

Affleck William, nail maker
Armstrong John, tailor   [Urr
Beattie James, cartwright, Bridge of
Broadfoot Alex. miller, Bridge of Urr
Chartres David, stone mason
Dawson Isabella, shopkeeper
Douglas Joseph, joiner
Fergusson Samuel, master of paro-
  chial school
Fergusson Thomas, joiner
Flowers Janet, shopkeeper

SHOPKEEPERS, &c.—*Continued.*
Gray William, farrier
Hansley John, shopkeeper
Ker William, dyer, Bridge of Urr
Kirk John, draper
Leslie Jos. shopkeeper   [of Urr
M'Dougal Andw.blacksmith,Bridge

M'George Jas. flesher & shopkeeper
M'George John, blacksmith
M'Gill Thomas, tailor
M'William John, flesher
Milligan John, joiner
Milligan Robert, slater
Shaw Mary, baker

Sloan Robert and Thomas, shoe makers
Smith James, schoolmaster, Drumhumphry
Tait Joseph, blacksmith
Turner James, joiner,   [of Urr
Watson James, stone mason, Bridge

LAWRIESTON AND NEIGHBOURHOOD.

LAWRIESTON is a small village in the parish of Balmaghie, 23 miles w. of Dumfries, 10 N. of Kirkcudbright, the like distance s. s. E. of New Galloway, and 7 N.W. of Castle Douglas. On the north west the village is skirted by a mountainous district, which abounds with various kinds of game : on the east the land is more fertile. The parish has several small lakes and a number of mineral springs, among the latter Lochenbreck Well is a place of some resort in the summer. About a mile west of the village is the mansion of W. K. Lawrie, Esq. the principal proprietor of it. The parish kirk stands three miles to the east.

POST OFFICE, John Bennett, *Post Master.*—Letters from CASTLE DOUGLAS arrive (by foot post) every afternoon at half-past two, and are despatched every evening at six.

GENTRY AND CLERGY.
Cunningham John, esq. of Hensol
Gordon Capt. Jas. Balmaghie house
Henderson Rev. James, Balmaghie manse   [Woodhill
Lawrie William Kennedy, esq. of
INNKEEPERS & VINTNERS.
Black Bull, James Doig
Compass & Square, John Durham

Crown, David M'Crae
Lochenbreck Well, Robert Laudsborough, Lochenbreck
SHOPKEEPERS,TRADERS,&c.
Bean Samuel, slater
Burnet John, shopkeeper
Dalziell John, shoe maker
Lawrie John, joiner & cartwright
Liviston & Durham, joiners

M'Dowall Samuel, miller
M'Laudsborough Saml. shopkeeper
M'Vane Peter, shoe maker
M'Vittie William, master of parochial school
Miller Alexander, tailor
Muir Andrew, tailor
Sproat William, blacksmith
Strachan William, shopkeeper

NEW ABBEY AND NEIGHBOURHOOD.

NEW ABBEY is a small village in the parish of its name, 80 miles s. of Edinburgh, 12 E. of Dalbeattie, and 7 s. by w. of Dumfries, situate at the eastern extremity of the county, near to the mouth of the Nith. The parish, which was originally called Kirkinder, takes its present name from the once celebrated religious establishment of New Abbey, a monastery founded in the thirteenth century, for the Cistertian order of monks, by Dovergilla, daughter of Alan, lord of Galloway, niece to David, Earl of Huntingdon, spouse to John Baliol, lord of Castle Barnard, and mother of John Baliol, the imbecile competitor for the crown. The village derives its chief, indeed its only consequence, from the contiguity of the ruins of this once important religious establishment. From the dimensions of the abbey and church, as given by Grose, they must have been of great magnitude. Although much dilapidated for the sake of the stones, the remains of the structure are still very extensive, and form an interesting object of research to the antiquarian, while the beauty of the surrounding scenery is well calculated to gratify the most fastidious taste. On the north and south lie the woods of Shambelly, and on the south Loch Kindar, and the dark braes of Criffel, the lofty hill of which rises to the height of 2,000 feet above the sea, from which it is a mile distant. Besides that of Kindar, there are two other lakes in the parish, namely, Lochend and Craigend. The parish kirk stands on the south side of the abbey church, having been formed of that part of the ruins. In the village is a Roman catholic chapel and the parochial school.

POST OFFICE, Walter Miller, *Post Master.*—Letters from DUMFRIES and all parts arrive every afternoon at two, and are despatched every afternoon at three.

GENTRY & CLERGY.
Esbie John, esq. of Abbey bank
Hamilton Rev. James, Manse
Riddel J. R. esq. of Kintarvie
Smith Robert, esq. of Loch bank
Stewart William, esq. of Shambelly
Wightman John, esq. of Garlaff
SHOPKEEPERS & TRADERS.
The names without address are in NEW ABBEY.
Caid James, grocer
Calvert J. manager of saw mill

Connal David, tailor, Inglestonford
Copland James, blacksmith,Carbilly
Copland William, bacon curer, Old Shambelly   [Locharber
Harris Robert,blacksmith&vintner,
Ireland John, blacksmith
M'Kie S. master of parochial school
Mein Robert, mason and flesher
Millar Archibald, miller
Miller Walter, grocer
Mundel James, shoe maker

Nelson John, shoe maker, Gate end
Rankine James, blacksmith
Seaton James, joiner
Seeds Daniel, tailor   [mill
Thomson James,wool carder,Wauk
Thomson James, joiner
Turner John, vintner
Walker Samuel, shoe maker

CARRIER.
To DUMFRIES, John Thomson, every Wednesday and Saturday.

NEW GALLOWAY,
WITH THE PARISHES OF BALMACLELLAN, DALRY, AND CARSPHAIRN.

NEW GALLOWAY is a small town and royal burgh, in the parish of Kells ; 84 miles s. s.w. of Edinburgh, 25 w. of Dumfries, 18 N. E. of Newton Stewart, 14 N.W. of Castle Douglas, and 8 N. W. of Parton ; pleasantly situate on the west bank of the river Ken, over which, in the year 1822, an elegant stone bridge of five arches was erected ; this structure, lying in the valley below the town, has a very pleasing effect : at its completion a dinner was given, by Lord Viscount Kenmure, to fourteen of the oldest inhabitants of the town, whose united ages amounted to 1,264 years. The houses of the town stretch along the public road, and form a single tolerably well-built street ; the business of the place is confined to the local domestic retail and handicraft branches. Its burghal charter was conferred by Charles I, and the municipal government vested in a provost, two bailies, and fifteen councillors. A justice of peace court is held on the first Monday in every month, for the recovery of debts under £5 ; attached to the court is a criminal and debtors' gaol, with a steeple and town clock. The burgh unites with Wigvn, Strauraer and Whithorn in returning a member to parliament. On the north side of the town, within the distance of half a mile, is the parish church, a neat stone edifice, with a square tower in the centre, built in 1822 ; in the same year a Sunday-school was established, in which upwards of one hundred children are gratuitously taught by the inhabitants. At a short distance south of the town stands the ancient castle of Kenmure, once a place of considerable strength ; Mary Queen of Scots lodged in it one night, on her way from this country to England. Loch Ken, which joins the town, is four miles and a half long, and in many places more than a mile broad ; it abounds with pike and perch, and some of the former have been caught of the astonishing weight of 50 and 60 lbs. Fairs are held on the first Wednesday after the 12th of April, the first Wednesday after the 12th of July, the first Wednesday after the 12th of August, and the first Wednesday after the 12th of November.

DALRY is rather a populous village, in the parish of its name, lying on the east bank of the river Ken : the southern portion of the district is situate in a beautiful valley, composed of rich arable land ; the high grounds

3

are pastoral, and graze considerable numbers of cattle and sheep. The village of Dalry (the name of which signifies 'the dale of the king') is surrounded with delightful scenery. There are several lakes in the parish; the largest, called Loch Invar, covers an area of fifty acres: in the lake stand the remains of an ancient castle, formerly belonging to the Gordons, Knights of Lochinvar, and latterly Viscounts of Kenmure. Besides Dalry, there is a small village in the parish, called John's Clachan, agreeably situate on the margin of the Ken. The population of Dalry village amounts to about six hundred.

CARSPHAIRN village, which is situate near the river Deogh, contains a neat parish kirk, the manse, a pa-rochial school, and a few scattered houses. The parish is somewhat extensive, but thinly populated; it is the most northerly and mountainous district in the stewartry, and is chiefly devoted to grazing. This parish, with those of Dalry, Kells, and Balmaclellan, are designated the district of Glenkens—famed for the true breed of black-faced sheep and black cattle, as also for good horses of the Galloway breed.

The small village of BALMACLELLAN (in the parish of its name) is situate on the opposite side of the Ken to New Galloway, not far from the confluence of the stream with the head of Loch Ken, twelve miles south-west of Minnyhive. The parish is of a moory character, interspersed with some inconsiderable lakes.

POST OFFICE, NEW GALLOWAY, John Muir, *Post Master.*—Letters from CASTLE DOUGLAS and all parts arrive every afternoon at three, and are despatched every evening at seven.

POST OFFICE, DALRY, William M'Clellan, *Post Master.*—Letters from CASTLE-DOUGLAS arrive every afternoon at half-past three, and are despatched every afternoon at half-past one.

NOBILITY, GENTRY AND CLERGY.

Alexander John Shaw, esq. (of Glenhoul), Dalry
Baird Mr. James, Craighead, Dalry
Barber Mr. James, Dalshangan, Carsphairn [manse
Cullen Rev. Gavin, Balmaclellan
Dalziell Mrs. Ivy lodge, New Galloway
Gordon Mr. Anthony, Dalry
Hobbs Mrs. Meadow bank, New Galloway
Kenmure the Right Hon. Viscount, Kenmure castle [ling), Kells
Kennedy David, esq. (of Knocknal-M'Millan Mr. Jas. Lamloch, Carsphairn [phairn
M'Millan Mr. Robert, Holm, Carsphairn
Maitland Rev. Jas. Kells manse
Ritchie Rev. Alexander, Dalry
Spalding John Eden, esq. (of Holm) Balmaclellan
Welch Rev. —, Carsphairn manse

BLACKSMITHS.

M'Bride John, Balmaclellan
M'Kie James, Dalry
M'Lellan William, Dalry
M'Murtree Duncan, Carsphairn
M'Nish John, Balmaclellan
M'Queen James, Dalry
Turner Matthew, New Galloway
Turner William, New Galloway

BOOT AND SHOE MAKERS.

Chesters Robert, New Galloway
Crosbie John & Son, New Galloway
Murdoch Robert, Dalry

GROCERS AND DRAPERS.

(See also Shopkeepers, &c.)
Donaldson James, Dalry
M'Kay John, New Galloway
Regan Patrick (draper), Dalry
Wallace Alexander (and hardware-man), New Galloway

INN-KEEPERS & VINTNERS.

Commercial, Wm. M'Clellan, Dalry
Cross Keys, Jas. M'Crae, Carsphairn
Cross Keys, Thomas M'Kilvie, New Galloway
Dempster James, Carsphairn
Kenmure Arms, Isabella Wilson, New Galloway [Dalry
Kenmure Bridge, James M'Garva, M'Millan Daniel, Balmaclellan
Plough, John Cowan, Dalry
Shoulder of Mutton, James Donaldson, Dalry [Galloway
Town's Arms, Wm. Turner, New

JOINERS.

Candlish John, Dalry
Corson Alexander, Dalry
Douglas John, New Galloway
Gordon Peter, Balmaclellan
Johnston Robert, New Galloway
M'Candlish Wm. New Galloway
M'Culloch John, New Galloway
M'Gill James, (& cartwright) Dalry
M'Kay William, Carsphairn
M'Millan Robert, Carsphairn

SHOPKEEPERS & DEALERS IN SUNDRIES.

Marked thus * are also Spirit dealers.
Ballantyne James, Carsphairn
*Bell John, Dalry
*Black Joseph, Balmaclellan
Campbell Agnes, Carsphairn
*Cown John, Dalry
Hall John, Dalry
Hastings Robert, Carsphairn
Shannon John, Dalry
Sloane Sarah, Balmaclellan
Smyth James, New Galloway
Wood Cutler, Dalry

STONE MASONS.

Hawthorn William, New Galloway
Patterson Thomas, New Galloway

TAILORS.

Candlish James, New Galloway
Galloway James, New Galloway
Haining Peter, Dalry
Houston John, Dalry
Little Archibald, New Galloway
M'Kie Peter, Dalry
Patterson John, New Galloway

WRIGHTS—See Joiners.

Miscellaneous.

Andrew John, factor to Lord Glenlee, Glenlee park [New Galloway
Candlish Wm. ironmonger & spirit dealer, Douglas Archibald and Son, surgeons, New Galloway
Kennedy James, surveyor of taxes for East District of Stewartry, New Galloway
Lamont Jas. stocking makr. New Galloway
M'Call Thomas, auctioneer and sheriff's officer, Dalry
M'Gill James, flesher, New Galloway
M'Lean Ronald, turner, Dalry
M'Millan David, surveyor of taxes for West District of Stewartry, View field
M'Turk Robert & William, cattle dealers, Waterside, Kells
Martin Samuel, miller, New Galloway
Young Robert, excise officer, New Galloway

PAROCHIAL SCHOOLS.

BALMACLELLAN, Jas. M'Kay, master
CARSPHAIRN, — Sloane, master
DALRY, Peter Moore, master
KELLS, John Muir, master, New Galloway

COACHES.

To AYR, a Coach (from Dumfries), calls at the Cross Keys, Carsphairn, every Monday, Wednesday and Friday forenoon at eleven.
To DUMFRIES, a Coach (from Ayr), calls at the Cross Keys, Carsphairn, every Tuesday, Thursday and Saturday afternoon at four.

CARRIERS.

To CASTLE DOUGLAS, D. M'Clure or T. Wallett (from Glasgow), pass through Dalry, every Monday.
To DUMFRIES, Robert M'William, from New Galloway, & George Neilson, from Dalry, every Tuesday—and John M'Cutcheon, from New Galloway, once a fortnight.
To EDINBURGH, David Rorison, from Dalry, once a fortnight.
To GLASGOW, D. M'Clure or T. Wallett, pass through Dalry, every Monday.
To KIRKCUDBRIGHT, John M'Cutcheon, from New Galloway, every alternate Friday.

PALNACKIE,

OR GARDEN, is the principal village in the parish of Buittle, 18 miles s. w. of Dumfries, 14 N. of Kirkcudbright, and 6 s. of Castle Douglas; eligibly situate on the water of Urr, where there is a good harbour capable of receiving vessels of two hundred tons burthen, having, at ordinary spring tides, a depth of thirty feet water. It is the chief port for supplying the surrounding neighbourhood with coal and various other sea borne necessaries. The parish is bounded on the east by the Urr, on the south by the Solway Frith, and on the west by Kelton. It is a fertile and agricultural district, extending 8 miles in length by 3 in breadth.

POST OFFICE, Thomas Dalling, *Post Master.*—Letters from CASTLE DOUGLAS arrive (by foot post) every afternoon at two, and are despatched every evening at seven in summer and six in winter.

GENTRY AND CLERGY.

Crosby Rev. Alex. Buittle manse
M'Knight John, esq. of Barlochan
Maxwell Francis, esq. of Breoch
Reid John, esq. of Kirkinnan
Robinson Mrs. Mary, of Almorness

PUBLIC HOUSES.

Anchor, John Robson
Royal Oak, Thomas Dalling
Ship, William Candlish

SHOPKEEPERS & TRADERS.

Anderson Archibald, shoe maker
Black Maxwell, joiner
Candlish David, blacksmith
Dalling Joseph, stone mason
Dalling Thomas, shopkeeper
Heuchan James, joiner
Heuchan William, blacksmith
Horuel William, tailor
Kevan Janet, shopkeeper

M'Adam George, tide waiter
Palmer Jas. master of parish school
Raleigh John, joiner
Welch William, miller
Wright Joseph, cooper

CARRIERS.

To CASTLE DOUGLAS, GLASGOW, and KIRKCUDBRIGHT, David M'Clure, once a fortnight.
To DALBEATTIE, Hugh Milligan, every Thursday.

WIGTONSHIRE.

THIS county, which forms the western part of the ancient district of Galloway, occupies the south-western extremity of Scotland: it is bounded on the east by the stewartry of Kirkcudbright (or Eastern Galloway), also by Wigtown bay; on the south and west it is girded by the Irish Sea, and on the north by the county of Ayr. The extent of the shire from north to south is about thirty miles, and (including Luce Bay) its breadth from east to west is about thirty miles: the superficial contents of the county (adopting a medium calculation betwixt conflicting authorities) may be taken at 484 square miles, or 309,760 statute acres—of which about one-third, perhaps, is cultivated. The Bay of Luce indents the land to the extent of fifteen miles, and forms two promontories; at the southern extremity of the western projection is the Mull of Galloway, while the apex of the eastern is called Burrow Head; these two peninsular headlands are also known by the Celtic name of the *Rhinns* (*Rhyns* or *Rinos*) of Galloway. On the north another promontory is formed by the intersection of Loch Ryan. At the epoch of the Roman power obtruding itself into North Britain, the ancient British tribe of the *Novantes* inhabited the whole of eastern and western Galloway, having *Leucophibia* (the modern Whithorn) for their principal town, and *Rerigonium* (Loch Ryan) for their principal port. The Anglo-Saxons overran the district in the sixth century; and Oswie, the Northumbrian king, settled at Whithorn. During the ninth and tenth centuries the country on the west was inhabited by the Picts from Ireland and the Isle of Man; and hence the name of *Galloway*, or 'the country of the Gael,' was conferred on the territory. About the twelfth century Galloway passed into the hands of the Scottish king, Alexander II. In the sanguinary contests which originated in the competition of Bruce and Baliol, the chieftains of Galloway long remained attached to the party of the latter, whose family they sheltered after Edward Bruce had subdued the whole country. The family of Douglas subsequently became possessed of the lordship of Galloway; but, on the attainder of the nobleman of that name in 1455, the title became extinct: it was revived, however, and now bestows an earldom on the distinguished family of Stewart and Garlies.

SOIL, CLIMATE, PRODUCE, &c.—This shire is one of the most level districts in Scotland; and the hills, of which there are none of great altitude, are generally pretty free from the encumbrance of rocks. The best lands lie near the shores—the inland divisions being more elevated, and largely mixed with heath and moss. The major part of the SOIL is of a hazel colour, and is of that kind sometimes called a dry loam, though it often inclines to a gravelly nature. The county presents an exposure to the south, and its waters mostly descend to the Irish Sea. The CLIMATE is moist, with winds from the south-west, which prevail during the greater part of the year, usually accompanied with rains; yet, when proper attention is exercised by the agriculturist, the moisture of the climate is but seldom injurious to the products of the earth: snow rarely lies long, and frosts are not generally severe or of tedious duration. In early times this district of Galloway, like most other sections of the country, was covered with woods; and in modern days planting has been pursued most extensively: it is said that, during twenty years, the Earl of Stair annually planted twenty thousand trees. The salutary improvements that have been effected in the agriculture of this county have been, with some justice, ascribed to the efforts of the agricultural society of Dumfries; the spirit and practice of husbandry gradually spread from that shire to Kirkcudbright, and thence penetrated into Wigtonshire: since that period, rents have risen rapidly; and corn and other products of tillage, black cattle, wool, sheep and swine, are now largely exported. The district has long been celebrated for its breed of horses, distinguished by the appellation of 'Galloways;' they are of the Spanish or rather Moorish race, and, when the breed is pure, of a dun colour with a black line along the back: these animals are small, but active, sinewy and spirited. The mineral resources of this county are by no means extensive: there is no coal, at least for any useful purpose; and, although there is plenty of iron ore, the absence of the former article renders the latter of comparatively little value: in the northern part of the

'Rhinns' the existence of sandstone has been ascertained; quarries of slate, of different qualities, are found in various places; and lead mines were formerly wrought within the district.

RIVERS and MOUNTAINS.—This county has no considerable rivers; the principal are the CREE, the BLADENOCH and the TARF, with a few of smaller size. The Cree, which is a boundary river between this county and the stewartry of Kirkcudbright, rises in Carrick, in Ayrshire; after forming a lake at the head of Wigtonshire, it flows again as a stream, and, passing Newton-Stewart on the east, falls into a creek at the head of Wigtown Bay. The Bladenoch also has its source in Carrick, and, after running a course of twenty-four miles, falls into Luce Bay. The Tarf issues from a small lake, called Loch Whinnoch, in the parish of Girthon, Kirkcudbright; and, after a course of twenty-one miles, unites with the Dee. The MOUNTAINS, with their elevations above the level of the sea, are, Lang, 1,758 feet; Mochrum Fell, 1,020; Knock of Luce, 1,014; and Barhullion, 814.

Wigtonshire comprehends seventeen parishes, and has three Royal and Parliamentary Burghs, namely, WIGTOWN, STRANRAER and WHITHORN; with these is associated New Galloway in returning a member to parliament, and the COUNTY sends another representative. The burghs of barony in the shire are Newton-Stewart, Garlieston, Glenluce and Portpatrick: it has several thriving villages, and a number of small sea-ports or natural harbours; and is ornamented by many splendid mansions and elegant seats of its nobility and gentry.

———oo———

POPULATION OF WIGTONSHIRE,

IN THE YEARS 1801, 1811, 1821, AND 1831, WITH THE INCREASE IN THIRTY YEARS.

The Italic letters, b. and p. respectively signify Burgh and Parish.

	1801.	1811.	1821.	1831.	Increase in 30 Years.		1801.	1811.	1821.	1831.	Increase in 30 Years.
Glasserton..............p.	860	1047	1057	1194	334	Mochrum..............p.	1113	1345	1871	2105	992
Inch ....p.	1577	1831	2386	2521	944	Penningham and........p.	} 1569	2847	3090	3461	1892
Kirkcolm ....p.	1191	1465	1821	1895	705	Newton-Stewart ..town					
Kirkcowan ....p.	787	1006	1283	1374	587	Portpatrick ....p.	1090	1302	1818	2239	1149
Kirkinner ....p.	1160	1433	1488	1514	354	Sorby..................p.	1091	1265	1319	1412	321
Kirkmaiden ....p.	1613	1719	2210	2051	438	Stoneykirk ....p.	1848	2364	3133	2966	1118
Leswalt................p.	1329	1705	2332	2636	1307	Stranraer..........b. & p.	1722	1923	2463	3329	1607
Luce, New ... .p.	368	457	609	628	260	Whithorn ....b. & p.	1904	1935	2361	2415	511
Luce, Old..............p.	1221	1536	1957	2180	959	Wigtown ....b. & p.	1475	1711	2042	2337	862
						TOTAL POPULATION OF WIGTONSHIRE........	21918	26891	33240	36258	14340

The total annual value of Real Property in this county, as assessed in April, 1815, amounted to £143,425.

GARLIESTON AND SORBY.

GARLIESTON is a sea-port village in the parish of Sorby, finely situate at the head of Garlieston bay (a small haven on the west side of Wigton bay), and opposite Fleet bay. The place is built in the form of a semicircle, facing the sea, with a safe and commodious harbour, capable of receiving a great number of vessels; and if a breakwater was carried out to a rock called the Allen, which could be effected at an expense comparatively trifling with the benefit that would result from the improvement, vessels might here take shelter, when wind-bound, at all times of the tide, which at the spring-flow rises eighteen feet. A regular communication is now maintained between this port and Liverpool, by the 'Countess of Galloway' steam-packet, once a fortnight. The Broughton and Poutenburn streams, which here flow into the bay, are crossed by several bridges. Galloway House, a splendid mansion, the seat of the Earl of Galloway, erected in 1740, is adjacent on the south; it is surrounded by beautiful plantations and pleasure-grounds, and the walks about it, for several miles, are extremely picturesque, and the prospects on every side delightful.

SORBY (or *Sorbie*) is a village in the parish of its name, 39 miles E. of Portpatrick, 30 s E. of Stranraer, 13 s. of Newton Stewart, and 6 s. of Wigtown; situate in a fine part of the county, and surrounded by land in a high state of cultivation. The parish is of an irregular figure, extending along the shore about twelve miles, and varying in breadth from two to six miles inland. The chief bays in the parish are Garlieston (above described) and Rigg, with the ports of Allan, Whaple and Innerwell: these bays and ports are very convenient for shipping, and well adapted for the prosecution of the fisheries. The headlands are Crugleton and Eagerness: upon these are the remains of two strong castles; and about a mile to the east of the kirk are the gradually mouldering outlines of Sorby tower, formerly belonging to the Hannay family. The places of worship are the parish church at Sorby, and an independent chapel at Garlieston.

POST OFFICE, GARLIESTON, John Marshall, Post Master.—Letters from all parts arrive every morning at seven in summer and eight in winter, and are despatched every day at twelve.

NOBILITY, GENTRY AND CLERGY.
Davidson Rev. Elliot Wm. of Sorby
Forrester Rev. Alexdr. Garlieston
Galloway the Earl of, Galloway hse
Gowan Mr. Allen, R. N. Garlieston
Grant Capt. George, H.E.I.C.S. Culderry house
Young Rev. Thomas, Garlieston

ACADEMIES AND SCHOOLS.
Harriet Miss, Pier cottage
M'Kie David, Garlieston [master
PAROCHIAL, Sorby—Wm. M'Culloch

BAKERS.
Broadfoot John, Garlieston
Wylie Margaret, Garlieston

BLACKSMITHS.
Huchan James, Sorby
Wither Thomas, Garlieston

BOOT AND SHOE MAKERS.
Conner Michael, Sorby
Malone Thomas, Garlieston
Rennie John, Sorby
Robb Alexander, Garlieston

GROCERS.
Brown Alexander, Garlieston
Drysdale George, Sorby
Hannah Janet, Garlieston [lieston
M'Adam Michael (& flesher), Gar-
M'Cutcheon Jno.(& spirit dlr.)Sorby
M'Whinnie Mary, Garlieston
Pollock John (& draper),Garlieston
Sloan Rebecca, Garlieston
Thomson Eliz. Sorby [lieston
Walker Mary (& corn dealer),Gar-
Wylie Margaret, Garlieston

JOINERS AND WRIGHTS.
Dick Alexander (& ship carpenter), Garlieston

M'Clure Andrew, Sorby
M'Credie John, Sorby
M'Gowan George (& cartwright), Garlieston

MILLERS.
M'Dowall James, Ramestone
White William, Sorby
Wild William, Garlieston

NAIL MAKERS.
Maxwell John, Garlieston
Nelson Hugh, Garlieston

STONE MASONS.
Harg Peter & Son, Garlieston
Hyslop William, Garlieston

TAILORS.
M'Cutcheon John, Sorby
Nish Hugh, Sorby
Nish William, Sorby
Rennie John, Garlieston
Rennie Samuel, Garlieston

VINTNERS.

Coltran Jane, Garlieston
Kevan Elizabeth, Sorby
M'Credie John, Sorby
Narin Janet, Garlieston
Shaw Anthony, Garlieston

WRIGHTS.
See Joiners and Wrights.

Miscellaneous.

At GARLIESTON *if not otherwise expressed.*

Bain James, whitesmith
Douglas William, principal coast officer
Hannah Thomas, cooper
Hannah William, cabinet maker
Kippie John, damask manufacturer, Sorby
M'Clary William, dyer, Waulk mill
M'Gill James, clog maker

Marshall John, timber merchant
Shaw Jas. solicitor in the supreme court
Shaw John, rope and sail maker

CARRIER.
To WIGTON, Alexander Dick, from Garlieston, every Saturday.

CONVEYANCE BY WATER.
To LIVERPOOL, the *Countess of Galloway* steam-packet, once a fortnight.

GLENLUCE AND NEW LUCE.

GLENLUCE is a thriving village in the parish of Old Luce, 19 miles E. by N. of Portpatrick, 17 w. of Wigton, 16 s. w. of Newton Stewart, and 10 E. by s. of Stranraer; beautifully situate on the banks of the river Luce, and on the public road at the head of Luce bay, which here forms a tolerably good harbour for small vessels. The country around is interesting and picturesque, and abounds with game of almost every kind. The church is a neat edifice, remarkable only for its simplicity; there is but one other place of worship—a chapel for an united secession congregation. About a mile to the north of the church, farther up the vale (from which the village takes its name), are the ruins of Luce Abbey, founded by Rolland, Lord of Galloway, in 1190: it must have been, in its perfect state, an extensive pile of building—its vast mass of prostrate fragments at present cover about an acre and a half of ground, notwithstanding the vast quantities that have been carried away. The only part that now remains entire is a small apartment on the east side of the square, within which latter stood the cloisters; in the middle of this apartment stands a pillar, about fourteen feet high, from which eight arches spring, and have their terminations in the surrounding walls. Tradition reports Michael Scott, of cabalistic memory, to have been at one time abbot of this establishment, and adds that his magical library still exists under a particular part of the ruins. An annual fair is held at Glenluce on the Tuesday before the 26th of May; and there is a monthly fair or market, from the first Friday in April to the first Friday in December.

The village of NEW LUCE is five miles north of Glenluce, pleasantly situate on the Luce, where the Cross water falls into that river. This district, which until the year 1646 formed part of the parish of Old Luce, extends about ten miles in length by from five to six in breadth. It consists partly of high and partly of low ground: of the former, the greater proportion is covered by rocks or heath; the arable land, which is not of great extent, lies principally on the banks of the rivers. In the village stand the parish church and school, the former a plain but commodious edifice.

POST OFFICE, GLENLUCE, Alexander M'Crackan, *Post Master.*—Letters from LONDON, &c. arrive every evening at six, and are despatched every evening at a quarter before eight.—Letters from STRANRAER, part of Ayrshire and Ireland arrive every evening at eight, and are despatched every evening at six.

GENTRY AND CLERGY.

Adair John, esq. Balkail
Cathcart Mrs. Genoch
Hay Sir James Dalrymple, Bart. Dunraggit
M'Crackan Mr. John, Glenluce
M'Crackan Mr. John, jun. Glenluce
M'Dowall Rev. John, Luce Abbey
M'Kergo Rev. William (justice of the peace), New Luce
Puller Rev. James, Glenluce

BAKERS.

Gibson William, Glenluce
M'Dowall James, Glenluce

BLACKSMITHS.

Blackwell John, New Luce
Campbell Hugh, New Luce
Leech David, Glenluce
M'Clelland David, Glenluce
M'Clure Peter, Glenluce
M'William John, Glenluce
Park John, New Luce

BOOT AND SHOE MAKERS.

Kelly Charles, New Luce
M'Cann James, Glenluce
M'Millan Hugh, Glenluce
Sproat Robert, Glenluce
Wilkins David, Glenluce

CARTWRIGHTS.

Agnew Alexander, New Luce
Douglas Peter (& joiner), Glenluce
M'Bryde James, New Luce
M'Clelland William, Glenluce
M'Credie James, Glenluce
M'Hurg Peter, Glenluce
Peacock Matthew, Glenluce

GROCERS.
Marked thus * are also Spirit Dealers.

Dougan John, Glenluce
*Douglas Alexander, New Luce
Douglas Peter, Glenluce
*M'Crackan Thomas, Glenluce
*M'Kenzie William, New Luce

*M'Micking Peter, Glenluce
M'Millan William, New Luce
Murchie Thomas (& iron monger), Glenluce
*Paul William, Glenluce
*Steven Christiana, New Luce
Withers Margaret, Glenluce

LINEN & WOOLLEN DRAPRS.

Saunders Robert, Glenluce
Withers Margaret, Glenluce

MILLERS.

Adair Alexander, Galdenoch mill
Findley James, Glenluce

MILLINERS AND DRESS AND STRAW HAT MAKERS.

Coleman Mrs. (straw hat), Glenluce
M'William Eliz. & Margt. Glenluce

SADDLERS.

M'Clew David, Glenluce
Murray Hugh, Glenluce

STONE MASONS.

Agar Robert, Glenluce
M'Micking Gilbert, Glenluce
Skimming John, Glenluce

SURGEONS.

Hannah Samuel, Glenluce
M'Clymont John, Glenluce
M'Crackan Alexander, Glenluce

TAILORS.

Hannah Thomas, Glenluce
M'Dowall Andrew, Glenluce
Milroy Thomas (& draper) Glenluce
Walker & Loughlin, New Luce

TANNER.

Wallace Thomas, Glenluce

VINTNERS.

Douglas John
Gracey Hugh
Hannay John
M'Clelland John
M'Kenzie Robert, King's Arms
M'Kie William
M'Tier Robert

Murray William
Templeton Margaret

WRIGHTS---See Cartwrights.

Miscellaneous.

Gibson James, factor, Glenluce
M'Culloch —, schoolmaster, Drochdool
Wales Andw. woollen manufacturer and dyer, Glenluce

PLACES OF WORSHIP.

ESTABLISHED CHURCH, Glenluce—Rev. John M'Dowall
ESTABLISHED CHURCH, New Luce—Rev. William M'Kergo
SECESSION CHURCH, Glenluce—Rev. James Puller

PAROCHIAL SCHOOLS.

GLENLUCE—William M'Moreland, master; John Ross, assistant
NEW LUCE—Andw. M'Lean, master

COACHES.

To DUMFRIES, the *Royal Mail* (from Portpatrick), calls at the King's Arms, every evening at eight; goes through Newton-Stewart, Gatehouse, &c.
To PORTPATRICK, the *Royal Mail* (from Dumfries), calls at the King's Arms, every afternoon at six; goes through Stranraer.

CARRIERS.

To NEWTON-STEWART, Alexander Telford, every Monday, and Isabella Agnew, every Saturday.
To PORT WILLIAM, William M'Culloch, every Wednesday.
To STRANRAER, William M'Millan and William M'Dowall, every Tuesday and Saturday.
To WHITHORN, H. Matthews, every Wednesday.
To WIGTOWN, John Simpson, Tuesday.

KIRKMAIDEN, STONEYKIRK AND NEIGHBOURHOODS.

THE parish of KIRKMAIDEN occupies nearly the whole of the western limb or peninsula of Wigtonshire—projecting into the mouth of the Solway Frith, and tapering to a point that inclines to the east. This parish, which comprehends the most southerly district of all Scotland, is about ten miles in length and from two to four and a half in breadth; it still has a wild appearance, but produces good crops of corn and potatoes, and feeds numbers of black cattle. The coast is generally bold, and indented by caves scooped out by the endless operations of the sea, and particularly by its furious lashings against this opposing barrier in stormy weather; on both sides of the peninsula, however, there are several good anchoring grounds. At PORTNISSOCK is an excellent harbour, constructed at the expense of the late Andrew M'Douall, Esq., then proprietor, who used every exertion in his power to improve this locality. There is also a tolerable harbour at DROMORE; here the coast-guard have a station, under the command of a lieutenant of the royal navy. The church, a plain edifice, is situate near the centre of the parish, not far from Dromore bay, at the distance of six miles from the Mull of Galloway, 35 from Wigton, 36 from Newton Stewart, 20 from Stranraer, and 16 from Portpatrick. On the estate of Captain M'Douall, of Logan, is a fish-pond well worthy of the inspection of visiters: it is hewn out of the solid rock, and has communication with the sea by means of an ingeniously contrived iron grating; some of the fish in this artificial reservoir have been rendered so tame that they will feed out of the hand.

The parish of STONEY KIRK (more properly *Steven's Kirk*) lies in the western peninsula of the county, to the north of Kirkmaiden, six miles from Stranraer and about the like distance from Portpatrick; on the east and south-east is the bay of Glenluce. The parish, which extends seven miles in length by from three to five in breadth, comprehends the three old parishes of Stoney Kirk, Clachshant and Toskerton. The surface is generally hilly, moorish, and of a pastoral character; the low grounds are arable, and in some places planted. On the estate of Captain Maitland, in this district, is an artificial mount, supposed to be of Roman origin, and used as a beacon in the time of war; there is likewise another, of a similar kind, on the estate of John M'Taggert, Esq., of Ardwell House.

POST OFFICE, KIRKMAIDEN, Wm. Todd, *Post Master.*—Letters from all parts arrive every Tues. Thurs. and Sat. afternoon at three, and are despatched every Monday, Wednesday and Friday noon at 12.

GENTRY AND CLERGY.
Agnew Mr. Hugh (surgeon) Sandhd
Anderson Rev. James, Stoneykirk
Lamb Rev. John, Kirkmaiden
M'Douall Capt. James, Logan
M'Douall Mrs. Logan [house
M'Taggart John, esq. M. P. Ardwell
Maitland Capt. Patrick, Balgriggan
Thompson Lieut. Ts. R.N. Portnissock

ACADEMIES AND SCHOOLS.
Gibson William, Portnissock
M'Cormick John, Dromore
M'Master James, Sandhead
PAROCHIAL, Kirkmaiden—William Todd, master
PAROCHIAL, Stoneykirk——James Crum, master

BLACKSMITHS.
Gibson Charles, Stoneykirk
Hills James, Kirkmaiden
M'Crackan Alexander, Kirkmaiden
M'Nellie James, Sandhead
M'Nellie John, Portnissock
Thompson David, Ardwell Inn

BOOT & SHOE MAKERS.
Byers Francis, Stoneykirk
Cochrane Samuel, Sandhead
Davis William, Dromore
Groves John, Stoneykirk

M'Bryde William, Portnissock
M'Culloch James, Portnissock
M'Lean Robert, Portnissock
Maskell William, Dromore
Nibloe Peter, Dromore
Stevenson William, Dromore

CARTWRIGHTS.
Gunion James, Dromore
Gunion William, Dromore
M'Culloch John, Sandhead
M'Gowan Wm. (joiner) Stoneykirk

GROCERS
Marked thus * are also Spirit Dealers.
Allison Agnes, Stoneykirk
Campbell David, Sandhead
Campbell Hugh, Sandhead
Carney John, Dromore
Gaudy Peter, Portnissock
*M'Gaw Alexander, Dromore
*M'Gaw Margaret, Portnissock
*M'Nellie Alexander, Dromore
Paterson Andrew, Stoneykirk
Taylor William (and corn dealer) Dromore
Wallace John, Dromore

MILLERS.
Birkmyer Thomas, Ardwell mill
Kelton Matthew, Logan mill
Melville Alexander, Dromore

TAILORS.
Stevenson James, Dromore
Stevenson John, Dromore
Tellie Samuel, Sandhead

VINTNERS.
Carr Thomas, Ardwell Inn
Chesney Samuel, Stoneykirk
Douglas Peter, Sandhead
Hannay Mary, Dromore
Hunter Thomas, Stoneykirk
M'Colm John, Kirkmaiden
M'Colm Samuel, Dromore
M'Kelvie John, Portnissock
Milwie Jane, Portnissock
Muir James, Sandhead
Murray William, Dromore

WRIGHTS—See Cartwrights.

Miscellaneous.
Agnew Peter, stone mason, Sandhead
Allison James, corn merchant, Portnissock
Gibson John, factor, Logan
M'Harry John, dyer, near Sandhead
Robb William, nail maker, Sandhead

CARRIERS.
To STRANRAER, William Stevenson, from Kirkmaiden, every Friday, and Daniel M'Clymont, every Mon & Fri.

KIRKOWEN,

OR *Kirkcowan*, is a village in the parish of its name, nine miles from Glenluce, eight from Wigton, and the like distance from Newton-Stewart; situate on the Tarf water, near its junction with the Bladenoch. Near the village is the extensive woollen manufactory of Messrs. Milroy, which furnishes employment to many of the inhabitants. The church, which is a very neat edifice, was erected in 1830; its site, as well as the ground occupied by the church yard, was mu- nificently given by Captain W. C. Hamilton, of Craiglaw. The old church was dedicated to St. Cowan, the original name of the parish. The surface of this district is various, consisting of moorland, interspersed with pieces of arable land. It extends from north to south fifteen miles, by a general breadth of about five; it is well watered by the Tarf and Bladenoch streams. There is a parochial school in the village, and lately a branch post office has been established in it.

POST OFFICE, Alexander Livingston, *Post Master.*—Letters from all parts arrive every evening at half-past six, and are despatched every afternoon at half-past four.

GENTRY & CLERGY.
Hamilton Captain William Charles, Craiglaw
Milligan Mr. John, Tannilaggie
Milligan Mr. William, Kilbockadale
Stewart Rev. Anthony, Kirkowen

VINTNERS.
M'Keand James
M'William George
Milligan John
Telfour Alexander, Halfway House

SHOPKEEPERS & TRADERS.
Fulton Michael, grocer

Gibson James, tailor
Hannah Alexander, miller, Spittal
Hannah Andrew, miller
Hannah William, baker
Livingston Alexander, master of the parochial school
M'Caig John, baker
M'Cubbin William, joiner
M'Fadden John, grocer
M'Kie Alexander, grocer
M'Lean Jas. tailor
M'William Alexander, joiner and cartwright

M'William James, blacksmith
M'William William, blacksmith
Milligan David, boot & shoe maker
Milligan John, grocer
Milligan Robert, grocer
Milroy William & Thomas, woollen manufacturers [dealer
Murphy David, grocer and spirit
Robb William, boot & shoe maker
Steele William, stone mason

CARRIER.
To NEWTON STEWART, Wm. Nicholson, every Monday & Fri.

NEWTON-STEWART,
AND THE PARISH OF PENNINGHAM, WITH MINNIEGAFF AND NEIGHBOURHOODS.

NEWTON-STEWART is a thriving town and burgh of barony, 121 miles s.w. of Edinburgh, 82 s. of Glasgow, 52 w. of Dumfries, 26 w. of Stranraer, and 8 N. of Wigton; situate on the high road from Dumfries to Portpatrick, on the right bank of the river Cree, in the parish of Penningham, with a small portion on the opposite side of the stream in the parish of Minniegaff. It owes its origin to a younger branch of the Stewarts, Earls of Galloway, who possessed the estate of Castle Stewart, and founded the village upon it, to which he gave the name of Newton-Stewart. About the year 1778 the estate fell into the hands of William Douglas, Esq., when it was created a burgh of barony under the title of Newton Douglas; but it subsequently resumed its original name. 'Not much longer than sixty years since, the houses consisted of but one story, and were covered with thatch; but the greater portion are now two stories in height, and slated. The town is principally composed of one long street, in the centre of which is the town-house, forming the chief ornament of the place. The Cree is crossed by a very handsome bridge of five arches, connecting the larger division of the town with the lesser part on the other side of the river. The government of the town is vested in the hands of justices of the peace, who meet once a month. The cotton manufacture was carried on here, and in the neighbourhood, to a considerable extent, but it has been in a declining state for some years: the staple at present is the trade in wool furnished from the surrounding country, and mostly purchased for the Lancashire markets; among the other prominent branches may be mentioned the tanning of leather, for which there are two yards, and an extensive brewery.

The places of worship are a church of the establishment, and chapels for the relief synod, Cameronians, and Roman catholics. The institutions, educational and otherwise, consist of two sabbath schools, the Douglas endowed charity school, a reading and coffee room, a weavers' society, and a masonic lodge. Agri-cultural improvement has been carried to a great and beneficial extent in this district; and a society entitled the 'Galloway Union Horticultural Society' has been recently formed, which, from the situation of the village, bids fair to prosper. At the upper extremity of that part of the town in Minniegaff parish, there is a large moat hill, where David Graham, brother to Claverhouse, and superior of this district, used, immediately before the revolution, to administer justice. About three miles to the north of the town are the remains of Castle Stewart, formerly belonging (as before stated) to a branch of the Galloway family—now to James Blair, Esq. The weekly market is held on Friday, and cattle markets, which are well attended, on the first Friday in every month; the annual fairs are held on the last Wednesdays of March, July and October, and on the first Wednesday after the 15th of June, all old style.

The parish of Penningham (or *Penninghame*) extends along the right bank of the river Cree for about fifteen miles, by a breadth of from three to five; bounded by Wigton on the south and Kirkowen on the west. The greater part of the district is moorish and uncultivated, chiefly adapted to pasture.

Minniegaff is a large parish in the western part of the stewartry of Kirkcudbright; bounded on the west by the Cree, over which is a bridge (before noticed), forming the communication with the parish of Penningham and the town of Newton-Stewart. The parish is fourteen miles in length, and eight in breadth. In the lower parts the land is a good deal improved, especially towards the margin of the Cree, which stream being navigable for several miles up, has been of much benefit in an agricultural point of view; this river likewise produces excellent fish of different kinds, but the best and most abundant is the salmon. By far the greater portion of the parish is devoted to pasturage; it is covered by large flocks of sheep and numerous herds of black cattle.

POST OFFICE, Newton-Stewart, Marion Paterson, *Post Mistress*.—Letters from London and all parts of England and Scotland (west of Wigtonshire excepted) arrive every afternoon at four, and are despatched every night at half-past ten.—Letters from Glenluce, Stranraer, Portpatrick and Ireland arrive every night at half-past ten, and are despatched every afternoon at four.

*** The names without address are in Newton-Stewart.

NOBILITY, GENTRY AND CLERGY.

Alexander Mrs. Margt. Cree bridge
Blair James,esq. Penningham house
Campbell Mr.Geo. Newton-Stewart
Campbell Rev. Jno. Newton-Stewart
Dill Miss Elizabeth, Newton-Stewart
Douglas the Misses Sarah & Jessie, Cree bridge
Galloway the Right Hon Earl of, Cumloden cottage
Jamieson Mrs. J. Newton-Stewart
Kelly Mrs. Isabella, Cree bridge
Kevan Mrs. Grace, Bellvue
Lees Mr. James, Newton-Stewart
M'Caa Mrs. Boyd, Cree bridge
M'Cornack the Misses, Cree bridge
M'Kean Mrs. Jane, Cree bridge
M'Kenzie Mrs. Capt. Cree bridge
M'Kerlie Capt. Jno. R.N. Corvisel hse
M'Lean Mrs. Mary, Cree bridge
M'Laurin Mrs. Dnl. Newton-Stewart
M'Laurin Mrs. Jas. Newton-Stewart
M'Lurg the Misses, Newton-Stewart
M'Millan the Misses Helen & Willie, Newton-Stewart
Maxwell Lady Heron, Kirrouchtree
Maxwell Jno. Heron,esq. Kirrouchtree
Porter James, esq.(justice of peace) Newton-Stewart
Reston Rev. Jas. Newton-Stewart
Richardson Rev. Sml. Newton Stewrt
Simpson Miss Mary, Newton-Stewart
Sinnott Rev. Richd. Newton-Stewart
Stewart Miss Dunlop, Corvisel house

Stewart James, esq. Cavinsmoor, Minniegaff
Stewart Hon. Montgomery, Cursbie
Thomson C. W. D. esq. (justice of peace) Newton-Stewart
Wason E. Sidney, esq. Merton hall

ACADEMIES AND SCHOOLS.
DOUGLAS ACADEMY—James Low, A. M. master
Ferguson Peter, Cree bridge
Gordon Mrs. (ladies' boarding&day)
PAROCHIAL, Penningham—John Martin, master [Scott, master
PAROCHIAL, Minniegaff—Archibald Sloan Miss Mary Ann(boarding and day) Cree bridge

BAKERS.
Kelly Alexander
Logan James (& spirit dealer)
Todd John

BANKERS.
BRITISH LINEN Co. (Branch)—(draw on Smith, Payne & Smiths, London)—James Newall, agent

BLACKSMITHS.
Crossan Andrew, Cree bridge
Donnan John
Erskine Charles
Erskine Charles, Cree bridge
M'Cormick John

BOOKSELLERS & STATIONRS
M'Nairn Joseph (and circulating library and printer) [buter)
Paterson Marion (& stamp distri-
Thomson Isabella

BOOT AND SHOE MAKERS.
Gray John
Hunter William
M'Cutchon John
M'Kie David, Minniegaff
M'Whae John, Minniegaff
Milligan John, Minniegaff
Murray John
Simpson James
Stewart Thomas
Summers Jane
Vernon James, jun.

CABINET MAKERS AND UPHOLSTERERS.
Kennedy Gilbert
M'Guffog William

CARPENTERS AND JOINERS
Bell John
Hannah Robert
M'Clellan Peter
M'Kinna Peter
M'Murray Robert
Smith Walker
Welsh James, Cree bridge

CARTWRIGHTS.
Bell John
Smith Walker

COOPERS.
Connel John
Geddes William

CURRIERS.
Gibson Hugh
Hunter William

DRESS AND STRAW HAT MAKERS.
Alexander Mary
Dunn Margaret

DRESS, &c. MAKERS—Contd.
McKie Jane
Robb Jane and Elizabeth
Wilson Mary and Elizabeth

FIRE, &c. OFFICE AGENTS.
CALEDONIAN, James Newall
HERCULES, William Dill

FLESHERS.
Campbell George
Craig William
McMiekan John
Maconochie David
Stewart John
Willoughby Charles

GLASS & CHINA DEALERS.
Brown William
McAdam Thomas
McKinna Peter

GROCERS & SPIRIT DEALRS
Adam Henry
Armstrong Robert, Cree bridge
Beck James
Brown William
Carson Robert
Douglas Edward
Gordon Wallace
Hannah John
Kelly James
McAdam Thomas
McDowell Alexander, Minniegaff
McDowell John, Cree bridge
McHaffie Alexander
McKinna Peter
McLaggan Catherine, Cree bridge
McLellan Alexander
McMillan Basil (& draper)
Murray Thomas
Paterson James
Scott Ann
Shaw Aexander
Stewart John
Strachan Mary
Thomson Isabella

HARDWAREMEN AND IRONMONGERS.
Gray Thomas
McNairn Joseph
Thomson Isabella

INNS.
Galloway Arms Inn (and posting house), John Craik
Grapes Inn, Samuel Maconochie

LINEN & WOOLLEN DRAPRS.
Auld Patrick
Craik William
Ewart James
Hughes Peter
McCubbin John
McMillan Basil

MERCHANTS.
Glover and Co.

MILLERS.
Cumming Samuel, Garlies mill
Hannah Robert
Johnstone George, Minniegaff mills
Auld James
McCormick David

NAIL MAKERS.

NURSERY & SEEDSMEN.
Mitchell John (nurseryman only)
Spark Robert

PAINTERS AND GLAZIERS.
Miller Daniel
Milligan William
Robertson John, Cree bridge

PLUMBERS & TIN-SMITHS.
Drynan Andrew
Moffat Joseph

SADDLERS AND HARNESS MAKERS.
Hannay John
Maconochie William
Murray William

SURGEONS.
McMillan Thomas
Smith Charles
Smith Charles, jun.
Thomson James

TAILORS.
Armstrong Frs.
Broadfoot James
Crawford James
Dickson James
Dowling William
McClymont Hugh
Paterson George
Paterson James

TALLOW CHANDLERS.
Gordon Margaret
Wilson Mary and Elizabeth

TANNERS.
Campbell Archibald
Cowan & Sinclair, Cree bridge

VINTNERS.
Andrew James
Brown William, jun.
Coid Charles
Cornak William
Dowall John   [gaff
Dowall Samuel, Black craig, Minnie-
Dunn Jane
Erskine Charles, Cree bridge
Good William
Gordon Nicholas
McBryde John, Cree bridge
McClellan Peter
McClement John
McConnel John
McConochie Samuel
McCullock Hugh
McCrakan Janet, Causewayend, Pen-
ningham
McHarg Gilbert
McHarg James
Macilwraith William

McMurray Robert
Nelson John
Robinson William
Thomson John
Underwood John
Vernon James

WINE & SPIRIT MERCHNTS
Glover and Co.
McBryde James

WRITERS.
Dill William (& notary, messenger, deputy clerk of the peace and procurator)
Douglas John
Good William
Jamieson Adam (and auctioneer)
McMillan John

Miscellaneous.
Adams Jas. precentor to the parish church
Andrew James, builder
Dunn John, hair dresser
Gilchrist Mary, clothes dealer
Gourlay James, watch and clock maker
Harding John, precentor to relief church
Kelly Bruce, bookbinder [Minniegaff
Laird David, brick maker, Machermore,
McChlery John, dyer, Minniegaff
McClymont Gilbert, cattle dealer, Challock
McGeoch James, wood turner
McLaurin Ludovic, brewer
McNab James, factor, Larg, Minniegaff
Nelson John, builder
Nicholson Peter, cotton agent

PLACES OF WORSHIP.
ESTABLISHED CHURCH, Penningham—Rev. Samuel Richardson
RELIEF—Rev. James Reston
CAMERONIANS—Rev. John Campbell
CATHOLIC—Rev. Richard Sinnott

COACHES.
To DUMFRIES, the *Royal Mail* (from Portpatrick), calls at the Galloway Arms, every night at half-past ten; goes through Creetown, Gatehouse & Castle Douglas.
To PORTPATRICK, the *Royal Mail* (from Dumfries), calls at the Galloway Arms, every afternoon at four; goes through Glenluce and Stranraer.

CARRIERS.
To DUMFRIES, Robt. Raeside, Monday.
To EDINBURGH, John Candlish, every alternate Monday.
To GIRVAN, Samuel Paterson, Tuesday.
To GLASGOW, Hugh Steel and William McLurg, every Monday.
To KIRKCUDBRIGHT, Isabella Agnew, occasionally.
To STRANRAER, Isabella Agnew, every Tuesday and Friday, and Alexander Telford, every Friday.
To WHITHORN, Adam McKeand, Tues.
To WIGTOWN, Hugh Steel and William McLurg, every Monday and Saturday.

PORTPATRICK

IS a sea-port town in the parish of its name, 133 miles s. w. of Edinburgh, 89 s. s. w. of Glasgow, between 34 and 35 w. of Wigtown, the like distance w. by s. of Newton-Stewart, and rather more than 8 s. by w. of Stranraer; it is 117 miles from Dublin, 38 from Belfast, and 21 from Donaghadee. It is situate on the coast of the North Channel, and has long been the great thoroughfare from the north of Ireland, being the nearest point of Great Britain to that country, and the best place for crossing from one kingdom to the other. The town is small, but delightfully situate, with a fine southern exposure, and surrounded on the other side by a ridge of small hills. It was formerly, with the estate of Dunskey, the property of Lord Mount-Alexander, whose residence was the old castle of Dunskey, which stands in the neighbourhood, on the brink of a tremendous precipice overhanging the sea, and was once a building of considerable strength, as appears from its interesting remains; the late Sir James Hunter

Blair subsequently became possessed of the castle, and it is to the exertions of that gentleman that the town and harbour are indebted for many improvements. There is now one of the finest quays in Britain, and a reflecting light house; in the construction of the quay the diving-bell has been most successfully employed. Of late years there have been extensive and important improvements carrying on at the harbour, under the auspices of government and direction of Sir John Rennie, for the accommodation of her Majesty's packets, and to ensure facilities for the embarkation of troops, at all times of the tide, for Ireland: when completed, these works will prove a great national convenience; while the establishment of steam-packets has secured a constant communication between this and the sister country. The commerce of the town and district has kept pace with the improvements as they progressed, and it is now a thriving little place. The principal imports are black cattle and horses from Ireland.

POST OFFICE, John Hannay, *Post Master.*—Letters from LONDON, &c. arrive every evening at nine, and are despatched every evening at six.—Letters from GLASGOW, &c. arrive every morning at five, and are despatched every afternoon at three.—Letters from Ireland arrive every afternoon at two, and are despatched every morning at twenty minutes past five.

GENTRY & CLERGY.

Blair Col. Ths. Hunter,c.b.Dunskey
Hannay Mrs. Mary
Little Capt. John, R. N.
M'Kenzie Rev. John, D. D.
Murdock Mr. John (factor to Col. Blair) Dinvin
Urquhart Rev. Andrew

INN-KEEPERS & VINTNERS.

Cumming Andrew
Gordon William (Downshire Arms)
Hogg Janet
Kennedy Jane
M'Cleary Jane & Margaret
M'Cormick John
Milroy Alexander
Montgomery Barbara
Niven Andrew

SHOPKEEPERS,TRADERS,&c.

Adair Thomas, cartwright
Adams David, miller, Spittal
Anderson John,wool carder,Spittal
Cunningham Janet, grocer
Fernie William,custom house officer
Gibson Hugh, master of parochial school
Groves William, schoolmaster
Hannay John,wine & spirit merchant
Hannay William, miller, Dinvin mill
Hay Hugh, flesher
Kerr Robert, grocer
Linn John, engineer to the commissioners of the harbour works
Lyburn John, blacksmith
Lyburn Peter, blacksmith
M'Carlie John, tailor
M'Clew John, grocer & spirit dealer
M'Cormick May,grocer&spirit dealr
M'Crea Mary, grocer
M'Dowall Andrew, blacksmith
M'Ewen Jane, grocer
M'Miekan John, baker
M"Taldrock James, grocer
Maltman Alexander, rope maker
Manderton James, flesher
Mills Robert, nail maker
Neilson Hugh, boot & shoe maker
Neilson John, boot & shoe maker
Park William, tailor
Scott Margaret, grocer
Tait Alexander, boot & shoe maker
Wright Thomas, baker

COMMISSIONERS OF THE HARBOUR WORKS OFFICE.

John Linn, engineer

COACHES.

To DUMFRIES, the *Royal Mail*, from the Downshire Arms, every evening at six; goes through Stranraer, Glenluce, Newton-Stewart, Gatehouse, &c.
To GLASGOW, the *Royal Mail*, from the Downshire Arms, every afternoon at three; goes through Stranraer, Girvan, Maybole, Ayr, and Kilmarnock.

CARRIER.

To STRANRAER, Davidson Rankin, every day.

CONVEYANCE BY WATER.

To DONAGHADEE,the post-office steam packet every morning at twenty minutes past five—Capt. John Little, agent.

PORT WILLIAM and MOCHRUM.

PORT WILLIAM is a prospering village in the parish of Mochrum, 24 miles s.e. of Stranraer, 15 s.s.e. of Glenluce, and 8 w. of Whithorn, situate in the bay of Glenluce. It possesses a harbour, which, though small, is commodious and safe; from it large quantities of grain and potatoes are exported for Liverpool and Lancaster. In the vicinity is Montrith, the handsome residence and demesne of Sir William Maxwell, Bart., the founder of the place and its present proprietor; the mansion, which stands on the bank of a fine lake, commands an extensive prospect of the bay of Glenluce, the shores of Galloway, the Isle of Man and the coast of Cumberland: near it is an old castle, surrounded by lofty trees.

The parish of MOCHRUM is about ten miles in length, and extends inland between four and five miles. The Castle or 'Old Place' of Mochrum, surrounded by lakes, is a very ancient picturesque building, in an inland part of the parish; it was formerly the family seat of the Dunbars, Knights of Mochrum, but has for many years been the property of the Earl of Galloway. The village of Mochrum, which is about a mile and a half from Port William, contains nothing worthy of mention except the parish church and school.

POST OFFICE, PORT WILLIAM, Anthony Dickson, *Post Master*.—Letters from all parts arrive every morning at eight, and are despatched every morning at ten.

GENTRY & CLERGY.

Cumming Mr. James, Arilour
Cumming Mr. Robert, Port William
M'Cormick Mr. — (surgeon)
Maxwell Sir William, bart. Montrith
Young Rev. Alexander, Mochrum

SCHOOLS.

Johnston James, Eldrick
PAROCHIAL, Mochrum—Alexander M'Nish, master
Withers William, Port William

VINTNERS.

Dickson Anthony, Port William
Gibson Peter, Port William
Kevand William, Mochrum
Kirby Robert, Port William
M'Conchie Robert, Mochrum
M'Culloch Elizabeth, Port William
M'Master John, Port William
Ross James, Port William

SHOPKEEPERS & TRADERS.

The names without address are in PORT WILLIAM.

Agnew Jane, grocer
Agnew William, boot & shoe maker
Broadshaw David,blacksmith,Mochrum
Campbell Andrew, shoe maker
Carr John, tailor, Eldrick
Clay Alexander, joiner, Eldrick
Cumming Jas. miller & corn dealer
Dalrymple Ths.cartwright,Mochrum
Drysdale Thos.cartwright,Mochrum
Ferguson Hugh, blacksmith & spirit dealer, Mochrum
Hannah John, grocer, Eldrick
Hartley James, grocer and spirit dealer, Eldrick
Hartley William,grocer,spiritdealer and boot& shoe maker, Mochrum
Innis P. tide waiter [Eldrick
M'Clure Alex. joiner & spirit dealer,
M'Cormick —, surgeon
M'Court Hugh, grocer
M'Credie William, cartwright
M'Guffie John, boot & shoe maker, Mochrum [Mochrum
M'Guffie William, grocer & draper,
M'Master Robert, blacksmith
Manson Wm. blacksmith, Eldrick
Milhiuch Mary, grocer & draper
Milhiuch Peter, tailor & draper
Paterson John, tailor, Mochrum
Robb Thomas, nail maker
Routledge John, miller & bone dust grinder, Eldrick
Simpson John, grocer, Mochrum
Skimming James, cartwright
Smith William, shoe maker,Eldrick
Templeton Alexander, saddler
Wallace James, grocer & draper

CARRIERS.

To STRANRAER, William M'Culloch, every Tuesday.
To WHITHORN, H. Matthews, every Wednesday.

STRANRAER,
AND THE PARISHES OF INCH, KIRKCOLM AND LESWALT.

STRANRAER is a thriving, respectable and ancient town, a royal burgh and the seat of a presbytery, as well as a parish within its bounds; rather more than eight miles (by the toll-road) from Portpatrick; eligibly situate at the inner extremity of Loch Ryan. The principal street is of great length, but the houses have not been erected on the most regular plan. In the centre of the town stands a building, originally a castle, but now used as the gaol: it is an edifice of considerable antiquity, but the date of its foundation has not been satisfactorily ascertained; it is mentioned, however, in the charter granted by James VI, and is called the 'tower, fortalice, and manor place of Chappel;' and was once the residence of the family of Kennedy of Chapel and Chrychan; in the year 1614 it was inhabited by John Kennedy, of Grennan, and Elizabeth his wife, then Lady Auchtriloor: the lands of Auchtriloor are immediately contiguous to the burgh of Stranraer, and now the property of the Earl of Stair. The town-hall, in George-street, is a neat structure; in it a justice of peace court is held on the first Monday of every month, also a burgh court every Saturday, and the sheriff of the county frequently holds criminal courts with a jury. If the bill now before parliament, for establishing district sheriff small-debt courts, pass into a law, such courts will be held in the burgh six times a year. As a royal burgh, the town is governed by a provost, a dean of guild, and fifteen councillors: it joins with Whithorn, Wigtown and New Galloway in parliamentary representation; the constituency of the burgh is about two hundred and twenty. Stranraer possesses a custom-house, of which all the creeks within the ' Rhinns' are members ; and there are likewise two coast-guard establishments, under the inspection and command of a captain of the royal navy.

The bay and harbour of Stranraer afford excellent anchorage ; and the pier, which is of considerable length, and has been constructed within the last eleven years, has proved a great convenience to the shipping. Cairn Ryan also presents safe anchorage ; and vessels from the West Indies, bound for the Clyde, frequently take shelter in this haven ; the depth of water is such as to allow a fleet of men of war to ride at anchor here with perfect safety. The bay affords a plentiful supply of fine oysters, the right of fishing for which belongs exclusively (by ancient charter) to Sir Alexander Wallace, of Loch Ryan, who annually lets it. There are likewise several kinds of white fish caught abundantly ; and occasionally some herrings are got, equal in quality to the finest obtained on any other part of the Scotch coast. The exports of the place consist of shoes and leather—also grain, cheese and all kinds of farm produce, and cattle, which are now conveyed to Glasgow regularly twice every week by steam-vessels, to Belfast once a week, and to Liverpool occasionally. Among other branches of business usually found in a flourishing town, there are in Stranraer three tanyards, two or three extensive nurseries in the neighbourhood, and some nail manufactories. There are four principal inns, and two banking houses; these latter are branches respectively of the Paisley Banking Company and the British Linen Company.

The edifices for public worship are a church of the establishment, three dissenting meeting-houses, and a Roman catholic chapel. The inhabitants support two news-rooms, a subscription and two circulating libraries, a savings' bank, and a dispensary. There are a debating and two friendly societies, a masonic lodge, and various clubs. Another society, which is advancing in importance, is the ' Stranraer and Rhinns of Galloway Agricultural Society ;' it has its exhibitions and

meetings twice annually. There are several seats in the neighbourhood adorned with all the charms of nature and art : Culhorn, now the residence of the Earl of Stair, is one mile and a half distant ; Castle Kennedy, four miles off, the property of the same nobleman, is surrounded by delightfully picturesque scenery. The following, situate in the vicinity of the burgh, are also worthy of notice :—Lochnaw Castle, the residence of Sir Andrew Agnew, Bart.; Corsewell House, J. Carrick Moore, Esq.; Loch Ryan House, Gen. Sir Alexndr. Wallace; Dunskey, Colonel Thomas Blair ; Balgriggan House, Captain P. Maitland ; Ardwell House, John M'Taggart, Esq.; Logan, Capt. M'Dowall ; Dunraggit, Sir Jas. Dalrymple Hay, Bart.; Gerroch, — Cathcart, Esq.; Balkail House, J. Adair, Esq ; Park House, Col. P.V. Agnew ; and North-west Castle, Sir Jno. Ross, R.N.

The market is held on Friday. The following are the annual fairs : Tuesday before the first Wednesday of January, for horses; third Friday of April, for cattle ; first Friday of May, cloth—and third Friday, cattle; Thursday before Midsummer, for horses—and Friday, for cattle ; and the third Fridays of July, August, September (and horse fair), October and November, are cattle markets.

The parish of INCH lies on the shore of Loch Ryan, extending nine miles in length by a breadth nearly as great. The parish church stands on the margin of a lake, in which there is a small beautifully wooded island. The lake is nearly divided by a neck of land, on which stand the ruins of a castle, formerly a seat of the Earls of Stair.

KIRKCOLM parish is bounded by Loch Ryan on the east, measuring a square of about five miles. The church is pleasantly situate near the shore of the lake, north of the bay called the Wig.

The parish of LESWALT lies betwixt the Irish channel on the west and Loch Ryan on the east ; it is about the same size, and of much the same form, as Kirkcolm. The surface of this district is most agreeably varied with hill and dale ; while from the sea the coast presents bold and rocky features.

POST OFFICE, Lewis-street, STRANRAER, Mrs. M'Nish, *Post Mistress.*—Letters from LONDON arrive every evening at eight, and are despatched every evening at seven.—Letters from Ireland arrive every afternoon at four, and are despatched every morning at four.—Letters from GLASGOW arrive every morning at four, and are despatched every afternoon at four.——The Irish mail is made up at ten the night previous, and the others half an hour before their departure.

NOBILITY, GENTRY AND CLERGY.

Agnew Sir Andrew, bart. M.P. Lochnaw castle
Agnew John, esq. George st
Atkin Miss Helen, Hanover st
Baird Mr. Samuel, Princes st
Caird Mrs. Hanover st
Christie Capt. R. N. Hanover st
Crane Lieut. Thos. R.N. Charlotte st
Ferguson Mrs. Hanover st
Ferguson Rev. James, Inch
Gillispie William, esq. Lewis st
Guthrie George, esq. (factor to the Earl of Stair) Culhorn
Hannah Mr. Samuel, Elm house
Kerr Mrs. Ann, Princes st
Kerr Mrs. Mary, King st
M'Crae the Misses, Charlotte st
M'Cubbin Rev. Andrew, Leswalt
M'Douall Colonel C. B. Lewis st
M'Douall Mrs. Helen, Church st
M'Gregor Rev. John, Glenville st
M'Kie Mrs. Helen, Glenluce road
Moore James Carrick, esq. Kirkcolm
Morrison Mrs. Elizabeth, King st
Paterson John, esq. Lewis st
Reid Sir John, bart. Park house
Ritchie Dav. esq. (of Airies) Challoch
Robertson Mrs. Hanover st
Rose Rev. William, Kirkcolm
Ross Captain Sir John, R.N. North-west castle
Smillie Rev. William, Glenluce road
Stair the Right Honourable the Earl of, Culhorn [kirk road
Symington Rev. William, Stoney-
Taylor John, esq. (justice of peace) Lewis st

Taylor Nathl. esq. Belmont cottage
Taylor Thomas, esq. (justice of peace) Lewis st [house
Wallace Genl. Sir Alex. Loch Ryan
Watt Mrs. Catherine, King st
Wilson Rev. David, Lewis st

ACADEMIES & SCHOOLS.

Blake Sarah (ladies' boarding and day) Queen street
Campbell Sarah, Princes st
M'Meikan Elizabeth (ladies' boarding and day) Princes st
M'Meikan Isabella, Queen st
PAROCHIAL SCHOOLS :—
INCH, James Boe, master
KIRKCOLM, Jas. Wallace, master
LESWALT, Alex. M'Ghee, master
STRANREAR(& gentlemen's boarding academy) Wm. Main, master

AUCTIONEERS.

M'Lean Peter, Bridge st
Robertson Wingate, George st
Sprott William, Church st
Warden Henry, Burn side

BAKERS.

Campbell John, Lewis st
Gartley Simon, Queen st
Johnston David, Hanover st
Kennedy Gilbert, Charlotte st
M'Crackan Alexander, Bridge st
M'Kie John, Castle st
M'Lelland Alexander, Fisher st
Melvin William, George st
Morrow Thomas, George st
Stevenson John, Hanover st

BANKERS.

BRITISH LINEN COMPANY (Branch) Princes street—(draw on Smith,

Payne and Smiths, London)—Alexander M'Neel, agent
PAISLEY BANKING COMPY. (Branch) King street—(draw on the Royal Bank of Scotland, Edinburgh, & on Smith, Payne & Smiths, London)—Charles Morland, agent

BLACKSMITHS.

Bruce William, Quay head
Johns James, Leswalt
M'Cubbin John, Kirkcolm
M'Dowall William, Harbour st
M'William John, Bridge st

BOOKSELLERS & STATIONRS.

Marked thus * are also Printers.
*Bryce Agnes, George st
Buchanan William, George st
Dick Janet, Lewis st
M'Coid James, Queen st
Walker Peter, George st
*Wylie Hugh, Church st

BOOT & SHOE MAKERS.

Bissett Thomas, George st
Black James, Castle st
Campbell Alexander, Kirkcolm
Findley John, George st
Galbraith William, George st
Hamilton Samuel, George st
M'Credie & Blyth, George st
M'Intyre Andrew, George st
M'Gill Alexander, Kirkcolm
M'Kie Peter, Leswalt
Ross David, George st
Stewart Alexander, Hanover st
Thomson William, George st
Wallace William, George st

BRICK MAKERS.

Rankin Alexander, Trade st
Wogan Samuel, Sun st

CABINET MAKERS.
Nibloe John, Bridge st
Ritchie John, Church st
Thorburn Alexander, Charlotte st

CARPENTERS & JOINERS.
Adair James (& builder) Charlotte st
Campbell William, Strand st
M'Crea John, Kirkcolm
M'Crackan Michael, Kirkcolm
M'Dowall William, Sun st
Ross James, Leswalt

CARTWRIGHTS.
Douglas Adair (and coach maker)
    Quay head   [Shuchan mill
Donglas James (and coach maker)
Gracey James, St. John st
M'Coid Alexander, Harbour st
Skimming Andrew, Hanover st

CHINA, GLASS & EARTHEN-WARE DEALERS.
M'Clean William, Charlotte st
M'Dowall William, Castle st
M'Farlane Alexander, George st
Warden Henry, Burn side

COOPERS.
Gullin James, Fisher st
Knox Peter, Queen st
M'Caig Robert, Glen st

CORN MERCHANTS.
M'Dowall Alexander, Church st
M'Kie John, Hanover st

CURRIERS.
Gibson Hugh, Castle st
Hill William, Mill hill st
M'Clymont Alexander, George st
M'Master Anthony, George st

FIRE, &c. OFFICE AGENTS.
HERCULES, Charles Morland, King st
INSURANCE COMPANY OF SCOTLAND,
    William Sprott, Church st
PROVIDENT, William Buchanan,
    George street
SCOTTISH AMICABLE and WEST OF
    SCOTLAND, John M'William,
    George street
SCOTTISH UNION, Wingate Robert-
    son, George street
STANDARD, Wm. Sprott, Church st

FLESHERS,
AT THE MARKET CROSS.
Boyle James | M'Harg Samuel
Donnan Andrew | M'Meikan Thos.
M'Harg Robert | Todd John

GROCERS & SPIRIT DEALERS
Agnew James, Castle st
Agnew John, Sun st
Beggs William & Co. George st
Biggam Barbara, George st
Buyers James, George st
Campbell Ezekiel, Kirkcolm
Cluckie Andrew, George st
Cowan Agnes, Castle st
Espie James, George st
Fernie & Co. Castle st
Fleming William, Hanover st
Gifford William, Charlotte st
Gunion Robert, George st
Henderson Alexander, Hanover st
Hunter James and Son (wholesale
    and retail) Church street
M'Caig Thomas, Queen st
M'Crea Hugh, Kirkcolm
M'Credie Hugh, King st
M'Culloch Hugh, George st
M'Dowall William, Castle st
M'Farlane Alexander, George st
M'Farlane Malcolm, George st
M'Kay Archibald, George st
M'Laughlin William, Kirkcolm
M'Meikan Archibald, George st
M'Nillie Charles, George st
M'Whinnie Alexander, George st
Muir John, Bridge st
Robertson John, Charlotte st
Robinson Robert, Kirkcolm

Thompson Samuel, Queen st
Turnbull Jean, Hanover st
Wallace Alexander, Princes st
Wilson David & Co. George st
Wither John, Hanover st

HARDWAREMEN AND IRONMONGERS.
Buchanan William, George st
Irving Andrew, George st
Kerr Charles, Castle st
M'Clean Hugh, George st
M'Clean William, Charlotte st
M'Cullock Alexander, Castle st
M'Dowall Alexander, Castle st

INNS.
Buck's Head, David Kennedy,
    Hanover st   [George st
George Hotel, Elizabeth Paterson,
King's Arms, Ths. King, Charlotte st
Stair's Arms, Stair Adair, Lewis st

LINEN & WOOLLEN DRAPERS
Auld William & Co. George st
Black Samuel, Charlotte st
Brown Alexander, Church st
Douglas Alexander, George st
Douglas John, George st
Douglas Peter, George st
Gordon James, Charlotte st   [st
Kirkpatrick R. (& merchant) George
M'Dowall James, Church st
Thompson James, George st
Todd George, George st
Wither John, Hanover st

MESSENGERS.
M'Kinnell William, Lewis st
M'Lean Peter, Bridge st
M'Neel Caird Alexander, Strand st
M'William John, George st

MILLINERS & DRESS MAKRS·
Cochrane Margt. & Eliz. Queen st
Crawford Sarah, Hanover st
M'Gaw Helen, Bridge st
M'Geoch Rosanna, Castle st   [st
Ritchie Mary, Helen & Eliz. Princes
Stewart Elizabeth, Queen st
Warden Jane & Eliza, George st

NAIL MAKERS.
Gourley John, Strand st
M'Culloch Alexander, Castle st
Millar George, Strand st

NURSERY & SEEDSMEN.
(See also Seedsmen.)
Nicol Ann, Sun st
Ross John, Broadstone garden
Wilson James, Rosefield cottage

PAINTERS.
Atkins Hugh (coach & house) Glen st
Gibson Samuel (& glazier) Sun st
Parker — (& glazier) Bridge st
Thurburn Peter (coach) Neptune st

SADDLERS AND HARNESS MAKERS.
M'Cleary Robert, Charlotte st
M'Gowan William, Charlotte st
M'Kie William, Hanover st

SEEDSMEN.
(See also Nursery and Seedsmen.)
M'Culloch Hugh, George st
Porteous George, Castle st

SHIP BUILDER.
Douglas James, Shuchan mill

STONE MASONS.
Brown & Cairns, Sun st
M'Cormick David, St. Andrew st
M'Crackan John, Stoneykirk road
M'Dowall Hugh, Hanover st
Wallace & Co. Kirkcolm

SURGEONS & APOTHECARIES
Agnew Charles, George st
Armour William, Charlotte st
Guilmette Alexander (apothecary)
    George street
M'Master John, George st
Orgill John, Princes st
Wilson Robert, George st

TAILORS.
Evans William, St. Andrew st
Gordon James, Charlotte st
Lister William, Burn side
M'Bride Peter, St. John st
M'Carlie Thomas, St. John st
M'Dowall James, Church st
M'Neel Matthew, King st
Morrow James, Queen st
Murray George, Hanover st
Savage William, Bridge st
Sprott Thomas, George st

TALLOW CHANDLERS.
Wallace Michael (and soap boiler)
    Castle street
Watt Henry, Charlotte st

TANNERS.
Dalrymple Thomas, Mill hill st
Kerr John, King st
M'Master Anthony, George st

TIN-PLATE WORKERS.
Christie Alexander, George st
Kerr Charles, Castle st
Kerr Francis, Castle st

VINTNERS.
Abernethy Jane, Bridge st
Alexander William, Kirkcolm
Biggam Samuel, Leswalt
Culloch Jean, Fisher st
Fleming Thomas, Neptune st
Gibson William, Hanover st
Gordon John, Charlotte st
Gracey James, St. John st
Hamilton John, St. John st
Hannah Thomas, King st
Jeffery Michael, Sun st
M'Crackan James, Neptune st
M'Crea Margaret, Kirkcolm
M'Cullock James, Stoneykirk road
M'Dowall John, King st
M'Gaw Alexander, King st
M'Harg John, Queen st
M'Ilwraith John, Mill hill st
M'Kie Mary, Castle st
M'Master John, Inch
Millar Robert, Bridge st
Nibloe John, Bridge st
Ross Jean, Kirkcolm
Stevenson Elizabeth, Hanover st
Stewart William, Castle st
Tunnick William, Kirkcolm
Wilson David, Church st

WATCH & CLOCK MAKERS.
Brown Charles, Lewis st
Garrick Fergus, Charlotte st
Garrick John, Castle st
Jamison James, Castle st
M'Credie Thomas, George st

WINE & SPIRIT MERCHANTS
Hunter James and Son, Church st
Morland William (and timber)
    Queen street

WRIGHTS.
See Carpenters & Joiners; and also
Cartwrights.

WRITERS.
Adair & M'Neel-Caird, Strand st
Guthrie David, Church st
M'Kinnell William, Lewis st
M'Lean Peter, Bridge st
Robertson Wingate, George st
Ross & M'William (James Hunter
    Ross, town clerk) George st
Sprott William, Church st

Miscellaneous.
Black William, leather dealer, George st
Brooks —, confectioner, Princes st
Brown Thomas, agent, Castle st
Campbell Abraham, agent to the Stranraer
    Steam Packet Company, Queen st
Hamilton John, sail maker, St. John st
Hood James, brewer, Strand st
Jeffery John, plasterer, Sun st
Irving John, hair dresser, &c. George st
Kennedy David, master of the Maid of
    Galloway steamer, Hanover st
M'Candlish William, dyer, Hanover st
M'Credie William, bookbinder, Fisher st
Mann Alexander, hat maker, George st
Savage John, turner, St. Andrew st

Public Buildings, Offices, &c.

PLACES OF WORSHIP.

ESTABLISHED CHURCH, Stranraer—Rev. David Wilson. [Wm. Rose.
ESTABLISHED CHURCH, Kirkcolm—Rev.
ESTABLISHED CHURCH, Leswalt—Rev. Andrew M'Cubbin. [Ferguson.
ESTABLISHED CHURCH, Inch—Rev Jas.
RELIEF—Rev. John M'Gregor.
SECESSION—Rev. William Smillie.
CAMERONIAN—Rev. William Symington.

CUSTOM HOUSE—Alexander M'Neel, esq. collector; John Semple, esq. comptroller; William Fernie, tide waiter at PORTPATRICK; and three officers.
EXCISE OFFICE—Moore & Smith, officers.
NEWS ROOM, George street—William Buchanan, manager.
STAMP AND TAX OFFICE, George st—R. Kirkpatrick, distributer and collector.

COACHES.

To DUMFRIES, the Royal Mail (from Portpatrick), calls at the King's Arms, every evening at seven; goes through Glenluce, Newton-Stewart and Gatehouse.
To GLASGOW, the Royal Mail (from Portpatrick), calls at the King's Arms, every afternoon at four; goes through Girvan, Maybole, Ayr, Kilmarnock, &c.
To KIRKMAIDEN, a Car, from the Buck's Head, every Friday.
To PORTPATRICK, the Royal Mail (from Glasgow), calls at the King's Arms, every morning at four, and (from Dumfries,) every evening at eight.

CARRIERS.

To AYR, John Steven, from the Buck's Head, every Thursday.
To GIRVAN, John Stratton, from the Buck's Head, every Saturday.
To GLENLUCE, William M'Dowall, from the George Hotel, and Wm. M'Dowall, from the Stair's Arms, Tues. and Sat.
To KIRKMAIDEN, B. Gilmore, from the Stair's Arms, every Tuesday.
To NEWTON-STEWART, Isabella Agnew, from the George Hotel, every Wed. and Sat.—and Alexander Telford, from Mrs. Abernethy's, Bridge st, Sat.

To PAISLEY, Hugh Reid, from Mrs. Abernethy's, Bridge st. once a fortnight.
To PORT WILLIAM, Wm. M'Culloch, from the Stair's Arms, every Wed.
To PORTPATRICK, James Rankin, from Mrs. Abernethy's, Bridge street, every Tuesday, Thursday & Saturday.
To WHITHORN, H. Matthews, from the Stair's Arms, every Wednesday.
To WIGTOWN, John Simpson, from the Stair's Arms, every Tuesday.

STEAM PACKETS.

To BELFAST and WHITEHAVEN, the Maid of Galloway, every Monday—Abraham Campbell, agent
To GLASGOW, the Loch Ryan, every Wednesday and Saturday morning, during summer, and on Friday in the winter—A. Campbell, agent; and the Nimrod, every Monday during the summer season—Thomas Brown, agent.
To GLASGOW & BELFAST, the Stranraer Company's vessels twice a week—A. Campbell, agent.

WHITHORN,

WITH THE ISLE OF WHITHORN, AND THE PARISH OF GLASSERTON.

WHITHORN (or *Whithern*) is a town of considerable antiquity and a royal burgh, in the parish of its name; 40 miles E. by s. of Portpatrick, 32 s.E. of Stranraer, nearly 20 s. of Newton-Stewart, and 10 s. of Wigton; situate not far distant from the shore of Wigton bay. It was originally inhabited by a tribe of Britons called the *Novantes*, and was then a town of some consequence: it is mentioned by Ptolemy under the name of *Leucophibia*; the Saxons called it *Hwitærn*, and from the latter the appellation *Whithern* is derived. St. Ninian built a church here in the fourth century, which Bede mentions as the first that was erected of stone. During the eighth century it was the seat of the bishops of *Candida Casa*, and it formed the episcopal capital of a bishopric of Galloway in the twelfth century. After the period of the reformation, however, it is seldom mentioned in public transactions, and seems to have sunk into obscurity. The trade of the place, at the present day, is inconsiderable; and, with the exception of tanning, it possesses no branch that can be classed under the head of manufactures. The town consists chiefly of one street, running from north to south, with diverging alleys; nearly in the centre it is intersected by a small stream, across which a bridge has been thrown for the public accommodation.

From successive kings Whithorn received various charters constituting it a burgh of barony; it is now a royal burgh, but the period when it attained that distinction does not appear. It is governed by a provost, two bailies, and fifteen councillors; and joins with Stranraer, and other burghs herein before mentioned, in returning a member to parliament. The places of worship are the parish church, and meeting-houses for Cameronians and seceders. The church is remarkably neat, as well as spacious, and much superior to most of the parish kirks in this county; it is erected partly on the venerable ruins of the priory, founded by the pious St. Ninian, who is said to have been the first who converted the Picts to the Christian faith. These ruins are remarkably grand and imposing; they contain several large vaults, a beautiful Saxon and some Gothic arches, also sculptured royal armorial bearings of Scotland, and the dilapidated arms of the bishops of Galloway. The inhabitants of this town support a subscription library, and the provident classes a savings' bank; there is also a bible society, and another for educating poor children of all denominations. An annual fair is held on the 7th July, and a monthly cattle market on the 2nd Thursday from April to December.

The ISLE OF WHITHORN is a pleasant village, about three miles from Whithorn, of which it is the port. The coast-guard has an establishment here, under the command of a lieutenant of the royal navy. Near the village stand the remains of an old church, said to be the first built in this part of the kingdom, or, as some affirm, the first founded in Scotland.

The parish of GLASSERTON lies on the east coast of Luce Bay, bounded by Whithorn on the east, Mochrum on the west, and Kirkinner on the north; it extends seven miles and a half in length by a general breadth of two and a half, except in its northern part, where it is nearly double that space. The church stands in the southern quarter of the parish. On the coast near its north-western confines is Lag Point, with a small haven on the north, called Monreith Bay; a little village at its head is termed the Milltown of Monreith.

POST OFFICE, WHITHORN, Ellen Kindal, Post Mistress.—Letters from all parts arrive every morning at seven in summer and eight in winter, and are despatched every forenoon at eleven.

GENTRY AND CLERGY.

Clauahan Rev. Samuel, Glasserton
Gibson Rev. James, Whithorn
Gourlay Mrs. Grace, Whithorn
Hathorn Hugh, esq. Castle wig
Johnston Lieutenant Henry (coast guard) Isle of Whithorn
Laurie Mr. Robert, Fine view
Maxwell the Misses, Physgill
Nicholson Rev. Christr. Whithorn
Sloan Mrs. Whithorn
Stewart Hugh Dunn, esq. Tundergie
Stewart Stair Hathorn, esq. Glasserton house

BAKERS.

Black Alexander, Whithorn
Campbell George, Whithorn
Gordon Alexander, Whithorn
M'Crea John, Whithorn

BLACKSMITHS.

Hannan John, Isle of Whithorn
Keand Robert, Whithorn
M'Dowall John, Whithorn
M'Guffie James, Whithorn
Peacock John, Whithorn

BOOT & SHOE MAKERS.

Hannah George, Whithorn
Kinnal Robert, Whithorn
Logan Peter, jun. Isle of Whithorn
M'Clure David, Isle of Whithorn
M'Clure John, Isle of Whithorn
M'Kelvie William, Whithorn
Wright David, Whithorn

CARTWRIGHTS.

M'Credie Hugh, Whithorn
Millar John, Whithorn
Wylie Robert, Whithorn

FLESHERS.

Douglas Andrew, Whithorn
Hannah James, Whithorn

GROCERS & TEA DEALERS.

Marked thus * are also Spirit Dealers.

Bell James, Whithorn
Broadfoot Jane, Isle of Whithorn
Carson Robert, Whithorn
Carter William, Whithorn
*Dickson William, Isle of Whithorn
Hannay James, Whithorn
*Jess James, Whithorn
Kugan Margaret, Isle of Whithorn

*Logan Peter, jun. Isle of Whithorn
M'Coid Jessie, Whithorn
M'Connel Margaret, Whithorn
M'Credie Margaret, Whithorn
M'Gaw Robert, Whithorn
*M'Guffie Margt. Isle of Whithorn
M'Kelvie John, Whithorn
M'Nonght Alexander, Whithorn
Marquis Agnes, Isle of Whithorn
Milne James, Isle of Whithorn
Nelson Mary, Isle of Whithorn
Stevenson John, Isle of Whithorn
Wilson Alexander, Whithorn

INN-KEEPERS & VINTNERS.

Carr Montgomery, Isle of Whithorn
Conning Caroline, Whithorn
Cumming George, Whithorn
Dickson John, Whithorn
Douglas Peter, Whithorn
Fortay Alexander, Isle of Whithorn
Hannah William, Whithorn
Hathorn Janet (Grapes) Whithorn
Hathorn Jno. (Commercial) Whithrn
Lawson Alexander, Whithorn

Logan Peter, Isle of Whithorn
M'Coskrie William, Whithorn
M'Credie Thomas, Whithorn
M'Culloch John, Whithorn
M'Millan Anthony, Whithorn
M'William Alex. Isle of Whithorn
Martin Jane, Whithorn
Reid John, Isle of Whithorn
Wallace John, Whithorn
Wilson William, Whithorn

IRONMONGERS.
Broadfoot John, Whithorn
Carson Robert, Whithorn

JOINERS & WRIGHTS.
Conning Andrew, Whithorn
Donnan John, Isle of Whithorn
M'Clelland John, Isle of Whithorn
M'Keand William, Whithorn
Millar George, Whithorn

LINEN & WOOLLEN DRAPERS
Blain Alexander, Whithorn
Dormon William, Whithorn
M'Donald Ronald, Whithorn
M'Kelvie William, Whithorn
Stewart Hugh, Whithorn

SADDLER.
Drape John, Whithorn

SPIRIT MERCHANTS.
Dinwoodie George, Whithorn
Lawson Alexander, Whithorn

SURGEONS.
Broadfoot Robert, Whithorn
Kindal Thomas, Whithorn
M'Millan Alexander, Whithorn

TAILORS.
Anderson William, Whithorn
Bell Samuel, Isle of Whithorn
Cannon Robert, Whithorn
Clanahan John (& draper) Whithorn
M'Dowall David, Whithorn
Simpson James, Whithorn
Simpson Thomas (& draper) Whithorn

TALLOW CHANDLERS.
Crawford James, Whithorn
Hannay James, Whithorn
Morrison Thomas, Whithorn

TANNER.
Brown William, Whithorn

WRIGHTS—See Joiners.

WRITERS.
Jorie John (& town clerk) Whithorn
Smith Robert Hannah, Whithorn

Miscellaneous.
Dinwoodie George, agent for the *Countess of Galloway* steam packet, Whithorn
Gibb William, watch maker, Whithorn
Gordon James, farrier, Whithorn
Hannah John, cooper, Whithorn
Laurie Sampson, hardwareman, Whithorn
Livingston Archbd. tide waiter, Isle of W.
M'Credie Wm. miller, Isle of Whithorn
M'Mekan Peter, ship carpenter, Isle of W.
Stewart William, nail maker, Whithorn
Thomson John, painter, &c. Whithorn
Walker Andrew, bookseller, &c. Whithorn
Wylie Jane, schoolmistress, Whithorn

PLACES OF WORSHIP.
ESTABLISHED CHURCH, Whithorn
—Rev. Christopher Nicholson
ESTABLISHED CHURCH, Glasserton
—Rev. Samuel Clanahan [son
SECEDERS, Whithorn—Rev. Js. Gibb
CAMERONIANS, Whithorn—(*Vacant*)

PAROCHIAL SCHOOLS.
GLASSERTON, James Gifford, master
WHITHORN, Robert Conning, master

CARRIERS.
To NEWTON-STEWART, Adam M'Keand, every Monday.
To STRANRAER, H. Matthews, Tues.
To WIGTOWN, Adam M'Keand, every Mon. and George Gardner, every Sat.

WIGTOWN,
AND THE PARISH OF KIRKINNER AND NEIGHBOURHOODS.

WIGTOWN (or WIGTON—the former mode of spelling, however, being now generally adopted, to distinguish this town from that of Wigton, in the county of Cumberland,) is a royal and parliamentary burgh, the seat of a presbytery, and the capital of the parish of its name; 105 miles s. s. w. of Edinburgh, 58 s. w. of Dumfries, 28 E. by s. of Stranraer, and 8 s. of Newton-Stewart; pleasantly situate on an eminence near the north side of the Bladenoch water, two miles from its junction with the Cree, or bay of Wigtown. It is a place of considerable antiquity, having come into existence, during the middle ages, from the erection of a castle on the spot by a band of successful Saxon invaders, who conferred on it the name of *Wig*, from the place having been contested in battle; the adjunct *ton*, or 'town,' was afterwards given when the town arose. The castle of Wigtown subsequently became a royal residence; but the town itself does not appear to have been conspicuous until the reign of David II, when it gave the title of earl to the family of Fleming. The principal street of the present town is a parallelogram, of which the internal space is laid out in shrubberies and inclosed by a rail, forming an agreeable promenade for the inhabitants. At the end of this is a very handsome modern cross, of granite, sculptured in an elegant and tasteful manner; at the other extremity is the town-house, having a tower of considerable height, which imparts a degree of dignity to the town. The building contains the court-room, an assembly-room, and a subscription library; the parish school is also accommodated beneath the same roof: the sheriff holds a debt court in it once a fortnight, for causes not exceeding £8. 6s. 8d.; and ordinary courts are held every Tuesday in time of session. Many new buildings have lately been erected, some of them of a very tasteful and costly description; and the burgh may, upon the whole, be considered in an improving condition. The inns and accommodations for strangers visiting the town are excellent; of the former there are two principal, one of which, the 'Commercial,' is an efficient posting-house. The harbour of Wigtown is safe, and has depth of water for vessels of three hundred tons burthen to approach the town. The principal exports from hence are corn and cattle; and there is a regular communication with Liverpool by steam-packets. An extensive brewery and a distillery (the latter at Bladenoch), with a private bank and a branch of the British Linen Company's bank, are the other leading pursuits in business. Wigtown is the seat of a custom-house, the members of which comprehend the creeks of Wigtonshire and those of the stewartry of Kirkcudbright, from the Mull of Galloway to the mouth of the river Fleet. In the year 1581 Wigtown was specified as one of the king's free burghs; it is (as a royal burgh) governed by a provost, two bailies, and fifteen councillors, and is associated with Stranraer, Whithorn and New Galloway in returning one member to the legislature; the constituency of the burgh is at present under one hundred.

The places of worship are a church of the establishment, and a meeting-house for seceders. A masonic lodge and a friendly society are in the town; the latter, which was established in 1795, possesses a capital of £600. There is a superior boarding establishment for young gentlemen, which is very ably conducted by the master of the grammar school. The parish of Wigtown extends five miles in length by four in breadth: it has several eminences throughout, but is in general flat and fertile. At the western extremity of the parish are nineteen large granite stones, placed in a circular form: they are supposed to have belonged to a druidic place of worship or sacrifice, while tradition points to the spot as the tomb of King Galdus. The market, which is, by charter, to be holden on Saturday, is now but little observed. Fairs are also entitled to be held at Candlemas, on the first Monday in April, and the first Fridays in July and August, all old style;—these are, however, in a great measure, discontinued.

The kirk town of KIRKINNER is about three miles from Wigtown, on the road to Garlies, and is remarkable for its beautiful and picturesque scenery. The principal ornament in this neighbourhood is the stately mansion of Col. P. V. Agnew. Here are also the remains of the ancient castle of Baldoun, formerly a residence of the Dunbars, an incident in which family is supposed to have served as the foundation of the 'Bride of Lammermuir,' by the late Sir. W. Scott. The parish extends three miles along Wigton bay, the Bladenoch water dividing it, on the north, from Wigtown, and Dowalton lake touching it on the south. The ruins of Longcaster church (the parish now incorporated with Kirkinner,) stand a mile from the lake.

POST OFFICE, WIGTOWN, Thomas Tait, *Post Master.*—Letters from LONDON, &c. arrive every afternoon at four, and are despatched every evening at nine.—Letters from PORTPATRICK, Ireland, &c. arrive every night at twelve, and are despatched every afternoon at two.—Letters from WHITHORN (by Garlieston) arrive every afternoon at twenty minutes before two, and are despatched every morning at four.

GENTRY & CLERGY.

Agnew Colonel P. V. Barnbarrouch
Blain Mrs. Helen, Wigtown
Boyd Capt. Robert, R. N. Wigtown
Briercliff Miss Martha, Wigtown
M'Donald Mrs. Johanna, Wigtown
M'Guffie John, esq. Barbadoes villa
M'Haffie Major, Torhouse muir
Murray John, esq. Wigtown
Reid Rev. James, Kirkinner
Towers Rev. James, Wigtown
Tweedale Mr. James, Wigtown
Young Rev. Peter, Wigtown

ACADEMIES AND SCHOOLS.

GRAMMAR SCHOOL & COMMERCIAL ACADEMY, Wigtown—Maxwell M'Master, master
M'Keand Jane, Wigtown
PAROCHIAL SCHOOL, Kirkinner—William Lewis, master
Porteous Joseph Baxter, Wigtown
Wylie Miss, Wigtown

BAKERS.

M'Jerrow David, Wigtown
M'Kie John, Wigtown
M'Queen Anthony, Wigtown
Shennan Peter, Wigtown

BANKERS.

BRITISH LINEN Co. (Branch) Wigtown—(draw on Smith, Payne & Smiths, London)—Jno. Black, agt
Donnan James, Wigtown

BOOKSELLERS, STATIONERS AND PRINTERS.

M'Minn Janet, Wigtown
Tait Thomas, Wigtown

BOOT AND SHOE MAKERS.

Carnochan John, Wigtown [town
Carnochan Thos. (& currier) Wig-
Dally John, Wigtown
Dally Thomas & Son, Wigtown
Douglas William, Bladenoch
M'Kinnal & Son, Kirkinner
M'Master John, Wigtown
M'Master William, Wigtown
M'Millan Thomas, Wigtown
Reid Arthur, Wigtown
Robinson Charles, Kirkinner
Roddy Thomas, Bladenoch
Scamble George, Wigtown

BREWER.

Fraser Gordon, Wigtown

CABINET MAKERS.

Bell John, Wigtown
Calderwood John, Wigtown
Reid Robert, Wigtown

COOPERS.

Forlow John, Wigtown
Melroy Alexander, Wigtown

DISTILLERS.

M'Clelland John and Thomas and Co. Bladenoch

FIRE, &c. OFFICE AGENTS.

INSURANCE COMPY. OF SCOTLAND, Andrew M'Master, Wigtown
NORWICH, John Black, Wigtown
PHŒNIX, Thomas Murray, Wigtown
SCOTTISH UNION, George M'Haffie, Wigtown

FLESHERS.

Adamson John, Wigtown
Chesney Robert, Wigtown
M'Geoch Anthony (& cattle dealer) Wigtown

GROCERS & SPIRIT DEALERS

Bennet Agnes, Bladnoch
Caffary John, Wigtown
Carnochan Agnes, Wigtown
Cuningham Peter, Wigtown
Gulline John (& glass dealer) Wigtn
Hannay Grace, Wigtown

Kelvie Peter, Wigtown
Kevand Alexander, Wigtown
Law Margaret, Wigtown [town
M'Geoch Wm. (& wholesale) Wig-
M'Keand Peter, Wigtown
M'Kie Susan, Wigtown
M'Kinnal Robert, Kirkinner
M'Minn Janet (& druggist) Wigtown
M'Queen Anthony, Wigtown
Milligan Agnes (& druggist) Wigtwn
Owen Michael, Wigtown
Skiming Elizabeth, Wigtown
Skimming William, Kirkinner
Thompson Elizabeth, Bladenoch
Wither Mary, Bladenoch

INNS.

Commereial Inn (& posting house) John M'Dowall, Wigtown
Red Lion, James Tait, Wigtown

IRONMONGERS.

Dickson James (and iron merchant) Wigtown
M'Master Andrew, Wigtown
Milligan Agnes, Wigtown

JOINERS & WRIGHTS.

Fraser William, Wigtown
Graham Robert, Kirkinner
Kelly Thomas, Wigtown
Kevan William, Wigtown
M'Kie Andrew, Wigtown
M'Kie Peter, Bladenoch
M'Murray John, Wigtown
M'Queen James, Wigtown
Parker Alexander, Kirkinner

LINEN & WOOLLEN DRAPERS

Donnan Alexander, Wigtown
M'Guffie James, Wigtown
Morison Alexander, Wigtown
Tait James M. Wigtown

MESSENGERS

Carson William, Wigtown
M'William William, Wigtown

MILLERS.

M'Gowan Margaret, Torhouse mill
M'Queen William, New mills
Routledge William, Kirkinner

PAINTERS.

Allison Joseph, Wigtown
Cowan David, Wigtown
Kelly William, Wigtown
Michael Samuel, Wigtown

SADDLERS AND HARNESS MAKERS.

Donnan Ebenezer, Wigtown
M'Master Andrew, Wigtown

SALT DEALERS.

Adamson John, Wigtown
M'Master Andrew, Wigtown
Owen Michael, Wigtown

SMITHS.

Anderson Peter, Bladenoch
Beddie David, Wigtown
Keughan William, Wigtown
M'Candlish Robert, Wigtown
M'Millan Alexander, Wigtown
Milroy William, Wigtown

SPIRIT MERCHANTS.

Dunn Henry (& seedsman) Wigtown
M'Geoch William, Wigtown
Owen Michael, Wigtown

SURGEONS & APOTHECARIES

Broadfoot David, Wigtown
Dalziel William, A. R. N. Wigtown

TAILORS.

Gardner Samuel, Wigtown
Henderson John, Wigtown
M'Clumpha Peter, Bladenoch
M'Cormick John, Kirkinner
M'Taggart William, Wigtown
Nelson Alexander, Bladenoch
Thompson William, Wigtown

TALLOW CHANDLERS.

M'Caudlish Robina, Wigtown
Milligan Agnes, Wigtown

TIMBER & SLATE MERCHNTS

Marshall, M'Master and Co. (and importers of tallow, herrings, &c.) Wigtown

VINTNERS.

Cowan John, Kirkinner
Cunningham John, Bladenoch
Dodds James, Wigtown
Harrison Robert, Wigtown
Harvey Janet, Wigtown
Johnston John, Kirkinner
M'Guffie John, Wigtown
M'Mekan Andrew, Bladenoch
M'William Robert, Wigtown
Murray Catherine, Wigtown

WATCH & CLOCK MAKERS.

Halliday Peter, Wigtown
M'Gowan William, Wigtown
Tait William, Wigtown

WOOL CARDER AND DYER.

Dunlop Robt. Torhouse waulk mill

WRIGHTS—See Joiners.

WRITERS.

Marked thus * are also Notaries.
*Agnew Geo. (& sheriff clerk) Wigtn
Beddie John, Wigtown
*Black John (clerk of the peace for the county and treasurer to the Galloway Steam Navigation Co.) Wigtown [Wigtown
Carson William (and town clerk)
*Hawthorn John (and joint town clerk) Wigtown [Wigtown
M'Donell Alex. (sheriff substitute)
*M'Haffie George (provost of the borough of Wigtown and general clerk of public meetings) Wigtown
M'Haffie John, Wigtown
*Simson John, Wigtown

Miscellaneous.

Brearcliffe Martha, boarding and lodging house, Wigtown
Cameron Alexander, nail maker, Wigtown
Gibson Jas. lint and saw mill, Kirkinner
Herron Robert, timber dealer, Bladenoch
Kilpatrick William; cartwright, Bladenoch
M'Candlish Eliz. straw hat mkr. Wigtown
M'Caul Anthony, farmer, Burrow moss
M'Clellan John, corn dealer, Wigtown
M'Taggart Margt. dress maker, Wigtown
Stevenson John, gardener, Wigtown
Tait Thomas, precentor to the Seceders' church, Wigtown
Wilson John, farmer, West Kirkland
Wyllie Mr. George, Bladenoch
Wyllie Mr. Samuel, Bladenoch

PLACES OF WORSHIP.

ESTABLISHED CHURCH, Wigtown—Rev. Peter Young. [James Reid.
ESTABLISHED CHURCH, Kirkinner—Rev.
SECEDERS, Wigtown—Rev. Jas. Towers.

CUSTOM HOUSE.

Collector—John Simpson, esq.
Comptroller—Thomas Young, esq.
Supervisor—Henry Carr.
Harbour Master—John M'Guffie.

CARRIERS.

To DUMFRIES, Wm. Raside, Monday.
To EDINBURGH, John M'Candlish, every alternate Monday.
To ELDRICK, Jas. Stanhope, Saturday.
To GARLIESTON, Alex. Dick, Saturday.
To GLASGOW, M'Clurg & Steel, every Tuesday and Saturday.
To MOCHRUM, Hugh Gibson. Saturday.
To PORT WILLIAM, Wm. M'Culloch, every Saturday.
To STRANRAER, John Simson, Monday.
To WHITHORN, Adam M'Keand, every Tues. and George Gardner, every Sat.

CONVEYANCE BY WATER.

To CREETOWN, a passage boat daily.
To LIVERPOOL, the Countess of Galloway steam packet, once a fortnight.
To WHITEHAVEN, vessels sail weekly.

Slater's Directory
1852

DUMFRIES-SHIRE.

THIS is a large and important shire, in the south of Scotland; bounded on the east by the counties of Roxburgh and Selkirk; on the north-west by Ayrshire; on the south-west by the stewartry (or county) of Kirkcudbright; on the north by the counties of Lanark, Peebles, and part of Selkirk; its south and south-eastern boundary is washed by the Solway Frith, and its south-eastern base is skirted by Roxburghshire and the English county of Cumberland. The length of the county, from north-west to south-east, is nearly fifty-five miles; and its extreme breadth, from the south to where it touches Peeblesshire on the north, is nearly thirty miles. According to the latest and best surveys, it embraces an area of one thousand, two hundred and twenty-eight square miles, or seven hundred and eighty-five thousand, nine hundred and twenty statute acres of land, and about ten square miles of lakes.

EARLY HISTORY.—At the epoch of the Roman invasion under Agricola, in the year 80, this part of Scotland was inhabited by a race called the *Selgovæ*, who spread themselves as far as the banks of the Dee, in Galloway: these people continued independent till the year 875, when they were overpowered by the Northumbrian Saxons, who retained the ascendancy for two centuries; during the lapse of this time, however, immense swarms of adventurers from Ireland and Cantyre effected a settlement; and from these intermixtures sprung the Picts, who progressively acquired the paramount sway. At this period Dumfries-shire is understood to have formed part of Cumbria, which district Edgar bequeathed to his youngest brother David, who encouraged the cupidity of many opulent Anglo-Norman barons, and the country was then divided into extensive baronies. The almost interminable border warfare was a frightful calamity to the inhabitants of Dumfries-shire and Cumberland, who for centuries were subjected to all the horrors attendant upon barbarous incursion and reckless feudal hostility. When the civil war broke out under Charles I, the common people entered heartily into the covenant, and the shire was disturbed by the exertions made by the loyal noblemen and gentlemen in quelling the insurrections. Attachment to the house of Stuart ruined several of the great families; and humbler causes have conspired to extinguish many names of great local interest. The Maxwells were completely ruined by the attainder of the Earl of Nithsdale in 1715. The Douglasses of Queensberry, and the Johnstons of Annandale, have merged in other families, and out of the general wreck the noble house of Buccleuch has risen to the greatest prosperity and influence of any family in the south of Scotland. From being thus so frequently subjected to the horrors of early invasion and predatory warfare, and being so partitioned into baronies, the shire exhibits, even to this day, the remains of some very important castles and places of security.

SOIL and SURFACE, PRODUCE, MANUFACTURES, &c.—The lower parts of Dumfries-shire are based with brown, red, yellow, or white sandstone, which dips generally to the Solway; a considerable body of limestone also lies in this quarter, and beds of ironstone are occasionally found to accompany the other strata. Coal prevails in great plenty in the upper portions of Nithsdale and lower parts of Eskdale, the two extreme points of the county. The limestone of the shire has been of great value in improving the lands; marl likewise abounds in various tracts, and of freestone and whinstone there is a sufficiency in all directions: marble is also procured for different useful and ornamental purposes; and near the northern confines of the county, at Wanlock head, there are inexhaustible mines of lead. As in most districts of the south of Scotland, there is a very general mixture of arable and pasture land. The upper part of the shire, or Annandale, Eskdale, and Ewesdale, is principally devoted to sheep-feeding; in the lower portion the farms are larger, and more adapted to agriculture; the plantations and pleasure grounds are consequently more numerous, and are remarkable for their beauty and richness. The following are the principal eminences in Dumfries-shire, with their altitude above the level of the sea:—

In Nithsdale District.	FEET.	*In Annandale District.*	FEET.	*In Eskdale District.*	FEET.
Wardlaw (in Caerlaverock)	826	Annan Hill	256	Moss Paul (Inn and Stage, Vale of Ewes)	820
Auchinleck	1,500	Repentance Tower	350		
Wanlockhead (village)	1,564	Brunswark Hill (Tunder-garth parish)	740	Langolm Hill	1,204
Cairn-Kennow(nr.Drumlanrig)	2,080			Tinnis Hill	1,366
Queensberry Hill	2,250	Erickstane Brae	1,118	Wisp (in Ewes)	1,910
Black Larg(border Ayrshire)	2,890	Loch-Skene	1,300	Etterick, or Phawhope Penn	2,220
Lowthers (nr.Wanlockhead)	3,150	Hartfell (near Moffat)	2,629		

In Annandale the improvement of the breed of cattle has been most apparent; at the Highland Society's meetings some of the choicest specimens of the pure breed of Galloway cows, heifers, and bullocks are exhibited. The number of oxen, sheep, and pigs nurtured in this county are invariably more than adequate to the demands of its population; an exportation, therefore, of the excess product takes place—and the same may be observed of corn, wool, hides, and skins. The condition of the county is represented as having been greatly improved within the last forty years, and at present its affairs may be considered in as prosperous state as those of any other district of Scotland. Dumfries-shire cannot be ranked as a manufacturing county: the principal branches under this head are the manufacture of hosiery goods and cotton spinning; the chief seat of the former is limited to the capital of the county—the latter to the town of Annan.

RIVERS, &c.—The chief, indeed the only rivers of consequence, are the Nith, the Annan, and the Esk: from these streams the principal divisions of the county obtain their names; from each of these greater divisions diverge vales, which likewise have denominations taken from the waters that are poured through them, such as Moffatdale, Dryfesdale, and Ewesdale. The Nith rises in the eastern hills of Ayrshire, enters Nithsdale by the foot of Carsoncone hill, in the parish of Kirkconnel, and descends into the valley of Sanquhar; having forced its way through the hills which surround this valley, it receives the Crawick water from the north, and the Euchan from the south. The river Cairn, which forms the western boundary of the county, unites its stream with the Nith a little above Dumfries, a short distance southward from which the latter river empties itself into the Solway Frith. Near to Jarborough castle, on the banks of the river Cairn, are to be seen those earthen mounds, called 'Bow-butts,' where the barons of Glencairn, with their vassals, used to practice archery. The river

Annan (as well as the Tweed and Clyde), takes its rise in the mountains above Moffat, and runs through the flat part of Annandale for upwards of twenty-three miles; in this course it receives the Evan and Moffat waters, and the Wamphray stream; which irrigates a pleasant valley of that name: passing Johnstone, some other tributary rivulets increase its volume; at Loch Maven it is enlarged by the Ae, and a little lower by the Dryfe, which courses through the vale of Dryfesdale, considered the termination of the vale of Annan.　The higher part of Eskdale, for nearly twenty miles, is mountainous: the Esk, in its progress through this district, is joined by the Black Esk, the Meggot, the Ewes, and the Wauchope—(almost the whole of this division belongs to the noble family of Buccleuch): after reaching Broomholm, the river traverses a flat country, and a part of Cumberland, before it reaches the Solway Frith; during this portion of its course it receives the Liddal from Roxburghshire, and the Line water from the county of Cumberland: the entire length of its race is about thirty-eight miles, thirty of which are in the shire of Dumfries.　The Solway differs very materially from other estuaries receiving in Scotland the appellation of ' Firths:' its waters are shallow, and have long sandy reaches at the ebbing of the tide.　The ebbs and flows of the Solway are proverbial for the rapidity of their action, and this is particularly the case during spring tides and the prevalence of gales from the south-west: the borderers, though well mounted, have, in numerous melancholy instances, been overwhelmed and drowned, when returning from the Cumberland fairs, in crossing the bed of this estuary—even the most experienced persons are liable to be overtaken by the tides, when they have the best expectation of fording it in safety: on one occasion, within these few years, a gentleman who had been thus engulphed was preserved by the sagacity and courage of his horse, which swam with him right across the Firth. The principal lines of RAILWAY now in operation, are, the ' Glasgow and South-Western,' and the ' Caledonian.' The first named includes in its route, the towns of Dumfries, Annan, Closeburn, Sanquhar and Thornhill.　The Caledonian goes to Gretna, Cummertrees, Lockerbie, Moffat and within a mile of Ecclefechan.

DIVISIONS and REPRESENTATION.—The whole county is now popularly apportioned into three districts, namely—ESKDALE on the east, ANNANDALE in the middle, and NITHSDALE on the west.　It is ascertained that Dumfries-shire was placed under the government of a sheriff in the thirteenth century, at which period it included the stewartry of Kirkcudbright; the district of Annandale, however, continued to be a stewartry from the period when it merged in the Crown, by the accession of Bruce, till the abolition of the heritable jurisdictions.　Up to the era of the reformation, Dumfries-shire formed part of the extensive diocess of Glasgow, and was divided into the two deaneries of Nithsdale and Annandale ; it now possesses forty-three parishes, which are divided into five presbyteries and one synod.　There are four royal burghs in the county,—Dumfries, Annan, Sanquhar, and Lochmaben; and six burghs of barony—Moffat, Lockerby, Langholm, Ecclefechan, Thornhill, and Minniehive.　The shire at large sends one member to parliament, and the royal burghs before named join with Kirkcudbright in returning another representative.

POPULATION OF THE SHIRE, IN THE YEARS, 1801, 1811, 1821, 1831 AND 1841.

The Italic letters b. p. and t. signify respectively Burgh, Parish, and Township.

	1801	1811	1821	1831	1841		1801	1811	1821	1831	1841
Annan ....*b. & p.*	2570	3341	4186	5033	5471	Kirkmahoe ....*p.*	1315	1464	1608	1601	1568
Applegarth ....*p.*	795	858	943	999	857	Kirkmichael ....*p.*	904	1035	1202	1226	1578
Canonbie ....*p.*	2580	2749	3084	2997	3032	Kirkpatrich—Fleming ..*p.*	1544	1664	1696	1666	1692
Caerlaverock ....*p.*	1014	1170	1200	1271	1297	Kirkpatrick—Juxta ...*p.*	596	821	912	981	934
Closeburn ....*p.*	1679	1762	1682	1680	1530	Langholm............*p.*	2039	2636	2636	2676	2820
Cummertrees ....*p.*	1369	1633	1551	1407	1277	Lochmaben ....*b. & p.*	2053	2392	2651	2795	2809
Dalton ....*p.*	595	691	767	730	638	Middlebie............*p.*	1507	1983	1874	2107	2150
Dornock ....*p.*	691	788	743	752	847	Moffat ....*p.*	1619	1824	2218	2221	2199
Dryfesdale ....*b. & p.*	1607	1893	2251	2283	2093	Morton ....*p.*	1255	1570	1806	2140	2161
Dumfries ....*b. & p.*	7288	9262	11052	11696	11409	Mouswald ....*p.*	705	769	795	786	683
Dunscore ....*p.*	1174	1325	1491	1488	1517	Mungo, Saint ....*p.*	644	727	709	791	618
Durisdeer ....*p.*	1148	1429	1601	1488	1145	Penpoint ....*p.*	966	987	1082	1232	1266
Eskdalemuir ....*p.*	547	581	651	659	616	Ruthwell ....*p.*	936	1184	1285	1216	1032
Ewes ....*p.*	358	348	314	335	328	Sanquhar............*b. & p.*	2350	2709	{ 1357	1527 }	3577
Glencairn ....*p.*	1403	1566	1831	2068	2094	Sanquhar ....*p.*			963	1066	
Graitney (or Gretna)....*p.*	1765	1749	1945	1909	1761	Wanlochhead ....*t.*	....	....	706	675	
Halfmorton ....*p.*	497	....	553	616	737	Tindwall ....*p.*	980	1204	1248	1220	1805
Hoddam ....*p.*	1250	1328	1540	1582	1627	Torthorwald ....*p.*	702	932	1205	1320	1346
Holywood............*p.*	839	830	1004	1066	1051	Tundergarth ....*p.*	484	522	518	530	524
Hutton and Corrie......*p.*	616	677	804	860	809	Tynron ....*p.*	563	574	513	493	474
Johnstone............*p.*	740	904	1179	1234	1072	Wamphray ....*p.*	423	481	554	580	509
Keir ....*p.*	771	993	987	1084	984	Westerkirk ....*p.*	638	698	672	642	638
Kirkconnel ....*p.*	1093	1017	1075	1111	1130						
						TOTAL POPULATION OF DUMFRIES-SHIRE........	54606	62960	70878	73770	74043

The total annual value of Real Property, in Dumfries-shire, as assessed in April, 1815, amounted to £295,621.; and the amount assessed to the Property Tax, in 1843, to £291,869. 15s. 6d.

ANNAN AND BRIDE-KIRK.

ANNAN the capital of the district of Annandale and of its parish, is an ancient royal burgh, 79 miles s. of Edinburgh, 87 s.e. of Glasgow, 43 n.e. of Kirkcudbright, 27 s. of Moffat, 16 s. e. of Dumfries, and 6 from Ecclefechan; situated on the east or left bank of the river Annan, rather more than a mile above its influx into the Solway Frith; and upon the Carlisle, Dumfries and South Western railway, for which line there is a station here. The name is derived from that of the river, whose appellation is traced to the Celtic *An*, signifying simply water. It is a town of considerable antiquity, and is one of the most ancient burghs in Scotland. Annan was a Roman station, and the *Verorutm* of the geography of Ravenna. It seems to have been held by the Britons after the departure of the Romans, till they were subdued by the Saxons of Northumbrian kingdom, when it came to the Scotch. It afterwards became a principal port, and was granted, with the territory of Annandale and the port of Lochmaben, to the ancestors of Robert Bruce, by some of whom a castle was erected, which was once occupied as a church, but afterwards went to ruins, and the original wall now forms part of the gaol and town hall. Upon the death of David II., in 1371, this castle, Lochmaben, and the lordship of Annandale, came to Thomas Randolph, Earl of Murray, and went, with his sister Agnes, to the Dunbars, Earls of March; after their forfeiture it went to the Douglasses, who lost it by similar conduct, and then, having come to Alexander, Duke of Albany, he, for rebelling against his brother, king James III, and plundering the fair of Lochmaben, in 1484, also forfeited it. Since that period it continued in the hands of the king, and became the great key of the western border. By the accession of the Bruce family to the throne, it became a royal burgh. The existing charter was granted by James VI. of Scotland, and is dated July 10th, 1612; it confirms previous charters, and particularly recites one conferred by James V, dated 1st March, 1538, which had with others been burned and destroyed by sieges and the inroads of the English, particularly in 1298, when they entered Annandale, and burnt the town with its church. The burgh is governed by a provost, three bailies and fifteen councillors, a treasurer, a dean of guild, and a town clerk. It unites with Dumfries, Sanquhar, Lochmaben and Kirkcudbright, in returning one member to parliament.

The port or harbour of Annan is free, and vessels of two hundred and fifty tons can come within half a mile of the town, but vessels of much larger burthen can enter the river at its confluence with the Solway, distant little more than a mile from the town; at this place two new wooden wharfs or jetties have recently been erected by rival steam boat companies, whose vessels generally make the passage between Annan and Liverpool within twelve hours, that is, in one tide only, from harbour to harbour; and a vessel belonging to each company makes, at least, one trip to and from weekly. The convenience afforded by this rapidity of communication with Liverpool, has greatly increased the trade, and a considerable quantity of bacon, grain, live stock, and other commodities, are thus weekly conveyed to the Liverpool market; while, by return of these steam vessels, the principal supply of general merchandize is imported for the consumption of the town, and adjoining country to a very considerable distance, as the harbour of Annan is much preferable to that of Dumfries. Among the other branches of trade are those of shipbuilding, tanning, brewing, and malting; and there is an extensive distillery a short distance from the town, up the river. Branches of the 'Commercial Bank of Scotland,' of the 'British Linen Company,' and of the Western Bank of Scotland,' are settled here; there is also a Bank for savings. Limestone and freestone is abundant in many parts of the parish, which has been long famed for the superior quality of potatoes cultivated within it. Annan, of late years, has been much improved by new streets and buildings. The old bridge, which consisted of five arches, was removed some years since, and a new one erected on its site, towards which a grant £3,000 was obtained from government, and the remainder supplied by the county. On the west are the town-house and market-place, and at the east end of the town is a fine new church, built of stone, with a tower and spire. A free church, and united presbyterian, episcopal, independent, and Roman catholic chapels are the other places of worship. Parochial and infants' schools, and several private schools are well conducted; but the principal educational establishment is a classical academy: the building, a very, handsome one, was erected in 1820; in it are taught most of the elegant and all the useful branches of education. It is governed by the magistrates and a committee of heritors, and the preceptors consist of a rector, and teachers in the several branches.

The market is held on Thursday, at which, during the season, large quantities of pork are sold. There are fairs on the first Thursday in February, the first Thursday in May, the third Thursday in August, the first Tuesday after the 29th of September, the third Thursday in October, and the first Thursday after the 11th of November.

BRIDE-KIRK is a modern village, 3 miles N. from Annan, situated on the west bank of the Annan river. The proprietor is Mrs. General Dirom, through whose interest it was erected into a *QuoadSacra* parish in May, 1836; and the same lady built the kirk in 1835; she is looked upon as the responsible supporter of the minister. The remains of Bride-Kirk Tower are in this parish. Annan is the post town.

POST OFFICE, High-street, ANNAN, George Pool, *Post Master.*—Letters from CARLISLE and the SOUTH, arrive every morning at a quarter past nine, and are despatched at half-past three in the afternoon, and six in the evening.

Letters from DUMFRIES, &c. arrive every afternoon at a quarter past three, and are despatched at a quarter before nine in the morning.

Letters from places NORTH arrive (from ECCLEFECHAN), every morning at seven, and are despatched at twenty minutes before seven in the evening.

NOBILITY, GENTRY AND CLERGY.

Armstrong Mrs. Agnes, Scotch st
Beattie Mr. John, Church place
Beck Mrs. —, Port st
Bell Mrs. —, Greencroft
Bell Capt. Thomas, English st
Carruthers Mr. Andrew, English st
Carruthers Mr. D. A, Warmanbie
Clapperton Miss Georgiana, the Lodge
Clapperton Mrs. Mary, Thomas st
Clapperton Mr. John, Carlyle place
Connel Mr. —, Bloomfield
Cooke Rev. Henry Bowen, Moat
Dalgliesh Mrs. Margaret, Bruce st
Dickson Miss Jane, High st
Dickson the Misses Margaret & Isabella, Scotch street
Dickson Mrs. Mary, Church st
Dirom Mrs. Capt, Cleughheads

Dirom Mrs. General, Mount Annan
Dobbie Mrs. Jane, Johnston st
Drumlanrig Visct, M.P., Glen Stewart
Edgar Miss Janet, Johnston st
Foot Miss Margaret, Butt st
Forrest John Esq, Long Meadow
Forrest Mrs. Mary, Church st
Gailey Rev. James, Church st
Gardiner Rev. —, the Manse
Geddes Capt. William, Scotch st
Hannah the Misses Jane & Margaret Solway Cottage
Herrington Miss Ann, Downie's wynd
Hudson Mrs. Capt. John, Port st
Irving Mrs. Dorothy, Ednam st
Irving Miss Janet, Wellington st
Irving Rev. John, Bonshaw
Irving Mr. Nathaniel. High st
Irving Robert, Esq. Plumdon
Jackson Mrs. Margaret, High st
Johnston Mrs. Jane, Watch hill

Johnston Miss Janet, High st
Johnston Mr. William, Shaw hill
Keswick Mr. Thomas, Beech Grove
Lawson Mr. Wm, Colonel's wynd
Lenton Mrs. Robert, Greencroft
Little Miss Janet, Wellington st
Little Mrs. Jessie, Ednam st
Monilaws Rev. James, Port st
Nelson Mr. Philip, M.D, High st
Patterson Mr. John, Watch Hall
Richardson Mrs. Ann, Ednam st
Rodgerson Mr. James, North st
Rutherford Mr. James, Violet bank
Saunders James, Esq, Scotch st
Scott Mr. John, Ednam st
Scott Mrs. Martha, Green bank
Smith Miss Margaret, Wellington st
Thomson Mr. John, Beckfoot
Torbron Mrs. Ann, Downie's wynd
Wilson Mrs. Agnes, Watch hill
Young Rev. Ebenezer, Carlyle place

ACADEMIES AND SCHOOLS.

ACADEMY, Ednam st — Theodore Crosbie, classical master; Thomas White, mathematical master
Fell Jane, High st
Carlyle James, Lady st
Herbertson George, English st
INFANTS' SCHOOL, Solway st
Ireland Mary, Port st
Lorimer Matthew, Butt st
PAROCHIAL SCHOOL, Greenknow— William Sewell, master
PAROCHIAL SCHOOL, Bride-Kirk— William Jeffrey, master

BACON CURERS.

Forrest William, High st
Reidford John, Lady st
Steel David, English st

BAKERS & FLOUR DEALERS.

Baxter William, High st
Cartner Thomas, Murray st
Dixon John & Robert, High st
Hay David, High st
Hornel William, High st
Irving Jane, North st
Irving William, High st
Kay James, North st
Lottimer Charles, Scotch st
Lowrey Wm, Lodge wynd, High st
M'Donald Norman, High st
Patterson Andrew, High st
Reidford John, Lady st
Thomson George. North st
Waugh Ann, High st
Williamson John, North st
Wright George, High st

BANKERS.

BRITISH LINEN COMPANY (Branch), Bank st—(draw on the parent establishment, Edinburgh, the Bank of England and branches, and Smith, Payne & Smith's, London)—John Brand, agent
COMMERCIAL BANK OF SCOTLAND (Branch), High st—(draws on the parent establishment, Edinburgh, and Jones, Loyd & Co, London)—James Simpson and James S. Skelton, agents
WESTERN BANK OF SCOTLAND (Branch), High st—(draws on the parent establishment, Glasgow, and Jones, Loyd & Co, London)—John Forrest & Alexander Downie, agents
SAVINGS' BANK, High st—James Simpson & James S. Skelton, agents

BLACKSMITHS.

Blacklock Deborah, High st
Chalmers John, Port st
Cock James, George st
Dalgliesh James, High st
Holmes John, Port st
Jamieson Ebenezer, Bride Kirk
Johnstone James, Lodge walk
Johnstone Thomas, Ednam st, Lodge
Marshall John, Bride-Kirk
Smith Heron, Carlyle place

BOOKSELLERS & STATIONERS

Cuthbertson William, High st
Richardson Wellwood, High st
Watt Robert (binder), Murray st

BOOT AND SHOE MAKERS.

Bell William, Port st
Carrick William, Bride-Kirk
Farish Robert, Downie's wynd
Farish William, Downie's wynd
Firash Edward, Colonel's wynd
Graham John, Bank st
Halliday James, High st
Hannah James, High st
Irving John, Poplar cottage
Linton Robert, Butt st
Martin William, Bride-Kirk
Morton Thomas, Port st
Murdoch Thomas, High st
Rae Thomas, High st
Richardson James, High st
Scott John, Bride-Kirk
Shannon William, Colonel's wynd
Thomson James, Thorns, Bride-Kirk
Thomson John, Queensberry st
Waugh George, Butt st

CHEMISTS AND DRUGGISTS.

Halbert John Potts, High st
M'Kinnell Robert, High st
Robison William, High st
Williamson Ann, High st

CLOG MAKERS.

Bell Thomas, Bride-Kirk
Burnie William, Bank st
Dalrymple James, Colonel's wynd
Graham James, Lady st
Ross Thomas, Bride-Kirk

CLOTHES BROKERS AND DRAPERS.

Dobie John F., High st
Park William, High st
Petit Adam, George st
Scott John, High st
Thomson John, High st

COAL DEALERS.

Beattie James, Railway station
Little John, Port st
Moffat Thomas, Railway station
Scott Henry, Railway station
Watson Charles, Railway station
Weightman Robert, Railway station

CONFECTIONERS.

Hornel William, High st
Irving Margaret, Port st
M'Donald Norman, High st
Norval Isabella, Church st
Waugh Ann, High st

COOPERS.

Aitchison Andrew, Lodge wynd
Crawford Daniel, Nelson's close
King Jonathan, Downie's wynd

CURRIERS.

Baxter William, Ednam st
Moffatt John, Butt st

FIRE, &c. OFFICE AGENTS.

ABERDEEN, William Cuthbertson, High st [Bank st
BRITISH GUARANTEE, John Brand,
CALEDONIAN, Nathaniel Wield, Bank st [High st
EXPERIENCE, William Cuthbertson,
FARMERS', Alexander Downie, High st [High st
KENT MUTUAL, John Cunningham,
NATIONAL, William Carruthers, High st [High st
NORTH BRITISH, Simpson & Skelton,
SCOTTISH UNION, John Thomson, High st [High st
STANDARD, A. B. Bogie, M.D.
UNITED DEPOSIT, John Cunningham, High street

FLESHERS.

Hill Francis, Thomas st
Irving John & George, High st
Lindsay George, High st [st
Moffatt John & William, High

GROCERS.

Marked thus * are Spirit Dealers.
Bell Robert, Butt st
Brown Jane, Johnstone st
Carlyle James, Lady st
Carlyle Martin, Watch hill
Cartner Thomas, Murray st
*Chalmers Thomas, High st
Clark William, High st
Cuthbertson Thomas, Bride-Kirk
Dean Margaret, Scotch st
*Ewart James, High st
Fairbie John, Butt st
Farries James, High st
Forrest James, High st
Forsythe John, Bride-Kirk
*French David, High st
Graham Sarah, Bride-Kirk
Halliday Andrew, Bride-Kirk
Hamilton Robert, High st
*Hodgson Isaac, High st
*Irving Esther, Murray st
Irving Jane, Bride-Kirk
*Irving John, Port st
Irving Mary, Close st
*Irving Thomas, High st
*M'Lean Campbell, Port st
M'Lean Thomas, High st
Mill Janet, Wellington st
*Pool George, High st
Reid Adam, Port st
*Richardson John, High st
*Richardson Robert, High st
Scambler Henry Christr. High st
Scott James, High st
Scott Mrs. —, High st
Scott Robert, Bride-Kirk
*Scott Thomas, High st
*Smith William, Lady st
Steele James, Scotch st
*Swan John, High st
Turnbull Robert, High st
*Vivers William, High st
Williamson Ann, High st
*Wilson Andrew, Watch hill
Wright George, High st

HAIR DRESSERS.

Blaylock John, High st
Rule William, Downie's wynd

HATTERS.

Bonner James (manufacturer) High st
Nicholl Helen, High st

INNS.

(See also Vintners.)
Blue Bell, Jane Beattie, High st
Commercial, Robert Watson, High st
Queen-berry Arms Hotel, Henry Pilkington, High st
Steam Packet, William Smith, Port st

IRON MERCHANTS.

Cunningham John, High st
Forrest William, High st
Gunning Mary, High st
Hamilton Robert, High st

IRONMONGERS.

Cunningham John, High st
Gunning Mary, High st
Halliday Walter, High st
Hamilton Robert, High st

JOINERS AND CARPENTERS

Aitcheson Adam, Carlyle place
Dixon James, Butt st
Edgar Adam, High st
Ewart William, Bride-Kirk
Gass James, Downie's wynd
Graham George, Ednam st
Harkness Robert, Bride-Kirk
Irving William, High st
Johnstone Douglas, Scotch st
Kerr George, Butt st
Little Andrew, Johnstone st
Rome William, High st
Thompson John, New dyke

LINEN & WOOLLEN DRAPERS

Bell Simon (travelling), High st
Johnston George, High st
Montgomery John, High st
Thomson John, High st
Waugh William, High st

MANUFACTURERS.

Graham James, Thorns, Bride Kirk
Hall Francis, Bride-Kirk
Story & M'Gibbin (ginghams) Lodge
  wynd—James Wilson, agent

MASONS AND BUILDERS.

Beattie James, Bride-Kirk
Black James, Bride-Kirk
Brown Robert, Port st
Irving John, Carlyle place
Johnstone William, Carlyle place
Kerr Hugh, Rose st
M'Douie John L. Murray st
Pain George, Rose st

MILLERS.

Brown Robert, Bride-Kirk
Elliott William & John, North st
Richardson William, High st

MILLINERS AND DRESS MAKERS.

Burnett Isabella, North st
Holmes Ann, Butt st
Irving Jessie, Ednam st
Little Jane, High st
Lotimer Jane, High st
Nelson Maria, High st
Richardson Mary & Jane, High st
Wilson Helen, High st

NAIL MAKERS.

Baxter William, Close head
Forrest William, High st
Irving James, George st

NURSERY AND SEEDSMEN.

Bogie William, Downie's wynd
Glendinning John, Butt st
Hill Thomas, Johnstone st
Johnston John, Church st
Palmer John, Lady st

PAINTERS, GLAZIERS AND GILDERS.

Blacklock Joseph, High st
Cleminson John, Carlyle place
Gunning —, High st
Moyes David, Lodge wynd
Wadeson Robert, Murray st

PRINTERS.

Cuthbertson William, High st
Lorimer John (copper-plate), Lady st

ROPE MAKERS.

Irving John, Butt st
Lawson John, Scotch st. & Murray st

SADDLERS.

Hill James, High st
Johnstone William, High st

SHERIFF'S OFFICERS.

Hill Thomas, High st
Little William, Johnstone st
Smith John, High st

SHIP BUILDERS.

Brown James, Port st
Irving Robert, High st
M'Cubbin James, Port st
Mundie George, Port st
Nicholson John & Co. Port st

SHIP OWNERS.

Forrest William, High st
Johnstone Joseph, Watch hill
Lawson William, High st
Nicholson John & Co. Port st
Richardson Robert, High st
Weild David, High st

STRAW BONNET MAKERS.

Bell Jane, Church st
Calvert Elizabeth, Port st
Howe Mary, High st
Little Margaret, High st
Robertson Jessie & Jane, High st
Rome Mary, High st
Wilkinson Jane, High st

SURGEONS.

Bogie Agnew, Downie's wynd
Edgar William, Port st
Edie John, Vine cottage
Johnstone Robert, R.N. Wellington st
Williamson Thomas, Hill top

SURVEYORS.

Carruthers George, English st
Corsan William, Scotch st
Marshall Thomas, Ednam st
Nelson James, High st

TAILORS.

Drummond Thomas, Annan wall
Farish John, Carlyle place
Henderson John, High st
Irving George, High st
Jeffrey Adam, High st
Johnston George, High st
Lackie James, Rose st
Palmer John, Lady st
Pettit Adam, George st
Rae William, Bride-Kirk
Richardson James, Scotch st
Seaton James, Downie's wynd

VINTNERS.

Bell Jane (Britannia), Port st
Brough Joseph, Kenziel [High st
Campbell John (Old King's Arms), Clark William, Port st
Graham William (Coach & Horses),
  High street   [street
Harkness Francis (Old Bush), High
Hodgson Isaac (Shoulder of Mutton), High st
Lawson William, Waterfoot
Nicholson Jane (Shoulder of Mutton), Watch hill
Pool William, Port st
Pool William (Buck), High st
Robinson John (Crown & Thistle), High street
Rome William (Spear), High st
Scott Jane, Hill top   [High st
Shankland John (Burns' Tavern), Telford David, High st
Turnbull George, Close head

WATCH AND CLOCK MAKERS.

Hodgson John, Port st
Little John, High st
Wilkinson Joseph, High st

WRIGHTS.

See Joiners and Carpenters.

WRITERS.

Brand John (and notary), Bank st
Carruthers William, High st
Downie Alexdr. (& notary), High st
Little James, High st
M'Lellan John, High st

MISCELLANEOUS.

Baxter Charles, tallow chandler, High st
Burnie Wm. temperance hotel, Bank st
Burton Anthony, block maker, Port st
CUSTOM HOUSE, Port street—Robert
  Chalmers, coast waiter
Donald George, distiller, Annandale
Ewart Wm. manager of gas works, Rose st
Ferguson Wm. Ross, auctioneer, Bank st
Forrest James, tin-plate worker, High st
Forrest James, plumber, High st
Foster John, town officer, Gaol
Goss Elizabeth, brewer & maltster, Port st
Graham William, plasterer, Hope st
Little John, jeweller, High st
Lockerbie Wm. general dealer, Northgate
M'Kay Joseph, flax dresser, Bride-Kirk
M'Lellan John, messenger-at-arms High st
Moffatt John, tanner, Butt st
Nicholson John & Co. timber and slate
  merchants, Port street
Park William, plasterer, North st
POLICE STATION, High street—John
  Robertson, officer
Romney Geo. & Robt. sail makers, High st
Shaw Henry, skinner, Butt st
STAMP AND TAX OFFICE, Commercial
  bank, High street—James Simpson, distributer
Tait John, veterinary surgeon, High st
Turnbull John, castle dlr. Colonel's wynd
Turnbull Robert, cattle dealer, High st
Wilson Robert, weaver, Nelson's close

PLACES OF WORSHIP,

AND THEIR MINISTERS.

ESTABLISHED CHURCH—Rev. James Monilaws
FREE CHURCH—Rev. James Gailey
EPISCOPAL—Rev. Henry Bowen Cooke
PRESBYTERIAN, Green know
UNITED PRESBYTERIAN..Rev. James Gardiner
UNITED PRESBYTERIAN..(vacant)
INDEPENDENT, Colonel's wynd..Rev. Ebenezer Young
CATHOLIC, Close head..Rev. Henry Small

CONVEYANCE BY RAILWAY,

ON THE GLASGOW AND SOUTH-WESTERN LINE.

Station, about a quarter of a mile from the town..John Stevenson, collector
An Omnibus, from the Queensberry Arms, awaits the arrival, and attends the departure of the several trains

CARRIERS.

From the SPUR INN, High street.

To CARLISLE, John Davidson, Monday and Saturday, and John Moffatt, Wednesday and Saturday.
To DUMFRIES, John Davidson, Wed.

CONVEYANCE BY WATER,

STEAM PACKETS.

To LIVERPOOL, the Cumberland, every Wednesday and Saturday....David Baxter, agent

---

CAERLAVEROCK PARISH,

INCLUDING THE VILLAGES OF BANK-END, KELTON, GLENCAPLE-QUAY, AND NEIGHBOURHOODS.

THE parish of CAERLAVEROCK occupies a sort of Peninsula, formed by the Solway Firth, the river Nith, and Lochan water. The magnificent ruin of Caerlaverock castle, stands on a level plain, between 8 and 9 miles from Dumfries. It is an ancient possession of the Maxwells, once a powerful family in this part of Scotland, and wardens of the western marches. It was besieged and captured by Edward I., in 1300, and by Cromwell in 1651. After this it ceased to be a tenable fortress, and fell into decay: it now presents a ruin massive and picturesque, eminently worthy the notice of the tourist. This ancient fortalice was the scene of a foul and remarkable murder, about the middle of the fourteenth century, which has furnished the theme of a very beautiful ballad by K. Sharpe, Esq. published in the 'minstrelsy of the Scottish border.' The tragical event was connected with the assassination of the Red Cumine (a powerful chieftain, who formerly held the regency of Scotland), by Robert Bruce, attended by Kirkpatrick and Lindsay, two of his adherents.

BANK-END is a clean, pleasant village, about 7 miles from Dumfries, containing the parochial and grammar school, which is also a boarding academy.

POST OFFICE, BANK END, Ellen F. M'Morine, *Post Mistress.*—Letters from all parts arrive every afternoon at three, and are despatched at four.

POST OFFICE, GLENCAPLE QUAY, Susannah Thomson, *Post Mistress.*—Letters from all parts arrive every afternoon at one, and are despatched at half-past four.

GLENCAPLE QUAY, on the banks of the Nith, in this parish, is where numbers of coasting traders discharge and take in their cargoes, for various parts of the united kingdom; and when the tide serves, the steamers from Liverpool land their passengers here. KELTON is likewise a small seaport village on the Nith

GENTRY AND CLERGY.

Connell James, Esq. Cow heath
Loden Mrs. Mary Ann, Glencaple Quay
Loraine Rev. Joseph Currie, Caerlaveron Manse

INNKEEPERS & VINTNERS.

AT GLENCAPLE QUAY

Armstrong John
Edgar John
Heughan Margaret
Thomson Susannah

SHOPKEEPERS & TRADERS.

Anderson James, grocer, Bank End
Anderson John, shoe mkr, Bank End
Beattie George, spirit dealer, Kelton
Beattie John, tailor, Kelton
Bird Thomas, cartwright, Troughoughton
Brisbane Alex., miller, Bank End
Brown Wm, shoe maker, Bank End
Carson John, grocer, Glencaple Quay
Chalmers James, tailor, Glencaple Quay
Clarke Elizabeth, grocer, Glencaple
Edgar David, joiner, Trohoughton
Fleming Thos, blacksmith, Bank End
Geddes James, weaver, Bank End
Geddes John, weaver, Bank End
Hill John Edward, master of parochial school, Bank End
Irving Benjamin, blacksmith, Kelton
Lowry John, grocer, Kelton [ton
M'Lean William, grocer, Trohough-
Millan Mary, spirit dealer, Kelton
Moffat John, ship carpenter, Kelton
Muir Thomas, blacksmith, Bank End
Reid John, shopkeeper, Bank End
Richardson Mary, grocer, Glencaple Quay
Scales George, shoe mkr, Bank End
Scott John, smith, Sherrington
Slaba Thomas, cartwright, Trohoughton
Slater Thos, shoe maker, Bank End
Thomson Robert, grocer, Glencaple Quay
Thomson Robert, shipwright, Glencaple Quay

CLOSEBURN, GLENCAIRN, DUNBEGGAN, MINNIEHIVE,
KEIR, KIRKMICHAEL AND TYNRON.

CLOSEBURN is an inland parish in the district of Nithsdale; it has incorporated with it the parish of Dalgarno, and is about ten miles in length, by about eleven and a half in breadth. The annual produce of the parish amounts to £40,300. of which £3,500 arises from the sale of lime only. The ruins of the ancient Castle of Closeburn, the property of Sir James Stewart Monteath, Bart., form an interesting object in the scenery here, which derives additional beauty from some romantic waterfalls, within two miles of the castle, and some caverns, in one of which latter the hunted covenanters used to take up their abode, to evade pursuit: it is considered to be the place alluded to by the author of 'Waverley,' in his description of the cave occupied by Balfour of Burley. A school was most amply endowed in 1723, by one John Wallace, a native of the parish; it is placed under the government of the presbytery of Penpont, and in it all the children of the parish are taught the elements of education, free of expense.

The parish of GLENCAIRN is also in Nithsdale, and extends eleven miles in length, by from three to five in breadth. Several small rivulets meander beautifully through it, enriching the scenery, to which the elegant mansion and grounds of H. Ferguson, Esq. contribute greatly. On the south-west verge of the parish is Loch Urr, whence issues the river of that name. A new church has been erected a short distance from the site of the old edifice.

DUNBREGGAN is a small well-built village, in the parish of Glencairn, five miles and a half south-east of Penpont, situated on the north bank of the Dalwhat water, where it is crossed by a bridge to MINNIEHIVE,

a small but pleasant village, in the same parish as Dunbreggan, half a mile therefrom, and sixteen from Dumfries. This is a place of some antiquity, and formerly of more consequence than it now is, having been a burgh of barony, chartered in the reign of Charles I. It was in this district that several martyrs suffered at the time of the Reformation, and in this neighbourhood may be seen various but decent testimonials to their memory.

KEIR is a small parish, possessing a considerable quantity of plantation and limestone; it is bounded on the east by Closeburn, on the north-west and north by Tynron and Penpont, and on the south by Dunscore; it is about two miles and half in breadth, and seven and a half in length.

KIRKMICHAEL, united with Garren, in the district of Nithsdale, is about ten miles long, and four broad. The parish of Kirkpatrick-juxta bounds it on the north-west, Johnstone on the north-east, Lochmaben on the south east, Tinwald and Kirkmause on the south, and Closeburn on the west. Many remains of ancient fortifications and Roman roads are visible in this district. The parish kirk is near the Ae river, which bounds the parish on the west.

TYNRON parish lies between Penpont on the north and north-east, and Glencairn on the south, and extends nine miles in length, by a breadth of from two to three. It is watered partially by the Shinnel rivulet, along the banks of which there is some pleasing scenery. Near the eastern extremity of the parish rises the Doon of Tynron, a conspicuous pyramidical hill, near the summit of which is an ancient Castle. A new church has been erected on the site of the old structure.

POST OFFICE, CLOSEBURN, John Coltart, *Post Master.*—Letters from parts SOUTH arrive (from DUMFRIES) every evening at half-past three, and are despatched thereto at eight in the morning. Letters from parts NORTH arrive (from SANQUHAR) every morning at eight, and are despatched thereto at half-past three in the afternoon.

POST OFFICE, MINNIEHIVE, Margaret Collow, *Post Mistress.*—Letters from various places arrive (from THORNHILL) every evening at half-past six, and are despatched thereto at half-past five in the morning.

GENTRY AND CLERGY.

Arundel James H., Esq. (of Barjay Tower), Keir
Boarwick Rev. Robert, the Manse. Minniehive
Borrowman Rev. Patrick, Free Church Manse, Minniehive
Brown William, Esq. (of Dalwhat), Glencairn [Glencairn
Collow Miss —, (of Auchenchain),
Collow Gilbert, Esq. (of Upper Kirkcudbright), Glencairn
Copeland William, Esq. (of Black Wood), Keir [cairn
Corson Miss Mary (of Hill), Glen-
Dobie Rev. Hugh, the Manse, Kirkmichael
Fector William, Esq. (of Maxwelltown House), Glencairn
Ferguson Sir Adam, Kirkmichael
Ferguson Minor, Esq. (of Craigdarrock) Glencairn
Ferguson Lieut.-General, of (Craigdarrock House), Glencairn
Gibson Alexander, Esq. (of Gilchrist Land), Closeburn
Graham Colonel Nicholas Graham, (of Jarbruck), Glencairn
Grierson James, Esq. (of Copenach), Keir [Penpont
Hewitson John, Esq. (of Grennan),
Hoggan Edward, Esq. (of Belleview), Keir
Hoggan Geo. M'Murdo, Esq. Waterside, Keir [Tynron
Hunter James, Esq. (of Miltown),

Kennedy John, Esq. (of Kirkland), Tynron

Kennedy William, Esq. (of Dalmakerran), Tynron   [Closeburn

Leadbetter John, Esq. (of Shaws),

Lennox Charles Adam, Esq. R. N, Minniehive   [Glencairn

M'Call Samuel, Esq. (of Cairhlock)

M'Turk Robert, Esq. (of Hastings Hall), Glencairn

Mairland Lauderdale, Esq. (of Eccles), Penpont

Mather John, Esq., Nith side

Menzies Rev. Wm, the Manse, Keir

Moffat Samuel, Esq. (of Auchenhastine), Tynron

Moffat Thomas, Esq. (of Barrondennock), Glencairn

Monteath Sir James Stewart, Bart. Closeburn Hall   [cairn

Park Rev. John, the Manse, Glen-

Pringle Andrew, Esq. (of Land), Tynron   [Keir

Smith Mr. Thomas (of Penfil an), Glencairn   [Tynron

Stewart Mrs. — (of Younneston),

Wilson Rev. Robert, the Manse,

ACADEMIES & SCHOOLS.

Dalziel Justina & Sarah. Miniehive

GRAMMAR SCHOOL, Closeburn — Crawford T. Ramage, master

PAROCHIAL SCHOOL, Keir—James Blackstock and James M'Kinnell, masters

PAROCHIAL SCHOOL, Kirkmichael— James Hislop, master

PAROCHIAL SCHOOL, Minniehive— David Morine, master

PAROCHIAL SCHOOL, Tynron — Robert Newal and James Hunter, masters

SURGEONS.

Moffat John, M D. Minniehive

Stitt Hugh, M.D. Minniehive

INNS.

Brown Hill Inn, Thomas Ferguson, Closeburn

Craigdarrock Arms, John Donald-Minniehive

George, John Cranstoun, Minniehive

King's Arms, William Todd, Minniehive

SHOPKEEPERS & TRADERS.

Amos Robert, flesher and meal dealer, Minniehive

Black George, blacksmith, Tynron

Brown William, saddler, Minniehive

Chambers John, blacksmith, Minniehive   [niehive

Collow & Thomson, joiners, Min-

Collow Robert, joiner, Minniehive

Coltart John, shopkeeper, Closeburn

Coltart Thomas, joiner, Closeburn

Dalziel Jno. blacksmith, Minniehive

Dalziel Samuel, grocer, Minniehive

Douglas Walter, shoe maker, Minniehive   [niehive

Ferguson Robert, flesher, Min-

Gordon James. joiner, Minniehive

Gordon Wm. joiner, Minniehive

Harper John, shoe maker, Minniehive   [niehive

Harper William, shoe maker, Min-

Henderson James, Minniehive   [Minniehive

Hiddleston James, blacksmith,

Hiddleston Jas joiner, Minniehive

Hunter William, agent to the Scottish Union Insurance Company, Minniehive

Kennedy Adam, miller, Gaps Mill Minniehive

M'Bryer George, draper and grocer, Minniehive

M'Call William, blacksmith, Minniehive   [Minniehive

M'Chain William, shoe maker,

M'Kay James, baker, Minniehive

M'Turk James, draper and grocer, Minniehive

M'Whirter Thos. baker, Minniehive

Melross Janet, draper and grocer, Minniehive   [niehive

Morton Walter, shopkeeper, Min-

Muirhead John, tailor, Minniehive

Mundell Andw. blacksmith, Closebrn

Murry William, shoe maker, Minniehive   [burn

Newton David, shopkeeper, Close-

Park William, tailor, Closeburn

Proudfoot George, shoe maker, Closeburn

Proudfoot James, joiner, Glencairn

Proudfoot John & Samuel, woollen manufacturers and dyers, WAUK MILLS, Minniehive

Proudfoot Robert. draper and grocer, Minniehive   [niehive

Reid Thomas, nail maker, Min-

Smith Thomas, joiner, Tynron

Smith William, tailor, Minniehive

Wallace Thomas, draper and grocer, Minniehive

Williamson James, grocer and spirit merchant, Tynron

Wilson David Miller, Craigdarrock, Minnichive   [burn

Wright William, shopkeeper, Close-

PLACES OF WORSHIP,
AND THEIR MINISTERS.

ESTABLISHED CHURCH, Glencairn.... Rev. John Park

ESTABLISHED CHURCH, Keir....Rev. William Menzies

ESTABLISHED CHURCH, Tynron..Rev. Robert Wilson

ESTABLISHED CHURCH, Kirkmichael.. Rev. Hugh Dobie

FREE CHURCH, Minniehive..Rev.Patrick Borrowman

UNITED PRESBYTERIAN CHURCH, Minniehive..Rev. Robert Boarwick

COACH.

To DUMFRIES, a Coach, from the Craigdarrock Arms, Minniehive, every morning at half-past seven

CONVEYANCE BY RAILWAY, ON THE GLASGOW AND SOUTH-WESTERN LINE.

Station, in Closeburn village

CARRIERS.

To AYR. William Ferguson, on Monday

To DUMFRIES, Michael Hunter & Jas. Reid, from Minniehive, Wednesday and Saturday

---

CUMMERTREES, POWFOOT, DALTON, MOUSWALD,
RUTHWELL, AND NEIGHBOURHOODS.

CUMMERTREES is a parish and village—the latter clean and neat, is 84 miles s. of Edinburgh, the same distance s. E. of Glasgow, 22 N. W. of Carlisle, 13 s. E. of Dumfries, 10 s. E. of Lochmaben, the same distance s. from Lockerbie, 6 from Ecclefechan, and 4 from Annan, situated on the Caledonian Railway, for which line there is a station at the village. The parish, which is about four miles in length by three in breadth, is bounded on the north-east by the river Annan, and on the south by the Solway Frith. It is a flat, fertile, and well cultivated district, and is now well enclosed. The name is derived from the British words Cum-ber-tree, signifying the hamlet at the short valley, and is sufficiently descriptive of the local situation of the village—About a mile south-east of Cummertrees is POWFOOT, a fishing hamlet, situated on the shore of the Solway.

DALTON is a small village between three and four miles from Cummertrees. The parish of which now comprehends the two ancient ones of Meikle Dalton and Little Dalton, is four miles in length by three in breadth. Its general appearance is that of high cultivation, which has been extended over once unprofitable moors and commons. The village contains the kirk and parochial school, together with a female day and Sunday school.

MOUSWALD village stands six miles from Dumfries, lying between that town and Annan. The kirk, which is about a quarter of a mile from the village, on an elevated site, contains a dilapidated effigy of Sir Simon Carruthers, since laird of Mouswald. Sir Richard Grierson, Baronet, of Lagg, has a mansion in the parish.

RUTHWELL is a village about three miles from Cummertrees; this place is a barony, and is privileged to hold markets and fairs, but it is long since the inhabitants availed themselves of these rights. It was in early days celebrated for the manufacture of salt; but this art has not been practised for some time. Near the shore is the Brow well and hamlet, where Burns spent several of the last weeks of his existence. The kirk and manse of Ruthwell stand about a quarter of a mile from that village. The gardens of the manse, which are extensive and laid out with great taste, contain a very ancient Runic monument, in a good state of preservation. The parochial school is at Clarencefield.

About a mile from Ruthwell, in the parish of Mouswald, is mount Kedar, where a monument has been erected to the memory of the Rev. Henry Duncan, D.D. late minister of Ruthwell. The memorial which is of stone, consists of an arched base and pyramid forty feet in height; on the base an inscription states that he was the founder of the system of savings' banks and was born in 1774, and died in 1846, after being minister of Ruthwell parish forty four years, when he closed in communion with the free church of Scotland. A free church and school-house have been erected here.

POST, CUMMERTREES.—Letters from ANNAN arrive and are despatched three days a week.

POST, DALTON.—Letters arrive from and are despatched daily to ECCLEFECHAN.

POST, MOUSWALD and RUTHWELL.—Letters from DUMFRIES arrive and are despatched three days a week.

NOBILITY, GENTRY AND CLERGY.

Broach Mr. William, (surgeon), Margaret's field
Brown Rev. Alex., Mount Kedar, Manse, Ruthwell [Dalton
Buchannan Rev. James, Hetland,
Carruthers Wm. Esq., Dormont Dalton [Cottage
Dickson Miss Isabella, Clarence
Dobie Wm. Esq., Glenholm st, Mungo
Drumlanrig the Rt. Hon. Viscount M. P., Glen Stewart
Gillespie Rev. George, the Manse, Cummertrees
Grierson Charles, Esq., Rook Hall
Hatherton Richard, Esq., Denbie House
Lorimer Thos. Esq., Lockerwoods
M'Cheyne Wm. Esq., Clarencefield
M'Donald Wm. Bell, Esq., Rammerscales [wald
Murray Rev. A.B., the Manse, Mouswald
Murray John Dalrymple, Esq., Murraythwaite, Dalton
Newton James Ewen, Esq., White croft, Dalton [Cottage
Patterson Robt. Esq., Brocklehirst
Patterson Robert, Esq., Mouswald
Philips Walter, Esq. Comlongan Castle
Queensberry the Most Noble the Marquess of, Kinmount
Sandeman David, Esq. Kirkwood, Dalton
Stevenson Rev. Alex., Ruthwell
Thomson Rev. Thos.H., the Manse, Dalton [place
Threshie Robert, Esq., Mouswald

SCHOOLS.

Dalrymple Robert, Ruthwell
FREE CHURCH SCHOOL, Mount Kedar—Thos.Wrightman, master
Frood David, Cummertrees
INFANTS'SCHOOL, Ruthwell—Agnes —M'Lean, mistress
PAROCHIAL SCHOOL, Cummertrees —John Herberton, master
PAROCHIAL SCHOOL, Dalton—John Rae, master
PAROCHIAL SCHOOL, Mousfield— Francis Halliday, master
PAROCHIAL SCHOOL, Clarencefield —James Scott, master

INNKEEPERS & VINTNERS.

Brown Andrew, Flosh, Ruthwell
Dalgliesh Edward, (Queensberry Arms Inn), Cummertrees
Dixon John, Dolbeck, Mouswald
Henderson James, (Castle Inn), Clarencefield
Kennedy Waltr.,(Royal Oak), Dalton
Thomson James, (Tam O' Shanter Inn), Carruthersone

SHOPKEEPERS & TRADERS.

Beck John, shoe maker, Ruthwell
Boyd William, joiner, Ruthwell
Brown Andrew, grocer, Flosh, Ruthwell [mertrees
Coulthart Christopher, joiner, Cummertrees
Dixon James, grocer & spirit dealer, Mouswald
Duncan Arthur, shoe maker, Margaret's field [Mouswald
Edgar David, miller, Wood-ide,
Fele John, joiner and cartwright, Mouswald

Fergusson Edw. grocer, Clarencefld
Graham John, miller, Ruthwell
Graham Robert, bacon curer, Cummertrees
Grierson Mattw. joiner, Ruthwell
Grierson Murray, tailor, Ruthwell
Henderson Jas. grocer, Clarencefield
Jackson —, bacon curer, Ruthwell
Johnstone John, blacksmith, Cummertrees
Kennedy David, miller, Cummertrees
Marshall Francis, grocer and blacksmith, Cummertrees
Maxwell William, joiner and cartwright, Mouswald
Mundell Edw.shoe maker, Ruthwell
Niven Thomas, tailor, Cummertrees
Richardson Jane, grocer, Clarencefield [trees
Scott John, shoe maker, Cummertrees
Smith Helen, shopkeeper, Ruthwell
Tweddie Thos. grocer, Cummertrees
Thomson William, lime burner, Kelhead, Cummertrees
Wade Janet, shopkeeper, Ruthwell
Watt Wm. lime burner, Kelhead-Cummertrees
Wield James, grocer and blacksmith, Cummertrees

CONVEYANCE BY RAILWAY,

ON THE CALEDONIAN LINE.
Station at Cummertrees..Donald M'Allister, station master, and another station about one mile from Ruthwell..John Morehead, station master
CARRIER.
To ANNAN, James Richardson, on Thursday [Wednesday
To DUMFRIES, James Richardson, on

DORNOCK, GRAITNEY (or GRETNA),

WITH SPRINGFIELD, KIRKPATRICK-FLEMING AND NEIGHBOURHOODS.

DORNOCK is a parish and village—the latter a small one, is 84 miles s. of Edinburgh, 18 s. of Langholm, 17 s.e. of Dumfries, 12 s.e. of Lockerbie, 7 s. of Ecclefechan, and 2 e. of Annan; situated on the high road from the latter town to Carlisle, and about a quarter of a mile from the shore of the Solway Frith, where there is good sea-bathing. The parish, which is about two miles and a half square, is washed on its southern part by the Solway. An ancient erection, called Stapleton tower, stands on the estate of Stapleton, in this parish; as is Robgill tower, formerly belonging to the Irvings, of Robgill. The Duke of Buccleuch and the Earl of Mansfield are the principal owners of the land, which for the most part is in a high state of cultivation. The kirk and the parochial school, are in the village

GRAITNEY (more popularly called Gretna) is a parish in the south part of the county, lying on the west side of the small river Sark. The present parish comprehends the old parishes of Gretna and Redkirk, which were united in 1609. The village of Gretna, or Gretna-Green, is situated on the road from Annan to Carlisle, by Longtown—eight miles and a half from the former, nine miles and a half from the latter town; and is the first stage on entering Scotland from England. The Caledonian railway passes through the parish, and there is a station contiguous to the village. This place has long been noted for the celebration of clandestine marriages: any person can perform the ceremony, which merely amounts to a declaration, before witnesses, that the parties are man and wife—such an acknowledgement being sufficient to constitute a valid marriage in Scotland; by a certificate being subscribed by the officiating priest and witnesses, the union becomes quite indissoluble. The fee charged varies according to circumstances, and the means of the party—from half a guinea to £40, and even £50 has been paid. Recently bills were brought

into the House of Lords to alter the law of Scottish marriage, and more especially the Gretna Green contracts, but they were not carried. The first of these 'convenient priests' was a fisherman named Coulthard; he kept a ferryboat before any high roads were made through the country; after him a farmer, named Peter Graham, succeeded to the office; the next was Joseph Paisley; the present marriage functionary is Mr. John Linton, of Gretna Hall, an innkeeper. The following is the form of the marriage certificate, which, if required, is furnished:—

"KINGDOM OF SCOTLAND, COUNTY OF DUMFRIES,

PARISH OF GRETNA.

"These are to certify to all to whom these presents may come, that A. B, from the parish of ——, in the county of ——, and C. D. from the parish of ——, in the county of ——, being now here present, and having declared themselves single persons, were this day married agreeable to the laws of Scotland.

AS WITNESS our hands at Gretna Hall," &c. &c.

About a quarter of a mile from Gretna is the village of SPRINGFIELD, which participates in this matrimonial trade; this village is held on long lease from Sir J. H. Maxwell; that of Gretna belongs to Colonel William Maxwell. At SARKFOOT, about a mile from the latter village, is good bathing ground. About two miles west from Gretna is the small village of RIGG, where there is a dissenting chapel.

The parish of KIRKPATRICK-FLEMING, interesting in Scottish legend and song, is bounded on the east by Graitney; the kirk and parochial school, which stand at the southern end of the parish, are about three miles from Gretna. Lime and freestone abound in this district, in which are likewise several mineral springs, possessing medicinal properties similar to those of Hartfield spa, near Moffat.

POST OFFICE, GRETNA, Margaret Morrison, *Post Mistress.*—Letters from various places SOUTH arrive (from CARLISLE) every morning at ten, and afternoon at four, and are despacthed thereto at nine in the morning, and afternoon at three.

Letters from places NORTH arrive (from DUMFRIES) every afternoon at twenty minutes past two and are despatched thereto at twenty minutes before ten in the morning.

GENTRY AND CLERGY.

Anderson Rev. John, the Manse, Dornock
Bell John, Esq. Kirkpatrick
Carlyle John, Esq. Dornock
Crow Miss A. Newton
Graham Lieut. Colonel William, Moss Know   [Kirkpatrick
Hastie Rev. George, the Manse,
M'Gill Rev. Matthew, Rigg
MorganMiss ElizaR.Burn-ideCottge
Murdoch Rev. John, the Manse, Kirkpatrick
Ogilvie George, Esq. Cove
Rea Matthew, Esq. Newton
Roddick Rev. James, the Manse, Gretna
Small William A. Esq. Robgill
Thompson Mrs. Agnes. Woodhouse

SCHOOLS.

Anderson Mary, Dornock
Bell Mary, Rigg
INFANTS' SCHOOL, Graitney—Helen Morrison, mistress
INFANTS' SCHOOL, Springfield—Carruthers, mistress
PAROCHIAL SCHOOL, Dornock—William Purdie, master
PAROCHIAL SCHOOL, Kirkpatrick—John Carruthers, master
PAROCHIAL SCHOOL, Graitney—William Duff, master
PAROCHIAL SCHOOL, Rigg—James Barclay, master
Tinning John, Lowthertown

PROFESSIONAL PERSONS.

Birrell James, land valuer, Sarkfoot
Carruthers John, surgeon, Rigg

INNKEEPERS & VINTNERS.

Baxter Robert (Green), Gretna
Beattie John (Crown Inn), Dornock
Bell Elizabeth (Drove Inn), Louninehead
Bell William, Allisons bank, Gretna
Davidson Ann & Isabella (Solway Inn), Rigg

Davidson John, Lowthertown
Fulton John, Springfield
Gloven John (Brow), Gretna
Irving William, Rigg
Linton John (posting house, and marriage functionary),GretnaHall
Little Mrs. —. Springfield
Montgomery John (Blue Bell Inn), Dornock
Wannop Isaac, Springfield
Young Christopher (Cross Keys), Dornock

SHOPKEEPERS & TRADERS.

Armstrong Francis, grocer, Dornock
Beattie David, flesher, Rigg
Beattie James, blacksmith and grocer, Springfield
Bell Robert, joiner, Springfield
BlytheMary, shopkeeper,Springfield
Blythe Wm, shopkeeper,Springfield
Carlyle John, miller and bacon curer, Dornock   [field
Carlyle Paisley, blacksmith, Spring-
Carruthers William, joiner and cartwright, Rigg   [thertown
Clarke Andrew, blacksmith, Low-
DavidsonJohn,grocer,Lowthertown
Edgar David, joiner and cartwright, Lowthertown
Gordon Robert, blacksmith, Rigg
Gordon William, grocer, Rigg
Graham Wilhelmina, straw bonnet maker, Springfield
Graham William,clogger,Springfield
Harkness James, blacksmith,Gretna
Irving John, shoe maker and clogger, Springfield
Jardin William, shoe maker and clogger, Gretna   [Dornock
Jarding William, travelling grocer,
Johnson Christopher, joiner and cartwright, Gretna
Johnson John, shoe maker and grocer, Springfield
Johnston Andrew, shoe maker,Rigg

JohnstonChristophr, joiner, Gretna
Johnston Wm, draper, Springfield
Kennedy Elizabeth, straw bonnet maker, Rigg
Kerr Bryce, saddler, Rigg
Lattimer William, joiner and cartwright, Dornock
Little Richard, miller, Guards Mill
M'Crackan Jas.blacksmith,Dornock
Maxwell William, shoe maker, Lowthertown
Murray John, miller, Redkirk
Nicholson David, shoe maker, Dornock   [town
Nicholson Peter, tailor, Lowther-
Nicholson William, tailor, Rigg
Richardson John, shopkeeper, Lowthertown
Scott Simon, tailor, Springfield
Scott Thomas, tailor, Springfield
SteeleJames,blacksmith,Springfield
Steele Wm. clogger, Lowthertown
Syme Catherine, grocer and flour dealer, Dornock
Wallace Jane, dress maker, Rigg
Wallace John, shopkeeper, Rigg

PLACES OF WORSHIP,

AND THEIR MINISTERS.

ESTABLISHED CHURCH, Dornock—Rev. John Anderson
ESTABLISHED CHURCH, Kirkpatrick-Fleming—Rev. John Murdock
UNITED PRESBYTERIAN, Rigg—Rev. Matthew M'Gill

CONVEYANCE BY RAILWAY,

ON THE CALEDONIAN LINE.

Station, adjoining the village of GRETNA W. M. Williamson, *collector*

CARRIERS.

To ANNAN.— Moore, Thursday
To CARLISLE, Francis Foster, Tuesday and Saturday

DUMFRIES, MAXWELLTOWN & NEIGHBOURHOODS.

DUMFRIES, the capital of its county and parish, a royal burgh, the seat of the synod and presbytery of Dumfries, is 338 miles from London (by the route of Manchester), 71 s. of Edinburgh, 72 s.e. of Glasgow, 180 s. by w. of Aberdeen, 60 s. e. of Ayr, 33 n. w. of Carlisle, (by railway), 15 n.n.w. of Annan, and 8 s. w. of Lochmaben: it is situated on the Glasgow and South-Western railway, and there is a station for the line about a quarter of a mile from the town. Dumfries, which may be considered as the metropolis of the south-west quarter of Scotland, is seated on the left bank of the river Nith, about nine miles above its confluence with the Solway Frith, and navigable for vessels of light tonnage, the tide flowing as high as the old bridge. There exists no record whereby to ascertain the date when the town was founded, or the etymology of its name *Drium-a-frish—Dun-fries—Drum-fries* and 'Dumfries' have successively been its appellations—*Dun* a castle, and *fries* shrubs, is a plausible compound for the original name. The site of this queen of Nithsdale is singularly picturesque, stretching along the banks of the Nith at an elevation sufficient to command a rich prospect terminating at the distance of a few miles in a chain of lofty hills, either cultivated or umbrageous to their summits. There are so many attractions in and around Dumfries that the gentry of the neighbouring counties resort to it, imparting vivacity and all the delights of good society.

Amongst the improvements of modern times may be named the erection of a suite of assembly-rooms, new market-places, the widening of Bank-street, and lighting the town with gas; a spacious quay has been constructed along the side of the town; and a fine Doric column, raised by the county of Dumfries to the memory of Charles Duke of Queensberry who died in 1778, adorns the centre of the burgh. The Court-House is a large elegant edifice, comprising a very capacious court-room and other offices; nearly opposite stands the gaol, whence the prisoners are conveyed for trial through a subterraneous passage which communicates with the court-room. Circuit courts of justiciary are held in April and September for Dumfries-shire and the stewartry of Kirkcudbright; there are also ordinary and small debt, sheriff's and justiciary burgh courts. The station of the Glasgow and South-Western railway is an important erection, giving animation to the south-eastern suburb of the town. The commodious cottages or alms-houses, founded by the benevolence of Mrs Carruthers, are an interesting memorial to her philanthropy. The Theatre is rather a handsome building of stone, with a project ing portico; the interior, which is tastefully decorated is lighted with gas: it is generally open a few weeks in the winter. It was here that Kean first emerged, from obscurity to fame, and he never forgot the early patronage of the denizens of Dumfries.

The trade of Dumfries will be greatly benefited when the projected plans are achieved for confining the current of the river within walled embankments, which will not only deepen the channel but prevent the expansion of the tide, and thereby reclaim large tracts of land from the tidal submersion. The principal imports are timber, hemp, tallow, coals, slate, iron, and wine; the exports consist of wheat, barley, oats, potatoes, wool, and freestone. Considerable business is done in the manufacture of hosiery, hat-making, brewing, tanning, and the glue manufacture; and on the east bank of the river is a large mill for the manufacture of tweeds and checks, conducted by R. Scott and Sons. Dumfries was for many years the leading market for hare-skins in Scotland, and even regulated the price of home fur in England; and it is still looked to as the arbiter of prices. Several branch banking companies afford facilities to the monetary transactions of the town. The principal Hotels are the 'King's Arms,' and the 'Commercial,' both highly respectable and well-conducted establishments. Three Newspapers issue weekly, on Tuesday, Wednesday, and Thursday, respectively, their names are the 'Dumfries Courier,' the 'Dumfries and Galloway Standard,' and the 'Dumfries-shire and Galloway Herald.'

The municipal government of the burgh is vested in a provost, three baillies, a dean of guild, a treasurer, a town-clerk, and nineteen councillors. The craftsmen were formerly divided into seven corporations, with each a deacon chosen from their respective trades, who elected one of their own number to be convenor, and another to be general box-master; all of whom formed what was termed a grand committee of the seven trades: these distinctions, however, (for distinctions of considerable importance they were in former times), were virtually abolished by the reform bill; some of the trades possessed considerable property, which has since been publicly sold, and the proceeds equitably divided among the respective parties. Dumfries unites with Annan, Lockmaben, and Sauquhar, in returning one member to parliament. The numerous nursery grounds around the town are both useful and ornamental to the suburbs. The great desideratum of a copious supply of pure water has now been attained, and the inhabitants have an abundance brought from ample sources, about five miles from the town, and as a rate is laid upon all, no housekeeper will hesitate to secure to himself an ample supply.

The places of worship, including Maxwelltown, comprise three churches of the establishment, two of the free church, several united presbyterian and cameronian churches, an episcopal, an independent, a baptist, and a catholic chapel. Saint Michael's, or the mother church, claims peculiar notice on account its cemetery, which contains numberless elegant and curious monuments, many of them very ancient; but the most attractive is the fine mausoleum raised to the memory of the Scottish bard, Burns: the design for the mausoleum was by F. Hunt, Esq., of London; and Turnerelli modelled the sculpture. By the erection of this monument, it may be said that Scotland has repaid the debt so long due to the memory of him of whose natural genius his countrymen may well be proud. Burns died at Dumfries on the 21st July, 1796, aged 37 years, and his remains were deposited in the churchyard of Saint Michael's. This mausoleum and the profusion of funeral sculpture which adorn this cemetery, are so attractive that it is a pity free ingress is not at all times permitted; the fee doubtless prevents many a stranger from inspecting these beautiful memorials to the dead. The tasteful new free church of Saint Mary, on the north side of English-street, is a graceful ornament to this approach to the town, and the cemetery around it is gradually being enriched with finely executed monumental sculpture.

CHARITABLE, EDUCATIONAL AND SCIENTIFIC INSTITUTIONS.—The infirmary was founded in 1776, at a period when very few charities, of a similar nature, were in Britain; and this is still the only one in the South of Scotland. Medical advice and medicines are gratuitously afforded to every applicant who is an object of charity. It is supported by annual subscriptions, legacies, donations, benefactions, &c., and is under the management of governors There is also the Crichton Institution for lunatics, a noble foundation upon a lofty site. The Poors' Hospital is for the purpose of supporting aged and indigent poor, and destitute children, who are taught to read and write. It is governed by the magistrates, town council, &c., and is supported by a part of the collections from the church doors, numerous benefactions, donations and annual subscriptions. It was founded in 1753, by Messrs. J. and W. Moorhead, merchants. Dumfries is not behind other towns in its support of numerous religious and educational societies—both an infant and a ragged school are amongst the latter institutions.—The Academy. This elegant and useful seminary was founded in 1802: the expenses of the ground, and of building and finishing the fabric, were entirely defrayed by voluntary subscription. In October, 1814, the structure was formally delivered over to the magistrates as patrons and guardians of the institution, who, along with other members of the town council, have the exclusive privilege of appointing the masters. The New Club House, in Assembly-street, was formerly the Old Assembly-rooms. The Exchange-rooms and a Farmers' Club are among the projected novelties. The Dumfries and Maxwelltown Astronomical Society have erected, on Corbelly hill, on the Maxwelltown side of the river, an observatory, which is regarded as a highly ornamental feature in one of the most unique half-urban half-sylvan landscapes: and commands an extensive view of beautiful and varied scenery; the cost which exceeded one thousand guineas, was raised in £5 shares. The plans were by Mr. Newall, architect, and the building was completed in little more than twelve months. It contains four stories,—the lower one for the use of the keeper; three others for the accommodation of the subscribers and strangers, which are furnished with globes, mathematical instruments, newspapers and periodicals; and the upper story is set apart for a camera-obscura and prism. The grounds, which consist of more than half an acre, are laid out with much taste, containing flowers and shrubs of various kinds.

The market days are Wednesdays. The two principal half-yearly markets take the name of the Candlemas and rood fairs. Besides the usual commodities that change hands at these periods, many thousand head of black cattle are bought and sold; and vast quantities of pork also find purchasers in Dumfries from the beginning of December to the end of February. The fairs are held on the first Wednesday in February, the third Wednesday in March, the third Wednesday in April, the 26th May or the Wednesday after; the third Wednesday in June, the third Wednesday in July, the third Wednesday in August, the third Wednesday in October and the third Wednesday in November, for cattle (all old style).

MAXWELLTOWN, formerly a village, is now a burgh of barony, in the stewartry of Kirkcudbright, and connected with Dumfries by two bridges across the Nith. In no instance have the good effects of erecting a village into a burgh of barony been more conspicuous than in Maxwelltown. The charter was obtained from the crown in 1810, and since that time, from being a poor village, notorious for disorderly conduct,—(for it was a remark of the late Sir John Fielding, that he could trace a rogue over the whole kingdom, but always lost him at the bridge-end of Dumfries, now Maxwelltown, or in the Gorbals of Glasgow),—it has improved in value and extent of houses, and increased considerably in the number and respectability of its inhabitants: it is governed by a provost, two baillies and councillors. Among the trading establishments are a brewery, two foundries and several corn mills. The church here, is handsome and of modern erection.

POST OFFICE, ENGLISH-STREET, DUMFRIES.

Mr. JOHN THORBURN, Post Master.

TOWNS, &c.	ARRIVAL OF MAILS.	BOX CLOSES.	DESPATCH OF MAILS.
LONDON and the SOUTH, EDINBURGH, GLASGOW, &c. also IRELAND (via LOCKERBIE)	2. 30 a.m.	7. 45 p.m.	8. 0 p.m.
LONDON, &c., also IRELAND (via GRETNA)	9. 55 a.m.	2. 15 p.m.	2. 40 p.m.
PORTPATRICK, &c.	1. 0 p.m.	9 45 a.m.	10 25 a.m.
KIRKCUDBRIGHT, CASTLE DOUGLAS, DALBEATTIE, &c.	6. 0 p.m.	7 30 a.m.	8. 0 a.m.
SANQUHAR, &c.	1. 0 a.m.	9 45 a.m.	10. 25 a.m.
PARKGATE, &c.	7. 0 p.m.	6. 30 a.m.	7. 0 a.m.
DALSWINTON, &c.	9. 30 a.m.	9. 45 a.m.	10. 25 a.m.
GLENCAPLE, NEW ABBEY, &c.	7. 0 p.m.	9. 45 a.m.	10. 25 a.m.

The *Office is Open* from the fourth of November to the fourth of March, at half-past seven in the morning; and from the fourth of March to the fourth of November, at seven in the morning; and the *Office Closes* at nine at night (Sundays excepted).

On *Sundays* the Office is open from a quarter before one noon till a quarter before two.

Late Letters may be posted with an *additional stamp*, through the late letter-box, until within five minutes of the despatch of each mail.

Money Orders are granted and paid daily (Sundays excepted), from nine in the morning till six in the evening.

.*.* *When the letter* M. *occurs at the end of an address it signifies* MAXWELLTOWN.

NOBILITY GENTRY AND CLERGY.

Aird Thomas, Esq., Irish st
Aitken Mrs. Ann, Queensberry st
Anderson Allen, Esq., Allen bank
Anderson Mrs. Mary, Shakspere st
Babington Mrs. Catherine, George st
Baird Charles, Esq , Irish st
Bell Benjamin, Esq., High st
Bell Mrs. Jane, Terrogles st, M.
Berwick Mrs. Margaret, Albany bank
Biggar James, Esq., Maryholme
Biggar Mrs. Margaret, 18 Buccleuch st
Black Mas. Jessie, 4 Greyfriars st
Blount Miss Mary, Galloway st, M.
Brown James, Esq. Corberry, M.
Brown Mrs. Jessie, Nith bank
Brown Mr. John, Galloway st, M.
Bucanon Mrs Mrct. Glasgow st. M.
Burnside Miss Janet, 12 Buccleuch st
Cannon Wm. Esq , Mill bank
Carruthers Miss Mary, English st
Cavan Douglas, Esq., Nith bank
Charters George, Esq.. High st
Christie John, Esq., Goldielea
Clark Miss Christiana, Castle st
Clerk Mr. John, Galloway st, M.
Clarke Mrs. Jane, 13 Buccleuch st
Clarke Miss Mary, Castle st
Clyde the Misses —, High st
Colton Miss —, Irish st
Copeland Miss Janet, 2 Bridge st
Corrie John Kirkpatrick, Pleasance
Corson Miss Jane, Galloway st, M.
Corson Mrs. —, Flosh Cottage
Costine John, Esq., Gleason, Southwick
Coulthard Mr. Jos. Galloway st, M.
Cowans Rev. Geo., St. Michael st
Craik John, Esq., Bank st
Creig Miss Sarah, Assembly st
Creighton Mrs. Agnes T. Union st
Cumrie Mrs. Janet, Ladyfield
Dalziel Mrs. Catherine, 3 Castle st
Davies Major Wm., Castle st
Dickson Mrs. Eliz. B, Laurieknowe, M
Dickson Mrs. Margaret, King st, M.
Dickson Mrs. Mary Carruthers, Galloway st, Maxwelltown
Dinwiddie Mr. James P. Buccleuch st
Douglas Mrs. Eliz. Galloway st, M.
Drummond Mrs. Major, Castle st
Dugeon Henry H. Esq., Drungans Lodge and Woodheave
Duncan Rev. Thomas, M.D., Moathouse, Townhead
Ferguson the Misses Janet & Margaret, 10 Buccleuch st

Finley Miss Jane. 2 Buccleuch st
Forsyth Mrs. Christian, George st
Forsyth Philip, Esq. (factor), Nithside, Troqueer
Gilchrist Mrs. John, Irish st
Goldie Miss Margaret, Castle st
Goldie Miss —, Summer hill, M.
Goold Rev. Marshall N. Queen st
Gordon Miss —, Glasgow st, M.
Gordon Miss Janet, Galloway st, M.
Gordon Mrs. Nicholas, 14 Buccleuch street
Grierson Lieu. Col., St. Michael st
Grierson the Dowager Lady, Rock Hall Cottage
Hairstens Mrs. —, Galloway st, M.
Hairstens Mrs. Annie, 6 Portland place, Maxwelltown
Hairstens the Misses Barbara and Jane, Laurieknowe place
Hairstens Mrs. Little, 9 Buccleuch st
Halliday Mm. Esq., Rose bank
Hammond Mrs. Mary Ann, Waterloo place
Harkness Robert, Esq., Albany place
Harley Miss Agnes, George st
Hepburn John Buchen, Esq., Castle dykes
Heron Mrs. Catherine, 5 Buccleuch street
Heron James, (of Duncow), Galloway st, Maxwelltown
Herron Mrs. —, Laurieknowe place
Hoeg Mrs. Ann S. Terrogles st, M.
Hood Mrs. Elizabeth A. George st
Howat Mrs. Ellen, 5 Castle st
Howat Miss Helen, Assembly st
Hutton Mrs. Margaret, Charter House, Troqueer
Hyslop Miss Helen Stewart, Irish st
Jackson David, Esq., Newton House
Johnston Miss Agnes, George st
Johnston Adml. Charles James, Waterloo place and Cowhill
Johnston Walter, Esq., George st
Kennedy Mrs. Eliz. 18 Academy st
Kennedy Cap. John, 18 Academy st
Kirkpatrick Mrs. Roger, Irish st
Laidlaw the Misses Sarah & Jessie, Castle street
Lawrie Mrs. Jane, Mill bank, M.
Lenv J. Macalpine, Esq., Dalswinton
Litle John McFarlane, Esq. Maryfield
Litt Mrs. —, 2 Castle st
Livingstone William, Esq., Nithmount, Townhead
Lookup Mrs. —, Galloway st, M.
McCracken Alexander, Esq. Millbank Cottage

McDermid Rev. John, Maxwelltown
McDonald Wm., Terrogles st, M.
McEwen Rev. Archibald, 5 Portland place, Maxwelltown
McFarline Rev. Walter, Troqueer
McGhie the Misses —, Castle st
McGhie Mrs. Cicely, Portland pl, M.
McHarg Robert William, Esq., of Rose Hall, Loreburn st
McKune James, Esq., Netherwood
McMorrien Miss Eliza, Castle st
McMurdo Mrs. Catherine, 9 Castle st
McMurdo Captain —, Mavies grove
McNeillie David, Esq., Castle hill
McRobert James, Palmerstone Cottage, Maxwelltown
Mann Rev. James, Albany place
Martin Miss —, Galloway st, M.
Martin Miss Catherine, 4 Portland place, Maxwelltown
Martin Wm. Esq. Noblehill Cottage
Maxwell Mrs. —, Terraughty
Maxwell Francis, Esq. (factor), Terrogles banks, Maxwelltown
Maxwell Miss Isabella, 11 Buccleuch street
Maxwell Marmaduke Constable, Esq., Terrogles, near Maxwelltown
Maxwell the Misses Mary & Lucy, 1 Buccleuch street
Maxwell Wellwood Esq, of the Grove
Maxwell Wm. Esq., of Carruchan
Maxwell Wm. Esq. jun., Cardoness
Melville Mrs. Agnes, Castle st
Mitchelson William, Esq., Castle st
Montgomery Mrs. Mary, 5 Buccleuch street
Murray Peter, Esq., 1 Portland place, Maxwelltown [Corberry
Neilson James, Esq., Bank House,
Newall Adam, Esq., Loreburn st
Nicholson William, Esq., 2 Queensberry street
Patty Mrs. —, (of Crosslands), Long close, 53 High street
Primrose Wm. Esq., Primrose hill, Maxwelltown
Reid Mr. James, 71 High st
Rutherford Captain James, Isaac Park, Craig road [burn st
Scott Rev. David L., Manse, Loreburn st
Simpson T. Esq., Dalawiddie
Sloan John, 3 David street, M
Small Rev. Henry, Shakspere st
Staig John, Esq , Castle st
Stewart Rev. James, Irving st
Stewart Mrs. Jessie, 18 Buccleuch st

Stott John, Esq., Netherwood
Swan Miss —, Waterloo place
Swanson Captain Francis, Albany place, Townhead
Symons Mrs. Harriet, Nith House, Irish street
Thompson Miss Agnes, George st
Thompson Wm. Esq. Pleasance
Thorburn John, Esq., Assembly st
Thorburn the Misses —, Bank House, Troqueer
Thorburn Kenneth, Esq., Moat of Troqueer [Troqueer
Thorburn Mrs Mary, Mountain Hall
Thorburn Thomas, Esq., Ryedale,
Turner Mrs. Mary, 2 Bridge st
Walker James, Esq., Woodlands
Wallace Rev. Robert, D.D., the Manse, St. Michael street
Whigham David, Esq., Kelton Mains
Whigham Miss —, Cartuchan
Wood Rev. James Julius, George st
Wood Thomas, Esq., Hannah field
Young Miss Henrietta, High st
Young the Misses — Terregles st, M
Young the Hon. Lady of Lincluden, Terrogles

ACADEMIES AND PRIVATE TEACHERS.

Burns Robert, Three Crowns close
Campbell Walter, Loreburn st
DUMFRIES ACADEMY, Academy st —Charles Maxwell, rector; William Armstrong, mathematical teacher; Louis Griellmette, French; Campbell Forbes, English; John Craik, writing
Edgar John, Gasston
Fell Jane. Castle st
Forbes Duncan Campbell (boarding), Pear mount
FREE CHURCH SCHOOL, King st, Maxwelltown — Adam Boddie, master
Gallaher John, Loreburn st
Gemmill William, Irish st
GREENSANDS SCHOOL—HenryShaw, master; Jane Thomson, mistress
INFANTS' SCHOOL, Shakspere st— Margaret Burnie, mistress
Laurie James, Anchor Inn close
Martin William, Trades land
NATIONAL SCHOOL, Glasgow st, Maxwelltown—John Marchbank, master
Neaison Eliza, Newmarket st
PAROCHIAL SCHOOL, Lockabriggs —James M'Lellan, master
PAROCHIAL SCHOOL, Trohoughton —James Grev, master
RAGGED SCHOOL, Burns street— Charles Eadie Hall, master
Riddick Euphemia, High st
ST. ANDREW'S CATHOLIC SCHOOL, Shakspere st — Michael John O'Sullivan, master
SALTMARSH SCHOOL, Irish st— John M'Burney, master
Turner Joseph, Maxwelltown
Waugh Isabella, Castle st
White Jane, St. Andrew's st
Wilson Joseph, Gasston

AGENTS.

(See also Fire, &c. Office Agents.)
Beck James (for Traitflatt Bleach Work), Union st [Bridge st
Caird Ellen (for Anderson's pills),
Lamb P. K. (general and mineral), Bank st
Sinclair John (news), High st

AGRICULTURAL IMPLEMENT MAKER.

Hamilton John, Torthorwald

ARCHITECTS.

M'Gowan William, Irving st
Newall Walter, George st

ARTISTS.

Currie John (sculptor), Queensberry st [13 Academy st
Dacre Jas Murray (portrait painter),

AUCTIONEERS.

Crichton David, Gasston
Dunbar George, Church crescent
Nelson John, 1 Bridge st
Smart James, 44 Friars' vennel

BAKERS & FLOUR DEALERS.

Allan John, 102 High st
Allan William, 75 English st
Armstrong Andrew, 74 English st
Arnott John, 37 Friars' vennel
Barns William, Queensberry st
Brown John, Old Fleshmarket st
Carnan Robert, Galloway st, M.
Clarke James, 25 Friars' vennel
Coltart Thomas, High st
CO-OPERATIVE PROVISION SOCIETY —Robert Nicholson, agent
CO-OPERATIVE SOCIETY, Glasgow st, Maxwelltown—James Holmes, agent
Dickson James, High st
Dickson James, Nith place
Forsyth William, Maxwelltown
Kelley Thomas & John, Bridge st
M'Brown John C. Loreburn st
M'Lellan George, High st
Mennies John, 19 Friars' vennel
Murray Francis, 79 High st
Porteous Charles, Galloway st, M.
Ronald William, 60 High st
Thompson John, 2 Friars' vennel

BANKERS,

BANK OF SCOTLAND (Branch), Irish st—(draws on the parent establishment, Edinburgh, and Coutts & Co. London)—Robert Threshie, agent
BRITISH LINEN COMPANY (Branch), Irish st—(draw on the head office, Edinburgh, and Smith, Payne & Smiths', London)— Robert Adamson, agent
COMMERCIAL BANK OF SCOTLAND (Branch) Irish st—(draws on the head office, Edinburgh, and Jones, Loyd & Co. London)—William Goldie, agent
EDINBURGH AND GLASGOW BANK (Branch), Irish st—draws on the head office, Edinburgh, and the Union Bank of London)—William M'Gowan, agent
NATIONAL BANK OF SCOTLAND (Branch), Bank st—(draws on the head office, Edinburgh, and Glyn, Halifax & Co. London)— Alexander Hannay, agent
WESTERN BANK OF SCOTLAND (Branch), Buccleuch st—(draws on the parent establishment, Glasgow, and Jones, Loyd & Co. London)—William Primrose and James Gordon, agents

BASKET MAKERS.

Gordon Thomas, Flesh market
Kennedy James, St. David st

BLACKSMITHS.

Bell John, Queensberry st
Burgess William, M'George's close
Byers John, St. Andrew st
Campbell George, Loreburn st
Dixon David, Nith bank
Glindinning William, 53 High st
Haining William, M'George's close
Haugh & Pearce, 50 High st
Irving John, Friars' vennel
Kirkpatrick Robert (frame smith), Loreburn street

M'Naes Alexander, Galloway st, M.
M'Quennell Allen, Pleasance
Mofft Wm. King st, Maxwelltown
Nicholson Robert, Shakspere st
Smart William, Irish st
Wilson John, Newmarket st

BOOKBINDERS.

(See also Booksellers, &c.)
Henry James, Irish st
Maxwell James, Mid steeple

BOOKSELLERS, STATIONERS AND BINDERS.

Anderson Allan, 70 High st
Anderson John, 74 High st
Halliday David, Old Council chambrs
Johnstone Wm. Francis, 44 High st
M'Robert John, 92 High st
Maxwell James, Mid steeple
Montgomery & Co. (and newspaper agents), 102 High street; residence 13 Academy street

BOOT & SHOE MAKERS.

Aitken Alexander, Friars' vennel
Beck Alexander, Queensberry st
Brown James, Queensberry st
Corrie John, Old Bridge street, M.
Crawford James, 23 Academy st
Eller James, Glasgow street, M.
Fleming James & Co. 10 English st
Gass Joseph, 28 Buccleuch st
Gibson Robert, Shakspere st
Gordon John, Friars' vennel
Gordon William, Friars' vennel
Harkin John, Bank st
Henderson William, High st
Irving John, 91 Friars' vennel
Irving William, 108 High st
Johnston Andrew, Mill st
Kirk T. Glasgow st, Maxwelltown
M'Clellan John, 13 Friars' vennel
M'Clure John, 7 English st
M'Cormack John, 50 High st
M'Haig Peter, Queensberry st
M'Lellan James, Bank st
Moore William, 42 Friars' vennel
Mouncey William, 80 Friars' vennel
Nibloe William, 86 High st
Richardson John, 76 Friars' vennel
Scott Robert, High st
Scott Robert, 22 English st
Shaw John (and leather cutter), 8 Queensberry street
Todd Archibald, Glasgow street, M.
Todd John, Glasgow street, Maxwelltown [welltown
Todd William, Market square, Max-
Walker John, 11 English st
Wallace William, 18 Castle st
Watson John, Church place
Wilson John, 12 Friars' vennel
Wilson John, Shakspere st

BREWERS AND MALTSTERS.

Corson Margaret, Irish st
Edgar John, White sands
Turner Mary, Green sands

BUILDERS.

See Masons and Builders.

CABINET MAKERS.

Marked thus * are also Upholsterers.
*Aitchison Wm, Church crescent
*Burnside William, 7 Church place
Charteris Jas, (and turner), Nith pl
Donaldson George, Queen-berry st
*Dunbar George, Church crescent
Forsyth James, Galloway st, M
Graham Thomas, Loreburn st
Grecan William, High st; works, Clark hill
Herries Robert, Friars' vennel
Lowry James, High st
Robb Elizabeth, 4 Castle st

CARVERS AND GILDERS.
Barry Alexander, St. Michael st
M'Kay John, 27 Buccleuch st
M'Pherson Thomas, Bank st
Spence William, St. Andrew st
Watson Joseph, Academy st

CHAIR MAKER.
Alexander John Todd (rustic), 8
  Galloway st, Maxwelltown

CHEMISTS & DRUGGISTS.
Carruthers Richard Virren, High st
Duncan Walter, 11 Church place,
  and Glasgow st, Maxwelltown
Low & Morris Church place
Rodan David, 88 High st
Sinclair James, 95 High st

CLOG & PATTEN MAKERS.
Davidson John, Galloway st, M.
Kennedy James, St. David st
Moffat John, Glasgow st, M.
Moodie James, Galloway st, M.
Richardson John, 24 Friars' vennel
Wyper David 8 Grey friars' st

CLOTHES DEALERS AND BROKERS.
Farmer John, Friars' vennel
Hay Mary Ann, Friars' vennel
M'Closkay, —, Chapel st
O'Neil Henry, Friars' vennel
Richardson Burnside, Church place
Shields Catherine, Queensberry st
Stewart Charles, Queensberry st
Wallace James, 39 Friars' vennel
Weemys —, 26 Buccleugh st

COACH MAKERS.
Campbell Frederick, Nith place
Beck Joseph, jun, (and harness),
  St. David st
Sloan David, Irish st

COAL MERCHANTS.
Begg John, Railway station
Lamb P. K., Bank st
M'Mackin James, Railway station
Maxwell William, Railway station
Scott John, Railway station
Watson James, Railway station

COFFEE HOUSES.
M'Nish Jessie, High st
Muir Maxwell, High st
Swan James, Bank st

CONFECTIONERS.
Dick Charlotte, 13 English st
Irving Jane, 66 High st
M'Grigor James, 75 High st
Shaw Alexander, 65 High st

COOPERS.
Afflerg Samuel, Bank st
Beattie Margaret, Irish st
Kerr William, Irish st
M'Burnie John, Galloway st, M.
Maxwell Samuel 75 Friars' vennel
Walker David, Queensberry st

CORK CUTTERS.
Grindal Dorothy, Queensberry st
Lacey Joseph, Shakspere st

CORN MERCHANTS AND GRAIN DEALERS.
Bennett Mary, English st
Brown Robert, Bridekirk
Chalmers William, Dumfries Mills
Irving William, St. Michael st
Lowry James, St. Michael st
M'Lellan George, High st
Melbourne Henry, Church crescent
Thompson William, Queensberry st

CURRIERS AND LEATHER CUTTERS.
Currie Thomas, White sands
Farrer John, 18 English st
Irving James, Nith place
Taylor Alexander, Clark hill

CUTLERS.
Hinchliffe Joseph Walker, 126
  High street
Love William, Friars' vennel

392

DRESS MAKERS.
See Milliners and Dress Makers.

DYERS.
Armstrong William, White sands
Brown John (& woollen manufac-
  turer), Market st, Maxwelltown
Shortridge Thomas (and cleaner),
  St. Michael st
Thompson Andrew, 44 St.Michael st
Wilson Janet, College street, Max-
  welltown

EARTHENWARE AND CHINA DEALERS.
Brisbane Jane, 6 Friars' vennel
Crosbie Robert, 7 Castle st
Hepburn Jemima, 4 St. Andrew st
Maxwell John, St. David st
Moffats Janet & Mary, 22 Friars'
  vennel
Robinson Thomas, 7 St. David st
Whitewright John, Galloway st, M.

EATING-HOUSE KEEPERS.
Aitken Alexander, Friars' vennel
Charteris Margaret, Brewery st
Gunson Thomas, 77 Friars' vennel
Murray Jane, Brewery st
Nixon Rachael, Brewery st

FIRE, &c. OFFICE AGENTS.
ATLAS, John Anderson, 74 High st
FARMERS' (life), J. Bell, Church st. M
FARMER' AND GRAZIERS', Joseph
  Bell, 10 Bank st
INSURANCE OF SCOTLAND, M'Gowan
  & Hairstens, High st
NORTHERN, John Goodall, 3 Bank
  street; and Robert K. Walker,
  Galloway st, Maxwelltown
NORWICH UNION, John M'Diarmid
  & Son, Irish st
PROFESSIONAL (life), Thomas
  Symth, 65 English st
SCOTTISH INSURANCE, James Gor-
  don & William Primrose, Castle st
SCOTTISH PROVIDENT, John Rob-
  son, Irish st   [Bank st
STANDARD (life), William Brown
SUFFOLK, Christopher Harkness, 150
  High street
SUN, James M'Kie, Long close
UNITED KINGDOM (life), Christo-
  pher Harkness, 150 High st
YORKSHIRE, J. G. Montgomery &
  Co. High st

FLESHERS.
Barbour James, Galloway st, M.
Campbel Andrew, High st
Glendining Andrew, Glasgow st. M.
Hughan James, Queensberry st
Kerr Jane, Bank st
Kerr Robert W. 53 Friars' vennel
M'Cormack Alexdr. Friars' vennel
M'Holm James, 61 High st
Milligan David, Mid steeple
Milligan Robert, High st
Murphie Jane, 121 High st
Palmer Joseph, Mid steeple
Payne James, 1 Friars' vennel
Payne John, 85 High st
Selkirk Robert, Friars' vennel
Selkirk Robert, High st
Smith Hugh, Galloway st
Thompson Edward, 55 Friars' vennel

FURNITURE BROKERS.
Shiels Catherine, Queensberry st
Todd Robert, Queensberry st
Wilson James, Queensberry st

GROCERS AND TEA DEALERS.
Marked thus * are also Spirit Dealers.
(*See also Shopkeepers, &c. and also
Spirit Dealers.*)
Allison Helen, Glasgow st. M.
*Bell John, Galloway st. M.
Bendall James, 68 Friars' vennel
*Black John, 73 English st

*Brash Thomas, 87 High st
Clark John, 1 Glasgow st. M.
Clarke James, High st
Crackston John, 12 Glasgow st. M.
Crosbie John, 17 English st
Davidson John Qu eensberry square
Dickson William, 57 High st
Dobie Robert J. High st
*Dodd Joseph, High st
Dunbar —, 92 High st
*Dykes William, 36 Glasgow st. M.
*Erving David, 32 Friars' vennel
Ferguson & Co. High st
Ferguson David, 6 Queensberry st
Glendinning Thomas, 141 High st
*Glover Thomas, 8 Church place
Gray Matthew, 5 Bank st
Grindall Robert, 29 Friars' vennel
Hastings Margaret, 1 English st
Heron James, Glasgow st. M.
*Hetherington Jno. 1 Queensberry sq
Jamieson Charles, David st. M.
*Johnston James, 80 Queensberry st
*Kennedy John, 1 Queensberry st
Leighton Miles & Sons (and dry-
  salters), Shakspere st
M'Kaig John, 5 Castle st
*M'Kerr Adam, Bridge st
*M'Naught James, 48 High st
*M'Turk —, Galloway st. M.
Milligan Samuel, 81 High st
Moffat Hannah, 48 Glasgow st. M
Moffat Robert, Glasgow st. M.
*Muir George, 80 High st
Mundell Peter, High st
*Murray William Millar, 1 New-
  market st   [berry st
*Nicholson Frs. (wholesale) 2 Queens-
*Paterson Joseph, Queensberry st
Paterson Robert, Glasgow st. M.
Paterson Samuel, Queensberry st
*Rae George, 43 Friars' vennel
*Robson Marion, 3 Friars' vennel
Shepherds Jonathan & Joseph, 7
  Church place   [square
*Sloan Brothers, 4 Queensberry
*Smart James, 44 Friars' vennel
*Smith Robert, 79 English st
Smith William, 104 High st
*Smith William, Galloway st. M.
*Stitt Robert, 11 English st
*Swan William, Bank st
Tait Mary, Queensberry st
Toppin Isaac, 125 High st
Walker Robert, Galloway st. M.

GUN MAKERS.
Hume George, 81 English st
Turner James, 3 English st

HAIR DRESSERS.
Coupland John, 118 High st
Dykes Thomas, 10 Castle st
King Peter, Queensberry st
Knight Edward, 25 Buccleuch st
Macaskie John, 17 Friars' vennel
Maxwell John, English st
Porteous George, Friars' vennel
Smith William, 2 English st
Wilkinson Andrew, 24 English st

HAT MANUFACTURERS AND DEALERS.
Balieff John, 123 High st
Thomson Elizabeth (late Beattle
  & Co.) High street
Tibbetts Alexander, 82 High st
Tweddle George, 111 High st

HAY DEALERS.
Ferries Hugh, Queensberry st
Hollis Edmund, Queen st
Johnston James, Queensberry st
Watson William, Galloway street, M.

HOSIERY MANUFACTURERS.
Dinwiddie William, High st
Milligan & Dinwiddie, Buccleuch st
Pagan John & Sons, Irish st
Scott R. & Sons, English street

HOTELS.
(*See also Vintners.*)

Commercial (and family and posting), William Clark, High st
King's Arms (family, commercial and posting), John Fraser, High street   [Bank st
Swan's Hotel, William Swan,

IRON FOUNDERS.
Affleck James & Co. High st
Affleck John & Co. King street, M.
Maxwell John, Stakeford, M.

IRONMONGERS.
Bell John, 109 High st
Bell Robert, High st
Frazer William, 63 High st
Halliday James (aud smith), 9 Church place
Watt John. 38 High st

JEWELLERS AND SILVER-SMITHS.
Dickson Samuel, 126 High st
Halliday James, 9 Church place
Johnstone James (working), Glasgow street, Maxwelltown
Thomson James C. (working), High street

JOINERS & CARPENTERS.
Callender George, High st
Claughton Henry, 81 Friars' vennel
Corson Thomas, College street, M.
Forsten William, Nith place
Forsyth James, Galloway st, M.
Forsyth John, Glasgow street, M.
Geddies William, Galloway st, M.
Gillies William, King street, M.
Halliday William, College street, M.
Herries Robert, Friars' vennel
King William, St. Michael st
Lowry James, High st
M'Laughlen Wm. Redlion st, M.
Thomson & M'Courty, Loreburn st
Thorlborn William, Academy st

LIBRARIES.
(*See also Booksellers, &c. and also Reading Rooms.*)

Anderson Allan(circulating),High st
Anderson John(circulating),High st
Commercial, High st —— Francis Nicholson, secretary
Dumfries Book Club, High st— John Anderson, secretary
Dumfries Library, Irish street— James M'Robert, secretary
Law Library, Court-house, Buccleuch st—— Robert M'Lellan, secretary
Mechanics' Institute Library, High st—Alexander M'Crombie, secretary

LINEN & WOOLLEN DRAPERS.
Anderson Andrew, 101 High st
Boyd Samuel, 51 High st
Brown William & Co. 42 High st
Dickie Thomas, 2 Queensberry square
Grierson Walter, 59 High st
Hogg Ann, 53 High st
Howat William, High st
Irving Mary, 90 Friars' vennel
M'Gowan John, 37 High st
M'Kay William, Glasgow street, M.
Moffat Thomas, 96 High st
Moffat William, 100 High st
Potter William, Bank st
Smith & Jamieson, 52 High st
Swan James, 54 High st
Wylie Ann, Assembly st

MALTSTERS.
See Brewers and Maltsters.

MASONS AND BUILDERS.
Crombie Alexander, New road, St. Michael street
Crombie Andrew. St. Michael st

Grierson Edwd. & Son, White sands
Montgomery Robert & Son, 7 David street, Maxwelltown
Thompson Janet, 13 Glasgow st, M.
Watson Thomas (and stone engraver), Queen st

MESSENGERS AT ARMS
Corrie Thomas, County buildings
Hainning Thomas, 42 High st
Hamilton Archibald, Assembly st
Kemp Robert, High st
M'George Charles, Queen st
Wallace Robert, Dumfries

MILLERS.
Chalmers William, Dumfries Mills and West Clauden
Charlton Thomas & Son, Clauden bank Mills

MILLINERS & DRESS MAKRS.
Arnott Margaret C. Galloway st, M.
Brydone Ann & Catherine, 119 High street
Campbell Mary, 15 Castle st
Crockett A. & J. Church crescent
Duff Margaret, Queen st
Hannah Elizabeth, Irish st
Henderson Mary, English st
Hunter Agnes & Mary & Jessie, Galloway st, Maxwelltown
Hunter Jane & Euphemia, 3 Queensberry square
Irvine Jane & Margaret & Elizabeth, 83 English street
Johnstone Agnes, 18 High st
Kerr Elizabeth, Irish st
M'Burney Maria, 3 Buccleuch st
M'Dowel Mary, 21 Academy st
Milligan Mary, Queensberry st
Montgomery Agnes, Long close, 53 High street
Murray Isabella, 97 High st
Nicholson Janet & Annie, 64 High st
Pagan Elizabeth, 21 Academy st
Patterson William, 79 Friars' vennel
Sandland Jane, Mundell's close, Queensberry st
Simpson Mary, Buccleuch st
Thomson Elizabeth, 93 High st
Underwood Isabella, High st

MUSIC & MUSICAL INSTRUMENT SELLERS.
Fryer John (piano-forte), Queen st —William Gregan, agent
Potts Henry, Castle st

NAIL MAKERS.
M'Kinnell John, Fergusou's close
M'Naren —, Queensberry st
Paterson William, Queensberry st
Russell Thomas, King st

NEWSPAPERS.
Dumfries & Galloway Standard, (Wednesday), 117 High st— William Burgess, publisher
Dumfries Courier, (Tuesday,) Irish st—John M'Diarmid & Son, publishers
Dumfries-shire and Galloway Herald, (Tuesday), High st— William C. Craw, publisher

NURSERY & SEEDSMEN.
Agar Thomas, Nunholm
Bogie James, Glasgow st, M.
Irving Mary & James, Galloway st, M.
Kennedy James, 107 High st
Kennedy Thomas. & Co., Midrow, High street
Kennedy William, Strawfield
Learmont John, Townhead st
Learmont John, 49 English st
Richardson George, Galloway st, M.
Thorp John, English st
Waugh John, 94 High st

PAINTERS & GLAZIERS.
Aitken James (and paper hanger), English street

Coltart Robert, Bank st
Coston Thomas, Galloway st, M.
Dinwiddie John (& paper hanger), 98 High street
M'Morine —, Castle st
M'Pherson Thomas, Bank st
Smith Thomas, Queen st

PAWNBROKERS.
Hammond Mary Ann, Queensberry st
Trevitt James, Queensberry st

PERFUMERS.
Coupland John, 118 High st
Dykes Thomas, 10 Castle st
Smith William, 124 High st

PHYSICIANS.
Barker William, Old Assembly st
Grieve James, 20 Buccleuch st
M'Culloch James Murray, Castle st
Scott William, Castle st

PLASTERERS.
Crocket Thomas. Friars' vennel
Dickson John, St. Michael st
Fraser James, College st, M
Parke William, 58 Friars' vennel

PLUMBERS.
Fergusson John, Friars' vennel
Little John, 6 St. David st
Milligan Thomas, 91 High st
Thomson David (and brazier), 106 High street

PRINTERS—LETTER-PRESS.
Burgess William, 117 High st
Craw William C. High st
Halliday Dav. Old Council chambers
Harkness Thomas, 150 High st
M'Diarmid John & Son, Irish st

PROFESSORS & TEACHERS.
Potts Henry (music), 9 Castle st
Roberts Mary (music), Friars' vennel
Shaw —, (music). 25 English st
Watson Joseph (drawing), Academy street

READING ROOMS.
Subscription, High street—Jane Swan, keeper
Working Men's, Queensberry st

ROPE & TWINE MAKERS.
Knight John, 78 Friars' vennel
Little William, 70 Friars' vennel
Turner Geo. Mark, 44 Glasgow st, M

SADDLERS.
Lancaster John, Friars' vennel
Milligan Peter, 1 Frars' vennel
Perry James, High st
Weir John 78 English st

SHERIFF'S OFFICERS.
Rae David
Smith James Thompson

SHIP OWNERS.
Blaind Samuel, Church place
Sinclair John, High st
Turner William, 25 Castle st
Walker James, George st

SHOPKEEPERS & DEALERS IN GROCERIES & SUNDRIES.
Bell J, Old Bridge st, Maxwelltown
Carruthers Sarah, 14 Friars' vennel
Clarke David, Friars' vennel
Crawford Susan, College st, M.
Dinwiddie Mary, English st
Given George, Queensberry st
Halliday Mary, 62 College st, M.
Hellon Jacob F. English st
Hope Wm, 45 College st, M.
Irvine Peter, 60 Glasgow st, M.
Johnson Wm, Market st, M.
Johnston James. English st
Liddie John, Friars' vennel
Lookup Janet, High st, M.
Macaskie Mary, 18 Friars' vennel
Macaskie Mary, 16 Friars' vennel
M'Ken Adam, Bridge st
M'Kie Gerard, English st
Menzies Margaret, Market st, M.
Mundell David, College st, M.

SHOPKEEPERS, &c—Continued.

Neilson Ann, 16 Academy st
Rain John, Friars' vennel
Rogerson Mary, 96 Friars' vennel
Smith Margaret, 35 Friars' vennel
Thompson Millar, Friars' vennel
Thomson Agnes, St. Michael st
Thomson John, 82 Friars' vennel
Turner John, 41 Friars' vennel
Watson James, Old Bridge st, M.
Welsh Elizabeth, Galloway st, M.

SLATERS.

Adair Thomas, English st
Briggs John, English st
Irving Margaret, 50 High st
Kirk James, 80 Friars' vennel
M'Quhae Alexander, Friars' vennel
M'Quhae James, English st
Maisie Richard, 5 David st, M.
Sloan Brothers (dealers), Bank st
Thomson Wm. & Son (dealers), White sands

SMALLWARE DEALERS.

Crockett Janet, 38 Friars' vennel
Knight Sarah, 5 English st
M'Gill James, Market st, M.
Richardson Catherine, Friars' vennel

SPIRIT DEALERS.

Marked thus * are also Provision Dealers.
(See also Wine & Spirit Merchants.)

*Beattie Agnes, St. Michael st
*Bell William, Irish st
*Brown James, Old Bridge st, M.
Cameron Jane, Market st, M.
*Colvart James, Queensberry st
Currie Ephraim, St. Andrew st
Devlin Peter, Market st, M.
Dickson Agnes (and tea), 2 Bank st
Dickson James, Bank st
*Dobie Robert, Queensberry st
*Fergusson Rebecca, 5 Queensberry st
*Hellon Joseph, 62 English st
*Hill William, Queensberry st
*Irving Ann, Market st, M.
*Jardine Alexander, 67 English st
*Johnston David, Queensberry st
*Knight Rickleby, St. Michael st
*Locke David, 142 High st
M'Clure Samuel, New quay
M'Kinnel James, Market st, M.
*M'Turk Mrs, Galloway st, M.
*Millar Isabel, Loreburn st
*Millar John, St. Michael st
Robinson Martha, Queensberry st
Scott Thomas, Shakspere st
*Shanks Robert, Queensberry st
Shorthouse John, St. Michael st
Thompson —, Nith place
Touns Mary, Newmarket st
Watson Mary, Irish st
Wilson William, Milldam head

STAY MAKERS.

Brydone Ann & Catherine, 119 High st
Graham Isabella, High st
Haining Jessie, 51 Friars' vennel
M Culloch Mary, English st
M'Dowal Douglas, 46 High st
Muir Mary, Friars' vennel

STRAW BONNET MAKERS.

Campbell Martha, 5 St. Andrew st
Corson Mary, Glasgow st, M.
Easton Mary Ann, 23 English st
Hannah Agnes, Queensberry st
Maxwell Margaret, 22 Academy st
Muir Mary, Friars' vennel

SURGEONS.

Blacklock Archibald, R.N., Castle st
Borthwick Alexander, Castle st
Burgess Robert, 4 Buccleuch st
Burnside Jno, 19 Buccleuch st
Clinahan Mark, 167 High st
Fyfe James Carson, Buccleuch st
Grieve James, M.D., 20 Buccleuch st
M'Culloch James M, M.D., Castle st
Marshall Wm, M. D., Buccleuch st

TAILORS.

Marked thus * are also Clothiers.

(See also Woollen Drapers and Clothiers.)

Aitken John, Nith place
Anderson Samuel, Old Bridge street, Maxwelltown
*Balieff John, 123 High st
Beck Joseph, Anchor close
Graham Thomas, High st
Halliday John, English st
*Hellon Jacob, 103 High st
Hunter John, 62 High st
*Jackson Thomas, 130 High st
Johnston Alexander, 17 English st
Johnston William, 53 High st
Ker John, 97 High st
Lawson William, 124 High st
Little Thomas, 39 High st
*Lockerbie William, 1 Church place
Martin David, Queensberry st
Martin John, 97 High st
Muir James, Queensberry square
*Oney Benjamin, 82 English st
Richardson John, Queensberry st
Riddick J, Castle st
Roxburg Alexander, 67 High st
Shankland William, English st
*Thomson George, 90 High st
Tweedie George, St. Michael st

TALLOW CHANDLERS.

Ferguson & Co., High st
Logan John, 69 High st
Nicholson Francis, 2 Queensberry st
Riddick Samuel, 77 Friars' vennel

TANNERS.

Crosbie Robert, Shakspere st
Wallace Thomas, High st
Watt William & Son (and glue manufacturers), Mill st

TIMBER MERCHANTS.

Gillies Wm & Son, Glasgow st, M.
Sloan Brothers, Bank st
Thompson William & Son, White sands
Willet Saml. Balmoa, Maxwelltown

TIN-PLATE WORKERS AND BRAZIERS.

Fergusson John, Friars' vennel
M'Gregor James, Queensberry st
M'Quhae Edward, Mid steeple
M'Quhae John (and gas fitter), 28 Queensberry st
Milligan Thomas (and gas fitter), 91 High street
Smith John, 15 English st

TWEED & CHECK MANUFRS.

Scott R. & Sons, KINGHOLME MILLS

UMBRELLA MAKERS.

Clark Daniel, Castle st
Glover William, 54 Friars' vennel

UPHOLSTERERS.

See Cabinet Makers.

VETERINARY SURGEONS.

Lauder Charles, White sands
Paterson Robert, Queensberry st
Wilson John, Newmarket st

VINTNERS.

Admiral Duncan, Mary Grierson, Queensberry st
Admiral Napier, Francis Bell, High
Anchor, Maret. Jardine, English st
Bay Horse, John Muirhead, 97 Friars' vennel
Black Bull, Mary Paple, Brewery st
Black Horse, Janet Farries, 58 High st
Blue Bell, Elizabeth Munsie, 92 Friars' vennel
Buck, Francis Hogg, White sands
Bush, Margaret Anderson, Queensberry street

Caerlaverock Castle, William Briggs, 39 High street
Coach & Horses, Thomas Jardine, English street
Coach & Horses, — Kirkpatrick, White sands
Coach & Horses, — Mitchell, High
Cross Keys, Alexander Robson, Queensberry st
Crown, Euphemia Grierson, High st
Douglas Arms, Margaret Wilson, St. David st
Dumfries Arms, W. A. Moffat, High
Durham Ox, Agnes Dunbar, Bridge st
Eagle, James M'Merkan, Bridge st
Edinburgh Castle, William Ferries, 56 Friars' vennel sands
Ewe & Lamb, William Duff, White
Ewe & Lamb, Mary Johnson, Queensberry st
Farmers, Jane Muir, White sands
Fleshers, Jane Beggs, White sands
Flying Spur Inn, William M'Caul, White sands
George, Peter Milligan, High st
Globe, Mary Graham, High st
Golden Bull, Thomas Dalrymple, High street
Grapes, Martha Affleck, High st
Grapes, — Shankland, White sands
Grey Horse, John Laurie, 40 Friars' vennel sands
Grey Horse, Michael Teenan, White
Hare & Hounds, William Ferguson, 53 High street
Hole in the Wall, Archibald M'Kie, 93 High st
Hound & Hare, William Nicholson, Queensberry street
King's Arms, Elizabeth Pagan, Glasgow st, Maxwelltown
Lion & Lamb, John C. Kennedy, Queensberry st
New Bridge, Margaret Pagan, Bridge
Nithside, Thomas Ross, Bridge st
Old Bridge, James M'Adam, Maxwelltown berry st
Old Spur, Andrew Beattie, Queens-
Pine Apple, James Hunter, High st
Red Lion, James Hunter, Chapel st
Royal Oak, Thomas Deucher, Brewery street st
Royal Oak, Thomas Dobbie, 62 High
Sailor's Return, John Young, New quay st, M.
Salutation, James Dixon, Market
Ship, Sarah Anderson, New quay
Ship, James Paton, White sands
Smiths' Arms, James Fallas, 64 High street
Spur, Mary Johnston, Loreburn st
Sun, Henry Dornon, 49 High st
Swan, Wm. Mathers, Queensberry st
Thistle & Crown, James Mundell, Queensberry st
Three Crowns, Thomas Gowanloch, Queensberry st
Turk's Head, John M'Gowan, Irish
White Hart, Joseph Bowman, Brewery street st
Woolpack, John Smith, Loreburn

WATCH AND CLOCK MAKERS.

Charters William, Nith place
Duncan James, 56 Friars' vennel
Gunter Jos. (German clock), High st
Law Samuel, 49 Friars' vennel
M'Adam Robert, 105 High st
Todd John, St. Andrew st
Todd Robert, Queensberry st

WHITESMITHS AND BELL-HANGERS.

Fallas James, 64 High st
Haugh & Pearse, 50 High st

WINE & SPIRIT MERCHANTS.

Bryden John (and tea dealer), 25 English st
Cockburn & Campbell (of Edinburgh), 159 High st — David Whigham, agent
Dickie William, English st
Fraser William, 17 Irish st
Gray William, Friars' vennel
Jardine John, Bridge st
M'Naught John, 98 Friars' vennel
Rankine Adam, Bridge st
Sloan Brothers, Bank st
Swan William, 13 Bank st

WOOLLEN CARDER AND SPINNER.

Smith James, Market street, Maxwelltown

WOOLLEN DRAPERS AND CLOTHIERS.

Hellon Jacob, 103 High st
Oney Benjamin, 82 English st and Hollybush House

WRIGHTS.

See Joiners and Carpenters.

WRITERS.

Marked thus * are also Notaries.

*Adamson Robert, Irish st
Blacklock Jacob, Glasgow st, M.
*Brown William, Bank st
Crichton James M'Millan, Queen st
Dinwiddie William, Church crescent
Goodall John, 3 Bank st
*Gordon & Whitelaw, Bank st
*Hamilton Archibald, Assembly st
*Hannay Alexander, Bank st
Harkness Christopher, 150 High st
Jackson & Symons, Nith place
Johnstone David, Castle st
*Kemp Robert, High st
M'George Charles, Union st
M'Gowan & Hairstens, Irish st
M'Kie James, Long close, 53 High st
M'Lellan Robert, Laurieknowe, M.
Muir Robert, Maxwelltown
*Primrose & Gordon, Buccleuch st
Sanders John, Queen st
Smith T. F. Shakspere st [town
*Smyth John, Galloway st, Maxwell-
Smyth John Alexander, 65 English st
Smyth Thomas Robinson, 65 English st
*Thomson Alexander, Buccleuch st
*Thorburn John, Assembly st
*Threshie & Simpson, Bank st
Walker Robert K. Galloway st, M.
Whigham David, Keiton mains
Wright James, High st
Young Alexander (and procurator fiscal), Castle st

MISCELLANEOUS.

Benson Saml. needle maker, 65 English st
Brown John, cattle dealer, Laurieknow, Maxwelltown
Coulthard David, accountant, Irish st
FISHMONGERS' DEPÔT, 2 Castle street.. James Lockie, manager
Gillies Robert, engraver and printer, Coffee close
Gordon Thomas, basket maker, 108 High st
Hill Robert, soda water manufacturer, Queensberry street
Jones John, superintendent of county police, English street
Langhorn Joseph, livery stable keeper, Shakspere street
Little Wm. flax dresser, 70 Friars' vennel
Norris Mary, fruiterer, High st
Teasdale Joseph, mail contractor, 34 Friars' vennel
Teenan Michael, horse dealer, White sands
Welsh Joseph, inspector and collector of poor rates, Glasgow st. Maxwelltown

Public Buildings, Offices, &c.

PLACES OF WORSHIP, AND THEIR MINISTERS.

SAINT MICHAEL'S, CHURCH — Rev. Robert Wallace, D.D.
NEW CHURCH — Rev. Thos. Duncan, M.D. and Rev. A. Shepherd
SAINT MARY'S CHURCH — Rev. James Stewart
TROQUEER CHURCH, Troqueer — Rev. Walter M'Farlane
FREE CHURCH, Dumfries - Rev. James Julius Wood
FREE CHURCH, Maxwelltown — Rev. W. B. Clarke
UNITED PRESBYTERIAN, Queensberry street — (vacant)
UNITED PRESBYTERIAN, Loreburn st — Rev. David Scott
UNITED PRESBYTERIAN, Buccleuch st — Rev. Marshall N. Gould
REFORMED PRESBYTERIAN — Rev. John M'Dermid
EPISCOPAL — Rev. Archibald M'Ewen
INDEPENDENT CHAPEL, Irving st — Rev. James Mann
WESLEYAN METHODIST CHAPEL, Queen street — (ministers various)
BAPTIST CHAPEL, Irish st —
ROMAN CATHOLIC CHAPEL — Rev. Henry Small
INFIRMARY AND GAOL CHAPEL..Rev. George Cowans

LUNATIC ASYLUM,
CRICHTON ROYAL INSTITUTION.

Resident Physician..William Alexander Francis Brown, M.D.
Chaplain..Rev. George Cowans
Matron..Jane Sandeman

DUMFRIES AND GALLOWAY ROYAL INFIRMARY,
ST. MICHAEL ST.

Matron..Jessie Connell
House Surgeon..Dr. Rogers
Chaplain..Rev. George Cowans

CUSTOM HOUSE, BANK ST.

Comptroller..John M'Kenzie, Esq.
Collector — Alexander Rose M'Clay, Esq.
Searching and Landing Waiter..Thomas Duncan
Coast and Tide Waiter..Robt. Ferguson

INLAND REVENUE OFFICE,
NITH PLACE.

Collector..Thomas Smith [teous
Deputy Collector..Chas. Dalrymple Por-
Supervisor..Thomas Nichols

DUMFRIES & MAXWELLTOWN ASTRONOMICAL SOCIETY.
CORBERY, MAXWELLTOWN.

Secretary..John Jackson
Treasurer..James Caldoo
President..John Haig, Esq.

ASSEMBLY ROOMS, George st
BUTTER MARKET, New Market street
CARRUTHER'S ALMHOUSES, New road
COUNCIL CHAMBER, High st..Robert Kemp, *town clerk*
COUNTY GAOL and BRIDEWELL,..Mr. John Kidd, *governor*; Rev. George Cowans, *chaplain*; .... M'Knight, *surgeon*
COUNTY TAX OFFICE,159 High street.. David Whigham, *collector*
COURT HOUSE, Buccleuch st..Charles Baird, *sheriff's clerk*; John Jones and William M'Nab, *inspectors of police*
DISPENSARY, Irish street
GAS WORKS, Shakspere street..... Marvine, *manager*
MECHANICS' INSTITUTE, Council chambers, High st..Alexander M'Crombie, *secretary*
POLICE OFFICE, Mid steeple..William M'Nab, *superintendent*
POOR'S OFFICE, St. Michael street..... Eliza Richardson, *matron*
STAMP OFFICE, High street....David Stewart, *distributer*; and Galloway st, Maxwelltown....Robert K. Walker, *distributer*

THEATRE, Shakspere street
TOWN HALL, Glasgow st, Maxwelltown ..Robert Walker, *clerk*

COACHES.

To BEATOCK & MOFFATT, a *Coach* from the King's Arms, High st, every afternoon at half-past nine
To KIRKCUDBRIGHT and CASTLE DOUGLAS, a *Coach*, from the King's Arms, High street, every morning at eight, and afternoon at twenty minutes before five
To LOCKERBIE, a *Coach*, from the Commercial Inn, High street, every afternoon at half-past one
To PORTPATRICK and CASTLE DOUGLAS, a *Coach*, from the King's Arms, High st, every forenoon at eleven

CONVEYANCE BY RAILWAY,
ON THE GLASGOW AND SOUTH-WESTERN LINE.

Station, a quarter of a mile from the town..John Fairfull Smith, *secretary*; Balfour Balsillie, *station master*
Omnibuses, from the King's Arms, and Commercial Inns, to the Station, await the arrival, and attend the departure of the trains

CARRIERS.

To ANNAN and RUTHWELL, James Richardson, from the Admiral Duncan, Wednesday and Saturday
To APPLEGARTH, James Bayes, from the Hound and Hare, Wednesday
To AUCHENCAIRN, Andrew Carter, from the Old Spur, Wednesday
To BERRESCARR, James Scott, from the Three Crowns, Wednesday
To CARSETHORN, Joseph Kirk, from the Grey Horse, Wednesday and Sat.
To CASTLE DOUGLAS, John Palmer, from the Admiral Duncan, Wednesday and Saturday
To DALBEATIE, Hugh Thomson, from the Thistle and Crown, & John Hyslop, the Grey Horse, Wednesday & Saturday
To GATEHOUSE, Peter Comelin, from the Admiral Duncan, Wednesday
To HARDGATE URR, John Craig, from the Black Horse, Wednesday
To KILPATRICK. William Barkley, from the Buck, Wednesday & Saturday
To KIRKCUDBRIGHT, Thos. Wallace, from the Admiral Duncan, Wednesday
To KIRKMICHAEL, Joseph Byatt, from the Three Crowns, Wednesday
To LOCHMABEN, Janet Hall, from the Admiral Duncan, Wednesday and Sat.
To LOCKERBIE, James Thomson, from the Admiral Duncan, Wednesday
To MINNIEHIVE, James Reid, from the Bay Horse, and Michael Hunter, from the Grey Horse, Wednesday and Saturday
To MOFFATT, Alexander Denham, Wed
To NEW GALLOWAY, John Chartris, from the Royal Oak, Wednesday
To PENPONT. Thomas M'Ken, from the Grey Horse, Wednesday
To PIERPONT,.. Finley, from the Blue Bell, Wednesday and Saturday
To PRESTON MILL, Jas. Walles, from the Grey Horse, Wednesday & Saturday
To SOUTHWICK, John Penn, from the Buck, Wednesday
To SPRINGHORN & KIRKPATRICK, John Dempster, from the Old Spur, Wednesday
To WIGTON & HETTONSTEWART, James Raeside, from the Admiral Duncan, Wednesday

CONVEYANCE BY WATER.

To LIVERPOOL, the Arab Steam Packet, Captain Richard Fullarton, from Glencaple quay, every Wednesday & Saturday one week, and Friday in the following week

COASTING VESSELS.

To GLASGOW, the Robert and Helen.. James Little, agent, Bank street, and the Jane and Margaret..Wm. Turner agent, Castle street
To LIVERPOOL, the Grace, the Joseph, and the Jane..William Thomson, agent, White sands
To WHITEHAVEN, the Active..William Turner, agent, Castle street
The above Coasting Vessels, sail at uncertain periods

DUNSCORE, HOLYWOOD AND KIRKMAHOE.

DUNSCORE, a parish in the district of Nithsdale, is bounded by Glencairn and Keir on the north, and Holywood and Kirkcudbrightshire on the south. It is twelve miles in length, and its breadth varies from one to four miles. The land is arable on the banks of the Nith, which irrigates its eastern part; it is also intersected by the Cairn. Sheep and black cattle are reared off these lands, for the southern markets; and oats, barley, wheat, potatoes, and turnips are produced in great quantities. The kirk of the parish is about nine miles from Dumfries, and seven from Minnichive. Robert Burns, at one time, held a farm in this parish, near the Nith, named Friars' carse; and it was while here that he had an opportunity of eulogizing the Cluden river, which is a continuation of the Cairn water. At this period he took charge of a village library, instituted by his landlord, Robert Riddel, Esq.

HOLYWOOD parish, which is bounded by Dunscore on the north and west, extends for ten miles along the right bank of the Nith, its breadth being from two to three miles. The district derives its name from a sacred grove, to which, it is said, the Druids resorted to perform their rites. The temple of these pagans was succeeded by the cell of a hermit, which was subsequently changed into a house for monks of the premonstratenses, in the beginning of the twelfth century; and the ruins of an old abbey in the churchyard are supposed to be remains of that building. The church, an exceedingly neat erection, and much admired, stands in a most delightful part of the country, about three miles from Dumfries.

KIRKMAHOE is a small modern village in the parish of its name, and district of Nithsdale, five miles from Dumfries, situate on a rivulet, tributary to the Nith, near the southern extremity of the parish. The church is a handsome gothic edifice of recent erection. The lands of the parish are well cultivated, and there are several plantations.

GENTRY AND CLERGY.

Anderson Rev. William, Kirkmahoe
Armstrong —, Esq. Duneslin
Crichton Mrs. Elizabeth, Dunscore
Johnstone Admiral James Charles, (of Cawhill), Holywood
Lawrie James, Esq. Milliganton, Dunscore
Macalpineleny James, Esq. Dalswinton, Kirkmahoe
M'Kinnell John, Esq. (of M'Murdoston), Dunscore
Maxwell Francis, Esq. (of Gribton), Holywood
Morin John, Esq. Allanton, Dunscore
Robinson William, Esq. (of Kemyss Hall), Kirkmahoe
Wilson Johnstone, Esq. (of Strouquhan), Dunscore

PAROCHIAL SCHOOLS.

DUNSCORE, John Thomson, master
HOLYWOOD, John Russell, master
KIRKMAHOE, Adam Robson, James Maclellan and James Blacklock, masters

SHOPKEEPERS, TRADERS, &c.

Bell Agnes, dress maker, Kirkmahoe
Broatch Wm. blacksmith, Dunscore
Corrie John, grocer and spirit dealer, Holywood
Coupland James, tailor, Kirkmahoe
Crosbie Margaret, King's Arms Inn, Dunscore [mahoe
Crosbie Robert, blacksmith, Kirk-
Dalziel Robt. shopkeeper, Dunscore
Dalziel William, blacksmith, Kirkmahoe
Dempster James, grocer, Kirkmahoe
Dickson Newton, grocer, Holywood
Fisher John, cartwright, Kirkmahoe
Graham Samuel, joiner, Dunscore
Henderson John, grocer, Kirkmahoe
Hunter James, blacksmith, Dunscore
Johnston John, mason, Kirkmahoe
Kirk James, joiner, Dunscore
Kirkpatrick John, stocking maker, Holywood [Holywood
Lansbery James, stocking maker,
M'Bibby James, stocking maker, Holywood
M'Cullom John, tailor, Kirkmahoe

M'George William, stocking maker, Holywood
M'Haig James, clog maker, Dunscore
M'Nae James, stocking maker, Holywood
Maxwell Janet, grocer, Dunscore
Miller Janet, spirit dealer, Kirkmahoe [Kirkmahoe
Riddick John, shoe and clog maker,
Smith James, grocer, Kirkmahoe
Stott William, surgeon, Dunscore

PLACES OF WORSHIP, AND THEIR MINISTERS.

ESTABLISHED CHURCH, Dunscore..Rev. John Hope
ESTABLISHED CHURCH, Holywood.... Rev Robert Davison
ESTABLISHED CHURCH, Kirkmahoe.. Rev. David Hoeg
FREE CHURCH, Dunscore..Rev. Robert Bryden
FREE CHURCH, Kirkmahoe..Rev.Wm. Anderson
UNITED PRESBYTERIAN, Dunscore.. Rev. Matthew Beattie

RAILWAY.

The nearest *Station* is at DUMFRIES, about nine miles distant

ECCLEFECHAN

WITH THE VILLAGE OF WATERBECK IN MIDDLEBIE AND NEIGHBOURHOODS.

ECCLEFECHAN is a considerable village, in the parish of Hoddam, 71 miles s. of Edinburgh, 75 s. E. of Glasgow, 19 N. W. of Carlisle, 16 E. of Dumfries, and 6 N. of Annan: lying in a fine situation, near the foot of Annandale, and on the road from Glasgow to Carlisle, within a mile of the station on the Caledonian Railway. The land of Hoddam parish is of the very best quality, under a superior system of cultivation, and the district is perhaps one of the most healthy and pleasant in the south of Scotland. The principal employment of the inhabitants is weaving cotton goods for the Carlisle manufacturers, who have constantly a demand for the labours of the loom, and which enables the operatives to enjoy many comforts which they would otherwise be deprived of. Ecclefechan contains many respectable shops, in which a variety of trades is carried on, the prosperity of which is mainly sustained by the extensive cattle markets, for which this village has been so long noted. These great marts are held on the first Fridays after the 11th in the months of January, February, March, April, and July; the Friday before the 26th of August, the 18th of September (or the Friday before), the 26th of October, the Friday after the 11th of November, and the Friday after the 11th of December. The first Friday after the 11th of May and the 26th of October are hiring days for servants, the latter being also a cattle market; and the first Tuesday after the 11th of June is a fair for cattle and general merchandise. On the two fair days in June and October, the Duke of Buccleuch, as superior, claims certain customs for all standings, and for all cattle exposed for sale. Ecclefechan can boast of being the birth-place of two persons of considerable celebrity — namely, the Rev. Edward Irvine, founder of that section of Christians called Irvinites; and Thomas Carlyle, renowned for his quaint but powerful writing.

MIDDLEBIE is a parish lying on the road between Langholm and Ecclefechan: it is about seven miles in length by four in breadth, abounds in red freestone, and is valuable for its lime quarries; but much of the land is of rather poor quality. The village—a small one. is about two miles from Ecclefechan, and about twelve from Langholm.

WATERBECK village, in Middlebie parish, is two miles from thence, on the road to Langholm. It is a pretty little rural place, and has been much improved by the late Mr. Robert Carlyle and his sons.

POST OFFICE, ECCLEFECHAN, William Johnstone, *Post Master.*—Letters from the SOUTH arrive every forenoon at half-past ten, and are despatched at half-past three in the afternoon, and morning at one.

Letters from the NORTH arrive every afternoon at half-past three, and morning at one, and are despatched at half-past ten in the morning.

396

GENTRY AND CLERGY.

Armstrong George, Esq. Castlemilk
Arnott Archibald, Esq. M.D. Hall of Kirkconnell
Bell George, Esq. Minsca
Bell John, Esq. Torbeck hill
Bell William, Esq. Ecclefechan
Blacklock Mrs. Helen Smith, Middlebie
Carruthers John, Esq. Breckon hill
Davidson Miss Jean, Braes
Dobie William, Esq. Ecclefechan
Evison Rev. Richard, Middlebie Manse
Graham James, Esq. Dumaby
Hamilton Rev. Robert, Waterbeck
Hepburn David, Esq. Hoddamtown
Hunter John, Esq. Meinfoot, Ecclefechan
Irving John, Esq. Middlebie
Irving John Ball, Esq. Bankside
Irving William Ogle, Esq. Bankside
Little Mrs, Mary, Cresfield House, Ecclefechan
Lockhart Norman, Esq. Newlands
Maxwell Sir John H, Bart. Springkell
Menzies Rev. Robert, Luce Manse
Murray Mrs. Catherine, Norwood
Murray Mrs. Isabella, Kirtleton
Nevison Rev. Richd, Middlebie Manse
Roy William, Esq. Millbank
Scott Mr. William, Ecclefechan
Sharp Mr. W. Esq. Knock hill
Smith E. B. Esq. Lockwood House
Smith P. de Irving, Esq. Langshaw

SCHOOLS.

FREE CHURCH, Ecclefechan—William Duff, master
PAROCHIAL, Ecclefechan — David Galbrath, master
PAROCHIAL, Waterbeck — John Brown, master
PAROCHIAL, Middlebie — Charles Borthwick, master

BLACKSMITHS.

Haddon Robert, Ecclefechan
Irving John, Waterbeck
Irving John, Ecclefechan
Miller James, Waterbeck
Tait William, Ecclefechan

BOOT AND SHOE MAKERS.

Elliot James, Ecclefechan
Johnston David, Ecclefechan

Johnston George, Waterbeck
Murray John, Middlebie
Thompson William, Waterbeck

CLOG MAKERS.

Corrie Robert, Ecclefechan
Elliot James, Ecclefechan
Moffat John, Waterbeck
Steel James, Ecclefechan

GROCERS & SPIRIT DEALERS.
(See also Shopkeepers, &c.)

Broatch Mary, Ecclefechan
Carlyle Thomas & Robert (and seedsmen), Waterbeck
Carruthers John, Ecclefechan
Dunn William, Waterbeck
Ferguson Janet, Ecclefechan
Jackson Janet, Ecclefechan
Johnstone William, Ecclefechan
Muir Peter & Co. Ecclefechan
Murray William, Ecclefechan
Trotter Robert, Ecclefechan
Wright William, Ecclefechan

JOINERS AND WRIGHTS.

Forsyth Robert, Ecclefechan
Hysslop Charles, Waterbeck
Latimer David, Waterbeck
Scott George, Middlebie
Scott John, Ecclefechan
Wright William, Ecclefechan

LIME BURNERS.

Byers Andrew, Blackwoodridge
Fergusson John, Middlebie
Murray Peter, Blackwoodridge Works, Middlebie

LINEN & WOOLLEN DRAPERS.

Carlyle Thomas & Robert (and woolstaplers), Waterbeck
Graham John (and iron merchant), Ecclefechan

MASONS.

Bell George, Ecclefechan
Burnet Robert, Waterbeck
Easton George, Ecclefechan
Tannant John, Ecclefechan

SHOPKEEPERS & DEALERS IN SUNDRIES.

Burton H. Middlebie
Byers Andrew, Blackwoodridge
Ferguson John, Donkins, Burnhead
Henry John, Ecclefechan
Rae Jane, Ecclefechan
Tweedie Jane, Ecclefechan

SURGEONS.

Little George, Ecclefechan
Simpson John, Ecclefechan
Wilson John, Waterbeck
Young William, Ecclefechan

TAILORS.

Graham James, Ecclefechan
Hall James, Ecclefechan
Wells John, Waterbeck
Wells William jun. Waterbeck

VINTNERS.

Bell Andrew (Carlyle Arms), Waterbeck [fechan
Broatch Janet (Commercial), Ecclefechan
Carruthers Wm. (Crown), Waterbeck
Farriers Isabella (Globe,) Ecclefechan
Johnston Edward, Ecclefechan
Kennedy Thos. (Swan), Ecclefechan
Rogers William (Bush), Ecclefechan

WRIGHTS.

See Joiners and Wrights.

MISCELLANEOUS.

Ewart David, writer. and agent to the English and Scottish Assurance Company. Ecclefechan
Irving George, farmer. Middlebie
Macconnel James, carver and gilder, Ecclefechan
Manderson George, saddler. Ecclefechan
Murray Matthew, flesher, Ecclefechan
Park James,, baker, Ecclefechan
Tennant Mary Paterson, straw bonnet maker, Ecclefechan
Watson Isaac, tinsmith, Ecclefechan
Wright Walter, watch maker, Ecclefechan

PLACES OF WORSHIP,
AND THEIR MINISTERS.

ESTABLISHED CHURCH, Ecclefechan.. Rev. Robert Menzies
ESTABLISHED CHURCH, Middlebie.. Rev. Robert Evison
FREE CHURCH, Ecclefechan.. Rev. Thos. Mathieson
UNITED PRESBYTERIAN, Ecclefechan.. Rev. William Tait
UNITED PRESBYTERIAN, Waterbeck.. Rev. Robert Hamilton

CONVEYANCE BY RAILWAY,
ON THE CALEDONIAN LINE.
Station, one mile from the town

CARRIER.

To DUMFRIES, John Jardine, Tuesday and Saturday, and to LANGHOLM, on Monday and Thursday

---

LANGHOLM,

AND THE PARISHES OF CANONBIE, ESKDALEMUIR, EWES, WESTERKIRK & NEIGHBOURHOODS.

LANGHOLM is a thriving market town and burgh of barony, in the parish of its name; 73 miles S. from Edinburgh, 80 S. W. from Glasgow, 30 E. by N. from Dumfries, the like distance S. E. from Moffat, 21 N. from Carlisle, 18 N. E. from Annan, and 12 N. from Longtown (in Cumberland), delightfully situated on the left or east bank of the Esk, over which there is a stone bridge of three arches. This parish and the adjoining ones of Canonbie, Ewes, Westerkirk and Eskdalemuir are known as the 'five kirks of Eskdale.' The town of Langholm owes its origin to a border house or tower, which was formerly the property of the all-powerful Armstrongs, but is now only seen in a state of ruin. Langholm was long famed for an ingeniously formed iron instrument, called the 'branks,' which fitted upon the head of a shrewish female, and, projecting a sharp spike into her mouth, fairly subdued the more annoying weapon within; this instrument was deemed more effectual than the ducking (or cucking) stool, used in some parts of England, as the latter permitted liberty to the unruly member between every dip. The author of the 'Picture of Scotland' says—'Eskdale derives more than common charm from the memory of Johnnie Armstrong, whose name is associated with many of its localities;' his tower of

Gilnockie still stands, though converted into a cow-house, a few miles below Langholm, on the left bank of the Esk. It was on 'Langholm Holm' that, when going to meet the king, he and his 'gallant companie' of thirty-six men 'ran their horse and brak' their spears.' Johnnie terminated his mortal career at Carlenrig, a place not far distant from Moss-Paul, on the road between Langholm and Hawick: the story of the judicial execution of this borderthief and his companions, by James V., is well known; the graves of the whole of the marauding band are to be seen in a deserted church-yard at Carlenrig. In the present day Langholm does not seem to partake of any of the peculiarities which distinguished the country in the 'riding times', or in the ages of superstition, being now one of the most thriving towns of its size in Scotland. It is built in the bosom of a lovely woodland scene, along the Edinburgh and Carlisle road; and is composed generally of good stone houses, roofed with blue slate. The bridge connects the ancient town with a more modern suburb on the opposite side of the river, called New Langholm or New Town. In the market-place of the old town stands the town-hall, jail, and county police station, ornamented with a neat spire and clock. The annually increasing woollen trade more than compensates for the decrease of cotton manufacture, which formerly flourished here. The town contains a number of respectable shops, a branch each of the 'National Bank of Scotland' and the 'British Linen Company', two distilleries, a brewery, dyehouse, tannery, and some excellent inns. The government of the town is vested in a baron baillie, appointed by the Duke of Buccleuch, who is superior. Sheriff's small debt and justice of peace courts are held at stated periods.

The parish church, recently erected, is allowed to be one of the most elegant and substantial in the south of Scotland ; the other places of worship are a free church and two united presbyterian chapels. A good parochial school, one endowed by the late Capt. George Maxwell of Broomholm, and one connected with the free church are the institutions for instruction ; and there are two extensive well supported libraries, one of which derives considerable advantage from a munificent bequest of the late Thomas Telford, Esq. A monument to Sir John Malcolm has been erected on the highest hill at a cost of £1,300, and more recently, one has been raised in the market place, in memory of his brother Sir Poulteney Malcolm. The market day is Wednesday ; the fairs are held on the 16th April, the last Tuesday in May (old style), 26th July (for lambs) 18th September, and in November : there are also two hiring days—one in May, the other in November.

CANONBIE (or *Canonby*) is a village and parish delightfully situated on the banks of the Esk, halfway between Longtown and Langholm, and on the southern border of the county ; it is separated from England by the river Liddal, whose romantic banks

present some pleasing scenery. This parish is about nine miles long and six broad ; the high road from Edinburgh to London runs through it. The kirk is a very large stone building, and will accommodate 1,400 persons. There are inexhaustible mines of coal and lime-quarries of excellent quality in the parish, but only a small portion of them is wrought. The scenery along the Esk is considered to be the finest in the south of Scotland. The HOLLOWS is a small village, about a mile and a half from Canonbie ; near to which on the north is Gilnockie tower. The Duke of Buccleuch is sole proprietor of the parish.

ESKDALEMUIR is a mountainous pastoral parish, on the north-eastern border of the county, and in the district of Eskdale ; the manse, which is about the centre of the parish, is thirteen miles from Langholm. A very small portion of Eskdalemuir is under cultivation ; the principal land proprietor is the Duke of Buccleuch.

The parish of EWES, situated on the eastern extremity of the county, is remarkable for its beautiful ranges of green hills, covered with verdure to their summits, and the clearness of the river, which affords excellent trouting. Numerous plantations on the properties of the Duke of Buccleuch and the late Mr. Beattie (of Meikledale), add additional beauty to the lovely appearance of the sweet dale of the Ewes.

WESTERKIRK parish is also situated near the eastern boundary of the county, about six miles from Langholm. Nearly the whole of this portion of the district is devoted to pasture for sheep and black cattle ; but there are several elegant villas, which in some degree relieve its otherwise monotonous appearance. The church stands on the left bank of the river Esk.

POST OFFICE, High-street, LANGHOLM, John Nicol, *Post Master.* The LONDON mail, with letters from all parts of the SOUTH, arrives every forenoon at a quarter before eleven, and is despatched at half-past one in the afternoon. The EDINBURGH mail, with letters from all parts of the NORTH, arrives every afternoon at half-past one, and is despatched at a quarter before eleven in the morning. Letters from NEWCASTLE arrive (by penny post) every forenoon at a quarter past ten, and are despatched at ten minutes past two in the afternoon. Letters from ESKDALEMUIR arrive every Wednesday and Saturday forenoon at eleven, and are despatched every morning on the arrival of the South mail.

POST OFFICE, Bowholme, CANONBIE, Miss Donaldson, *Post Mistress.* Letters from the SOUTH arrive every morning at ten, and are despatched at twenty minutes past two in the afternoon. Letters from the NORTH arrive every afternoon at twenty minutes past two and are despatched at ten in the morning,

---

*** When the initials N. L. occur they signify* NEW LANGHOLM.

NOBILITY, GENTRY AND CLERGY.

Ballantyne Rev. Wm. Buccleuch sq
Bell Mrs. —, Woodhouse lees
Bell George Graham (of Crurie and Castle o'er), Eskdalemuir
Borthwick Miss Jane, New Langholm
Borthwick Thomas Chalmers, Esq., (justice of the peace), Housrig
Borthwick Lieut. Col. William, (justice of the peace), Georgefield, Westerkirk
Brown John, Esq. M.D., (justice of the peace), Milltoun
Buccleuch his Grace the Duke of, Langholm Lodge
Church James, Esq. (justice of the peace), Park House, Canonbie
Connell James, Esq. (chamberlain to the Duke of Buccleuch), Irving House
Connell James, Esq. (justice of the peace), Broomholme
Connell James, Esq., Longwood
Cross Mrs. —, Langholm
Dickson Mrs. —, Buccleuch square
Dobie Mrs. —, Townhead [nie
Donaldson Rev. Jas. Manse, Canonside, Westerkirk [head
Dunbar Rev. William, Manse, Burnside, Westerkirk
Elliot Mrs. Captain Alison, Clint-
Elliot Mrs. Scott, Woodslie, Canonbie
Irving Miss Janet, Market place
Irving John Esq R. N. Oak Cottage
Irving Miss Mary, Market place
Johnstone Miss—, Buccleuch square
Keir Mrs. —, Rose vale
Little Mrs. —, High st

Little James, Esq. (justice of the peace), Carlesgill, Westerkirk
Malcolm the Misses —, Burnfoot
Malcolm Miss Margaret, Milnholm
Malcolm Wm. Elpinstone, Esq. (justice of the peace), Burnfoot, Westerkirk
Maxwell George, Esq. (justice of the peace), of Broomholm
Maxwell George, Esq. (justice of the peace), Priors lyne, Canonbie
Maxwell Mrs. Jane, Buccleuch sq
Maxwell John Esq. (justice of the peace), Westwater
Mein George A. Esq. M.D. of Marsh House, Canonbie
Mein Pulteney, Esq. Glencortholm, Canonbie
Murray Mrs. Eliza, High st
Richardson Mrs. C., Forge, Canonbie
Scott Charles, Esq., Bush Ewes
Scott Mrs. Helen, Buccleuch place
Shaw Rev. Robert, Manse, Ewes
Shaw Rev. William Berry, Manse
Stevenson Alexander, Esq., (justice of the peace), High st
Strathearn Rev. John, Manse, Eskdalemuir
Thomson Mrs. Jane, High st
Watson Rev. Chas. Manse, Townhead
Watson Rev. Wm., Esk Cottage
Wilson John, Esq. (justice of the peace), Billholm, Westerkirk
Yates Mrs. L. D. & Miss C. Esk Cottage

ACADEMIES & SCHOOLS.

Not otherwise described are Day Schools.
BROOMHOLM FREE SCHOOL, Langholm—Thomas Wilson, master

Brown Elizabeth, Church wynd
Carruthers Mary & Janet, Meikleholm
ESKHOGG SCHOOL, Canonbie—Robert Murray, master
FREE CHURCH SCHOOL, Charles street—William Eston, master
GLENZIER SCHOOL, Claygate, Canonbie—James Leishman, master
HAIRLOWHOGG SCHOOL, Claygate, Canooby—Adam Foster, master
INFANTS' SCHOOL, Langholm—Thompson, mistress
LANGHOLM ENDOWED SCHOOL, Buccleuch square—George Johnson Todd, master
Macdonald Ellen Charlotte, (boarding), Holm foot

PAROCHIAL SCHOOLS.—
Buccleuch square—George Johnson Todd, head master
Claygate, Canonbie—Wm. Hunter, master
Eskdalemuir—James Yool, master
Ewes—John Little, master
Westerkirk—James Brice, master

TAIL SCHOOL, Claygate, Canonbie—Thomas Heard, master
Todd —, (girls'), Canonbie
Yeoman Jane, Henry st, New Langholme

BAKERS.

Davidson James, Canonbie
Grieve James, High st
Hyslop William, Market place,

BANKS.

BRITISH LINEN COMPANY (Branch), High st—(draw upon the parent establishment, and on the Bank of England and Edinburgh, Smith, Payne & Smiths, London)—Alexander Stevenson, agent

NATIONAL BANK OF SCOTLAND (Branch) High st—(draws upon the parent establishment, Edinburgh, and on Glyn, Hallifax, & Co., London)—Robert Wallace, manager

SAVINGS' BANK, High st—Robert Wallace, treasurer ; George Maxwell, secretary

BLACKSMITHS.

Anderson William, Elizabeth st, N.L.
Porteous James, John st
Scoon Walter, Langholm
Scott George, Hollows, Canonbie

BOOKSELLER, STATIONER, BINDER & PRINTER.

Rome Thomas Laidlaw, (and news agent), High street

BOOT & SHOE MAKERS,

Atchinson Thomas (& last maker), Charles street
Beattie John, Charles st
Bell James, High st
Grieve Thomas, Charles st, N.L.
Hairstanes John, Langholm
Kershaw John, David st
Little Andrew, High st
Murray Thomas, Canonbie
Porteous Thomas, John st
Turnbull Thomas, Buccleuch square
Watt Joseph, Canonbie
Whillans Robert (and last maker), Market place

BREWER & MALTSTER.

Chalmers Walter, Langholm

CHEMIST & DRUGGIST.

Rome Robert Moncrieff, High st

CHINA, GLASS, &c. DEALERS.

Bell David (earthenware), High st
Coulthard Matthew Jameson, (glass), High street
Knox John, Market place
Scott David, (earthenware), High st

CLOG MAKERS.

Atchinson Thomas, Charles st, N.L.
Grieve James, High st
Hounam Thomas, Charles st, N.L.
Platoff William, Henry street
Watt Joseph, Canonbie
Whillans Robert, Market place

DISTILLERS.

LANGHOLM DISTILLERY, — John Connell, proprietor
GLENTARRAS DISTILLERY,—James Kennedy, proprietor

FIRE, &c. OFFICE AGENTS,

AGRICULTURIST, (cattle), John Nicol, High street
CALEDONIAN, John Nicol, High st,
COUNTY, (fire) & PROVIDENT (life), George Scott, Market place
EDINBURGH, (life), Robert Wallace, High street
NORTH BRITISH, Alexander Stevenson, High street
LIFE ASSOCIATION OF SCOTLAND, Thomas Laidlaw Rome, High st
ROYAL FARMERS' AND GENERAL, Robert Moncrieff, Rome, High st
STANDARD, (life), John Nicol, High street
TEMPERANCE & GENERAL PROVIDENT, William Little

FLESHERS

Anderson Walter, Buccleuch square
Bell Andrew, High st
Davidson Wm. Claygate, Canonbie
Lunn Robert, Market place
Scott George, Langholm

GROCERS AND PROVISION DEALERS.

Marked thus * are also Spirit Dealers.

*Archibald Francis, Market place
Bell Andrew, Market place
Bell George, Claygate, Canonbie
Bell John, High st
*Cuningham James, High st
Forsythe Mary, Martin st, New L.
Grieve James, High st
Hairstens Joseph, High st
Hyslop William, Market place
Little William, Langholm
Pasley Robert, Langholm [holm
Reid Thomas, Henry st, New Lang-
*Scott George, Market place
*Scott James, Claygate, Canonbie
Smellie Robert, High st
Young Mary, Langholm

INNS.

(See also Vintners, &c.)

Buck, John Glendining, (and wine and spirit merchant), High st
Commercial, William Grieve (and horse and gig owner for hire), High street
Cross Keys, (and livery stables), Walter Glendining, Canonbie
Crown (and posting house), Clement Brown, High street
Salutation, John Young, High st

IRONMONGERS.

Marked thus * are also Bar Iron Merchants

Bell David, High st
*Glendining Archibald (and hardwareman), Market place
Knox John (and hardwareman), Market place
*Scott James, Claygate, Canonbie

JOINERS AND CABINET MAKERS.

Armstrong Thomas, Brewery close
Knox John (& upholsterer,) Market place, (& cartwright), Martin st
Irving William, Hollows, Canonbie
M'Vittie Thomas (and cartwright), Henry st, New Langholm
Milligan Robert, (joiner), Eskrow, New Langholm
Wilson John, High st [st
Wilson Ninian (& cartwright), Mary

LIBRARIES.

GENTLEMEN'S SUBSCRIPTION, High-street—Thomas Laidlaw Rome, librarian
TRADESMEN'S SUBSCRIPTION Charles st, New Langholm—Wm. Little, treasurer ; Walter Bell, librarian
WESTERKIRK LIBRARY — James Bryce, librarian

LINEN & WOOLLEN DRAPERS.

Archibald Francis (Scotch tweeds, &c.), Market place
Armstrong Isabella, High street
Bell George, Claygate, Canonbie
Bell John, High st
Dalgliesh William, High st
Little William, Langholm
Reid Thomas, Henry st, N. L
Scott George, Market place
Scott James, Claygate, Canonbie
Smellie Robert, High st

MANUFACTURERS.

Anderson Adam (tweed), George st
Archibald James & Francis (woollen) Whitshiels Mill, Ewes
Bowman James & Son (woollen and patent thread, and dyers), Henry st, New Langholm

Bowman William (tweed, and dyer) Martin st, New Langholm
Byers Andrew & Son, (Scotch tweeds, linseys, plaids, scarfs, &c), Charles street, New Langholm
Easton, Cairns & Co., (woollen goods and hosiery), Ewes Mill, Langholm
Frater John (tweeds) Charles st, N.L
Lightbody Thomas (tweed), N. L
Reid David & Son (Scotch tweeds, shepherds-plaids, linseys, &c.), Henry street, New Langholm
Renwick Thomas and Alexander Walter (Representatives of the late — hosiery and wool spinners), Woollen Mills, N.Langholm

MASONS AND BUILDERS.

Byers Robert, Charles st, N. L
Hotson Alexander, George st
Hotson James, Elizabeth st, N.L
Irving William (mason), Langholm
M Vittie Thomas (builder), Henry street, New Langholm
Scott George & James, Langholm
Scott Robert, Langholm

MEAL DEALERS.

Armstrong James, Charles st, N.L
Atchinson John, Langholm
Bell George, Claygate, Canonbie
Douglas Robert, High st
Grieve James, High st
Hairstens Joseph, High st
Hope James, High st
Hyslop Jane, Langholm
Hyslop William, Market place
Little John, Martin st, N. L
Little Mary, High st
Oliver James, Charles st, N.L
Scott James, Claygate, Canonbie

MILLERS.

Graham John, Hollows, Canonbie
Irving John, Langholm Corn Mills
Millar William & John, Meikleholm Water Mills

MILLINERS AND DRESS MAKERS.

Armstrong Isabella, High street
Brown & Park, Market place
Carruthers Mary & Janet, Meikleholm, New Langholm
Dalgliesh Janet, Charles st
Esplin Grace & Margaret & Elizabeth, Langholm,
Hairstens Ann, High st
Hastie Elizabeth, Market place
Irving Margaret, High st
Park Ellen, Buccleuch square
Pasley Margaret, Brae, Langholm
Slack Miss Margaret, High st
Telford Hannah, Langholm
Yeoman Jane, Henry st, N. L.

NAIL MAKERS.

Glendining Archibald, Market place
Lightbody William, David st
M'Millan Samuel, High st

NEWSPAPER OFFICE, &c.

ESKDALE AND LIDDESDALE ADVERTISER (Monthly Journal & Railway Travellers' Guide, first Wednesday in the month—Thomas Laidlaw Rome, proprietor and publisher, High st

OIL AND COLOURMEN

Glendining Archibald, Market place
Johnstone William, High st
Scott George, Market place

PAINTERS & GLAZIERS.

Coulthard Matthew Jameson, High st
Harkness William, High st
Irving John, (glazier), High st
Johnston William, High st

PLUMBER & GAS FITTER.

Duncan Andrew (& zinc worker and bell hanger), High st

SADDLER.

Clark John (and trunk maker), High street

SEEDSMEN.

Bell George, Claygate, Canonbie
Cunningham James, High st
Glendining Archibald, Market place
Scott James, Claygate, Canonbie

SHOPKEEPERS & DEALERS IN SUNDRIES.

Armstrong Mary, New Langholm
Bell John, Henry st, N. L
Borthwick Matthew, Henry st, N.L
Byers Robert, Charles st, N. L
Foster Francis, Church wynd
Graham George, Charles st, N. L
Harkness William, High st
Hill David, Martin st, N. L
Hope James, High st
Hudson Nancy, Langholm
Johnstone Jessie, Esk row, N. L
Nicol Isabella, David st
Oliver James, Charles st, N. L
Scott George, Langholm
Scott James, Charles st, N.L
Slacks John, Charles st, N. L
Sutton Anne, John st
Thomson Isabella, Henry st, N. L
Wilson Margaret, Hollows, Canonbie

STRAW BONNET MAKERS.

Armstrong Isabella, High st
Brown & Park, Market place

SURGEONS.

Carlyle Dr. Wm. Johnston, High st
Maxwell William, Langholm

TAILORS.

Anderson Robert, Charles st
Beattie Hugh, Charles st
Dalgliesh John, Henry st, N. L
Foster Francis, Church wynd
Hill John, Charles st, N. L
Johnstone Andw, Claygate, Canonbie
Oliver John, Church wynd
Rickerby Alexander, High st
Sanders Andrew, John st
Tait Martin, High st

TANNERS.

Scott and Niven (and skinners), Elizabeth st, New Langholm

TEA DEALERS.

Beattie William, Charles st
Dalgliesh William, High st

VINTNERS & SPIRIT DEALERS

Davidson Wm, Claygate, Canonbie
Grenwell William, (Gilnockie Inn), Hollows
Jackson Henry (King's Arms), Market place
Jackson John (Shoulder of Mutton), High st

Murray David, High st
Park Mary (Royal Oak), High st
Yeoman James, Elizabeth st, N. L

WATCH & CLOCK MAKERS.

Carruthers Charles (and cutler), Well close
Carruthers George, High st

WRIGHTS.

See Joiners.

WRITERS & NOTARIES.

Henderson George, High st
Nicol John, Elizabeth st
Stevenson Alexander (baron baillie), High st

MISCELLANEOUS.

Borthwick Matthew, carter, Henry st
BRITISH GUARANTEE ASSOCIATION—Alexander Stevenson, agent, High st
Brown Robert, inland revenue officer, Buccleuch square
Carruthers Charles, hair dresser, Well close
Doughty William, wood forester to the Duke of Buccleuch. Canonbie
Douglas Robert, inland revenue officer, High street
Duncan Wm. tin-plate worker, High st
Esplin James, stocking makers' needle maker, Henry street, New Langholm
Foster John, coal dealer & carter, Henry st
GAS WORKS—John Murray, manager; John Nicol clerk and collector
Harkness William, horse and gig owner for hire, High street
Henderson George, sheriff's clerk, and deputy for small debt summonses, High st
INLAND REVENUE OFFICE, Salutation Inn, High street—John Miller, supervisor; Thomas Hartley and Robert Brown, officers
Irving Jane, temperance coffee-house and reading room, High street
Jamieson Matthew, overseer for the Duke of Buccleuch, Saw Mills, Milltown
M'Vittie Thos. saw mills, Henry st
Moffat John, currier and leather cutter, David street—William Gray, agent
MUTUAL ACCUMULATION SOCIETY—Stevenson, agent, High street
Nichol James, turner, Langholm
Pasley Robert, coffee room, Brae
READING ROOM (Subscription), at Jane Irving's temperance coffee house, High street
ROYAL ASSOCIATION FOR THE PROMOTION OF THE FINE ARTS IN SCOTLAND—George Scott, agent
Scott David, carter, High st
STAMP AND TAX OFFICE, Market place..George Scott, sub-distributer and collector
Stevenson Thomas, deputy justice of the peace clerk, High street
Telford Peter, cooper, Langholm
Telford William, cooper, David st
Todd George Johnson, heritor's clerk, inspector of poor, collector of poor's rates and session clerk, Buccleuch square

TOWN HALL, GAOL & COUNTY POLICE STATION, Market place..William Ingram, resident police officer
Wilkin William, inland revenue officer, Glentarras Distillery
Witherington William, tile and brick maker, Canonbie

PLACES OF WORSHIP,

AND THEIR MINISTERS.

ESTABLISHED CHURCHES:—
New Langholm—Rev. Wm. Berry Shaw
Canonbie—Rev. James Donaldson
Ewes..Rev. Robert Shaw
Eskdalemuir..Rev. John Stratheam
Westerkirk..Rev. William Dunbar
FREE CHURCH, Charles street..Rev. Charles Watson
FREE CHURCH, Canonbie..Rev. Alexander Milne
UNITED PRESBYTERIAN CHAPEL (North) Townhead..Rev. William Ballantyne
UNITED PRESBYTERIAN CHAPEL (South) Townfoot..Rev. William Watson

COACH.

To CARLISLE, the Engineer Mail Coach from Hawick, calls at the Crown Inn, every afternoon at half-past one
To HAWICK, the Engineer Mail Coach (from Carlisle), calls at the Crown Inn, every forenoon at a quarter before eleven

RAILWAY.

The nearest Station is at ECCLEFECHAN, on the CALEDONIAN LINE, about twelve miles from Langholm

CARRIERS.

To ANNAN, David Murray, from High street, and W. Wightman, from the Shoulder of Mutton, on Friday
To CARLISLE, Walter Scott, from the Buck Inn, Tuesday and Thursday; George Hope & David Telford, from their houses, Tuesday and Friday, and James Armstrong, from the Buck Inn, Wednesday and Saturday
To DUMFRIES, John Jardine, from the Buck Inn, Tuesday and Friday
To ESKDALEMUIR, Michael Byers, from the King's Arms, Wednesday, and E. Dixon, Saturday
To HAWICK, David Murray, Robert Douglas, and James Veitch, from their houses, Monday & Wednesday; Robert Wintrop, from the Commercial Inn, Tuesday & Friday; W. Wightman, from the Shoulder of Mutton, Wednesday, & Walter Scott, from the Buck Inn, Thursday and Saturday
To LOCKERBIE, John Jardine, from the Buck Inn, Monday and Thursday, and Robert Irving, from the same place, once a week
To NEWCASTLETON and LIDDESDALE, James Nicol, from the King's Arms, Tuesday and Friday

LOCHMABEN,

WITH THE PARISHES OF TINWALD AND TORTHORWOLD, AND THE VILLAGES OF COLLIN, ROUCAN AND NEIGHBOURHOODS.

LOCHMABEN is a town of considerable antiquity, a royal burgh, the seat of a presbytery, and capital of the parish of the name, 65 miles s. from Edinburgh, 70 s.e. from Glasgow, 33 s. E. from Sanquhar, 30 N. W. from Carlisle, 21 s. E. from Thornhill, the same distance w. from Langholm, 15 s. from Moffat, 13 N. W. from Annan, 10 w. N. w. from Ecclefechan, 8 N. by E. from Dumfries, and 4 w. from Lockerbie—the last named a railway station on the Caledonian line—situated in a level country, surrounded by a beautiful amphitheatre of hills, and by all the charms which wood and water can bestow. It traces its origin to a very early age, and derives its name from the loch on which it is so delightfully placed, the word Lochmaben signifying, in the Scoto-Irish, the lake on the white plain. The loch, which is about three miles in circumference, abounds with several sorts of fish—among others the vendace (or vendise), which is peculiar to these waters, and is

said not to be met with any where else in Britain. The town owes its rise to the protection of a castle of vast strength, which was built by Robert Bruce, lord of Annandale, and was the chief residence of the Bruces till the end of the thirteenth century. It stood on the north-west of the lake, which was called the Castle Loch, and the castle was surrounded by a deep moat. This ancient castle was succeeded by a much larger fortress, built on a peninsula on the south-east side of the loch. This edifice, with its outworks, covered about 16 acres; after different grants to various relations of the Bruces, it was annexed by parliament, in 1487, to the crown. Some of the walls still exist; they are of great thickness, and, with the melancholy firs which mingle with them, present a gloomy yet interesting mass of ruins. The period of the first erection of Lochmaben into a royal burgh is of too remote a date for conjecture; its present charter was granted b y James VI., and bears date 16th of July, 1612, from which it appears that the town was more than once destroyed and burnt during the civil wars, its public edifices plundered, and its ancient records, &c. totally lost; but although the whole of the former privileges have been regained, the place itself has never recovered its former consequence. The municipal government is vested in a provost, three baillies, a dean of guild, and treasurer, all of whom are chosen out of fifteen councillors. The burgh unites with Dumfries, Annan and Sanquhar, in returning one member to parliament. The town-house, with its tower and clock, stands at the end of the principal street. A subscription library affords literary and other information to the gentlemen by whom it is supported, and there are freemasons lodges and a savings' bank; but it is a place of narrow trade, and, with the exception of a few stockings that are made, is unconnected with manufacture; it is, in fact, a rural town, solely dependant upon its own resources.

The parish church is a handsome and convenient building in the pointed style, with a bold square tower, in which are two well-toned bells. An edifice has been recently erected for the free church, and there is a chapel for the united presbyterians. The market is held during the winter months, every fortnight, for the sale of pork, &c.; and fairs on the first Tuesdays

in January, April, July and October, (all old style.)

The small village of TINWALD, which is situated about six miles from Lochmaben, was the birth-place of Paterson, the projector of the Bank of England, and the planner of the disastrous Darien expedition. The parish is of a triangular figure, each side of which is about four miles and a half in length; its northern boundary is watered by the pleasant river Ae. The greater part of the parish is arable; within its precincts, five miles from Dumfries, is Amisfield Castle, the seat of the ancient family of Charteris.

The parish of TORTHORWOLD lies near the foot of Nithsdale, and is bounded by Tinwald on the north, by Lochmaben and Mouswald on the east, and separated on the west from Dumfries parish by the Lochar water. It extends six miles in length from north to south, by a breadth, at the northern extremity, of about two miles and a half, tapering to a point on the south. The village, which is situated in the north of the parish, is about four miles from Lochmaben, and the same distance from Dumfries. In this village is an excellent classical and commercial academy; and in the vicinity are the ruins of the ancient castle of Torthorwold, supposed to have existed since the thirteenth century. On the road between Dumfries and Annan is COLLIN, and near the parish church is ROUCAN, both villages belonging to this parish.

POST OFFICE, LOCHMABEN, Robert Henderson, *Post Master*—Letters from all parts arrive (from LOCKERBIE), every morning at eight, and are despatched thereto at a quarter before six in the evening.

GENTRY AND CLERGY

Brown Rev. Hugh M'Bride, Lochmaben
Dalziel David, Esq. Glenœ House
Duncan Rev. Joseph Roger, Torthorwold Manse
Jackson John Esq. Amesfield House
Jardine Sir William, Bart. of Jardine Hall, Applegarth
Johnstone Andrew, Esq. Halbeaths
M'Naughten Mrs. Agnes, Lochmaben
Majoribanks Rev. Thos. Lochmaben
Martin Rev. John, Lochmaben
Vallance Rev. James, Tinwald Manse

ACADEMIES AND SCHOOLS.

HIGH TOWN SCHOOL, Trailflat—James Smith, master
INFANTS' SCHOOL, Lochmaben—Mary Poole, mistress
INFANTS' SCHOOL, Collin——Sarah, Grierson, mistress
PAROCHIAL SCHOOL, Lochmaben—(master not appointed)
PAROCHIAL SCHOOL, Collin—Joseph Kirkpatrick, master
PAROCHIAL SCHOOL, Tinwald—Jas. Smith, master
TORTHORWOLD CLASSICAL & COMMERCIAL BOARDING ACADEMY, Torthorwold—William Lithgow, master

BANK.

NATIONAL BANK OF SCOTLAND (Branch), Lochmaben—(draws on the parent establishment, Edinburgh, and Glyn, Hallifax & Co. London)—Adam Waugh, agent

BLACKSMITHS.

Dalziel William, Tinwald
Glendinning James, Tinwald
Hamilton John, Torthorwold
Lockerby William, Collin
Reid James, Roucan
Rogerson Thomas, Tinwald
Smail William, Lochmaben
Smith William, Lochthorn
Thomson James, Tinwald
Thomson John, Lochmaben
Wells William, Lochmaben
Young Robert, Lochabriggs

BOOT AND SHOE MAKERS.

Bell Andrew, Roucan
Caesar William, Amesfield
Coupland James, Roucan
Fargay Andrew, Lochmaben

Fergusson John, Collin
Halliday Robert, Collin
Hunter Walter, Lochmaben
Johnson John, Lochthorn
Johnston John, Tinwald
Lowry James, Amesfield
Lowry William, Tinwald
M'Bride William, Collin
Reed John, Torthorwold
Smith William, Collin
Thompson James, Roucan
Wells Thomas, Collin
Wells Walter, Lochmaben
Wright David, Torthorwold
Wright Johnson, Amesfield

CLOG MAKERS.

Blaxland James, Collin
Halliday John, Lochmaben
Jardine James, Lochmaben

GROCERS AND SPIRIT DEALERS.

(See also Shopkeepers, &c.)

Adamson William, Collin
Austin James, Lochmaben
Craig Elizabeth, Lochmaben
Dinwoodie William, Lochmaben
Eskdale John, Collin
Gibson James, Collin
Graham William, Lochmaben
Henderson Robert, Torthorwold
Hetherington John (and druggist), Lochmaben
Imrie Peter, Lochmaben
Jardine John, Lochmaben
Johnston Thomas, Lochmaben
M'Kenzie Peter, Roucan
Mellor William, Collin
Neiven William, Tinwald
Richardson William, Torthorwold
Scott Joseph, Lochmaben
Smith James, Roucan
Waugh Thomas (and ironmonger), Lochmaben
Wright Janet, Lochmaben
Wright John, Lochmaben

INNKEEPERS & VINTNERS.

Commercial Inn, Agnes Wilkin, Lochmaben
Crown, William Mitchell, Lochmaben
King's Arms, James Austin, Lochmaben

JOINERS.

Henderson James, Lochmaben
Henderson James, Amesfield
Henderson John, Lochmaben

Mundell John, Collin
Rule Thomas, Collin
Rule Thomas, jun. Collin
Sloan James, Lochthorn
Smith William, Collin

MILLWRIGHTS.

Cowen George, Ames-field
Johnstone —, Amesfield

SHOPKEEPERS & DEALERS IN SUNDRIES.

Ballintyne John, Lochmaben
Burnie Elizabeth, Lochmaben
Clark David, Lochabriggs
Imries James, Lochmaben
Shaw John, Lochmaben
West William, Amesfield

SLATERS.

Gibson Alexander, Lochmaben
Gibson David, Lochmaben

STOCKING MAKERS.

Cambell John, Lochmaben
Ferguson Thomas, Lochmaben
Johnstone David, Collin
Lindsay John, Lochmaben
Murphy Robert, Stoop
Paton James, Torthorwold
Scott James, Lochmaben
Tweedie William, Torthorwold

SURGEON.

Wright Alfred, Lochmaben

STONE MASONS'

Ellison James, Lochthorn
Emery William, Lochmaben
Kilpatrick Thomas, Lochthorn
Scott Joseph, Lochmaben

TAILORS.

Aggin Matthew, Collin
Creighton David, Roucan
Dickson John, Amesfield
Dickson Robert, Amesfield
Morrison George, Roucan
Rogerson James, Lochmaben
Watt John, Lochmaben

MISCELLANEOUS.

In LOCHMABEN.

Armstrong James, baker
Bell Andrew, wheelwright
Byers Jane, dress maker
Creighton Mary, straw bonnet maker
Crincan Robert, linen draper
Dougan Janet, dress maker
Hope Thomas, flesher
Martin John, baker
Thomson Benjamin, miller, Steam Mill
Wells William, cooper

PLACES OF WORSHIP, AND THEIR MINISTERS.		CONVEYANCE BY RAILWAY, ON THE CALEDONIAN LINE.
ESTABLISHED CHURCH, Lochmaben—Rev. Thomas Majoribanks	FREE CHURCH, Lochmaben—Rev. Hugh M'Bride Brown	*Station* at LOCKERBIE, four miles distant A *Coach*, from the Crown Inn, to the Station, every afternoon (Sunday excepted) at half-past two
ESTABLISHED CHURCH, Tinwald—Rev. James Vallance	UNITED PRESBYTERIAN, Lochmaben—Rev. John Martin	
ESTABLISHED CHURCH, Torthorwold—Rev. Joseph Rogers Duncan	**COACH.** To DUMFRIES, a *Coach* from the Crown Inn, every forenoon (Sunday excepted) at eleven	**CARRIER.** To DUMFRIES, John Boyes, from Townhead, Wednesday and Saturday

LOCKERBIE,
AND THE PARISHES OF DRYFESDALE, SAINT MUNGO, TUNDERGARTH AND APPLEGARTH.

LOCKERBIE is a neat small market town, in the parish of Dryfesdale, 65 miles s. of Edinburgh, 12 N.E. of Dumfries, 11 N.W. of Annan, 6 N.W. of Ecclefechan, and 4 E. of Lochmaben; situated on the great mail road betwixt Glasgow and Carlisle, 72 miles S.E. of the former, and 26½ N.W. of the latter, and on the Caledonian railway, for which line there is a station here. The town occupies a considerable space of ground; the buildings have a regular and clean appearance, and the surrounding country presents some fine scenery. The origin of this place is remote, and probably, for a long period, its character was only that of a small hamlet, attached to, and protected by the residence or stronghold of a family of some power. It is within the last century that improvements have manifested themselves to some extent, which may be mainly ascribed to the liberality of the proprietors, who have granted long terms to the tenants on their estates. Manufactures have not made their appearance in Lockerbie, but the trade in articles of general and domestic consumption is good, and progressively augmenting with the increasing prosperity of its fairs and public markets. A branch of the Western Bank of Scotland, and of the Edinburgh and Glasgow bank, are established here; and there are several good inns: a bank for savings opened in 1824, has been eminently successful.

The parish church stands about thirty yards off the High-street, and is centrically placed in relation to the parish generally, the extreme points not being at a greater distance than three miles and a half. The free church, erected in 1843, is a handsome ornament to Bridge-street, and the chapel, belonging to the united presbyterian congregation, is a convenient building. There is a female society for the relief of the occasional poor, a masonic lodge, and two libraries—one parochial, the other circulating.

The market is held on Thursday; from the commencement of October till the end of April it is extensively supplied with pork, at which there is sometimes sold, in a single day, from £1,000 to £2,000 worth; there is also a market for hiring servants on the second Thursday of October, (old style.) Fairs are held on the second Thursday in January, February, March, April, and May, the third Thursday in June, and the second Thursday in August, (all old style;) the last fair, which is for lambs, is the largest and last lamb fair in Scotland—the number of lambs on the ground being, in some years, from 30 to 40,000; the remaining fairs are a new one (established for the sale of cattle) in September, the second Thursday in October for cattle and horses, the second Thursday in

November, and the Thursday before Christmas, (all old style.) These fairs add much to the prosperity of the town, being well attended; the new one in September takes place the Thursday before the large fair on Brough Hill. The day following the lamb fair in August, races occasionally take place.

DRYFESDALE parish is in the district of Annandale; the extreme length from north-east to south-west is about seven miles; the average breadth of the upper part is about three miles, and of the lower half about one and a half; about two-thirds of the parish is lowland, and the rest is hilly. There is also a considerable extent of holm land towards the junction of the Annan and the Dryfe. Of the whole extent of ten thousand acres in this parish, about eight thousand are either cultivated or have occasionally been in tillage, the remainder being in moor and pasturage. The point which assumes the greatest height is Whitewoollen hill, the elevation of which is 650 feet above the level of the sea.

SAINT MUNGO parish is in the district of Annandale, through which the road to Glasgow and Carlisle passes, and at a short distance from the villages of Ecclefechan and Lockerbie. Castlemilk is one of the most beautiful mansions in this part of Scotland, being romantically situated in the midst of pleasure grounds, and in the bosom of a fine valley: it is now without a resident proprietor. This was originally the seat of the ancient Lords of Annandale. Much later it belonged to the Maxwells and the Douglasses. In the minority of Edward VI. it was besieged by the Duke of Somerset, and some of the balls fired upon that occasion were found in 1771, when planting a spot afterwards called 'The Cannon Holes.'

TUNDERGARTH is a parish in which a great number of sheep are pastured, and is separated from that of Saint Mungo's on the west, is nearly 13 miles in length, by a breadth of only about two miles at its widest part. The old castle, now in ruins, is deserving of notice, as it was formerly the residence of the Marquesses of Annandale. The conspicuous hill, called Brunswark, overlooks the district from the south.

APPLEGARTH (or *Applegirth*) is a parish in the presbytery of Lochmaben; in length northwards it extends nearly five miles and a half, and its breadth eastward the same. It is bounded by Wamphray on the northeast, by Hutton on the east, by Johnstone and Lochmaben on the west, and by Dryfesdale on the south. The village lies on the banks of the Annan, about eleven miles from Dumfries.

POST OFFICE, High-street, LOCKERBIE, Robert Newbigging, *Post Master.*—Letters from LONDON and the SOUTH, arrive every morning at a quarter past ten, and night at half-past twelve; and are despatched at a quarter before three in the morning, and night at half-past twelve.

Letters from EDINBURGH and the NORTH, arrive every morning at a quarter before three, and night at twenty minutes past twelve, and are despatched at a quarter past ten in the morning, and night at half-past twelve.

Letters from DUMFRIES and neighbourhood, arrive every night at ten, and are despatched at half-past twelve.

NOBILITY, GENTRY AND CLERGY.		BANKERS.
Carmichael Mrs. Jane, High st	Stewart Charles, Esq.. Hillside	EDINBURGH AND GLASGOW BANK (Branch), High st—(draws on the parent establishments and the Union Bank, London)——John Baird, agent
Douglas Rev. Hugh, High st	Stewart James Hope, Esq. Gillinbie	
Dunbar Rev. William, Applegarth	**SCHOOLS.**	
Graham George, Esq., of Shaw	Dunbar Rev. William (boarding), Applegarth	
Jamieson Rev. Andrew, St. Mungo	PAROCHIAL SCHOOL, top of Bridge st—Alexander Ferguson, master	
Jardine Sir William, Bart., Jardine Hall, Applegarth	**BAKERS.**	WESTERN BANK OF SCOTLAND (Branch), High st—(draws on the head office Glasgow, and on Jones, Loyd & Co., London)—William Richardson, agent
Little Rev. Thomas, Tundergath	Hardie John, High st	
Rogerson William, Esq., Gillesbie	Johnstone Archibald, High st	
Roy William, Esq., St. Mungo	Shankland Mary, High st	
	Wright John, High st	

402

SAVINGS' BANK, High st (open daily)
—William Richardson, treasurer;
Thomas Monteath, cashier; David
W. Stewart, secretary

BLACKSMITHS.

Bryden John, High st [st
Edgar Robt. (and whitesmith), High
Robertson Radford (and bellman),
High street
Smith John, High st
Steel Robert, Bridge st

BOOKSELLERS, STATIONERS AND PRINTERS.

Halliday David (and library), High st
Rule Robert Little, High st

BOOT & SHOE MAKERS.

Bell John, High st
Dinwoodie William, Bridge st
Gladstone Thomas, High st
Johnston William, High st
M'Guire Alexander, Bridge st
Wright Alexander J., High st

CARPENTERS AND JOINERS.

Backlock William, High st
Glendinning John, High st
Irving James, High st
Paterson John, Bridge st
Rae John, High st
Stoddart Thomas, High st

CLOG MAKERS.

Johnston William, High st
Wright Alexander J., High st
Wyper Joseph, High st

FIRE, &c., OFFICE AGENTS.

ACCIDENTAL DEATH, Wm. Richardson, High st [High st
CALEDONIAN, William Richardson,
LIFE ASSOCIATION OF SCOTLAND,
David Halliday, High st
STANDARD (life), John Baird, High st
UNION, John Baird, High st

FLESHERS.

Bell Thomas, Bridge st
Carruthers Andrew, Bridge st
Douglas Robert, High st
Rae William, High st

GROCERS & SPIRIT DEALERS.

Bell Christopher, High st
Boyes David, High st
Carruthers David, High st

Creighton David, High st
Irving Janet, High st
Johnston William, High st
M'Colom Major, High st
Moffat Adam, High st
Moffat Francis, High st
Murray Mary, High st
Paterson John, Bridge st
Sanders Jane, Bridge st
Smith Sarah, High st
Wallace Alexander, High st
Wilson Joseph, Bridge st
Wright Alexander Jardine, High st
Wright David, Bridge st

INNKEEPERS & VINTNERS.

Black Bull, Elizabeth Smith, Bridge st
Commercial, David Little, High st
Cross Keys, Frances Forster, Bridge st
Crown, Frances Johnston, High st
Ewe & Lamb, James Barton, High st
Globe, James Scott, High st
King's Arms Hotel, Mary Gracie,
High st

IRONMONGERS.

Bryden William, High st
Farries William Carlisle, High st

LINEN & WOOLLEN DRAPERS

Dobie William, High st
Edgar John, High st
Pagan John, High st

MASONS AND BUILDERS.

Black William, Bridge st
Creighton George, Bridge st
Irving Matthew, Bridge st
Lawson George, High st

MESSENGERS.

Baird John, High st
Richardson William, High st

MILLINERS & DRESS MAKERS

Gardiner Agnes & Margaret, High st
Mundell Elizabeth, High st
Williamson Margaret Dempster,
High st

NAIL MAKERS.

Jardine John, High st
Johnston Andrew, High st

SADDLERS.

Turner Comrie, Bridge st
Wyper Joseph Taylor, High st

SURGEONS.

Newbigging Robert, High st
Rae Matthew, High st
Wilson James Thomson, High st

TAILORS.

Elvin Daniel, High st
Gardner John, High st
Sanders Joseph, Bridge st
Thomson John, High st

WATCH & CLOCK MAKERS.

Forrester Charles, High st
Fritschler William, High st

WRIGHTS.

See Carpenters and Joiners.

WRITERS.

Baird John, High st [st
Richardson Wm. (and notary), High

MISCELLANEOUS.

Douglas Robert, bacon curer, High st
Easton George, road contractor, High st
Jardine Alexander, turner, High st
Johnston Thomas, tinsmith, High st
M'Naughton Thomas, stocking maker,
High street
Newbigging Robert, sub-distributer of
stamps and tax collector, High st
PAROCHIAL LIBRARY, High st
Smith John, auctioneer, High st
Thomson Francis, tanner, High st
Wilson Grace, straw bonnet maker,
High st [High st
Wilson Matthew, temperance coffee house,

PLACES OF WORSHIP,
AND THEIR MINISTERS.

ESTABLISHED CHURCH, Applegarth—
Rev. William Dunbar
ESTABLISHED CHURCH, High street—
Rev. Robert Hill White
ESTABLISHED CHURCH, Saint Mungo—
Rev. Andrew Jamieson
ESTABLISHED CHURCH, Tundergarth—
Rev. Thomas Little
FREE CHURCH, Bridge st, Lockerbie—
Rev. Thomas Duncan
UNITED PRESBYTERIAN, High street—
Rev. Hugh Douglas

COACH.

To DUMFRIES, a Coach, from the Blue
Bell, High street, every morning (Sunday excepted), at twenty minutes past
ten; goes through Lochmaben

CONVEYANCE BY RAILWAY,
ON THE CALEDONIAN LINE.

Station, at the foot of Bridge street

MOFFAT,

WITH THE PARISHES OF JOHNSTONE, KIRKPATRICK,-JUXTA, AND WAMPHRAY.

MOFFAT is a parish in the interesting district of Annandale—the town, which is small and very respectable, is 51 miles s. of Edinburgh, and 21 N. of Dumfries; situated two miles from the Beatock station, on the Caledonian railway. It stands upon rising ground gently declining towards the south, immediately at the foot of a chain of mountains, which form the northern boundaries of Dumfries-shire, with the adjacent counties of Lanark, Peebles, and Selkirk. and which completely environ it on the west, north, and east; the huge summits of this elevated region reach to various altitudes; some covered with wood—others beautifully chequered and skirted with plantations of unequal size, and natural clumps of birch, oak, and mountain ash, affording shelter and enclosure to the intervening grounds, which are partly cultivated and partly in pasture. The principal street of the town (High-street) is wide and spacious, laid down upon the principle recommended by the late Mr. M'Adam, and is clean and dry, even within a few minutes after the heaviest fall of rain. It commands an extensive and fine prospect of a delightful valley, stretching towards the south, interspersed with edge-rows, meadows and corn-fields, and pleasingly diversified by the windings of the river Annan, which first makes its appearance in an extraordinary ravine in this district, and

runs at the distance of about two hundred yards from the town; the surrounding plantations, every year increasing in extent and beauty, are within view from the street. The houses are modern and commodious, well suited for the accommodation of visitors, and there are four principal inns, admirably conducted by their respective proprietors—their names are, the 'Annandale Arms,' the 'Beatock Bridge,' the 'Black Bull,' and the 'Star.'

Moffat has long and justly been celebrated as a fashionable summer resort, and for the medicinal virtues of its mineral waters. The springs are three in number, one sulphureous and two chalybeate; the sulphureous spring is distinguished by the name of 'Moffat well,' and is about a mile from the town; a very good carriage-road leads to it. There are likewise in the town well frequented bath-rooms, to which a spacious news-room is attached for the use of visiters. It is now upwards of two hundred years since the discovery of the valuable qualities of this spring, during which time it has been much frequented from all parts of Scotland, the northern counties of England, and in some instances from Ireland. In all scrofulous and scorbutic cases it is a powerful remedy, being seldom known to prove ineffectual when the lungs were not diseased; in the removal of bilious complaints, also, it is eminently successful, as well as in creating appetite and promoting digestion; and it is an excellent specific for gravel and rheumatism: it sparkles in the glass like champagne, but is so volatile that it can be drunk in perfection only at the fountain. Hartfell spa was first discovered in the year 1748, by a man named John Williamson: it issues from a rock of alum slate, in the side of Hartfell mountain, near Moffat; it may be carried to any distance, and will keep for years; it is a potent restorative, highly beneficial in all complaints peculiar to the fair sex, and may be advantageously used as a wash in the healing of obstinate cutaneous eruptions. The other chalybeate is of a peculiar nature, and obtained in a very curious manner, viz. by pouring water upon a rock in the side of a savage dell, called 'Gartpool Linn,' in the vicinity of the town: the surface of this rock is strongly impregnated with sulphate of allumina and iron; the water is much stronger than that of Hartfell, and consequently is taken in smaller portions—not more than a wine-glass full at a time. About four miles north-west from hence there is a petrifying spring, and there are others that do not attract so much notice. To the antiquary the neighbourhood of Moffat presents many objects of gratification, and to these are attached traditions worthy of attention, but too numerous and prolix for detail in a work like the present. The celebrated road maker, John Loudon M'Adam, died in this town on the 26th November, 1836, in his eighty-first year: he was a native of Ayrshire, but was much attached to the locality of Moffat, where he spent a great portion of his early life; upon one of his sons was conferred the honour of knighthood, which his father had declined on account of his age, and growing infirmities. Mr. M'Adam received from government £10,000, in two separate instalments; to his credit it is recorded that, during the whole career of his honourable independent service, he never contracted for works, deeming such a method of acquiring wealth incompatible with the duties of an engineer.

The parish and town of Moffat derive their name from the principal stream, the vale of which is deep, and of a very romantic and pastoral character; it was formerly densely wooded, and must, therefore, have well accorded with the appellation it received—Moffat being a corruption of *Oud vat*, which signifies, translated from the Gaelic, 'the long deep mountain hollow.' The parish is the highest in the entire district of Annandale; its greatest length is about fifteen miles, and its breadth from eight to nine. The different rivers supply abundance of amusement to the trout-angler; and the celebrated alpine lake, Lochakeen (whose elevation is upwards of one thousand feet above the level of the sea), contains the finest species of that fish in the south of Scotland. The outlet of the waters of this lake is by the lofty and magnificent cascade called the 'Grey Mare's Tail,' tumbling over precipitous rocks, computed to be about four hundred feet above the level of the vale, and which appears, from the opposite side of the glen, to be one unbroken fall. The market is held on Friday, and the fairs on the third Friday in March, the second Friday in September, and on the 20th of October, or the Tuesday after.

JOHNSTONE parish is in the district of Annandale, adjoining Kirkpatrick Juxta; it is six miles in length and three in breadth. The remains of Lochwood tower, situate at the northern end of the parish, in the centre of a venerable and picteresque wood, and surrounded by impassable bogs, are the only vestiges of antiquity, sufficiently interesting to attract attention, in the parish: regarding the (now unknown) personage by whose order it was originally erected, James VI is recorded to have remarked, that, "however honest he might have been in outward appearance, he must have been a rogue at heart;' Robert, natural brother to the chieftan, Lord John Maxwell, of Nithsdale, burnt it down in savage glee in the sixteenth century. John Hope Johnstone, Esq., of Raehills, is proprietor, and occupies an elegant mansion, the only notable residence in the parish. There is nothing peculiar to be observed respecting this local portion of the district, further than that (on the authority of the present reverend minister) in this populous rural parish there is neither public-house nor meeting-house, nor resident surgeon, nor village, nor prison, nor lawyer, nor beggar.'

The parish of KIRKPATRICK JUXTA derives its name from its vicinity to a chapel formerly dedicated to the famous missionary, meaning the 'lands nigh to the kirk of Saint Patrick;' it is situate in the upper district of Annandale—bounded on the north by Moffat, and on the east by Wamphray. The celebrated Gartfel Linn is in this parish; likewise the castle of Auchincass, the ruins of which cover a considerable extent of ground: it was erected by Randolph, Earl of Murray, during the minority of David 'the Bruce; and subsequently was in the possession of Douglas of Morton: its antiquity, therefore, is unquestionable; the old tower of Loch-house is supposed to have been rebuilt by James Johnstone, of Corehead, chamberlain to Bishop Whiteford, of Brechin, whose daughter the chamberlain married, and with her obtained possession of the extensive lands belonging to the bishop in Kirkpatrick Juxta and Moffat. Loch-house is now inhabited by a cottier or herd, who has his cot within its walls. Their are other ruins of ancient edifices, which excite some interest and are worthy of survey. The summer residence of William Younger, Esq., Craigland, is the only modern mansion of any note in the parish, with the exception of the Beatock Inn, about a mile and three quarters from Moffat. About one-third of the land is under tillage; the larger portion is unimproved and pasture.

The parish of WAMPHRAY received its name from its situation, emphatically expressed by the Gaelic word *Uamh-fri*, signifying 'the den in the forest.' Agreeably to this etymology, the church stands in a deep woody recess, by the side of Wamphray water, which brawls and thunders its way through a most romantic and picturesque glen, formed on both sides either by high steep banks, clad with thriving plantations—or by lofty basaltic columns, mantled with ivy, and sportively adorned by saplings of ash rising from their interstices. This parish adjoins Kirkpatrick and Johnstone; it is of an oblong figure, six miles and a half in length by three in breadth. There are but four resident proprietors.

POST OFFICE, MOFFAT, Thomas Grieve, *Post Master.*—Letters from LONDON and all parts SOUTH arrive every morning at one, and forenoon at half-past eleven, and are despatched at half-past one afternoon, and ten at night.

Letters from EDINBURGH and the NORTH, arrive every morning at one and a quarter past three in the afternoon, and are despatched at ten in the morning, and the same hour at night.

.*. *The names without address are in* MOFFAT.

NOBILITY, GENTRY, AND CLERGY.		
Appleyard Robert B. Esq. Langshaw-bush	Dickson Rev. Charles, the Manse, Wamphray [Wamphray	Johnstone James, Esq. Laich hill
Barrie Mr. Thos. Poldean, Wamphray	Hope Rev. Peter, the Manse and Jardine Thomas, Esq. of Granton	Johnstone John James Hope, Esq. (of Annandale), Raehills
Beatson David, Esq. Glassmont	Jardine Miss —, of Meikleholmside	Johnstone William Hope, Esq. jun. (of Annandale), Moffat House
Bennett James C. Esq. R.N., Mill Meadows Cottage	Johnston Mr. John, Hunterheck	Kinnear Rev. Robert, Old Well rd
Carruthers William, Esq. (of Senerish hill), Wamphray	Johnston Mr. Michael, Archbank	Little Rev. William, the Manse, Kirkpatrick Juxta
Colvin Rev. Dr. Robert, the Manse, Johnstone [Wamphray	Johnston Mr. Peter, of Harthope	Marjoribanks Mrs. Mary, Moffat
Corrie Mr. Hope, Pumplewburn,	Johnston Walter, Esq.(of Bodesbeck), Copplegill [haugh	Maxwell Mrs. Johanna Mary, Sidmount Cottage
	Johnstone Rev. Alexander, Heathery	Moffat Mr. William, of Craigbeck
	Johnstone, the Honourable Henry Butler, Auchin Castle	Pennie, the Misses —, Old Well rd

Proudfoot Mrs. Jane, Craigburn
Purves Miss Magdalene (daughter of Sir Alexander Purves, Bart. of that Ilk)
Riddle Rev. John, the Manse, Moffat
Rogerson David, Esq. (of Leitenhall,) Wamphray
Rogerson John, Esq. (of Girthead), Wamphray
Rollo the Right Honourable Lord, Dumcrieff House
Singers Mrs. Ann, Moffat
Stewart Rev. John, the Manse
Tod Mr. James, Raecleuch
Tod Mrs. Janet, Moffat
Tod Mrs. Robert, Heathery haugh
Tod William, Esq. Heathery haugh
Welsh James, Esq. Braefoot
Welsh James, Esq. of Errectston
Younger Willam, Esq. Craigielands

ACADEMIES AND SCHOOLS.

Infants' School — Jane Maria Wilson, teacher
Johnstone Ebenezer
Mitchell Mary
Moffat Academy (boarding), —James Auld, rector ; Thomas Rome, usher
Morrison's School—Archibald Crawford, teacher

BAKERS.

Brown James L. (and confectioner)
Wilson Henry

BANKERS.

Union Bank of Scotland (Branch —draws on the head offices, Edinburgh and Glasgow, and Glyn, Hallifax & Co. London)— David Jardine, agent
Western Bank of Scotland, (Branch—draws on the head office, Glasgow, and Jones, Loyd, & Company, London)—Samuel M'Millan, agent
Savings' Bank, Moffat—James Anderson, cashier; Saml. M'Millan, treasurer

BLACKSMITHS.

Brown William
Dalling George
Halliday George
Little Michael
Tait Joseph

BOOT AND SHOE MAKERS.

Borrowman Jas. | Henderson Hugh
Cootes William | Henderson Jas. J.
Coutts Andrew | Little George
Davidson Thos. | Little John
Earsman Wm. | Neilson Thomas
Grieve George | Tait William

FIRE, &c. OFFICE AGENTS.

Alliance, Alexander Johnstone
Caledonian, James M'Millan
Insurance Company of Scotland William Tait
Life Association of Scotland, Thomas Reid
National, Robert Burnie

FLESHERS.

Edgar James
Halliday William
Moffat William

GROCERS AND SPIRIT DEALERS.

Brown Margaret
Campbell James
Crosbie John
Gothwell William

Henry David
Jackson Robert
Jardine Robert & Co.
Kerr Jane
Little James
M'Millan James (wine merchant and stamp distributer)
Russell John
Stewart Samuel
Stodart Elizabeth
Tait Allison

INNS.

(*See also Vintners.*)

Annandale Arms (family, commercial & posting), Jane Cranstoun
Beatock Bridge (family, commercial and posting), Margaret Holmes
Black Bull, Ann Anderson
Star, George Ramsay

IRONMONGERS.

Carruthers David & Co.
M'Millan James (& iron merchant)
Russell Hugh

JOINERS & CABINET MAKERS.

Aitchison Adam | Henderson Thos.
Brown George | Sanderson James
Carruthers James | Thomson Hugh
Earsman James | Thomson James
Grieve Thomas | Thomson John
Hamilton & Williamson

LINEN & WOOLLEN DRAPERS

Anderson James
Burnie Robert
Johnstone Archibald & Alexander
Tait William

LODGING HOUSES.

Allen Mary | Henderson Ann
Anderson Mary | Henderson Janet
Aitcheson Adam | Hyslop Christina
Beattie John | Hyslop Mary
Bell John | Johnston Alex.
Bowes Jane and Eliza | Johnstone Isabilla
Brown Jane | Johnstone Jessie
Brown Margaret | Johnstone John
Campbell Helen | Little John
Cowan William | Little Michael
Cranstoun Jane (Annandale Arms Inn) | Little William
Cumming Janet | M'Millan James
Dalling Peter | March Janet
Denholm Alex. | Menzies Adam
Dickson James | Mitchell James
Dinwoodie David | Morrison Alex.
Edgar James | Morrison Archbl
Fleming Margt. | Moffat Adam
Gilchrist Jane | Mounsey Janet
Grieve Jane C. | Proudfoot Jane
Grieve John | Russell Hugh
Grieve Margaret Cowan | Russell John
Gunning Elspeth and Mary | Scott William
Halliday Ann | Smith Wm. Geo
Hamilton Agnes | Stephenson Rsina
Hamilton James | Tait William
 | Turner Cathrine
 | Watt Catherine
 | Williamson Jas.
 | Wilson Isabella,
 | Wilson John

MASONS AND BUILDERS.

Brown William | Morrison Archibl
Halliday James | Murray John
Morrison Alex. | Turnbull Robert

MEAL DEALERS.

Bell John
Burgess Isabella

MILLINERS & DRESS MAKERS

Earsman Jane | Kerr Sophia and Agnes
Johnston Isabel. |
Kennedy Martha and Elizabeth | M'Knight Margt.
 | Proudfoot Misses
 | Wilson Jane

SURGEONS AND DRUGGISTS.

Dalglish James
Hetherington Thomas
Scott William
Smith William George

TAILORS.

Carruthers Saml. | Dalling Peter
Cowan James | Hastie John
Cowan Samuel | Moffat Adam

WATCH & CLOCK MAKERS.

Graham John
Leithhead James
Russell Hugh (and jeweller)
Wightman Alexander

MISCELLANEOUS.

Bell John, woolstapler
Denholm Thomas, saddler
Dickson James, woollen manufacturer
Easton John, clog maker
Finnis John, plasterer
Geddes Ellen, circulating library
Graham Mary, straw bonnet maker
Grieve William, hosier
Hamilton & Williamson, millwrights
Hyslop James, clogger
Johnstone John, baron officer to the Duke of Buccleuch
Kerr Jane, provision dealer
Martin Matthew, auctioneer and sheriff's officer
Moffat Bath Company's Reading Room---William Tait, secretary
Moffat Gas Light Company---Robert Burnie, treasurer; Jas. M'Millan, clerk
Reid Thomas, writer and notary public
Richardson James, slater
Sanderson James, wood turner
Scot Janet, straw bonnet maker
Sheriff's Court (held three times a year)—William Tait, clerk depute
Stewart James, bookseller and stationer
Subscription Library—James M'Millan, secretary
Syme Robert, hosier
Tait Thomas, writer and notary public
Thomson James, painter and glazier
Youdle Hugh, gaol & court-house keeper

PLACES OF WORSHIP,
AND THEIR MINISTERS.

Established Church, Moffat— Rev. John Stewart
Established Church, Kirkpatrick— Rev. William Little
Established Church, Johnstone— Rev Dr. Robert Colvin
Established Church, Wamphray— Rev. Charles Dickinson
Free Church, Moffat—Rev. Robert Kinnear
Free Church, Johnstone—Rev. Peter Hope
United Presbyterian Chapel, Moffat—Rev. John Stewart

COACH.

To Dumfries, the *Hero*, from the Annandale Arms, every morning at twenty minutes past nine

CONVEYANCE BY RAILWAY,
ON THE CALEDONIAN LINE.

Beatock Station, two miles s.w. from Moffat—George W. Powell, *station master*
An *Omnibus* awaits the arrival of the different trains for the conveyance of parties to the town, and there is likewise at the station an excellent refreshment room

CARRIERS.

To Dumfries, Alexander Denham, on Tuesday
To Selkirk, James Johnston & Robt. Borrowman, on Monday, and Thomas Davidson, on Wednesday

SANQUHAR,

WITH THE VILLAGES OF CRAWICK, KIRKCONNEL AND NEIGHBOURHOODS

SANQUHAR is a parish in the district of Nithsdale—the town an ancient one, and burgh of barony, is 56 miles s.s.w. of Edinburgh, the same distance s. by E. of Glasgow, 32 E. S. E. of Ayr, and somewhat about 26 N. W. of Dumfries; situated on the road, up the left bank of the Nith, passing into Ayrshire, and on the Glasgow and South-Western railway, for which line there is a station on the east side of the town. Sanquhar, it is supposed, owes its origin to a castle of considerable importance, the ruins of which are now to be seen at a short distance to the south-east, on a high bank overlooking the river Nith. It must have been a building of great strength, having towers at the angles, and was surrounded by a ditch. It formerly belonged to a branch of the family of Creighton (or Crichton), ancestors to the Earl of Dumfries. The castle, as well as greater part of the land in the neighbourhood, is now the property of the Duke of Buccleuch. About a mile from it stands the house of Eliock, the residence of the family of Veitch, which gave a senator to the college of justice in the last century; this mansion lays claim (which is disputed by some authorities) to the dignity of being the birthplace of the 'admirable Crichton.' The town consists chiefly of one main street. The family of Queensberry has been great patrons of this town, particularly in improvements on the roads which pass through or approach to it. The late duke also erected the town hall, at his sole expense; it stands at the end of High-street, and has a tower, with a clock. Sanquhar is the principal coal mart in the county, and large quantities are supplied to Dumfries and other parts. In this parish, as well as that of Kirkconnel, the seams are most valuable; the coal-field extends seven miles in length and two and a half in breadth, and the veins are from three feet eight inches to four feet six inches in depth. The Duke of Buccleuch is the chief proprietor. At the eastern extremity of the parish, about nine miles from the town, are the valuable lead mines of WANLOCKHEAD, belonging likewise to that nobleman. They are said to have been discovered in the minority of James VI., by some Germans, who were employed in searching for gold about this spot: at present, employment, by these works, is furnished to a considerable number of miners, artisans and others. At the village of CRAWICK MILL, half a mile north-west of the town, on the banks of the Crawick stream, is a considerable manufactory for carpets, in which upwards of sixty men, forty women, and a number of children of both sexes are employed; and from the looms in the town twenty thousand yards of tartan cloth are generally produced annually for the Carpet Company. There are also about one hundred and fifty cotton weavers employed by the Glasgow manufacturers, and upwards of three hundred females of the neighbourhood are occupied in embroidering muslins for the same market. In the town is a large manufactory for spades, shovels, and other agricultural implements. A branch of the British Linen Company's bank is settled here, and one of the Western Bank of Scotland; there is also a Savings' Bank and a Mechanics' Institute.

Sanquhar was erected into a burgh of barony in 1184, and advanced to the dignity of a royal burgh, by charter from James VI., in 1596. It is governed by a provost, three baillies, a dean of guild, and eleven councillors, and, in connexion with Dumfries, Annan, and Lochmaben, sends one member to parliament. A sheriff's small-debt court is held here four times a year.

The places of worship, in the town, are the parish church, a free church, and two for united presbyterians. The parish church, which was erected in 1823, on the site of the old one, is a very handsome edifice, with a square tower, and stands on elevated ground at the west end of the town. At Wanlockhead is a chapel, in connexion with the establishment, for the accommodation of the miners and others employed in the lead works. The executors of the late James Crichton, of Friars' carse, in this county, and a native of Sanquhar, have appropriated £2,000 for the purpose of erecting and endowing a free school in Sanquhar: the interest of the money, since it was set apart for this design, has been laid out in purchasing a site for the school, and the surplus, after the building is completed, will be invested for its endowment. The weekly market, formerly held on Friday, is no longer continued, but there are four cattle markets held in the year—namely, on the third Friday in April; on the Friday before Tarbolton fair, in June; on the Friday before Falkirk tryst, in October, and on the Friday before Mauchline fair, in November. Fairs on the first Friday after the twelfth day in the months of February, May, August and November (old style); and a large fair for lambs, sheep and wool on the 17th July, or the first Friday after.

KIRKCONNEL village is four miles from Sanquhar, and eight from New Cumnock; situate on the high road between Dumfries and Glasgow. It contains the parish church and parochial school. The parish, which is bounded by that of Sanquhar on the south and east, is fifteen miles in length and eight in breadth. In it are two mineral springs, one possessing medicinal properties similar in effect to those of Hartfield spa, near Moffat; the other similar to the Kirkland spa, in Galloway. The village inhabitants are almost all employed in the lead mines. The Duke of Buccleuch is proprietor of nearly the whole of this parish.

POST OFFICE, SANQUHAR. John Halliday, *Post Master.*—Letters from LONDON, EDINBURGH and all parts NORTH and SOUTH, arrive every evening at half-past five, and are despatched at six in the morning.

.*. *The names without address are in* SANQUHAR.

GENTRY AND CLERGY.

Barber Mrs. William, Sanquhar
Bramwell Mr. John, Blackeddie, Sanquhar
Croom Rev. David, Sanquhar
Donaldson Rev. John, the Manse, Kirkconnel
Hutchinson Miss Margaret, Killoside, Kirkconnel
Ingles Rev John, the Manse, Sanquhar
Logan Rev. William, Free Church Manse, Sanquhar
Macqueen J. W. Esq., (justice of peace), Sanquhar
Otto Mrs. James, Newark, Sanquhar
Simpson Rev. Robert, Sanquhar
Veitch James, Esq, Eliock, Sanquhar
Veitch Jas, jun., Esq. Eliock, Sanquhr
Whigham Mrs. George, Burnfoot, Sanquhar

ACADEMIES & SCHOOLS.

CRICHTON SCHOOL—James Lawrie, master
M'Arthur John, Wanlockhead
M'Cullum John, Mennock bridge
PAROCHIAL SCHOOL, Sanquhar—James Orr, master
PAROCHIAL SCHOOL, Kirkconnel—William Hastings, master
Thomson Mary & Janet, Sanquhar

AGENTS FOR MNFACTURERS AT SANQUHAR.

Henderson William
Kirkhope William
Russell William
Whigham Samuel

BAKERS.

Lorimer William
Stoddart Robert
Todd Daniel

BANKERS.

BRITISH LINEN COMPANY'S BANK (Branch — draws on the head office, Edinburgh, and Smith, Payne & Smith', London)—J. W. Macqueen, agent

WESTERN BANK OF SCOTLAND (Branch — draws on the head office, Glasgow and Jones, Loyd & Co., and the Union Bank, London)—James Veitch. jun., agent

SAVINGS' BANK—John Halliday, agent and treasurer

BLACKSMITHS.

Coltart James
Hyslop John
Kerr John
Turnbull Wm
Williamson Robt

BOOT & SHOE MAKERS.

Fingland Walter | Pennan Edwd.
Henderson John | Simpson Alexr
Kirkconnel | Sloane Augns
Kerr William | Stoddart John
Lawrie James | Wallace James
M'Cranick Wm | Wilson George

CARPET MANUFACTURERS.

SANQUHAR CARPET COMPANY—
John Halliday, managing partner

DRESS AND STRAW BONNET MAKERS.

Anderson Sarah, | Fingland Jane
Kirkconnel | Gilmour Mary
Austin Agnes | Irving Catherine
Bell Ellen | Kerr Jane
BlairEllen (and | Kerr Mary
milliner) | Lorimer Mary
Colvin Jane | M'Math Agnes
Corson Mary, | M'Night Isabella
Kirkconnel | Thomson Agnes
Edgar Janet | Wire Margaret

FIRE, &c. OFFICE AGENTS.

CALEDONIAN, J. W. Macqueen
EDINBURGH (life), John Halliday
NORTHERN, John Williamson
SCOTTISH UNION, John Halliday
UNITEDDEPOSIT, John Williamson

GROCERS & SPIRIT DEALERS.

(See also Shopkeepers.)

Brown Archibald | Kirkhope James
Crow Wm, Kirk- | Ritchie Gilbert,
connel | Kirkconnel
French William, | Russell William
Kirkconnel | Scott John
Halliday John. | Taylor James
Harkness Thos. | Wigham Edw.

INNS.

(See also Vintners.)

Crown Inn, Christina Taylor
Nithsdale Inn, John Dickson
Queensberry Hotel, (family, com-
mercial & posting), Thomas Gibb

JOINERS & CARPENTERS.

Duff William | M'Millan Andw
Hair Alexr, Jas. | Shankland Wm.
& John | Kirkconnel
Howat James | Weir Alexr, (and
KerrJno Louden | cabinet maker)

LINEN & WOOLLEN DRAPERS.

Ballantine Jane | Telfer Jane
Henderson Wm | Weir Margaret
Ritchie Gilbert | Whigham Saml
Kirkconnel | Wigham Edward
Sloane Alexr | Williamson John

MASONS & BUILDERS.

Gilchrist James & Sons [head
Hair Alexr. & James & John, Green
Hair James
Murdock James

SHOPKEEPERS & DEALERS IN SUNDRIES.

Blair Bryce | Rae David (and
Carmichael Jno, | flesher)
Kirkconnel | Scott John
Harkness Thos | Shaw Robert,
Hunter Thomas | Kirkconnel
Kerr Margaret | Tait Sarah
Hyslop Barbara | Weir John, Kirk-
Kirkhope James | connel
Pyle Adam | Whigham Eliz.
| Crawick Mill
| Wilson Margt.

SPADE & SHOVEL MANFCTRS.

Rigg James & Charles (and scrap
iron, and agricultural implement
makers), CRAWICK FORGE.

SURGEONS & DRUGGISTS.

Ewing Josh.&Co. | Kay William
Gibb William. | M'Leod Jas.M.D.
Hair Archd.M.D. | Osborne George

TAILORS.

Black Jno, Kirk- | Lawrie William
connel | Crawick Mill
Broadfoot Jas, | M'Kay William
Broadfoot Wm | Murdock David
Brown Robert | Samson William,
Fingland Wm | Kirkconnel
Hyslop John, | Walker Andrew
Kirkconnel | Wigham James

VINTNERS.

Borthwick William
Gilmour John
Somerville John, Kirkconnel

WATCH & CLOCK MAKERS.

Cunningham William
Duncan James
Howatson James

WRITERS AND NOTARIES.

Anderson William
Jenkins David
Macqueen J. W. (and town clerk,
stamp distributer and collector of
taxes), Bank

MISCELLANEOUS.

Anderson Robert, miller, Kirkconnel
Barker Ann, farmer, Whitehill, Crawick
Blair William, woollen carder & spinner,
and engineer, Yochen Mill
Campbell James, tallow chandler
Colvin John. miller, Mennock Mill
Donaldson John, sheriff's officer
Douglas Peter, earthenware dealer
Edgar James, saddler and harness maker
GASCOMPANY—J.W.Macqueen, treasurer
Gibson Daniel, tinsmith and ironmonger
Hair John, architect, Greenhead
Hastings Thomas, hair dresser
Hunter Michael, meal dealer
Kerr Andrew, painter and glazier
Kerr John, miller, Crawick
Kerr William, clog maker
M'Call David, saddler & harness maker
M'Crone James, flesher
M'Iver John, cooper
MECHANICS' INSTITUTION—William
Anderson, secretary
Moffat James, depute clerk of the peace
Niebolt Peter, railway contractor
Oliver David, clog maker [tary
READING ROOM—Wm. Anderson, secre-
Semple Miss — teacher of music
SHERIFF'S SMALL DEBT COURT—J.
Macqueen, clerk
Sloane James, tinsmith and ironmonger
Spalding Samuel, stay and corset maker
SUBSCRIPTION LIBRARY—Jonathan
Clark librarian
Weir William, earthenware dealer

PLACES OF WORSHIP, AND THEIR MINISTERS.

ESTABLISHED CHURCH, Sanquhar—
Rev. John Inglis
ESTABLISHED CHURCH, Kirkconnel—
Rev. John Donaldson
FREE CHURCH, Sanquhar—Rev. William
Logan
UNITED PRESBYTERIAN CHAPEL
(South)—Rev. David Croom
UNITED PRESBYTERIAN CHAPEL,
(North)—Rev. Robert Simpson

CONVEYANCE BY RAILWAY, ON THE GLASGOW AND SOUTH-WESTERN LINE.

Station, on the east side of the Town

CARRIERS.

To AYR, Thomas Adlleck, Monday,Wedn-
nes day and Friday
To DUMFRIES, Thomas Glencorse, on
Tuesday [Monday
To EDINBURGH,John Slimmon, on
To GLASGOW, John Baird and James
Cook, from the Crown Inn, on Friday

THORNHILL,

AND THE PARISHES OF MORTON, DURISDEER, AND PENPONT, THE VILLAGE OF CARRON BRIDGE, AND NEIGHBOURHOODS.

THORNHILL is a very respectable and considerable village, in the parish of Morton, 66 miles s. by E. of Glasgow, 48 N.W. of Carlisle, 40 N.E. of Newton Stewart, 34 S.E. of Kilmarnock, 30 N.W. of Annan, the same distance S.E. of Cumnock, 22 N.E. of New Galloway, 14 N.W. of Dumfries, 12 S.E. of Sanquhar, and 7¼ N.E. of Minniehive. It is a station on the Glasgow and South-Western railway, and is charmingly seated upon an eminence rising from the banks of the Nith, and on the great road from Carlisle to Dumfries and Glasgow. The country around Thornhill is exceedingly beautiful, the hills bounding in the scene as with an immense wall. The vale of the Nith is here very spacious, and the hills spring suddenly up from the plain, at such a distance, as to suggest no idea of sterility. From the rising grounds a little way up the hills to the west of the village, the noble massive castle of Drumlanrig, the property of the Duke of Buccleuch, looks down upon the plain. The scenery is also ornamented by Cowenoch, the property and residence of J. Grierson, Esq.; Eccles House, Lauderdale Maitland, Esq.; Waterside, belonging to James Hoggan, Esq.; Closburn Hall, Sir James S. Monteath, Bart.; Dabton, William Maxwell,

Esq.; Nith bank, the Misses Yorstown; Baitford, Samuel Moffat, Esq. &c. The Duke of Buccleuch is sole superior of this thriving village. Since his majority, the Duke has expended very considerable sums in its improvement, and it is now lighted with gas by a company.

Thornhill formerly ranked as a burgh of barony, and within the last fifty years the ruins of the old gaol were to be seen: the site is now covered by a handsome house, the property of Mr. James Dalziel. The streets are wide and airy: in the centre of the village is a handsome monument or cross (erected by the late Duke of Queensberry), surmounted by the figure of a winged Pegasus, associated with the arms of that noble family. The trade of the village is chiefly of a domestic nature; there are, however, a tannery and a brewery, and it can boast of two of the most respectable and comfortable hotels that can be met with in the south of Scotland—they are the 'Buccleuch and Queensberry Arms,' and the 'George.' A subscription library of 600 volumes; a literary and philosophical society; an elegant freemasons' hall, erected in 1834, and two or three benevolent societies are here established, and well sustained.

The parish church, which was erected in 1781, was so inconveniently situated, as regarded the accommodation of the majority of the inhabitants, that it was taken down, and a new one in 1840-1 erected, in a handsome style, contiguous to the village. Fairs are held on the second Tuesdays in the months of February, May, August, and November (old style); and on the last Friday in June; the latter chiefly for hiring reapers and agricultural labourers.

About two miles to the north of Thornhill, on the road to Sanquhar, and seated on the banks of the rivulet from which it derives its first appellative, is the small romantic village of CARRON-BRIDGE, lying partly in the parish of Morton, and partly in that of Duri-deer.

The parish of MORTON extends from the left bank of the Nith north-eastward to the borders of Lanarkshire, a distance of between six and seven miles by a breadth of about four; it is bounded on the north and north-west by Penpont and Durisdeer, and on the east and south by Closeburn: it is both pastoral and arable, and, where cultivated, is well enclosed and fertile. In addition to the Nith, the Carron and Cample streams pass through the parish, nearly the whole of which is the property of the Duke of Buccleuch. Within the district is the large ruin of Morton Castle, the ancient residence of the Earl of that title.

PENPONT parish, which gives name to a presbytery, is an extensive agricultural district, of irregular form and uneven surface, having comparatively little flat or low grounds: the latter description of land is found chiefly upon the verge of the rivers which flow through it. The village is about two miles from Thornhill; the church, which is contiguous to the village, was built in 1782; it underwent a thorough repair in 1834, when a session-house was annexed to it. There are two other places of worship in the parish, one for the relief congregation (erected in 1800); the other belonging to the reformed presbytery. The stupendous Glenquhargen Craig, rising perpendicularly one thousand feet, and one of the greatest natural wonders in Scotland, is in this parish; there are likewise the remains of Roman encampments, causeways, and a castle. The Duke of Buccleuch is nearly the sole proprietor of this parish. Three hiring markets are held annually on the third Tuesdays of March, June, and October.

The parish of DURISDEER is bounded on the south and south-east by Morton, on the north and north-east by the parish of Crawford, on the south and south-west by Penpont, and on the north-west by Sanquhar; it is eight miles in length, and six in breadth. In this parish is Drumlanrig Castle, the superb and noble residence of the Duke of Buccleuch; it was erected towards the close of the seventeenth century. About a mile above the church the traces of a Roman encampment are obvious. Exclusive of three small properties, the entire parish belongs to the nobleman before-mentioned.

POST OFFICE, THORNHILL, Samuel M'Kinnell, *Post Master.*—Letters from LONDON and places SOUTH arrive every afternoon at a quarter past three, and are despatched at half-past seven in the morning.

Letters from EDINBURGH and the NORTH arrive every morning at half-past seven, and are despatched in the afternoon at a quarter past three.

NOBILITY GENTRY AND CLERGY.

Buccleuch His Grace the Duke of, Drumlanrig Castle
Carmichael Rev. Peter, Penpont
Crawford Rev. Robert, the Manse, Virgin Hall, Penpont
Dobbin Rev. Edward, South Drumlanrig street [ton
Douglas Miss —, Holm hill, Morton
Ewart Mrs. Alison, Nith bank
Graham Rev. James, the Manse, Penpont [Penpont
Hewitson John, Esq. (of Grennan),
Kennedy Robert, Esq. Riddings
Lawson Mrs. —, Nith bank
M'Kelvie Mr. William, Thornhill
Maitland Lauderdale, Esq. Eccles House, Penpont
Maxwell William, Esq. of Dabton
Moffat Saml.Esq.Grove hill,Penpont
Murray Rev. John, the Manse, Morton
Richardson James, Esq (of Slongabar), Chapel st
Rogerson Rev. Wm.West Morton st
Smith Rev. John, Burnhead Manse, Penpont [Durisdee r
Wallace Rev. George, the Manse,
Yorstoun the Misses —, Nith bank

ACADEMIES AND SCHOOLS.

M'Dargavil John, Grass yards
M'Night Robert, Penpont [st
Melross Agnes, South Drumlanrig
PAROCHIAL SCHOOL, Durisdeer—Thomas Davidson and Alexander Gibson, masters
PAROCHIAL SCHOOL, Morton—Alexander Hewison, master
PAROCHIAL SCHOOL, Penpont—C. H. Banytine, master
Skinner Isabella & Agnes, New st
Underwood Thomas, Carron bridge
Wallace Elizabeth, New st

BAKERS.

Henderson Wm.NorthDrumlanrig st
Kellock JamesHunter,SouthDrumlanrig st [street
Melross James, North Drumlanrig

BANKS.

UNION BANK OF SCOTLAND, Thornhill—(draws on the parent office, Glasgow; and Glyn, Hallifax & Co. London)——David Crichton, agent
SAVINGS' BANK, Thornhill—John Webster, manager and treasurer

BLACKSMITHS.

Brown John, Penpont
Duncan James, East Morton st
Findlater John, Carron bridge
Kerr William,North Drumlanrig st
Kirk James, East Morton st
M'Millan James, Penpont
MaxwellWalker,Burnhead,Penpont
Shankland John, Sth.Drumlanrig st
Wilson Robert, West Morton st

BOOT AND SHOE MAKERS.

Brown Robt. North Drumlanrig st
Carson James, West Morton st
Davidson Jas. North Drumlanrig st
Edgars Halbert, Penpont
Hodson John, Penpont
Hunter Thos. North Drumlanrig st
M'Caig Wm. South Drumlanrig st
Martin William, Carron bridge
Milligan James, Grass yards

CHEMISTS AND DRUGGISTS.

Russell & Fingland(and perfumers) South Drumlanrig st
Smart Thomas William, North Drumlanrig st

CLOG MAKERS.

Easdale Thos. North Drumlanrig st
Moffat William, Penpont

DRESS MAKERS.

Beck Jane (and milliner), North Drumlanrig st
Biggins Jane, New st
Dickson Nicholas (and milliner), North Drumlanrig st [st
Dow Hannah, North Drumlanrig
Lawrie J. & M. Penpont
Nisbet Mary, South Drumlanrig st

Rae Margaret, New st
Shankland Elizabeth (and milliner), North Drumlanrig st
Sharp Harriet,North Drumlanrig st
Taet Mary, New st
Walker Euphemia, West Morton st
Williamson Jessie, South Drumlanrig street [street
Williamson Margaret,West Morton

FARMERS.

Blackley Jno. Cleughead,Durisdeer
Corson George, Marr, Durisdeer
Gracie Robert, East Morton
Grierson James, Morton mains
Harper William, Breckonside, Durisdeer
Hastings John, Chapel, Durisdeer
Hewitson Robert, Auchenkenzie, Penpont [deer
Hunter John, Glenougher, Durisdeer
Hunter John, Morton Mill
Hyslop William, Cooshogle, Durisdeer [deer
Kennedy Adam, Hapland, Durisdeer
Kerr James, Castle hill, Durisdeer
Lorimer George,Druincork,Morton
Maxwell John, Muiryhill,Durisdeer
Maxwell William, Ingleston,Durisdeer [Durisdeer
Meggat Alexander, Muirclough,
Meggat William,Ardoch, Durisdeer
Milligam Wm,Craigpark, Durisdeer
Milligan James, Hayfield, Morton
Nivison Thomas, Burn, Morton
Patterson William, Crazynow, Durisdeer [deer
Patterson William,Crazyhill, Durisdeer
Rae William, Gateslack, Durisdeer
Smith Thomas, Penfillan, Morton
Smith William, Campbell green
Wilson John, Dalvin, Durisdeer

FIRE, &c., OFFICE AGENTS,

IN THORNHILL.

NATIONAL, William Smith
SCOTTISH PROVIDENT, John Webster
SCOTTISH UNION, David Crichton

FLESHERS.

Hewitson William, Carron bridge
Kellock Robert, New st
Laidlaw Robert & William, North Drumlanrig st
Lorimer Robert, New st

GROCERS AND SPIRIT DEALERS.

Armstrong William, Penpont
Davidson William (and wine merchant), North Drumlanrig st
Grierson Robert, Penpont
Hastings Margaret, North Drumlanrig street   [Morton st
Hay John (and meal dealer), East
Hewetson William, Carron bridge
Kellock James Hunter, South Drumlanrig street
Kellock Robert, New st
Kennedy Mary (and seed merchant), North Drumlanrig st
Laidlaw Robert & William, North Drumlanrig st
Lawrie James, Penpont
M'Caig Elizabeth, North Drumlanrig st   [rig st
M'Lachlan James, North Drumlan-
Mather John, North Drumlanrig st
Meggat John, Carron bridge
Pearson Jane, Carron bridge
Pearson Patrick, Penpont
Shankland William, North Drumlanrig street
Waugh Robert, West Morton st

INNS.

(See also *Vintners*.)
Buccleuch & Queensberry Arms, John M'Intyre
George (family and commercial), Mary Ann M'Kinnell

JOINERS & CARTWRIGHTS.

Bell Samuel, Carron bridge
Coltart John, Carron bridge
Harkness John, Penpont
Hunter Thomas, Penpont   [st
Lorimer George, North Drumlanrig
M'Caig William (builder), North Drumlanrig street
M'Millan James, Burnhead, Penpont   [street
M'Morine John, South Drumlanrig
Morine John, New st
Shankland James, East Morton st

LINEN & WOOLLEN DRAPERS

Dalziel Peter & James, South Drumlanrig street
Grierson John, North Drumlanrig st
Hastings Margaret, North Drumlanrig street
Hiddleston John, West Morton st
Meggat John, Carron bridge
Sloane Robert, Penpont   [st
Thomson John, North Drumlanrig
Webster John, North Drumlanrig st

MASONS.

Grierson Alexander, North Drumlanrig street
M'Cubbin James, Penpont
M'Lachlan Jas. North Drumlanrig st
M'Lachlan Thomas, West Morton st

NAIL MAKERS.

Allen James, East Morton st
Nisbet John & Co. East Morton st

NURSERYMEN, SEEDSMEN AND FLORISTS.

Hamilton John, West Morton st
Pringle James, New st

PLASTERERS AND SLATERS.

M'Kenzie James, New st
M'Lachlan John, West Morton st
Nickol George, West Morton st
Wallace William, New st

SADDLERS.

Brown James, East Morton st
Brown William, South Drumlanrig st

SAW MILLS.

Buccleuch His Grace the Duke of, CARRON-BRIDGE SAW MILLS—Doughty, manager

STATIONERS.

Doig David, Drumlanrig st
Russell & Finglaud, South Drumlanrig street   [street
Young John (and bookbinder), New

STRAW BONNET MAKERS.

Lawrie J. & M. Penpont
Lorimer Susan, North Drumlanrig st
Patterson Janet, South Drumlanrig st
Rae Mary, New st   [st
Shankland Mary, North Drumlanrig
Williamson Ann, North Drumlanrig street

SURGEONS.

Anderson Andrew, West Morton st
Dalziel John, M.D. Penpont
Grierson Thomas B., M.D. North Drumlanrig street
Mounsie John, M.D. Grass yards
Russell James, M.D. South Drumlanrig street

TAILORS.

Cairns William (& clothier), New st
Hastings John, South Drumlanrig st
Hiddleston Robert, West Morton st
Kellock Thomas, West Morton st
Kennedy James, East Morton st
Laidlaw James, West Morton st
M'Kay Peter, Penpont
Morrison James, Penpont
Ramsay John, Penpont
Sharp James, Carron-Bridge
Sharp Robert, North Drumlanrig st
Williamson James & Co. (and clothiers), South Drumlanrig st
Yarker William, South Drumlanrig st

VINTNERS.

Clark Samuel, Penpont
Grierson Robt. South Drumlanrig st
Kellock Geo. North Drumlanrig st
Pearson Elizabeth, Penpont

WATCH MAKERS.

Bennock James, Penpont
Hird Henry, North Drumlanrig st
Scott William, South Drumlanrig st

WINE MERCHANTS.

Armstrong William, Penpont
Davidson William, Drumlanrig st

WOOLLEN MANUFACTURERS

Davidson William (and spinner), Drumlanrig street
Wallace James & Son (& weavers), New street

WRITERS & MESSENGERS.

Jenkins David, North Drumlanrig street
Smith William (and notary public and stamp distributer), West Morton street

MISCELLANEOUS.

Baxter John, hosier, Drumlanrig st
Brown Thomas, cattle dealer, Grass yards
Burgess David, millwright, New st
Carse & M'Caig, brewers, Nith Bridge Brewery
Douglas John, architect to his Grace the Duke of Buccleuch, Drumlanrig mainse
Duns James, cooper, Drumlanrig st
Eskdale Thos. clogger, West Morton st
Ferguson Archibald, earthenware dealer, South Drumlanrig street
Gas Works, Thornhill..Daniel Mathieson, manager   [Morton st
Gilchrist James, sheriff's officer, West
Kerr Elizabeth, currier and tanner, South Drumlanrig street
M'Kinnell Robert, coach proprietor, George Hotel
Maxwell Archibald, hosier. West Morton st
Nisbet John & Co. ironmongers, North Drumlanrig street
Reading Room, Thornhill..Alexander Hewson, president
Richardson David, gauger, Drumlanrig st
Saddler William, provision dealer, West Morton street   [st
Shanks David, road surveyor. Drumlanrig
Subscription Library, Thornhill.. Agnes Shankland, librarian
Thomson John, tin-plate worker, Drumlanrig street   [Penpont
Wood Alexander, painter and glazier,

PLACES OF WORSHIP, AND THEIR MINISTERS.

Established Church, Durisdeer.. Rev. George Wallace
Established Church, Morton..Rev. John Murray
Established Church, Penpont..Rev. James Graham
Free Church, Virgin hall..Rev Robert Crawford
United Presbyterian Chapel, Penpont..Rev. John Smith
United Presbyterian Chapel, Thornhill..Rev. William Rogerson
Reformed Presbyterian Chapel Penront..Rev. Peter Carmichael

COACHES.

To AUCHINLECK, the *Standard* (from Dumfries), calls at the George Hotel, daily, at half-past twelve noon
To DUMFRIES, the *Standard* from Auchinleck), calls at the George Hotel, every afternoon at half-past two
To ELVANFOOT RAILWAY STATION, a *Coach*, from the Buccleuch and Queensberry Arms, every afternoon (Sundays excepted) at one
CONVEYANCE BY RAILWAY, on the GLASGOW AND SOUTH-WESTERN LINE.
Station, about a quarter of a mile from the town

CARRIERS.

To DUMFRIES, Robert Patterson, Robt. Mulligan, & David Kirkpatrick, Wednesday and Saturday
To ELVANFOOT RAILWAY STATION, William M'Dougall, Tuesday and Thursday

KIRKCUDBRIGHTSHIRE,

COMMONLY called a STEWARTRY, but in reality and to all intents and purposes a sheriffdom or shire, lies on the south of Scotland, and forms the eastern and by far the most extensive portion of the ancient district of Galloway. It is bounded by Dumfries-shire on the east and north-east; on the south by the Solway Frith and the Irish Sea; by the county of Ayr on the north and north-west, and by Wigtonshire (or Western Galloway) and Wigton bay on the west. In extent it measures, from south-east to north-west, about forty-four miles, by a breadth varying from twenty to thirty miles, the narrowest part being on the north and towards its north-western limits: it comprises a superficies of 834 square miles, or 525,760 statute acres, including twelve square miles of lakes: about one-third of the whole surface may be said to be brought into cultivation.

EARLY HISTORY.—It appears that the denomination of 'stewartry' originated at the period when, by the forfeiture of the possessions of the Baliols, the Cummins, and their various vassals, this district became the property of the Crown, when it is understood to have been first put under the authority of a royal STEWART; in subsequent times the office of stewart, in the appointment of the king, was one of much honour, and was often the subject of contest. For a considerable lapse of time, however, after the establishment of a separate stewartship, the district was still in some measure esteemed to be politically attached to Dumfries-shire, but this nominal connexion was formally dissolved before the civil wars in the reign of Charles I. From the force of ancient usage, the appellation of stewart, instead of that of sheriff, has, down to the present day, been popularly continued, although, by the civil arrangements of modern times, there is not the least difference in the two offices. Events in early times, possessing considerable interest, are more immediately connected with Kirkcudbright, its capital—which was frequently visited by, and occasionally became the abode of, royalty. Edward I. spent some time there during the warfare of 1300; and in 1455 it was visited by James II. in the course of his march through Galloway. A few years later, in 1461, Henry VI. with his queen and court, fled thither after his defeat at Towton; and in 1508 James IV. was hospitably entertained in that town.

SOIL, SURFACE, PRODUCE and MANUFACTURES.—The soil of the county is principally composed of a thin mould, or a brownish loam mixed with sand—and is incumbent sometimes on gravel, and in many places on rock; the whole surface is interspersed with meadows, and mingled with moss. The shire has no statistical subdivisions, except that four of the most northerly parishes—Carsphain, Dalry, Kells and Balmaclellan—are commonly designated the district of 'Glenkins.' The aspect of the country, however, forms a very natural distinction into two divisions: if a line be drawn from the centre of Kirkpatrick-Iron-Gray parish to the Gatehouse of Fleet, all to the north-west, with little exception, is so mountainous, that it may with propriety be termed a Highland district; while the south and east parts exhibit a fine champaign and cultivated country—a contrast strikingly obvious. The principal eminences in the shire are, Criffill (or Crawfell), 1,800 feet; Cairnsmuir, 1,728; Bencairn, 1,200, and Cairn, 1,000, above the level of the sea. Anciently the greater proportion of the land was covered with a forest, which is now eradicated, or to be traced only in trifling remnants on the banks of the streams. It appears that, so early as the twelfth and thirteenth centuries, this hilly territory was under a productive process of agriculture, originated and improved by the assiduity of the monks of the different abbeys in the district; and it is upon record that in the memorable year 1300, when Edward I. subdued Galloway, he caused considerable quantities of wheat to be exported from the harbour of Kircudbright to Cumberland, and even to Dublin, to be manufactured into flour, in which state it was brought back to victual the various strongholds and castles held by that monarch. In these times the staple products were wheat and oats—the culture of barley, pease and beans being very limited. This age of agricultural prosperity was succeeded by destructive intestine wars, fanaticism, improvidence, and consequent misery, which lasted four hundred years, and reduced the country to a desert. It was not until the beginning of the eighteenth century that any measures were adopted to effect a recuscitation of its agricultural capabilities, which for so long a period had lain dormant. The enclosure of the land with fences was the first attempt at a series of improvements; but this judicious preliminary was encountered by a riotous opposition from the rural population, who rose in considerable numbers, under the title of 'levellers,' and proceeded to demolish the newly-formed boundaries, under the influence of some extravagantly wild notions as to a natural general right in property; and they were not subdued until the most energetic measures were employed for that purpose: this mischievous result of ignorance having been overcome, however, and the 'levelling' delusion dissipated, the county steadily advanced in an accelerated progress of improvement; and towards the close of the same century the district could compete with Dumfries and other adjacent shires in agricultural prosperity. Planting has been introduced by several noblemen and gentlemen of the stewartry, and much has been accomplished in reclaiming moss-lands. The number of horses, cattle, and sheep reared in the county is sufficiently large to evince the possession of much practical knowledge, and consequent success, in this branch of productive economy; and the breed of swine has increased to a prodigious extent, these animals being now a staple commodity both for home consumption and exportation. The district is very nearly destitute of coal, which, as well as the greater part of the lime used, is brought from Cumberland; and there is very little freestone. Marl is found in great plenty, especially in the loch of Carlinwark, which contains an inexhaustible store of the best shell-marl; ironstone and lead ore also abound, but the deficiency of coal presents an obstruction to either being made available for the smelting process. Besides the salmon-fishings at the mouths of the rivers, the Solway Frith affords every opportunity for the capture of the inhabitants of the deep. The manufacture of linen, woollen, and cotton goods engages a considerable number of hands in the towns and villages.

RIVERS, &c.—Like other mountainous countries, this is intersected by numerous streams, which, uniting, form four considerable rivers; these are—the Dee, the Ken, the Cree, and the Urr. The Ken is considered the largest, receiving in its course numerous rivulets which drain the neighbouring hills, and even affording an asylum to the waters of the Dee, although the latter assumes the appellative privilege after entering the Ken. All these rivers rise in the north, and empty themselves into the Solway Frith or the Irish sea. The smaller streams are the Fleet, the Tarf, the Deogh, and the Cluden. The Solway Frith, in a circular form, washes the coast of the stewartry, from the Nith to the Cree, a space of forty-five miles; and along the shore of this beneficial estuary the coast is bold and rocky, the cliffs in some instances rising to a great height.

The shire, or stewartry, comprises twenty-eight parishes, and contains two royal burghs—Kirkcudbright and New Galloway; the latter, in conjunction with Wigtown, Stranraer, and Whithorn (in Wigtownshire), sends one member to parliament; and the Stewartry, like the other counties of Scotland, returns another representative.

POPULATION OF THE SHIRE, IN THE YEARS 1801, 1811, 1821, 1831 AND 1841.

The Italic letters b. and p. respectively signify Burgh and Parish.

	1801.	1811.	1821.	1831.	1841.		1801.	1811.	1821.	1831.	1841.
Anworth ....p.	637	740	845	830	883	Kirkgunzion ....p.	545	659	776	652	638
Balmaclellan ....p.	554	734	912	1013	1134	Kirkmabreck ....p.	1212	1264	1519	1779	1854
Balmaghie ....p.	969	1110	1361	1416	1252	Kirkpatrick-Durham ...p.	1007	1156	1473	1487	1484
Borgue ....p.	820	856	947	894	1117	Kirkpatrick-Iron-Gray..p.	730	843	840	912	927
Buittle ....p.	863	932	1023	1000	109	Lochrutton ....p.	514	563	594	650	659
Carsphairn ....p.	496	450	474	542	790	Minnigaff.............p.	1609	1 80	1923	1855	1826
Colvend & Southwick ..p.	1106	1298	1322	1358	149	New Abbey ....p.	842	1015	1112	1060	1049
Crossmichael ....p.	1084	1227	1299	1325	1321	Parton ....p.	426	569	845	827	808
Dalry ....p.	832	1061	1151	1246	121	Rerwick ....p.	1166	1224	1378	16 5	1692
Girthon ....p.	1727	1760	1895	1751	1874	Terregles ....p.	511	534	651	605	564
Kells ....p.	778	941	1104	1128	1121	Tongland ....p.	636	802	810	800	842
Kelton ....p.	1905	2263	2416	2877	2875	Troqueer ....p.	2774	3409	4391	4665	4351
Kirkbean ....p.	696	890	790	802	897	Twynholme ....p.	683	740	783	871	777
Kircudbright ....b & p.	2380	2763	3377	3511	3525	Urr..................p.	1719	2329	2862	3098	3096
						TOTAL POPULATION OF KIRKCUDBRIGHTSHIRE	29210	33681	38903	40590	41119

The total annual value of Real Property in Kirkcudbrightshire, as assessed in April, 1815, amounted to £213,308; and the amount assessed to the Property Tax, in 1843, £193,751.

AUCHENCAIRN AND DUNDRENNAN IN RERWICK.

AUCHENCAIRN, the principal village in the parish of Rerwick, is 18 miles from Castle Douglas, 14 E. from Kirkcudbright, and 22 s. w. from Dumfries; situated on the main road between the two last named towns. In the month of Auchencairn bay lies the small island of HESTON, which stands high out of the water, and affords excellent pasture for sheep, and there are rabbits in great numbers. A fair is held on the first Monday after the 16th of August.

DUNDRENNAN is a small village in the same parish as Auchencairn, four miles therefrom, deriving its chief, indeed only, importance from having in its vicinity the ruined abbey of Dundrennan, the greatest attraction in this part of the country. This abbey, the venerable remains of which stand about a mile and a half from the sea, was founded by Fergus, Lord of Galloway, in the year 1142. The church was built, as usual, in the form of a cross, with the spire rising two hundred feet from the centre. The body was one hundred and twenty feet in length; and on the south side of the church were the cloisters, with a grass plot in the centre. From what remains of the edifice, the whole must have been built in a style of great taste and architectural beauty. The buildings are now greatly dilapidated, and are almost entirely covered with a pale gray-coloured moss, which gives a character of peculiar and almost airy lightness to the lofty columns and gothic arches, many of which are entire. This sacred edifice afforded a temporary shelter to Mary Stuart during the last hours she spent in Scotland. Tradition has traced with accuracy her course from Langside to the scene of her embarkation for England. She arrived at this spot in the evening, and spent her last night within the walls of the monastery, then a magnificent and extensive building. The spot where she took boat next morning for the English side of the Solway is at the nearest point of the coast; the road from the religious establishment thither runs through a secluded valley of surpassing beauty, and leads directly to the shore, where the rock is still pointed out by the peasantry from which the hapless queen embarked on her death-destined voyage; it is situated in a little creek, surrounded by vast and precipitous rocks, and called 'Port Mary,' in commemoration of the event. The scene is analogously wild and sublime; and besides being inspirative of melancholy associations in the mind of the poet or romantic tourist, the coast here and in the neighbourhood merits the attention of the painter and the investigation of the mineralogist.

POST OFFICE, AUCHENCAIRN, Mary Kissock, *Post Mistress.* Letters from all parts arrive (from CASTLE DOUGLAS) every morning at ten minutes past five, and are despatched thereto at seven in the morning.

. *The names without address are in AUCHENCAIRN.*

GENTRY AND CLERGY.

Colton Miss Mary, Auchternburney
Culton Miss —, Natwood
Douglas Mrs. —, Collin
Gibson Rev. David, Auchencairn
Gordon Mrs. Colonel, Balcarrie
Henry Samuel, Esq. Auchenlech
Johnston Alexander, Esq. Blue hill
Maxwell Col.Christphr. Orchardton
Murray Rev. John Gray, Auchencairn
Thomson Rev. Jas. Berwick Manse
Welsh David, Esq. Collin

SCHOOLS.

Affie Ann, Auchencairn
FREE CHURCH SCHOOL, Auchencairn— W. Gibson, master
PAROCHIAL SCHOOL, Auchencairn— Robert Scott, master
PAROCHIAL SCHOOL, Dundrennan— Thomas Edger, master
PAROCHIAL SCHOOL, Dundrennan— Andrew Carter, master

VINTNERS.

Anchor, Mary M'Brioe, Dundrennan
Black Lion, James Scott
Commercial Inn, Adam Hunter
Commercial Inn, Samuel Kirkpatrick, Dundrennan
Cross Keys, Mary Kissock
Ship Inn, Anthony Millroy

SHOPKEEPERS & TRADERS.

Bell John, miller, Potterland
Bennett John, miller, Farem Mill
Blackstocks Jas.grocer, Dundrennan
Brown John, joiner, Dundrennan
Boddan James, joiner
Boyes John, draper
Caig John, joiner
Callan James, cartwright
Carter James, tailor, Dundrennan
Clark John, tailor
Coates John, grocer, Dundrennan
Craig Charles, stone mason
Craig Peter, grocer and shoe maker

Craig Peter, shoe maker
Crosbie Joan, grocer, Dundrennan
Fergusson Robert, shoe &clog maker
Geddies Robert, stone mason
Ghirr Maxwell, stone mason
Glover Wm.blacksmith,Dundrennan
Graham John & Geo. stone masons
Gunning Jane, baker and grocer
Hannay John, miller & millwright
Hunter Adam, grocer
Kettrick John, blacksmith, Chapel yard, Rerwick
Kinnel John, blacksmith
Kirkpatrick Samuel, Dundrennan
Kissock Mary, grocer
Kissock Thos. miller, Balmangan Mill
Lock James & Samuel, tailors
M'Clure William, stocking maker
M'Knight Andrew, meal seller
M'Knight William, shoe maker
M'Vittie Jacob, cartwright

Maxwell Colonel Christopher, saw mill, Slate row, Rerwick
Milroy Anthony, joiner
Murray Robert, tailor [drennan
Rae John, shoe & clog maker, Dun-
Rae William, shoe and clog maker
Robinson Isabella, dress maker and confectioner

Scott James, grocer
Scott James, tailor
Shannon Janet, milliner and draper
Sharp William, stone mason
Shaw Robert, tailor
Trotter Robert, surgeon [drennan
Woodrow James, shoe maker, Dun-

CARRIERS.

To CASTLE-DOUGLAS, James Kirk-patrick, on Monday

To DUMFRIES, Andrew Carter, on Tuesday

CASTLE DOUGLAS IN KELTON,

WITH THE VILLAGES OF KELTON-HILL, GILSTON AND NEIGHBOURHOODS.

CASTLE DOUGLAS is a modern, neat, thriving town and burgh of barony, in the parish of Kelton; 90 miles s.s.w. from Edinburgh, 18 w. by s. from Dumfries, 15 n.e. from Gatehouse, and 10 n.n.e. from Kirkcudbright; situated on the road between the two latter towns, and on that from Portpatrick to Carlisle, in a pleasant fertile district, on the banks of the Carlinwark water, from which lake the original name of the place was derived. In 1792 it was erected by the proprietor into a burgh of barony by its present appellation, and its government vested in a provost, two baillies, and seven councillors. Seventy years ago it was composed of but a few detached houses; it has now upwards of four hundred and fifty respectable dwellings, laid out in regular streets, the principal one lining the public road. Altogether Castle Douglas may be considered one of the most respectable and prosperous little towns, although not of remote origin, in the south of Scotland. In the town-house, which is a modern commodious edifice, with a good clock, a court is held on the first Monday, monthly, for the recovery of small debts. There are three principal inns, and several others of a respectable character, but less elevated pretensions. On the south-west side of the town are the ruins of the ancient Castle of Threave; and on its south-eastern quarter stands the modern and elegant mansion of Gilston Castle (formerly called Douglas Castle), now the residence of Mrs. Maitland. Carlinwark lake, before mentioned, is upwards of a mile in length, and occupies one hundred and eighteen acres; before it was partially drained, however, by the canal cut from it to the river Dee, its area was much greater. It contains a number of small islands, one of which, in the middle of the lake, has been bound round its base with huge frames of oak; but whether the island has been artificially formed upon them, as some think, or they have been placed there with intent to support some vast superstructure, cannot now be decided. The lake is plentifully stored with pike and perch, and at its bottom is an inexhaustible treasure of the best shell marl.

Nearly a mile beyond the lake, towards Kelton, stands the established church frequented by the inhabitants of Castle Douglas and neighbourhood, which with its burying ground at a short distance below the hill, are noted for their slovenly appearance; near the church is Kelton Manse, now occupied by the Rev. Samuel Cowan. A parochial school, and one connected with the free church, are in Douglas. Castle Douglas and its vicinity appear to have been the arena of much contest during the feudal system, when the ancient Douglasses dwelt in the castle of Threave and were lords of this district; for on the west side of the town are still visible encampments and breastworks, evidently thrown up against the castle; and on the south-west bank of the lake is a spot still termed the 'gallows lot' or 'plot,' said to have been the place of execution in former times. Near the head of the lake before noticed lived, it is said, three brothers, by trade smiths; they made the large cannon called 'Mons Meg,' shown at Edinburgh Castle: it was forged in staves, and hooped round like a cask. The market, a large one, for grain in winter, and cattle in summer, is held on Monday: the grain is sold monthly by sample, and exported, some to England and some to the north of Scotland. Fairs February 11th, or the following Monday, for horses; the last Monday in March for hiring servants: September 23rd, or the following Monday, for hiring and for horses; and November 13th, or the following Monday for horses.

KELTON-HILL (or *Roan house*), is a small village in the same parish as, and about two miles and a half from Castle Douglas. Of the extensive horse fairs, formerly held here, only one is now maintained—the others being transferred to its more fortunate neighbour Castle Douglas. The fair still retained is held June 17th (old style), or the following Tuesday, and is a considerable one for horses and hiring harvest servants.

Nearly two miles from Carlinwark lake, in Kelton parish, is the small village of GILSTON, and its castle, formerly called Douglas Castle, and then the seat of the proprietor, Sir William Douglas, the founder of Castle Douglas. The present building, modern and elegant, is the residence of Mrs. Maitland. About two miles on the road towards Kirkcudbright, is a small village called the BRIDGE OF DEE, of little, if any note, but that obtained from the number of Irish, there located and being the scene of frequent unseemly broils

POST OFFICE, CASTLE DOUGLAS, William Green, *Post Master.*—Letters from the NORTH of SCOTLAND, and from ENGLAND, arrive (from DUMFRIES), every afternoon at a quarter past ten, and are despatched thereto at two in the afternoon—Letters from KIRKCUDBRIGHT and Neighbourhood, arrive every afternoon at two, and are despatched at a quarter past ten in the forenoon.

POST OFFICE, KELTON-HILL, Nathaniel Morrison, *Post Master.*—Letters from all parts arrive (from CASTLE DOUGLAS), every afternoon at three, and are despatched thereto at eight in the morning.

POST OFFICE, GILSTON, James Brown, *Post Master.*—Letters from all parts arrive (from AUCHENCAIRN) every morning at eight, and are despatched thereto at three in the afternoon.

GENTRY AND CLERGY.

Anderson Mr. James, Cotton st
Barber Mrs. Margaret, Dunmuir House
Black Mrs. Catherine, King st
Brown Rev. George, Free church, Manse
Byron Mr. William, Cotton st
Charters Mrs. Margt. St. Andrew st
Cochrane Miss Isabella, St. Andrew st
Cowan Rev. Samuel, Kelton manse
Creagh Mrs. Margaret, Cotton st
Crosbie Mrs. Agnes, Queen st
Douglas Mr. John, Cotton st
Finlay James, M.D., King st
Freeland Rev. —, D.D. Balnagie Manse
Gillespie the Misses Margaret and Janet, King street

Gillespie Mrs. Marion, King st
Glendinning Miss Barbara, King st
Gordon Miss Agnes, Queen st
Gordon Rear Admiral —, Balnagie House
Grierson Miss Isabella, Queen st
Halliday Mrs. Isabella, King st
Inglis Colonel —, Carlingwork
Jenkins Rev. James, Cotton st
Johnson Mr. Samuel, St. Andrew st
Lawrie Mrs. Mary, Queen st
Lawrie W. K., Esq. Wood Hall
Litterdale James, Esq. Loch bank
M'Connel Mr. William, King st
M'Intyre Mrs. Hannah, King st
M'Keur Mrs. Ann, King st
Maitland Mrs. —, Gelston Castle
Morgan Mrs. S. M. the Grove
Richardson Mr. Samuel, Queen st

Robson Mrs. Margaret, Queen st
Simmington Rev. William, Queen st
Snodgrass Mrs. Sarah, King st
Train Mr. Joseph, Loch Vale Cottage
Wilson Mr. John, King st
Wilson Miss Mary, Queen st

ACADEMIES & SCHOOLS.

FREE CHURCH SCHOOL, Cotton st—William Lambie, master
PAROCHIAL SCHOOL, Academy st—William Johnson, master
PAROCHIAL SCHOOL, Kelton-Hill—John Johnston, master
M'Millan Jane, King st
SOCIETY HALL SCHOOL, Bridge of Dee—Samuel M'Lellan, master
Sproat James, Glenlochar bridge

AUCTIONEERS.
Carson David, Cotton st
Rain George, King st

BAKERS.
Green Jane, King street
Porteous James, King st
Thomson James, King st

BANKERS.
BANK OF SCOTLAND (Branch)—(draws on Coutts and Co. London)—Thomas Brown, agent
BRITISH LINEN COMPANY (Branch)—(draws on the parent bank, Edinburgh, the Bank of England, and Smith. Payne & Smiths', London)—John Sinclair, agent
NATIONAL BANK OF SCOTLAND (Branch)—(draws on Glyn, Halifax & Co. London)—James Lidderdale, agent

BOOKSELLERS & STATIONERS
Aitken Joseph, Cotton st
Gordon John (and printer), St. Andrew street [King st
M'Naught William (and binder),

BOOT & SHOE MAKERS.
Blacklock James, King street
Blacklock Matthew, Kelton-Hill
Blyth Alexander, King street
Blyth Samuel, King st
Craik James, King street
Haining Peter, Gelston
Kingstree David, Gelston
M'William Joseph, King st
M'William William, Cotton st
Palmer James. Kelton-Hill
Shaw Robert, King street
Sowerby Hester, King street

CABINET MAKERS AND UPHOLSTERERS.
Burnside William. King street
Fergusson Fergus, Calinwark cottage
Wilson John, Queen st

CHEMISTS & DRUGGISTS.
Blackley Peter, St. Andrew st
Patterson Joseph, King st

FIRE, &c. OFFICE AGENTS.
ABERDEEN. James Laidlaw, St. Andrew street
EDINBURGH (life), James Lidderdale, King street
EDINBURGH SCOTTISH UNION, Thomas Brown, King st
ENGLISH AND SCOTTISH LAW (life), Thomas Brown, King street
LIFE ASSOCIATION OF SCOTLAND, John Nicholson. King st
NORTHERN, Richd. Hewat. King st
PHŒNIX, William H. Lidderdale, Castle Douglas

FLESHERS.
Fleming William, King st
M'Adam Adam, King st

GRAIN DEALERS.
Craig Joseph, Queen st
Gracie William, King st

GROCERS.
Marked thus * are Spirit Dealers.
(See also Shopkeepers, &c.)
Affleet James, St. Andrew st
*Clarke & Wilson, St. Andrew st
*Green Jane, King st
Jardin James, King st
Morrison Nathaniel, Kelton-Hill
*Nicholson John, King st
Patterson Joseph, King st
Pattie James, Gelston

INNS.
(See also Vintners.)
Commercial, Agnes Macqueen, King street [street
Douglas Arms. Mary Douglas, King
King's Arms, Thomas Cowan, St. Andrew street

JOINERS & CARTWRIGHTS.
Christie William, Kelton-Hill
Gordon James, King st
Kelley Andrew, King st
M'William Adam, Gelston
Martin John, King st
Robinson John, Kelton-Hill
Thomson William, Kelton-Hill

LINEN & WOOLLEN DRAPERS
Black James, King st
Crosbie Thomas, King st
Green Joseph G. King st
Stitt Thomas, King st [st
Thomson Joseph & Robert, St Andrew

MILLERS.
Gibson Thomas, Kelton-Hill
M'Kie John, Gelston

MILLINERS AND DRESS MAKERS.
Black —, King st
Dundsmuir Margaret, King st
Fraser Sarah, St. Andrew st
Halliday Elizabeth, Cotton st
Landsburgh Margaret, King st
Lindsay Mary, King st
Lowry Isabella, Queen st
M'Vine Jane, King st
M'William Mary, King st
Maxwell Ann, King st
Parker Elizabeth, Cotton st
Rain Grace, King st
Wilson Mary, King st

SADDLERS AND HARNESS MAKERS.
Milligan John, King st
Parker Arthur, King st
Robertson Gordon, King st

SHOPKEEPERS & DEALERS IN GROCERIES & SUNDRIES.
Davidson John, King st
Delling Jane, Bridge of Dee
Delling Mary, Bridge of Dee
Duff James, Queen st
Gordon Nicholas, King st
Harper John, King st
Henney Matthew, King st
Irving Mary, Kelton-Hill
M'Clure William, King st
M'Connel Robert, Kelton-Hill
M'Vaue William, King st
Rae Alexander, King st
Robb William, Bridge of Dee
Thomson James, St. Andrew st
Thomson Mary, Gelston
Waters Ralph, King st

SLATERS.
Carson James, Underhill cottage
Clarke James, Step Inn
Jardine James, King st

SMITHS.
Brown James, Gelston
Burnie John, Queen st
Dempster James, St. George st
Fletcher William, St. George st
Glover John, Gelston
Halliday Hugh, King st
M'Adam Adam, King st
M'George James, Cotton st
Miller Nathaniel, Kelton-Hill
Shaw William, Queen st
Smith Robert, King st
Trainor James, Bridge of Dee
Tweedie James & Sons, Cotton st

STONE MASONS.
Cowan Samuel, St. Andrew st
Garland John, Kelton-Hill
Geddies David, Kelton-Hill
Geddies Samuel, Kelton-Hill
Ireland Robert, Bridge of Dee
Ireland William, Bridge of Dee
M'Connel Adam, Kelton-Hill

STRAW BONNET MAKERS.
Donkin Isabella, King st
Kerr Mary, St. Andrew st
Law Jessie, King st
Law Margaret, King st
M'Grier Nicholas, Square point
M'Naught Margaret, King st
Payne Agnes, King st

SURGEONS.
Anderson Patrick, St. Andrew st
Laidlaw James. St. Andrew st

TAILORS.
Beck William, St. Andrew st
Bland William. King st
Halliday David Queen st
Henry David, King st
Johnston James, Kelton-Hill
Kirk Robert, Cotton st
Morrison Thomas, Kelton-Hill
Sreds George, King st
Shaw John, King st

TANNERS & SKINNERS.
Robertson Gordon, Marlborough st
Robinson Samuel, Queen st
Sowerby Daniel (& currier) Queen st

VINTNERS.
Affleck Geo (Ewe & Lamb), King st
Armstrong Geo (Black Ball) King st
Aughterton Wm (Globe), King st
Carson Saml (George Inn) King st
Carter William, Gelston
Crosbie John, Buchan bar
Dalling James, Bridge of Dee
Geddies Robert, Kelton-Hill
Heron Maxwell (Crown) King st
Hunter Mary (Thistle) St. Andrew st
Hutton Margaret, Kelton-Hill
Jackson Smith (Grapes), King st
M'Caw John (Ram), King st
M'Nae James (George Inn) King st
M'Quhae James, St. Andrew st
Martin Robt. C (Bay Horse) Queen st
Muir Thomas, Kelton-Hill
Rain George (Crown) King st
Thomson James M., St. Andrew st
Thomson Margaret, King st
Tracey Edwd (Grey Horse) Step Inn
Tracey Philip, Bridge of Dee

WATCH & CLOCK MAKERS.
Burgess Adam, King st
Law James, King st
Yule James, King st

WRITERS AND NOTARIES.
Brown Thomas, King st
Hewat Richard, King st
Lidderdale James, King st
Nairne James Gordon, King st
Sinclair John. King st

MISCELLANEOUS.
Alexander William, cooper, King st
Beck Jane, confectioner, St. Andrew st
Blackley Thomas, road surveyor, Queen st
Borland Jas. painter and glazier, King st
Brown James, coach builder, Queen st
Brown James, stocking maker, Queen st
Brown John, inland revenue officer, King st
Brown Robert, manager of gas works, Cotton street
Borland James, painter & glazier, King st
Carson David, town officer, Cotton st
Colthart Robert, weaver, Kelton-Hill
Copeland Wm. hair dresser, St. Andrew st
Davidson Anthony, printer, Cotton st
Dobie Andrew, jeweller, ironmonger and plumber, King street
Forrest William, tin-plate worker, King st
Graham Andrew, weaver, Cotton st
Hewetson James, brewer, Queen street
Irving John, veterinary surgeon, Queen st
Kirk Alexander, clog maker, King st
M'Clean William, surveyor, King st
M'Clellan John, china and glass dealer, King st [Cotton st
Macken Jane, nursery and seedswoman,
Martin William, builder, St. George st
Rae William, sheriffs' officer, King st
SAINT JOHN'S LODGE OF FREEMASONS, St. Andrew street

STAMP OFFICE. King street—Richard Hewat, distributer
TOWN HOUSE. King street—Richard Hewat, town clerk

PLACES OF WORSHIP,
AND THEIR MINISTERS.

ESTABLISHED CHURCH—Rev. Samuel Cowan
FREE CHURCH—Rev. George Brown
REFORMED PRESBYTERIAN CHAPEL—Rev. William Simmington
UNITED PRESBYTERIAN CHAPEL—Rev. James Jenkins

COACHES.
Calling at the DOUGLAS ARMS.

To DUMFRIES, the *Royal Mail* (from Portpatrick), every forenoon at ten, and (from Kirkcudbright), every afternoon at three; and the *Perseverance* and the *Victoria* (from Kirkcudbright), every morning (Sundays excepted) at half-past seven

To KIRKCUDBRIGHT, the *Royal Mail* (from Dumfries), every forenoon at eleven, & the *Perseverance* & *Victoria* (from Dumfries), every evening (Sundays excepted), at seven

To PORTPATRICK, the *Royal Mai* (from Dumfries), every afternoon at two; and goes through Gatehouse, Glen luce and Stranraer

CARRIERS.

To DALBEATIE, Robert C. Martin and Thomas Wallet, Saturday
To DUMFRIES, John Palmer, Wednesday and Saturday
To GATEHOUSE, Robert C. Martin, Friday, and Thomas Wallet, Saturday
To GLASGOW, Robert C. Martin, Monday and Thursday
To KIRKCUDBRIGHT, Robert C. Martin, Monday, and Thomas Wallet, Monday and Friday

CREETOWN.

IS a small town and burgh of barony, in the parish of Kirkmabreck, 117 miles s. w. from Edinburgh, twelve w, from Gatehouse, about 6 s.e. from Newton-Stewart, and three from Wigton, across the ferry. It was formerly called *Ferry-Town of Cree*, and derived that appellation, doubtless, from its situation—the town being seated on the east side of the creek of the river Cree, at the head of Wigton bay, and opposite the peninsula, on which stands the town of Wigton. It is a place of but little consequence as connected with commerce, the only trade it possesees being almost confined to the importation of coal and lime, and the exportation of crain and granite; the latter of which is wrought by the trustees of the Liverpool docks, from a fine quarry contiguous. The mail road from Portpatrick to Dumfries passes through the town, which circumstance conduces, in some degree, to its importance. This place is the property of John M'Culloch, Esq. whose mansion is a great ornament to it; and there are some few o her handsome residences in the neighbourhood. The church, erected in 1834, is a neat building; connected with it is a public school.

POST OFFICE, Alexander M'Kean, *Post Master*.—Letters from all parts arrive (from PORTPATRICK) at twenty minutes before seven in the morning, and from DUMFRIES at five in the afternoon, and are despatched immediately after.

GENTRY AND CLERGY.
Aitken Mrs Jessie, Creetown
Dennerston Captain James Murray, Creetown
Hannah Mrs. Janet, Creetown
Hannay Miss —, Kirkdale
M'Culloch John, Esq. Barholm
M'Kean Captain John, Creetown
Muir Rev. John, Creetown
Scott Rev. James, Creetown

ACADEMIES AND SCHOOLS.
Birkett Jane
Cannon Michael
M'Coyd Sarah [master
PAROCHIAL SCHOOL, John Moore,
Simpson James
Weatherhead Margaret

BLACKSMITHS.
Candlish William
M'Nish Samuel
Tait James

BOOT AND SHOE MAKERS.
Cochren Hugh   M'Kie Peter
Harcomb Hugh   Rodgers Daniel
M'Kean Thomas   Rogan Edward

CARPET MANUFACTURERS.
Blair & Dunlop

GROCERS.
See Shopkeepers, &c.

INN-KEEPERS & VINTNERS.
Barber Margaret (M'Culloch's Arms)
Heron Margaret
Kevan John
M'Kean Alexander
Michael Thomas
Rogan Charles
Scott John (Commercial Inn)
Stroyan William (Plough Inn)
Vernou Alexander

JOINERS & CARTWRIGHTS.
Lennox William
M'Credie Hugh
Mitchell John

LINEN DRAPERS.
Cowan Robert
Hyslop Andrew
Kenyon D. B

SHOPKEEPERS & DEALERS IN GROCERIES AND SUNDRIES.
Blaen John   M'Dowall Janet
Boyle William   M'Kean Alexdr.
Heron John   (ironmonger)
Irving William   Michael Thomas
Kerr James   Scott John
M'Coschrie Janet Simp-on James
M'Culloch Alex.   Steen John

TAILORS.
Lennox James   M'Nish Andrew
M'Dowall John   M'Nish George

WRIGHTS.
See Joiners and Cartwrights.

MISCELLANEOUS.
Cameron David, nailer
Candlish William, blacksmith
Crichton Alexander, surgeon
Edgar James, cooper
Irving Peter & Sons, fishmongers
Keachie Lewis, miller
Kermey Fanny, straw bonnet maker
Kevan John, flesher
M'Clellan Samuel, weaver
M'Kenzie Edward, plasterer
M'Nish Samuel, blacksmith
Michael Thomas, bookseller
Parker John, flesher
Tait James, blacksmith
Tait John, baker   [foot
Templeton William, stone mason, Burn
Thomson James, stone mason
Welsh William, agent to Liverpool Dock Co. Kirkmabreck

MAIL.
To DUMFRIES, the *Royal Mail* (from PORTPATRICK) every morning at twenty minutes before seven.
To PORTPATRICK, the *Royal Mail* (from DUMFRIES), every evening at five

CROSSMICHAEL AND PARTON.

CROSSMICHAEL is a parish and village—the latter a small one, 91 miles s.s.w. from Edinburgh, 19 s.w. from Dumfries, and 9 s.s.e. from New Galloway; pleasantly situated on the banks of the Dee, which river is crossed, about a mile and a half from the village, by an elegant stone bridge, over which passes the high road leading to Lawrieston and Castle Douglas; Crossmichael being distant five miles from the former town and three and a half from the latter. In the village is the parish church, the patron saint of which, prior to the reformation, was Saint Michael, and hence the name, though of the cross there are neither remains or tradition preserved. The parish lies nearly in the centre of the stewartry, having the Urr water on the east, and the Dee or Loch Ken on the west. Two small lakes which have an outlet to the Dee water furnish good perch and pike fishing. A fair is held on the 29th October if it falls on a Thursday, if not, then on the Thursday after.

PARTON parish lies along the banks of the Dee, that water and the Urr being its western boundary; it extends from six to seven miles in length, its breadth varying from four to six. A large portion of the parish is hilly, heathy, and pastoral, especially in the northern quarter—towards the Dee the land is flat and arable, and under cultivation. What may be called the village, which contains but a few houses, the church (a neat building erected in 1834), and the manse, is about three miles from Crossmichael. The manse occupies a very pleasant situation fronting the river, and is surrounded by hills and wood. In the vicinity is an excellent slate quarry.

POST OFFICE, CROSSMICHAEL, Samuel Walker, *Post Master*.—Letters from all parts arrive (from CASTLE DOUGLAS) every afternoon at three and are despatched thereto at nine in the morning.

POST OFFICE, PARTON, William Fraser, *Post Master*.—Letters from all parts arrive (from CASTLE DOUGLAS) every afternoon at half-past three and are despatched thereto at half-past eight in the morning.

GENTRY AND CLERGY.

Bell Allen, Esq., Hillerton
Crosby James, Esq., of Markland, Parton
Fletcher Capt. Edward, of Corsock, Parton
Glendinning Miss Xeveria, of Parton
Gordon William, Esq., of Greenlaw
Lawrence G. W. Esq., of Largnane
Leeckie Rev. Thomas, the Manse, Parton
Maxwell Clark, Esq., of Nether Corsock, Parton
Rennie Wm. Esq., of Denvale Park
Sanderson Capt. Archibald, Glenlocher Lodge
Shaw Ebenezer, Esq., of Drumrash, Parton
Whitson Rev. John, M.D., the Manse, Crossmichael

SCHOOLS.

Crocket John, Crossmichael
M'George John, Crossmichael
PAROCHIAL SCHOOL, Crossmichael —Robert Murray, master
PAROCHIAL SCHOOL, Parton—Jas. Johnstone, master

SHOPKEEPERS & TRADERS.

In CROSSMICHAEL unless otherwise stated.

Callander Ebenezer, blacksmith, Clarebrand
Dickson Abraham, clog maker
Fraser William, shopkeeper, Parton
Green William, shopkeeper, Parton
Hannah Andrew, blacksmith, Parton
Heslop James, blacksmith
Hornal James, shoe maker
Kirkpatrick John, shopkeeper
Lock William, shoe maker

M'Caig Alexander, tailor
M'George William, miller
M'Night William, joiner
Middleton Christopher, well sinker
Milligan John, vintner
Mitchell John, joiner
Mountree James, joiner & engraver
Mountree John, letter cutter
Patterson David, shopkeeper
Porter James, farmer
Richardson William, miller, Parton
Stewart James, tailor, Parton
Sturgeon John, joiner
Taylor Robert, shopkeeper
Walker John, joiner, Clarebrand
Walker Samuel, vintner
Walker Samuel, shopkeeper
Wilson Samuel, shopkeeper, Clarebrand
Wright David, shoe maker, Maxwellfield

DALBEATTIE-IN-URR AND NEIGHBOURHOOD.

DALBEATTIE, the principal village in the parish of Urr, is 87 miles s.s.w. from Edinburgh, 13½ N. by E. from Kirkcudbright, the like distance s.w. from Dumfries, and 6 from Castle Douglas; most eligibly situated on the Dalbeattie burn, a rivulet which falls into the water of Urr; which latter is here navigable for vessels of seventy or eighty tons. This harbour, which is called Dub-o'-Hass, is about five miles from the Solway firth, and is now being greatly improved. The village possesses great advantages, in respect to situation, for a maritime trade, having a communication by sea with the western ports, and it possesses some large falls of water, capable of turning any kind of machinery. The mills now in operation are a paper, a flax, a corn and a waulk mill, and two for sawing timber—the whole propelled by water; there is also an extensive smithy, the hammers of which are also worked by the same power. In the village are places of worship for presbyterians and Roman catholics, and a comfortable inn. About 4 miles N.E. from Dalbeattie is Corra Castle, formerly the residence of Lord Herries, but now the property of the Maxwells, of Terreeles. It is a fine old ruin, and mentioned as the place where Mary Queen of Scots passed a night on her way for embarkation at the Solway Firth to England, after the battle of Langside moor; the remains of the bed in which she slept is still in Terreeles house. Within the parish, on the banks of the river, about a mile below Urr church, is the Mote of Urr, an artificial mount rising from the centre of elevated circles, and used in primitive times as a court of judicature by the petty chiefs of this district of Galloway.

POST OFFICE, DALBEATTIE, Sarah M'Nish, Post Mistress.—Letters from various places arrive (from DUMFRIES) every morning at a quarter before ten, and from KIRKCUDBRIGHT at four in the afternoon, and are despatched to those towns immediately after.

POST OFICE, HAUGH OF URR, James Lowden, Post Master.—Letters from various places arrive (from PORTPATRICK) every forenoon at eleven, and are despatched thereto at twenty minutes past twelve noon.
Letters from DUMFRIES and various places SOUTH and EAST arrive every afternoon at half-past one, and are despatched at ten in the morning.

GENTRY & CLERGY.

Bain Mr. William, Fore st
Bennett William, Esq., Mill bank, Haugh of Urr
Black Mrs. Martha, Rose bank
Burnside Rev. George, Urr
Crocket Rev. Jno. Kirkgunzeon manse
Dudgeon Rev. George, Maxwell st
Falls Mr. James, Fore st
Herries William Young, Esq (of Spottes), Urr
Kerr Alexander, Esq. Haugh of Urr
M'Knight Robert, Esq. (of Barbchan) Urr
Maxwell Mr. Francis, Summer bank
Maxwell Wellwood, Esq. Munches
Rawline Miss Janet, Fore st
Rigg Mr. George, Fore st
Simpson Samuel, Esq. King's Grange
Sinclair John, Esq. Ried castle, Haugh of Urr
Stewart Rev. Duncan, the Manse
Strain Rev. John, St. Peter's Catholic chapel

SCHOOLS.

FREE CHURCH SCHOOL, Fore st—William Gibson, manager
Johnston John, Middle st
M'Neilie Thomas, Urr
PAROCHIAL SCHOOL, Fore st—Jas. Farish, master
PAROCHIAL SCHOOL, Haugh of Urr —William Allan, master

BAKERS.

Houstin James, Fore st
Patterson David, Maxwell st

BLACKSMITHS.

Anderson John, Fore st
Clark Peter, Urr
Donaldson John, Middle st
Elliott John, Bar
Heughan William, Fore st
Kim Robert, Urr
M'Quae —, Urr

BOOT & SHOE MAKERS.

Anderson William, Urr
Blacklock William, Urr
Dornan James, Middle st
Henderson John, Urr
Kaig James, Urr
Kelly Edward, Middle st
M'Gowan Wood, Maxwell st
Mitchell James, Fore st
Murdoch John, Fore st
Telfor John, Fore st

CARTWRIGHTS & JOINERS.

Clarke Robert, Maxwell st
Copeland John, Middle st
Elliott Robert, Fore st
Haugham James, Middle st
Heuchan James
Hyslop James, Spot's Saw Mill
Murdoch John, Urr
Ragg John, Middle st
Reid William, Fore st
Wilson Robert, Fore st

CLOG MAKERS.

Aitken John, Fore st
Beattie James, Middle st
Blacklock William, Urr
Donaldson John, Middle st
Ker James, Fore st

DRUGGISTS.

Lowden John, Fore st
Nisbet George (and ironmonger and stationer), Fore st

GROCERS.

See Shopkeepers, &c.

INN-KEEPERS & VINTNERS.

Blain Thomas, Fore st [well st
Graham Jane (King's Arms Inn) Maxwell st
M'Gowan William, Urr
M'Laurin James (Copeland Arms), Fore st [Dalbeattie
M'Nish Sarah (Maxwell's Arms), Milligan Robert Swan, Urr
Slimmon Hugh, Maxwell st

LINEN DRAPERS.

Brown Samuel, Fore st
Hodgson Lawson, Maxwell st
Rawline Thomas, Fore st

MILLERS.

Breadfoot James, Maxwell st
Carswell John (and bone merchant) Fore street
Harris Alexander, Urr

NAIL MAKERS.

Halliday James, Fore st
Houstin William, Fore st
Nairne James, Fore st

SHIP OWNERS.

Brown Thomas	Reddick Charles
Carswell John	Shaw John
Rawline Thomas	Sloane John

578

SHOPKEEPERS & DEALERS IN GROCERIES.

Carswell John, Fore st
Cunningham Alexander, Middle st
Elliot Robert, Fore st
Farish Margaret, Fore st
Hair Alexander, Fore st
Houstin James, Fore st
Kirkpatrick Margaret, Fore st
Kirkpatrick Samuel, Maxwell st
Lowden James, Urr
Lowden John, Fore st
M'Gowan William, Urr
M'Laurine Jas (& spirit dealer) Fore [st
Milligan John, Maxwell st
Mulligan Robert Swan, Urr
Newall Charles, Fore st
Porter George, Middle st
Robinson James, Fore st
Stimmon Hugh, Maxwell st
Telfer William, Fore st
Weir William, Middle st
Wilson Robert, Fore st

STONE MASONS.

Carter John, Urr
Colvend William, Middle st
Conchie William, Middle st
Copeland James
Crocket William, Fore st
Garney John, Urr
Hyslop William, Urr
Kim James, Urr
M'Nish John, Back st

Newall Andrew, Fore st
Newall Horner, Fore st
Rain Robert, Fore st
Reid John, Fore st

SURGEONS.

Currie James, Maxwell st
Smith William, Fore st
Smith William, Urr

TAILORS.

Gibson James, Urr
Johnson George, Fore st
M'George Thomas, Urr
M'Kinnal Robert, Fore st
M'Leod William, Green head
Porter Eleazer, Mill st
Smith Robert, Hill st

WRIGHTS.

See Cartwrights and Joiners.

MISCELLANEOUS.

Alexander John, artist, Urr
Beattie Jonathan, cooper, Middle st
Cambell David, police officer, Middle st
Carmont John, flesher, Fore st
Carson Wm. teacher of dancing, Middle st
Caven James, slater, Middle st
Copeland Samuel, weaver, Maxwell st
Coverley Elizabeth, dress maker, Hill st
Donaldson Robert, cooper, Middle st
Hamilton John, weaver, Middle st
Helm Thos. & Wm. bobbin manufacturers
Johnston W. weaver, Urr
Lewis William, paper maker

Lindsay Hugh, dyer and wool carder, Isle croft
M'Cornack John, flesher, Maxwell st
M'Morlin James, grain dealer, Hill st
Matthewson Alexander, travelling tea dealer, Middle street
Millican Wm. manufacturer, Maxwell st
Rain Robert, weaver, Fore st
SAW MILL, Munches—Wellwood Maxwell, Esq. proprietor
Stewart John, china dealer, Middle st
Thomson William, skinner, Port st
Whirr Margaret, straw bonnet mkr. Fore st
Wright John, painter, Hill head

PLACES OF WORSHIP, AND THEIR MINISTERS.

ESTABLISHED CHURCH, Dalbeattie—Rev. Duncan Stewart
ESTABLISHED CHURCH, Urr—Rev. George Burnside
FREE CHURCH, Dalbeattie—Rev. George Dudgeon
UNITED PRESBYTERIAN CHURCH, Urr—Rev. David Bain
SAINT PETER'S CATHOLIC CHAPEL—Rev. John Strain, *priest*

COACHES.

To DUMFRIES, two Coaches (from Kirkcudbright), every morning at eight
To KIRKCUDBRIGHT, the *Royal Mail* (from Dumfries), every forenoon at ten, and two Coaches, at six in the evening

CARRIER.

To DUMFRIES, John Hyslop, from Mill street, Wednesday and Saturday

GATEHOUSE-OF-FLEET AND NEIGHBOURHOOD.

GATEHOUSE is a neat modern town partly in the parish of Anwoth, but chiefly in that of Girthorn, 105 miles s. s. w from Edinburgh. 50 E. from Portpatrick, 33 s. w. from Dumfries, and 8 w. from Kircudbright; charmingly seated in a romantic and fertile vale, embosomed within hills and lofty eminences, which form a spacious and delightful amphitheatre. Some of the hills have their sides clothed, and their summits crowned with woods, interspersed with rich pasturage; while the higher and more distant mountains penetrate the clouds. The town is well built, regular, and clean, the houses being generally of the same height, the streets running in straight lines, and crossing each other at right angles. A good stone bridge crosses the Fleet, connecting the principal part of the town with that in Anworth parish. At the foot of the town flows the small river Fleet, which here meets the tide, and becomes navigable for vessels of sixty tons burthen; and the navigation of the river has been considerably improved by the late Mr. Murray, who, at a cost of £3600 cut a canal in a straight line, which, besides deepening the river, reclaimed many acres of land, since which a commodious quay has been constructed by Mr. M'Adam, at an expense of £600, and has received the thanks of the ship owners of Kirkcudbright for his spirited enterprize by which their shipping has been so greatly benefitted. The exports of Gatehouse are principally grain; and its imports lime and coal; but the chief business is the spinning and manufacture

of cotton goods, by water power, by which also two saw mills are propelled. Mines of lead and copper have been discovered in the neighbourhood, which have been wrought to some advantage. Gatehouse was erected into a burgh of barony in 1795, through the interest of the late Mr. Murray. Its municipal government is vested in a provost, two baillies, and four councillors. A burgh court for the recovery of small debts not exceeding five pounds, is held every fortnight, and a justice of peace court sits every month for the parishes of Girthon and Anworth.

The parish church which is a commodious building, was erected in 1817, and its site well chosen. The free church, at the other end of the town, is also a spacious and handsome building, and contiguous to it is a chapel for the united presbyterians. A good parochial school is well attended, and a news room and library, and a masonic lodge have their respective members and supporters. In this neighbourhood, in the parish of Anworth, are the ancient castles of Rasene and Cardoness; a mile south of the town stands Caliv, the noble residence of the proprietor, Mr. Murray; and at the distance of about two miles, are the neat villas of Ardwall and Cardoness. The market is held on Saturday; and fairs on the first Monday after the 17th of June (old style), and a cattle market, or fair, commencing on the third Saturday in September, and continuing on that day for eight weeks.

POST OFFICE, High street, GATEHOUSE, Samuel Blythe, *Post Master.* Letters from LONDON and the SOUTH. and from EDINBURGH and the NORTH, arrive every afternoon, at a quarter-past three, and are despatched at half-past eight in the morning.

GENTRY AND CLERGY.

Brown Mr. John, High st
Brown Mrs. Mary, Fleet st
Campbell Mrs. Thomas, High st
Campbell Mr. William, Roseville
Hannay Miss —, of Kirkdale
Johnston Rev. Thomas, Anworth
M'Cartney Mrs. Jean, Rose bank
M'Culloch Mr. Henry, Knockbrex
M'Culloch James Murray, Esq. of Ardwall
M'Culloch Walter, Esq. Kirkclough
M'Nish Miss Martha, Rose bank
Maxwell Sir David, Cardoness
Murray Rev. George, Gatehouse
Robertson Rev. John, High st

Shiriff David, Esq. High st [Calley
Stewart the Honble. Montgomery,
Stewart Mrs. Horatia, Calley

ACADEMIES AND SCHOOLS.

FREE SCHOOL, Black street—Peter Young, master
M'Adam Alexander, Croft st
PAROCHIAL, Fleet street — John Thomson, master
Wilson Eliza, High st

AGENTS.

M'Adam David (shipping), Fleet st
Shiriff David (and factor to H. G. S. Murray, Esq.), High st

BAKERS.

Brown George, High st [st
Hunter Margt. (confectioner), High
Porter Janet, High st

BANK.

WESTERN BANK OF SCOTLAND—(draws on Jones, Lovd & Co. London)—David Shirriff, agent

BOOKSELLER, STATIONER AND PRINTER.

M'Millan William Douglas, Fleet st

BOOT AND SHOE MAKERS.

Biggam Peter, Back st
Blacklock Robert, High st
Buchanan Joseph, Fleet st
Dryburgh Charles, High st

BOOT, &c. MAKERS—Continued.
M'Kinnall John, High st
M'Lean William, Fleet st
M'Leilan Robert, Back st
Taylor George, High st
Telfer Samuel, High st

FIRE, &c. OFFICE AGENTS.
LIFE ASSOCIATION OF SCOTLAND, M. C. Thomson, High st
NORWICH UNION, Thos. Kirkpatrick, High street   [High st
SCOTTISH UNION, Samuel Blythe.

FLESHERS.
M'Clellan Alexander, High st
M'Cornick Thomas, High st
M'Michael John, Cross st
Wilson Peter, High st

GROCERS & SPIRIT DEALERS.
(See also Shopkeepers, &c.)
Baird James (and smith and ironmonger), High st
Campbell Thomas, Front st
Coltart Robert, High st
Fowler Thomas, High st
Porter James, High st
Slimmon Hugh, High st
Stewart David H. High st

INN-KEEPERS & VINTNERS.
Angel, Peter Wilson, High st
Bay Horse, Jas. Cowan. Rose bank
Black Swan James Roy, Front st
Blue Bell, Jane Munro, Back st
Commercial Inn, Jas. Wilson, High st
Crown, Agnes Stewart, Anworth
Mason's Arms, Robert Johnston, Rose bank
Murray Arms, Henry Forster, High st
Old Bay Horse, Janet Duncan, Rose bank
Ship, Mary Shannon, Fleet st
Shoulder of Mutton, Alexander M'Clellan, High street

JOINERS & CABINET MAKERS
Cunningham John, High st
Gordon James (and cartwright), Back street
Graham John, Rose bank   [st
Henry Samuel (& cartwright), Fleet
Kelly James, High st
M'Kearn Samuel, Cross st
Murray James, Cross st

LINEN & WOOLLEN DRAPERS.
Campbell James, High st
Kirkpatrick Thomas, High st

M'Geoch Catherine, High st
Mason Andrew, High st
Menzies William, High st

MILLINERS & DRESS MAKERS
Campbell Isabella, High st
Carson Janet, Back st
M'Geoch Catherine, High st

SAW MILLS.
Halliday & Co. Calley Mills
M'Master Robert, Barlay Mill

SHOPKEEPERS & DEALERS IN GROCERS AND SUNDRIES.
Dalzell Agnes, Back st
Edgar Thomas, Cross st
Gibson Dickson, High st
Hanning Lillies, Cross st
Hornsby James, Back st
Hyslop John, High st
Kennedy John, Anworth
Kirk John, Fleet st
Lightbody James, Fleet st
M'Haffie John, High st
M'Millan John, Back st
M'Taggart James, High st
Porter Janet, High st
Thompson Mary, High st
Waugh Thomas, Anworth
Wright Elizabeth, Back st

SMITHS.
Bain James, High st
Campbell Hugh, Fleet st
Halliday Archibald, High st
M'Donald Alexander, Cross st
Turner James, Back st

STONE MASONS.
Cairns John, Back st
Hume Robert, Fleet st

SURGEONS.
Baird William, High st
Kennedy Charles, High st
M'Lean John, M D. High st

TAILORS.
Garraway John, High st
Graham William, Cross st
Kennedy John, High st
M'Bride Peter, High st
Walker David, Fleet st
Walker James, High st

TINSMITHS.
Brown Robert, High st
M'Nellie Charles, Anworth
Pollock Hugh, Cross st

WRIGHTS.
See Joiners and Cabinet Makers.

WRITERS.
Darling Thomas, High st
M'Minn Charles, High st

MISCELLANEOUS.
Armour John, painter, High st
Credie Grier, nurseryman, Rose bank
CUSTOM HOUSE, Fleet st—Hugh Milligan, principal coast officer
Douglas James, saddler, High st
Faie William, miller, Barlay Mill
Finlay Andrew, watch maker, High st
GAS WORKS, Fleet street —— Charles M'Nellie, manager
Gordon William, auctioneer, High st
Halliman Thomas & William, bobbin turners, Bobbin Mill
INLAND REVENUE OFFICE, High street — John Roberts, officer
Kelvie David, cutler, High st
Kirk Andrew, brewer, High st
M'Adam David, harbour master, Port M'Adam   [High st
M'Dougall John, manager to John M'Kie
M'Kie John, cotton spinner, High st
Menzies Samuel, tanner, Anworth
Nelson Alexander, hair dresser, Back st
Sproat Agnes, dyer, Back st
STAMP OFFICE, High street—Thomas Kirkpatrick, sub-distributer
Swanson John, timber merchant, Port M'Adam   [street
Whitewright Thomas, druggist, High

PLACES OF WORSHIP, AND THEIR MINISTERS.
ESTABLISHED CHURCH, Gatehouse—— Rev. George Murray.
ESTABLISHED CHURCH, Anworth—Rev. Thomas Johnston.
FREE CHURCH, Gatehouse—Rev. John Robertson.
UNITED PRESBYTERIAN CHAPEL, Gatehouse—(ministers various.)

MAIL.
Calling at the Murray Arms.
To DUMFRIES, the *Royal Mail* (from PORTPATRICK), every morning at half-past eight.
To PORTPATRICK, the *Royal Mail* (from DUMFRIES), every afternoon at a quarter-past three.

CARRIERS.
To CREETOWN & NEWTON-STEWART, Peter Walker, from the Commercial, Tuesday, and — Gorman, from the Angel, Thursday.
To KIRKCUDBRIGHT, James Coltart, from Cross st, Friday.

KIRKCUDBRIGHT,

WITH THE PARISH OF TWYNHOLME AND NEIGHBOURHOODS.

KIRKCUDBRIGHT is a royal burgh, the seat of a presbytery, and capital of the stewartry and a parish; 100 miles s.s.w. from Edinburgh, 55 E. from Portpatrick, and 28 s.s.w. from Dumfries. It occupies a peninsular situation on the east of the Dee, about six miles from the confluence of that river with the Solway Frith, is a town of considerable antiquity, but of its origin there is no authentic or even traditionary record; but that Saint Cuthbert's church was erected so long ago as the eighth century is unquestionable. The establishment of this church was followed by the construction of a small fort by the lords of Galloway, which in after-times was superseded by a castle in the proprietary of the Crown, by whose authority the place was put under the government of a constable. During the domination of the Douglasses in Galloway, Kirkcudbright became a burgh of regality under their influence: on their forfeiture, James II. erected the town into a royal burgh, by charter dated at Perth, 26th October, 1455: this grant was renewed and confirmed by Charles I., on the 20th July, 1633; and the burgh has since been under the government of a provost, two bailies, and thirteen councillors, with a treasurer and chamberlain; it joins with Dumfries, Annan, Sanquhar and Lochmaben in returning a member to parliament. The revenue of the corporation is considerably increased by the salmon fishings in the Dee; and the town derives a certain degree of consequence and advantage from being the seat of the stewartry courts.

Kirkcudbright which has been materially improved, at the present day presents an aspect remarkably pleasing: within, it is regular, clean and neat; and externally it appears embosomed in the beautiful foliage of a fine sylvan country. It is composed of six or seven distinct streets, built at right angles with each other; the houses, which are for the most part two stories high, have a respectable and comfortable appearance, and at once bespeak the taste and easy circumstances of the inhabitants. The stewartry buildings and gaol, erected in 1816, exhibit a highly imposing appearance; and from one of the lofty towers which surmount the latter an extensive view may be obtained of the beautiful environs of the town, including the ruins of the ancient castle of Kirkcudbright, built in 1582, by M'Clellan, ancestor of the Lords Kirkcudbright. The former gaol and court-house is a very curious old edifice (with the market cross stuck up against it), supposed to have been erected about the middle of the sixteenth century. The burgh has a little shipping trade, and a productive fishery, and the intercourse with Liverpool, by steam navigation, gives animation to the town, and a stimulus to its trade. The manufacture of cotton goods and hosiery exists here to a limited extent, and the shops and inns are very respectable—of the latter, the 'Commercial' and the 'George' are the principal—both posting hous s, and the proprietor of the former has private apartments to let. The harbour is the best in the stewartry; at ordinary spring-tides the depth of water is thirty feet, and at the lowest neap tides eighteen feet. The river is navigable for two miles above the town, to the bridge of Tongland, which is constructed of one arch of one hundred and ten feet span, and picturesquely blends with the surrounding landscape. As yet there is no bridge across the Dee at Kirkcudbright, and passengers and carriages have to be ferried over in a flat-bottomed boat, or sort of floating bridge of peculiar formation; in stormy weather, however, or when there is an excessive current, this mode of conveyance is not without danger; and the construction of a drawbridge, to admit of vessels passing through, would be esteemed a great improvement as well as advantage to the district. There is a regular communication kept up between this place and Liverpool, by means of a steamvessel, at least once a week.

The established church is of recent erection, with nave and transepts, and a fine tower surmounted by a spire; it is a very tasteful structure, built wholly of stone, and stand- in the centre of a beautiful plantation through which are public walks. The tree church is a handsome buil ing adjoining the Johnstone academy. In High-street is a next chapel in which the united presbyterian congregation worship. The ancient church has been pulled down, with the exception of a fragment, enclosing a venerable monument in memory of a former Lord Kirkcudbright; a recumbent figure of whom is in fine preservation. This portion of the ancient church is now appropriated to the Countess of Selkirk's school. The academy, or grammar school, is a handsome edifice, comprising a spacious room for a public subscription library. The Johnstone's free school is a chaste stone building with centre wings, and a handsome tower it is for the tuition of both sexes, and was opened September 12th, 1848. There are in the town news and billiard rooms and a masonic lodge. The environs of Kirkcudbright are truly delightful: the rising grounds on each side of the river, from Tongland to the sea, are embellished with thriving plantations; and the general prospect, both marine and inland, is really lovely. St. Mary's Isle, a beautiful spot, the seat of the Earl of Selkirk, is about a mile from the town. The burgh is amply supplied with all domestic necessaries, and provisions are comparatively cheap. The market day is Friday, and there are two fairs, namely, on the 12th of August or following Friday, and the 29th September or Friday after.

TWYNHOLME is a parish and village, the latter a small one, is situated three miles from Kirkcudbright, on the main road from Gatehouse to Castle Douglas. The soil is fertile, and the surface of the district rises into many small hills, partly arable. Of the extensive woods with which this part of Galloway was formerly covered, the only remains now existing are around the old castle of Campstone, a building pleasantly situated on an eminence nigh the junction of the rivers Dee and Tarf. The village contains a small neat church of the establishment, and a parochial school.

POST OFFICE, Castle-street, KIRKCUDBRIGHT, Charles James Finlayson, *Post Master*.—Letters from all parts NORTH and SOUTH arrive (from DUMFRIES) daily, at twelve noon, and afternoon at four, and are despatched thereto (except those for EDINBURGH) every morning at a quarter before eight, and to EDINBURGH and other places NORTH at two in the afternoon.

Letters from TWYNHOLME and BORGUE arrive every morning at a quarter past seven and are despatched thereto at half-past four in the afternoon.

NOBILITY, GENTRY AND CLERGY.

Bell the Misses —, St. Cuthbert st
Biglam Mrs. John, Union st
Caig Miss Barbara. Castle st
Carson the Misses —. High st
Cavan Mrs. Barbara. Union st
Cavan Miss Mary, Union st [park
Davidson Mrs. Margaret, Neptune
Drew Miss Margaret, High st
Dunbar Wm.Hyacinth, Esq.Jauefield
Durn Mrs. Margery, Castle st
Erskine Mr. Robert. Castle st
Gordon Rev. Jno,Twynholme manse
Gordon Mr. Alexander, High st
Gordon, Rear Admiral —, Balmachie House
Gordon Robert M. Esq., Rattra
Gordon Mr. Thomas, Castle st
Gordon Lady, Earlstone
Grant Mr. John, St. Mary st
Guthrie Mrs. Jane, High st
Hamilton Mrs. Jane, High st
Hanny Mrs. John, Castle st
Hart Mr. John, High st
Irving General —, Balmea
Johnstone the Misses —, High st
Kis-ock Mrs. John, Castle st
Kerr Robert, Esq., Argrennan
M'Courtie Mrs. Jane, High st
M'Culloch Henry, Esq., Knockbrex
Mackenzie Mrs. Catherine, Castle st
M'Knight Mr. Samuel, High st
M'Lellan Mrs.David, St. Cuthbert st
M'Millan Rev. John, Free manse
M'Millan Mrs. P. L., Barwhinnock
M'Millan Miss Helen, Mill Burn
M'Minn the Misses—, St. Cuthbert st
M'Culloch Walter, Esq., High st
Maitland David, Esq., Barcaple
Maitland Miss Elizabeth, Fludha Cottage [Castle
Maitland Thomas, Esq., Campstone
Mure William, Esq., High st
Murray Mr. Andrew, St. Cuthbert st
Niven Miss Eliza, Union st

Paul Miss Agnes, High st
Rankine Mrs.Margaret,Castlegarden
Roy Thomas, Esq., St. Cuthbert st
Reid Rev. Mr., Borgue
Selkirk the Right Honble. the Earl of, St. Mary's Isle
Sims Mrs Elizabeth, Castle st
Smyth Rev. Samuel. Borgue
Threshie Mrs. Major, High st
Underwood Rev.John,Oakley House
Welsh Mrs. Jane, Union st
Williamson Rev. Dougald Stewart, Tongland manse
Wood Rev. George, St.Cuthbert st

ACADEMIES & SCHOOLS.

Ballantyne John, High st
COUNTESS OF SELKIRKS SCHOOL—Jane Beck, mistress
Copland Margaret, High st
GRAMMAR SCHOOL—James Simpson classical tutor; Charles Mackintosh, mathematical and commercial tutor; E. B. Fleming, English tutor
JOHNSTONES FREE SCHOOL, St. Mary st—John M'Laren, master; Isabella Kay. mistress
PAROCHIAL, Borgue — Maxwell M'Master, master
PAROCHIAL, Tongland—Robt.Shaw master
PAROCHIAL, Twynholme — John Watson, master

AGENTS.

Cairns Elizabeth (to manufacturers) Millharn
Mure William, Esq., (and factor to the Earl of Selkirk), High st
Wh-shart Thomas (to the fishery), Fish House

BAKERS.

Bell William, Castle st
Douglas Ellen, High st
Greive John, High st

BANKS.

BANK OF SCOTLAND (Branch), High st—(draws on the Bank of England, Coutts & Co. and Smith, Payne and Smiths', London)—William Hanny M'Lellan, agent
WESTERN BANK OF SCOTLAND (Branch), High st—(draws on Jones, Loyd & Co. London)—John Ferguson, agent

BOOKSELLERS, STATIONERS AND PRINTERS.

Cannon John, High st
Nicholson John & James Castle st
Stewart James, Castle st

BOOT & SHOE MAKERS.

Angus John, Union st
Cairn George, St. Cuthbert st
Dalzell James, Twynholme
Gibb William, High st
Hornel James, Union st
Hornel John, St. Cuthbert st
Hornel John, Castle st
Hornel William, High st
Horne. William Leatherdale,High st
Jamieson William, Castle st
Kirkpatrick William. St Cuthbert st
Leatherdale James, Twynholme
Milroy Thomas, Castle st

COOPERS.

Anderson John, High st
Brown David, High st

EARTHENWARE DEALERS.

Cannon John, High st
M'Whinnie Thomas, High st

FIRE &c. OFFICE AGENTS.

CROWN (fire), Gavin M'Master, Castle st
MERCANTILE, William Campbell Low, St. Mary st [High st
SCOTTISH UNION, David Gordon,

FLESHERS.

Barber John, Castle st
Elgar Mary, Castle st
Frater George, Castle st

FLESHERS.—Continued.

Gourlay Henry, Castle st
Guthrie Hugh, High st
Stewart John, High st

GROCERS & SPIRIT DEALERS.
(See also Shopkeepers, &c.)

Cavan Samuel, St. Cuthbert st
Cruikshanks Robert, St Cuthbert st
Cunningham Samuel, Castle st
Goodman William, Union st
Gordon Andrew, Castle st
Gordon Thomas, St. Mary st
Houston James, Twynholme
M'Kay Samuel, High st
M'Kinnell William, High st
Macmurray James, St. Cuthbert st
M'Whinnie Jane, High st [High st
M'Whinnie Thomas (& merchant),
Rain John (& merchant) Twynholme
Sproat Thomas, High st

INNS.
(See also Vintners.)

Commercial Hotel (& posting house),
Jane Kissock, St. Cuthbert st
George Inn, Robert Maxwell, St.
Mary st [High st
King's Arms, Margaret Malcomson,
Selkirk Arms, Elizh. Tyson, High st

IRONMONGERS.

Finlayson Charles James, Castle st
Muir Adam, St. Cuthbert st
Sproat Thomas, High st

JOINERS & CABINET MAKERS.

Bland John, Twynholme
Gordon John, High st
Kerr William, High st
M'Cracken John, High st
M'Ewen James, St. Cuthbert st
M'Master Gavin, Castle st
Rae Alexander, Castle st
Murray John, Bank of Bishoptown
Robertson James, Castle st
Robertson Samuel, Castle Dykes
Stitt Thomas, Union st

LINEN & WOOLLEN DRAPERS

Brown William, St. Cuthbert st
Craig David, High st
Hewitson James, Castle st
Rankine William & Adam, Castle st

MILLINERS AND DRESS MAKERS.

Callie Margaret & Jane, Castle st
Duncan Mary, Millburn
Erskine Janet & Ann, Castle st
M'Ewen Grace, High st
M'Lachlan Jane & Mary, Millburn
Milligan Elizabeth. St Mary st
Morgan Mary & Eliza, Castle st
Rae Margaret, Castle st

NAIL MAKERS.

Gordon William, High st
Gourlay James, High st
M'Knight Alexander, Castle st
Price John, High st
Wilson Andrew, High st

PAINTERS & GLAZIERS.

Chrystal Robert, Castle st
Erskine John, High st
Fergusson Robert, Castle st
Macmurray James, St. Cuthbert st
M'Murray William, Castle st
Mounsie John, High st

PHYSICIANS.

Shand John, High st
Shand John S. High st

SHIP OWNERS.

Bee Robert, St. Cuthbert st
Conning James, Castle st
Dickson James, High st
GALLOWAY STEAM NAVIGATION
COMPANY, St. Cuthbert st—Saml.
Cavan, agent
Hart William, High st

M'Keachie James, High st
M'Murray Robert, Castle st
Mitchell John, Castle st
Rankine William & Adam, Castle st
Sproat Thomas (and timber merchant), High st
Whishart Thomas, Twynholme

SHOPKEEPERS & DEALERS IN SUNDRIES.

Alexander Jane, High st
Beck Jane, High st
Cairns Agnes, High st
Cairns Elizabeth, Old Millburn
Cowan Phillis, Castle st
Dickie Thomas, High st
Doud John. St. Cuthbert st
Graham Barnet. St. Mary st
Hart Isabella, Castle st
M'Candlish Thomas, High st
M'Crae William, High st
M'Whinnie William, St. Cuthbert st
Marshall Helen, St. Mary st
Milligan Henrietta, High st
Munro Mary, High st
Rae Alexander, Castle st
Wilson Jane, St. Cuthbert st

SMITHS.

Anderson Thomas, High st
Elbot William, Castle st
Hunter James, Twynholme
Purves Thomas, Twynholme
Seggie John, Union st
Stevenson Samuel, High st
Wasson Wm., Bank of Bishoptown

STONE MASONS.

M'Keachie James, High st
M'Murray John, Castle st
Milligan James, St. Mary st

STRAW BONNET MAKERS.

M'Cymmyp Mary, Millburn
Munro Mary, High st
Thomson Helen, High st

SURGEONS.

Blair David, High st
Campbell Archibald, High st
Johnstone William, Castle st

TAILORS.

Carter James, High st
Gibson William, St. Mary st
Gourlay Alexander, High st
Leatherdale William, Highmilnburn
Maxwell James, Union st
M'Conchie Robert, St. Mary st
M'Kinnell Alexander, High st
Mitchellhill James, Castle st
Nairn Joseph, High st
Ritchie John, Union st
Trainer James, High st
Walker Samuel, Twynholme

TINSMITHS.

Macmurray James, St. Cuthbert st
Sommervill James, High st

VINTNERS

Beattie Eliza (Ship), the Shore
Bell Janet (Freemason's Arms), Castle st
Candlish George, (Steam Packet),
St. Cuthbert's place
Davies Robert, Twynholme
Gordon Agnes (Grapes), High st
Gray Jane, High st
Jolly William (Crown). St. Mary st
Knox John (Mason's Arms) High st
M'Kay Samuel (Coach & Horses),
High st
M'Robert J., Quay
Mitchell John, Tongland Bridge
Sibbald William, Castle Sod

WATCH & CLOCK MAKERS.

Halliday Robert, High st
Low William, High st

WRITERS & NOTARIES.

Fergusson John, High st
Gordon David Hutchinson, (procurator fiscal of the steward court of Kirkcudbright, and clerk to the road trustees), High st
Gordon Robert M., High st
Low William Campbell, (and procurator fiscal for the justices of the peace, and for the commissary court for the stewartry and burgh of Kirkcudbright), St. Mary street
Mackean William, High st
M'Culloch Walter, High st
Mackenzie John, St. Cuthbert st [st
M'Lellan & Mackenzie, St. Cuthbert
Skeoch Anthony, St. Cuthbert place

MISCELLANEOUS

Beck Samuel, weaver. St. Cuthbert st
Broadfoot James, miller, Mill burn
Broom James, secretary to the incorporations, Castle street
Callie John, harbour master, St. Mary st
Christal Robert, tallow chandler, Castle st
Clarke David, slater, Highmilnburn
COUNTY GAOL, High street—William Clark, governor
COURT HOUSE, High street—William Hanny M'Lellan, town clerk
CUSTOM HOUSE, High street—William Gray, collector
Dryden John, sheriff's officer, Union st
Dunlop John, hair dresser, High st
Finlayson Charles James, wine and spirit merchant, Castle street
GAS WORKS—William Elliott, manager
Hannah John, saddler, High st
Hay Peter, plumber, Old Mill burn
M'Candlish James, builder, High st
M'Conchie Alex. precentor, St. Mary st
POLICE OFFICE, High street—Duncan Grant Macdougall, superintendent of the police force
Rae James, clog maker, Union st
Smith William, clog maker, St. Cuthbert st
STAMP OFFICE, High street—John Cannon, sub-distributer
Stitt & Campbell, ship builders, Quay
Thomson James, inspector of weights and measures, Castle street

PLACES OF WORSHIP
AND THEIR MINISTERS.

ESTABLISHED CHURCH, Kirkcudbright—Rev John Underwood
ESTABLISHED CHURCH, Twynholme—Rev. John Gordon
ESTABLISHED CHURCH, Borgue—Rev. — Reid
ESTABLISHED CHURCH, Tongland—Rev. Dugald Stewart Williamson
FREE CHURCH, St. Mary street—Rev. John M'Millar
FREE CHURCH, Borgue—Rev. Samuel Smyth
UNITED PRESBYTERIAN CHAPEL—Rev. George Wood
ROMAN CATHOLIC CHAPEL. St. Cuthbert street—Rev. John Strain, priest

COACHES, &c.

To DUMFRIES, a Coach, from the Commercial Hotel, every morning at a quarter before seven, and two in the afternoon, and the Perseverance, from the George, at a quarter before seven in the morning; all go thro' Castle-Douglas and Dalbeattie
To GATEHOUSE, an Omnibus, from the Commercial Hotel, weekly, on the arrival of the Steamer from LIVERPOOL.

CARRIERS.

To DUMFRIES, Peter Comlin, from High street, Tuesday and Friday
To GLASGOW, William Glendinning from the George, Tuesday

CONVEYANCE BY WATER.
STEAM VESSEL.

To LIVERPOOL, the Countess of Galloway, Captain Hugh M'Queen, weekly—Samuel Cavan, agent
SAILING VESSELS.

To GLASGOW, the Marion, and to WHITEHAVEN, the Skerdon, occasionally

KIRKPATRICK-DURHAM AND OLD BRIDGE OF URR.

KIRKPATRICK-DURHAM is a parish and village —the latter a small one. is 85 miles s.s.w. from Edinburgh, 14 s.e. from New Galloway, 13 w. from Dumfries, 7 e. from Parton, and 6 n. from Castle Douglas. The parish, which is skirted by the Urr water on its western side, derives its name from the old church dedicated to St. Patrick, and Durham, a hamlet where it stood—the latter appellation signifying the 'hamlet on the water.' A new church in the Gothic style with a handsome tower, has been erected on the site of the old church. built two centuries ago. Formerly, a woollen mill furnished employment to many inhabitants of the village, but it is now undistinguished by manufactures of any kind, and is a place of no trade but that which belongs to a few shops for the reciprocal accommodation of the inhabitants. The parish, which is between nine and ten miles in length, and about four miles in breadth, is partly pastoral and partly arable; the former character prevailing in the north, the latter in the south of the district. A fair is held on the first Thursday after the 17th of March, (old style.)

OLD BRIDGE OF URR is a very inconsiderable village in the parish of, and two miles from Kirkpatrick-Durham; seated on the banks of Urr Water and contains but a few houses and no business worthy of notice.

POST OFFICE, KIRKPATRICK-DURHAM, Joseph Leslie, *Post Master.*—Letters from various places NORTH and SOUTH arrive (from DUMFRIES) every afternoon at one and are despatched thereto at twelve noon.

Letters from places WEST and the neighbourhood of CASTLE DOUGLAS arrive from that town every forenoon at eleven and are despatched at ten in the morning.

*_*_* *The names without address are in* KIRKPATRICK-DURHAM.

GENTRY AND CLERGY.
Campbell Colonel —, Walton park
Craig Rev. George, Manse
Crosbie James, Esq., Hoimehead
Dixon Colonel —, Durham hill
Fergusson John, Esq., Kilwhanity
Greig Rev. George, Manse
Jones Mrs. —, Brooklands
M'Math John, Esq., Woodpark
M'Queen John, Esq., Crofts
Mairland Mrs. —, Chipperkyle
Milligan Rev. John, Corsock
Skirving Adam, Esq., Croys
Willis Rev. Benjamin, Kirkpatrick-Durham
Wood William, Esq., Culshand

ACADEMIES AND SCHOOLS.
FREE SCHOOL—John Brown, master
INDUSTRIAL SCHOOL—Maria Taylor, mistress
Mitchell —, Crocketford
PAROCHIAL SCHOOL—Samuel Fergusson, master
PAROCHIAL SCHOOL, Drumbumphry—John Knox, master
Welch John, Corse

INN-KEEPERS & VINTNERS.
Affleck Mary, Crown Inn
Barkley Janet, Plough

Clinghan Andrew, Commercial Inn
M'Neil Mary, Swan
Murdoch Margaret,

SHOPKEEPERS, TRADERS, &c.
Affleck Mary, grocer
Affleck William, shoe & clog maker
Aitken William, tailor
Allen Robert, surgeon
Armstrong John, grocer
Bell James, inspector
Bland Elizabeth, grocer
Broadfoot Alexander, draper
Canning William, joiner & cartwright
Carson James, mason
Carson John, tailor
Carson William, shoe maker
Clingan Andrew, grocer
Clinghan John, mason
Craig Mary, grocer
Fergusson Thomas, joiner
Gibson James, miller, Lochpatrick
Gillespie Peter, surgeon
Greirson James, mason
Hansley John, shopkeeper
Houslin Alexander, miller, Old Bridge of Urr
Leslie Joseph, shopkeeper
M'Clarance Daniel, draper
M'Cubbing John, joiner
M'Douxal William, blacksmith, Old Bridge of Urr
M'George John, blacksmith
M'George John, farrier
M'Gill William, tailor
M'Gowan William, mason, Old Bridge of Urr [bank
M'Millan Robert. manufacturer, New
M'Vane James, painter & plasterer
Milligan John, joiner
Milligan John, slater
Milligan Robert, slater
Milligan William, slater
Murdoch Margaret, grocer
Oliver John, joiner and cartwright
Sloan Robert & Thomas, shoe makers
Tait John, blacksmith, Lochpatrick
Tait Joseph, blacksmith
Thomson James, joiner and cartwright, Old Bridge of Urr
Turner James, joiner

CARRIERS.
To DUMFRIES, Thomas Barkley, Wednesday and Saturday, and John Armstrong, Wednesday

LAWRIESTON IN BALMAGHIE, AND NEIGHBOURHOOD.

LAWRIESTON is a small village in the parish of Balmaghie, 23 miles w. from Dumfries, 10 n. from Kirkcudbright, the like distance s. s. e. from New Galloway, and 7 n. w. from Castle Douglas. On the north west the village is skirted by a mountainous district, which abounds with various kinds of game : on the east the land is more fertile. The parish has several small lakes and a number of mineral springs, among the latter Lochenbreck Well is a place of some resort in the summer ; and the village is a good and comfortable inn—the 'Black Bull.' About a mile west of the village is the mansion of William Kennedy Lawrie, Esq. the principal proprietor of it ; and three miles to the east stands the parish church, with which a school is connected. A free church is in the village, and that also has a school.

POST OFFICE, LAWRIESTON, William M'Vittie, *Post Master.*—Letters from all parts arrive (from CASTLE DOUGLAS) every afternoon at half-past four, and are despatched thereto at half-past seven in the morning

GENTRY AND CLERGY.
Bean Mr. David, Lawrieston
Cochrane Rev. Thomas, Manse, Lawriston
Cunningham John, Esq., of Hensol
Freeland Rev. William, Manse, Balmaghie [hie House
Gordon Admiral James, of Balmaghie
Lawrie William Kennedy, Esq., of Wood Hall

INN-KEEPERS.
Black Bull Inn, James Doig
Crown, Robert Landsborough
Dolphin, Alexander Miller
Lochenbreck Well, Auton M'Millan, Lochenbreck

SHOPKEEPERS, TRADERS, &c.
Bean David, slater
Byron Andrew, tailor
Campbell David, tailor
Campbell Walter, shopkeeper
Carson Henry, librarian of the parish library
Carson Henry, joiner, Balmaghie
Clark David M'Lellan, shopkeeper
Clark John, master of the free church school
Dodds Andrew, millwright
Lawrie John, joiner and cartwright
Lindsey Henrietta, shopkeeper
Livinson Alexander, joiner
M'Landsborough James, weaver
M'Myn John, shopkeeper
M'Vane Peter, shoe maker
M'Vittie William, master of the parochial school
Miller Alexander, tailor
Muir Andrew, tailor
Murdock Hetrick, bleach mill
Stewart James, shoe maker
Scott James, saw mill
Sprout William, blacksmith

CARRIERS.
To AYR. — Glendinning, Tuesday
To CASTLE-DOUGLAS, Hugh M'Hingie, Monday and Thursday, and to KIRKCUDBRIGHT, Monday, Thursday, and Friday

NEW ABBEY, KIRRBEAN AND NEIGHBOURHOODS.

NEW ABBEY is a parish and village—the latter a small one, is 80 miles s. from Edinburgh, 12 E. from Dalbeattie, and 7 s. by w. from Dumfries, situated at the eastern extremity of the county, near to the mouth of the Nith. The parish, which was originally called Kirkinder, takes its present name from the once celebrated religious establishment of New Abbey, a monastery founded in the thirteenth century, for the Cistercian order of monks, by Dovergilla, daughter of Alan, lord of Galloway. The ruins which occupy an area of two hundred and forty by one hundred and fifty feet, are supported on arches and Gothic pillars; and the area itself is used as a burial ground for Roman catholics. The extreme outer walls, or precincts are traced to an extent of fourteen acres. To the north-east are seen the ruins of the Abbot's house, and the foot-path between the two buildings a mile long is still the kirk road. On the north and south lie the woods of Shambelly, and on the south Loch Kindar, and the dark braes of Criffle, the lofty hill of which rises to the height of two thousand feet above the sea, from which it is a mile distant. Besides that of Kindar there are two other lakes in the parish—namely Lochend and Craigend. Near the former is the spot where one of the early Covenanters of this district met an untimely end. The school of Kessock stands on the edge of the lake; and the parish kirk which was built with part of the ruinous materials of the abbey, is situated on the south of the ruins. On the Glen hill, a continuation of the Criffle range stands a monument erected in commemoration of the battle of Waterloo. It is of spiral form, ninety feet high, with a winding stair within. The base bears an inscription, laudatory of the British troops and there allies.

KIRKBEAN is a parish and village—the latter very inconsiderable is situated in the northern part of the parish, about a mile from the sea on the road to Dumfries. This little place possesses some notoriety, if not distinction, from having been the birth-place of John Paul, otherwise Paul Jones, a 'sea adventurer,' who was born here in 1745, and was the son of an honest gardener in the place. The conspicuous mountain called Criffle stands partly within this parish, and within that of New Abbey; and there are within the former traceable ruins of the castle of Cavens and Weaths, both, of which were the property and occasional residence of the Regent Morton. There are two other small villages belonging to this parish, called PRESTON and SALTERNESS.

POST OFFICE, Margaret Newall, Post Mistress.—Letters between NEW ABBEY, DUMFRIES, and KIRKBEAN arrive and are despatched twice a day, at uncertain hours.

GENTRY & CLERGY.
Boyd the Misses Elizabeth & N., Catholic Chapel
Craik John Hamilton, Esq., Arbigland, Kirkbean
Esbie John, Esq., of Abbey bank
Fraser Rev. Charles, Colvend
Gibson Rev. James, Mainsriddle, Kirkbean
Grierson Rev. Thomas, Kirkbean
Hamilton Rev. James, Manse
Kirk John, Esq., Drumstinchill, Kirkbean
Laing Robert, Esq., Kindar Lodge
Lowden John, Esq., Clonyard Crolven
M'Naughton Rev. James, New Abbey [bean
Mercer Rev. M. Mainsriddle, Kirkbean
Murray Rev. William, Kirkbean
Oswald James, Esq., Cavens, Kirkbean
Riddel Mrs. Agnes, of Kintarvie
Smith Robert, Esq., Loch bank
Stewart Mark, Esq., Southwick, Kirkbean
Stewart William, Esq., Shambelly
Thrishie Robert, Esq., Barnbarroch
Witham Robert, Esq., Kirkconnel, Troqueer [Troqueer
Witham Rev. Thomas, Kirkconnel,

SCHOOLS.
PAROCHIAL SCHOOLS:—
Barnbarroch—Jno Smith, master
Colvend—John Johnston, master
Crigmoorine—Francis Coldwall, master [master
Kirkbean—Rev. William Murray,
Kirkbean—James Lindsay Preston. master
Kissock—Thos. Kenney, master
New Abbey—Thomas Porteous, master
Southwick—Wm. Wilson, master

INN KEEPERS & VINTNERS.
Blair James, Carsthorne, Kirkbean
Brown William, (Crown), New Abbey [New Abbey
Caven Nathanial, (Breswing Inn),
Clark —, Carsthorne, Kirkbean
Hyslop John, Mainsriddle, Kirkbean
Lewis Thomas New Abbey
Millar Archibald, (King's Arms), New Abbey [Abbey
Newall Jane, (Commercial)), New
Scott John, Kirkbean
Turner John, New Abbey

SURGEONS.
M'Donald John, New Abbey
Maxwell John, Kirkbean
Morrison Thomas, New Abbey

SHOPKEEPERS & TRADERS.
Bell John, blacksmith, Troqueer
Bounar Mary, grocer, New Abbey
Caird James, grocer, New Abbey
Calvert J., manager of saw mill
Cavan Thomas, slater, Troqueer
Connal David, tailor, Inglistonford
Copeland James, blacksmith Carbilly
Copeland John, bacon curer, Old Shambelly [Abbey
Corrie Nathaniel, ship owner, New
Curlie James, tailor, New Abbey
Dempster William, blacksmith, Kirkbean [arter
Harris Robert, blacksmith, Loch-
Hunter James, keeper of lighthouse, Saturness, Kirkbean
Ireland Joseph, blacksmith, New Abbey [Abbey
Kinzan John, ship owner, New
Lewis Thomas, mason, New Abbey
M'Cloud Still, cooper, New Abbey
M'Kinnell Joseph, shoe maker, New Abbey
M'Kune Robert, grocer, Kirkbean
M'Lellan John, joiner, Kirkbean

M'Murray John, weaver, Locharter
Martin Lewis, blacksmith, Preston-mill
Mein Janet, grocer, New Abbey
Mein Robert, flesher and mason, New Abbey
Millar Archibald, miller NewAbbey
Mundell Andrew, blacksmith, Kirkbean [Abbey
Mundell James, shoe maker, New
Neilson John, shoe maker, Gate end
Newall Margt., grocer, New Abbey
Pagan J. grocer, Kirkbean
Rankine James, blacksmith, New Abbey [burn
Robinson Joseph, mason, Drum-
Seaton James, joiner & cartwright, New Abbey
Seeds Daniel, tailor, New Abbey
Smith Elizabeth, grocer, Locharter
Thomson James, wool-carder, Wauk Mill
Thomson James & John, joiners and cartwrights, New Abbey
Walker Samuel, shoe maker, New Abbey
Wallace James, grocer, Preston-mill

PLACES OF WORSHIP,
AND THEIR MINISTERS.
ESTABLISHED CHURCH, New Abbey—Rev. James Hamilton.
ESTABLISHED CHURCH, Kirkbean—Rev. Thomas Grierson.
ESTABLISHED CHURCH, Colvend ——Rev. James Fraser.
FREE CHURCH, New Abbey —— Rev. James M'Naughton.
FREE CHURCH, Kirkbean—Rev. James Gibson.
CATHOLIC CHAPEL, New Abbey.

CARRIERS.
To DUMFRIES, James Stewart, from New Abbey; James Wallace, from Preston-Mill. and Joseph Kirk, from Carsthorne, Wednesday and Saturday.

NEW GALLOWAY,
WITH THE PARISHES OF BALMACLELLAN, DALRY AND CARSPHAIRN.

NEW GALLOWAY is a small town and royal burgh, in the parish of Kells; 84 miles s.s.w. from Edinburgh, 25 w. from Dumfries, 18 N.E. from Newton Stewart, 14 N.w. from Castle Douglas, and 8 N.w. from Parton: pleasantly situated on the west bank of the river Ken, over which was thrown, in 1822, an elegant stone bridge of five arches; this structure, lying in the valley below the town, has a very pleasing effect; at its completion, a dinner was given by the late Lord Viscount Kenmure, to fourteen of the oldest inhabitants of the town, whose united ages amounted to 1,261 years. The houses of the town stretch along the public road, and form a tolerably well-built-street. The business of the place is confined to the local domestic retail and handicraft branches; and there is a very comfortable inn—the 'Spalding Arms.' Galloway's burghal charter was conferred by Charles I., and the municipal government rested in a provost, two baillies and fifteen councillors. A justice of peace court is held in the first Monday in every month, for the recovery of debts under £5; attached to the court is a criminal and debtors' gaol, with a steeple and town clock. The burgh unites with Wigtown, Stranraer and Whithorn in returning one member to parliament.

On the north side of the town, within the distance of half a mile, is the parish church, a neat stone edifice, with a square tower in the centre, built in 1822; in the same year a Sunday school was established, in which upwards of one hundred children are gratuitously taught by the inhabitants. At a short distance south of the town stands the ancient castle of Kenmure, once a place of considerable strength; Mary Queen of Scots lodged in it one night, on her way from this country to England. Loch Ken, which joins the town, is four miles and a half long, and in many places more than a mile broad; it abounds with pike and perch, and some of the former have been caught of the astonishing weight of fifty and sixty pounds. Fairs are held on the first Wednesday after the 12th of April, the first Wednesday after the 12th of July, the first Wednesday after the 12th of August, and the first Wednesday after the 12th of November.

DALRY is rather a populous village, in the parish of its name, lying on the east bank of the river Ken: the southern portion of the district lies in a beautiful valley, composed of rich arable land; the high grounds are pastoral and graze considerable numbers of cattle and sheep. The village of Dalry (the name of which signifies 'the dale of the king,') is surrounded with delightful scenery; and there is a good inn (the Plough) at the command of the visiter. There are several lakes in the parish; the largest, called Loch Invar, covers an area of fifty acres: in the lake stan ds the remains of an ancient castle, formerly belonging to the Gordons, Knights of Lochinvar, and latterly Viscounts of Kenmure. Besides Dalry, there is a small village in the parish, called JOHN's CLACHAN, agreeably situated on the margin of the Ken.

CARSPHAIRN village, which is situated near the river Deogh, contains a parish kirk, the manse, a parochial school and a few scattered houses. The parish is somewhat extensive, but thinly populated; it is the most northerly and mountainous district in the stewartry, and is chiefly devoted to grazing. This parish, with those of Dalry, Kells and Balmaclellan, are designated the district of Glenkens—named for the true breed of black-faced sheep and black cattle, as also for good horses of the Galloway breed.

The small village of BALMACLELLAN, stands on the opposite side of the Ken to New Galloway, not far from the confluence of the stream with the head of Loch Ken, twelve miles south west of Minniehive. The parish is of a moory character, interspersed with some inconsiderable lakes.

POST OFFICE, NEW GALLOWAY, John Muir, Post Master.—Letters from all parts arrive (from CASTLE DOUGLAS), every afternoon at half-past four; and are despatched thereto at half-past seven in the morning.

POST OFFICE, DALRY, William Smith, Post Master.—Letters from all parts arrive (from CASTLE DOUGLAS), every evening at five; and are despatched thereto at seven in the morning.

NOBILITY, GENTRY AND CLERGY.

Alexander Mackilston, Esq. Glenhaul, Dalry   [Balmaclellan
Bannister Mr. Edward, Holm House.
Barber Thomas, Esq. Muirdrochwood, Carsphairn
Barber William, Esq. Muirdrochwood, Carsphairn
Blair Rev. Samuel, the Manse, Dalry
Bowman Mrs. —, Craighead, Dalry
Gordon the Honble. Mrs. Bellemay, Kenmure Castle
Haining Rev. —, the Manse, Balmaclellan   [phairn
Jennison Mr. Richard, Holm   [Carsphairn
Kenmure the Right Honble. Dowager Viscountess, Meadow-bank House, New Galloway
Kennedy Mrs. —, Knocknalling, Kells
Lee Tottenham, Esq. Glenlee Park, Kells   [Dalry
M'Turk Mr. Alexander, Burlen, Kells   [Dairy
Maitland Rev. James, the Manse, Kells
Patterson Rev. —, the Manse, Taylor Mrs. —, Kenmure Castle
Welch Rev. David, the Manse, Carsphairn   [Balmaclellan
Wilson Rev. William, the Manse, Yourston William G. Esq. Balamgarr, Kells

SCHOOLS.

Cowan James, New Galloway
PAROCHIAL SCHOOLS:—
Balmaclellan—Henry Symington, master
Carsphairn—James Sloane, master
Dalry—Peter Muir, master
Kells—John Muir, master

BAKERS.

Douglas John, Dalry
Kerr Andrew, Dalry
Muir William, New Galloway

BANK.

EDINBURGH AND GLASGOW BANK (Branch) New Galloway—(draws on the parent bank, Edinburgh and Glasgow, and on the Union Bank, and Williams, Deacon & Co. London)—Adam Corrie, agt.

BLACKSMITHS.

M'Bride John, Balmaclellan
M'Murtree Duncan, Carsphairn
M'Queen James, Dalry
Turner Matthew, New Galloway
Turner William, New Galloway

BOOT AND SHOE MAKERS.

Bland Nathan, New Galloway
Charters Robert, New Galloway
Coltart William, New Galloway
Crosbie John & Son, New Galloway
M'Kay Anton, Dalry
M'Queen James, Balmaclellan
Murdok Robert, Dalry
Stephenson James, Dalry

FIRE &c. OFFICE AGENTS.

ABERDEEN, John Muir, New Galloway   [New Galloway
MERCANTILE (life), Adam Corrie, New Galloway

GROCERS AND DRAPERS.

(See also Shopkeepers, &c.)
Campbell David, New Galloway
Campbell Gilbert, New Galloway
Douglas Archibald, Dalry
M'Gill David, Dalry
Mackay David, New Galloway

INN-KEEPERS & VINTNERS.

Charters John, Balmaclellan
Cowan William (Plough Inn), Dalry
Dempster James, Carsphairn
M'Adam Robert (Spalding Arms), Dalry   [Dalry
M'Clellan Isabella (Commercial),
M'Crea Jane (Cross Keys), Carsphairn   [Galloway
M'Kelvie Thomas (Cross Keys), New
Mitchell Henry (Spalding Arms Inn), New Galloway

Turner William, New Galloway
Wilson John (Kenmure Arms), New Galloway

JOINERS.

Corson Alexander, Dalry
Douglas John, New Galloway
Gordon Peter, Balmaclellan
M'Caudlish William (and architect), New Galloway
M'Culloch John, New Galloway
M'Gill James (& cartwright), Dalry
M'Kay William, Carsphairn
M'Millan Robert, Carsphairn

MILLERS.

Andrew John, Glenlee Mill, Kells
Grier Robert, New Galloway

SHOPKEEPERS & DEALERS IN SUNDRIES.

Ballantyne James, Carsphairn
Bell Jane (and spirit dealer), Carsphairn
Black Joseph (and draper, and spirit dealer), Balmaclellan
Candlish Ann, New Galloway
Cowan David, Dalry
Haining Adam, Dalry
Hall John, Dalry
Hastings Robert, Dalry
Murray Agnes, New Galloway
Shannon James, Dalry
Shannon John, Dalry
Slowne Marian, Balmaclellan
Smith William, Dalry

STONE MASONS.

Hawthorn William, New Galloway
Patterson Thomas, New Galloway
Smith Alexander, New Galloway

TAILORS.

Garraway James, New Galloway
Little Archibald, New Galloway
M'Kie Peter, Dalry
Patterson John, New Galloway

WRIGHTS.
See Joiners.

MISCELLANEOUS.

The names without address are in NEW GALLOWAY.

Archibald Joseph, factor to Sir William Miller, bart.
Clark James B. painter
Cowan James, woollen weaver
Gallocher William, weaver
Halliday Matthew, tea dealer
Halliday James, tea dealer
Jamont James. stocking maker
M'Call Thomas, auctioneer and sheriff's officer, Dalry

M'Gill Samuel, flesher
M'Janet Andrew, cooper   [field
M'Millan David, surveyor of taxes, View-
M'Night William, saddler
M'Queen Jas. millwright, Balymaclellan
Millencen Alfred, M.D. surgeon
Sibthorpe Jno. excise officer, Balmaclellan
Turner Seria, dress maker

PLACES OF WORSHIP,
AND THEIR MINISTERS.

ESTABLISHED CHURCH, Kells — Rev. James Maitland.
ESTABLISHED CHURCH, Balmaclellan — Rev. William Wilson.

ESTABLISHED CHURCH, Dalry — Rev. Samuel Blair.
ESTABLISHED CHURCH, Carsphairn — Rev. David Welch
UNITED PRESBYTERIAN CHAPEL, Dalry — Rev. Alexander Patterson.
FREE CHURCH, Bog, Balmaclellam — Rev. John Haining.

CARRIERS.

To DUMFRIES, Jno. Charters. Monday
To GLASGOW, Thomas Wallett and Robert Martin. from Dalry, every alternate week on Monday and Thursday.

PALNACKIE,

OR GARDEN, is the principal village in the parish of Buittle, 18 miles s.w. from Dumfries, 14 N. from Kirkcudbright, and 6 s. of Castle Douglas; agreeably situated on the water of Urr, where there is a good harbour, having, at ordinary spring tides, a depth of thirty feet water, and capable of receiving vessels of two hundred tons burthen. It is the chief port for supplying the surrounding neighbourhood with coal and various other sea borne necessaries. The parish is bounded on the east by the Urr, on the south by the Solway Frith, and on the west by Kelton. It is a fertile and agricultural district, eight miles in length, three in breadth.

POST OFFICE, Thomas Dalling, *Post Master.*—Letters arrive from and are despatched twice a day between PALNACKIE and DALBEATTIE, except on Sunday, when there is one arrival and despatch only.

GENTRY & CLERGY.

Grant the Rev. Wm. R. Buittle
M'Knight Robert, Esq. Barlachan
Robinson Mrs. Mary, Almorness
Wyms Robert, Esq. Kirkinnan

SCHOOLS.

PAROCHIAL SCHOOL, Palnackie — James Mackie, master
PAROCHIAL SCHOOL, Buittle — John Tait, master

PUBLIC HOUSES.

Bell James, vintner
Black Helen, vintner
Black John (Commercial)
M'Quhae William (Royal Oak)

SHIP OWNERS.

AT PALNACKIE.

Black Helen
Black John
Carswell James
Gibson Elizabeth

M'Knight Robt. Esq.
Wilson John
Wilson Samuel

SHOPKEEPERS & TRADERS.

Anderson Archibald, shoe maker
Black Maxwell, joiner
Candlish James, blacksmith
Halliday Matthew, miller
Hannah Neilson, blacksmith
Henghan William, shopkeeper
M'Adam Alexander, tide waiter
M'Caughee William, tailor
M'Quhae M., joiner
Robson Grace, shopkeeper
Wright Joseph, cooper

WIGTONSHIRE.

THIS county, which forms the western part of the ancient district of Galloway, occupies the south-western extremity of Scotland. It is bounded on the east by the stewartry of Kirkcudbright (or Eastern Galloway), also by Wigtown bay; on the south and west it is girded by the Irish Sea, and on the north by the county of Ayr. The extent of the shire from north to south is about thirty miles, and (including Luce Bay) its breadth from east to west about the same: the superficial contents of the county (adopting a medium calculation betwixt conflicting authorities) may be taken at four hundred and eighty square miles, or three hundred and nine thousand, seven hundred and sixty statute acres—of which about one-third, perhaps, is cultivated. The Bay of Luce indents the land to the extent of fifteen miles, and forms two promontories; at the southern extremity of the western projection is the Mull of Galloway, while the apex of the eastern is called Burrow Head; these two peninsular headlands are also known by the Celtic name of the *Rhinns* (*Rhyns* or *Rinos*) of Galloway. On the north another promontory is formed by the intersection of Loch Ryan. In ordinary language the district is divided into Upper and Lower Galloway, which designates the northern or high and the southern or low parts of the shire.

EARLY HISTORY.—At the epoch of the Roman power obtruding itself into North Britain, the ancient British tribe of the *Novantes* inhabited the whole of Eastern and Western Galloway, having *Leucophibia* (the modern Whithorn) for their principal town, and *Rerigonium* (Loch Ryan), for their principal port. The Anglo-Saxons over-ran the district in the sixth century; and Oswie, the Northumbrian king, settled at Whithorn. During the ninth and tenth centuries the country on the west was inhabited by the Picts from Ireland and the Isle of Man; and hence the name of *Galloway*, or 'the country of the Gael,' was conferred on the territory. About the twelfth century Galloway passed into the hands of the Scottish king, Alexander II. In the sanguinary contests which originated in the competition of Bruce and Baliol, the chieftains of Galloway long remained attached to the party of the latter, whose family they sheltered after Edward Bruce had subdued the whole country. The family of Douglas subsequently became possessed of the lordship of Galloway; but, on the attainder of the nobleman of that name in 1455, the title became extinct: it was revived, however, and now bestows an Earldom on the distinguished family of Stewart and Garlies. The Maxwells of Nithsdale received a portion of the estates. The proximity to Ireland and the Isle of Man caused the country of the Gael to remain for a long period a separate community from the rest of Scotland, and the Gaelic dress, manners and language lingered here long after they fell into desuetude in the rest of the Lowlands. Whilst these distinctions remained, the inhabitants were conspicuous for rudeness bordering on ferocity. Their chief derived his authority sometimes from the kings of Scotland and at others from the kings of Northumbria, but neither could subdue the turbulence and insubordination of the chieftain and his vassals, who were very troublesome neighbours, inflicting the mischiefs of reckless incursions into the territories of those that had the misfortune to dwell in the proximity of these half civilized marauders.

SOIL, CLIMATE, PRODUCE, &c.—This shire is one of the most level districts in Scotland; and the hills, of which there are none of great altitude, are generally pretty free from the encumbrance of rocks. The best lands lie near the shores—the inland divisions being more elevated, and largely mixed with heath and moss. The major part of the soil is of an hazel colour, and is of that kind sometimes called a dry loam, though it often inclines to a gravelly nature. The county presents an exposure to the south, and its waters mostly descend to the Irish Sea. The climate is moist, with winds from the south-west, which prevail during the greater part of the year, usually accompanied with rains; yet, when proper attention is exercised by the agriculturist, the moisture of the climate is but seldom injurious to the products of the earth: snow rarely lies long, and frosts are not generally severe or of tedious duration. In early times this district of Galloway, like most other sections of the country, was covered with woods; and in modern days planting has been pursued most extensively: it is said that, during twenty years, the Earl of Stair annually planted twenty thousand trees. The salutary improvements that have been effected in the agriculture of this county have been, with some justice, ascribed to the efforts of the agricultural society of Dumfries; the spirit and practice of husbandry gradually spread from that shire to Kirkcudbright, and thence penetrated into Wigtonshire: since that period, rents have risen rapidly; and corn and other products of tillage, black cattle, wool, sheep and swine, are now largely exported. The district has long been celebrated for its breed of horses, distinguished by the appellation of 'Galloways;' they are of the Spanish or rather Moorish race, and, when the breed is pure, of a dun colour with a black line along the back: these animals are small, but active, sinewy and spirited. This district has long been pre-eminent as being an excellent pastoral one and for the superiority of its wool. The mineral recources of this county are by no means extensive: there is no coal, at least for any useful purpose; and although there is plenty of iron ore, the absence of the former article renders the latter of comparatively little value; in the northern part of the 'Rhinns' the existence of sandstone has been ascertained; quarries of slate, of different qualities, are found in various places; and lead mines were formerly wrought within the district. The shipping trade of Wigtonshire has felt, like all maritime counties, the impetus of steam navigation. The ports of Stranraer, Wigtown and Whithorn derive considerable benefit from this mighty power; and till recently Portpatrick was the station for the mail steam packets communicating with Ireland: the removal of which to Glasgow and Greenock has been a severe blow to the prosperity of this interesting little port. The coasting trade of this county is considerable and is steadily increasing, giving employment to a large number of mariners. In 1688 the number of boats belonging to this shire was four, and in 1851 this insignificant number is augmented to hundreds. There is also considerable activity in the fisheries connected with the numerous ports and lochs, so that combining the various sources of agriculture, commerce and the fisheries, Wigtonshire may be pronounced an active and prosperous county.

RIVERS AND MOUNTAINS.—This county has no considerable rivers; the principal are the Cree, the Bladenoch and the Tarf, with a few of smaller size. The Cree, which is a boundary river between this county and the stewartry of Kirkcudbright, rises in Carrick, in Ayrshire; after forming a lake at the head of Wigtonshire, it flows again as a stream, and, passing Newton-Stewart on the east, falls into a creek at the head of Wigtown Bay. The Bladenoch also as its source in Carrick, and, after running a course of twenty-four miles, falls into Luce Bay. The Tarf issues from a small lake, called Loch Whinnoch, in the parish of Girthon, Kirkcudbright; and, after a course of twenty-one miles, unites with the Dee. The mountains, with their elevations above the level of the sea, are, Lang, 1,758 feet; Mochrum Fell, 1,020; Knock of Luce, 1,014; and Barhullion, 814.

Wigtonshire comprehends seventeen parishes, and has three royal and parliamentary burghs, namely, WIGTOWN, STRANRAER and WHITHORN; with these is associated New Galloway in returning one member to Parliament, and the county at large sends another. The burghs of barony in the shire are Newton-Stewart, Garlieston, Glenluce and Portpatrick; it has several thriving villages, and a number of small sea-ports or natural harbours; and is ornamented by many handsome mansions and elegant seats of its nobility and gentry.

POPULATION OF THE SHIRE IN THE YEARS 1801, 1811, 1821, 1831 AND 1841.

The Italic letters, b. and p. signify respectively Burgh and Parish.

	1801.	1811.	1821.	1831.	1841.		1801	1811.	1821.	1831.	1841.
Glasserton ....p.	860	1047	1057	1194	1253	Mochrum ....p.	1113	1345	1871	2105	2539
Inch ....p.	1577	1831	2386	2321	2950	Penninghame and ......p. } Newton-Stewart ..town. }	1569	2847	3090	3461	3672
Kirkcolm............p.	1191	1465	1821	1896	1973						
Kirkcowan ....p.	787	1006	1253	1374	1423	Portpatrick ....p.	1090	1202	1818	2239	2043
Kirkinner ....p.	1160	1433	1488	1514	1709	Sorbie ....p.	1091	1265	1319	1412	1700
Kirkmaiden ....p.	1633	1719	2210	2051	2202	Stoneykirk ....p.	1848	2364	3133	2966	3062
Leswalt............p.	1329	1705	2332	2636	2712	Stranraer ....b. & p.	1722	1923	2463	3329	3440
Luce, New ....p.	368	457	609	628	652	Whithorn............b. & p.	1904	1935	2361	2415	2795
Luce, Old............p.	1221	1536	1957	2190	2448	Wigtown............b. & p.	1475	1711	2042	2337	2562
						TOTAL POPULATION OF WIGTONSHIRE............	21918	26891	33240	36258	39195

The total annual value of Real Property in Wigtonshire, as assessed in April 1815, amounted to £143,425; and the amount assessed to the Property Tax, in 1843, to £131,277 5s. 1½d.

GARLIESTON AND SORBY.

GARLIESTON is a sea-port village in the parish of Sorby, finely situated at the head of Garlieston bay (a small haven on the west side of Wigton bay), and opposite Fleet bay (distances *see* SORBY). The place is built in the form of a seminircle, facing the sea, with a safe and commodious harbour, capable of receiving a great number of vessels; and if a breakwater was carried out to a rock called the Allen, which could be affected at an expense comparatively trifling with the benefit that would result from the improvement, vessels might here take shelter, when wind-bound, at all times of the tide, which at the spring-flow rises eighteen feet. A regular communication is now maintained between this port and Liverpool, by the 'Countess of Galloway' steam-packet, once a fortnight, and there are traders occasionally. The Broughton and Pouenburn streams, which here flow into the bay, are crossed by several bridges. Galloway House, a fine mansion, the seat of the Earl of Galloway, erected in 1740, is adjacent on the south; it is surrounded by beautiful plantations and pleasure-grounds, and the walks about it, for several miles, are extremely picturesque, and the prospects on every side delightful.

SORBY (or *Sorbie*) is a parish and village—the latter 39 miles E. from Portpatrick, 30 s. E. from Stranraer, 13 s. from Newton Stewart, and 6 s. from Wigtown; situated in a fine part of the county, and surrounded by land in a high state of cultivation. The parish is of an irregular figure, extending along the shore about twelve miles, and varying in breadth from two to six miles inland. The chief bays in the parish are Garlieston (above described) and Rigg, with the ports of Allan, Whaple and Innerwell: these bays and ports are very convenient for shipping, and well adapted for the prosecution of the fisheries. The headlands are Crueleton and Eagerness: upon these are the remains of two strong castles; and about a mile to the east of the kirk are the gradually mouldering outlines of Sorby tower, formerly belonging to the Hannay family. The places of worship are the parish church at Sorby, and a free church and an independent chapel at Garlieston.

POST OFFICE, GARLIESTON, John Pollock, *Post Master.*—Letters from all parts arrive (from WIGTOWN) every evening at nine, and are despatched thereto at two in the morning.

POST OFFICE, SORBY, William Campbell, *Post Master.*—Letters from all parts arrive and are despatched at the same hours as those of the GARLIESTON office.

NOBILITY, GENTRY, AND CLERGY.

Blair Rev. Samuel, Garlieston
Galloway The Right Honble. the Earl of, Galloway House
Grant Captain George, Castle Wig
Nun Rev. John, Garlieston
Sloan Rev. Edward K., the Manse, Sorby
Young Rev. Thomas, Garlieston

SCHOOLS.

FREE SCHOOL, Sorbie——David M'Kie, master
INFANTS' SCHOOL, Garlieston—— Harriet Herbert, mistress
PAROCHIAL SCHOOL, Garlieston— Robert Anderson, master
Wilson Ebenezer, Garlieston

BLACKSMITHS.

Huchan James, Sorby
Mauson Andrew, Sorby
Simson John, Garlieston

BOOT AND SHOE MAKERS.

Connor Michael, Sorby
M'Keachie John, Garlieston
Paul John, Sorby
Robb Alexander, Garlieston
Robb Alexander, jun. Garlieston

GROCERS AND DEALERS IN SUNDRIES.
Campbell William, Sorby
Conpetbite James, Garlieston
Dunse James, Sorby
Hannah Elizabeth, Garlieston
M'Cutcheon John, Sorby
M'Queen Margaret, Sorby
Pollock John, Garlieston
Scott William, Sorby
Stewart Thomas, Garlieston
Wild Robert, Garlieston

JOINERS & WRIGHTS
Dick Alexander, Garlieston
M'Clure Andrew, Sorby
M'Clure John, Garlieston
M'Credie John, Sorby
M'Gowan George, Garlieston
M'William Archibald, Sorby
Paton James, Garlieston

MILLERS.
White Alexndr.Creech Mills, Sorby
Wild William, Garlieston

NAIL MAKERS.
Halliday James, Garlieston
Nelson James, Garlieston

STONE MASONS.
Harg George, Garlieston
Harg Peter, Garlieston
Hyslop William, Garlieston
Robinson William, Garlieston

TAILORS.
M'Cutcheon John (and clothier), Sorby
M'Millan John, Sorby
Rennie John, Garlieston
Rennie John, jun. Garlieston
Rennie Samuel, Garlieston
Rennie William, Garlieston

VINTNERS
Coughtrie Margaret, Sorby
Henderson Andrew, Garlieston
Highet Robert, Garlieston
M'Cutcheon John, Sorby
Paton James, Garlieston
Stewart Thomas, Garlieston

WRIGHTS.
See Joiners and Wrights.

MISCELLANEOUS.
Allen Robert, painter, Garlieston
Brice James, ship broker, Garlieston
Callow William, painter, Garlieston
Douglas William, tide waiter, Garlieston
Dunsmore Jas. master mariner, Garlieston
Forlow Alexander, saddler and harness maker, Sorby
Hannah Wm. master mariner, Garlieston
M'Harg Janet, baker, Garlieston
Marshall William, ship owner & timber merchant, Garlieston
Wild Robert, baker, Garlieston

CARRIER.
To WHITHORN. Alexr. Dick, Tuesday
To WIGTOWN, Alexander Dick, Mond.

CONVEYANCE BY WATER
To LIVERPOOL, the *Countess of Galloway* steam packet, once a fortnight
Coasting Vessels leave regularly for all parts.

GLENLUCE and NEW LUCE,

GLENLUCE is a village in the parish of Old Luce, 19 miles E. by N. from Portpatrick, 18 w. from Wigton 16 s.w. from Newton-Stewart, and 10 E. by s. from Stranraer; situated on the banks of the river Luce, and on the public road, at the head of Luce bay, which here forms a tolerably good harbour for small vessels, and affords employment for many fishermen. The country around is interesting and picturesque, and abounds with game of almost every kind. The church is a neat edifice, remarkable only for its simplicity; there are also a free church, and a chapel for an united secession congregation. About a mile to the north of the church, farther up the vale (from which the village takes its name) are the ruins of Luce Abbey, founded by Rolland, Lord of Galloway, in 1190: when in its perfect state it must have been an extensive building. The vast mass of prostrate fragments at present cover about an acre and a half of ground, notwithstanding the quantities that have been carried away. The only part now remaining entire is a small apartment on the east side of the square, within which latter stood the cloisters; in the middle of this apartment stands a pillar, about fourteen feet high, from which eight arches spring, and have their terminations in the surrounding walls. Tradition reports

Michael Scott, of cabalistic memory, to have been at one time abbot of this establishment, and adds that his magical library still exists under a particular part of the ruins. To ascertain this a person excavated a part of the ground and found many curiosities, together with several skeletons in an upright position; the explorer however having been seized with insanity, farther search by him was interrupted, and the superstitions of the people here prevented others from from pursuing the examination. An annual fair is held at Glenluce on the Tuesday before the 26th of May; and there is a monthly fair or market, from the first Friday in the month of April to the first Friday in December.

The village of NEW LUCE is five miles north from Glenluce, situated on the Luce, where the Cross water falls into that river. This district, which, until the year 1646 formed part of the parish of Old Luce, extends about ten miles in length by from five to six in breadth. It consists of high and of low ground : of the former, the greater proportion is covered by rocks or heath; the arable land, which is not of great extent, lies principally on the banks of the rivers. The parish church—a plain building, and an united presbyterian chapel, are the places of worship.

POST OFFICE, GLENLUCE, Sarah Hawthorn, *Post Mistress.*—Letters from various places arrive (from PORTPATRICK) every morning at four, and from DUMFRIES and various parts at half-past seven in the evening, and are despatched at the same hours.

GENTRY AND CLERGY.
Adair John, Esq. Balkail
Blain Mr. Andrew, Glenluce
Hannay Mr. William, Glenluce
Hay Sir James Dalrymple, Bart., Dunraggit
Hood Mr. David, Glenluce
Kelley Lieutenant —, R.N. Glenluce
M'Caw Mrs. Susan, Glenluce
M'Cormack Mr. William, Glenluce
M'Cracken Captain John, Glenluce
M'Dowall Mrs. —, Genock
M'Dowall Capt.James,Logan House
M'Dowall Rev. John, Luce Abbey
M'Kergo Rev. William, New Luce
Milroy Mr. James, Glenluce
Pullar Rev. James, Glenluce
Rodin Miss Helen, Glenluce
Saunders Mrs. Maria, Glenluce
Wilson Rev. George, Glenluce

ACADEMIES AND SCHOOLS.
FREE CHURCH SCHOOL——James Holbourn, master
Kelly Sarah
M'Colm Isabella   [master
PAROCHIAL SCHOOL—John Ross,
PAROCHIAL SCHOOL, New Luce—Andrew M'Lean, master

BANK.
WESTERN BANK OF SCOTLAND (Branch), Glenluce—(draws on the head office, Glasgow, and its branches, and on the Union Bank, London)—James Gibson, agent

BLACKSMITHS.
Blackwell Hugh, New Luce
Blackwell John, New Luce
Cambell Hugh, New Luce
M'Clelland David, Burnside
M'Clure Peter, Glenluce
M'William John, Glenluce
Park John, New Luce

BOOT AND SHOE MAKERS.
Carson James, Glenluce
Gilston James, Glenluce
Kelly Charles, New Luce
King David, New Luce
M'Caun James, Glenluce
M'Ewen James, New Luce
M'Vae John, Glenluce
Wilkins David, Glenluce

CARTWRIGHTS & JOINERS.
Buyers John, Bridge of Park
Cumming Charles, Glenluce
Douglas Peter, Glenluce

M'Credie James, Glenluce
M'Gaw Samuel, New Luce
M'Mekin Robert, New Luce
Sproat Edward, Glenluce

FIRE, &c. OFFICE AGENTS.
FARMERS' AND GRAZIERS MUTUAL (cattle), James Gibson
LONDON INDISPUTABLE(life),David Bell
NORTH BRITISH, James Gibson

GROCERS
Marked thus * are also Spirit Dealers.
Hannah Samuel, Newland
M'Carlie Thomas, Newland
M'Kenzie David, Newland

AT GLENLUCE.
Canse Andrew	M'Micking Jane
Coleman Helen	M'Quaid Terance
*M'Chlery Alexr.	*Milligan James
*M'Claymont Ptr	Mitchell John
M'Cowen James	Saunders Isabella
*M'Gill James	Skimming Grace
*M'Kenzie Janet	Stroyan William
M'Lellan John	Walls Henry
M'Master Margaret & Helen	Withers Margrt.

LINEN & WOOLLEN DRAPERS
AT GLENLUCE.

M'Caw James
M'Master Margaret & Helen
Milroy Thomas
Saunders Elizbth
Withers Margt.

MILLERS.

Adair Alexander, Bridge of Park
Duggan William, Mill Town Mill
Finlay John (and carder), Galdanoch Mill

MILLINERS AND DRESS AND STRAW BONNET MAKERS.
AT GLENLUCE.

Coleman Mrs. —,
Kelly A. & J.
M'Creadie Margt
M'Cubbin Elzth
M'Dowall Elzbth
M'Nish Margt.
Rennie Eliza
Smith Janet
Wallace Margt.,
New Luce

SADDLERS.

M'Clew David, Glenluce
Main James, Glenluce

STONE MASONS.

Agar Robert, Glenluce
Gordon William, New Luce
M'Bratnie John, Glenluce
M'Creadie James, Glenluce
M'Micking Gilbert, Glenluce
M'Neilie Charles, New Luce
Skimming John, Glenluce

TAILORS

Hannah Thomas, Glenluce
M'Cubbin John, New Luce
M'Dowall Andrew, Glenluce

M'Lauchland James, New Luce
Milroy Thomas, Glenluce

VINTNERS.

Gracey Hugh, Woodside
Hannah Samuel, New Luce
Hannay John, Glenluce
M'Carlie Thomas, New Luce
M'Chlery Alexander, Glenluce
M'Claymont Peter, Glenluce
M'Gill James, Glenluce
M'Kenzie Janet, New Luce
M'Kenzie John, New Luce
M'Kenzie Robert, Glenluce
M'Micking James, Glenluce
Miller John, Glenluce
Milligan James, Glenluce
Peaterson Mrs. —, Glenluce
Templeton Mary, Glenluce

WEAVERS.

Duggan John, New Luce
M'Clew William, Glenluce
M'Gill John, Glenluce
M'Neilie John, New Luce
Murray James, New Luce
Wallace William & John, Glenluce

WRIGHTS.
See Cartwrights.

MISCELLANEOUS,
At GLENLUCE.

Dinwiddy Samuel, nail maker
Fisher Thomas, police officer
Gowdie George, cooper
King John, veterinary surgeon
M'Clelland James, chandler & tea dealer

M'Dowall James, baker
M'Micking James, auctioneer
Saunders Elizabeth, stamp office
Stroyan William, flesher
Thompson Thomas, inland revenue officer
Wales Andrew, manufacturer and dyer
Walls Henry, travelling draper

PLACES OF WORSHIP
AND THEIR MINISTERS.

ESTABLISHED CHURCH——Rev. John M'Dowall.
ESTABLISHED CHURCH, New Luce—Rev William M'Kergo.
FREE CHURCH—Rev. George Wilson.
UNITED PRESBYTERIAN CHAPEL——Rev. James Pullar.
UNITED PRESBYTERIAN CHAPEL——New Luce

COACHES,

To DUMFRIES, the Royal Mail (from Portpatrick) calls at the King's Arms morning at four; goes through Newton Stewart
To PORTPATRICK, the Royal Mail (from Dumfries), calls at the King's Arms every evening at seven
To STRANRAER, the Union (from Wigtown) calls every alternate evening at a quarter before seven.
To WIGTOWN, the Union (from Stranraer) calls every alternate morning at half-past seven

CARRIERS.

To STRANRAER, Gilbert M'Mekin, from Glenluce, Tuesday, Thursday and Saturday, and John Waugh and Helen Wilson, from New Luce, Tuesday and Friday

---

KIRKMAIDEN, STONEYKIRK AND NEIGHBOURHOODS.

THE parish of KIRKMAIDEN occupies nearly the whole of the western limb or peninsula of Wigtonshire—projecting into the mouth of the Solway Frith, and tapering to a point that inclines to the east. This parish, which comprehends the most southerly district of all Scotland, is about ten miles in length and from two to four and a half in breadth; it still has a wild appearance, but produces good crops of corn and potatoes, and feeds numbers of black cattle. The coast is generally bold, and indented by caves scooped out by the endless operations of the sea, and particularly by its furious lashings against the opposing barrier in stormy weather; on both sides of the peninsula, however, there are several good anchoring grounds. At PORTNISSOCK is an excellent harbour, constructed at the expense of the late Andrew M'Douall, Esq., then proprietor, who used every exertion in his power to improve this locality. There is also a tolerable harbour at DROMORE; here the coast-guard have a station, under the command of a lieutenant of the royal navy. The church, a plain edifice, is situate near the centre of the parish, not far from Dromore bay, at the distance of six miles from the Mull of Galloway, 35 from

Wigton, 36 from Newton-Stewart, 20 from Stranraer, and 16 from Portpatrick. On the estate of Colonel M'Douall, of Logan, is a fish pond well worthy of the inspection of visiters: it is hewn out of the solid rock, and has communication with the sea by means of an ingeniously contrived iron grating; some of the fish in this artificial reservoir have been rendered so tame that they will feed out of the hand.

The parish of STONEYKIRK (more properly Steven's Kirk) lies in the western peninsula of the county, to the north of Kirkmaiden, six miles from Stranraer and about the like distance from Portpatrick; on the east and south-east is the bay of Glenluce. The parish, which extends seven miles in length by from three to five in breadth, comprehends the three old parishes of Stoneykirk, Clachshant and Toskerton. The surface is generally hilly, moorish, and of a pastoral character; the low grounds are arable, and in some places planted. On the estate of Major Maitland, in this district, is an artificial mount, supposed to be of Roman origin, and used as a beacon in the time of war; there is likewise another, of a similar kind, on the estate of Sir John M'Taggart, of Ardwell House.

POST OFFICE, KIRKMAIDEN, Helen Brown, Post Mistress.—Letters from all parts arrive every afternoon at a quarter before one and are despatched at a quarter past nine in the morning.

GENTRY AND CLERGY.

Agnew Mr. Hugh, Drummontrae
Lamb Rev. John, Kirkmaiden
M'Douall Colonel James, Logan
M'Douall Mrs. Mary Ann, Logan
M'Taggart Sir John, M.P. Ardwell
Maitland Major Patrick, Balgriggan
Todd Mr. William, Drumore

SCHOOLS.

FREE CHURCH SCHOOL, Drumore —George Cowan, master
FREE CHURCH SCHOOL, Kirkmaiden —Archibald Kirkland, master
PAROCHIAL SCHOOL, Kirkmaiden— James Mackenzie, master
PAROCHIAL SCHOOL, Stoneykirk— James Crum, master
Thompson George, Port Logan

BLACKSMITHS.

Gibson Charles, Stoneykirk
Hills James, Port Logan
M'Cracken Alexander, Kirkmaiden
M'Millan Anthony, High Drumore
M'Millan John Curghie
M'Nellie James, Sandhead

BOOT & SHOE MAKERS.

Cochrane Samuel, Sandhead
Davis William. Drumore
M'Culloch James, Port Logan
M'Lean Robert, Port Logan
Maxwell William, Drumore
Nibloe Peter, Drumore

CARTWRIGHTS.

Gunion George, Drumore
Guuion William, Drumore
M'Gaw Peter (& joiner), Drumore

GROCERS.
Marked thus* are also Spirit Dealer

Cairnie John, Drumore
Cochrane Ann, Port Logan
Edgar William, Port Logan
Gibson Charles, Stoneykirk
*M'Chlery John, Drumore
*M'Gaw Alexander, Drumore
M'Nellie Alexander, Drumore
Rainey John, Drumore
Sproat Robert, Stoneykirk
Stewart Alexander, Sandhead
Taylor William (& corn merchant), Drumore

MILLERS.

Birkmyer Thomas, Ardwell Mill
Kelton Matthew, Logan Mill
Murray Alexander, Drumore

SURGEONS.
Agnew Hugh, Drumontrae
M'Bride George, Drumore
Sloan John Charles, Sandhead

TAILORS.
M'Vie Archibald, Drumore
Stevenson James, Drumore
Stevenson John, Drumore
Tellie Samuel, Sandhead

VINTNERS.
Annan James (Ship), Drumore
Chesney Jane, Stoneykirk
Corkran Wm. (New Inn), Port Logan
Hannay Mary, Drumore
M'Colm Samuel, Drumore
M'Gaw William, Drumore
Milwie Jane, Port Logan

Robb William, Port Logan
Stewart Hugh (Ship Inn), Sandhead

WRIGHTS.
See Cartwrights.

MISCELLANEOUS.
Agnew Peter, mason, Sandhead
Cameron David, chief officer of customs, Drumore
Chesn-y James, saddler, Stoneykirk
Hannay James, bookseller, Curghie
Higgin Mary, straw bonnet mar. Drumore
Kain William, saddler, Drumore
M'Bryde William, draper, Port Logan
M'Culloch David, factor to Col. M'Douall
M'Harry John, dyer, Sandhead
M Nellie Robert, baker, Drumore
Watson James, corn dealer, Drumore

PLACES OF WORSHIP,
AND THEIR MINISTERS.
ESTABLISHED CHURCH, Kirkmaiden—
Rev. William Williamson.
ESTABLISHED CHURCH Stoneykirk—
Rev. John Campbell.
FREE CHURCH, Kirkmaiden—Rev. John Lamb.
FREE CHURCH, Kirkmaiden——Rev. Robert M'Neel.

CARRIERS.
To STRANRAER, a Car (for passengers) from the New Inn, every Monday, Wednesday & Friday morning at eight, and Daniel M Clymont, from Kirkmaiden, and William Corkran and John Little, from Port Logan, Saturday

KIRKOWEN,

OR *Kirkcowan*, is a parish and village—the latter ten miles from Glenluce, eight from Wigton, and seven from Newton-Stewart; situated on the Tarf water, near its junction with the Bladenoch. Near the village is the extensive woollen manufactory of Messrs Milroy, which furnishes employment to many of the inhabitants. The church, which is a very neat edifice, was erected in 1830; its site, as well as the ground occupied by the churchyard, was munificently given by Captain W. C. Hamilton, of Craiglaw. The old church was dedicated to Saint Cowan, the original name of the parish. The surface of this district is various, consisting of moorland, interspersed with pieces of arable land. It extends from north to south fifteen miles, by a general breadth of about five; and it is well watered by the Tarf and Bladenoch streams.

POST OFFICE, David M'Gill, *Post Master.* Letters arrive (by foot post) from all parts every morning at ten, and are despatched at two in the afternoon.

GENTRY AND CLERGY.
Gilespie Mr. James, (surgeon), Kirkowen [Craiglaw
Hamilton Captain William Charles,
Milligan Mr. John, Tannilaggie
Milligan Mr. William, Kilhockadale
Smail Rev. Thomas, Kirkowen

SHOPKEEPERS & TRADERS.
Burdett Thomas, schoolmaster
Carlie James, grocer
Coulther William, flesher
Court William, draper
Court William, tailor
Davidson David, shoe maker
Faggin Thomas, tailor
Findlay John, mason
Kevan John, grocer, draper and spirit dealer

Hannah Alexander, miller, Spital
Hannah Andrew, miller
Hunter Thos. grocer & spirit dealer
Hutchinson Alexander, shoe maker
Hutchinson Hugh, draper
Parker Wm. joiner and cartwright
M'Dowall William, grocer
M'Gall William, weaver
M'Kechnie Eliz. straw bonnet maker
M'Kechnie James, baker
M'Lellan Thomas, shoe maker
M'William Alexander, joiner and cartwright
M'William George, vintner
M'William James, blacksmith
M'William John, blacksmith, joiner and cartwright

M'William William, blacksmith
Martin Martha, shoe maker
Milligan David, boot & shoe maker
Milligan Peter, tailor
Milligan Robert, vintner,
Milroy James, grocer
Milroy William & Thomas, woollen manufacturers
Sloane Agnes, dress maker
Telfour Agnes, vintner, (Half-way House.)

CARRIERS.
To NEWTON-STEWART. Mary and Margaret Nicholson, Monday & Friday

NEWTON-STEWART,
AND THE PARISH OF PENNINGHAM, WITH MINNIEGAFF AND NEIGHBOURHOODS.

NEWTON-STEWART is a thriving town and burgh of barony, 121 miles s.w. from Edinburgh, 82 s. from Glasgow, 52 w. from Dumfries, 26 w. from Stranraer, and 8 N. from Wigton; situated on the high road from Dumfries to Portpatrick, on the right bank of the river Cree, in the parish of Penningham, with a small portion on the opposite side of the stream in the parish of Minniegaff. It owes its origin to a younger branch of the Stewarts, Earls of Galloway, who possessed the estate of Castle Stewart, and founded the village upon it, to which he gave the name of Newton-Stewart. About the year 1778 the estate fell into the hands of William Douglas, Esq., when it was created a burgh of barony under the title of Newton Douglas; but it subsequently resumed its original name. Not much longer than sixty years since, the houses consisted of but one storey, and where covered with thatch; but the greater portion are now two stories in height, and slated. The town is principally composed of one long street, in the centre of which is the town house. The Cree is crossed by a very handsome bridge of five arches, connecting the larger division of the town with the lesser part on the other side of the river. The government of the town is vested in the hands of justices of the peace, who meet once a month. The cotton manufacture is carried on here, and in the neighbourhood, to a considerable extent, but it has been in a declining state for some years: the staple at present is wool furnished from the surrounding country, and mostly purchased for the Lancashire markets; among the other prominent branches may be mentioned the tanning of leather (for which there are two yards), and an extensive brewery.

The places of worship are a church of the establishment, and chapels for the reformed and united presbyterians and Roman catholics. The educational establishments comprise parochial and sabbath schools, the Douglas academy; industrial and infants' schools, and two or three private schools. Agricultural improvement has been carried on to a great and beneficial extent in this district. At the upper extremity of that part of the town in Minniegaff parish, there is a large moat hill, where David Graham, brother to Claverhouse, and superior of this district, used immediately before the revolution, to administer justice. About three miles to the north of the town are the remains of Castle Stewart, formerly belonging (as before stated) to a branch of the Galloway family. Cattle markets, which are well attended, are held on the first Friday in every month; and the annual fairs on the last Wednesdays of March, July and October, and on the first Wednesday after the 15th of June, (old style). The parish of PENNINGHAM (or *Penninghame*) extends along the right bank of the river Cree for about fifteen miles, by a breadth of from three to five; bounded by Wigton on the south and Kirkowen on the west. The greater part of the district is moorish and uncultivated, chiefly adapted to pasture. MINNIEGAFF is a large parish in the western part of the stewartry of Kirkcudbright; bounded on the west by the Cree, over which is a bridge (before noticed), forming the communication with the parish of Penningham and the town of Newton-Stewart. The parish is fourteen miles in length, and eight in breadth. In the lower parts the land is a good deal improved, especially towards the margin of the Cree, which stream being navigable for several miles up, has been of much benefit in an agricultural point of view; this river likewise produces excellent fish of different kinds, but the best and most abundant is the salmon. By far the greater portion of the parish is devoted to pasturage; it is covered by large flocks of sheep and numerous herds of black cattle. There are two places of worship —one each of the established and the free churches. Within a mile of Newton-Stewart, but in the parish of Minniegaff, is 'Heron-Kirouchtree,' the charming seat of Lady Heron Maxwell; beautifully situated on the side of a hill, surrounded by fine woods, and intersected by tasteful serpentine walks; access to the grounds and a grotto or hermitage is courteously granted by Lady Maxwell, whose general urbanity is ever so conspicuous to strangers. The grotto, of exceedingly romantic appearance, is curiously formed out of an old stone quarry, and is well worth inspection.

POST OFFICE, NEWTON-STEWART, Jessie M'Lean, *Post Mistress.*—Letters from WIGTOWN an WHITHORN, &c., arrive every morning at ten minutes past five and are despatched at half-past six in the evening.

Letters from PORTPATRICK,&c., arrive every morning at six and are despatched at the same hour in the evening.

Letters from GIRVAN, &c., arrive every afternoon at half-past four and are despatched at a quarter past one in the afternoon. Letters from DUMFRIES arrive every evening at twenty minutes before six and are despatched at six in the morning.

₊ *The names without address are in* NEWTON-STEWART.

NOBILITY, GENTRY AND CLERGY.

Blair Colonel Stopford, Penningham House
Campbell Mr. Geo.Newton-Stewart
Cowan Mrs. Jane, Culpee Cottage
Craik Mrs. Christian, Newton-Stewart
Douglas Miss Sarah, Cree bridge
Ewart Miss Agnes,Newton-Stewart
Galloway the Right Honble. the Earl of, Cumloden Cottage
Good Miss Ann, Newton-Stewart
Goold Rev. James, Newton-Stewart
Hamilton Captain W. Craighlaw
HannahMrs. Mary,Newton-Stewart
IrvingMrs. Margat.Newton-Stewart
Jamieson Mrs. J. Newton-Stewart
Kelly Mrs. Isabella, Cree bridge
Lees Mrs. Elizabeth, Glenluce row
Lees Mr. James, Newton-Stewart
M'Adam Mrs. Hannah, Newton-Stewart
M'Conchie John, Newton-Stewart
M'Cormack the Misses Mary and Eliza, Ivy bank
M'Dowall Mr. Samuel, Cree bridge
M'HaffieMr.Alexr.Newton-Stewart
M'Kenzie Mrs. Capt. Cree bridge
M'Kerlie Mrs. —, Corvisal House
Mackie John, Esq. Bargally
M'Laurin Mrs. Elizabeth, Newton-Stewart
M'Lean Miss Robina, Cree bridge
M'Millan Miss Helen, Newton-Stewart [ton-Stewart
M'Millan Mr. John, factor, New-
M'Way Thomas, Esq. Larg
Matthews Mr. John, Newton-Stewart [Kirouchtree
Maxwell the Lady Heron, of Heron
Patterson Mrs. Marion, Mill bank Cottage
Pollock Mr. Hume, NewtonStewart
PorterMiss ElizabethNewtonStewart
PorterMissIsabella,Newton Stewart
Raven Mrs. Grace, Corsby
Reid Rev. Wm, Presbyterian Manse
Richardson Rev. Samuel, Manse
Ryan Rev. Michael, Roman Catholic Church
Scamble Mr. George, New-ton-Stewart [art
Simpson Miss Mary,Newton-Stewart
Spark Miss Margaret, Newton-Stewart [House
Stewart Miss Dunlop, Corresel
Stewart Henry, Esq. Corsby West
Stewart James, Esq. Cairnsmore
Thomson C. W. Esq. Machermore
Walker Rev. John, Munniegaff
Wallace Mrs. Margaret, Newton-Stewart
Williams Capt. Richard, Cree bridge

ACADEMIES & SCHOOLS.

Aitkin Helen
DOUGLAS ACADEMY — William G. Cumming, rector; John Hepburn, English teacher
Gordon Fanny
INDUSTRIAL SCHOOL—Jane Rankine, mistress
INFANTS' SCHOOL — Isabella Henderson, mistress
PAROCHIAL SCHOOL,Newton-Stewart—John M'Callum, master
PAROCHIAL SCHOOL, Minniegaff—Archibald Scott, master

AGENTS.

Jordan John
Nicholson Peter

AUCTIONEERS.

Jamieson Adam
M'Chlery Charless

BAKERS.

Kelly Alexander
M'Kechnie James
Todd John

BANKERS.

BRITISH LINEN COMPANY'S BANK (Branch), Newton - Stewart — (draws on the parent bank, Edinburgh, andSmith,Payne&Smiths', London)—James Newall, agent
EDINGBURGH AND GLASGOW BANK (Branch—draws on the parent establishments, and Williams, Deacon & Co., and the Union Bank, London)—Peter Dargie, agent
NATIONAL BANK OF SCOTLAND —(Branch—draws on the parent establishment and its branches, and on Glyn, Hallifax & Co. London)—William Dill, agent

BLACKSMITHS.

Crossan Andrew, Cree bridge
Erskine Charles
Erskine John, Minniegaff
M'Cormick John
Thomson John
Thomson Nicholas

BOOKSELLERS & STATIONRS.

Kelley Bruce
Martin Margaret
Watson Agnes

BOOT & SHOE MAKERS.

Aitken John	M'CutcheonJohn
Barkley John	M'Whae John
Chesney Hugh	Minniegaff
Diamond James	Murray John
Girvan Thomas	Sillers David
Gray John	Simpson James
Hunter William	Stewart Thomas
M'Calauchlan	Thomson James
Nathaniel	Vernon James
M'Craken Leslie	Wilson Robert

BROKERS.

Benn James
Collins Daniel
Hughs James
M'Chlery Charles
Smith John

CABINET MAKERS AND UPHOLSTERERS.

Kennedy Gilbert
M'Gill Jane
M'Guffog William
Snodgrass Peter
Young Robert

COACH MAKER.

Bell John

DRESS AND STRAW BONNET MAKERS.

Brown Sarah	M'Kay Jane
Gourlay Margret.	M. Kie Sarah
Hannah, Jane &	M'Lachlan Eliza
Helen	Robb Sarah
Kirk Isabella	Robson Elizabth
Lockhart Elizabth	Wallace Mary &
M'Cornick Agnes	Jane

FIRE, &c OFFICE AGENTS.

CALEDONIAN, James Newall
COLONIAL (life), William Dill
ENGLISH AND SCOTTISH LAW (life), William Dill
GRESHAM (life), William Dill
SCOTTISH UNION (fire), Wm. Dill
STANDARD, Peter Dargie

FLESHERS.

Craig John	M'Conchie David
Findley Thomas	Vernon James
Kelley Andrew	Willoughby Chs.

GROCERS & SPIRIT DEALERS.

Adam Henry	M'Cutcheon Sarah.
Beck James	M'Dowall--,Min-
Carmont Grace	niegaff
Carson James	M'Dowall John,
ChesneyEbenzr	Cree bridge
Coid Charles	M'Ewen Walter
Douglas Edwd.	M'LagganCathrn
Galbraith Peter	Cree bridge
Galbraith Robt.	M'Lellan Alexr
Gibson Margrt.	Martin John
Gibson Michael	Martin Margaret
Good James	Murray Mary
HannahEsther	Reid John
Hunter Alexr.	Robinson Joseph
Kennedy John	Stewart Martha
M'Cartney Violet	Vernon James
M'Crea Peter	Wilson James

HARDWAREMEN & IRONMONGERS.

Gray Thomas (and ship owner), Newton-Stewart
Rowatt Thomas, Newton-Stewart

INNS.

(See also Vintners.)
Black Horse, Barbara M'Clement
Galloway Arms, John Munby
Grapes Hotel(commercial and posting house) William Thomson

966

JOINERS & CARTWRIGHTS.

Andrew James
Bell Alexander
Hannah Robert
M'Clellan Peter
M'Crea Peter
M'Kinnell John
Murray Nathan

LINEN & WOOLLEN DRAPERS

Armstrong Frncs | Hughes Peter
Craik William | M'Cubbins John
Ewart James | M'Deade Hugh

MANUFACTURERS.

Cumming William, Newton-Stewart
Hammond James, Cumloden Mill

MASONS.

Andrew James (& builder) Newton-Stewart
Litterick Alexndr, Newton-Stewart
M'Dowall David, Minniegaff
M'Dowall William, Minniegaff
Tait William, Cree bridge

MERCHANTS.

Glover J. & Co (and bacon curers),
M'Ewen Walter
M'Millan Peter & William

MILLERS.

Hannay Alexander, Minniegaff Mill
Hannay Robert, Newton Stewart

NURSERY & SEEDSMEN.

Mitchell John, Newton-Stewart
Webster Wm. Holme Park cottage

PAINTERS & GLAZIERS

Hinds John, Newton-Stewart
Robertson John, Cree bridge

PLUMBERS & TIN-SMITHS

Drynan Andrew, Newton-Stewart
Moffatt Joseph, Newton-Stewart

SADDLERS

Hannah John
Murray William
Rae David (and harness maker)

STATIONERS.

Kelley Bruce (and printer and bookbinder)
Watson Agnes (and druggist)

SURGEONS.

Erskine William
M'Knight Thomas
Smith Charles

TAILORS.

Adams James | M'Deade Hugh
Armstrong Francis | M'Gregor Wm
Broadfoot James | Patterson Jas.
Dickson James | Patterson John
Dowling William | Simpson John,
M'Claymont Hugh | Cree bridge
Tallas James

TANNERS

Campbell Archbld, Newton-Stewart
Sinclair George C. (and leather seller) Minniegaff

VINTNERS

Coid Charles | M'Clellan Peter
Cornack William | M'Clement —,
Douglas Edward | M'Connol John
Dowall John | M'Cullock Hugh
Dowall Samuel | M'Laggan Cathro
Minniegaff | Cree bridge
Erskine Janet, | M'Lellan James
Cree bridge | M'Whae John,
Galbraith Peter | Minniegaff
Glover Ebenezer | Milroy James
Hunter Alexander | Nelson John
Litterick Alexr. | Rennie James,
M'Bryde James | (Plough)
M'Caul Robert | Shennon Andrew
Thomson John

WATCH & CLOCK MAKERS

Gurlay James, Newton-Stewart
M'Lachlan Wm., Newton-Stewart

WOOL DEALER.

Porter Samuel, Minniegaff

WRITERS

Dill William (and notary) Newton-Stewart
Good William, Newton-Stewart
Martin David, Newton-Stewart

MISCELLANEOUS.

Adams James, precentor
Andrew James & Co. Minniegaff Saw Mill
Andrews Susan & Grace, stay makers
Auld James, nail maker
Brand Matthew, clogger
Crawford William, grain dealer
Cubbin James, plasterer
Cuthbertson William, skinner
Dargie Peter, distributer of stamps
Dunn Thomas, police officer, Cree bridge
Erskine James, gun maker

Geddies William, cooper
Gordon Margaret, tallow chandler
Harding John, precentor
Kirk John, pig dealer
M'Chlery John, dyer
M'Keand James, weaver
M'Kinnel Matthew, game & general dealer
M'Laurin Ludovick, brewer, maltster and soda water manufacturer
M'Millan James, manager of Lord Galloway's Saw Mill
Murphy Cornelius, town officer
Neilson Elizabeth, stay maker
Nelson John, builder
Robinson Thomas, fisherman

PLACES OF WORSHIP,

AND THEIR MINISTERS.

ESTABLISHED CHURCH, Minniegaff—Rev. Michael S. Johnstone.
FREE CHURCH, Minniegaff—Rev. John Walker.
UNITED PRESBYTERIAN CHAPEL—Rev. William Reid.
REFORMED PRESBYTERIAN CHAPEL,—Rev. James Gould.
ROMAN CATHOLIC CHAPEL——Rev. Michael Ryan, priest

COACHES.

Calling at the GALLOWAY ARMS.

To AYR, the *Hero* (from Wigtown) every alternate evening at seven
To DUMFRIES, the *Royal Mail* (from Portpatrick) every morning at six
To PORTPATRICK the *Royal Mail* (from Dumfries) every evening at twenty minutes before six
To WIGTOWN, the *Hero* (from Ayr every alternate morning at seven

CARRIERS.

To AYR, GLASGOW & EDINBURGH, William M'Lurg, Tuesday & Thursday
To GARLIESTON and WHITHORN, William M'Lurg, Monday, Thursday and Friday
To GATEHOUSE, James Thorburn, Monday and Thursday
To STRANRAER, Thomas Alexander, Tuesday and Friday, and Wm. M'Lurg, Tuesday
To WIGTOWN, William M'Lurg, Monday and Saturday, and Jas. Thorburn, once a fortnight to meet the Liverpool steamer

PORT WILLIAM AND MOCHRUM.

PORT WILLIAM is a prosperous village in the parish of Mochrum, 2½ miles s. E. from Stranraer, 15 s.s.E from Glenluce, and 11w. from Whithorn, situated in the bay of Glenluce. The harbour here, though small, is commodious and safe, and from it large quantities of grain and potatoes are exported for Liverpool and Lancaster. In the vicinity is Montrith, the handsome residence and demense of Sir William Maxwell, Bart., proprietor of the place and its founder. The mansion, which stands on the bank of a fine lake, commands an extensive prospect of the bay of Glenluce, the shores of Galloway, the Isle of Man, and the coast of Cumberland: near it is an old castle, surrounded by lofty trees; and contiguous are the remains of the old parish church,

now occupied as a place of sepulture by a family named M'Culloch, whose ancestors formerly possessed the estate, and which was wrested from them when power was law.

The parish of MOCHRUM is about ten miles in length, and extends inland between four and five miles. The Castle or 'Old Place' of Mochrum, surrounded by lakes, is a very ancient picturesque building, in an inland part of the parish; it was formerly the family seat of the Dunbars, Knights of Mochrum, but has for many years been the property of the Earl of Galloway. The village of Mochrum, which is about a mile and a half from Port William, contains nothing worthy of mention except the parish church and school.

POST OFFICE, PORT WILLIAM, James Ross, *Post Master.*—Letters from all parts arrive (from WIGTOWN) every morning at eight, and are despatched thereto at half-past three in the afternoon.

GENTRY AND CLERGY.

Cumming Mr. James, Arilour
Cumming Mr. Robert, Port William
Dunlop Rev. Mr.— Port William
M'Cormick Mr.— (surgeon) Port William
Maxwell Sir William Bart. Monteith
Young Rev. Alexander, the Manse, Mochrum

SCHOOLS.

Anderson John, Port William
Johnston James, Eldrick
PAROCHIAL SCHOOL, Mochrum—M'Farlane, master

VINTNERS

Ferguson Hugh, Mochrum
Gibson Peter, Port William
M'Conochie Robert, Mochrum
M'Culloch Alexander, Port William
M'Master John, (Noble Science Inn) Port William
Ross James, Port William
Wallace James, Port William

SHOPKEEPERS & TRADERS

Agnew William, shoe maker, Port William
Beggs James, grain dealer, Port William
Broadshaw David, blacksmith, Mochrum
Campbell Andrew, shoe maker,

Carr John, tailor, Eldrick [William
Clark J. P. grocer and draper, Port
Clay Alexander, joiner, Eldrick
Dalrymple Thomas, cartwright, Mochrum
Dickson Adam, miller, Port William
Douglas John, baker, Port William
Drysdale Thomas, cartwright Mochrum [rum
Ferguson Hugh, blacksmith, Mochrum
Galloway Peter, ship wright, Port William
Goodwin Samuel, tailor & clothier, Port William
Hannah John, grocer, Mochrum

SHOPKEEPERS, &c.—Continued.

Hartley James, grocer & spirit dealer, Eldrick
Hartley William, grocer, spirit dealer, and boot maker, Eldrick
Heron Thomas, grocer, Port William
Innis Peter, tide waiter, Port William
Lang William, blacksmith, Port William
Little J. blacksmith, Port William
M'Clure Alexander, joiner & spirit dealer, Eldrck [William
M'Credie William, cartwright, Port
M'Dowel Janet, baker & grocer, Port William
M'Farlane Thomas, mill wright & hardwareman, Port William

M'Guffie Jon. shoemaker, Mochrum
M'Master Robert, blacksmith, Port William [Eldrick
Manson William, blacksmith,
Milhinch Peter, tailor & draper, Port William [William
Mulroy James, blacksmith, Port
Nosh Hugh, flesher, Port William
Patterson John, tailor, Mochrum
Robb Thos. nail maker, Port William
Rontledge John, miller & bone dust grinder, Eldrick [William
Simm Robert, watch maker, Port
Simpson John, grocer, Mochrum
Skimming James, cartwright, Port William
Smith William, shoe maker, Eldrick

Templeton Alexander, saddler, Port William
Wallace James, joiner, Port William

COACH.

To STRANRAER, a Coach, from the Noble Science Inn, every Monday morning at half-past five (in time for the steamer to Ayr) and on Tuesday, Wednesday and Friday afternoons at three.

CARRIERS.

To STRANRAER, William M'Culloch, and Andrew M'Master, Monday, & H. Matthews, Tuesday
To WHITHORN, William M'Culloch, Wednesday
To WIGTOWN, Andrew M'Master, Saturday

PORTPATRICK

IS a parish and sea-port town—the latter 133 miles s.w. from Edinburgh, 89 s.s.w. from Glasgow, between 34 and 35 w. from Wigtown, the same distance w. by s. from Newton-Stewart, and rather more than 8 s. by w. from Stranraer: it is distant from Dublin 117 miles; from Belfast 36; and from Donaghadee 21. It is situated on the coast of the North Channel, and has long been the great thoroughfare from the north of Ireland, being the nearest point of Great Britain to that country, and the best place of crossing from one kingdom to the other. The town is small, but its position delightful—having a fine southern exposure, and surrounded on the other side by a ridge of small hills. It was formerly, with the estate of Dunskey, the property of Lord Mount-Alexander, whose residence was the old castle of Dunskey, which stands in the neighbourhood, on the brink of a tremendous precipice overhanging the sea, and was once a building of considerable strength, as appears from its interesting remains; the late Sir James Hunter Blair subsequently became possessed of the castle, and it is to the exertions of that gentleman that the town and harbour are indebted for many improvements. There is now one of the finest quays in Britain, and a reflecting light-house; in the construction of the quay the diving-bell has been most successfully employed. Of late years extensive and important improvements have been carried on at the harbour, under the auspices of government and direction of Sir John Rennie, for the accommodation of her Majesty's packets, and to ensure facilities for the embarkation of troops, at all times of the tide, for Ireland. These works will prove a great national convenience; while the establishment of steam-packets has secured a constant communication between this and the sister country. The commerce of the town and district has kept pace with the improvements as they progressed, and it is now a thriving little place. The chief imports are black cattle and horses from Ireland. The Gordon Hotel and the Commercial Inn, are upon a superior scale.

The places of worship are the parish church, and one for the free communion of Scotland; and the schools are one connected with each. The parish church is a remarkably neat edifice, with an embattled tower, and from its advantageous site is a conspicuous, as well as an ornamental object.

POST OFFICE, Alexander Niven, Post Master.—Letters from all parts arrive (from DUMFRIES) every evening at half-past eight, and are despatched thereto at half-past four in the morning.

GENTRY AND CLERGY.

Balmer Rev. Stephen
Boyer Captain Alexander
Gardner Captain
Gillespie Captain James
Hawes Commander Edward, R.N.
Murdock John, Esq. (factor to the late W. Blair), Dinven
Oke Lieut. William Walter, R.N.
Ross Captain Andrew
Urquhart Rev. Andrew

PROFESSIONAL PERSONS.

INCLUDING SCHOOLS.

Davidson Adam, civil engineer
Davidson Mrs. —, teacher
Elder William, master of the free school
Gibson Hugh, master of the parochial school
M'Clymont Elizabeth, teacher
M'William Andrew, civil engineer
Robertson Alfred, M.D. surgeon

INNS.

Commercial Inn, Mary M'Cleary
Cross Keys, Andrew Cumming

Crown, James Gillespie
Gordon Hotel, Jane Gordon

SHOPKEEPERS, TRADERS, &c.

Adair Jane, tea dealer
Adair Martha, grocer
Alexander John, carpenter
Anderson John, wool carder, Spittal Mill
Boyd John, grocer and spirit dealer
Campbell Robert, steward to steamer
Douglas Barbara, grocer and spirit dealer
Fernie William, tide surveyor
Hannah Alexander, overseer of the works [Mill
Hannay William, miller, Dinvin
Haselot Jacob, tailor
Hay David, flesher
Lyburn John, blacksmith
Lyburn Peter, blacksmith
M'Carlie John, tailor
M'Clymont James, stone mason
M'Crea Elizabeth, draper
M'Cubbin Andrew, grocer
M'Douall Andrew, blacksmith
M'Ewen Jane, shopkeeper

M'Mikine Ellen, spirit dealer
Manderson James, flesher
Milmine John, grocer and spirit dealer
Mills Robert, nail maker
Nelson John, spirit dealer
Nill William, grocer
O'Neill William, baker
Park William, tailor
Rankin John, tailor
Scott Margaret, grocer
Wallace James, keeper of the Northern lighthouse
Wallace John, carpenter
Wright William, baker

MAIL.

To DUMFRIES, the Royal Mail, from Gordon's Hotel, every morning at half-past one; goes through Stranraer, Newton Stewart, Glenluce, Gatehouse and Castle Douglas

CARRIER.

To STRANRAER, Wm. Johnston, daily

CONVEYANCE BY WATER

To DONAGHADEE, the Post Office Steam Packets every morning at five.

STRANRAER,

AND THE PARISHES OF INCH, KIRKCOLM, LESWALT, CAIRN RYAN & NEIGHBOURHOODS.

STRANRAER (or Stranrawer), is a thriving, respectable and ancient town, a royal burgh and the seat of a presbytery as well as a parish within its bounds; nearly ten miles N. from Glenluce and rather more than eight miles (by the toll-road) from Portpatrick; eligibly situated at the inner extremity of Loch Ryan. The principal street is of great length, but the houses have not been erected on the most regular plan. In the centre of the town stands a building, originally a castle, but now used as the police office; an edifice of considerable antiquity, but the date of its foundation has not been satisfactorily ascertained. It is mentioned in a charter granted by James VI, and and is called the 'tower, fortalice, and manor place of Chappel;' and was once the residence of the family of Kennedy of Chapel and Chrychan; in the year 1614 it was inhabited by John Kennedy, of Grennan, and Elizabeth his wife, then Lady Auchtriloor; the lands of Auchtriloor are immediately contiguous to the burgh of Stranraer, and now the property of the Earl of Stair. The town-hall, in George-street, is a neat structure; in it a justice of the peace court is held on the first Monday of every month, also a burgh court every Saturday, and the sheriff of the county frequently holds criminal courts with a jury, and also courts for the recovery of small debts. The new prison is a handsome and substantial erection possessing the requisite adaptation both for confinement and discipline. The academy is a large and commodious building, and measures are taking to provide for the necessary educational masters. As a royal burgh, the town is governed by a provost, a dean of guild, and fifteen councillors; and it joins with Whithorn, Wigtown and New Galloway in parliamentary representation.

The bay and harbour of Stranraer afford excellent anchorage; and the pier, which is of considerable length, and has been constructed within the last twenty-five years, has proved a great convenience to the shipping; the depth of water is such as to allow a fleet of men of war to ride at anchor here with perfect safety. The bay affords a plentiful supply of fine oysters, the right of fishing for which belongs exclusively (by ancient character) to General Sir Alexander Wallace, of Loch Ryan, who annually lets it. There are likewise several kinds of white fish caught abundantly; and occasionally some herrings are got, equal in quality to the finest obtained on any other part of the Scotch coast. There are two coast guard establishments here under the command of a captain of the Royal Navy; and a custom-house the jurisdictional duties of which includes all the creeks within the 'Rhyuns' as members. The exports of the place consist of shoes and leather—also grain, cheese and all kinds of farm produce, and cattle, which are now conveyed to Glasgow regularly twice every week by steam-vessels; to Belfast once a week, and to Liverpool occasionally. Among other branches of business usually found in a flourishing town, there are in Stranraer, tan-yards, two or three extensive nurseries in the neighbourhood, some nail manufactories, and three banking companies—branches of the British Linen Company, the Union Bank of Scotland and the Edinburgh and Glasgow Bank. The principal inns are the 'King's Arms,' the 'King's Hotel' and the 'George.' A news room, subscription libraries and various societies, literary, benevolent and religious are among the institutions, maintained by the denizens of Stranraer.

The new church, in church street, is a very handsome structure in the pointed style of architecture; the front lofty, and surmounted with pinnacles; the interior is capacious, with galleries and a commanding pulpit, and the whole as an aspect of chaste neat-ness. The second church connected with the establishment, is situated at the western extremity of the town on a lofty eminence, and with its tower, is a conspicuous landmark from the Loch. There are eight other places of worship for various denominations, inclusive of two free churches—a list of all these is given in the directory, with their localities and ministers.

Numerous seats adorned with all the charms of nature and art ornament the neighbourhood of Stranraer. Culhorn, now the residence of the Earl of Stair, is one mile and a half distant, and Castle Kennedy, four miles off, the property of the same nobleman, is surrounded by delightfully picturesque scenery. The following, situate in the vicinity of the burgh, are also worthy of notice:—Lochnaw Castle, the residence of Sir Andrew Agnew, Bart.; Corsewell House, J. Carrick Moore, Esq.; Loch Ryan House, Gen. Sir Alexander Wallace; Dunskey, General Thomas Hunter Blair; Balgreggan, Major Maitland; Logan, Colonel M'Dowall; Genoch, Mrs. M'Dowall; Calloch, David Ritchie, Esq.; Rephad, George Guthrie, Esq.: Laurel Bank, John Adair, Esq.; Belmont, Nathan Taylor, Esq., &c. The market is held on Friday. The following are the annual fairs: Tuesday before the first Wednesday of January, for horses; the third Friday of April, for cattle; the first Friday of May, cloth—and the third Friday, cattle; the Thursday before Midsummer, for horses—and Friday for cattle; and the third Fridays of July, August, September (and horse fair), October and November, are cattle markets.

The parish of INCH lies on the shore of Loch Ryan, extending nine miles in length by a breadth nearly as great. The parish church stands on the margin of a lake, in which there is a small beautifully wooded island. The lake is nearly divided by a neck of land, on which stands the ruins of a castle, formerly a seat of the Earls of Stair.

KIRKCOLM parish is bounded by Loch Ryan on the east, measuring a square of about five miles. The church is pleasantly situate near the shore of the lake, north of the bay called the Wig.

The parish of LESWALT lies betwixt the Irish channel on the west and Loch Ryan on the east; it is about the same size, and of much the same form, as Kirkcolm. The surface of this district is most agreeably varied with hill and dale; while from the sea the coast presents bold and rocky features.

CAIRN RYAN is a small group of houses on the eastern margin of Loch Ryan, six miles from Stranraer; the harbour affords safe anchorage for vessels which frequently take refuge here, and there is a lofty lighthouse for their guidance—General Sir Alexander Wallace has a residence here.

POST OFFICE, STRANRAER, Alexander Mann, *Post Master.*—Letters from EDINBURGH, GLASGOW and the NORTH, arrive every evening at twenty-five minutes before eight and are despatched at a quarter past one in the afternoon.

Letters from LONDON and the SOUTH, arrive (from DUMFRIES) every afternoon at a quarter past four, and are despatched at a quarter before five in the morning.

NOBILITY, GENTRY AND CLERGY.

Agnew Sir Andrew, Bart. Locknaw Castle
Aitken Mrs. Agnes. Charlotte st
Aiken Miss Helen, Hanover st
Baird Miss Jane, Princes st
Bathgate Rev. William, Stranraer
Bell Rev. Blizard, Leswalt
Black Mrs. Isabella, George st
Caldwell Mrs. Cathrne. Hanover st
Charles Rev. George Hanover st
Donald Rev. Robert, Stranraer
Emmerson Mrs. Eliz. Hanover st
Ferguson Rev. James, Inch
Ferguson Rev. Peter, Inch
Guilmette Mrs. Mary, George st
Guthrie George, Esq. (factor to the Earl of Stair), Rephad
Hall Rev. John, Cairn Ryan
Hannah Samuel, Esq. Elm House
Hannay Mrs. Mary, Hanover st
Howarth Rev. Robert, Hanover st
Hyslop Rev. Robert, Kirkcolm
Kay Mr. John, Hanover st
Kerr Mr. Charles, Church st
Kerr Miss Helen, King st
Kirkmichael Mr. John, Hanover st

Lister Mrs. —, King st
M'Bryde Miss Rosanna, Hanover st
M'Cubbin Rev. Andrew, Leswalt
M'Creuie Mr. James, Hanover st
M'Cririe Rev. Archbld. Cairn Ryan
M'Culloch James, Esq. Belleviila
M'Douall Mrs. Helen, Church st
M'Douall Mrs. James, Church st
M'Douall Mrs. Jane, Hanover st
M'Dowall Rev. Andrew, Kirkcolm
M'Gregor Rev. John, George st
M'Kie Mrs. Agnes, Hanover st
M'Kie Mrs. Helen, Hanover st
M'Nae Mrs. Hannay, Ivy House, Hanover st
Millar Mr. James, Hanover st
Moore Rev. —, Stranraer
Morland Miss —, King st
Morrison Mrs. Elizabeth, King st
Perryman Mrs. —, Church st
Ritchie Dav. Esq. (of Arries) Challoch
Robertson Mrs. Wingate, Hanover st
Ross the Misses Euphemia & Annie, Church st [West Castle
Ross Captain Sir John, R.N. North
Ross Mrs. Margaret, George st
Simpson Rev. William, Church st
Smeilie Rev. William, Hanover st

Stair Rt. Hon. the Earl of, Culhorn
Stewart James, Esq. Church st
Stewart Rev. James, Shuchan
Taylor Nathan, Esq. Belmont House
Taylor Mrs. Thomas, Church st
Torrence Mrs. —, Church st
Vans Miss —, Park House [House
Wallace Gen. Sir Alex. Lochryan st
Wallace Mrs. Jean Taylor, Hanover
Watt Rev. Robert John, High st
Watt Mrs. William, King st

ACADEMIES AND SCHOOLS.

ACADEMY, Stranraer—Wm. M'Neil, master
FREE CHURCH SCHOOL, Cairn Ryan—Richard Pearson, master
FREE CHURCH SCHOOL, Leswalt—John Adam, master
FREE CHURCH SCHOOL, Stranraer—James Wylie, master
M'Clymont Miss —, King st
M'Meikan Isabella, Queen st
PAROCHIAL SCHOOL, Cairn Ryan—Robert Lupton, master
PAROCHIAL SCHOOL, Kirkcolm—James Wallace, master
PAROCHIAL SCHOOL, Leswalt—William Main, master

AUCTIONEERS.
Douglas John, Hanover st
M'Culloch David, Broadstone

BAKERS.
Brown James, Hanover st
Gartly Simon, Queen st
Johnston David, George st
M'Clelland Alexander, King st
M'Cracken Alexander, Church st
M'Evoy William, Church st
M'Kie William, George st
M'William Peter, King st
Shaw James, Castle st

BANKERS.
BRITISH LINEN COMPANY (Branch)
Princes st—(draw on Smith, Payne
and Smiths', London) — Charles
Kerr and Thomas M'Caig, agents
EDINBURGH AND GLASGOW BANK
(Branch), George st—(draws on
Williams, Deacon & Co. and the
Union Bank, London) — John
Kerr, Esq. agent
UNION BANK OF SCOTLAND (Branch)
Church st—(draws on the head
offices in Edinburgh & Glasgow;
Glyn, Hallifax & Co., and Jones,
Loyd & Co. London)—Alexander
M'Douall, Esq. agent

BLACKSMITHS.
Doag John, Castle st
Jones James, Leswalt
M'Douall William, Harbour st
M'William John, Bridge st
Millar Robert, Bridge st
Watson Alexander, Cairn Ryan

BOOKSELLERS & STATIONERS
Marked thus * are also Printers.
*Dick Robert, Church st
M'Cuid James, Church st
Robertson Jane, George st
*Walker Peter, George st

BOOT AND SHOE MAKERS
Beattie Robert, George st
Bisset Robert, George st
Black James, Stoneykirk road
Campbell William, Castle st
Cummin William, Kirkcolm
Galbraith William, George st
Gribbin Michael, Cairn Ryan
Hutcheson James, Hanover st
Kennedy Henry James, George st
M'Caull John, Castle st
M'Intyre Andrew, High st
M'Kie Peter, Leswalt
Reid James, Fisher st
Stewart Robert, Hanover st
Young Alexander, Charlotte st

CABINET MAKERS.
M'Douall John, George st
Nibloe Elizabeth, Bridge st
Thorburn Alexander, Charlotte st

CARPENTERS AND JOINERS.
Adair Jas. (& builder), Charlotte st
M'Cune William, Stoneykirk road
M'Meikan Robert, Leswalt
Taylor Samuel, Hanover st

CARTWRIGHTS.
Douglas James (and coach builder),
Shuchan Mill
Douglas John, Sun st

CHEMISTS & DRUGGISTS.
Fleming James, George st
M'Gregor Robert, George st

CHINA, GLASS & EARTHEN-
WARE DEALERS.
Boyle Agnes, Fisher st
Kaily Philip, George st
M'Meikam Archibald, George st

COOPERS.
Knox Peter, Fisher st
Torrance Robert, Fisher st

CORN MERCHANTS.
Gibson William, Hanover st
SHUCHAN MILL COMPANY, Shuchan
Mill

CURRIERS.
M'Clymont Alexander, King st
M'Master Anthony, North Strand st

FARINA MANUFACTURERS.
Rankin Alexander, Stoneykirk road
SHUCHAN MILL COMPANY (& flour),
Shuchan Mill—James M'Ewing,
manager

FIRE &c OFFICE AGENTS.
AGRICULTURAL (cattle), Murdoch
Jeffray, Church st
HERCULES (fire), Chas. Kerr. Lewis st
MERCANTILE (life), R. Kirkpatrick,
George st
LONDON, William Black, George st
MUTUAL (life), John M'William,
George st
NORTH BRITISH (life), David Guth-
rie, Church st
NORTH OF SCOTLAND, William
Stewart, Neptune st
NORTH AND SOUTH OF SCOTLAND,
Murdoch Jeffray, Church st
SCOTTISH UNION, David M'Clean,
Church st   [Church st
STANDARD (life), Murdoch Jeffray,

FLESHERS.
Barber Joseph Mason, George st
Boyle James, George st
Boyle James, Hanover st
Dounan George, George st
King John, George st
M'Harg Andrew, Castle st
M'Harg Robert, Queen st
M'Meikan James, Church st

GROCERS & SPIRIT DEALERS.
(See also Shopkeepers, &c.)
Allison James, St. John st
Armstrong Robert, George st
Bell James, Queen st
Bell Thomas, Neptune st
Biggam Barbara, George st
Byers James, George st
Cairns James, Cairn Ryan
Cluckie Andrew, George st
Cowan Thomas, Hanover st
Cummin John, Kirkcolm
Davidson Samuel, Hanover st
Drynan James, George st
Edgar Thomas, Hanover st
Espie Jean, George st
Ewing James, Hanover st
Fleming Margaret, High st
Galbraith Thomas, South Strand st
Grove William, George st
Hannah Elizabeth, North Strand st
Hunter Mary, St. John st
Kerr Samuel, George st
M'Credie Moses, Church st
M'Culloch Hugh (and seedsman),
George st
M'Gill John, Cairn Ryan
M'Keand Michael, Queen st
M'Kinzie Agnes, Fisher st
M'Meikan Archibald, George st
M'Michan Hugh, Queen st
M'Queen James, Hanover st
Milne James, George st
Murdoch William, Castle st
Paterson Alexander, George st
Robertson John, Charlotte st
Sinclair Alexander, Church st
Stewart James (& carriage owner
for hire), St. John st
Taylor Niven, Hanover st
Taylor William, Fisher st
Thomson William, George st
Wither John, Hanover st

HAIR DRESSERS.
Blair Millar, Princes st
Mason Joseph, George st

HARDWAREMEN AND IRON-
MONGERS.
Irving Andrew, George st
Kerr Charles, Hanover st
M'Clean Hugh, George st
M'Culloch Alexander, Castle st
M'Dowall Jane, Castle st
iller John, George st

INNS.
(See also Vintners).
Albion Hotel, William Thomson,
George st   [nover st
Buck's Head, John Maclure, Ha-
George Hotel, Jas. Byres, George st
King's Arms, Andrew M'Robert,
Castle st   [st
King's Hotel, George King, George
Stair Arms, Stair Adair, Church st

LIBRARIES
Dick Robt. (circulating), Charlotte st
NEWS ROOM, Queen st—Samuel
Gordon, secretary
STRANRAER LIBRARY, George st—
Jane Robertson, librarian
THEOLOGICAL LIBRARY, George st
—Jane Robertson, librarian
Walker Peter (circulating), George st

LINEN & WOOLLEN DRAPERS.
Auld Margaret, King st
Cavan Thomas, George st
Douglas Alexander, George st
Gordon Samuel, George st
Hutchison William, Queen st
Kirkpatrick Robert (and silk mer-
cer, and merchant), George st
M'Douall James, George st
Malcolm David, George st
Todd George & Edward, George st
Wither John, Hanover st

MESSENGERS.
M'Lean David, Church st
M'Neel Caird Alexander, Church st
M'William John, George st

MILLINERS & DRESS MAKERS
Brown Charlotte, Sun st
Lindsey Helen, Hanover st
M'Gill Marian, Church st
M'Master Grace, Princes st
M'Master Jessie, Hanover st
Ritchie H. M. H. & D. Princes st
Sproule Mary, Church st
Thomson Mary, High st
Watt Elizabeth, George st

NURSERY AND SEEDSMEN.
M'Arther Angus (and market gar-
dener), Rosenfield Cottage
Robinson Samuel, Castle st

PAINTERS.
Brown Thomas, Castle st
Inglis Alexander, Castle st
Lynas Andew, Hanover st
Snodgrass James (and paper-hanger
Church street
Thorburn Peter, Castle st

SADDLERS AND HARNESS
MAKERS.
Crawford John, George st
Kennedy John, Hanover st
M'Cleary Robert, Bridge st
M'Gowan William, Charlotte st
M'Kie Alexander, Hanover st

SHOPKEEPERS & DEALERS
IN SUNDRIES.
(See also Grocers & Spirit Dealers.)
Adair James, Hanover st
Davidson William, High st
Harris Peter, High st
M'Caig Agnes, Cairn Ryan
M'Caul John, Castle st
M'Kittock Mary, High st
Wemys Margaret, High st

STONE MASONS.
Cairns David, George st
M'Cracken John, Stranraer
M'Dowall Hugh, Church st
Ross William, Cairn Ryan
Wallace Edward, Kirkcolm

SURGEONS & APOTHECARIES
Bogan Robert Hughes, George st
Orgill John, George st
Wilson Robert, George st

TAILORS.
Carlie Thomas, St. John st
Fernon Hugh, High st
Henney Edward, High st
Logan Archibald, Stoneykirk road
M'Bryde Peter, St. John st

Marshall John, Princes st
Murray George, Stranraer
Roney William, George st
Savage William, North Strand st
Sproat Thomas, South Strand st
Thompson James, Hanover st
Thorburn Robert, South Strand st

TALLOW CHANDLERS.
Cameron Jane, Castle st
Thompson James, Bridge st

TIMBER MERCHANTS.
Adair & Thorburn, Charlotte st
Irving Andrew, George st

TIN-PLATE WORKERS.
Alison Sarah, Charlotte st
Christie Alexander, George st
Kerr Francis (and copper-smith), Castle street

VINTNERS.
Bark Andrew, Stoneykirk road
Biggam John, Bridge st
Brown Alexander, George st
Douglas Alexander (Cross Keys), Hanover street
Findlay Hugh (and owner of horses for hire), Queen st   [High st
Fleming Grace (Loch Ryan Tavern),
Gordon John (Cross Keys), Cairn Ryan
Hannah Margaret, George st
Hughes Lawrence, Hanover st
Hunter Mary (Crown), St. John st
Huston George, Hanover st
Kennedy David, Charlotte st
Kerr Alexander (Crown), King st
M'Culloch James, Pier
M'Garva Alexander, Neptune st
M'Gaw Alexander, King st
M'Master Grace, North Strand st
M'Whinnie Marian, Fisher st
M'Whirter Robert, Cairn Ryan
M'William Alexander, Kirkcolm
Millar Chas (Railway Inn), George st
Millar Robert, Bridge st
Murphie Wm. (Crown), St. John st
Simpson William, North Strand st
Stewart Robert Sun st
Stewart William (Eagle), Neptune st
Taylor Alexander (Bay Horse), Hanover st

WATCH & CLOCK MAKERS.
Garrick Fergus (and jeweller), Charlotte street
Kay John, George st
M'Credie Thomas, George st

WRIGHTS.
See Carpenters and Joiners; and also Cartwrights.

WRITERS AND NOTARIES.
Adair John (and factor to R. V. Agnew, Esq.), North Strand st
Black William (and town clerk), George street
Caird Alexander M'Neel (and procurator fiscal), Church st
Guthrie David, Church st
Ingram William Forbes, Castle st
Jeffray Murdoch (and justice of the peace clerk), Church st
M'Clean David, Church st
M'William John, George st

MISCELLANEOUS.
Bruce William, iron and coal merchant, Neptune st
Campbell John, brewer. North Strand st
Christie Alexander, inspector of weights and measures, 1 George st
COAST GUARD STATION, Cairn Ryan—John Campbell, chief officer
Dalrymple Thomas, tanner. Hanover sq
Eaglesome John, veterinary surgeon North Strand st
Finlay Agnes, coffee house, Queen st
GAS WORKS Harbour st—Robert Morland, manager   [st
Gourlay Elizabeth, nail mkr. North Strand
Haswell John D. captain of the Albion steamer, Queen st   [George st
Irving Elizabeth, toy dealer & fruiterer,
Kelly Robert George, artist, George st
LIGHT HOUSE, Cairn Ryan—Thomas Dawson, keeper
Lynass John, pawnbroker, George st
M'Candlish Grace, dyer, Mill st
M'Lean Robert, umbrella makr. Bridge st
Nochar John, clothes dealer, High st
POLICE OFFICE, George st—William Ross, superintendent
Ross Mary, stay maker, St. John st
STAMP OFFICE, George st—David Guthrie, distributer
STEAM PACKET OFFICE, Queen st—Abram Campbell, agent
Taylor William, harbour master, Fisher st
Wallace David & Co. wine and spirit merchants, Charlotte st
Wright Brice, plumber, Charlotte st

PLACES OF WORSHIP,
AND THEIR MINISTERS.
ESTABLISHED CHURCHES:—
Church st—Rev. William Simpson.
Stranraer—Rev. James Stewart.
Cairn Ryan—Rev. John Hall.
Inch—Rev. James Ferguson.
Kirkcolm—Rev. Robert Hyslop.
Leswalt—Rev. Andrew M'Cubbin.
FREE CHURCHES:—
Church st—Rev. George Charles.
Stranraer—Rev. Robert Donald.
Cairn Ryan—Rev. Archibald M'Cririe.
Inch—Rev. Peter Ferguson.
Kirkcolm—Rev. Andrew M'Dowall.
Leswalt - Rev. Blizard Bell.

UNITED PRESBYTERIAN CHAPEL, Hanover st—Rev. Robert Hogarth.
UNITED PRESBYTERIAN CHAPEL, Chapel st—Rev. William Smellie.
UNITED PRESBYTERIAN CHAPEL, Bridge st—Rev. John M'Grigor.   [Stranraer.
REFORMED PRESBYTERIAN CHAPEL, ORIGINAL SECESSION, Stranraer—Rev. Robert John Watts.   [Bath ate.
MORRISONIAN, Stranraer—Rev. William
ROMAN CATHOLIC CHAPEL, Stranraer:—Rev. — Moore, priest.

CUSTOM HOUSE,
PRINCES-STREET.
Collector—Alexander M'Neel, Esq.
Comptroller—Mr. John Semple.
Coast Waiter at Portpatrick—William Fernie.   [ron
Coast Waiter at Drumore—David Came-

NEW PRISON,
CHURCH STREET.
Keeper—James Moorhead.
Matron—Elizabeth Moorhead.
Chaplain—Rev. Robert Simpson.
Surgeon—Robert Wilson.

MAILS, &c.
To DUMFRIES, the *Royal Mail* (from Portpatrick) calls at the King's Hotel, every morning at three ; goes through Glenluce, Newton Stewart, Gatehouse and Castle Douglas
To PORTPATRICK, the *Royal Mai* (from Dumfries) calls at the King's Hotel, every night at half-past eight
To STONEYKIRK & KIRKMAIDEN, a *Car*, from the George, every Monday, Wed. and Friday afternoon at three

CARRIERS.
To GIRVAN; Hugh Clark, from the Stairs Arms, once a fortnight
To GLENLUCE, Gilbert M'Meikan, from the George, Wednesday & Saturday
To KIRKMAIDEN, William Corkran, and Daniel M'Clyment, from the George Hotel. Saturday
To NEWTON STEWART James Cluad from the Stairs Arms, Saturday
To PORT WILLIAM, Wm. M'Culloch, from the King's Arms, Tuesday
To PORT PATRICK, William Johnson, from Alexander Brown's, George st, Tuesday, Thursday and Saturday
To WIGTON, William Simpson, from Alexander Brown's, George st, Tuesday and Saturday

CONVEYANCE BY WATER.
STEAM PACKETS.
To GLASGOW, AYR, GIRVAN and CAMPBELTOWN & BELFAST, the *Albion*, Captain Haswell; the *Briton*, Captain Cumming; and the *Scotia*, Captain Hogarth, from Stranraer pier, three days a week during Summer
To GLASGOW, GREENOCK and GIRVAN, the *Ayrshire Lass*, two or three times a week

---

WHITHORN,
WITH THE ISLE OF WHITHORN, AND THE PARISH OF GLASSERTON.

WHITHORN (or *Whithern*) is a town of considerable antiquity and a royal burgh, in the parish of Whithorn, 40 miles E. by S. from Portpatrick, 32 s. from Stranraer, 21 s. from Newton-Stewart, and nearly 13 s. from Wigton ; situated not far distant from the shore of Wigton bay. It was originally inhabited by a tribe of Britons called the *Novantes*, and was then a town of some consequence : it is mentioned by Ptolemy under the name of *Leucophibia*; the Saxons called it *Hwitaern*, and from the latter the appellation *Whithern* is derived. St. Ninian built a church here in the fourth century, which Bede mentions as the first that was erected of stone. During the eighth century it was the seat of the bishops of *Candida Casa*, and it formed the episcopal capital of a bishopric of Galloway in the twelfth century. After the period of the reformation, however, it is seldom mentioned in public transactions, and seems to have sunk into obscurity. The town consists chiefly of one street, running from north to south, with diverging alleys ; nearly in the centre it is intersected by a small stream, which is crossed by a bridge.

From successive kings Whithorn received various charters constituting it a burgh of barony; it is now a royal burgh, but the period when it attained that distinction does not appear. It is governed by a provost two baillies, and fifteen councillors ; and joins with Stranraer, and other burghs herein before-mentioned, in returning one member to parliament. The trade of Whithorn is very inconsiderable, and that which it does enjoy is merely of a retail and domestic character; independent of this, however, there are two banking establishments, and four insurance agencies. The places of worship are the parish church, a free church and one each for united and reformed presbyterians and seceders. The parish church is remarkably neat as well as spacious, and much superior to most of the parish kirks in this county; it is erected partly on the venerable ruins of the priory, founded by Saint Ninian before-mentioned, and who is said to have been the first who converted the Picts to the Christian faith. These ruins are remarkably grand and imposing; they contain several large vaults, a beautiful Saxon, and some Gothic arches, also sculptured royal armorial bearings of Scotland, and the dilapidated arms of the bishops of Galloway. The inhabitants support a subscription library, and a bible society, and parochial and infants' schools are the other institutions of the town. A cattle market is held on the second Thursday in each month from April to December, and an annual fair on the 7th of July.

The ISLE OF WHITHORN is a pleasant village, about three miles from Whithorn, of which it is the port. Near the village stand the remains of an old church, said to be the first built in this part of the kingdom, or, as some affirm, the first founded in Scotland, and its preservation is desirable from its venerable age and interesting origin.

The parish of GLASSERTON lies on the east coast of Luce Bay, bounded by Whithorn on the east, Mochrum on the west, and Kirkinner on the north; it extends

seven miles and a half in length by a general breadth of two and a half, except in its northern part, where it is nearly double that space. On the coast near its north-western confines is Lae Point, with a small haven on the north, called Monreith Bay; a village at its head is termed the Milltown of Monreith. The church stands in the southern quarter of the parish.

POST OFFICE, WHITHORN, Alexander MacCulloch, *Post Master.*—Letters from all parts arrive (from WIGTON) every night at ten, and are despatched thereto at half-past one the morning.

GENTRY AND CLERGY.
Anderson Rev. Frederick, Whithorn
Broadfoot Robert. Esq. Fine view
Fleming Rev. James, Whithorn
Gibson Rev. James, Whithorn
Gourley Mrs. Grace, Whithorn
Lawrie Mr. Robert, Whithorn
Lawson Mr. James, Whithorn
Macindoe Rev. Thomas, Whithorn
Maxwell Misses —, Physgill
M'Cullach Mr. James, Isle Whithorn
Nicholson Rev. Christopher, the Manse, Whithorn
Sloan Miss Elizabeth, Whithorn
Stewart Rev. Archiould, the Manse, Glasserton
Stewart Mr. Hugh, Whithorn
Stewart Mrs. Janet, Whithorn
Stewart Mrs. Peter, Whithorn
Stewart Stair Hawthorn, Esq. Glasserton House
Thomson Mrs. Jane, Whithorn

ACADEMIES AND SCHOOLS·
Hannah Grace, Whithorn
INFANTS'SCHOOL, Whithorn—Ellen Stark, mistress
PAROCHIAL SCHOOL, Isle Whithorn —Isaac M'Connell, master
PAROCHIAL SCHOOL, Whithorn— Robert Conning, master
PAROCHIAL SCHOOL, Glasserton— J. Gifford, master
Patterson James, Isle Whithorn

AUCTIONEERS.
Dalrymp'e Alexander (and appraiser), Whithorn
Hawthorn Douglas M. Whithorn

BAKERS.
M'Crea John, Whithorn
Martin Alexander, Whithorn
Stevenson John, Whithorn
Wood Francis, Isle Whithorn

BANKS.
EDINBURGH AND GLASGOW BANK (Branch), Whithorn—(draws on the head offices Edinburgh and Glasgow; on Williams, Deacon and Co. and Union Bank, London)—John Broadfoot, agent
NATIONAL BANK OF SCOTLAND (Branch), Whithorn—(draws on the head office. Edinburgh; Glyn, Hallifax and Co. and the Union Bank, London)—George C. Dinwoodie, agent

BLACKSMITHS
Campbell William, Isle Whithorn
Cholm James, Whithorn
Keand Robert, Whithorn
M'Credie David, Whithorn
M'Guffie James, Whithorn
Peacock John, Whithorn
Ross David, Isle Whithorn

BOOT AND SHOE MAKERS.
Black John, Isle Whithorn
Blaind John, Whithorn
Hannah George, Whithorn
M'Clure David, Isle Whithorn
M'Clure James, Isle Whithorn
M'Clure John, Isle Whithorn
M'Ewen Peter, Whithorn
M'Kinnel John, Whithorn
Wright David, Whithorn

CARTWRIGHTS.
M'Credie Hugh, Whithorn
Millar John, Whithorn
Wylie Robert, Whithorn

FIRE, &c. OFFICE AGENTS
ABERDEEN, Robert H. Smith, Whithorn
ASSOCIATION OF SCOTLAND (life), Alexander M'Culloch, Whithorn
CALEDONIAN, Geo. E. Main, Whithorn
NORTHERN (fire; Ronald Macdonald, Whithorn   [Whithorn
NORTHERN (life), George E. Main, Whithorn

GROCERS & TEA DEALERS.
Marked thus * are also Spirit Dealers.
Bell Jael, Whithorn
Byron Agnes, Whithorn
Carter William, Whithorn
Chesney John, Whithorn
Chesney William, Whithorn
Clokie John, Whithorn
Crawford James, Whithorn
Dickson Elizabeth, Isle Whithorn
*Dougan David, Whithorn
Douglas George, Whithorn
Drysdale George, Whithorn
Gibb Wm. (& perfumer), Whithorn
Gordon Isabella, Whithorn
Hannah James, Whithorn
*Logan Charlotte, Isle Whithorn
M'Clelland Elizabeth, Isle Whithorn
M'Coid Helen, Whithorn
M'Credie Margaret, Isle Whithorn
M'Kelvie John, Whithorn
Mickan Peter, Isle Whithorn
Muir James, Whithorn
Reid Jane, Isle Whithorn
Walker Andrew, Whithorn

INN-KEEPERS & VINTNERS.
Broadfoot Thomas, Isle Whithorn
Chesney Charlotte, Whithorn
Conning Carolina (Red Lion), Whithorn
Dempster Robert (Grapes, and posting-house), Whithorn
Dinnel Alexander, Whithorn
Gibb Joseph, Whithorn
Kerr Montgomery, Isle Whithorn
Logan Charlotte, Isle Whithorn
M'Queen Mary (Commercial), Whithorn
M'William Jane, Isle Whithorn
Snodden Matthew (Plough), Whithorn   [horn
Wallace Ann (King's Head), Whit-

IRONMONGERS·
Carter William, Whithorn
Drysdale George, Whithorn

JOINERS AND WRIGHTS.
Chesney John, Whithorn
Jardine David, Whithorn
M'Adam William, Whithorn
M'Keand William, Whithorn
M'William William (and shipwright) Isle Whithorn
Millar George, Whithorn

LINEN & WOOLLEN DRAPERS
Fenwick John, Whithorn
Hawthorn Charles, Whithorn
Macdonald Ronald, Whithorn
M'Kelvie William, Whithorn
Simpson Thomas, Whithorn
Simpson William, Whithorn

MASONS.
Broadfoot James, Whithorn
Clokie John, Whithorn
Irving William, Whithorn
M'Clelland Alexander, Whithorn

MILLINERS & DRESS MAKERS
Broadfoot Grace, Whithorn
Hawthorn Grace & Agnes, Whithorn

M'Kelvie Agnes (and bonnet maker) Whithorn
Mackie Margaret, Whithorn
Sloan Grace, Whithorn   [horn
Stevenson Jane & Margaret, Whit-

PAINTERS.
Allen Alexander, Whithorn
Miller George, Whithorn
Thomson John, Whithorn

SURGEONS.
Broadfoot Robert, Whithorn
M'Millen James, M.D. Whithorn
White Dunbar. M.D. Whithorn

TAILORS.
Bell Samuel, Isle Whithorn
Cannon Robert, Whithorn
Kelly John, Whithorn
M'Clelland David, Whithorn
Morrison Anthony, Whithorn
Simpson James, Whithorn
Simpson Thomas, Whithorn
Simpson William, Whithorn
Smith George, Whithorn

TALLOW CHANDLERS.
Lawrie Peter, Whithorn
M'Dowie William, Whithorn

WATCH MAKERS.
Gardiner Samuel, Whithorn
Gibb Joseph, Whithorn

WRIGHTS.
See Joiners and Wrights.

WRITERS.
Jorie John (and town clerk), Whithorn
Smith Robert H. Whithorn

MISCELLANEOUS.
In WHITHORN *when the address is not stated.*
Christie James, cabinet maker and upholsterer
Clark James, seedsman   [horn
Crichton John, master mariner, Isle Whit-
Cumming Peter, master mariner & cattle dealer, Isle Whithorn
Dickie Adam, tin-plate worker
Drape John, saddler
Dunse Alexander, cooper
Findley John, flesher
Gordon James, veterinary surgeon
Hannah James, flesher
Heron John, master mariner [Whithorn
Livingston Archibald, coast waiter, Isle
M'Coid John, slater
M'Credie William, miller, Isle Whithorn
M'Culloch Alexander, wine & spirit mercht
M'Dowel Isabella, meal dealer
M'Kelvie Grace, teacher of music
M'Millan John, slater
Mickan Peter, ship builder, Isle Whithorn
Milne James, earthenware dealer
Stewart William, nail maker
Walker Andrew, bookseller & stationer

PLACES OF WORSHIP·
AND THEIR MINISTERS.
ESTABLISHED CHURCH, Whithorn— Rev. Christopher Nicholson.
ESTABLISHED CHURCH, Glasserton— Rev. Archibald Stewart.
FREE CHURCH, Whithorn—Rev. Frederick Anderson.
UNITED PRESBYTERIAN CHAPEL, Whithorn—Rev. James Fleming.
REFORMED PRESBYTERIAN CHAPEL—Whithorn—Rev. Thomas Macindoe.
SECEDERS CHAPEL, Whithorn——Rev James Gibson.

CARRIERS.
To NEWTON STEWART, Adam M'Kean, Monday   [turday
To WIGTOWN, Alexander Dinnel, Sa-
To PORT WILLIAM, William M'Culloch, Wednesday   [day
To STRANRAER, H. Matthews, Tues-

WIGTOWN,
AND THE PARISH OF KIRKINNER AND NEIGHBOURHOODS.

WIGTOWN or WIGTON—(the former mode of spelling is, however, now generally adopted, to distinguish this town from that of Wigton, in the county of Cumberland,) is a royal and parliamentary burgh, the seat of a presbytery, and the capital of its parish; 105 miles s. s. w. from Edinburgh, 58 s. w. from Dumfries, 28 x. by s. from Stranraer, and 8 s. from Newton-Stewart, pleasantly situated on an eminence near the north side of the Bladenoch water, two miles from its junction with the Cree, or bay of Wigtown. It is a place of considerable antiquity, having come into existence, during the middle ages, from the erection of a castle on the spot by a band of successful Saxon invaders, who conferred on it the name of *Wig*, from the place having been contested in battle; the adjunct *ton*, or 'town,' was afterwards given when the town arose. The castle of Wigtown subsequently became a royal residence; but the town itself does not appear to have been conspicuous until the reign of David II. when it gave the title of Earl to the family of Fleming.

The principal street of the present town is a parallelogram, of which the internal space is enclosed by a wall and iron palings, and the centre laid out in walks and a bowling green, forming an agreeable promenade for the inhabitants. At the end is a very handsome modern cross, of granite, sculptured in an elegant and tasteful manner, and enclosed with an iron railing. At the other extremity is the court house, having a tower of considerable height, which imparts a degree of dignity to the town. The building contains the court-room, an assembly-room, and a subscription library, the sheriff's small-debt court, and the ordinary courts—which latter are held every Tuesday in time of session; and the sheriff's court sits once a fortnight, for deciding claims not exceeding £3 6s. 8d. Many new buildings have lately been erected, some of them of a very tasteful and costly description; such as the parochial borough, and grammar school, the new county jail, and the banks—the latter are branches from the respectable establishments of the 'British Linen Company' and the 'Edinburgh and Glasgow.' The inns and accommodation for strangers visiting the town are excellent, and the burgh altogether may be considered in an improving condition. The harbour of Wigtown is safe, and has depth of water for vessels of three hundred tons burthen to approach the town. The principal exports are corn and cattle; and there is a regular communication with Liverpool by steam-packets. An extensive brewery and a distillery (the latter at Bladenoch); a large manufactory for farina, and another for agricultural implements (at Bladenoch) are the other principal branches. Wigtown is the seat of a custom-house, the members of which comprehend the creeks of Wigtonshire and those of the stewartry of Kirkcudbright, from the Mull of Galloway to the mouth of the river Fleet. In the year 1581 Wigtown was specified as one of the 'King's Free Burghs' it is (as a royal burgh) governed by a provost, two baillies, and fifteen councillors, and is associated with Stranraer, Whithorn and New Galloway in returning one member to the legislature.

The places of worship are a church of the establishment, a free church, and one for united presbyterians. A masonic lodge and a friendly society are in the town—the latter established in 1795. The parish of Wigtown extends five miles in length by four in breadth; it has several eminences throughout, but is in general flat and fertile. At the western extremity of the parish are nineteen large granite stones, placed in a circular form: they are supposed to have belonged to a druid place of worship or sacrifice, while tradition points to the spot as the tomb of King Galdus. The market, entitled by charter, to be holden on Saturday, is now but little observed. Fairs are also chartered to be held at Candlemas, on the first Monday in April, and the first Fridays in July and August, all old style,—they are, however, in a great measure, discontinued, but there is an annual cattle show, which is numerously attended.

The kirk town of KIRKINNER is about three miles from Wigtown, on the road to Garlies, and is remarkable for its beautiful and picturesque scenery. The principal ornament in this neighbourhood is the stately mansion of Col. P. V. Agnew. Here are also the remains of the ancient castle of Baldoun, formerly a residence of the Dunbars, an incident in which family is supposed to have served as the foundation of the 'Bride of Lammermoor,' by the late Sir W. Scott. The parish extends three miles along Wigton bay, the Bladenoch water dividing it, on the north, from Wigtown, and Dowalton lake touching it on the south. The ruins of Longcaster church (the parish now incorporated with Kirkinner,) stand a mile from the lake.

POST OFFICE WIGTOWN, Grace Tait, *Post Mistress.*—Letters from all parts (except WHITHORN) arrive (from NEWTON-STEWART) every evening at half-past seven, and are despatched thereto at a quarter-past four in the morning. Letters from WHITHORN, &c. arrive every morning at four, and are despatched at eight in the evening.

☞ The proprietor claims the attention of the public to the mode necessary to be observed in directing to this town—which should be ' Wigtown, North Britain,' or ' Wigtown, Wigtonshire, not *Wigton* (only) as, in the latter case letters, &c. will be forwarded to Wigton, in *Cumberland,* instead of to their proper destination.

NOBILITY, GENTRY AND CLERGY.
Agnew Col. P. V. Barnbarrouch Kirkinner
Barrett John, Esq. Wigtown
Beddie Mr. David, Wigtown
Boyd Robert, Esq. Wigtown
Briercliff Miss Martha, Wigtown
Dickson Mrs. Margaret, Wigtown
Dunn Mr. Henry, Wigtown
Falconer Rev. James, Wigtown
Hannay Rev. Peter, Wigtown
M'Clelland Charles, Esq. Ford bank
M'Clelland Mrs. Isabella, Wigtown
M'Donald Mrs. Johanna, Wigtown
M'Guffie John, Esq. (justice of peace), Barbadoes Villa
M'Haffie George, Esq. of Corsemabsie
M'Haffie Col. Torhouse Muir
Murray John, Esq. Kilwhim Cottage
Palmer Capt. George, R.N. Wigtown
Rainsford Capt. Thomas, Wigtown
Reid Rev. James, Kirkinner
Rhurd M'Duff, Esq. (under sheriff), Wigtown
Simpson John, Esq. of Barraclun,
Young Rev. Peter, Mance, Wigtown
Young Thomas, Esq. Wigtown

ACADEMIES & SCHOOLS.
CHARITY SCHOOL, Wigtown—Elizabeth M'Taggart, mistress
Douglas Jessie, Bladnoch
Gulline Ann, Wigtown
M'Keand Janet, Wigtown
M'Queen Grace, Wigtown
NORMAL SCHOOL. Wigtown—Jas. W. Husband, master
PAROCHIAL, BOROUGH AND GRAMMAR SCHOOL, Wigtown—Joseph Watson, master
PAROCHIAL SCHOOL, Kirkinner—William Lewis, master
Wylie Grace & Elizabeth, Wigtown

BAKERS.
Griffin James, Wigtown
M'Jerrow David, Wigtown
M'Kie John, Wigtown
Shennan Peter, Wigtown

BANKERS.
BRITISH LINEN COMPANY (Branch) Wigtown—(draw on the head office, Edinburgh, and on Smith, Payne & Smiths', London)—John Black, agent
EDINBURGH AND GLASGOW BANK, Wigtown—(draws on the head offices in Edinburgh and Glasgow, and on the Union Bank of London)—Thomas Murray, agent

BOOKSELLERS, STATIONERS AND PRINTERS.
Malcolm Walker (and druggist), Wigtown
Morrison Alexander, Wigtown
Tait Thomas, Wigtown

BOOT AND SHOE MAKERS.
Blackiock Joseph F. Wigtown
Carnochan John, Wigtown
Carnochan Thomas, Wigtown
Cronney Francis, Wigtown
Dally James, Wigtown
Dally Thomas, Wigtown
Kennedy David, Wigtown
M'Kenna James Wigtown
M'Kinnell Robert, Kirkinner
Marshall John, Wigtown
Martin William, Wigtown
Powel John, Bladenoch
Richardson John, Wigtown
Robinson Charles, Kirkinner
Roddy Thomas, Wigtown
Roney James, Wigtown

CABINET MAKERS AND UPHOLSTERERS.
Bell John, Wigtown
M'Queen Peter H. & Co. Wigtown
Reid Robert, Wigtown

COOPERS.
Dickson Thomas, Wigtown
Forlaw Isaac, Wigtown
Maxwell John, Bladenoch

DISTILLERS.
M'Clelland J. T. & A. & Co. Bladenoch

FARINA MANUFACTURERS.
M'Clelland George, FORD BANK MILLS, Wigtown

FIRE, &c. OFFICE AGENTS.
IN WIGTOWN.
AGRICULTURISTS (cattle), Thomas Murray
GENERAL, Alexander Cowper
INSURANCE COMPANY OF SCOTLAND Andrew M'Master
LAW (life), James M'Lean
LIVERPOOL, William Carson
NATIONAL, George C. Black
NORTHERN (life), Thomas Murray
NORWICH UNION, John Black
PHŒNIX (fire), Thomas Murray
SCOTTISH UNION (fire), Geo. M'Haffie
STANDARD (life), Andrew M'Master

FLESHERS.
Adamson John, Wigtown
Doyle Michael, Wigtown
M'Candish Alexander, Wigtown
M'Geoch Anthony (& cattle dealer) Wigtown
Pollock Peter, Wigtown

GRAIN DEALERS.
Broadfoot Peter, West Mains, Wigtown
Jardine John, Wigtown
M'Gowan William, Bladenoch

GROCERS & SPIRIT DEALERS.
Bennet Agnes, Bladenoch
Bennett Robert, Bladenoch
Brown Samuel, Wigtown
Campbell Andrew, Kirkinner
Comrie William, Wigtown
Cowper Alexander (and druggist), Wigtown
Dunlop James, Wigtown
Graham John (and tea dealer), Wigtown
Gulline John (& glass dealer), Wigtown
M'Donald Anthony (& smallwares) Wigtown
M'Guffie Sarah, Wigtown
M'Keand Peter, Wigtown
M'Kinnell John A. Wigtown
M'Laughlan Margaret, Kirkinner
M'Taggart Margaret, Wigtown
M'William James, Wigtown
Owen Alexander, Wigtown
Skiming Elizabeth, Wigtown
Skimming William, Kirkinner
Thompson Elizabeth, Bladenoch
Walker Mary, Wigtown

INNS.
(See also Vintners.)
Commercial Inn (and posting house) Archibald Bigham
Craig Inn, Agnes Kelly
Queen's Arms Hotel (and posting house), Robert Martin
Ship, Janet M'Cracken

IRONMONGERS.
Cowper Alexander (and oil and colourman), Wigtown
M'Master William, Wigtown

JOINERS & WRIGHTS.
Dunn John, Bladenoch
Fraser William & Sons (& glaziers), Wigtown
Galloway Thomas, Wigtown
Kelly Thomas, Wigtown
Kevan Samuel, Wigtown
M'Kie William, Wigtown
M'Queen James, Wigtown
Neilson James, Wigtown
Neilson William, Wigtown
Parker Alexander, Kirkinner
Russell George, Wigtown
Withers William, Bladenoch

LINEN & WOOLLEN DRAPERS
Donnan Alexander, Wigtown
Geory William, Wigtown
Kevan Peter B. Wigtown
M'Geoch William, Wigtown
M'Guffie Jane, Wigtown
Morrison Alexander, Wigtown

MASONS.
Brown Alexander, Wigtown
Brown James, Wigtown

Kelly Peter, Wigtown
Kelly William, Wigtown
Martin James, Wigtown
Stewart Archibald, Wigtown

MEAL DEALERS.
Fraser Alexander, Wigtown
O'Hair Francis, Wigtown
Stitt John, Wigtown

MESSENGER.
Carson William (and auctioneer and appraiser), Wigtown

MILLERS.
M'Dowel William, Kirkinner
M'Queen William, New Milis
Rae John, Torhouse Mills

MILLINERS & DRESSMAKERS.
Cameron Mary Ann, Wigtown
Gibson Anna, Wigtown
Hannah Isabella, Wigtown
Hunter Mary, Bladenoch
M'Millan Isabella, Wigtown
Owen Janet (and straw bonnet maker), Wigtown
Owen Mary & Margaret, Wigtown
Scott Mary, Wigtown
M'Queen Margaret, Wigtown
M'Taggart Martha, Wigtown

NAIL MAKERS.
Baxter James, Wigtown
Cameron Alexander, Wigtown

PAINTERS.
Cowan David, Wigtown
Gibson Samuel, Wigtown
Michael Samuel, Wigtown

SALT DEALERS.
Adamson John, Wigtown
M'Master Andrew (and general merchant), Wigtown

SMITHS.
Anderson William (and agricultural implement maker), Bladenoch
M'Candish Robert, Wigtown
M'Whirter Thomas, Wigtown

SPIRIT MERCHANTS.
Beddie David (and seedsman), Wigtown
Graham John (and wine merchant), Wigtown
Letterick William, Wigtown

SURGEONS & APOTHECARIES.
Broadfoot David, Wigtown
M'Master John, Wigtown
M'Millan Thomas, M.D. Wigtown

TAILORS.
Dally William, Wigtown
Dinnell William, Wigtown
Gardiner Samuel, Wigtown
Lennox Samuel, Wigtown
M'Clumpha Peter, Bladenoch
Murraw William, Wigtown
Neilson Alexander, Bladenoch
Spark William, Kirkinner
Thomson William, Wigtown

TALLOW CHANDLERS.
Cowper Alexander, Wigtown
M'Candish Mary, Wigtown

TIMBER & SLATE MERCHNTS.
Marshall M'Master & Co. (and importers of tallow, herrings, &c.), Wigtown

VINTNERS.
Cowan John, Kirkinner
Dodds James, Wigtown
Johnston John, Kirkinner
Kelly Thomas, Wigtown
M'Ilwraith John, Wigtown
M'Kenna Agnes, Bladenoch
M'Mekan Andrew, Bladenoch
M'William Janet, Wigtown
Martin Primrose, Wigtown

WATCH & CLOCK MAKERS.
Halliday Peter, Wigtown
M'Gowan William, Wigtown
Tait William, Wigtown

WRIGHTS.
See Joiners and Wrights.

WRITERS
Marked thus * are also Notaries.
*Agnew George, Wigtown
*Black George Couper, Wigtown

*Black John (procurator fiscal of sheriffs court, clerk of lieutenancy, and of the peace, secretary to the police committee for the county, clerk to the lower district committee of the county prison board, and treasurer to the Galloway Steam Navigation Co.), Wigtown
*Carson William (town clerk and licensed procurator), Wigtown
*M'Haffie George, Wigtown
M'Lean James (and county clerk), Wigtown
Shaw James, Wigtown
*Simson John, Wigtown
Smith John, Wigtown

MISCELLANEOUS.
In WIGTOWN when the address is not stated.
Alexander Margaret, provision dealer
Anderson Peter, ship owner, Bladenoch
BIBLE SOCIETY, Wigtown—Thomas Murray, secretary and treasurer
Carnochan Peter, tanner and currier
COUNTY GAOL, Wigtown——Thomas M'Narney, governor; Rev. Peter Young, chaplain
Craigie William, officer of customs
Findley —, borough and sheriff's officer
Fraser Gordon, brewer
Fulton William, veterinary surgeon
GAS WORKS, Wigtown—Wm. M'Master, manager
Gulline Robert, inland revenue officer
Kelly James, stone cutter
Knox Matthew, jeweller
Leacy James, cattle dealer
M'Candish Elizabeth, straw hat maker
M'Candish William, wool carder & dyer, Waulk Mill, Torhouse
M'Knought Thomas, tin-smith
M'Lachlan Alexander, bookbinder
M'Master John, sub-distributer of stamps and agent to the Steam Packet Co.
M'Master Wm. saddler & harness maker
Marshall John, sheriff's officer
SHERIFF'S OFFICE, Wigtown—George Agnew, clerk
Stewart Jane, confectioner
Tilly James, inland revenue officer, Bladenoch
Wagstaff William, inland revenue officer
Walls Michael, broker
Withers Charles, coach builder

PLACES OF WORSHIP,
AND THEIR MINISTERS.
ESTABLISHED CHURCH, Wigtown—Rev. Peter Young.
ESTABLISHED CHURCH, Kirkinner—Rev. James Reid.
UNITED PRESBYTERIAN CHAPEL, Wigtown—Rev. Peter Hannay.
FREE CHURCH, Wigtown—Rev. James Falconer.

CUSTOM HOUSE.
Collector—John Simpson, Esq.
Comptroller—Thomas William Clark, Esq.
Supervisor—John Moor.
Harbour Master—Alexander Fraser.

COACHES.
To AYR, the Hero, from the Queen's Arms, every Monday, Wednesday and Friday morning at six
To STRANRAER, the Union, from the Queen's Arms, every Tuesday, Wednesday and Friday afternoon at three, and on Monday mornings at four

CARRIERS.
To DUMFRIES, William Raeside, Mon.
To ELDRICK, James Stanhope, Saturday
To GARLIESTON, Alex. Dick, Saturday
To GLASGOW, — M'Clurg, Tuesday and Saturday
To PORT WILLIAM, William M'Culloch, Saturday
To STRANRAER, Andrew M'Master, Monday
To WHITHORN, Adam M'Keand, Tuesday, and Geo. Gardner, Saturday

CONVEYANCE BY WATER.
To CRUTOWN, a Passage Boat, daily
To GLASGOW, the Lord Garlieston and the Glarion, alternately
To LIVERPOOL, the Countess of Galloway, once a fortnight
To WHITEHAVEN, Vessels sail weekly

ROUTE TO ENGLAND, VIA DUMFRIES.

GLASGOW AND SOUTH-WESTERN RAILWAY.

PASSENGER AND GOODS TRAFFIC.

THIS COMPANY'S TRAINS FROM CARLISLE,

Are in connexion with those of the London & North-Western, Midland, Lancashire and Yorkshire, and Lancaster and Carlisle Railways.

Passengers and Goods are Booked throughout from MANCHESTER, LIVERPOOL, LONDON, BIRMINGHAM, PRESTON, BOLTON, AND ALL STATIONS ON THESE COMPANIES' LINES,

To GLASGOW, PAISLEY, KILMARNOCK, AYR, &c.

Goods carried without Transference or Re-Invoicing, and at through Rates as low as charged by any similar Route.

Parties will please Address their Goods to the "CARE OF THE GLASGOW & SOUTH-WESTERN RAILWAY COMPANY, *via* DUMFRIES."

There are GOODS TRAINS daily from LONDON, BRADFORD, MANCHESTER and all places to GLASGOW, PAISLEY, &c., and the same *from* GLASGOW and PAISLEY, Southward.

Any information as to Rates will be immediately furnished by Mr. LAUDER, Goods Manager here.

GLASGOW, 1 *July,* 1851.   **J. FAIRFULL SMITH,** Secretary.

The following parties are authorised to collect GOODS IN GLASGOW—*Mr. George Gordon, Buchanan Street and Glassford Street; Messrs. Mackie, Stockwell Street, and Mr. Charles Robb, Brunswick Street.*

IN LONDON,—*Messrs. Chaplin & Horne, 13, Aldersgate Street; Cross Keys, Wood Street; and Golden Cross, Charing Cross.*

JOSEPH ELLIS,

(LATE CLULEY,)

SURGICAL INSTRUMENT

AND   CORPORATE

Truss Manufacturer,

41, SPRING STREET, SHEFFIELD.

WHOLESALE AND FOR EXPORTATION.

MARK.

BUXTON & RUSSELL,

DUKE PLACE, SHEFFIELD,

MANUFACTURERS OF

EXTRA HARD BRITANNIA METAL,

AND

ELECTRO-PLATED GOODS,

Nickel Silver and Electro-Plated Spoons, Forks, &c.

OF SUPERIOR QUALITY.

Subscribers

001	Mr K H Dobie	Dumfries, Scotland
002	Dumfries Archive Centre	Dumfries, Scotland
003	Dumfries Archive Centre	Dumfries, Scotland
004	Mrs S M W White	Dyfed, South Wales
005	Ian M Aitcheson	Formby, England
006	Mrs L L Sanderson	Edinburgh, Scotland
007	Ian T Millar	South Croydon, England
008	Norman Douglas Of Dundarrach	Arrochar, Scotland
009	Mrs A A Taylor	Kirkcudbright, Scotland
010	J E Brough	Lockerbie, Scotland
011	Malcolm J Adamson	Birmingham, England
012	Miss Margaret Banner	Birkenhead, England
013	Robert A Bonner	Chelford, England
014	Mrs Rita Thorne	Lichfield, England
015	Mr Robert Douglas	Corbridge, England
016	Mr Francis J Priestley	Farnborough, England
017	Mr & Mrs P B Richards	Newton Stewart, Scotland
018	Dr J C Little	Dumfries, Scotland
019	Mrs Jean Weir	Cansdale, Harlow, England
020	J Conchie	Copmere End, Staffordshire, England
021	Rev W & Mrs H M Holland	New Abbey, Dumfries, Scotland
022	Wm J Dougan	Hatfield, Hertfordshire, England
023	Mrs Anna Campbell	Carsphairn, Castle Douglas, Scotland
024	Mr David Birkmire	Urmston, Manchester, England
025	Mrs M G Ramsay	Troon, Scotland
026	John Thomson	Kirkpatrick-Durham, Scotland
027	Dr Edgar F Morris PhD LLB FFA	Stourbridge,West Midlands, England
028	Mrs Hilary Newton	Helston, Cornwall, England
029	Mrs J A Pepper	Bromley, Kent, England
030	Mr Hugh Norman	Orpington, Kent, England
031	Alastair Penman	Castle Douglas, Scotland
032	D R Torrance	Edinburgh, Scotland
033	Mr A McColm	Coventry, West Midlands, England
034	Francis N Ryan	Islesteps, Dumfries, Scotland
035	Colin M Newall	Eastbourne, Sussex, England
036	R H Earsman	Mill Hill, London, England
037	Mr W W & Mrs D M Brown	Wirral, Merseyside, England
038	Mrs M M Leggett	Reigate, Surrey, England
039	Alison M Mitchell	Bath, Avon, England
040	Mrs Caroline MacGregor Lockhart	Durrington, Wilts, England
041	Mr A Bullimore	Loughborough, Leics, England
042	Mrs Jean Stoddart	Durham City, County Durham, England
043	J Pagan	Dumfries, Scotland
044	Mrs M B West	Hanley Swan, Worcester, England
045	Mr Donald Whyte JP FSG	Kirkliston, Waet Lothian, Scotland
046	Mrs Margaret Kennedy	Shepparton, Victoria, Australia
047	Kathleen Grebneff	Torbay, Newfoundland, Canada
048	W J McDowall	Parry Sound, Ontario, Canada
049	Mr James B Nodwell	Dumfries, Scotland
050	J Thom	Dumfres, Scotland

051	Neil Chalmers Beattie	Altrincham, Cheshire, England
052	Mr David B Brow	Ipswich, Suffolk, England
053	Aberdeen Family History Society	Aberdeen, Scotland
054	Miss R J McCallum	Perth, Scotland
055	Ruth W Appleby	Bedhampton, Hampshire, England
056	S A McColm	Drummore, Stranraer, Scotland
057	Mrs Pauline Humphrey	Rotorua, New Zealand
058	J E D Smith	Poltmore, Exeter, England
059	Mrs A Thomas	Heathhall, Dumfries, Scotland
060	Janet W Aitken	Newton Stewart, Scotland
061	Neil McLean Gordon	Pinner, Middlesex, England
062	Warren McKean Gordon	Issaquah, Washington, USA
063	F & J Hunter Blair	Carshphairn, Castle Douglas, Scotland
064	Elizabeth D Allen	Strathhaven, Lanarkshire, Scotland
065	Mrs Margaret Concha Harris	Edinburgh, Scotland
066	Mrs Moira Aitken	New Abbey, Dumfries, Scotland
067	Dumfries and Galloway Family History Society	New Abbey, Dumfries
068	Dr G O Airley	Mobberly, Knutsford, England
069	A Younger	Hightae, Lockerbie, Scotland
070	Edward H Stewart	Willowdale, Ontario, Canada
071	Mrs M Kirkpatrick	Dumfries, Scotland
072	DGRC Economic Development Dept	Dumfries, Scotland
073	DGRC Economic Development Dept	Dumfries, Scotland
074	Mr R Britton	Kelloholm, Sanquhar, Scotland
075	Everell Cummins	San Raffael, California, USA
076	Ian Shankland	Colden Common, Winchester, England
077	St. Peter's Primary School	Dalbeattie, Scotland
078	Louisa Knight	Cookham Dean, Maidenhead, England
079	Pamela Knight	Cookham Dean, Maidenhead, England
080	Frank Gibson	Lockerbie, Scotland
081	Hugh Taylor & Moira McCrossan	Moniaive, Scotland
082	B K Edward	Winghcombe, Cheltenham, England
083	Ms R I Murdoch	Dalry, Castle Douglas, Scotland
084	Duncan Adamson	Dumfries, Scotland
085	J R Luff	Laurieston, Castle Douglas, Scotland
086	Mr & Mrs T A G Dalgliesh	Upstreet, Canterbury, England
087	Elizabeth Miles	St. Eleanor's, Prince Edward Is., Canada
088	Leswalt Primary School	Leswalt, Stranraer, Scotland
089	Springfield Primary School	Gretna, Carlisle, England
090	F W Oakes	Bradley Grange, Huddersfield, England
091	Loreburn Primary School	Dumfries, Scotland
092	Loreburn Primary School	Dumfries, Scotland
093	John F McGarva	St John's Town of Dalry, Scotland
094	Penninghame Primary School	Newton Stewart, Scotland
095	Closeburn Primary School	Closeburn, Thornhill, Scotland
096	W J Thoma	Dunbar, East Lothian, Scotland
097	Ronald H Ball	Castle Douglas, Scotland
098	St. Ninian"s Primary School	Dumfries, Scotland
099	Noblehill Primary School	Dumfries, Scotland
100	Miss I B Woods	Liverpool, England

101	N Z Society of Genealogists	
	Canterbury Group	Christchurch, New Zealand
102	Mr William Cowan	Sunderland, England
103	Castle Douglas High School	Castle Douglas, Dumfries
104	Mr K Haywood	Bishopthorpe, York, England
105	Lockerbie Academy	Lockerbie, Dumfries
106	Mr J G Oswald	Lockerbie, Dumfries
107	Colin McBurney	Croydon, Victoria, Australia
108	Dr Betty J Iggo	Edinburgh, Scotland
109	Langholm Primary School	Langholm, Scotland
110	Archie Miller	New Westminster, Canada
111	Brian W Hutchison	Calgary, Alberta, Canada
112	Miss J P S Ferguson	Edinburgh, Scotland
113	Scottish Genealogy Society	Edinburgh, Scotland
114	W J MacDonald	Dumfries, Scotland
115	Manchester & Lancashire Family	
	History Society	Manchester, England
116	Jane Marchbank	Thornhill, Dumfries, Scotland
117	Dr M McWilliam	Edmonton, Alberta, Canada
118	Dr M McWilliam	Edmonton, Alberta, Canada
119	Mrs Isabel M B Taylor	Annan, Scotland
120	Mrs Elma Wickens	Bangor, Co. Down, N Ireland
121	James R Douglas	Witney, Oxfordshire, England
122	Mr & Mrs G Snowden	Hubbert's Bridge, Boston, England
123	Ian McDowall	Dumfries, Scotland
124	David Melville	Waterbeck, Lockerbie, Scotland
125	Tundergarth Primary School	Lockerbie, Scotland
126	Hightae Primary School	Hightae, Lockerbie, Scotland
127	Miss Y Lind	Dumfries, Scotland
128	Mr Fraser Hamilton	Renfrew, Scotland
129	Anonymous	
130	Borgue Primary School	Kirkcudbright, Scotland
131	Palnackie Primary School	Castle Douglas, Scotland
132	Mrs Dorothy Cairns	Stranraer, Scotland
133	M C Clark	Dumfries, Scotland
134	Alex McCracken	Annan, Scotland
135	Society of Genealogists	London, England
136	Beattock Primary School	Beattock, Dumfries, Scotland
137	Joyce Dalziel Taylor	Manchester, England
138	Miss V L Dixon	Ashton-Under-Lyne, Lancashire, England
139	Emma Blore	Castle Douglas, Scotland
140	Elizabeth M Hogg	Dumfries, Scotland
141	Mrs M R Sparkes	Crowthorne, Berkshire, England
142	T R Jardine	Dumfries, Scotland
143	J G Marchbank	Dumfries, Scotland
144	Lockerbie Primary School	Lockerbie, Scotland
145	Lockerbie Primary School	Lockerbie, Scotland
146	John Wilson	Whithorn, Newton Stewart, Scotland
147	Torthorwald Primary School	Dumfries, Scotland
148	Maxwelltown High School	Dumfries, Scotland
149	Ian F Clowe	Dumfries, Scotland
150	Sheena Maxwell	Tundergarth, Lockerbie, Scotland

151	Deirdre Cook	Dumfries, Scotland
152	Mrs Georgina B Davis	Dumfries, Scotland
153	Mr John Hyslop	Tasmania, Australia
154	Mrs Helen F Vicary	Thornhill, Scotland
155	Mrs Helen F Vicary	Thornhill, Scotland
156	J N H Brown	Dumfries, Scotland
157	St Joseph's College	Dumfries, Scotland
158	K Johnston	Auldgirth, Dumfries, Scotland
159	James Dalzell	Annan, Scotland
160	Maureen Over (nee Anderson)	Maidenhead, Berkshire, England
161	Mrs Marjory Keiller	Dalkeith, Midlothian, Scotland
162	Mrs E M Graham	Whithorn, Scotland
163	Shelagh C Scott	Bootle, Merseyside, England
164	Mrs Mary E Dixon	Peterborough, England
165	Miss R J Moffatt	Beccles, Suffolk, England
166	G J L Coltart	Edinburgh, Scotland
167	Wallace Hall Academy	Thornhill, Scotland
168	Wallace Hall Academy	Thornhill, Scotland
169	Mrs Janette Copland	Dunblane, Scotland
170	Mrs M L Paine	Stanmore, Middlesex, England
171	Fred W Carswell	Ste Anne de Bellevue, Que, France
172	N Z Society of Genealogists Dunedin Group	Dunedin, New Zealand
173	Mr E H Robinson	Port Ling, Dalbeattie, Scotland
174	Ms Christine Murray	Crocketford, Dumfries, Scotland
175	Dinwiddie Grieve Ltd, Printers	Dumfries, Scotland
176	T C Farries	Dumfries, Scotland
177	Joseph Ian Craik	Boreland, Lockerbie
178	The Barony College	Parkgate, Dumfries, Scotland
179	Philip M Rain	Melbourne, Victorian, Australia
180	Miss L A E Knight	Mossdale, Castle Douglas, Scotland
181	Mrs S A Brennan	Cheadle, Cheshire, England
182	Mr A W Crichton	Ewhurst, Surrey, England
183	Patricia M Jeffs	Great Missenden, Bucks, England
184	Largs and North Ayrshire Family History Society	Largs, Ayrshire, Scotland
185	Kenneth Dallas	Barnwood, Glouscester, England
186	Carloyn Jane McCubbin	Dumfries, Scotland
187	Dumfries High School	Dumfries, Scotland
188	Mrs J Kellar	Wells, Somerset, England
189	Mr B Graham/Moffat Academy	
190	Mrs M Fisher	Reading, England
191	C John Halliday	Edinburgh, Scotland
192	H Slaven	Dumfries, Scotland
193	Mrs C M Powell	Cambridge, England
194	Mrs H Brown	Anna Valley, Andover, England
195	Mrs Margaret T Maxwell	Gatehouse of Fleet, Scotland
196	W McRobert	Ayr, Scotland
197	James and Pauline Williams	Dumfries, Scotland
198	Robert H McEwen	Lockerbie, Scotland
199	Miss M Grierson	Dumfries, Scotland
200	Philip Tweedie	Newmarket, Suffolk, England

201	David Dinwoodie	Carlton, Nottingham, England
202	Mrs Linda Galloway	Wigtown, Scotland
203	R J Martin	Ringwood 3134, Victoria, Australia
204	Douglas Ewart High School	Newton Stewart, Scotland
205	J W Hunter	Stranraer, Scotland
206	A R Johnston	Dumfries, Scotland
207	Queensland Family History Society Inc	Indooroopilly, Queensland, Australia
208	Angela McCormick	Troon, Ayrshire, Scotland
209	Mrs D Haining	Dumfries, Scotland
210	John Preston	Dumfries, Scotland
211	The Genealogical Society of Victoria	Melbourne, Victoria, Australia
212	Ian Anderson	Gribton, Dumfries, Scotland
213	Ian Anderson	Gribton, Dumfries, Scotland
214	Ian Anderson	Gribton, Dumfries, Scotland
215	Ian Anderson	Gribton, Dumfries, Scotland
216	Ian Anderson	Gribton, Dumfries, Scotland
217	Ian Anderson	Gribton, Dumfries, Scotland
218	Ian Anderson	Gribton, Dumfries, Scotland
219	Ian Anderson	Gribton, Dumfries, Scotland
220	Ian Anderson	Gribton, Dumfries, Scotland
221	Ian Anderson	Gribton, Dumfries, Scotland
222	Ian Anderson	Gribton, Dumfries, Scotland
223	Ian Anderson	Gribton, Dumfries, Scotland
224	James Halliday	Broughty Ferry, Dundee, Scotland
225	Castle Point Press	Colvend Scotland
226	Castle Point Press	Colvend Scotland
227	Castle Point Press	Colvend Scotland
228	Castle Point Press	Colvend Scotland
229	Castle Point Press	Colvend Scotland
230	Castle Point Press	Colvend Scotland
231	Castle Point Press	Colvend Scotland
232	Castle Point Press	Colvend Scotland
233	Castle Point Press	Colvend Scotland
234	Castle Point Press	Colvend Scotland
235	Castle Point Press	Colvend Scotland
236	Castle Point Press	Colvend Scotland
237	Castle Point Press	Colvend Scotland
238	Castle Point Press	Colvend Scotland
239	Castle Point Press	Colvend Scotland
240	Castle Point Press	Colvend Scotland
241	Castle Point Press	Colvend Scotland
242	Castle Point Press	Colvend Scotland
243	Castle Point Press	Colvend Scotland
244	Castle Point Press	Colvend Scotland

PATENT GELATINE WORKS.

GORGIE MILLS, Near EDINBURGH.

COX'S
PATENT REFINED SPARKLING
GELATINE
STANDS UNRIVALLED FOR QUALITY AND CHEAPNESS,
BEING STRONGER THAN THE BEST LONDON
ISINGLASS,
And only ONE-THIRD the Price.
In a few minutes it can be Converted into the Richest and Purest
CRYSTALLINE JELLY,
AND IS PECULIARLY WELL ADAPTED FOR
BLANC-MANGE, SOUPS, GRAVIES, LOZENGES, &c.

To be had of all the Principal DRUGGISTS, GROCERS, &c. in *Packets only*, at the following cheap rates :—

	6d.	9d.	1s.	1s.6d.	3s.	5s. and 10s. each Package.
Yielding......	1	1½	2	3	6½	11 and 24 Quarts of Rich Crystalline Jelly.

Directions for Use and a Copy of Dr. Ure's Testimonial is enclosed in each Packet.

CONFECTIONERS, INNKEEPERS & LARGE CONSUMERS
ARE PARTICULARLY RECOMMENDED TO TRY
COX'S

PALE AMBER GELATINE,
REFINED AMBER GELATINE, } **Sold in Bulk.**

As very Economical and Advantageous for General Purposes.

Shipping and Wholesale Orders punctually attended to.

(59)